Contemporary
Readings
in
Child
Psychology

Contemporary Readings in Child Psychology

E. Mavis Hetherington
Department of Psychology, University of Virginia

Ross D. Parke
Department of Psychology, University of Illinois

McGraw-Hill Book Company
New York St. Louis San Francisco Auckland
Bogotá Düsseldorf Johannesburg London
Madrid Mexico Montreal New Delhi
Panama Paris São Paulo Singapore
Sydney Tokyo Toronto

Contemporary Readings in Child Psychology

1 2 3 4 5 6 7 8 9 0 D O D O 7 8 3 2 1 0 9 8 7 6

This book was set in Times Roman by Black Dot, Inc. The editors
were Richard R. Wright and John M. Morriss; the cover was designed
by Scott Chelius; the production supervisor was Angela Kardovich.
The drawings were done by ANCO/Boston.
R. R. Donnelley & Sons Company was printer and binder.

See Acknowledgments on pages 439–441. Copyrights
included on this page by reference.

Library of Congress Cataloging in Publication Data
Main entry under title:

Contemporary readings in child psychology.

    Bibliography: p.
    1. Child psychology. I. Hetherington,
Eileen Mavis, date   II. Parke, Ross D.
[DNLM: 1. Child psychology. WS105 H589ca]
BF721.C62   155.4   76-27250
ISBN 0-07-028425-3

To John and Sue
and our children:
Grant, Eric, and Jason
Jill, Tim, and Megan

Contents

CHAPTER SEVEN   THE FAMILY AS A PRIMARY AGENT OF SOCIALIZATION

CHAPTER EIGHT   EXTRAFAMILIAL AGENTS OF SOCIALIZATION: PEERS, THE SCHOOL, AND THE MASS MEDIA

Preface

The field of child psychology has undergone radical changes in the past decade and change is still the clearest characteristic of this exciting area of study. The purpose of this volume is to provide students a firsthand opportunity to share some of the recent research findings of child psychologists.

A number of themes run throughout the field of child psychology and we have tried to choose articles that will illustrate these themes. One of the most important themes is our revised view of the child and the important role that the child plays in his or her own development. We recognize that infants and children are more capable, more influential, and more effective at earlier ages than ever before. The shift is best described by the view of the child as "competent." Recent research in infancy illustrates the shift very dramatically. Gone forever is our old view of infants as passive creatures of limited sensory, perceptual, and social capacities, awaiting the imprint of the adult world. Instead we now recognize that infants have much greater capacity to see, learn, and even socialize; the articles on infancy in this volume have helped dispel our earlier myths by demonstrating the wide range of perceptual and social competence that infants display. Infants are more prepared to respond and to interact with their environment than we previously imagined. Part of the shift in our views of infancy can be credited to our revised recognition of the contribution of biological and genetic factors in child development. We have not shifted back to a one-sided biological view of development; rather we now appreciate the important interactions between genetics and environment in shaping the course of development. In this volume, this interaction is illustrated in a host of different ways, including the IQ controversy, the role of nutrition in cognitive development, and the influence of hormones on sex role development.

Nor is it only our views of the *infant's* competence that have changed: children at *all levels of development* are increasingly recognized as competent, active, and influential. In both cognitive and social development, the child is viewed as an active participant. Children are curious, information-seeking, and information-processing organisms and no longer just passive actors in the learning process as the recent research represented in this book on both language and cognition illustrates so well. Similarly in the social sphere, our views of the child have changed. One shift is the recognition of the important relationship between cognitive and social development; the child's cognitive capacities are viewed as playing an influential role in shaping his or her social behavior and vice versa; social skills may play a role in modifying cognitive development.

A most dramatic change concerns our recognition of the child's role in his or her own socialization. As Bell reminds us in his article, our unidirectional view of development whereby adults influence children, but children do not alter adult behavior, is inadequate. Children play an active role in modifying and altering adult behavior—even in early infancy. A bidirectional view of socialization is now widely accepted with children playing an influential part in their own social and cognitive development.

There are other themes as well. A current concern is the study of the child from a developmental perspective so that the age-related changes and transformations in motor, social, and cognitive spheres can be described and understood. In this search, there are two aims: (1) to describe the nature of the child's development and (2) to explain the processes that account for the developmental progression.

These two aims have led to a recognition that a wide variety of methodological strategies are necessary. No single method will suffice. On the one hand child development specialists have been influenced by recent trends in other fields, such as ethology which emphasizes the study of the organism in its natural environment. Under this influence, there has been a renewed interest in describing the behavior of children at different ages in a variety of naturalistic settings, including homes, schools, and playgrounds. It is hoped that this trend will yield important data concerning how children in different cultures and subcultures develop in their own unique real-life environments.

At the same time, researchers continue the important task of understanding the processes of development. To a large extent, the preferred methodology for achieving this goal is the laboratory experiment. Using a well-controlled situation, this method allows the manipulation of relevant variables in order to establish clear cause-effect relationships. Increasingly, developmental psychologists are combining observational and experimental approaches; the observations yield hypotheses or clues concerning possible processes; in turn, these hunches can be systematically assessed in the laboratory. The importance of this trend is that the laboratory experiments are more likely to be testing hypotheses that will be of relevance to the ways in which children develop in their naturalistic environment.

Just as there are multiple methods, there are multiple theories. Although the grand theoretical scheme of Piaget is still influential, child psychologists are increasingly becoming more modest and restricted in the scope of their theories. As the complexity and multifaceted nature of development become apparent, minitheories that aim to explain smaller pieces of the developmental puzzle are becoming more popular. Theories of sex-typing, aggression, memory, and grammar development are more likely than elaborate theories aimed at explaining all social development or the total range of cognitive-language development.

Finally, child development is recognizing the culture-bound and even time-bound nature of its findings. As a number of articles in this book clearly show, no single picture of development is accurate for all cultures, social classes, or racial and ethnic groups. Children develop different skills and competencies in different cultural milieus; and no sweeping generalizations concerning children's development can be made without careful specification of a child's cultural background. Similarly, much of our knowledge about children is time-bound. As Bronfenbrenner so eloquently details in his article on "The Changing American Family," children and families are in a state of transition and change. It is our job not only to constantly monitor these changes, but to be aware of the very temporary nature of many of our "facts" about children.

Another theme of child psychology today is that it is influenced by and influences social policy concerning children. Just as government programs such as Head Start and day care programs alter the lives of children, the findings of child psychologists often give impetus and support to new types of government intervention on behalf of children. A significant shift over the past decade has been the increasing interdependence of child development as a scientific discipline and government policy.

PLAN OF THE BOOK

It is the aim of this volume to illustrate these contemporary themes in child psychology. An understanding of children must take into account both developmental changes that occur over the span of childhood as well as the processes underlying developmental changes and transitions. Therefore, we have organized this volume to reflect this viewpoint. Our topic-oriented organization permits us to achieve both of our goals. Each chapter deals with both the processes of development as well as the ways in which children change over age.

In the first two chapters, biological and genetic influences on development are represented by a wide range of topics including the impact of maternal medication on the infant, the effects of early mother-infant contact, and the role of hormones in sex role development. The second chapter highlights the recent controversy concerning the genetic and environmental determinants of intelligence. The next chapter deals with a special period: infancy; it is recognition of the virtual outpouring of research in this area over the past decade that led to a separate chapter for this age period. Recent advances in social, cognitive, and perceptual development during infancy are illustrated by these selections. In addition, the importance of early experience in determining later development is discussed in two articles.

Chapters Four and Five are devoted to language, learning, and cognition. In some selections the development of grammar in our own culture as well as in other countries is discussed. In another article, the special problems associated with language development in deaf children are illustrated while in other articles, communication in different settings and subcultures is discussed. To lead off the cognitive development chapter, an overview of Piaget is provided and recent experimental investigations illustrate Piaget's continuing influence. Learning is illustrated by articles on modeling and punishment while a final article addresses the topic of cognitive and intellectual training programs for children.

The remaining sections are devoted to socialization and social development. First, a series of topical issues such as altruism, aggression, and sex typing are illustrated. Next, a variety of agents that play important roles in childhood socialization are represented. The family remains an influential socialization agency as illustrated by papers on father-infant interaction, the effects of parental discipline, the impact of divorce, changes in the American family, and finally, an overview of alternative childrearing arrangements. In the final chapter, three other socializing forces are represented: (1) the peer group, (2) the school, and (3) the mass media. These agencies represent important and often neglected socialization influences. As our selections illustrate, peers exert an important influence on the child's intellectual and social development. Similarly schools affect children not only through the curriculum, but as the articles in this chapter illustrate, through their physical environment and through the sex of their teachers as well. In the last selections, the multiple effects—both good and bad—that television plays in children's social and cognitive development are illustrated. The socializing role of textbooks is illustrated in our final chapter.

It is our hope that you will not only learn from these articles some of the recent findings, methods, and theories of child psychology, but that through these articles you will share the excitement of our contemporary efforts to understand children.

Statistical Guide

Many students who read this volume will be unfamiliar with the common statistical terms used in research articles. So let us briefly identify and define some of these terms.

Mean and Median: The mean $(\overline{X})$ and median (M) are both measures of central tendency; the mean refers to the *arithmetic average* and so the mean height of children in a classroom would be the sum of the heights of individual children divided by the number of children in the class. The median, on the other hand, refers to the *middle number* when a group of values are arranged from smallest to largest. Therefore, the median height would be the height of the child who is in the middle of the group if all the students lined up from shortest to tallest.

Standard Deviation: (SD) is a measure of the variability or range of the values in a group of scores. For example, if the heights of the children in a class were all within 1 inch of each other, the standard deviation would be small; if the range was 8 inches, the standard deviation would be larger.

Correlation is an index of the relationship between two variables and is expressed in terms of the direction and size of the relationship. Height and weight are related in a positive direction since as height increases, so does weight typically rise. On the other hand, if one factor increases while the other factor decreases, the correlation is a negative one. Finally, if no relationship exists between two factors, such as eye color and IQ, then we speak of a zero order correlation. This means that changes in one factor are not related in any systematic way to changes in another factor.

Statistical Tests: A variety of tests will be found in the selections such as analysis of variance, t-tests, and chi-squares. Each of these represents different ways of determining whether differences among groups of subjects are due to chance factors. For the analysis of variance, a value of F will be given followed by another value that indicates the level of significance; for t-tests, a t value is provided, and for chi-square, a X^2 value is given. The important issue for your understanding the articles is the *level of significance* associated with each of these tests. Next we provide an explanation of this term.

Levels of Statistical Significance: The purpose of statistical tests is to permit the investigator to determine whether the results of his or her investigation were due to chance factors. For example, two groups of subjects may have received different treatments and the results of the statistical test yielded the following: $p < .05$ or $p < .01$. These values mean that the differences between the groups could have occurred by chance alone only 5 times out of 100 ($p < .05$) or 1 time out of 100 ($p < .01$). Most investigators in child psychology accept a finding as reliable and trustworthy if the difference is at the .05 level of significance.

This is a limited survey of common statistical terms, but we trust that it will help in understanding the articles presented in this book.

Reference Works

We have listed below a series of common reference sources in child psychology. For students who wish to pursue a topic in greater depth, this list will be a helpful guide to the literature.

Advances in child behavior and development. Volumes 1–10. New York: Academic Press, 1963–1975.

Caldwell, B.M., and Ricciuiti, H. N. (Eds.) *Review of child development research.* Volume 3. Chicago: University of Chicago Press, 1973.

Goslin, D. (Ed.) *Handbook of socialization theory and research.* Chicago: Rand McNally, 1968.

Hartup, W. W., and Smothergill, N. (Eds.) *The young child: Reviews of research.* Volume 1. Washington: National Association for the Education of Young Children, 1967.

Hartup, W. W. (Ed.) *The young child: Reviews of research.* Volume II. Washington: National Association for the Education of Young Children, 1972.

Hetherington, E. M. (Ed.) *Review of child development research.* Volume 5. Chicago: University of Chicago Press, 1975.

Hoffman, M. L., and Hoffman, L. W. (Eds.) Volumes 1–2. *Review of child development research.* New York: Russell Sage, 1964–1966.

Horowtiz, F. G. (Ed.) *Review of child development research.* Volume 4. Chicago: University of Chicago Press, 1975.

Lewis, M., and Rosenblum, L. A. *The origins of behavior series.* Volumes 1–3. New York: Wiley, 1974, 1975, 1976.

Minnesota symposia on child psychology. Volumes 1–10. Minneapolis: University of Minnesota Press.

Mussen, P. H. (Ed.) *Carmichael's manual of child psychology.* Volumes 1–2. New York: Wiley, 1970.

Stone, L. J., Smith, H. T., and Murphy, L. B. (Eds.) *The competent infant: Research and commentary.* New York: Basic Books, 1973.

E. Mavis Hetherington
Ross D. Parke

Contemporary
Readings
in
Child
Psychology

Chapter One

The Biological Basis
of Behavior

Some concepts, theories, and controversies in developmental psychology appear briefly, stimulate a flurry of research activity, and disappear having made little lasting impact on the field. Other questions continue to provoke psychologists and to be studied in a relatively unmodified and often unproductive form. Still other problems maintain a tenacious hold on the curiosity of developmental psychologists, but the questions asked about the issues change, new methods of studying them become available, the controversies remain in a changed form. The interaction between biological[1] and environmental factors in development is a topic that clearly falls in the last category.

Although the historical antecedents of this problem might be said to go back to the interests of the ancient Chinese and Greeks in the relation between body types and temperament, a more modern and directly relevant antecedent is Galton's book *English Men of Science; Their Nature and Nurture,* published in 1874. Galton reported that there was an unusually high incidence of intellectually and professionally outstanding persons among the relatives of eminent scientists. Until the interest in learning theory starting early in this century, and notably the rise of behaviorism in the 1930s and 1940s, the predominant emphasis was on the role of heredity as the important determinant of development, particularly intellectual development.

In many ways this biological determinism is a philosophy incompatible with American social and political thought, which emphasizes equality, social mobility, and the value of

---

[1]In our discussion the term "biological factors" will subsume both genetic factors and changes in the anatomy or physiology of the child resulting from external agents or events.

education. In a culture imbued with the Horatio Alger story that a poor boy, if he is virtuous and works hard, can be a success, and the notion that any American can grow up to be president, the emphasis on experience and environment by the behaviorists held great appeal. It is interesting to note that in more rigidly socially structured societies such as in Great Britain and some of the European countries the genetic position found a more hospitable milieu and has been maintained more vigorously than in the United States. The following famous statement by John B. Watson, the leader of behaviorism, is more compatible with the American dream than are "folksy" maxims such as "Blood will tell" or "You can't make a silk purse out of a sow's ear":

> Give me a dozen healthy infants, well-formed, and my own specified world to bring them up in, and I'll guarantee to take any one at random and train him to become any type of specialist I might select—doctor, lawyer, artist, merchant-chief and yes, even beggar-man and thief, regardless of his talents, penchants, tendencies, abilities, vocations, race of his ancestors. (Watson, 1959, p. 104)

Such extreme genetic or environmentalist positions led to what was called "the nature-nurture controversy" where proponents on each side of the controversy championed either biological or experiential factors to the exclusion of others. In the past twenty years such irrational extremism has yielded to the view that behavior is determined by the interaction of biological and experiential factors and the question of whether heredity or environment determines a characteristic is no longer being asked. Instead we are asking "how" and "when" genetic and environmental factors and transactions affect development.

These transactions occur throughout the course of development. The expression of the genotype, the biological inheritance of the individual, as a phenotype, the observable characteristics of an individual, is constantly being modified. The impact of the environment in shaping phenotypical expression of the genotype varies with the kind, the amount, and the timing of experiences. In addition some individuals may be genetically predisposed to be more vulnerable to certain environmental factors than are others. Some individuals and some fetuses may be more likely to alter in response to such things as drugs, malnutrition, anoxia, disease, stress, and sensory or social stimulation or deprivation. Some behaviors are also more difficult to modify than are others. Responses such as smiling, babbling, crawling, and walking in infants seem to be strongly genetically programmed. Blind infants smile at about the same time as seeing infants, the emergence of babbling occurs in a similar fashion in deaf and hearing infants, and children who spend much of their time restrained in swaddling clothes or on a cradle board, crawl and walk at about the same time as infants reared under more mobile conditions. Such behaviors where there are fewer possible alternative paths from phenotype to genotype, or where the behavior is difficult to deflect under extreme variations in experience, are said to be highly "canalized" (Waddington, 1966).

At one time psychologists interested in genetic-environmental transactions were concerned with the child only after birth. It is now recognized that some of the most powerful of these transactions may occur prenatally while the infant is developing rapidly in utero and that some of the adverse effects of such transactions can be averted. Innovations in genetics and perinatology and new techniques in the detection and treatment of genetic disorders have led to an increased interest in prenatal development. Many of the papers in this section deal with very recent advances in our understanding of transactions between genetic and environmental factors and also to a considerable extent with the control over these factors. In many the underlying question is whether through genetic engineering or through the manipulation of environments we can develop more competent individuals.

The paper by Albert Rosenfeld presents new findings on sex determination and anticipates parental preselection of the sex of their children. The remaining four papers discuss modification of development associated with prenatal drugs, prematurity, nutrition, and fetal androgens.

In all these papers the transactions between social, environmental, and biological factors in shaping development are stressed. It is not just the direct physical and neurological impact of such biological factors that affect development; it is the associated experiential and social factors that modify or sustain their effects. The subtle influence on parent-child interaction of a drugged neonate concerns Brazelton. The sensory and social isolation of the premature baby in an isolette and the effects of the infant's early separation from its mother are regarded as the critical deleterious factors for low-birth-weight babies by Klaus and Kennell. Ricciuti is concerned with the influences of various social, educational, family, and child-rearing conditions found in the environment of the economically deprived malnourished child. Ehrhardt and Baker conclude that the quality of the specific behaviors exhibited by fetally androgenized children will depend to a large extent on the interaction between prenatal hormone levels and the child's environment. In none of the papers is the biological or environmental extremism prevalent twenty years ago apparent. All the authors present a transactional model of development which reflects the thinking of contemporary scientists working on human development.

REFERENCES

Waddington, C. H. *Principles of development and differentiation*. New York: Macmillan, 1966.
Watson, J. B. *Behaviorism*. Chicago: University of Chicago Press, 1959.
Galton, F. *English men of science: Their nature and nurture*. London: Macmillan, 1874.

Reading 1

If Oedipus' Parents Had Only Known

Albert Rosenfeld

Monarchs have traditionally wanted a boy first (so, indeed, have most parents), as heir to the throne. But King Laius of Thebes and his queen, Jocasta, really, *really* would have preferred a girl. They had been warned by the oracle that they would have a son who would kill his father and marry his mother. Sure enough, they did go ahead and have Oedipus—as we know from Freud in case we missed Sophocles.

If Laius and Jocasta had known what we know today about sperm and egg, or if they had had the contemporary equivalent of Dr. Landrum B. Shettles of New York to consult . . .

Among the facts we now know about the human sperm cell is that it is a packet of genetic material propelled by the energetic lashings of its tail—which it discards once it has reached and penetrated the egg. In the process of fertilization, it unites its 23 chromosomes with the egg's 23 to make up the 46 required to complete the manual of genetic instructions for the procreation of a human being.

Egg and sperm each carries, among its 23 chromosomes, a specific sex-determining chromosome, designated as X or Y. The egg's is always an X chromosome. An XX combination results in a female offspring; an XY, in a male. Because only the sperm can carry a Y chromosome, it is the sperm that determines the child's gender. An X-carrier is a gynosperm, or female-producer; a Y-carrier is an androsperm, or male-producer.

Dr. Shettles, who now does his research at the New York Fertility Foundation, has been a pioneer investigator in procreative biology. He has particularly sought to distinguish the differences between the two types of sperm—and to use the knowledge to help prospective parents predetermine the sex of their children. Photographs he produced a few years ago were not so clear to other scientists as to him; hence they were controversial and not universally accepted. But these new photographs, especially that below, taken by the scanning electron microscope, distinctly show the differences.

In each picture the sperm with the smaller, rounder head is the male-producing Y-carrier, and the larger, more oval head belongs to the female-producing X-carrier (hereinafter to be called Y and X and referred to as *he* and *she* as a space-saving convenience—though it does seem a bit strange to be calling a sperm *she*). X carries more genetic material; the male apparently gets short-changed genetically. In addition to being lighter, Y has a longer tail. Thus he is speedier. (Shettles has confirmed this difference by racing them.) But X is more durable. If the egg is ready and waiting, Y has a better chance of getting there first. But if ovulation is still a couple of days away, Y is more likely to have used up his energy, switching the odds to X, who, moving at a more stately pace, picks up the prize.

Other factors that favor Y are an alkaline environment and the presence of the secretions that follow female orgasm. X does better when conditions are slightly acidic. She doesn't necessarily *like* the acid—which in fact slows down both X and Y—but X is apparently better equipped to "tough it out." These discoveries are not all Shettles's by any means, but he uses them—as do a few other doctors—to give parents an opportunity to call the shots with claims of 80 to 85 percent accuracy (see box).

Shettles has for years been interested in those families that have all girls or all boys. In the fathers of all-boy families that he investigated, the spermatozoa were almost exclusively Ys, and in the all-girl cases, they were predominantly Xs.

Dr. Shettles's Advice for Improving Nature's Odds

TO FAVOR FEMALE OFFSPRING: (1) intercourse ceasing two to three days before ovulation, preceded by an acid douch of water and vinegar; (2) intercourse without female orgasm; (3) shallow penetration by the male at emission.

TO FAVOR MALE OFFSPRING: (1) intercourse at the time of ovulation, with prior abstinence during a given cycle, preceded by an alkaline douche of water and baking soda; (2) intercourse with female orgasm; (3) deep penetration at the time of emission.

In normal sperm, by the way, Ys are present in greater quantities. Nature seems to have provided the added quantity to offset the Y's greater fragility. Though Shettles estimates, from a study of the literature, that 160 males are conceived for every 100 females, so many male embryos are spontaneously aborted that only 105 males are actually born for every 100 females. This handicap appears necessary because more males die at almost every age until, toward the end of life, women outnumber men, reversing the original ratio.

Many researchers have sought ways to separate Xs from Ys, and, by using artificial insemination, to ensure the outcome 100 percent. They have tried centrifugation, electrophoresis, and sedimentation, as well as immunologic and other methods to separate Xs from Ys—and with fair success.

Other methods, too, exist for predetermining the sex of offspring, but they cannot be used until *after* conception, which makes them more controversial and less acceptable ethically. Not that tampering with Xs and Ys is free of controversy. Many people feel that this line of research should not be pursued at all, that people should not have this kind of power and choice. Some fear that passing fads and préférences could drastically overbalance the population one way or the other, thus affecting everything from the economy to the crime rate to the incidence of homosexuality. Others favor this option as a population reducer, arguing that most families that might otherwise go on and on "trying for a girl" or boy might be content with two children—a boy and a girl.

Parents do, in general, seem to welcome the opportunity to preselect the sex of their children; and once the choice is available, they will undoubtedly take advantage of it.

Reading 2

Effect of Prenatal Drugs on the Behavior of the Neonate

T. Berry Brazelton, M.D.

I have been interested in the genesis of individual differences in infant behavior and their ultimate outcome as the infant meets with an environment that may reinforce these particular assets and deficits. Having started my infant work with a group of psychoanalysts at the Putnam Children's Center in Boston, I first became aware of the analytic concern with the importance of the environment in "shaping" the infant. More recently Fries (15), Escalona and Heider (12), and Chess (9) have furthered research that appealed to me as a pediatrician—that of taking cognizance of the shaping influence on the environment of the particular kind of neonate with which it is presented. I have little question but that the kind of infant he is is fully as important in determining the outcome of the mother-infant interaction as is the mother's personality structure.

Two aspects of the genesis of individual behavior

Read at the 125th anniversary meeting of the American Psychiatric Association, Miami Beach, Fla., May 1969.

in the neonate need further attention from all of us who are concerned with this question. The first is the structure of the genotype as it defines the infant's potential for behavior. The second is the importance of the first nine months *in utero* in shaping the genotype's expression. The formula for behavioral phenotype becomes genotype X environment, and the first important environment is intrauterine.

Recent studies show rather conclusively that the expression of the genotype is heavily influenced by prenatal factors. These factors affect the genes in a lasting fashion, which later environmental influences cannot overcome. The "critical period" for influencing cellular development and its potential for expression in the developing organism may be a limited one; it usually occurs early in pregnancy.

Money and associates (23) studied ten patients who had the typical XY chromosomes of a male but who had the external appearance of females at birth and developed as females into adulthood. When they presented themselves for sterility studies, their blind vaginal pouches, absence of uterus or ovaries, and abdominal undeveloped testicles proved their potential maleness. As adults, functioning as females, they were studied for female gender roles and identity. Other than an inability to reproduce or lactate, they were healthy normal females in their adjustment to life—sex life, mothering of adopted children, etc.

This condition is now known as "fetal feminization of a male." It is brought about by an insensitivity of the fetus to androgen at a cellular level at a critical period in prenatal development—probably in the first few weeks. Lack of response to male hormones leaves the fetus sensitive to female hormones circulating from his mother. A neural organization is set in motion at a hypothalamic level that produces female genitalia, breast development at puberty, and adult female sexual behavior and cycling. When administered after birth, androgens do not reverse this. Thus the intrauterine conditioning of female hormones essentially changes *for life* the male genotype into a female phenotype—behavior and all.

Another example of this has been demonstrated in rats. Androgens given to mothers during pregnancy masculinize the infants even though they are female in genotype (13). In humans, a commonly used female hormone, progesterone (used to prevent abortion in the female), has been reported by Russell of Jerusalem (29) to "overmasculinize" male infants, with mild to moderate hypertrophy of the penis and scrotum and exceptional muscularity and accelerated neuromuscular development, accompanied by some hyperkinesis. He reports that these are tense, irritable male infants who demonstrate gastrointestinal difficulties. Female infants may have an enlarged clitoris and a comparable "pseudomasculine" increase in neuromuscular tissue and behavior.

Since the dosage is not large enough to produce more disturbing clinical symptoms, such as the sterility that results from large doses of androgens given female rats, these transient subclinical effects that Russell demonstrates have not changed the common practice of administering large doses of hormones to mothers during pregnancy. Smaller doses of such drugs and discontinuance of oral contraceptives as soon as pregnancy is suspected (since they may cause similar disturbances) might surely be safer. One wonders whether there might not indeed be behavioral residua of these commonly used drugs in the human infant, such as is seen in colicky, restless, driving infants who give their mothers a difficult first few months. Certainly the impact of their behavioral symptoms on a new mother could lead to profound disturbances in the mother-infant adjustment.

DIETARY INADEQUACY

The effect of dietary inadequacy on fetal development is becoming more clear-cut. Zamenhof and associates (33) fed pregnant rats an eight percent protein-insufficient diet from the time of conception and the control group a normal diet. At birth, the offspring of the hypoproteinemic group had fewer brain cells (as demonstrated by DNA content of the brains), half the protein that could have been expected for the size of the brain, smaller brains, and decreased birth weights. This decrease in brain cell number *and* in qualitative protein content of each cell confirms the hypothesis for central nervous system underdevelopment that has been raised in human groups beset with malnutrition in pregnancy. These quantitatively and qualitatively deficient brains are poorly adapted to normal development and must be more susceptible to any insult, however mild, of hypoxia, maternal depressant drugs, and other paranatal events. So here is a double potential for change of the genotype's expression—the numerically inadequate, undernourished brain cells coupled with hypersensitivity to insult.

Growth hormone given pregnant rats by Block and associate (4) seemed to increase the number of brain cells and the problem-solving capacities of the rats. Again, this hormone's influence seems to be laid down in the early weeks of fetal development.

DRUG EFFECTS

Drug abuse in the adolescent and adult female raises issues about influencing fetal development that must be faced. The clinical defect demonstrated by thalidomide babies paved the way for more extensive investigation. Maternal ingestion of LSD resulted in infants with persisting chromosomal defects of their own that tended to repair incompletely, according to Berlin (3). No gross structural or central nervous system defects were demonstrated in the 16 neonates, but no analysis of their behavior other than a gross neurological examination was done. Future sterility and reproduction of congenital defects in *next* generation offspring may result from such unrepaired chromosomal defects. Jacobsen (19) found a strikingly high incidence of abortion (50 percent) in 75 LSD users, and major abnormalities of the fetuses were demonstrated at post mortem. He also confirmed the chromosomal flaws in mothers and infants who survived. The chromosomal defects and rate of abortion did not seem to depend on the dosage of LSD but did relate to the time of its use in pregnancy.

Many cases of narcotic addiction (morphine, heroin) in mothers are reported in the literature (10, 16). Withdrawal symptoms of restlessness, irritability, tremors, convulsions, sleeplessness, fever, gastroenteritis, yawning, and sneezing occur in the neonate in the first week. Unless the appropriate drug is given to counteract these symptoms, serious illness and death of the baby may result. Codeine withdrawal symptoms similar to those mentioned above have been reported by Van Leewen and associates (31). Acute alcohol withdrawal in women in this country (24) and in a Yukon Indian mother (30) led to fever, alternating hyperirritability and lethargy, and severe hyperbilirubinemia in the neonate. The influence of these substances is a result of their continuous use to the end of pregnancy.

Aspirin in large doses given the mother just prior to delivery has been demonstrated to cause a decrease in albumin binding capacity and to increase the danger of brain damage from hyperbilirubinemia in the infant (26).

Tranquilizers such as reserpine, meprobamate, and chlorpromazine given to pregnant animals have been demonstrated by Hoffeld and associates (18) to affect both the birth weight and response to learning tasks of their infants. The time in pregnancy of administration of the drugs had an important influence—controls>mid>late>early. Young (32) showed that these animals were markedly susceptible to stress in the neonatal period. Any stress added to their environment in the first 30 extrauterine days (another critical period) resulted in animals who had permanent and more severe learning defects. Ordy and associates (25) showed a decrease in liver glycogen as a result of prenatal chlorpromazine; this might result in an impaired response of the organism to stress reaction and mobilization of glycogen stores. Too few of these investigations have been applied to human pregnancies and off-

spring. All of these drugs are in common usage as tranquilizers during pregnancy and are even more commonly used as premedicants just prior to delivery.

My interest in medication effects on the neonate was first stimulated by observing neonates who had excellent Apgar scores (1) in the delivery room and remained clinically responsive for half an hour—long enough to be sent to the nursery downstairs. After this initial period of responsiveness (which I now postulate is largely due to the neonate's ability to mobilize his resources to respond to the stimulating of labor, delivery, and the onslaught of new environmental stimuli), these babies shifted rapidly into a frightening state of relative unresponsiveness. They became unresponsive to any but very disturbing stimuli, with little spontaneous motor activity; they also had very slow heart and respiratory rates. Diffuse acrocyanosis demonstrated their poor circulatory response to the hypoxia that was present, and their ability to clear mucous from their airways became impaired. This depressed behavior lasted for a period of a few hours to a day and then tapered off not-so-gradually; subclinical behavior manifestations could be demonstrated for as long as a week in many infants.

The ready transmission of barbiturates to the fetus from the mother is well known. When the cord is cut his circulating level is 70 percent of hers (2), but his liver, kidneys, and tissue storage differs markedly from hers. His immature kidneys excrete drugs poorly and his liver is taken up with deconjugation of bilirubin and maternal hormones for which barbiturates must compete for detoxification (14, 20). Ploman and Persson (27) found that the selective tissue storage of depressant drugs such as barbiturates was many times higher in the midbrain than in the circulating blood. This selective storage lasted for as much as a week in the immature brain, affecting the CNS reactions and the midbrain-mediated behavior of the neonate for the entire time. Since the neonate's behavior is primarily midbrain in origin, this means that his behavioral repertoire is influenced for the entire important first week of his life. But since the infants survive and there is no clinical evidence of CNS damage demonstrable with our grossly inadequate neurological techniques, premedication of mothers in labor is an accepted obstetrical practice; little is done to change it.

Recent studies conclusively demonstrate subtle

but transient effects of medication on the neonate. Borgstedt and Rosen (5) found meperidine (50-100 mg.) and promethazine (25-50 mg.) in accepted premedicating doses caused impairment of behavioral states (on Prechtl and Beintema's scale [28]) in 29 of 33 babies of medicated mothers, versus one of eight babies of nonmedicated mothers at one to two days of age (table 1). EEG alterations were present in 28 of these, versus one of the eight controls. Behavioral impairment disappeared two days later in all but three, but EEG alterations persisted for a week in ten. All of these infants had had excellent Apgar scores at delivery, and all were found normal later in a neurological evaluation. Again, this kind of evidence is too subtle to change obstetrical practice.

Kron and associates (22) demonstrated that newborn sucking behavior was depressed for four days after delivery by routine maternal medication. The depression applied to sucking rate, pressure, and amount of consumption. Conway and Brackbill (11) found that perceptible effects on avoidance response to a conditioned stimulus could be still seen in one-month-old neonates whose mothers had been drugged at delivery.

I found a 24-48 hour lag in the neonate's ability to adapt to breast feeding as a result of maternal medication. This was reported by 41 multiparous mothers who had nursed before(14 were on low and 27 on high medication—scopolamine > .04 mg., barbiturates > 150 mg. one to six hours prior to delivery [7]). (See figure 1.) A 24-hour delay in weight gain confirmed this (figures 2 and 3). The

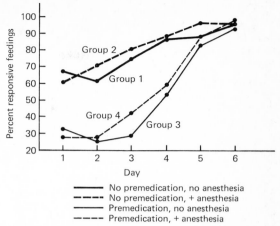

Figure 1 Responsive Feedings in Neonates. *(From Brazelton, T. Berry: Psychophysiologic Reactions in the Neonate II. Effects of Maternal Medication on the Neonate and His Behavior, J. Pediat. 58: 513–518, 1961.)*

inhalant anesthesia given mothers affected the infant relatively little. Mothers were asked to score the infants for: 1) initial alertness, 2) difficulty in rousing to institute active nursing, 3) length of time they could maintain a state appropriate for feeding, with only the usual stimulation. All of these infants were found neurologically normal on subsequent follow-up. I reported this study in 1961 (7), but there has been little change in the premedication given mothers at the institution where the work was done *except* by obstetricians who care about breast feeding.

Effects on Mother-Infant Relationship

My present concern is with the subtle effects on the early mother-infant relationship and how much this relationship may be affected by depressant drugs. Each member of the diad may be affected at a critical time in the mother-infant interaction, when such processes as "imprinting" and/or "sets of mind for the future" may be involved. This was demonstrated by two mothers and their infants whom we studied in detail over the first week as part of a longitudinal study.

Marked differences in their recovery rates were noted despite similar doses of premedication given the mothers: 200 mg. of seconal at three hrs. and 125 mg. of demerol in one and 24 mg. of thorazine in the other; 25 mg. of phenargan intramuscularly

Table 1 Effect of Premedication on the Neonate

	Medicated Mothers	Nonmedicated Mothers
Behavioral state		
Impaired	29	1
Not impaired	4	7
Newborn EEG		
Altered	28	1
Not altered	5	7
Both behavior and EEG		
Altered	24	1
Not altered	1	7

Reprinted from the *American Journal for Diseases of Children* 115: 21, 1968.

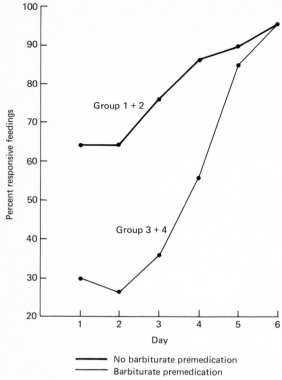

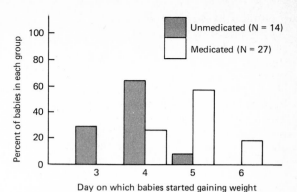

Figure 3   Weight Gain in Babies. *(From Brazelton, T. Berry: Psychophysiologic Reactions in the Neonate II. Effects of Maternal Medication on the Neonate and His Behavior,* J. Pediat. *58: 513–518, 1961.)*

Kovach (21) found that sympathetic drugs (amphetamine and epinephrine) given early facilitated initial following behavior and increased the strength and duration of the imprinting. They postulated that any agent which produced general activation of the CNS would lead to an increase in strength and

Figure 2   Responsive Feedings in Neonates. *(From Brazelton, T. Berry: Psychophysiologic Reactions in the Neonate II. Effects of Maternal Medication on the Neonate and His Behavior,* J. Pediat. *58: 513–518, 1961.)*

one and one-half hours prior to delivery in the alert mother (figure 4). The mothers had a paradoxical reaction compared with their infants. The more "depressed" infant was delivered by a wide awake mother and vice versa. This paradoxical drug action raises some questions: 1) Is there a difference in tissue storage and receptivity, both in mother and infant? 2) Does storage by the mother protect the infant, and so on? There was little doubt but that the drugs affected the imprinting responses in both of these mothers and infants—not necessarily for the worse, but in a fashion observed by them and by us.

Animal experiments suggest the importance of such a critical period on the mother-infant relationship. Hess (17) has demonstrated a delayed latency of acquisition of initial imprinting performance when meprobamate is given the neonatal chick.

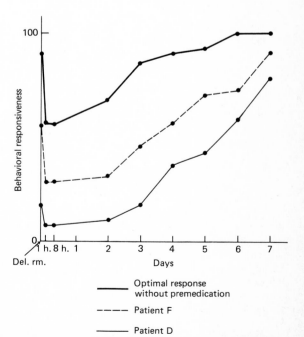

Figure 4   Behavioral Responsiveness of Neonates. *(Reprinted from the* American Journal for Diseases of Children, *volume 115, page 21, 1968.)*

conversely, that any depressant drug might delay and reduce the strength of the imprinting behavior.

We are all familiar with Bowlby's (6) concept of imprinting as it affects maternal behavior and the early mother-infant attachment. Watching a drugged mother and a depressed infant who must make a "go" with each other should stimulate us to reevaluate the routine use of premedication and anesthesia in pregnancy and delivery in the light of its effect on early mother-infant interaction as well as its lasting effect on their lives together.

In short, perhaps it is the combined responsibility of pediatricians and psychiatrists, who share a longer view of the effects of such intrauterine and postnatal experiences, to work together toward a more scientific, documented, and justified use of drugs, diets, and hormones in pregnancy.

REFERENCES

1 Apgar, V.: A Proposal for a New Method of Evaluation of the Newborn Infant, Current Researches in Anesthesia and Analgesia 32:260-268, 1960.
2 Baker, J. B. E.: The Effects of Drugs on the Fetus, Pharmacol. Rev. 12:37-90, 1960.
3 Berlin, C. M.: Effects of LSD Taken by Pregnant Women on Chromosomal Abnormalities of Offspring, Pediatric Herald, January and February 1969, p. 1.
4 Block, J. B., and Essman, W. B.: Growth Hormone Administration During Pregnancy: A Behavioral Difference in Offspring Rats, Nature 205:1136-1137, 1965.
5 Borgstedt, A. D., and Rosen, M. G.: Medication During Labor Correlated with Behavior and EEG of the Newborn, Amer. J. Dis. Child. 115:21-24, 1968.
6 Bowlby, J.: Attachment and Loss, vol. 1 of Attachment. New York: Basic Books, 1969.
7 Brazelton, T. B.: Psychophysiologic Reactions in the Neonate II: Effect of Maternal Medication, J. Pediat. 58:513-518, 1961.
8 Brazelton, T. B., Robey, J. S., and Collier, G. A.: Infant Development in the Zinacanteco Indians of Southern Mexico, Pediatrics 44:274-280, 1969.
9 Chess, S.: Individuality in Children, Its Importance to the Pediatrician, J. Pediat. 69:676-680, 1966.
10 Cobrinik, P. W., Hood, R. T., Jr., and Chusid, E.: Effect of Maternal Narcotic Addiction on the Newborn Infant, Pediatrics 24:288-290, 1959.
11 Conway, E., and Brackbill, Y.: Effect of Obstetrical Medication on Infant's Sensorimotor Behavior, read at the meeting of the Society for Research in Child Development, Santa Monica, Calif., March 1969.
12 Escalona, S. K., and Heider, G. M.: Prediction and Outcome. New York: Basic Books, 1959.
13 Feder, H. C., Phoenix, C. H., and Young, W. C.: Suppression of Feminine Behavior by Administration of Testosterone Propionate to Neonatal Rats, J. Endocr. 34:131-132, 1966.
14 Fouts, J. R., and Adamson, R. H.: Drug Metabolism in the Newborn Rabbit, Science 129:897-898, 1959.
15 Fries, M.: Psychosomatic Relationships Between Mother and Infant, Psychosom. Med. 6:159-162, 1944.
16 Henley, W. L., and Fitch, G. R.: Newborn Narcotic Withdrawal Associated with Regional Enteritis in Pregnancy, New York J. Med. 66:2565-2567, 1966.
17 Hess, E. H.: Effects of Meprobamate on Imprinting in Waterfowl, Ann. NY Acad. Sci. 67:724-733, 1957.
18 Hoffeld, D. R., McNew, J., and Webster, R. L.: Effect of Tranquilizing Drugs During Pregnancy on Activity of Offspring, Nature 218:357-358, 1968.
19 Jacobsen, C. S.: Association Between LSD in Pregnancy and Fetal Defects, personal communication, 1969.
20 Jondorf, W. R., Maickel, R. P., and Brodie, B. B.: Inability of Newborn Mice and Guinea Pigs to Metabolize Drugs, Biochem. Pharmacol. 1:352-354, 1958.
21 Kovach, J.: Effects of Autonomic Drugs on Imprinting, J. Comp. Physiol. Psychol. 57:183-187, 1964.
22 Kron, R. E., Stein, M., and Goddard, K. E.: Newborn Sucking Behavior Affected by Obstetric Sedation, Pediatrics 37:1012-1016, 1966.
23 Money, J., Ehrdardt, A. A., and Masica, D. N.: Fetal Feminization Induced by Androgen Insensitivity in the Testicular Feminizing Syndrome: Effect on Marriage and Maternalism, Johns Hopkins Med. J. 123:105-114, 1968.
24 Nichols, M. M.: Acute Alcohol Withdrawal Syndrome in a Newborn, Amer. J. Dis. Child. 133:714-715, 1967.
25 Ordy, J. M., Samarajski, T., and Collins, R. L.: Prenatal Chlorpromazine Effects on Liver, Survival, and Behavior of Mice Offspring, J. Pharmacol. Exp. Ther. 151:110-125, 1966.
26 Palmisano, P., and Cassidy, G.: Aspirin Linked to Diminished Binding Capacity in Neonates, Psychiatric Herald, January 10, 1969, pp. 1 & 7.
27 Ploman, L., and Persson, B.: On the Transfer of Barbiturates to the Human Fetus and Their Accumulation in Some of its Vital Organs. J. Obstet. Gynaec. Brit. Comm. 64:706-711, 1957.
28 Prechtl, H., and Beintema, D.: The Neurological Examination of the Full Term Normal Infant, Little Club Clinics in Developmental Medicine, No. 12. London: Heineman, 1964.
29 Russell, A.: Progesterone is Harmful to Male Fetus, Pediatric News, January 1969, p. 1.

30 Schaeffer, D.: Alcohol Withdrawal Syndrome in a Newborn of a Yukon Indian Mother, Canad. Med. Ass. J. 87:1333, 1962.

31 Van Leewen, G., Guthrie, R., and Stange, F.: Narcotic Withdrawal Reaction in a Newborn Infant Due to Codeine, Pediatrics 36:635-636, 1965.

32 Young, R. D.: Effects of Differential Early Experiences and Neonatal Tranquilization on Later Behavior, Psychol. Rep. 17:675-680, 1965.

33 Zamenhof, S., Van Marthens, E., and Margolis, F. L.: DNA (Cell Number) and Protein in Neonatal Brain: Alteration by Maternal Dietary Restriction, Science 160:322-323, 1968.

Reading 3

Care of the Mother

Marshall Klaus, M.D.
John Kennell, M.D.

"Mothers separated from their young soon lost all interest in those whom they were unable to nurse or cherish."

Pierre Budin, *The Nursling*

The significance of the early postpartum days to the mother infant relationship has recently been the focus of detailed investigation. Behavioral studies in humans and a wide range of animal studies[2,9,11,21] indicate that the events before and immediately following delivery may greatly influence later maternal behavior. This chapter reviews the recent human and animal studies and provides historical background which explains how mothers have been isolated from their infants in this country. Five cases are used to illustrate how presently available knowledge can be applied clinically.

HISTORY

The role of the mother in the hospital nursery for full-term and low-birth-weight infants has changed greatly during the last century. In the 1880s, rooming-in (still the popular mode in Europe) was prevalent in American hospitals.

The mother was welcomed into the premature nurseries of the Frenchman Pierre Budin (the first modern neonatologist) and was allowed to assist in her infant's care, for as Budin recognized in his book, *The Nursling*,[5] published in 1907, "Unfortunately . . . a certain number of mothers abandon the babies whose need they have not had to meet, and in whom they have lost all interest. The life of the little one has been saved, it is true, but at the cost of the mother." Mothers were therefore encouraged to breast feed their premature infants and

were advised in addition to nurse full-term infants to increase their milk production.

Ironically, Budin's desire to publicize his methods resulted in the exclusion of the mother from the nursery, Martin Cooney, a young pupil of Budin's, went to the Berlin Exposition of 1896, where his "Kinderbrutanstalt" (child hatchery), to which premature infants were brought and raised, became both commercially and clinically successful. After exhibiting at fairs in England and the United States, Cooney settled on Coney Island, successfully raising more than 5000 prematures during the next four decades. Mothers were not permitted to participate in their infant's care at Cooney's exhibits, and it is of significance that on some occasions Cooney experienced difficulty in persuading parents to take their infants back. In spite of the commercial aspect of Cooney's example, the early hospital nurseries in the United States adopted many of his methods of newborn care.

The high rate of morbidity and mortality of hospitalized patients in the early 1900s led to the development of strict isolation for patients with a large number of diseases. Visitors were strongly discouraged. Unfortunately, Cooney's example and the measures introduced to prevent the spread of infection were thus combined to totally exclude the mother from hospital nurseries.

The Sarah Morris Hospital in Chicago developed the first hospital center for premature care in 1923. Following the precepts of Budin, the director,

Hess, encouraged the production of breast milk at home and invited mother's assistance in caring for the infants.

However, in premature units created after the Sarah Morris Center, a standard set of stringent regulations was followed, including only essential handling of the infants, a policy of strict isolation, and the total exclusion of visitors.

During the period after World War II, several innovative approaches to newborn care appeared. In a study of the home-nursing of prematures in Newcastle-on-Tyne, Miller[22] noted that the mortality rate was only slightly greater than that of a control group nursed in hospital. A shortage of skilled personnel was the impetus for an arrangement created by Kahn et al[13] at Baragwanath Hospital, Johannesburg, South Africa. Here mothers were able to participate in supervised care and feeding of their infants while themselves remaining in hospital. This innovation was accompanied by a sharp decline in infant mortality.

Although mothers are still not admitted into most premature nurseries, many centers have recently begun to permit them to do so.

THE HUMAN MOTHER

Since the human infant depends entirely upon his mother to satisfy all his needs, emotional as well as physical, his mother's attachment to him is absolutely necessary for his optimal growth and development. Just exactly how these affectional bonds are formed and what influences may distort them are therefore of major importance. The actual process of attachment or bond formation is not yet completely understood, but a wide diversity of observations are beginning to piece together some of the various phases. The time periods which are apparently crucial for this process are shown in Table 1.

Pregnancy

Behavioral changes in the mother during this period have been described in detail.[2,3] Pregnancy for a woman has been considered as a process of maturation,[6] with a series of adaptive tasks, each dependent upon the successful completion of the preceding one. There are two general time periods during the pregnancy and another in the neonatal period during which a wide range of stressful factors may profoundly influence a woman's subse-

Table 1   Steps in Attachment[15]

Planning the pregnancy
Confirming the pregnancy
Accepting the pregnancy
Fetal movement
Accepting the fetus as an individual
Birth
Seeing the baby
Touching the baby
Caretaking

quent mothering behavior and ultimately the developmental outcome of her child.

Many mothers are initially disturbed by feelings of grief and anger when they become pregnant, because of factors ranging from economic and housing hardships to intrapersonal difficulties. However, by the end of the first trimester, the majority of women who initially rejected pregnancy have accepted it. This initial stage, as outlined by Bibring,[3] is the mother's identification of the growing fetus as an "integral part of herself."

The second stage is *a growing perception of the fetus as a separate individual,* usually occurring with the awareness of fetal movement. After quickening, a woman will generally begin to have some fantasies about what the baby may be like, will attribute to him some human personality characteristics, and will develop a sense of attachment and value toward him. At this time, further acceptance of the pregnancy and marked changes in attitude toward the fetus may be observed; unplanned, unwanted infants may now seem more acceptable. Objectively, the health worker will usually find some outward evidence of the mother's preparation by such actions as the purchase of clothes or a crib, selecting a name, arranging space for the baby.

Cohen[7] suggests the following questions to learn the special needs of each mother:

1   How long have you lived in this immediate area and where does most of your family live?
2   How often do you see your mother or other close relatives?
3   Has anything happened to you in the past (or do you currently have any condition) which causes you to worry about the pregnancy or the baby?
4   What was your husband's reaction to your becoming pregnant?

5 What other responsibilities do you have outside the family?

It is important to inquire about how the pregnant woman herself was mothered—did she have a neglected and deprived infancy and childhood or grow up with a warm and intact family life?

Delivery

Oddly enough, little data are available for this period. In agreement with veterinary experience, those mothers who remain relaxed in labor, who are supported and have good rapport with their attendants, are more apt to be pleased with their infants at first sight.[24] Unconsciousness during delivery does not seem to result in the rejection of the infant, as has been observed in some animals.

First Week after Delivery

The human mother after delivery appears to have a routine behavior pattern, as do other animal species. Filmed observations[24] show that a mother presented with her nude, full-term infant begins with fingertip touching of the infant's extremities and within a few minutes proceeds to massaging, encompassing palm contact of the infant's trunk. Mothers of premature infants also follow this sequence but proceed at a slower rate. We have observed that fathers go through some of the same routines. A strong interest in eye-to-eye contact was expressed by mothers of both full-term and premature infants. It has been suggested that eye-to-eye contact appears to initiate or release maternal caretaking responses. Coinciding with the mother's interest in the infant's eyes is the early functional development of his visual pathways; the infant is alert, attentive, and able to follow during the first hour of life.

In the immediate newborn period, the maternal affectional ties which have formed during pregnancy may easily be disturbed and affected permanently[16,25] by such minor problems as poor feeding, slight hyperbilirubinemia, and mild respiratory distress, even though the infant's problems are totally resolved before discharge.

The care of the mother at this early stage requires further study. When compulsory rooming-in was introduced at Duke University, the incidence of breast feeding increased (from 35 per cent to 58.5 per cent) and the number of anxious phone calls after discharge decreased 90 per cent. This suggests that close continual contact between mother and infant may indeed be an important factor in encouraging more relaxed maternal behavior.

Two long-term studies[2,15,19,21] are underway to attempt to evaluate the results of the prolonged mother-infant separation which is a routine procedure in premature and high-risk nurseries. Shortly after birth, mothers in one group (Early Contact) are admitted into the nursery, permitted to touch their infants, and, as the infant's condition permits, perform simple caretaking duties. Another group of mothers (Late Contact) is not permitted into the nursery until after their infants reach 20 days of age. If enforced long-term separation does affect the strength of attachment, then the results of this separation might be reflected in altered maternal behavior. Results to date reveal detectable differences in mothering performance as late as six months after birth. No increase in infection or disruption of nursery procedure has been noted when parents are allowed to visit their infants in the nursery.

In another study, one group of mothers of full-term infants were given 16 additional hours with their infants during the first four days of life and compared with mothers who had routine contact with their infants (20 to 30 minutes at a feeding every four hours). Maternal behavior was measured one month later using a standardized interview, an examination of the baby, and a filmed bottle feeding. . . .

These studies revealed that extended contact mothers showed greater soothing behavior and engaged in significantly more eye-to-eye contact and fondling during feeding, were additionally more reluctant to leave their infants with someone else, and usually stood and watched during the examination (Figure 1*A* and *B*). Interestingly enough, eleven months later the mothers were again significantly different during a physical examination. This simple modification of care shortly after delivery appeared to alter later maternal behavior and is support for a sensitive period in the human mother. This is of additional significance when taken in light of several observations[26] which show that increased maternal attentiveness facilitates later exploratory behavior in infants. Thus, these differences in mothers may have a potent influence on the later development of their infants.

Once these and similar studies have been completed, the evidence may reveal that widespread

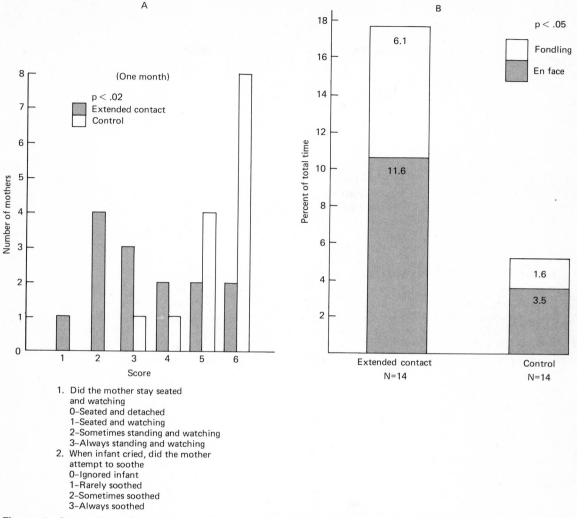

Figure 1 Summation of scores at one month.[18] *A.* Scores of performance from the observation of the mother during an office visit at one month post partum. *B.* Filmed feeding analysis at one month, showing percentage of "en face" and fondling times in mothers given extended contact with their infants and in the control group. (Fondling is defined as any spontaneous interaction initiated by the mother not associated with feeding, such as stroking, kissing, bouncing, or cuddling.)

alterations in hospital policies are required. There must be careful consideration of all the effects on the parents and babies before any changes are recommended. Most normal hospital deliveries result in several days during which the mother is deprived of many hours of contact with her healthy full-term infant; the mother of a premature must endure severe deprivation often until the 8th week of her baby's life. Using the levels of deprivation as categorized by Barnett[2] (Tables 2 and 3), it appears that only those mothers who room in or deliver at home have no period of deprivation.

The reactions of a mother to premature birth have been considered by some observers[14] as an

Table 2 Levels of Interactional Deprivation and Component Variables[2]

Levels of deprivation	Duration of deprivation	Sensory modalities of interaction	Caretaking nature of interaction
No deprivation	Full time	All senses	Complete
Partial deprivation	Part time	All senses	Partial
Moderate deprivation	Part time	All senses	None
Severe deprivation	Part time	Visual only	None
Complete deprivation	None	None	None

acute emotional crisis. Four psychological tasks have been postulated, through which a mother must progress: (1) anticipatory grief, or preparing for the death of the infant, (2) the realization and acceptance of her failure to deliver an infant at term, (3) resumption of the process of relating to her infant, and (4) learning the special needs of a premature and how he differs from full-term infants. It is not known at present if these four tasks would remain the same if the mother were able to live in close contact with her infant.

A great multitude of factors influence a mother's ability to endure emotional stress, her need for solicitous care, and ultimately her maternal behavior. Some of these major influences and the resultant distortions which may occur are outlined in

Figure 2. Some of these factors are already implanted and fixed at the time of delivery (e.g., how the mother herself was mothered as an infant, her cultural traditions, and her family relationships). Those influences which may be altered (indicated by dotted lines) include the physician's attitudes, policies, and statements; separation from the infant; and the infant himself, his personality as well as the state of his health. Obviously, one of the simplest variables to manipulate is whether or not a mother is separated from her infant after birth.

Also shown on this diagram are disorders or distortions of maternal behavior, which range from severe (the battered child syndrome) to mild (undue persistent concerns about a minor illness long since completely resolved). It is our contention that

Table 3 Deprivation Levels over Time, Related to Birth Situation[2]

Birth situation	Deprivation level. Days and weeks post partum					
	Day 0	Day 1	Day 3	Day 7	Week 8	Week 9
Home, full term	Partial deprivation	No deprivation	No deprivation	No deprivation	No deprivation	No deprivation
Hospital, full term, rooming-in	Moderate deprivation	No deprivation	No deprivation	No deprivation	No deprivation	No deprivation
Hospital, full term, regular care	Moderate deprivation	Partial deprivation	Partial deprivation	No deprivation	No deprivation	No deprivation
Premature, mother allowed in nursery	Complete deprivation	Severe deprivation	Moderate deprivation	Partial deprivation	Partial deprivation (discharge nursery)	No deprivation
Premature, regular care (separated)	Complete deprivation	Severe deprivation	Severe deprivation	Severe deprivation	Partial deprivation (discharge nursery)	No deprivation
Unwed mother, refuses contact	Complete deprivation	Complete deprivation	Complete deprivation	Complete deprivation	Complete deprivation	Complete deprivation

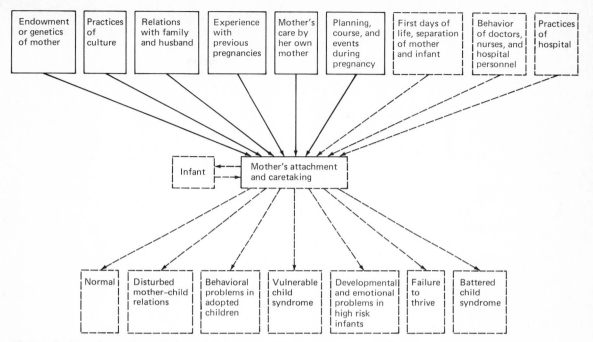

Figure 2 Disorders of mothering: A hypothesis of their etiology. Solid lines indicate determinants which are ingrained; dashed lines indicate factors which may be altered or changed.[17]

separation in the immediate newborn period may be a major component in these mothering disorders. Support for this hypothesis is the high number of premature infants who later return to the hospital with failure-to-thrive with no organic cause for the problem. Studies of failure-to-thrive infants have shown 15 to 30 per cent to have no organic disease; 25 to 41 per cent of this group were premature. Green and Solnit,[8] reporting on the vulnerable child syndrome (children whose parents expect them to die prematurely), noted that 44 per cent of these children were either born prematurely or were severely ill and separated from their mothers in the immediate newborn period.

In this country, adoptions generally take place when the infant is three to six weeks old. Perhaps if adoptions occurred at one day of life, the behavioral problems of the adopted child (which are far out of proportion to the incidence of adoption) would be decreased. In many societies, a substitute mother is ready at hand to take over when a mother dies at birth.

Probably the most dramatic manifestation of a mothering disorder is the battered child syndrome.[10] Unfortunately, authors reporting studies of the battered child usually fail to note whether or not the mothers and infants were separated following delivery. Combining two studies (totalling 44 patients) which did report birth weight or gestational age, 39 per cent of the patients were either premature or had suffered serious illness. The authors have recently learned of several cases in which battering occurred following the discharge of healthy normal prematures. These infants had been seriously ill after birth and separated from their parents for extended periods. Obviously, multiple influences are contributing to this problem, but one of the more significant factors may be separation. If prolonged separation occurs and anticipatory grief advances unduly, close affectional ties may never be securely established for the mother of a sick infant.

The relationship between prematurity, along with the question of prolonged separation of the mother from the child, and subsequent child battering has received considerable attention recently. In our own experience, we have found that the incidence of prematurity (with prolonged separation of the mother from the infant after birth) is three times as high among children who have subsequently been battered than among the general low-birth-weight incidence in the Province of Quebec. The difference is statistically highly significant and the contribution of this factor to what ultimately causes child battering should probably be taken into close consideration. It is understood that many other factors go into the ultimate relationship which results in this form of child abuse, but when viewed in this light, the early separation may play a crucial role in development of this disastrous situation.

L. STERN

It is of interest that study of behavior patterns in other cultures indicates that every society has some standard method of introducing a new member. In most cases, the mother and infant remain together, apart from other members, during the period required for the navel to heal. The mother has few if any responsibilities at this time apart from caring for her infant. There is no cultural practice except in the premature and high-risk nurseries of the Western world which routinely and completely separates a mother from her infant during the first days after birth.

ANIMAL STUDIES

As in other areas of neonatology, it has been useful to study mothers and infants of many species during the neonatal period. Although certain aspects of behavior differ from species to species, there are some overall patterns and trends which can be discerned. Despite the reluctance of many investigators to accept the concept that these patterns may apply to humans, the possibility of their extension to the human should not be neglected when they are found in a large number of species.

First, in goats, sheep, and cattle, when a mother is separated from her young in the first hour or the first few hours after delivery and then the two are reunited, the mother will show disturbances of mothering behavior, such as failure to care for her young, butting her own offspring away, and feeding her own and other babies indiscriminately.[11,20,23] In

contrast, if the mother and infant are kept together for the first four days and are separated on the fifth day for an equal period of time, the mother quickly returns to the maternal behavior characteristic of her species when the pair is reunited. It thus appears that there is a sensitive period immediately after delivery; if the animal mother is separated from her young during this interval, deviant maternal behavior may result. (It is important to note that not all mothers are equally affected by these early separations and that the disturbed mothering performance can be modified by special handling.) Surprisingly, in spite of this sensitive period, adoptions can be arranged. Sheep and goats can be induced to adopt strange lambs and kids—between as well as within species.[12] This requires delicate arrangements to prevent the mother from destroying the strange infant. The effects of early separation vary with the species. Harlow studied rhesus monkey mothers deprived of tactile contact but allowed to see and hear their infants.[9] After two weeks without any tactile contact, these mothers rapidly decreased the amount of time they spent viewing their infants. This indicated that viewing alone is not enough stimulus to maintain maternal interest.

Secondly, clear-cut, species-specific maternal behavior patterns such as nesting, retrieving, grooming, and exploring, have been observed in nonhuman mammalian mothers immediately after delivery. For example, in the cat during labor and just before delivery, the mother licks the genital region; then, following delivery, the mother licks the kitten completely, eats the membranes and placenta, and remains in close, almost constant physical contact through the first three to four days. This perinatal behavior may be severely distorted if the mother herself has received abnormal care as an infant,[4,9] or if the normal sequence of behavior is altered, as shown in Birch's experiments with rats. Noting the increased amount of self-licking (especially in the anogenital region) in the pregnant rat and hypothesizing that this self-licking might extend to the pups after delivery, Birch fashioned high collars which were placed on the necks of pregnant rats to prevent self-licking.[4] The collars were removed shortly before birth. These rats subsequently exhibited abnormal maternal behavior, such as waiting a long interval before initial licking of the pups, consuming them once licking began, and in the instance of pups surviving the licking period, refusing to allow them to suckle. No offspring survived the nursing period. Control mothers and mothers wearing collars similar to those described but notched to permit self-licking did not exhibit this aberrant behavior.

Thirdly, for some period after delivery, usually weeks or even months, animal mothers have characteristic patterns and orders of behavior. For example, the rhesus monkey mother grooms her infant more at one month than at other times. At five months she spends little time retrieving, whereas at 1½ months retrieving is maximum.[9] Recurring patterns of maternal behavior within a species can be distinguished in a large number of animal species. Careful observations in Uganda suggest that repeating sequences are also found in human mothers.[1]

REFERENCES

1　Ainsworth, M.: *Infancy in Uganda*. Baltimore, The Johns Hopkins Press, 1967.

2　Barnett, C., Leiderman, P., Grobstein, R., et al.: Neonatal separation: the maternal side of interactional deprivation. Pediatrics *45*:197, 1970.

3　Bibring, G.: Some considerations of the psychological processes in pregnancy. Psychoanl Stud Child *14*:113, 1959.

4　Birch, H.: Sources of order in the material behavior of animals. Amer J Orthopsychiat *26*:279, 1956.

5　Budin, P.: *The Nursling*. London, Caxton Publishing Co., 1907.

6　Caplan, G.: *Emotional Implications of Pregnancy and Influences on Family Relationships in the Healthy Child*. Cambridge, Harvard University Press, 1960.

7　Cohen, R.: Some maladaptive syndromes of pregnancy and the puerperium. Obstet Gynec *27*:562, 1966.

8　Green, M., and Solnit, A.: Reactions to the threatened loss of a child: a vulnerable child syndrome. Pediatrics, *34*:58, 1964.

9　Harlow, H., Harlow, M., and Hansen, E.: The maternal affectional system of rhesus monkeys. *In* Rheingold, H., Ed.: *Maternal Behavior in Mammals*. New York, John Wiley and Sons, 1963.

10　Helfer, R., and Kempe, C., Eds.: *The Battered Child*. Chicago, University of Chicago Press, 1968.

11　Hersher, L., Richmond, J., and Moore, A.: Maternal behavior in sheep and goats. *In* Rheingold, H., Ed.:

Maternal Behavior in Mammals. New York, John Wiley and Sons, 1963.

12　Hersher, L., Richmond, J., and Moore, A.: Modifiability of the critical period for the development of maternal behavior in sheep and goats. Behavior *20*: 311, 1963.

13　Kahn, E., Wayburne, S., and Fouceh, M.: The Baragwanath premature baby unit-an analysis of the case records of 1,000 consecutive admissions. South African Med J *28*:453, 1954.

14　Kaplan, D., and Mason, E.: Maternal reactions to premature birth viewed as an acute emotional disorder. Amer J Orthopsychiat *30*:359, 1960.

15　Kennell, J., and Klaus, M.: Care of the mother of the high-risk infant. Clin Obstet Gynec *14*:926, 1971.

16　Kennell, J., Slyter, H., and Klaus, M.: The mourning response of parents to the death of a newborn. New Engl J Med *283*:344, 1970.

17　Klaus, M., and Kennell, J.: Mothers separated from their newborn infants. Pediat Clin N Amer *17*:1015, 1970.

18　Klaus, M., Jerauld, R., Kreger, N., et al.: Maternal attachment: Importance of the first post-partum days. New Eng J Med *286*:460, 1972.

19　Klaus, M., Kennell, J., Plumb, N., et al.: Human maternal behavior at the first contact with her young. Pediatrics *46*:187, 1970.

20　Klopfer, P., Adams, D., and Klopfer, M.: Maternal "imprinting" in goats. Proc Nat Acad Sci USA *56*: 911, 1964.

21　Leifer, A., Leiderman, P., Barnett, C., et al.: Effects of mother-infant separation on maternal attachment behavior. Child Develop *43*:1203, 1972.

22　Miller, E.: Home nursing of premature babies in Newcastle-on-Tyne. Lancet *2*:703, 1948.

23　Moore, A.: Effects of modified care in the sheep and goat. *In* Newton, G., and Levine, S., Eds.: *Early Experience and Behavior*. Springfield, Charles C. Thomas, 1968, pp. 481–529.

24　Newton, N., and Newton, M.: Mothers' reactions to their newborn babies. JAMA *181*:206, 1962.

25　Rose, J., Boggs, R., Jr., Alderstein, A., et al.: The evidence for a syndrome of "mothering disability" consequent to threats to the survival of neonates: a design for hypothesis testing including prevention in a prospective study. Amer J Dis Child *100*:776, 1960.

26　Rubenstein, J.: Maternal attentiveness and subsequent exploratory behavior in the infant. Child Develop *38*:1089, 1967.

Reading 4

Malnutrition and Psychological Development

Henry N. Ricciuti

During the past 6 years or so, psychologists have become increasingly interested in the problem of nutritional influences on behavior and psychological development with particular reference to the question of whether nutritional deprivation early in life impairs the development of intellectual, social and motivational competencies in children. This growing interest developed in part as a consequence of the heightened social concern with malnutrition as a major public health problem in developing countries in Latin America, Africa and Asia and, more recently, in parts of the United States as well. At the same time, as a scientific question, the influence of nutritional deprivation on behavior development represents an issue of considerable importance for those investigators concerned with the broader problem of the interaction of biological, experiential and social influences on early development, in both human and infrahuman species.

A substantial body of evidence has been accumulating for some time now, indicating that children's health, physical growth and biological development may be seriously and even permanently impaired by the combination of severe malnutrition, infection and parasitic disease which are endemic in many regions of the world where conditions of extreme poverty prevail (32, 36). Public concern about malnutrition as a social problem, both in this country and elsewhere, has been accentuated considerably by the more recent but growing view that malnutrition early in life is not only a serious threat to children's health and physical development, but may also have adverse effects on the development of intellectual functions, social competence and adaptive behavior generally. By the mid 1960's, as this point of view was becoming quite prominent, it was based primarily on the following factors: growing evidence concerning reduced brain size and number of brain cells in seriously malnourished children (40, 41); animal studies indicating similar brain changes in early malnutrition, along with some impairment of performance in learning situations (1, 14); clinical observations by pediatricians

of psychological changes as well as pronounced motor retardation in children with protein-calorie malnutrition (17); and early reports of malnourished infants and children with markedly reduced developmental quotients (D.Q.'s) or intelligence quotients (I.Q.'s) on standardized tests (2, 7, 16).

During the period from approximately 1967 to 1969, when the White House Conference on Nutrition was held, and public concern with hunger and malnutrition in the United States was at a peak, there was a tendency in some circles at least to move rather prematurely from research findings indicating an association between malnutrition and impaired intellectual functioning, to somewhat oversimplified and, in some instances, rather exaggerated conclusions concerning a direct causal relationship between nutritional deprivation and mental retardation (33). Since that time, there has grown an increasing recognition of the fact that the relationships between nutritional deprivation and psychological development in children are quite complicated ones, involving a variety of associated social, environmental and biological factors, so that the problems are methodologically difficult to investigate and are not yet clearly understood.

What is the status of our present knowledge concerning the influence of malnutrition on intellectual development, learning and behavior in children? This paper focuses primarily on an identification of some of the major issues and questions which are of concern to investigators in the field, and through a selective review of representative studies, an attempt is made to indicate some of the major conclusions suggested by the research done thus far.

SOME DEFINITIONAL COMMENTS

The major concern of this review is with *undernutrition,* or malnutrition produced essentially by an insufficiency of protein and calories in the child's diet, commonly referred to as "protein-calorie malnutrition," which is regarded by many as the most serious nutritional problem on a world-wide basis (19). Some considerations will also be given, however, to recent research on specific nutritional deficiencies and intellectual development.

Protein-calorie malnutrition includes the conditions of *nutritional marasmus,* or starvation, usually beginning in the earliest months of life and continuing for an extended period, producing infants whose physical growth and motor development are grossly impaired; and *kwashiorkor,* due primarily to an insufficiency of protein, typically occurring as a rather acute illness toward the end of the 1st year or in the 2nd year of life, frequently after the birth of a younger sibling. Many combinations or mixtures of these two conditions are found in practice, and they vary greatly in severity and duration (35).

One of the important methodological problems in this area is that it is difficult to secure accurate assessments of nutritional status in children, particularly if one is concerned with measurement throughout a broad range of nutritional variation and not simply with clinically obvious and severe malnutrition. Three types of measures are usually employed: assessment of food intake from detailed dietary information; clinical or physical evaluations, including various anthropometric measures, particularly height, weight and head circumference; and biochemical evaluations of specific nutrients from blood and urine samples. The interpretation of such measures is considered quite difficult, particularly if one attempts to judge the adequacy of an individual's nutritional status from a single index, and many nutritionists feel that these assessments are most valid when used in combination with one another (39).

A final definitional comment has to do with the importance of distinguishing between hunger and malnutrition. The school child who frequently misses breakfast or lunch may perform poorly because of inattentiveness and distractibility associated with hunger. However, these potential influences on school performance and learning, about which we know very little, clearly need to be differentiated from those effects which are the result of long term protein-calorie malnutrition. Many severely malnourished children are characterized by apathy, withdrawal and loss of appetite, rather than by the increased activity and restlessness associated with hunger (12).

MAJOR QUESTIONS AND RESEARCH STRATEGIES

The specific research questions which are of major concern to investigators in this field may be summarized as follows:

1 Does malnutrition adversely influence learning, behavior and psychological development in children? How severe are these effects? Are they reversible with nutritional rehabilitation, or through the provision of enriched experience and stimulation?

2 How do the effects of malnutrition vary as a function of severity, age of onset, duration and the particular type of malnutrition involved?

3 Can the influence of malnutrition as such be isolated from the associated effects of those social, environmental and biological conditions typically involved in the ecology of human malnutrition? Perhaps more importantly, how do such conditions interact with malnutrition in jointly influencing psychological development?

4 Can we identify the particular behaviors and psychological processes which are most sensitive and those which are least sensitive to nutritional deprivation?

5 Finally, how are the behavioral effects of malnutrition mediated—for example, through brain changes leading to impaired ability to learn even under conditions of appropriate motivation and responsiveness or through dysfunctional changes in arousal thresholds or responsiveness to the environment?

Given these major questions, let us briefly consider some of the principal research strategies that have been employed by investigators in attempting to deal with them. Most studies of protein-calorie malnutrition and psychological development have been based on samples of children from poor populations in Latin America, Asia and Africa. A majority of them have involved the behavioral assessment of infants and children with a known or presumed history of malnutrition, whose performance is compared against some sort of standard or control group. Some of these investigations have dealt with protein-calorie malnutrition severe enough to require hospitalization and treatment some time in the first 2 or 3 years of life. Others have focused on children who presumably have been exposed to more moderate, chronic malnutrition, usually judged on the basis of restricted growth in stature and/or brain circumference.

The second major research strategy, employed increasingly in recent years, involves an essentially longitudinal approach, with major emphasis on the effects of various types of experimental intervention. Groups of children in situations where chronic malnutrition is endemic are provided with nutritional supplementation and improved medical care, and an evaluation is made of the behavioral consequences, as well as the nutritional and growth effects. More recently, we are beginning to see environmental stimulation included as an additional intervention.

A third approach, also longitudinal and considerably less common than those already mentioned, involves ecologically oriented, relatively detailed studies of the growth and development of samples of children from birth in settings where a good many children are clearly at risk with regard to malnutrition. The assumption here is that because of natural variation in such a population, it will be possible to study prospectively those conditions which lead to the development of malnutrition in some children and not in others in the same environment (10).

STUDIES OF SEVERE MALNUTRITION

Let's consider first studies of protein-calorie malnutrition severe enough to markedly curtail physical growth and to require hospitalization in the first several years of life. In general, these investigations have found early and severe malnutrition to be associated with substantially reduced levels of intellectual performance, even in the early preschool years.

One of the early and well known studies of this kind was carried out in Mexico City in the early 1960's by Cravioto and Robles (13). Twenty infants hospitalized for severe protein-calorie malnutrition were examined with the Gesell Infant Test every 2 weeks during treatment, which lasted as long as 6 months for some children. All infants were well below age norms on the Gesell scale shortly after admission, with developmental quotients mainly below 60. Moreover, children who had been admitted for treatment between 15 and 42 months of age showed considerable improvement in Gesell per-

formance during rehabilitation whereas those admitted between 3 and 6 months of age, whose weight retardation seemed more severe, showed virtually no recovery of their developmental deficit during the period of nutritional rehabilitation.

In a similar study conducted more recently in Beirut, Yaktin and McLaren (42) administered the Griffiths Mental Development Scale every 2 weeks to a sample of hospitalized infants during a 4-month period of treatment for severe marasmus. At the time of hospitalization, when the children were between 2½ and 16 months of age, their average developmental quotient was approximately 50. During treatment there was a steady improvement in the D.Q.'s, which reached the low 70's after the 4 months of rehabilitation. While one-half of the children were cared for in an ordinary five-bed pediatric ward with the usual caretaking routines, the other half were provided with environmental and social stimulation through a more complex material environment and additional caretaking and play activities. The stimulated infants showed a slightly greater degree of improvement than the nonstimulated group, although this differential was not significant.

Several very recent studies of hospitalized malnourished children have utilized carefully matched, nonmalnourished control groups and have begun to examine nutritional consequences on specific cognitive or learning functions, as well as on developmental test performance. Chase and Martin (9), working in Colorado, studied 20 children who had been hospitalized for protein-calorie malnutrition before the age of 1 year. When these children were examined approximately 3½ years later with the Yale Revised Developmental Examination, those who had been admitted and treated some time during the first 4 months of life had essentially normal developmental quotients, equivalent to the control group mean of 99. On the other hand, the children who had been hospitalized and treated some time between 4 and 12 months of age had a significantly lower development quotient with a mean of 70. The latter group, which presumably had been malnourished for a longer period of time without treatment, was also more retarded in physical growth, both at the time of hospitalization and on follow-up 3½ years later. It should be mentioned that the infants in this investigation, who were hospitalized for 16 days on the average, were not as severely malnourished as most infants included in the previously mentioned studies from Latin America and Lebanon.

While the aforementioned study involved a careful matching of malnourished and control subjects on social, family and environmental factors, the authors point out the great difficulty of separating undernutrition from the influence of these associated environmental factors. This caution is based on the fact that despite the careful matching, there was a higher incidence of social problems and stress in the homes of the malnourished children, whose mothers also had significantly lower scores on an index of home stimulation.

A careful controlled study still underway in Chile, conducted by Kardonsky and co-workers (20), also provides evidence of reduced intellectual functioning in preschool children hospitalized for severe malnutrition in the 1st year of life. At about 3 to 4 years of age, these children had a mean I.Q. of 73, although when reexamined 2 years later, there was a considerable improvement in their intellectual functioning. Moreover, children whose malnutrition occurred earlier, as judged by weight deficit, and whose recovery was more rapid, tended to have less marked I.Q. deficits, a finding consistent with those of Chase and Martin. In a series of other tests of specific psychological functions, the Santiago group are finding that malnourished children show increased excitability and reduced exploratory behavior, results consistent with recent behavior studies with pigs, rats and rhesus monkeys (25).

Another investigation of specific cognitive functioning in severely malnourished children was done by Brockman and Ricciuti (6), working with children from 12 to 43 months of age who had been hospitalized for severe marasmus in Lima, Peru, sometime between $2^{1}/_{2}$ and 42 months of age. Using simple sorting tasks to assess categorizing behavior, it was found that the malnourished children performed substantially and significantly less well than a control group selected from the same population on the basis of their greater height. Moreover, children with a longer period of nutritional treatment, with greater gains in body length and head circumference during treatment and with high medical ratings of nutritional recovery tended to perform better on the cognitive tasks.

Several studies in Mexico (11), India (8) and Jamaica (18) provide evidence that even school-age children hospitalized for severe malnutrition during the first 2 to 3 years of life do not perform as well as carefully matched control children without such a history. For the most part, however, the investigators themselves caution that while early malnutrition may well be implicated as an important determinant of the differences reported, the same environmental and social factors which contributed to the development of malnutrition in some children and not in others in the same environment may also contribute directly to the observed reduction in intellectual performance.

Generally speaking, then, there is reasonably good evidence that severe protein-calorie malnutrition in the 1st year of life may have adverse effects on intellectual development in children. The more severe the nutritional deprivation, and the longer it continues without rehabilitation, the greater the likelihood of substantial intellectual impairment, in some instances persisting into the early school years. On the other hand, if nutritional treatment and rehabilitation occur early in the 1st year, the chances of recovery of normal intellectual functioning appear very good. Although the data are not entirely clear, it appears as though severe malnutrition beginning in the 2nd or 3rd years of life produces effects which are less marked and more amenable to rehabilitation. In both instances, however, it is not yet entirely clear whether postnatal malnutrition, as such, is the primary determinant of impaired intellectual functioning, or how it may interact with socioenvironmental influences in producing such effects.

MODERATE MALNUTRITION

There have been a number of studies of children having experienced more moderate, chronic malnutrition, judged usually on the basis of restricted physical growth, particularly in height, weight or head circumference. While these children often manifest reduced levels of intellectual functioning, one cannot attribute these effects directly and solely to malnutrition. The problem is that differences in stature, which may well reflect differences in nutritional history, are also associated with a variety of other social characteristics of the environment, or biological characteristics of the individual, which are themselves capable of influencing intellectual development (15, 30, 31).

A frequently quoted study by Stock and Smythe in South Africa provides a good example of these interpretive difficulties (37). A small group of children between 1 and 3 years of age, who showed markedly reduced height, weight and head circumference, were followed over an 11-year period with periodic assessments of physical and intellectual development. These undernourished children scored consistently lower than a taller control group by 15 to 20 I.Q. points on various intelligence scales, and their educational placement was considerably behind average. However, since the control children came from more stable homes with markedly better living conditions and were attending an all day nursery school when the study began, it is impossible to determine to what extent the observed performance differences were attributable to malnutrition.

Several studies of tall and short school age children in Latin America raise similar interpretive problems. For example, in a Guatemalan village study of 6- to 11-year-old children (12), tall children tended to make fewer errors in identifying geometric forms on the basis of integrating visual, haptic and kinesthetic information, particularly in the younger age groups. Although tall and short groups were generally equivalent in a number of socioenvironmental background factors, maternal education was markedly higher in the case of the tall children, who may thus have had more opportunities for learning. In a more recent study of 1- to 5-year-old children in Chile (27), a substantial correlation ($r = 0.71$) was found between mother's I.Q. and the children's growth in height. Thus, while mother's intellectual competence may well influence the adequacy of nutritional care she provides her children, it may at the same time account at least in part for observed differences in the children's intellectual functioning, through genetic influences, and/or through the social and learning environments available to the children.

Several recent investigations of moderate malnutrition in preschool children are of particular interest because they provide additional examples of the growing trend toward the assessment and analysis of specific perceptual-cognitive, learning and motivational functions which might be influenced by nutritional deprivation. One of the best illustrations of this approach may be found in some preliminary

studies by Klein and co-workers in Guatemala (21), contrasting the performance of 5-year-old children previously treated for malnutrition at a rehabilitation clinic with the performance of taller control children from generally similar social backgrounds. The malnourished children performed more poorly than controls on two tests of short term memory and two perceptual discrimination tasks, all of which placed a high premium on sustained attention. On the other hand, the groups did not differ on 11 other tests, including measures of simple recall, vocabulary, visual-haptic matching, simple discrimination learning and exploratory behavior. A careful analysis of their results suggested to Klein and his colleagues that the performance differences observed in these children reflect primarily differences in attention and task concentration, rather than differences in perceptual-cognitive or memory capacity as such. This general view is compatible with other recent observations of malnourished preschool children in Colombia (23) and also with recent animal work (25).

With respect to the influence of moderate protein-calorie malnutrition, then, research thus far suggests that effects on psychological development are much less pronounced and consistent than is the case for severe and early malnutrition. Moreover, the particular contribution of nutritional factors, relative to the role played by concomitant social and environmental influences, is not at all clear. At the same time there is growing evidence indicating that the major influence of malnutrition may be upon attentional, arousal or motivational responses in children, rather than upon basic cognitive or learning competencies.

INTERVENTION STUDIES

Of increasing importance, from the point of view of both research and remediation, are the current efforts to evaluate the effects of various types of experimental intervention aimed at preventing or remedying the adverse consequences of malnutrition. For example, several rather elaborate studies of the long term effects of nutritional supplementation and improved health care on both the physical and psychological development of children at risk of malnutrition are presently underway in both Guatemala (22) and Colombia (23).

Some preliminary findings of considerable interest have been reported by the McKays in Colombia

(26), concerned with the effects of both nutritional remediation and cognitive enrichment. Preschool-age children identified as having been moderately malnourished were provided with nutritional supplementation and added health care. One group had in addition a 5-month preschool experience involving a program of cognitive stimulation as well as training in number and letter recognition skills. The preschool program of cognitive stimulation increased the intellectual performance of the malnourished children to about the same level as that achieved by nonstimulated, taller controls from the same environment, but considerably below the level achieved by controls who had also been cognitively stimulated. Nutritional and health care alone, without stimulation, produced no greater improvement in performance over the 5-month period than that shown by several normal and malnourished groups receiving no treatment of either kind. As one might expect, the greatest gains came from training on specific number and letter naming skills by both normal and malnourished children, who had virtually identical scores before and after training. Although this research has some methodological complications which make interpretation difficult, the results so far suggest that intellectual consequences of moderate malnutrition may be amenable to substantial remediation through nutritional supplementation and appropriate educational experiences, which may have a greater corrective impact than nutritional improvement and health care alone. Compatible with this view are the results of recent animal work suggesting that behavioral effects of early malnutrition can be greatly minimized or eliminated by additional stimulation early in life (24).

SPECIFIC DEFICIENCIES

In the past few years, with the increase in broad scale surveys of nutritional deficiencies in disadvantaged populations in this country (39), a number of investigators have examined relationships between intellectual functioning and specific deficiencies in such nutrients as iron or vitamins. In some instances, the intellectual consequences of nutritional treatment of these deficiencies has also been investigated. In a recent survey of nutritional deficiencies in disadvantaged preschool children in Nashville, Tennessee, Sandstead and co-workers (34) found no relationship between Stanford-Binet

I.Q. and a variety of biochemical indices of nutritional status. It should be mentioned, however, that these were children with mild degrees of malnutrition (only 5 per cent had hemoglobin values below 10.5 gm. per 100 ml.).

In a recent study by Beller and Howell (3), a variety of intellectual and perceptual tests were given to nearly 100 4- to 6-year-old children with mild to moderate iron deficiency anemia, who were enrolled in Philadelphia day care centers. No I.Q. differences were found between the anemic children and nonanemic controls from the same day care groups, a finding consistent with those of the Nashville study just mentioned. Moreover, relatively few differences were found between the two groups in the extensive battery of perceptual measures employed. It is of interest that these differences were in the areas of attention and task concentration, the same functions which appeared vulnerable to moderate nutritional deprivation in some of the previously mentioned studies. After 2 months of iron treatment administered to one-half of the anemic children, there were essentially no clear changes in intellectual or perceptive functioning which could be attributed to the nutritional remediation. It should be noted, however, that the iron treatment also failed to produce a significant increase in hemoglobin level for the treated as compared to the nontreated anemic children.

In contrast to the two studies just mentioned, Sulzer and co-workers (38) found that more severe iron deficiency anemia, when associated with growth retardation suggestive of longer term undernutrition, was related to reduced performance on several tests on intellectual functioning, including associative reaction time. No relationships were found with object sorting, short term memory and syntactic memory, however.

On the basis of research done thus far, it does not appear that moderate deficiencies in specific nutrients such as iron or vitamin B_1 have very substantial or lasting effects on psychological functioning in children, in the absence of more pervasive malnutrition; nor will nutritional supplementation with such specific nutrients alone produce appreciable changes in levels of performance. Whether more severe and prolonged dietary deficiencies in these nutrients might affect children's learning and intellectual development is not yet clear, and further research on the problem is certainly warranted.

In the interest of brevity, no attempt has been

made to deal with the important topic of maternal and fetal nutrition. Suffice it to say that severe maternal malnutrition during pregnancy and substantial deficiencies in the mother's previous nutritional and growth history, represent important contributing influences involved in the production of low birth weight, high risk infants whose subsequent psychological and behavioral development may be significantly impaired (4, 28). It is extremely difficult, of course, to isolate the influence of maternal nutritional deprivation as such from the many other complications and abnormalities of pregnancy, labor and birth which may have substantial adverse effects on the child's development. Nevertheless, severe deficiencies in the mother's nutrition, growth and health care during her previous life span, as well as during pregnancy, increase substantially the risk of behavioral and mental subnormality in the infant and child (5, 29).

SUMMARY AND CONCLUSIONS

Let me now try to summarize briefly the major points of this review, in the context of the main questions which were posed at the outset. Impairment of intellectual and psychological development in children as a consequence of protein-calorie malnutrition appears most likely to occur and to be rather severe and long lasting, to the extent that nutritional deprivation begins in the 1st year, is very severe and continues for an extended period of time without nutritional remediation. Extreme conditions of this sort are associated with borderline or more severe mental subnormality, sometimes persisting into the preschool and early school years. On the other hand, severe early malnutrition which is subject to adequate nutritional remediation within the first 5 or 6 months of life appears relatively unlikely to reduce intellectual functioning below normal or near normal levels. In contrast with nutritional marasmus, which typically begins in the 1st year, the condition of kwashiorkor, with typical onset in the 2nd year or later, seems to produce behavioral effects which are considerably less severe and more amenable to remediation. Psychological consequences of the mild to moderate malnutrition found in many socially disadvantaged populations are quite unclear and appear to be rather slight and relatively reversible. Effects of moderate deficiencies in specific nutrients like iron or vitamins upon intellectual functioning seem even more questionable.

While severe malnutrition seems clearly implicated as one determinant of impaired intellectual development, it has been extremely difficult to isolate this influence from that of various social, educational, family and child rearing conditions typically associated with malnutrition and capable of exerting major influences on psychological development of their own right. It seems reasonable to infer that when malnutrition is severe, early and enduring without treatment, it plays a substantial if not major role in shaping the course of subsequent psychological development, relative to the other conditions mentioned. On the other hand, it appears very likely that mild or moderate malnutrition plays a relatively minor part in determining children's intellectual development, in comparison with the substantial influence of various social, environmental and genetic factors.

It is not yet entirely clear what specific behavioral functions and psychological characteristics are most vulnerable to nutritional deprivation and how such effects are mediated, although current research with both animals and humans is addressed increasingly to precisely these questions. Evidence from these studies suggests that malnutrition may exert its major influence on behavior through dysfunctional changes in attention, responsiveness, motivation and emotionality, rather than through a more direct impairment of basic learning and cognitive competencies. It is also well recognized that some behavioral effects of severe malnutrition may be very indirect, brought about by changes in the way parents or other caregivers respond to and interact with the severely malnourished child.

The comments just made have clear implications with regard to the broad question of reversibility and remediation. Most of the evidence suggesting long term intellectual impairment in the case of severe malnutrition is based on studies in which remediation was directed primarily at the nutritional and health needs of the children and not at the social environment which contributed to the development of malnutrition and lower levels of intellectual functioning in the first place. It is in this environment that the severely malnourished children's I.Q.'s fail to show substantial improvement, although some gains do occur. Programs of remediation which provide an enrichment of the child's social and learning environment in day care, school, home and community settings, along with continuing nutritional and health care, may well reveal that the psychological and behavioral effects of even rather severe malnutrition may be amenable to substantial long term remediation and prevention. Programs of this sort are obviously of the highest priority from the point of view of human welfare and social action; they also represent the most fruitful research approach to the question of long term behavioral consequences of protein-calorie malnutrition.

REFERENCES

1 Barnes, R. H., Cunnold, S. R., Zimmerman, R. R., Simmons, H., MacLeod, R. B. and Krook, L.: Influence of nutritional deprivations in early life on learning behavior of rats as measured by performance in a water maze. J. Nutr., *89:*399–410, 1966.

2 Barrera-Moncada, G.: *Estudios sobre alteraciónes del crecimiento y del desarrollo psicologico del sindrome pluricarencial (kwashiorkor).* Editora Grafos, Caracas, 1963.

3 Beller, E. K. and Howell, D. A.: A study of anemia and mental functioning in underprivileged children. Presented at International Congress of Pediatrics, Vienna, 1971.

4 Bergner, L. and Susser, M. W.: Low birth weight and prenatal nutrition: An interpretative review. Pediatrics, *46:*946–966, 1970.

5 Birch, H. G. and Gussow, J. D.: *Disadvantaged Children: Health, Nutrition, and School Failure.* Harcourt-Brace Jovanovich Inc., New York, 1970.

6 Brockman, L. M. and Ricciuti, H. N.: Severe protein-calorie malnutrition and cognitive development in infancy and early childhood. Dev. Psychol., *4:*312–319, 1971.

7 Cabak, V. and Najdanvic, R.: Effect of undernutrition in early life on physical and mental development. Arch. Dis. Child., *40:*532–534, 1965.

8 Champakam, S., Srikantia, S. G. and Gopalan, C.: Kwashiorkor and mental development. Am. J. Clin. Nutr., *21:*844–852, 1968.

9 Chase, H. P. and Martin, H. P.: Undernutrition and child development. N. Engl. J. Med., *282:*933–936, 1970.

10 Cravioto, J., Birch, H. G., DeLicardie, E., Rosales, L. and Vega, L.: The ecology of growth and development in a Mexican pre-industrial community. Monogr. Soc. Res. Child Dev., *34:*1–65, 1969.

11 Cravioto, J. and DeLicardie, E. R.: Mental performance in school age children. Am. J. Dis. Child., *120:*404, 1970.

12 Cravioto, J., DeLicardie, E. R. and Birch, H. G.: Nutrition, growth and neurointegrative development: An experimental and ecologic study. Pediatrics, *38:*319–372, 1966.

13 Cravioto, J. and Robles, B.: Evolution of adaptive and motor behavior during rehabilitation from kwashiorkor. Am. J. Orthopsychiatry, *35:*449–464, 1965.

14 Dobbing, J.: Effects of experimental undernutrition on development of the nervous system. In *Malnutrition, Learning and Behavior,* N. S. Scrimshaw and J. E. Gordon, eds., pp. 181–202. Massachusetts Institute of Technology Press, Cambridge, 1968.

15 Douglas, J. W. B. and Blomfield, J. M.: Environmental influences on physical growth. In *Behavior in Infancy and Early Childhood,* Y. Brackbill and G. G. Thompson, eds., pp. 525–532. Free Press, Division of Macmillan Co., New York, 1967.

16 Gerber, M. and Dean, R. F.: Psychological changes accompanying kwashiorkor. Courier, *6:*3–15, Jan. 1956.

17 Gomez, F., Galvan, R. R., Crovioto, J. and Frenk, S.: Malnutrition in infancy and childhood, with special reference to kwashiorkor. In *Advances in Pediatrics,* S. Z. Levine, ed., Vol. 7, pp. 131–169. Yearbook Publishers, Chicago, 1954.

18 Hertzig, M. E., Birch, H. G., Richardson, S. A. and Tizard, J.: Intellectual levels of school children severely malnourished during the first two years of life. Pediatrics, *49:*814–824, 1972.

19 Jelliffe, D. B.: Protein-calorie malnutrition in tropical pre-school children. J. Pediatr., *54:*227, 1959.

20 Kardonsky, V., Alvarado, M., Undurraga, O., Manterola, A. and Segure, T.: Desarrollo intelectual y fisico en el niño desnutrido. Unpublished manuscript, Department of Psychology, University of Chile and Hospital Roberto del Rio, Santiago, 1971.

21 Klein, R. E., Gilbert, O., Canosa, C. and DeLeon, R.: Performance of malnourished in comparison with adequately nourished children (Guatemala). Presented at The American Association for the Advancement of Science meetings, Boston, December 1969.

22 Klein, R. E., Habicht, J. P. and Yarbrough, C.: Some methodological problems in field studies of nutrition and intelligence. In *Nutrition, Development and Social Behavior,* D. J. Kallen, Ed., pp. 61–75. United States Government Printing Office, Department of Health, Education and Welfare Publication NIH 73-242, Washington, D.C., 1973.

23 Latham, M. C. and Cobos, F.: The effects of malnutrition on intellectual development and learning. Am. J. Public Health, *61:*1307–1324, 1971.

24 Levitsky, D. A. and Barnes, R. H.: Nutritional and environmental interactions in the behavioral development of the rat: Long-term effects. Science, *176:*68, 1972.

25 Levitsky, D. A. and Barnes, R. H.: Malnutrition and animal behavior. In *Nutrition, Development and Social Behavior,* D. J. Kallen, ed., pp. 3–16. United States Government Printing Office, Department of Health, Education and Welfare Publication NIH 73-242, Washington, D.C., 1973.

26 McKay, H. E., McKay, A. and Sinisterra, L.: Behavioral intervention studies with malnourished children: A review of experiences. In *Nutrition, Development and Social Behavior,* D. J. Kallen, ed., pp. 121–145. United States Government Printing Office, Department of Health, Education and Welfare Publication NIH 73-242, Washington, D.C., 1973.

27 Monckeberg, F., Tisler, S., Toro, S., Gattas, V. and Vegal, L.: Malnutrition and mental development. Am. J. Clin. Nutr., *25:*766–772, 1972.

28 Osofsky, H.: Antenatal nutrition: Its relationship to subsequent infant and child development. Am. J. Obstet. Gynecol., *105:*1150–1159, 1969.

29 Ounsted, M.: Fetal growth and mental ability. Dev. Med. Child Neurol., *12:*222–224, 1970.

30 Pollitt, E.: Ecology, malnutrition and mental development. Psychosom. Med., *31:*193–200, 1969.

31 Pollitt, E. and Ricciuti, H.: Biological and social correlates of stature among children living in the slums of Lima, Peru. Am. J. Orthopsychiatry, *39:*735–747, 1969.

32 *Pre-school children malnutrition: Primary deterrent to human progress.* National Academy of Sciences, National Research Council, Washington, D.C., 1966.

33 Ricciuti, H. N.: Malnutrition, learning and intellectual development: Research and remediation. In *Psychology and the Problems of Society.* American Psychological Association, Washington, D.C., 1970.

34 Sandstead, H. H., Carter, J. P., House, F. R., McConnell, F., Horton, K. B. and Vander Zwaag, R.: Nutritional deficiencies in disadvantaged pre-school children: Their relationship to mental development. Am. J. Dis. Child., *121:*455–463, 1971.

35 Scrimshaw, N. S.: Malnutrition and the health of children. J. Am. Diet. Assoc., *42:*203–208, 1963.

36 Scrimshaw, N. S. and Gordon, J. E., eds.: *Malnutrition, Learning and Behavior,* Massachusetts Institute of Technology Press, Cambridge, 1968.

37 Stoch, M. and Smythe, P. M.: Undernutrition during infancy and subsequent brain growth and intellectual development. In *Malnutrition, Learning and Behavior,* N. S. Scrimshaw and J. E. Gordon, eds., pp. 278–288. Massachusetts Institute of Technology Press, Cambridge, 1968.

38 Sulzer, J. L., Hansche, W. J. and Koenig, F.: Nutrition and behavior in Head Start Children: Results from the Tulane study. In *Nutrition, Development and Social Behavior,* D. J. Kallen, ed., pp. 77–106. United States Government Printing Office, Department of Health, Education and Welfare Publication NIH 73-242, Washington D.C., 1973.

39 Ten State Nutrition Survey 1968–1970. United States Department of Health, Education and Welfare, Health Services and Mental Health Administration. Center for Disease Control, Atlanta, Georgia. Department of Health, Education and Welfare Publication (HSM) 72-8131, 1972.

40 Winick, M. and Rosso, P.: The effect of severe early malnutrition on cellular growth of the human brain. Pediatr. Res., *3:*181–184, 1969.

41 Winick, M. and Rosso, P.: Head circumference and cellular growth of the brain in normal and marasmic children. J. Pediatr., *74:*774–778, 1969.

42 Yaktin, U. S. and McLaren, D. S.: The behavioral development of infants recovering from severe malnutrition. J. Ment. Defic. Res., *14:*25–32, 1970.

Reading 5

Fetal Androgens, Human Central Nervous System Differentiation, and Behavior Sex Differences

Anke A. Ehrhardt
Susan W. Baker

The role of prenatal hormones in the central nervous system differentiation that mediates aspects of postnatal behavior of rats and monkeys has already been extensively reviewed. We now continue the discussion on prenatal hormone levels and their possible effects on behavior as relevant for *human* sex differences.

In the area of human behavior, evidence of fetal hormonal influences is much harder to obtain since it is impossible to design careful experiments analogous to planned animal research studies. Instead we are limited to research on spontaneously occurring clinical conditions with a known history of prenatal hormonal aberrations.

One such clinical condition will be the center of the next two chapters: the adrenogenital syndrome.

THE ADRENOGENITAL SYNDROME

The adrenogenital syndrome (AGS) is a condition in which the adrenal glands have a genetically determined defect in their function from fetal life on. The syndrome is transmitted as an autosomal recessive, which implies that both parents have to be carriers to produce one or several children with the illness. The genetic defect prevents the adrenal cortices from synthesizing cortisol. Instead the adrenal cortices release too much of another adrenal hormone that is androgenic in biological action, that is, a male sex hormone.

In the genetic female with AGS, excessive androgen production before birth masculinizes the external genitalia to varying degrees, in some cases only affecting the clitoris (enlargement) and in others also the formation of the labia (labial fusion). The masculinization of the genitalia is restricted to the external sex organs. The internal reproductive organs are differentiated as female. Postnatally, with proper endocrine management, the adrenal androgen output is regulated with life-long cortisone replacement therapy. With proper treatment, puberty, secondary sex characteristics, and female reproductive function are normal in female AGS patients, although menses tend to be of late onset (1). The masculinized external genitalia can be surgically feminized soon after birth.

The adrenogenital syndrome also occurs in genetic males, usually with no noticeable effect on the genitalia. Boys with AGS also have to be treated with cortisone; otherwise the excessive adrenal output of androgen will induce early male pubertal development. However, if corrected with early and regular cortisone replacement, boys with AGS will grow up looking like normal boys of their age.

Different subtypes of AGS occur, including one with an increased tendency to salt loss and another with hypertension. These additional traits of the clinical condition are not of particular concern here since the matter of interest in this context is the exposure to too much androgen before birth.

Genetic females with AGS are in many respects a human analogue to genetic female rats, guinea pigs, and monkeys who were experimentally exposed to androgens during the prenatal and/or neonatal critical period of central nervous system differentiation. Genetic males with AGS represent a human analogue to genetic male animals who were experimentally treated with additional amounts of androgens before and/or around birth.

Of special importance for the discussion of the effects of prenatal hormones on postnatal human behavior are those children with AGS who are regulated with cortisone at an early age, so that postnatal continuing developmental masculiniza-

tion is prevented. With early regular cortisone-replacement therapy and, in the case of females, after surgical correction of the external genitalia, children with AGS grow up looking like normal boys and girls.

PURPOSE

The studies concerning the effects of prenatal hormones on behavior in human females were started at The Johns Hopkins Hospital with John Money several years ago. At that time 10 girls with progestin-induced hermaphroditism and 15 girls with early-treated AGS, between 4 and 6 years old, were evaluated and compared with matched normal control girls (2–5).* In brief, the results of these earlier studies suggested that fetally androgenized females were different from normal control girls in that they displayed a higher level of physical energy expenditure in rough outdoor play and a lesser interest in dolls and other typical female childhood rehearsal of adult female roles in fantasy and play; they were also more often identified as long-term tomboys and preferred boys over girls as playmates. The question whether the behavior modifications were related to a group difference in fetal hormone history or to any other postnatal environmental variable is difficult to answer.

The goal of our more recent studies in Buffalo was to evaluate a comparable sample of fetally androgenized genetic females at another hospital to validate or disprove the findings at Johns Hopkins. In addition, we made a change in research design. In order to have both the experimental group and control group from a social environment as similar as possible, we evaluated complete families with one or more children with AGS. We also included not only genetic females but also genetic males with AGS. Females with AGS were compared with female siblings and mothers, and males with AGS were compared with male siblings. The project has two parts: one was aimed at behavior comparisons (the subject of this chapter), the other dealt with intelligence and cognitive abilities, and will be described in Chapter 4.

As to sexually dimorphic behavior, the following group comparisons will be reported: (1) genetic

---

*Progestin-induced hermaphroditism occurred in genetic daughters of mothers who had been treated with progestinic drugs during pregnancy to prevent miscarriage. The drugs sometimes had an unexpected virilizing effect on the daughters' external genitalia.

AGS females versus "unaffected" female siblings (i.e., female siblings who do not manifest AGS) and their mothers; (2) genetic AGS males versus "unaffected" male siblings (i.e., male siblings who do not manifest AGS).

The hypotheses can be formulated as follows:

1 Genetic females with a known history of high levels of prenatal androgen have been shown in previous studies at Johns Hopkins to differ as a group from normal control girls in some aspects of gender-related behavior. If similar differences in behavior can be documented for AGS females compared with unaffected female siblings and mothers who share many aspects of their social environment, this finding is more likely also related to a difference in prenatal history, rather than solely to social environmental factors.

2 Genetic AGS males may be exposed to even higher levels of prenatal androgen than normal males. If so, they may differ from unaffected male siblings in some aspects of typically masculine behavior. The underlying (unproved) assumption is that excessive androgen for the male fetus may affect the central nervous system and be related to a pronounced pattern of postnatal masculine behavior.

METHODS
Sample Selection and Characteristics

The sample for our family study in Buffalo consists of 27 patients—17 females and 10 males. This is clearly a representative sample of the clinical population seen in the Pediatric Endocrine Clinic, considering that at the time of our study only 31 patients with AGS had been seen since the clinic's inception 10 years before. The age range was 4.3 to 19.9 years for females and 4.8 to 26.3 years for males, with most of the children in middle childhood and early adolescence. Several families had more than one child with AGS. The total unaffected sibling sample consists of 11 females and 16 males with comparable age ranges (see Table 1). Eighteen mothers and 14 fathers participated in the study. Not all siblings and parents were available for all parts of the study. The respective numbers will be indicated for each comparison. The families came from social classes II to V according to the Hollingshead index (6), with a greater number from lower than from middle and upper classes.

All patients were under corrective treatment with cortisone replacement. Fourteen of the females

began receiving cortisone treatment during the first year of life, usually shortly after birth. The other three patients were started on cortisone in the second, third, and fourth year of life, respectively. Surgical correction of the external genitalia varied as follows: in six patients within the first year of life, in seven patients between ages 1 and 3 years, and in four patients later in life.

Six of the male patients began receiving cortisone treatment during the first month of life. The other four patients were started on cortisone in their fifth, sixth, seventh, and eighth year of life, respectively. The latter four patients had signs of precocious male puberty at the beginning of treatment. One of these late-treated boys was excluded from the behavior study, because both he and his mother were mentally retarded and detailed interview information could not be obtained.

Behavior Assessment

The methods and, in particular, the problems of getting good measurements of gender-related behavior are still largely the same as in the earlier studies. As in the Johns Hopkins project, we were interested in long-term childhood behavior that we could operationally define and assess in interviews with the mothers and the children themselves. These interviews were conducted with semistructured schedules. The areas included in the schedule were general developmental and play-behavior items intermixed with typical gender-related behavior.

Our interview schedule included items that are related to established sex differences in the normal population. Our choice was not influenced by a particular theory that the specific behavior item was clearly culturally determined or possibly also hormone-dependent. Our primary goal was to examine the kind of gender-related behavior that has been shown to differentiate between normal boys and girls consistently and over a wide age range. Next, we wanted to compare girls and boys with a specific atypical prenatal hormonal history to girls and boys with a presumably normal prenatal history.

One of the most consistent sex differences found in normal boys and girls has to do with rough-and-tumble play and aggression (7). From an early age on, boys tend to exert more energy in rough outdoor pursuits and become more frequently involved in fighting behavior. The results are not only

Table 1 Sample Characteristics

	Sex	Patients	Parents	Siblings
N	F	17	18	11
	M	10	14	16
Age range and mean	F	4.3-19.9	28-49	6.8-24.7
		10.8	37	12.93
	M	4.8-26.3	32-52	6.8-23.7
		11.8	40.5	13.22
Race	F	25 W, 2 B	29 W, 3 B	24 W, 3 B
	M			

remarkably consistent for our own culture but have also been noted in several cross-cultural comparisons and in nonhuman primate observations (8, 9). Thus we wanted to know whether fetally androgenized females are different from their normal sisters and mothers in this area of gender-related behavior and more similar to normal boys. Concerning boys with AGS, the question is whether, as a group, they show a higher level of intense energy expenditure and aggression than their normal brothers.

Preference of playmates is another gender-related childhood behavior in which girls, and boys typically differ. From about age 4 on, girls consistently prefer girls and boys prefer boys if they have a choice in playmates. At about the same age, sex differences in toy preferences occur. Girls typically like dolls, doll houses, toy stoves, and the like, whereas boys prefer cars, trucks, and guns. In spite of a considerable overlap between the sexes regarding play behavior, the sex differences in typical toy preferences, play activities, and choice of playmates remain fairly consistent throughout childhood (7).

Doll play probably has a very important function in preparation for the maternal role. Actually, we know very little about the response of human children to small infants or whether and when girls and boys differ in handling and care-giving behavior. Most of our evidence comes from animal studies or indirect nurturant behavior, as in response to baby dolls. Observations of free-living nonhuman primates indicate that adolescent females show more interest in infants than do males of the same age (10, 11). Numerous studies on human subjects show that girls play more and show more care-giving behavior with dolls than do boys of the same age. However, it is by no means the case that only girls respond to dolls or infants. Boys not only have the potential but often display care-giving behavior. The difference seems to be that females manifest increased readiness to respond to the young. For example, girls were found to show significantly greater nurturant responses to a baby doll than did boys of comparable ages (12). However, when the same group of children was subdivided by sex and ordinal position in their family, it was found that girls tended to be nurturant to the baby doll irrespective of having younger siblings or not, whereas boys tended to show nurturance only if they had younger siblings at home (13). This study suggests that boys may need more exposure to small infants than do girls in order to display nurturant behavior in the presence of a baby doll. The findings are in agreement with animal studies, which also suggest that males have a longer latency phase or a higher threshold before they respond to the very young of their species.

Since the response to infants is an important area in the study of sex differences, we compared AGS girls with their sisters and mothers in doll play, their attitude toward becoming a mother, and their response to infants. The question under study is whether fetally androgenized females have less interest in any aspect of maternal behavior suggestive of a higher threshold in their response to infants.

We also compared AGS males with their normal brothers on analogous items appropriately modified for boys, to see whether boys with a history of excessive androgen before birth differ in this respect from normal boys and show behavior modification toward an even higher degree of masculinity.

Another cluster of items in our interview schedule concerned gender-role preference and more arbitrary sex differences, such as interest in appearance, clothing, jewelry, and hairdo. Concerning gender-role preference, each subject was asked whether he or she would have preferred to be a boy or a girl if there had been a choice in the beginning of life and if boys or girls had more fun and advantages in society.

Concerning clothes, jewelry, and cosmetics, we were not interested in the preferred style, which obviously changes rapidly with different fashions, but rather whether the subject showed an interest in being attractive or clearly preferred functional outfits with little or no concern about looks.

The interview schedule also included specific items for adolescents—for example, dating, erotic attractions, love affairs.

Procedure

The families were referred by the Pediatric Endocrine Clinic and were asked to cooperate in our project. We informed them that we were interested in various aspects of child development in AGS patients and in their normal siblings. Furthermore, we proposed to do an intelligence study of all family members on the basis of a battery of cognitive-ability tests. The cooperation of the families was unusually good, which probably can be largely explained by their excellent rapport with the staff of the Pediatric Endocrine Division, whom they had often known for many years.

Originally we only collected data on the children. To obtain insight into the mothers' own developmental history and to ensure that we were not dealing with a sample of unusual mothers reinforcing their own attitudes and interests in their children, we asked the mothers to return and administered a standard interview about their own developmental history, comparable to the data we had collected on their children. We were able to collect data from 13 mothers (seven mothers of female, three mothers of male, and three mothers of both male and female patients).

The interview sessions were arranged on an individual basis and were scheduled according to the family's convenience. Data were collected over several sessions for each family. Each session lasted at least 2 to 3 hours.

Every subject and her or his mother was interviewed with the same interview schedule. The items were always consistent, although the sequence was flexible, so as to be unstilted in manner. All interviews were tape-recorded and subsequent-

ly transcribed. The transcribed interviews were rated according to coding scales, with a range from two to five verbally anchored points. Agreement between answers from mothers and from children as to the same aspect of the child's behavior has been found in the past to be very high (4), so that the answers can be pooled. Two raters tabulated the data from the transcribed interviews.

Statistical Analysis

Comparison of the patient and the various control groups were statistically tested with appropriate nonparametric tests after the rating scales for each item were dichotomized (for methodological details see ref. 4).

Data on the females are based on a comparison of the 17 patients versus the 10 mothers of females and 11 unaffected female siblings of all families in our study. Ideally we would have liked to use only the sisters of female patients. However, in order to increase sample size, we used all female siblings of AGS female and male patients.

Data were analyzed with a 3 X 2 chi-square test (14). In case of expected frequencies less than 5, the Freeman-Halton test was applied (15).

The behavior data on the males are based on 9 patients and 11 unaffected male siblings of all families. Comparisons of the two male groups were tested with the Fisher Exact Test for fourfold tables (14).

RESULTS

Fetally Androgenized Girls versus Unaffected Female Siblings and Mothers

Activity and Aggression We found that girls with AGS were significantly more often described by mothers, sisters, brothers, fathers, and themselves as having a high level of intense physical energy expenditure in comparison with the two other groups (Fig. 1). This behavior was long-term and specific in the sense of a high degree of rough outdoor play rather than a general elevation of activity level. This kind of energetic play and sport behavior has to be differentiated from hyperactivity, which interferes with the ability to focus attention and to concentrate and which was not typical for AGS females.

Girls with AGS also differed in choice of playmates. About 50% clearly preferred boys over girls

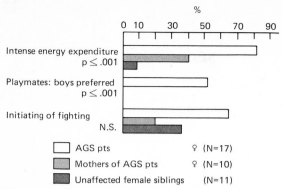

Figure 1 Comparison of female patients versus mothers and female siblings on activity and aggression. The bars represent the percentage of subjects from each group who were reported to exhibit the behavior specified by the category adjacent to the bars.

most or all of the time when a choice was available. This did not hold true for the other two groups, although some of the unaffected female siblings did play with boys and some of the mothers remembered having done so in their own childhood. However, if there was a choice, it was clearly for members of their own sex.

Our data on fighting behavior were initially quite crude and centered basically only around the question as to which member of the family usually instigated fights. There is a tendency for fetally androgenized girls to start fights more frequently than females in the other two groups, but the difference was not significant. Since fighting behavior appears to be one of the most consistent sex differences cross-culturally and in comparisons between various mammalian species, we studied this behavior again and have in the meantime obtained more detailed data on aggression (as yet unanalyzed). At this point it is not clear whether AGS females are in any way different from their sisters and mothers in respect to childhood fighting behavior.

Marriage and Maternalism The second cluster of pertinent results centers around toy preferences, response to infants, and rehearsal of adult female roles. As one can see from Figure 2, AGS girls show a conspicuously low interest in dolls. About 80% were rated as having had little or no interest in dolls at any time during their childhood, whereas

this was only true for a small number of sisters and mothers. The AGS girls tended to play with cars, trucks, and blocks. They also appeared to care little for future roles as bride and mother, but were much more concerned with future job roles. Female siblings and mothers, on the other hand, were described as being interested in childhood rehearsal of wedding and marriage as well as of various career roles and were in the latter aspect not different from the patients.

Girls with AGS were also more frequently characterized as being indifferent to small infants or expressing aversion to, and dislike of, handling babies. In contrast to their mothers and female siblings, they often avoided caring for a baby at home and preferred not to babysit. They did not exclude the possibility of becoming a mother one day; rather their attitude was noncommittal and matter-of-fact, with little or no rehearsal in daydreams or role play about motherhood—quite in contrast to the majority of unaffected female siblings and most of their mothers during childhood.

Gender Role, Appearance, and Adolescent Dating Behavior The next cluster of items has to do with gender-role preference and with more arbitrary sex

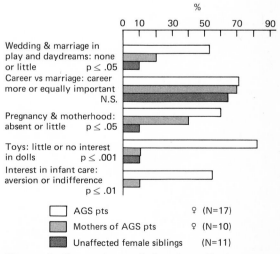

Figure 2 Comparison of female patients versus mothers and female siblings on marriage and maternalism. The bars represent the percentage of subjects from each group who were reported to exhibit the behavior specified by the category adjacent to the bars.

differences, such as interest in appearance (Fig. 3). If a girl tends toward rough-and-tumble play and prefers boys and boys' toys, then she is traditionally identified as a tomboy. Fifty-nine percent of the patients were identified by themselves and others as having been tomboys during all of their childhood. This was significantly different from the sample of unaffected siblings, none of whom demonstrated this complete and long-term pattern of tomboyism. However, 27% were rated as having manifested a limited episode of some tomboyish traits during their childhood. Girls with AGS were also significantly different from the sample of mothers, only two of whom described themselves as long-term tomboys.

To the question whether it was better to be a girl or a boy, 35% of the patients were undecided or thought that they might have chosen to be a boy if such a choice had been possible. However, it is important to see these results in the proper perspective: none of the AGS girls had a conflict with her female gender identity or was unhappy about being a girl. They were generally comfortable in the female role and liked to be tomboys.

The last two items relate to clothing and appearance. More girls in the patient sample preferred functional to attractive clothing and in general were not particular about their appearance. Consistently, they were also more frequently rated as having no

interest in jewelry, makeup, and hairdo than were the unaffected female siblings and the mothers during their childhood.

Our evidence on adolescent behavior is based on too few cases to make any definitive statement. Preliminary impressions tend to indicate that AGS patients are somewhat late in developing relationships with members of the opposite sex. They seem to be slow in starting to date and having their first crush on a boy. However, there is no evidence that homosexuality is increased in the patient sample. Several of the adolescent girls expressed interest in, and attraction to, boys, but were more reticent, not as eager, and possibly less skilled than the unaffected female siblings in becoming involved in a flirtatious relationship with a boy.

In summary, the comparison of female AGS patients with unaffected female siblings and mothers revealed several differences in childhood behavior. The patients tended to be long-term tomboys with a pattern of intense energy expenditure in rough-and-tumble outdoor activities, demonstrated a preference for boys over girls in peer contact, and showed little interest in clothing, hairdo, and jewelry. The patients were also less interested in playing with dolls, in taking care of small infants, and in playing bride and mother roles. They preferred trucks, cars, and building material as toys and were more concerned with the future in terms of a job or career role. They were significantly different in these respects from the other two groups. However, this behavior pattern was not considered abnormal and did not interfere in any way with the formation of a female gender identity.

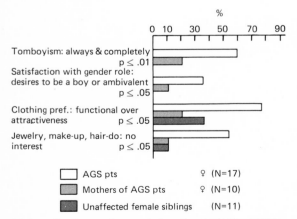

Figure 3 Comparison of female patients versus mothers and female siblings on gender-role and clothing preference. The bars represent the percentage of subjects from each group who were reported to exhibit the behavior specified by the category adjacent to the bars.

Male AGS Patients versus Unaffected Male Siblings

Activity and Aggression Boys with AGS manifested more frequently a high energy-expenditure level in sports and rough outdoor activities on a long-term basis, whereas more unaffected boys were rated as having a moderate or periodic interest in sports and physical activities (Fig. 4).

There were no significant differences in fighting behavior between the two groups as judged by the criterion of initiating fights in the family and elsewhere in their environment.

Almost all boys in both groups preferred boys over girls as playmates.

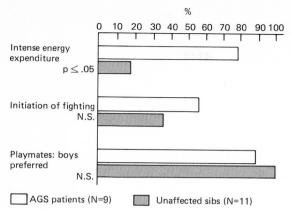

Figure 4 Comparison of male patients versus male siblings on activity and aggression. The bars represent the percentage of subjects from each group who were reported to exhibit the behavior specified by the category adjacent to the bars.

Marriage and Fatherhood No significant difference was found between AGS boys and unaffected brothers in toy preferences and rehearsal of future roles of husband and father (Fig. 5). In both groups

of males, very few boys were interested in dolls and other girls' toys. In both groups, some boys had thoughts and fantasies of becoming a father, although much less so than the unaffected girls who are concerned with becoming a mother. The same was true for the number of boys who liked to handle their little brothers or sisters and other small infants. The frequency was considerably lower than in the group of unaffected females, who scored 100% in the moderate and strong category.

Gender-Role Preference and Adolescent Dating Behavior The next cluster concerns satisfaction with the male gender role, which is 100% in both groups (Fig. 6). There was a total absence of effeminacy in both groups, and most of them were rated or rated themselves as extremely masculine rather than average in this regard. All boys preferred boys' clothes; approximately half in each sample had no interest in their appearance, whereas the other half had a moderate or strong interest in clothes and looking attractive. Interest in appearance *per se* is thus not specifically feminine but also a noticeable part of boys' behavior in childhood and adolescence.

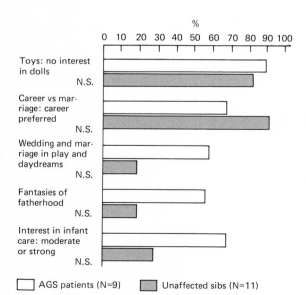

Figure 5 Comparison of male patients versus male siblings on marriage and fatherhood. The bars represent the percentage of subjects from each group who were reported to exhibit the behavior specified by the category adjacent to the bars.

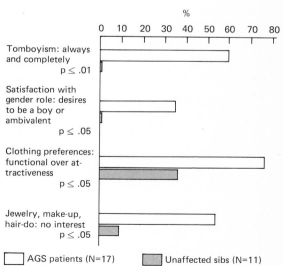

Figure 6 Comparison of male patients versus male siblings on gender-role and clothing preference. The bars represent the percentage of subjects from each group who were reported to exhibit the behavior specified by the category adjacent to the bars.

The number of adolescents was too small to make a definitive statement concerning erotic attraction and dating behavior. In both groups, some boys had begun dating and had become involved in adolescent love affairs—in all cases heterosexual and with no evidence of any conflict with the male sex role.

In summary, AGS males differed from the group of unaffected male siblings in only one aspect of gender-related behavior: intense energy expenditure in outdoor play and sports activities. Otherwise, both male groups followed the typical masculine behavior pattern of our culture, with no interest in dolls, preference for boys over girls in peer contacts, some interest in the future role of husband and father, and a clear-cut preference for the masculine role.

DISCUSSION

We found that girls with AGS differed from a sample of unaffected female siblings and their mothers in certain aspects of their sexually dimorphic behavior in childhood. They were significantly more often long-term tomboys with a profile of a high energy-expenditure level in rough outdoor play, showed a preference for boys over girls in peer contact, a low interest in playing with dolls and taking care of small infants, little rehearsal of the maternal adult role as wife and mother, and little concern about the attractiveness of their appearance in clothing, hairdo, and jewelry. However, AGS girls were clearly identified in the female role, and their behavior was not considered abnormal by them, by their parents, or by their peers. Rather, they presented an acceptable pattern of tomboyish behavior in this society, not unlike tomboyism in normal females except that it occurred significantly more often in the AGS sample than in either the sibling or the mother sample.

The patients were too young to make a definitive statement concerning homosexuality. Since most of the teenage girls were already romantically interested in boys, however, it seems unlikely that we shall find a significantly higher frequency of lesbianism in girls with a history of fetal hormonal androgenization.

Our findings are in agreement with previous studies on early- and late-treated AGS females (5). Thus we have confirmed in two different hospital populations that genetic females with an exposure to endogenous masculinizing hormones after birth are different in several aspects of their sexually dimorphic behavior in childhood from a matched group of normal unrelated girls, from a sample of unaffected female siblings, and from their mothers.

The results are also comparable to findings on subhuman female primates exposed to testosterone during intrauterine development. Fetally androgenized female rhesus monkeys were found to show more rough-and-tumble play as well as more dominance behavior; they were also more similar in some other aspects of their behavior to male monkeys than to normal female monkeys (16, 17).

The consistency of results in both earlier and more recent studies suggests strongly that it is the fetal exposure to androgens that contributes to the typical profile of behavior exhibited by AGS females. This conclusion is corroborated by the fact that girls with exogenous fetal androgenization by progestinic drugs showed a very similar behavior to that of AGS girls. In the progestin-treated group the hormonal abnormality was clearly limited to the prenatal phase. In the case of AGS, however, one cannot completely rule out the possibility that postnatal hormonal abnormalities may still affect behavior development in some way, although all girls in our sample were generally well regulated on cortisone, and, in most cases, treatment was initiated shortly after birth.

Girls with the progestin-induced condition and those with the early-treated AGS have abnormalities in their external genitalia. In spite of the fact that surgical correction to normal-looking sex organs usually took place early in infancy in our previous and present studies on children with either of the two conditions, one cannot completely exclude the genital abnormality as a factor that in some way might influence subsequent behavior. One way this effect could be transmitted would be by parental attitudes toward the affected child. It is undoubtedly a traumatic experience for parents to have a baby girl born with a genital abnormality. We interviewed the parents in great depth about their reactions and any possible lurking fears. Most parents had little persistent concern about the genital abnormality at birth, especially since the appearance of their daughter's genitalia had been normal for so many years. The tomboyish behavior was not seen as related to the genital abnormality. There was usually very little parental pressure toward more femininity, which is not surprising, since the behavior in the girls with AGS was not viewed as being abnormal or masculine.

The patients typically knew that their child's medical condition was one that was affected by cortisone levels. The older girls were informed about the clitoral enlargement at birth, which usually was accepted as a minor birth defect that had been corrected. As far as the behavior was concerned, girls with AGS typically enjoyed being tomboys without any fears of being different.

In summary, from our data it is unlikely that parental or patient attitude is a significant factor modifying the particular temperamental set of behavior toward tomboyism in either sample of girls with the progestin-induced or the adrenogenital condition.

The data on AGS males suggest no difference between the patient and male sibling sample in any area assessed, except for an increase in energy level in the patient group. The even higher level of physical strength and energy in sports and play activities in the AGS sample may be related to their prenatal history of a possibly even higher level of androgens compared with normal males; in three boys it may have also been due to postnatal androgen levels before treatment was initiated. The finding in the male sample also suggests that most aspects of masculine behavior development in male childhood are not affected by the prenatal hormone abnormality in the adrenogenital condition. This result is in agreement with earlier findings by Money and Alexander (18).

If prenatal exposure to androgens modifies behavior in genetic females as in the described clinical conditions, one may assume that similar hormonal factors contribute to the development of temperamental differences between males and females in general, and finer variations of fetal hormones may also possibly influence behavior differences within the sexes. We are obviously on speculative grounds with this theory at present, but let us assume for the sake of discussion that this was a proved fact. What implications and social consequences would such a finding have? We are aware that all sex differences in human behavior are much influenced by social-environmental reinforcement of appropriate behavior for girls and boys. Thus we are not suggesting that sexually dimorphic play, toy, and peer behavior is solely determined by prenatal and/or postnatal hormone levels. We rather suggest that prenatal

androgen is one of the factors contributing to the development of temperamental differences between and within the sexes. Undoubtedly it will depend to a large extent on the interaction between prenatal hormone levels and the particular environment of the child as to what quality the specific behavior will have.

We would like to close with one other point. If prenatal hormone levels contribute to sex differences in behavior, the effects in human beings are subtle and can in no way be taken as a basis for prescribing social roles. In fact, we rather like to make an argument from the opposite point of view. If it can be documented that prenatal hormone levels are among the factors that account for the wide range of temperamental differences and role aspirations with the female, and possibly also within the male, sex, a great variety of adult roles should be available and can be adequately fulfilled by both women and men, and they should be equally acceptable and respectable for either sex.

ACKNOWLEDGMENTS

The study was supported by a grant (C1-10-CH-71) from the United Health Foundation of Western New York, the Human Growth Foundation, and the Variety Club of Buffalo, Tent No. 7.

The patients in this sample were diagnosed and managed by Drs. Thomas Aceto, Jr., and Margaret MacGillivray of the Pediatric Endocrine Clinic at Children's Hospital of Buffalo, New York. Their clinical cooperation is greatly appreciated.

The data graphs were designed by the Department of Medical Illustrations, State University of New York at Buffalo.

REFERENCES

1 Jones, H. W., Jr. and B. S. Verkauf, *Am J Obstet Gynecol* **109:** 292, 1971.

2 Ehrhardt, A. A. and J. Money, *J Sex Res* **3:** 83, 1967.

3 Ehrhardt, A. A., R. Epstein, and J. Money, *Johns Hopkins Med J* **122:** 160, 1968.

4 Ehrhardt, A. A., in Duhm, E. (ed.), *Praxis der Klinischen Psychologie II*, Verlag für Psychologie, Dr. C. J. Hogrefe, Göttingen, 1971, p. 94.

5 Money, J. and A. A. Ehrhardt, *Man & Woman, Boy & Girl*, Johns Hopkins University Press, Baltimore, 1972.

6   Hollingshead, A. B., *Two Factor Index of Social Position,* privately printed, New Haven, Conn., 1957.

7   Maccoby, E. E. and C. N. Jacklin, *The Psychology of Sex Differences,* Stanford University Press, Palo Alto, Calif., 1974.

8   Harlow, H., *Am Psychol* **17:** 1, 1962.

9   Harris, G. W., *Endocrinology* **75:** 627, 1964.

10 DeVore, I., in Rheingold, H. L. (ed.), *Maternal Behavior in Mammals,* Wiley, New York, 1963.

11 Jay, P., in Rheingold, H. L. (ed.), *Maternal Behavior in Mammals,* Wiley, New York, 1963.

12 Sears, R. R., L. Rau, and R. Alpert, *Identification and Child Rearing,* Stanford University Press, Stanford, Calif., 1965.

13 Maccoby, E. E. and C. N. Jacklin, *Scientific American,* in press.

14 Lienert, G. A., *Verteilungsfreie Methoden,* Anton Hain, Meisenheim am Glan, 1962, p. 88.

15 Freeman, G. H. and J. H. Halton, *Biometrika* **38:** 41, 1951.

16 Goy, R. W., *Phil Trans Roy Soc London* **259:** 149, 1970.

17 Eaton, G. G., R. W. Goy, and C. H. Phoenix, *Nature New Biol* **242:** 119, 1973.

18 Money, J. and D. Alexander, *J Nerv Ment Dis* **148:** 111, 1969.

Chapter Two

Genetics, Culture, and IQ

Few topics have stimulated more controversy and research than that of the effects of transactions between biological and environmental factors on intellectual development. In most cases, studies in this area have involved the use of standardized intelligence tests and the obtained intelligence quotient, or IQ, as a measure of intelligence. Sometimes educational level, professional achievements, Piagetian tasks, and less frequently social problem-solving are also used to estimate cognitive level.

Many of the problems in interpretation of these studies rest in disparate views of what IQ scores represent, others are based on confusion about the concept of heritability. The layman tends to regard IQ as a measure of the innate capacity to learn that remains relatively stable throughout life. As the student will learn in reading the papers in this section this is not true. The IQ is a measure of performance on an intelligence test relative to the performance of a group of individuals on whom the test has been standardized. As the IQ goes above 100 it means the individual is performing better than the average person of his or her age in the standardization group; as it drops below 100 the individual is performing less well than the average person in the standardization group. The problem-solving performance measured on an intelligence test is most closely related to performance and achievement in academic settings and less closely to competence in social situations, practical problems in everyday life, and earning power.

The student should note first that IQ is a measure of performance, not innate capacity. This performance will be a result of the interaction between many variables: innate intellectual capacity, life experiences, the environment in which the individual is raised, condition at the time of testing, the particular items on the test, and the conditions under which the test is administered. Second the student should keep in mind that IQ is always a relative performance score. The group with whom we compare the performance of the individual should be one with a similar background and shared life experiences. Finally there are considerable fluctuations in IQ for the same individual over the life span. This is in part attributable to the fact that very different types of items which may be testing different cognitive competences are used with children of different ages. In the prelinguistic child under two years of age, items relying heavily on sensory or motor skills are used. With the onset of language, intelligence tests become more heavily weighted with items involving verbal skills. It has been argued that these early sensorimotor measures involve a different kind of cognitive competence than do verbal or abstract reasoning items. Some support for this position is found in the extremely low relationship between IQ scores obtained in the first two years of life and those from later ages. In addition the pattern and rate of intellectual development varies for different individuals. Just as children may show plateaus and spurts in physical growth at different ages, wide individual variations in patterns of cognitive development occur.

Closely related to misconceptions about the IQ is confusion about the meaning of heritability. In its simplest form, heritability is a statistical concept which reflects the percentage of variability that is associated with differences in the genetic composition of individuals in a group (McCall, 1975). Scarr-Salapatek in her article on unknowns in the IQ equation emphasizes that the heritability of IQ will vary in different populations. The percentage of variability in IQ associated with inherited factors and with experiential factors will vary for groups raised in different environments. Scarr-Salapatek uses this argument to rebut the positions of Jensen, Eysenck, and Herrnstein that the lower IQs obtained by blacks and lower-class whites relative to middle-class whites are largely based on genetic differences in intellectual abilities. If the heritability coefficient for IQ is lower for a group raised in one environment than those raised in another setting, it may mean that the environment may be suppressing or restricting the expressions of intellectual ability. Jensen's figure of 80 percent heritability of IQ, which is frequently cited, is largely based on twin and adoption studies of middle-class white populations. Scarr-Salapatek finds much lower proportions of heritability of IQ in black and lower-class white populations, which she attributes to the social and economic disadvantages suffered by these groups, particularly by the deleterious effects of the racial caste system imposed upon blacks.

Scarr-Salapatek and her colleague Richard Weinberg have extended her investigations on race and IQ in the interracial adoption study which is presented in the last paper in this section. In this paper they examine the effects of cross-fostering on the IQs of black children and find that the social and cognitive environment of middle-class white adoptive homes was associated with increases in IQ in black adopted children. They propose that *if* high IQs are considered desirable some restructuring of the social system within black homes is necessary to facilitate the development of intellectual skills measured by intelligence tests.

In both the Scarr-Salapatek and Weinberg paper and in the Banes and Jencks paper the need for social reorganization to help blacks is proposed. In both papers the usefulness of educational interventions alone is questioned. In the former paper, modifications in the black home environment considered in the larger social, economic, and cultural framework are proposed. In the latter paper the emphasis is more narrowly focused on equality of economic opportunities.

The issue of heritability in intelligence has not been resolved in these studies. However, a reasonable conclusion is that we should seek to improve existing environments in order to maximize the realization of individual competence for people in all groups in our society.

REFERENCES

McCall, R. B. *Heritability*. Homewood: Richard Irwin, 1975.

Reading 6

Unknowns in the IQ Equation

Sandra Scarr-Salapatek

IQ scores have been repeatedly estimated to have a large heritable component in United States and Northern European white populations (*1*). Individual differences in IQ, many authors have concluded, arise far more from genetic than from environmental differences among people in these populations, at the present time, and under present environmental conditions. It has also been known for many years that white lower-class and black groups have lower IQ's, on the average, than white middle-class groups. Most behavioral scientists comfortably "explained" these group differences by appealing to obvious environmental differences between the groups in standards of living, educational opportunities, and the like. But recently an explosive controversy has developed over the heritability of between-group differences in IQ, the question at issue being: If individual differences within the white population as a whole can be attributed largely to heredity, is it not plausible that the average differences between social-class groups and between racial groups also reflect significant genetic differences? Can the former data be used to explain the latter?

To propose genetically based racial and social-class differences is anathema to most behavioral scientists, who fear any scientific confirmation of the pernicious racial and ethnic prejudices that abound in our society. But now that the issue has been openly raised, and has been projected into the public context of social and educational policies, a hard scientific look must be taken at what is known and at what inferences can be drawn from that knowledge.

The public controversy began when A. R. Jensen, in a long paper in the *Harvard Educational Review,* persuasively juxtaposed data on the heritability of

IQ and the observed differences between groups. Jensen suggested that current large-scale educational attempts to raise the IQ's of lower-class children, white and black, were failing because of the high heritability of IQ. In a series of papers and rebuttals to criticism, in the same journal and elsewhere (*2*), Jensen put forth the hypothesis that social-class and racial differences in mean IQ were due largely to differences in the gene distributions of these populations. At least, he said, the genetic-differences hypothesis was no less likely, and probably more likely, than a simple environmental hypothesis to explain the mean difference of 15 IQ points between blacks and whites (*3*) and the even larger average IQ differences between professionals and manual laborers within the white population.

Jensen's articles have been directed primarily at an academic audience. Herrnstein's article in the *Atlantic* and Eysenck's book (first published in England) have brought the argument to the attention of the wider lay audience. Both Herrnstein and Eysenck agree with Jensen's genetic-differences hypothesis as it pertains to individual differences and to social-class groups, but Eysenck centers his attention on the genetic explanation of racial-group differences, which Herrnstein only touches on. Needless to say, many other scientists will take issue with them.

EYSENCK'S RACIAL THESIS

Eysenck has written a popular account of the race, social-class, and IQ controversy in a generally inflammatory book. The provocative title and the disturbing cover picture of a forlorn black boy are clearly designed to tempt the lay reader into a pseudo-battle between Truth and Ignorance. In this case Truth is genetic-environmental interactionism (*4*) and Ignorance is naive environmentalism. For the careful reader, the battle fades out inconclusively as Eysenck admits that scientific evidence to date does not permit a clear choice of the genetic-differences interpretation of black inferiority on intelligence tests. A quick reading of the book,

Scarr-Salapatek's paper is a review of three publications:

(1) "Environment, heredity, and intelligence," a collection of articles comprising a statement by Arthur R. Jensen and rebuttals by leading psychologists. *Harvard Educational Review,* Spring 1969 (subsequently published by the *Review* as a special reprint).

(2) H. J. Eysenck, *The IQ Argument,* New York: Library Press, 1971.

(3) Richard Herrnstein, "I.Q." *Atlantic* 288 No. 3 (1971): 44–64.

however, is sure to leave the reader believing that scientific evidence today strongly supports the conclusion that U.S. blacks are genetically inferior to whites in IQ.

The basic theses of the book are as follows:

1 IQ is a highly heritable characteristic in the U.S. white population and probably equally heritable in the U.S. black population.
2 On the average, blacks score considerably lower than whites on IQ tests.
3 U.S. blacks are probably a non-random, lower-IQ, sample of native African populations.
4 The average IQ difference between blacks and whites probably represents important genetic differences between the races.
5 Drastic environmental changes will have to be made to improve the poor phenotypes that U.S. blacks now achieve.

The evidence and nonevidence that Eysenck cites to support his genetic hypothesis of racial differences make a curious assortment. Audrey Shuey's review (5) of hundreds of studies showing mean phenotypic differences between black and white IQ's leads Eysenck to conclude:

All the evidence to date suggests the strong and indeed overwhelming importance of genetic factors in producing the great variety of intellectual differences which we observe in our culture, and much of the difference observed between certain racial groups. This evidence cannot be argued away by niggling and very minor criticisms of details which do not really throw doubts on the major points made in this book [p. 126].

To "explain" the genetic origins of these mean IQ differences he offers these suppositions:

White slavers wanted dull beasts of burden, ready to work themselves to death in the plantations, and under those conditions intelligence would have been counter-selective. Thus there is every reason to expect that the particular subsample of the Negro race which is constituted of American Negroes is not an unselected sample of Negroes, but has been selected throughout history according to criteria which would put the highly intelligent at a disadvantage. The inevitable outcome of such selection would of course be a gene pool lacking some of the genes making for higher intelligence [p. 42].

Other ethnic minorities in the U.S. are also, in his view, genetically inferior, again because of the selective migration of lower IQ genotypes:

It is known [sic] that many other groups came to the U.S.A. due to pressures which made them very poor samples of the original populations. Italians, Spaniards, and Portuguese, as well as Greeks, are examples where the less able, less intelligent were forced through circumstances to emigrate, and where their American progeny showed significantly lower IQ's than would have been shown by a random sample of the original population [p. 43].

Although Eysenck is careful to say that these are not established facts (because no IQ tests were given to the immigrants or nonimmigrants in question?), the tone of his writing leaves no doubt about his judgment. There is something in this book to insult almost everyone except WASP's and Jews.

Despite his conviction that U.S. blacks are genetically inferior in IQ to whites, Eysenck is optimistic about the potential effects of radical environmental changes on the present array of Negro IQ phenotypes. He points to the very large IQ gains produced by intensive one-to-one tutoring of black urban children with low-IQ mothers, contrasting large environmental changes and large IQ gains in intensive programs of this sort with insignificant environmental improvements and small IQ changes obtained by Head Start and related programs. He correctly observes that, whatever the heritability of IQ (or, it should be added, of any characteristic), large phenotypic changes may be produced by creating appropriate, radically different environments never before encountered by those genotypes. On this basis, Eysenck calls for further research to determine the requisites of such environments.

Since Eysenck comes to this relatively benign position regarding potential improvement in IQ's, why, one may ask, is he at such pains to "prove" the genetic inferiority of blacks? Surprisingly, he expects that new environments, such as that provided by intensive educational tutoring, will not affect the black-white IQ differential, because black children and white will probably profit equally from such treatment. Since many middle-class white children already have learning environments similar to that provided by tutors for the urban black children, we must suppose that Eysenck expects great IQ gains from relatively small changes in white, middle-class environments.

This book is an uncritical popularization of Jensen's ideas without the nuances and qualifiers that make much of Jensen's writing credible or at least responsible. Both authors rely on Shuey's review (5), but Eysenck's way of doing it is to devote some 25 pages to quotes and paraphrases of her chapter summaries. For readers to whom the original Jensen article is accessible, Eysenck's book is a poor substitute; although he defends Jensen and Shuey, he does neither a service.

It is a maddeningly inconsistent book filled with contradictory caution and incaution; with hypotheses stated both as hypotheses and as conclusions; with both accurate and inaccurate statements on matters of fact. For example, Eysenck thinks evoked potentials* offer a better measure of "innate" intelligence than IQ tests. But on what basis? Recently F. B. Davis (6) has failed to find any relationship whatsoever between evoked potentials and either IQ scores or scholastic achievement, to which intelligence is supposed to be related. Another example is Eysenck's curious use of data to support a peculiar line of reasoning about the evolutionary inferiority of blacks: First, he reports that African and U.S. Negro babies have been shown to have precocious sensorimotor development by white norms (the difference, by several accounts, appears only in gross motor skills and even there is slight). Second, he notes that by three years of age U.S. white exceed U.S. black children in mean IQ scores. Finally he cites a (very slight) negative correlation, found in an early study, between sensorimotor intelligence in the first year of life and later IQ. From exaggerated statements of these various data, he concludes:

> These findings are important because of a very general view in biology according to which the more prolonged the infancy the greater in general are the cognitive or intellectual abilities of the species. This law appears to work even within a given species [p. 79].

Eysenck would apparently have us believe that Africans and their relatives in the U.S. are less

highly evolved than Caucasians, whose longer infancy is related to later higher intelligence. I am aware of no evidence whatsoever to support a within-species relationship between longer infancy and higher adult capacities.

The book is carelessly put together, with no index; few references, and those not keyed to the text; and long, inadequately cited quotes that carry over several pages without clear beginnings and ends. Furthermore, considering the gravity of Eysenck's theses, the book has an occasional jocularity of tone that is offensive. A careful book on the genetic hypothesis, written for a lay audience, would have merited publication. This one, however, has been publicly disowned as irresponsible by the entire editorial staff of its London publisher, New Society. But never mind, the American publisher has used that and other condemnations to balance the accolades and make its advertisement (7) of the book more titillating.

HERRNSTEIN'S SOCIAL THESIS

Thanks to Jensen's provocative article, many academic psychologists who thought IQ tests belonged in the closet with the Rorschach inkblots have now explored the psychometric literature and found it to be a trove of scientific treasure. One of these is Richard Herrnstein, who from a Kinnerian background has become an admirer of intelligence tests—a considerable leap from shaping the behavior of pigeons and rats. In contrast to Eysenck's book, Herrnstein's popular account in the *Atlantic* of IQ testing and its values is generally responsible, if overly enthusiastic in parts.

Herrnstein unabashedly espouses IQ testing as "psychology's most telling accomplishment to date," despite the current controversy over the fairness of testing poor and minority-group children with IQ items devised by middle-class whites. His historical review of IQ test development, including tests of general intelligence and multiple abilities, is interesting and accurate. His account of the validity and usefulness of the tests centers on the fairly accurate prediction that can be made from IQ scores to academic and occupational achievement and income level. He clarifies the pattern of relationship between IQ and these criterion variables: High IQ is a necessary but not sufficient condition for high achievement, while low IQ virtually as-

---

*A measure of the electrical activity in the brain.

sures failure at high academic and occupational levels. About the usefulness of the tests, he concludes:

> An IQ test can be given in an hour or two to a child, and from this infinitesimally small sample of his output, deeply important predictions follow—about schoolwork, occupation, income, satisfaction with life, and even life expectancy. The predictions are not perfect, for other factors always enter in, but no other single factor matters as much in as many spheres of life [p. 53].

One must assume that Herrnstein's enthusiasm for intelligence tests rests on population statistics, not on predictions for a particular child, because many children studied longitudinally have been shown to change IQ scores by 20 points or more from childhood to adulthood. It is likely that extremes of giftedness and retardation can be sorted out relatively early by IQ tests, but what about the 95 percent of the population in between? Their IQ scores may vary from dull to bright normal for many years. Important variations in IQ can occur up to late adolescence (8). On a population basis Herrnstein is correct; the best early predictors of later achievement are ability measures taken from age five on. Predictions are based on correlations, however, which are not sensitive to absolute changes in value, only to rank orders. This is an important point to be discussed later.

After reviewing the evidence for average IQ differences by social class and race, Herrnstein poses the nature-nurture problem of "which is primary" in determining phenotypic differences in IQ. For racial groups, he explains, the origins of mean IQ differences are indeterminate at the present time because we have no information from heritability studies in the black population or from other, unspecified lines of research which could favor primarily genetic or primarily environmental hypotheses. He is thoroughly convinced, however, that individual differences and social-class differences in IQ are highly heritable at the present time, and are destined, by environmental improvements, to become even more so:

> If we make the relevant environment much more uniform (by making it as good as we can for everyone), then an even larger proportion of the variation in IQ will be attributable to the genes. The average person would be smarter, but intelli-

gence would run in families even more obviously and with less regression toward the mean than we see today [p. 58].

For Herrnstein, society is, and will be even more strongly, a meritocracy based largely on inherited differences in IQ. He presents a "syllogism" (p. 58) to make his message clear:

1 If differences in mental abilities are inherited, and
2 If success requires those abilities, and
3 If earnings and prestige depend on success.
4 Then social standing (which reflects earnings and prestige) will be based to some extent on inherited differences among people.

Five "corollaries" for the future predict that the heritability of IQ will rise; that social mobility will become more strongly related to inherited IQ differences; that most bright people will be gathered in the top of the social structure, with the IQ dregs at the bottom; that many at the bottom will not have the intelligence needed for new jobs; and that the meritocracy will be built not just on inherited intelligence but on all inherited traits affecting success, which will presumably become correlated characters. Thus from the successful realization of our most precious, egalitarian, political and social goals there will arise a much more rigidly stratified society, a "virtual caste system" based on inborn ability.

To ameliorate this effect, society may have to move toward the socialist dictum, "From each according to his abilities, to each according to his needs," but Herrnstein sees complete equality of earnings and prestige as impossible because high-grade intelligence is scarce and must be recruited into those critical jobs that require it, by the promise of high earnings and high prestige. Although garbage collecting is critical to the health of the society, almost anyone can do it; to waste high-IQ persons on such jobs is to misallocate scarce resources at society's peril.

Herrnstein points to an ironic contrast between the effects of caste and class systems. Castes, which established artificial hereditary limits on social mobility, guarantee the inequality of opportunity that preserves IQ heterogeneity at all levels of the system. Many bright people are arbitrarily kept down and many unintelligent people are artificially maintained at the top. When arbitrary bounds on mobility are removed, as in our class system, most of the bright rise to the top and most of the dull fall to the bottom of the social system, and IQ differences between top and bottom become increasingly hereditary. The greater the environmental equality, the greater the hereditary differences between levels in the social structure. The thesis of egalitarianism surely leads to its antithesis in a way that Karl Marx never anticipated.

Herrnstein proposes that our best strategy, in the face of increasing biological stratification, is publicly to recognize genetic human differences but to reallocate wealth to a considerable extent. The IQ have-nots need not be poor. Herrnstein does not delve into the psychological consequences of being publicly marked as genetically inferior.

Does the evidence support Herrnstein's view of hereditary social classes, now or in some future Utopia? Given his assumptions about the high heritability of IQ, the importance of IQ to social mobility, and the increasing environmental equality of rearing and opportunity, hereditary social classes are to some extent inevitable. But one can question the limits of genetic homogeneity in social-class groups and the evidence for his syllogism at present.

Is IQ as highly heritable throughout the social structure as Herrnstein assumes? Probably not. In a recent study of IQ heritability in various racial and social-class groups (9), I found much lower proportions of genetic variance that would account for aptitude differences among lower-class than among middle-class children, in both black and white groups. Social disadvantage in prenatal and postnatal development can substantially lower phenotypic IQ and reduce the genotype-phenotype correlation. Thus, average phenotypic IQ differences between the social classes may be considerably larger than the genotypic differences.

Are social classes largely based on hereditary IQ differences now? Probably not as much as Herrnstein believes. Since opportunities for social mobility act at the phenotypic level, there still may be considerable genetic diversity for IQ at the bottom of the social structure. In earlier days arbitrary social barriers maintained genetic variability throughout the social structure. At present, individuals with high phenotypic IQ's are often upwardly mobile; but inherited wealth acts to maintain genetic diversity at the top, and nongenetic biological and social barriers to phenotypic development act

to maintain a considerable genetic diversity of intelligence in the lower classes.

As P. E. Vernon has pointed out (10), we are inclined to forget that the majority of gifted children in recent generations have come from working-class, not middle-class, families. A larger percentage of middle-class children are gifted, but the working and lower classes produce gifted children in larger numbers. How many more disadvantaged children would have been bright if they had had middle-class gestation and rearing conditions?

I am inclined to think that intergenerational class mobility will always be with us, for three reasons. First, since normal IQ is a polygenic characteristic, various recombinations of parental genotypes will always produce more variable genotypes in the offspring than in the parents of all social-class groups, especially the extremes. Even if both parents, instead of primarily the male, achieved social-class status based on their IQ's, recombinations of their genes would always produce a range of offspring, who would be upwardly or downwardly mobile relative to their families of origin.

Second, since, as Herrnstein acknowledges, factors other than IQ—motivational, personality, and undetermined—also contribute to success or the lack of it, high IQ's will always be found among lower-class adults, in combination with schizophrenia, alcoholism, drug addiction, psychopathy, and other limiting factors. When recombined in offspring, high IQ can readily segregate with facilitating motivational and personality characteristics, thereby leading to upward mobility for many offspring. Similarly, middle-class parents will always produce some offspring with debilitating personal characteristics which lead to downward mobility.

Third, for all children to develop phenotypes that represent their best genotypic outcome (in current environments) would require enormous changes in the present social system. To improve and equalize all rearing environments would involve such massive intervention as to make Herrnstein's view of the future more problematic than he seems to believe.

RACE AS CASTE

Races are castes between which there is very little mobility. Unlike the social-class system, where mobility based on IQ is sanctioned, the racial caste system, like the hereditary aristocracy of medieval

Europe and the caste system of India, preserves within each group its full range of genetic diversity of intelligence. The Indian caste system was, according to Dobzhansky (*11*), a colossal genetic failure—or success, according to egalitarian values. After the abolition of castes at independence, Brahmins and untouchables were found to be equally educable despite—or because of—their many generations of segregated reproduction.

While we may tentatively conclude that there are some genetic IQ differences between social-class groups, we can make only wild speculations about racial groups. Average phenotypic IQ differences between races are not evidence for genetic differences (any more than they are evidence for environmental differences). Even if the heritabilities of IQ are extremely high in all races, there is still no warrant for equating within-group and between-group heritabilities (*12*). There are examples in agricultural experiments of within-group differences that are highly heritable but between-group differences that are entirely environmental. Draw two random samples of seeds from the same genetically heterogeneous population. Plant one sample in uniformly good conditions, the other in uniformly poor conditions. The average height difference between the populations of plants will be entirely environmental, although the individual differences in height within each sample will be entirely genetic. With known genotypes for seeds and known environments, genetic and environmental variances between groups can be studied. But racial groups are not random samples from the same population, nor are members reared in uniform conditions within each race. Racial groups are of unknown genetic equivalence for polygenic characteristics like IQ, and the differences in environments within and between the races may have as yet unquantified effects.

There is little to be gained from approaching the nature-nurture problem of race differences in IQ directly (*13*). Direct comparisons of estimated within-group heritabilities and the calculation of between-group heritabilities require assumptions that few investigators are willing to make, such as that all environmental differences are quantifiable, that differences in the environments of blacks and whites can be assumed to affect IQ in the same way in the two groups, and that differences in environments between groups can be "statistically con-

trolled." A direct assault on race differences in IQ is vulnerable to many criticisms.

Indirect approaches may be less vulnerable. These include predictions of parent-child regression effects and admixture studies. Regression effects can be predicted to differ for blacks and whites if the two races indeed have genetically different population means. If the population mean for blacks is 15 IQ points lower than that of whites, then the offspring of high-IQ black parents should show greater regression (toward a lower population mean) than the offspring of whites of equally high IQ. Similarly, the offspring of low-IQ black parents should show less regression than those of white parents of equally low IQ. This hypothesis assumes that assortative mating for IQ is equal in the two races, which could be empirically determined but has not been studied as yet. Interpretable results from a parent-child regression study would also depend upon careful attention to intergenerational environmental changes, which could be greater in one race than the other.

Studies based on correlations between degree of white admixture and IQ scores *within* the black group would avoid many of the pitfalls of between-group comparisons. If serological genotypes can be used to identify persons with more and less white admixture, and if estimates of admixture based on blood groups are relatively independent of visible characteristics like skin color, then any positive correlation between degree of admixture and IQ would suggest genetic racial differences in IQ. Since blood groups have not been used directly as the basis of racial discrimination, positive findings would be relatively immune from environmentalist criticisms. The trick is to estimate individual admixture reliably. Several loci which have fairly different distributions of alleles in contemporary African and white populations have been proposed (*14*). No one has yet attempted a study of this sort.

h^2 [HERITABILITY] AND PHENOTYPE

Suppose that the heritabilities of IQ differences within all racial and social-class groups were .80, as Jensen estimates, and suppose that the children in all groups were reared under an equal range of conditions. Now suppose that racial and social-class differences in mean IQ still remained. We would probably infer some degree of genetic difference between the groups. So what? The question now turns from a strictly scientific one to one of science and social policy.

As Eysenck, Jensen, and others have noted, eugenic and euthenic strategies are both possible interventions to reduce the number of low-IQ individuals in all populations. Eugenic policies could be advanced to encourage or require reproductive abstinence by people who fall below a certain level of intelligence. The Reeds (15) have determined that one-fifth of the mental retardation among whites of the next generation could be prevented if no mentally retarded persons of this generation reproduced. There is no question that a eugenic program applied at the phenotypic level of parents' IQ would substantially reduce the number of low-IQ children in the future white population. I am aware of no studies in the black population to support a similar program, but some proportion of future retardation could surely be eliminated. It would be extremely important, however, to sort out genetic and environmental sources of low IQ both in racial and in social-class groups before advancing a eugenic program. The request or demand that some persons refrain from any reproduction should be a last resort, based on sure knowledge that their retardation is caused primarily by genetic factors and is not easily remedied by environmental intervention. Studies of the IQ levels of adopted children with mentally retarded natural parents would be most instructive, since some of the retardation observed among children of retarded parents may stem from the rearing environments provided by the parents.

In a pioneering study of adopted children and their adoptive and natural parents, Skodak (16) reported greater *correlations* of children's IQ's with their natural than with their adoptive parents' IQ's. This statement has been often misunderstood to mean that the children's *levels* of intelligence more closely resembled their natural parents', which is completely false. Although the rank order of the children's IQ's resembled that of their mothers' IQ's, the children's IQ's were higher, being distributed, like those of the adoptive parents, around a mean above 100, whereas their natural mothers' IQ's averaged only 85. The children, in fact, averaged 21 IQ points higher than their natural mothers. If the (unstudied) natural fathers' IQ's averaged

around the population mean of 100, the mean of the children's would be expected to be 94, or 12 points lower than the mean obtained. The unexpected boost in IQ was presumably due to the better social environments provided by the adoptive families. Does this mean that phenotypic IQ can be substantially changed?

Even under existing conditions of child rearing, phenotypes of children reared by low-IQ parents could be markedly changed by giving them the same rearing environment as the top IQ group provide for their children. According to DeFries (17), if children whose parents average 20 IQ points below the population mean were reared in environments such as usually are provided only by parents in the top .01 percent of the population, these same children would average 5 points *above* the population mean instead of 15 points below, as they do when reared by their own families.

Euthenic policies depend upon the demonstration that different rearing conditions can change phenotypic IQ sufficiently to enable most people in a social class or racial group to function in future society. I think there is great promise in this line of research and practice, although its efficacy will depend ultimately on the cost and feasibility of implementing radical intervention programs. Regardless of the present heritability of IQ in any population, phenotypes can be changed by the introduction of new and different environments. (One merit of Eysenck's book is the attention he gives to this point.) Furthermore, it is impossible to predict phenotypic outcomes under very different conditions. For example, in the Milwaukee Project (18), in which the subjects are ghetto children whose mothers' IQ's are less than 70, intervention began soon after the children were born. Over a four-year period Heber has intensively tutored the children for several hours every day and has produced an enormous IQ difference between the experimental group (mean IQ 127) and a control group (mean IQ 90). If the tutored children continue to advance in environments which are radically different from their homes with retarded mothers, we shall have some measure of the present phenotypic range of reaction (19) of children whose average IQ's might have been in the 80 to 90 range. These data support Crow's comment on h^2 in his contribution to the *Harvard Educational Review* discussion (p. 158):

It does not directly tell us how much improvement in IQ to expect from a given change in the environment. In particular, it offers no guidance as to the consequences of a new kind of environmental influence. For example, conventional heritability measures for height show a value of nearly 1. Yet, because of unidentified environmental influences, the mean height in the United States and in Japan has risen by a spectacular amount. Another kind of illustration is provided by the discovery of a cure for a hereditary disease. In such cases, any information on prior heritability may become irrelevant. Furthermore, heritability predictions are less dependable at the tails of the distribution.

To illustrate the phenotypic changes that can be produced by radically different environments for children with clear genetic anomalies, Rynders (20) has provided daily intensive tutoring for Down's syndrome [i.e., so-called Mongoloid] infants. At the age of two, these children have average IQ's of 85 while control-group children, who are enrolled in a variety of other programs, average 68. Untreated children have even lower average IQ scores.

The efficacy of intervention programs for children whose expected IQ's are too low to permit full participation in society depends on their long-term effects on intelligence. Early childhood programs may be necessary but insufficient to produce functioning adults. There are critical research questions yet to be answered about euthenic programs, including what kinds, how much, how long, how soon, and toward what goals?

DOES h² MATTER?

There is growing disillusionment with the concept of heritability, as it is understood and misunderstood. Some who understand it very well would like to eliminate h^2 from human studies for at least two reasons. First, the usefulness of h^2 estimates in animal and plant genetics pertains to decisions about the efficacy of selective breeding to produce more desirable phenotypes. Selective breeding does not apply to the human case, at least so far. Second, if important phenotypic changes can be produced by radically different environments, then, it is asked, who cares about the heritability of IQ? Morton (21) has expressed these sentiments well:

Considerable popular interest attaches to such questions as "is one class or ethnic group innately superior to another on a particular test?" The reasons are entirely emotional, since such a difference, if established, would serve as no better guide to provision of educational or other facilities than an unpretentious assessment of phenotypic differences.

I disagree. The simple assessment of phenotypic performance does not suggest any particular intervention strategy. Heritability estimates can have merit as indicators of the effects to be expected from various types of intervention programs. If, for example, IQ tests, which predict well to achievements in the larger society, show low heritabilities in a population, then it is probable that simply providing better environments which now exist will improve average performance in that population. If h^2 is high but environments sampled in that population are largely unfavorable, then (again) simple environmental improvement will probably change the mean phenotypic level. If h^2 is high and the environments sampled are largely favorable, then novel environmental manipulations are probably required to change phenotypes, and eugenic programs may be advocated.

The most common misunderstanding of the concept "heritability" relates to the myth of fixed intelligence: if h^2 is high, this reasoning goes, then intelligence is genetically fixed and unchangeable at the phenotypic level. This misconception ignores the fact that h^2 is a population statistic, bound to a given set of environmental conditions at a given point in time. Neither intelligence nor h^2 estimates are fixed.

It is absurd to deny that the frequencies of genes for behavior may vary between populations. For individual differences within populations, and for social-class differences, a genetic hypothesis is almost a necessity to explain some of the variance in IQ, especially among adults in contemporary white populations living in average or better environments. But what Jensen, Shuey, and Eysenck (and others) propose is that genetic racial differences are necessary to account for the current phenotypic differences in mean IQ between populations. That may be so, but it would be extremely difficult, given current methodological limitations, to gather evidence that would dislodge an environmental hypothesis to account for the same data. And to assert, despite the absence of evidence, and in the present social climate, that a particular race is genetically disfavored in intelligence is to scream "FIRE! . . . I think" in a crowded theater. Given that so little is known, further scientific study seems far more justifiable than public speculations.

REFERENCES

1 For a review of studies, see L. Erlenmeyer-Kimling and L. F. Jarvik, *Science* 142, 1477 (1963). Heritability is the ratio of genetic variance to total phenotypic variance. For human studies, heritability is used in its broad sense of total genetic variance/total phenotypic variance.

2 The *Harvard Educational Review* compilation includes Jensen's paper, "How much can we boost IQ and scholastic achievement?," comments on it by J. S. Kagan, J. McV. Hunt, J. F. Crow, C. Bereiter, D. Elkind, L. J. Cronbach, and W. F. Brazziel, and a rejoinder by Jensen. See also A. R. Jensen, in J. Hellmuth, *Disadvantaged Child,* vol. 3 (Special Child Publ., Seattle, Wash., 1970).

3 P. L. Nichols, thesis, University of Minnesota (1970). Nichols reports that in two large samples of black and white children, seven-year WISC IQ scores showed the same means and distributions for the two racial groups, once social-class variables were equated. These results are unlike those of several other studies, which found that matching socio-economic status did not create equal means in the two racial groups [A. Shuey (*5*): A. B. Wilson, *Racial Isolation in the Public Schools,* vol. 2 (Government Printing Office, Washington, D.C., 1967)]. In Nichols's samples, prenatal and postnatal medical care was equally available to blacks and whites, which may have contributed to the relatively high IQ scores of the blacks in these samples.

4 By interaction. Eysenck means simply $P = G + E$, or "heredity and environment acting together to produce the observed phenotype" (p. 111). He does not mean what most geneticists and behavior geneticists mean by interaction; that is, the *differential* phenotypic effects produced by various combinations of genotypes and environments, as in the interaction term of analysis-of-variance statistics. Few thinking people are not interactionists in Eysenck's sense of the term, because that's the only way to get the organism and the environment into the same equation to account for variance in any phenotypic trait. How much of the phenotypic variance is accounted for by each of the terms in the equation is the real issue.

5 A. Shuey, *The Testing of Negro Intelligence* (Social Science Press, New York, 1966), pp. 499–519.

6 F. B. Davis, *The Measurement of Mental Capacity through Evoked-Potential Recordings* (Educational Records Bureau, Greenwich, Conn., 1971). "As it turned out, no evidence was found that the latency periods obtained . . . displayed serviceable utility for predicting school performance or level of mental ability among pupils in preschool through grade 8" (p. x).

7 *New York Times,* 8 Oct. 1971, p. 41.

8 J. Kagan and H. A. Moss, *Birth to Maturity* (Wiley, New York, 1962).

9 S. Scarr-Salapatek, *Science,* in press.

10 P. E. Vernon, *Intelligence and Cultural Environment* (Methuen, London, 1969).

11 T. Dobzhansky, *Mankind Evolving* (Yale Univ. Press, New Haven, 1962), pp. 234–238.

12 J. Thoday, *J. Biosocial Science* 1, suppl. 3, 4 (1969).

13 L. L. Cavalli-Sforza and W. F. Bodmer, *The Genetics of Human Populations* (Freeman, San Francisco, 1971), pp. 753–804. They propose that the study of racial differences is useless and not scientifically supportable at the present time.

14 E. W. and S. H. Reed, *Science* 165, 762 (1969); *Am. J. Hum. Genet.* 21, 1 (1969); C. MacLean and P. L. Workman, paper at a meeting of the American Society of Human Genetics (1970, Indianapolis).

15 E. W. Reed and S. C. Reed, *Mental Retardation: A Family Study* (Saunders, Philadelphia, 1965); *Social Biol.* 18, suppl. 42 (1971).

16 M. Skodak and H. M. Skeels, *J. Genet. Psychol.* 75, 85 (1949).

17 J. C. DeFries, paper for the C.O.B.R.E. Research Workshop on Genetic Endowment and Environment in the Determination of Behavior (3–8 Oct. 1971, Rye, N.Y.).

18 R. Heber, *Rehabilitation of Families at Risk for Mental Retardation* (Regional Rehabilitation Center, Univ. of Wisconsin, 1969), S. P. Strickland, *Am. Ed.* 7, 3 (1971).

19 I. I. Gottesman, in *Social Class, Race, and Psychological Development*, M. Deutsch, I. Katz, and A. R. Jensen, Eds. (Holt, Rinehart, and Winston, New York, 1968), pp. 11–51.

20 J. Rynders, personal communication, November 1971.

21 N. E. Morton, paper for the C.O.B.R.E. Research Workshop on Genetic Endowment and Environment in the Determination of Behavior (3–8 Oct. 1971, Rye, N.Y.).

Reading 7

The War over Race and IQ: When Black Children Grow Up in White Homes. . . .

Sandra Scarr-Salapatek
Richard A. Weinberg

Black children in this country, as a group, score lower on IQ tests than white children do. The difference between the two groups is about 15 points, a gap that generally corresponds to the white children's greater success in school.

The IQ difference is agreed upon by all parties in the continuing debate about race and intelligence. But there has been no resolution to the burning question of why it exists, and the efforts to explain it have generated anguish, bitterness and opprobrium among educators, makers of social policy, and laymen.

Three camps are now continuing the argument. One believes that the IQ is fixed genetically, and that efforts to change a child's score by changing his environment or giving him compensatory education must fail [see "The Differences Are Real," *pt,* December 1973]. This genetic view also maintains that IQ tests are valid because they reliably predict the academic success of all children, black and white, equally well. The second group, largely liberal and activist, retorts that black children show an IQ deficit because they live and grow in environments that are physically and intellectually impoverished. Change the environment, their argument runs, and the IQ will follow. The environmentalists consider IQ tests to be biased in favor of white middle-class children, and thus invalid measures of intelligence for minorities.

The third group, who might be called the pacifists, argues that no resolution of the debate is possible until black children are raised in exactly the same surroundings as whites. If equally rich environments close the IQ gap, then the genetic argument falls apart.

We have now completed a study on transracial adoption that provides a first look at what happens to the IQs of black children who live in white homes. Adoption changes a child's entire lifestyle around the clock, in contrast to compensatory-education programs or special classes that are wedged into the school curriculum and, at best, affect some part of the child's life between 9:00 and

3:00. If black children raised in white worlds do better on IQ tests than blacks raised in black environments, all groups in the controversy would have their answer.

White Parents, Black Children   In the mid-'60s thousands of white families adopted children of other racial and national origins, partly because few white infants were available for adoption, and partly because many of these families were personally committed to racial equality. We did not deal with the value judgment of whether transracial adoption is good or bad for the children and families involved; we simply seized the opportunity to see whether radical environmental change closes the IQ gap.

Over the past two years we have studied 101 white families who adopted black children. We reached them through the Minnesota Open Door Society, a group of such families, and the Adoption Unit of the Minnesota State Department of Public Welfare. In the Minneapolis area, where the black population is only 1.9 percent, black-white relationships are not as tense and troubled as they are in other states and cities. For this reason, parents can adopt children of different races easily, and the surrounding community exacts no social price, from parents or adopted children, for doing so.

A team of interviewers visited each family twice and gave every member over the age of four an IQ test: the Stanford-Binet for four- to eight-year-olds, the Wechsler Intelligence Scale for Children (WISC) for eight- to 16-year-olds, and the Wechsler Adult Intelligence Scale (WAIS) for children over 16 and their parents. The tests were all scored by an experienced psychometrician who was unaware of the children's race or adoptive status. We also interviewed the parents about the family's lifestyle, the circumstances of the adoption, and their experiences in raising children of different races.

The fathers in our transracial families tend to be professionals—ministers, engineers and lawyers. Nearly half of the mothers are employed at least part-time as secretaries, nurses, or teachers. Most of the parents are college graduates, but they are not especially wealthy. Many live in areas with a few black neighbors but most rarely see blacks in their daily lives. The households themselves often resembled miniversions of the United Nations, for a number of families adopted children of several races or nationalities in addition to having their own. The average number of children in a family was four, with a range from one to 14.

Of the 321 children in the study, 145 were natural and 176 adopted; 130 of the adoptees were black and 46 either white, Asian, or American Indian. Among the black children, 22 percent had two black parents, 52 percent had one black and one white parent, and 26 percent had one black parent and a parent of unknown or Asian ancestry.

Adoption and IQ The typical adopted child in these families—of any race—scored above the national average on standard IQ tests. But the child's age at adoption and his or her experiences before moving to the new family were strongly related to later IQ. The earlier a child was placed, the fewer disruptions in his life, and the better his care in the first few years, the higher his later IQ score was likely to be. The white adopted children, who found families earlier than any other group, scored 111 on the average; the black adopted children got IQ scores averaging 106; and the Asian and Indian children, who were adopted later than any other group, and more of whom had lived longer in impersonal institutions, scored at the national average, 100.

If the black adopted children had been reared by their natural parents, we would expect their IQ scores to average about 90. We infer these scores from the level of education and the occupations of their biological parents. The black adopted children, however, scored well above the national averages of both blacks and whites, especially if they were adopted early in life. In fact, the *lowest* score of an early-adopted black child, 86, was close to the average for all black children in the nation.

When we compare black and white adoptees, it seems that the white children still have an IQ advantage, 111 to 106. However, the black children had lived with their adoptive families for fewer years than the white children and were younger when we tested them. Adoption at an early age increased the scores of black children to an average

	IQ scores		
	Number	Average	Range
All adopted children			
Black	130	106	68–144
White	25	111	62–143
Other	21	100	66–129
Early adopted children			
Black	99	110	86–136
White	9	117	99–138
Other	only three cases		
Natural children	144	117	81–150

of 110. There was a trend for early adoption to increase the IQ scores of white children too, but we have only nine cases in that category.

True to their higher IQ scores, the black adopted children also did better at school, a real-life criterion of intellectual achievement. They scored above the average for Minnesota schoolchildren and above the national average as well on aptitude and achievement tests. In reading and math they scored in the 55th percentile; in comparison, the average ranking for all black children in the Minneapolis-St. Paul area is the 15th percentile.

The adoptive families are clearly doing something that develops intellectual skills in all of their children, adopted or not. These parents were a particularly bright group—with an average IQ of 121 for the fathers and 118 for the mothers—that is reflected in their high levels of education. Their natural children, who have lived in such enriched environments since their birth, scored above the adopted children and slightly below the parents.

The Influences of Birth vs. Breeding When it comes to explaining just why individual children differ in IQ, however, we still don't have a perfect way to separate genetic and environmental influences. Consider Daniel and Sara, two black children who were adopted before they were six months old. Daniel's adoptive father is a professor of biology and his mother is a high-school English teacher; both have high IQs. They had two children before adopting Daniel. The boy's black natural parents were college students. At the age of eight, Daniel tested out with an IQ of 123.

Sara's adoptive father is a minister, and her

mother a housewife; their IQs are average. They have four other children, two of whom were also adopted. Sara's black mother was a nurse's aide who had a 10th-grade education, and her father a construction worker who quit high school in the 11th grade. At the age of eight, Sara's IQ was 98.

Daniel and Sara had a different biological heritage and rearing environment. Which contributed more?

Children are not dealt randomly into adoptive homes like poker hands. Adoption agencies usually try to match the backgrounds of the natural and adoptive parents. As a result, children like Daniel, whose natural parents were well-educated, tend to get placed with adoptive parents who also are bright and have professional careers. So adopted children show an intellectual ability related to that of their natural parents, even though they were not raised by them.

To answer the genetic argument that blacks have lower IQ scores than whites because of their African ancestry, we compared the IQ scores of children who had had one black parent with those who had had two. The 19 children of two black parents got an average score of 97, while the 68 with only one black parent scored 109.

One might leap to the old genetic-deficiency explanation, but the confounding problem is that the two groups had very different placement histories and their mothers differed in amount of education. The children who had two black parents were significantly older when they were adopted, had been in their new homes a shorter time when we tested them, and had had more placements before being adopted. Further, their black natural mothers had less education than the white natural mothers and probably underwent more risks during pregnancy. Prenatal problems can affect a child's intellectual ability.

Intelligence, then—at least as measured by IQ tests—is a result both of environment and genetics, but overall, our study impressed us with the strength of environmental factors. Children whose natural parents had relatively little education and presumably below-average IQs can do extremely well if they grow up in enriched surroundings. If a different environment can cause the IQ scores of black children to shift from a norm of 90 or 95 to 110, then the views advanced by the genetic determinists cannot account for the current IQ gap between blacks and whites. Our work does not rule

Comparison of Adopted Children Having either One or Two Black Natural Parents:

	Children with two black parents (29)	Children with one black and one white parent (68)*
IQ	97	109
Age at adoption (in months)	32	9
Length of time in new family (in months)	42	61
Natural mother's education (in years)	10.9	12.4
Adoptive father's IQ	119.5	121.4
Adoptive mother's IQ	116.4	119.2

*Note in all but two of these cases, the pattern was a white woman and a black man.

out genetic contributions to intelligence, but it does demonstrate that a massive environmental change can increase black IQ scores to an above-average level. Social factors, such as age at placement and the adoptive family's characteristics play a strong role in accounting for this increase.

Cooling Out the Controversy The touchy and troubling question is, now what? Schools, as presently run, do not have the far-reaching, intensive impact of the family in the formation and enhancement of a child's intelligence. But no one would be so arrogant or foolhardy to endorse transracial adoption as social policy, shipping black children into white homes with the same furious effort now devoted to bussing them into white schools. On the contrary, many black-action groups are now putting pressure on adoption agencies to make sure that transracial adoption does not occur.

Now we need to find out what goes on in these adoptive families that enhances IQ. From personality tests and observations of the parents we worked with, we know they are generally warm, comfortable, free of anxiety, and relaxed with children. They run democratic households in which adults and kids participate in many activities together. These factors, along with the intellectual stimulation that the children are exposed to, are doubtless involved in their children's higher IQs. We need to look for other intangibles in the things parents give their children and do with them that increase intelligence.

And after we've found all the intangibles, we may want to ask whether IQ should be an overriding middle-class value at all. Intelligence tests do measure how well a child will get on in a white middle-class schoolroom, but tell us nothing about a person's empathy, sociability and altruism, a few blessed virtues that tend to get brushed off the psychologist's test battery.

But for the moment, at least, we have evidence that the black-white IQ gap is neither inevitable nor unchangeable. Smug whites have no cause to rest on biological laurels. The question no longer is why blacks do more poorly on IQ tests than whites. The question is what we are prepared to do about it.

Reading 8

Five Myths about Your IQ

Mary Jo Bane
Christopher Jencks

Standard IQ Tests purport to measure "intelligence," which is widely viewed as the key to adult success. As a result, children with low IQ scores* are the subjects of anxious solicitude from their parents, while groups that test badly, notably blacks, are constantly on the defensive. This is doubly true when, as usually happens, those who do poorly on IQ tests also do poorly on school achievement tests that measure things like reading comprehension and arithmetic skills.

Parents' and teachers' anxieties have been further intensified as a result of claims that IQ scores are largely determined by heredity. If an individual's genes determine his IQ, and if IQ then determines his chances of adult success, it is a short step to the conclusion that there is nothing he can do to improve his prospects. Moreover, if life chances are determined at birth, many recent efforts at social reform have obviously been doomed from the start.

The controversy over IQ and achievement tests has become so bitter that it is almost impossible to discuss the subject rationally. Neither social scientists nor laymen seem to have much interest in the actual facts, which are extremely complex. The best currently available evidence suggests that:

*An intelligence quotient is computed by ascertaining a person's mental age on the basis of a standardized intelligence test, and multiplying the result by 100. That result is then divided by the person's chronological age, to yield the IQ. Thus, the average IQ of the population is (and arithmetically must be) 100. About one person in six has an IQ under 85, and about one in six has an IQ over 115. About one in forty is under 70, and about one in forty is over 130.

1 IQ tests measure only one rather limited variety of intelligence, namely the kind that schools (and psychologists) value. Scores on the tests show remarkably little relationship to performance in most adult roles. People with high scores do a little better in most jobs than people with low scores, and they earn somewhat more money, but the differences are surprisingly small.

2 The poor are seldom poor because they have low IQ scores, low reading scores, low arithmetic scores, or bad genes. They are poor because they either cannot work, cannot find adequately paying jobs, or cannot keep such jobs. This has very little to do with their test scores.

3 Claims that "IQ scores are 80 percent hereditary" appear to be greatly exaggerated. Test results depend almost as much on variations in children's environments as on variations in their genes.

4 While differences in the environments that children grow up in explain much of the variation in their test scores, differences in their school experiences appear to play a relatively minor role. But even socioeconomic background has a quite modest impact on test scores. Many factors that influence the scores seem to be unrelated to either school quality or parental status. At present, nobody has a clear idea what these factors are, how they work, or what we can do about them.

5 If school quality has a modest effect on adult test scores, and if test scores then have a modest effect on economic success, school reforms aimed at teaching basic cognitive skills are likely to have minuscule effects on students' future earning power.

Each of these conclusions contradicts a commonly accepted myth about IQ.

MYTH 1: IQ TESTS ARE THE BEST MEASURE OF HUMAN INTELLIGENCE

When asked whether IQ tests really measure "intelligence," psychologists are fond of saying that this is a meaningless question. They simply define intelligence as "whatever IQ tests measure." This is rather like Humpty-Dumpty, for whom words meant whatever he wanted them to mean, and it was just a question of who was to be master. The trouble is that psychologists are *not* the masters of language, and they cannot assign arbitrary meanings to words without causing all kinds of confusion. In the real world, people cannot use a term like intelligence without assuming that it means many different things at once—all very important. Those who claim that "intelligence is what intelligence tests measure" ought logically to assume, for example, that "intelligence is of no more consequence in human affairs than whatever intelligence tests measure." But people do not think this way. Having said that "intelligence is what IQ tests measure," psychologists always end up assuming that what IQ tests measure *must* be important, because "intelligence" is important. This road leads through the looking glass.

What, then, does the term "intelligence" really mean? For most people, it includes all the mental abilities required to solve whatever theoretical or practical problems they happen to think important. At one moment intelligence is the ability to unravel French syntax. At another it is the intuition required to understand what ails a neurotic friend. At still another it is the capacity to anticipate future demand for hog bristles. We know from experience that these skills are only loosely related to one another. People who are "intelligent" in one context often are remarkably "stupid" in another. Thus, in weighing the value of IQ tests, one must ask exactly what *kinds* of intelligence they really measure and what kinds they do not measure.

The evidence we have reviewed suggests that IQ tests are quite good at measuring the kinds of intelligence needed to do school work. Students who do well on IQ tests are quite likely to get good grades in school. They are also likely to stay in school longer than average. But the evidence also suggests that IQ tests are *not* very good at measuring the skills required to succeed in most kinds of adult work.

MYTH 2: THE POOR ARE POOR BECAUSE THEY HAVE LOW IQS. THOSE WITH HIGH IQS END UP IN WELL-PAID JOBS

The fact is that people who do well on IQ and achievement tests do not perform much better than average in most jobs. Nor do they earn much more than the average. There have been more than a hundred studies of the relationship between IQ and people's performance on different jobs, using a wide variety of techniques for rating performance. In general, differences in IQ account for less than 10 percent of the variation in actual job performance. In many situations, there is no relationship at all between a man's IQ and how competent he is at his job. IQ also plays a modest role in determining income, explaining only about 12 percent of the variation. Thus, 88 percent of the variation in income is unrelated to IQ.

Nor do IQ differences account for much of the economic gap between blacks and whites. Phillips Cutright of the University of Indiana has conducted an extensive investigation of blacks who were examined by the Selective Service System in 1952. These men all took the Armed Forces Qualification Test, which measures much the same thing as an IQ test. In 1962, the average black in this sample earned 43 percent less than the average white. Blacks with AFQT scores as high as the average white's earned 32 percent less than the average white. Equalizing black and white test scores therefore reduced the income gap by about a quarter. Three quarters of the gap had nothing to do with test scores. This same pattern holds for whites born into working-class and middle-class families. Whites with middle-class parents earn more than whites with working-class parents, but only 25–35 percent of the gap is traceable to test-score differences between the two groups.

None of this means that a child with a high IQ has no economic advantage over a child with a low IQ, nor that a child with high reading and math scores has no economic advantage over a child with low scores. It just means that the economic effect is likely to be much smaller than anxious parents or educational reformers expect. Among white males, those who score in the top fifth on standardized tests appear to earn about a third more than the national average. Those who score in the bottom fifth earn about two-thirds of the national average. These differences are by no means trivial. But they do not look very impressive when we recall that the best paid fifth of all workers earns six or seven times as much as the worst paid fifth. Most of that gap has nothing to do with test scores, and cannot be eliminated by equalizing test scores.

How can this be? We know that test scores play a significant role in determining school grades, in determining how long students stay in school, and in determining what kinds of credentials they eventually earn. We also know that credentials play a significant role in determining what occupations men enter. Occupations, in turn, have a significant effect on earnings. But at each stage in this process there are many exceptions, and the cumulative result is that exceptions are almost commonplace. A significant number of students with relatively low test scores earn college degrees, for example. In addition, a significant number of individuals without college degrees enter well-paid occupations, especially in business. Finally, people in relatively low-status occupations (such as plumbers and electricians) often earn more than professionals (think of teachers and clergymen). Overall, then, there are a lot of people with rather low test scores who nonetheless make above-average incomes, and a lot of people with high IQs but below-average incomes.

The limited importance of test scores is also clear if we look at the really poor—those who have to get by on less than half the national average. Nearly half of all poor families have no earner at all, either because they are too old, because they are headed by a woman with young children, or because the father is sick, alcoholic, mentally ill, or otherwise incapacitated. These problems are a bit more common among people with low IQs, but that is not the primary explanation for any of them.

This does not mean that financial success depends primarily on socioeconomic background, as many liberals and radicals seem to believe. Socioeconomic background has about the same influence as IQ on how much schooling a person gets, on the kind of occupation he enters, and on how much money he makes. Thus we can say that neither socioeconomic background *nor* IQ explains much of the variation in adult occupational status or income. Most of the economic inequality among adults is due to other factors.

Unfortunately, we do not know enough to identify with much precision the other factors leading to economic success. All we can do is suggest their complexity. First, there is a wide variety of skills that have little or no connection with IQ but have a strong relationship to success in some specialized field. The ability to hit a ball thrown at high speed is extremely valuable, if you happen to be a professional baseball player. The ability to walk along a narrow steel beam 600 feet above the ground without losing your nerve is also very valuable, if

you happen to be a construction worker. In addition, many personality traits have substantial cash value in certain contexts. A man who is good at figuring out what his boss wants, or good at getting his subordinates to understand and do what he wants, is at a great premium in almost any large hierarchical organization. While these talents are doubtless related to IQ, the connection is obviously very loose. Similarly, a person who inspires confidence is likely to do well regardless of whether he is a doctor, a clergyman, a small businessman, or a Mafioso, and inspiring confidence depends as much on manner as on mental abilities.

Finally, there is the matter of luck. America is full of gamblers, some of whom strike it rich while others lose hard-earned assets. One man's farm has oil on it, while another man's cattle get hoof-and-mouth disease. One man backs a "mad inventor" and ends up owning a big piece of Polaroid, while another backs a mad inventor and ends up owning a piece of worthless paper. We cannot say much about the relative importance of these factors, but when it comes to making a dollar, IQ is clearly a small part of a big, complicated picture.

MYTH 3: YOUR IQ IS OVERWHELMINGLY DETERMINED BY YOUR GENETIC ENDOWMENT

Over the past decade, an enormous number of school reform programs have attempted to raise the scores of those who do poorly on standardized tests. These programs have involved preschool education, curriculum development, teacher training, compensatory education, administrative reorganization, and many other innovations. None appears to have produced the promised results on a permanent basis. This has led many people to the conclusion that variations in IQ scores must reflect innate genetic differences between individuals and groups. This is a logical non sequitur. But more important, the theory that IQ scores are determined at the moment of conception is not supported by the evidence. Genes clearly have a significant influence on IQ and school achievement scores, but so does environment. The reason reform programs have failed to improve test scores is not that the environment is irrelevant but that the reforms have not altered the most important features of the environment.

Much of the continuing furor over IQ scores derives from Arthur Jensen's controversial claim that genes "explain" something like 80 percent of the variation in children's performance on IQ tests. We have reviewed the same evidence as Jensen, and while it certainly shows that genes have *some* effect on IQ, we believe that his 80 percent estimate is much too high. The details of the argument are extremely complicated, but the basic reasons that Jensen overestimated the role of heredity and underestimated the role of environment are fairly easy to understand.

First, Jensen estimated the influence of genes on IQ scores largely by using data from studies of twins. Some of these studies dealt with identical twins who had been separated early in life and brought up by different parents. Identical twins have exactly the same genes. When they are brought up in different environments, all differences between them can be attributed to the effects of their environments.

Other studies compared identical twins who have been reared together with fraternal twins who had been reared together. Fraternal twins have only about half their genes in common; identical twins have all their genes in common. Thus if identical twins were no more alike on IQ tests than fraternal twins, we would have to conclude that genetic resemblance did not affect the children's test scores. But identical twins are in fact considerably more alike than fraternal twins, so it seems reasonable to suppose that genes have a significant effect on test scores. (Identical twins may also be treated somewhat more alike than fraternal twins, but the effect of this appears to be small.)

It is perfectly legitimate to use twin studies to estimate the relative influence of heredity and environment on test scores. But we can also estimate the effects of environment by measuring the degree of resemblance between adopted children reared in the same home. When we do this, environment appears to have somewhat more effect than it does in twin studies, while genes appear to have somewhat less effect. No one has ever offered a good explanation for this discrepancy, but that does not justify ignoring it. The most reasonable assumption is that the true effect of heredity is somewhat less than that suggested by twin studies but somewhat more than that suggested by studies of unrelated children in the same home.

A second difficulty with Jensen's estimate is that it is based on twin studies in England as well as in the United States. When we separate the American and English studies, we find that genetic factors appear to be more important in England than in America. This suggests that children's environments are more varied in the United States than they are in England. Other evidence, as well as common-sense observation of the two cultures, supports this interpretation. Consequently, when Jensen pools English and American data to arrive at his estimate of the effects of genes on IQ scores, he overestimates the relative importance of genes in America and underestimates their importance in England.

A third problem: Jensen assumes that the effects of genes and those of environment are completely independent of one another. In fact, since parents with favorable genes tend to have above-average cognitive skills, they tend to provide their children with usually rich home environments. Our calculations suggest that this double advantage accounts for about a fifth of the variation in IQ scores.

After correcting all these biases, our best estimate is that genes explain 45 rather than 80 percent of the variation in IQ scores in contemporary America. This 45 percent estimate could easily be off by 10 percent either way, and it might conceivably be off by as much as 20 percent either way. The estimate would change if the range of environments were to increase or decrease for any reason. Genes are relatively more important in small homogeneous communities, where children's environments are relatively similar, than in America as a whole. By the same token, genes are relatively less important among groups whose environments are unusually diverse. If, for example, there were a sharp increase in the number of children suffering from acute malnutrition, or if large numbers of children were excluded from schools, environmental inequality would increase, and the relative importance of genes in determining IQ scores would decrease.

While genes probably account for something like 45 percent of the variation in IQ scores, it does not follow that genetic differences in actual learning capacity account for anything like this much variation. Genes influence test scores in two quite different ways. First, they influence what an individual learns from a given environment. Placed in front of the same TV program, one child may remember more of what he sees than another. Confronted with subtraction, one child may "catch on" faster than another. These differences derive partly from genetically based differences in learning capacity.

In addition, however, genes can influence the environments to which people are exposed. Imagine a nation that refuses to send children with red hair to school. Under these circumstances having genes that cause red hair will lower your reading scores. This does not tell us that children with red hair cannot learn to read. It tells us only that in this particular situation there is a socially imposed relationship between genes and opportunities to learn. In America, the genes that affect skin color have an indirect influence on an individual's opportunities and incentives to learn many skills. So too hereditary appearance and athletic ability influence a youngster's chance of getting into many colleges, and thus affect his or her later test scores.

Beyond all that, a person's genes may influence his actual learning capacity, which may then affect his opportunities and incentives to learn. If an individual has low test scores for genetic reasons, he may be assigned to a "slow" class where he learns less. Or he may be excluded from college. Such practices tend to widen the initial test score gap between the genetically advantaged and the genetically disadvantaged. The resulting inequality is thus due *both* to genes *and* to environment. Yet conventional methods of estimating heritability impute the entire difference to genes.

When we say that genes "explain" 45 percent of the variation in test scores, we are talking about their overall effect, including their effect both on the capacity to learn and on opportunities and incentives to learn. No one has yet devised a method for separating these two effects. But if opportunities and incentives to learn were absolutely equal, genetically determined differences in learning capacity would account for considerably less than 45 percent of the variation in IQ scores.

MYTH 4: THE MAIN REASON BLACK CHILDREN AND POOR WHITE CHILDREN HAVE LOW IQ SCORES IS THAT THEY HAVE "BAD" GENES

Children from poor families tend to get lower scores on both IQ and school achievement tests than children from middle-class families. This difference is apparent when children enter school, and it does not seem to change much as children get older. Many liberals argue that the reason poor children do badly on these tests is that the tests are biased. Most of the tests contain items that are culturally loaded, in the sense that they presume

familiarity with certain objects or assume the correctness of certain attitudes. The bias in these items always appears to favor children from middle-class backgrounds. Yet when psychologists have examined children's answers to these "loaded" items, they have not found that poor children did particularly badly on them. Nor have they found that eliminating such items from tests reduced the disparity in overall performance between poor and middle-class children. Middle-class children outscore poor children by as much on "culture free" tests as on "culturally loaded" tests. This suggests that what poor children lack is not specific information but more basic skills that are relevant to many different kinds of tests.

These findings seem to support the theory that test-score differences between rich and poor derive from genetic differences between rich and poor children. Like the "cultural bias" explanation, this "genetic" explanation has considerable logical appeal. Everyone who has studied the matter agrees that genes have *some* influence on test scores, that test scores have *some* influence on education attainment, and that education has *some* influence on adult success. It follows that there must be *some* genetic difference, however small, between economically successful and unsuccessful adults. If this is true, there must also be some genetic difference between children with successful and unsuccessful parents.

The evidence suggests, however, that genetic differences between successful and unsuccessful families play a very minor role in determining children's IQs. Studies of adopted children indicate that genes may account for as much as half the observed correlation between parental status and children's test scores. Indirect evidence, derived from the relationship between test scores and parental success, suggests that the relationship is even weaker. Overall, our best guess is that genetic differences between social classes explain no more than 6 percent of the variation in IQ scores, while cultural differences between social classes explain another 6–9 percent.

This conclusion means that the average middle-class child may have a small genetic advantage over the average working-class child. But it also means that there are more working-class children than middle-class children with high genetic potential. This is because there are more working-class children to begin with. While their average score is a little lower than that of middle-class children, the difference is very small, and nearly half of all working-class children are above the middle-class average.

Furthermore, while differences between rich and poor whites are probably partly genetic, this tells us nothing about the origins of differences between whites and blacks. Blacks have lower IQ and achievement scores than whites, even when their parents have similar economic positions. But blacks also grow up in very different social and cultural environments from whites, even when their parents have the same occupations and incomes. We have no way of measuring the effects of these cultural differences. Our personal feeling is that black-white cultural differences could easily explain the observed IQ difference, which is only about 15 points. Differences of this magnitude are often found between white subcultures. Both black and white scores on military tests rose about 10 points between World War I and World War II, for example. Whites in eastern Tennessee improved by almost this much between 1930 and 1940, apparently as a result of the introduction of schools, roads, radios, etc.

The key point is that *it doesn't much matter whether IQ differences between blacks and whites are hereditary or environmental.* IQ accounts for only a quarter of the income gap between blacks and whites. Therefore, even if genes accounted for *all* the IQ gap between blacks and whites, which is hardly likely, they would account for only a quarter of the economic gap. In all probability their role is far smaller. The widespread obsession with possible genetic differences between races is thus a diversion from the real problem. We ought to worry about eliminating the discrimination that still accounts for most of the observed economic difference between blacks and whites. If this could be done, the average black would be earning almost as much as the average white, and the pointless debate about possible genetic differences would no longer seem important to most sensible people.

MYTH 5: IMPROVING THE QUALITY OF THE SCHOOLS WILL GO A LONG WAY TOWARD WIPING OUT DIFFERENCES IN IQ AND SCHOOL ACHIEVEMENT AND THEREFORE IN CHILDREN'S LIFE CHANCES

Whether we like it or not, the quality of a child's school has even less effect than his social class on his test scores. The best evidence on this still comes from the 1965 Equality of Educational Opportunity Survey, whose first and most famous product was the Coleman Report. This survey did not give individual IQ tests to children, but it did give "verbal ability" tests that are very similar. It also gave reading and math tests. The results of this survey have aroused all sorts of controversy, but they have been confirmed by several other large surveys, notably the national study of high schools conducted by Project Talent throughout the 1960s. These surveys show that the differences among students in the same school are far greater than the difference between the average student in one school and the average student in another.

The surveys also show that test score difference between the alumni of different schools are largely due to differences among the entering students. Those from high-status families who enter school with high test scores tend to end up with high scores no matter what school they attend. Conversely, students from low-status families with low initial scores tend to end up with low scores even in what most people define as "good" schools. It follows that even if all schools had exactly the same effects on students' scores, the variation in students' IQ and achievement scores would decline very little. Qualitative differences among elementary schools seem to account for less than 6 percent of the variation in IQ test scores. Qualitative differences among high schools account for less than 2 percent.

In theory, of course, we could give students with low initial scores *better* schooling than students with high initial scores. This would allow us to reduce initial differences by more than 6 percent. The difficulty is that nobody knows how to do this. There is no consistent relationship between the amount of money we spend on a school and the rate at which children's test scores improve after they enter. Indeed, while school expenditures nearly doubled during the 1960s, a recent Project Talent survey shows that eleventh graders' school achievement scores hardly changed at all during that decade. Nor is there a consistent relationship between any specific school resource and the rate at which students' test scores rise. Neither small classes, well-paid teachers, experienced teachers, teachers with advanced degrees, new textbooks, nor adequate facilities have a consistent effect on students' scores.

Compensatory educational programs aimed at boosting the test scores of disadvantaged students have also produced discouraging results. Some studies report big gains, but others show that students who were not in the program gained more than those who were. Taken as a group, these studies suggest that students' scores do not improve any faster in compensatory programs than elsewhere. Thus, while there are good theoretical reasons for assuming that we can improve the test scores of those who enter school at a disadvantage, there is also strong evidence that educators simply do not know how to do this at the present time. (Neither, we should add, do educational critics, including ourselves.)

Racial and economic segregation may have slightly more effect than school expenditures on IQ test scores. The evidence, however, is by no means conclusive. Blacks who attend what we might call "naturally" desegregated schools, that is, schools in racially mixed neighborhoods, generally have higher test scores than blacks who attend segregated schools. These differences are apparent when students enter first grade, but they increase over time. This suggests that attending a racially mixed school boosts test scores somewhat faster than attending an all-black school. But the cumulative difference over six years of elementary school is small enough so that the effect in any one year is likely to be almost undetectable.

When we turn from "naturally" desegregated schools to schools that have been desegregated by busing, the evidence is more ambiguous. Some busing studies report that blacks showed appreciable gains. Very few report losses. Most show no statistically reliable difference. Since most of the studies involve small samples and short periods of time, this is not surprising. Taken together, the studies suggest that *on the average* busing probably increases black students' test scores, but that there are plenty of exceptions. Our best guess, based on evidence from both studies of busing and studies of naturally desegregated schools, is that desegregated schools would eventually reduce the test score gap between blacks and whites by about 20 percent. This is, however, only an educated guess. The evidence on this question remains inconclusive, despite some recent extravagant claims to the contrary.

Nor is there any obvious reason to suppose that either decentralization or community control will improve students' test scores. Among whites, relatively small districts score at about the same level as large ones, once other factors are taken into account. Neither decentralization nor community control has been tried on a large enough scale in black communities to prove very much. But predominantly black suburban school districts, like Ravenswood and Compton in California, do not appear to have produced particularly impressive results. Neither have they done particularly badly.

None of this means that we should spend less on schools, stop trying to desegregate them, or reject decentralization or community control. Quite the contrary. If additional expenditures make schools better places for children, then they are justified regardless of their effects on reading comprehension, or IQ scores. If school desegregation reduces racial antagonism over the long run, then we should desegregate even though the students' test scores remain unaffected. And if community control gives parents the feeling that the schools belong to "us" rather than "them," this too is worthwhile for its own sake. Given the slim connection between test scores and adult successes, it would be myopic to judge any sort of school reform primarily in terms of its effect on either IQ or school achievement.

Because a student's mastery of the skills taught in school provides a very poor measure of how well he will do once he graduates, reforms aimed at teaching these skills more effectively are not likely to take us very far toward economic prosperity or equality among adults. We have noted that only 12 percent of the variation in men's earnings is explained by their test scores. We have also seen that reducing inequality in test scores is very difficult. Under these circumstances it makes little sense for economic egalitarians to concentrate on equalizing IQ and achievement scores. Instead, they should concentrate on eliminating the other sources of income inequality, which cause 88 percent of the problem.

To be sure, this is more easily said than done. Those who do well in the present economic system inevitably resist reforms that would reduce their privileges. Those who do poorly in the present system are for the most part too demoralized to protest in any effective way. So long as this persists, there will be little chance of reducing economic inequality.

The complacency of the rich and the demoralization of the poor are reinforced by theories that attribute economic success to genetic superiority and economic failure to genetic deficiency. These theories are nonsense. In 1968, the income difference between the best and worst paid fifth of all workers was about $14,000. Of this, perhaps $500 or $1000 was attributable to genetically determined differences in IQ scores. The idea that genetic inequality explains economic inequality is thus a myth. Like the divine right of kings, such myths help legitimize the status quo. But they should not be taken seriously by those who really want to understand the modern world, much less those who want to change it.

Chapter Three

Infancy and Early Experience

Few areas of research have undergone so radical a change as infancy in recent times. Gone is "the booming, buzzing confusion" that William James described as the world of the infant; nor is the infant viewed any longer as passive, helpless, and at the mercy of his environment. Rather, a new and more positive view of infancy has emerged with infants, characterized as active, competent, and very early ready to make their mark on both their social and physical environment. Owing to rapid and important advances in our methodology for investigating infants, many of the capacities of the infant are just being discovered. As Bower notes in his article in this section, many perceptual and cognitive capacities are available at an earlier age than had been previously assumed. In short, even newborn infants are ready to interact with their environment in a meaningful way.

Nor is the infant's precocity limited to his perceptual capacities; much evidence is accumulating to suggest that the infant is prepared for his social role as well. Infants' early preference for faces and voices over inanimate objects as well as their predisposition to react to human speech sounds are all indicators of the infant's readiness for social interaction. (See Freedman, 1974, in this section.)

However, the infant's social behavior undergoes important changes over the first year of life. One of the important accomplishments is the infant's ability to discriminate among different social situations and social objects. As the Lewis and Brooks-Gunn study in this section so nicely demonstrates, infants are highly discriminating social beings at an early age. However, in contrast to earlier beliefs that infants routinely show fear of strangers, these investigators show that the type of stranger and the manner in which the strange individual interacts with the infant are important determinants of the infant's reactions to strangers. Peer strangers may elicit smiles, while an abrupt and imposing adult stranger may elicit fear. Other investigators (Rheingold and Eckerman, 1973; Sroufe and Waters, 1975) have noted that the test setting is important as well; a mother who wears a strange mask may elicit laughter at home, while the infant may cry when he sees his masked mother in an unfamiliar laboratory.

As psychologists have shifted their views of the infant's competence, they have increasingly recognized that the infant plays an important role in determining his own course of development. During socialization, the influence process is bi-directional, with both the adult influencing the infant and the infant, in turn, modifying the behavior of his caretakers. No one who has been awakened at 3 A.M. by a crying infant would question the impact of infants on their parents. In an important attempt to formalize this process within a developmental framework, Sameroff (1975) in his article in this section proposes a transactional model which recognizes the mutual interplay between infants and adults and indicates how this two-way influence process affects the development of both the infant and his parents.

Finally, both Sameroff and Kagan and Klein (1973) remind us that the effects of early infant experiences are not irreversible. The human organism is adaptive and flexible and able to profit from experiences at a variety of age points. For example, early birth traumas and complications can be overcome by a stimulating and responsive child-rearing environment. Similarly, the timing of development in different cultures indicates that slowness in early development does not preclude catch-up advances at later ages. Different cultures, in short, have different timetables for development and demand certain skills at later times than in our American culture. The impressive aspect of the Kagan-Klein report is the reminder that early "deficits" can be overcome; early experience is important, but the early effects are neither inevitable nor irreversible.

Reading 9

Competent Newborns

Dr. Tom Bower

The human newborn is one of the most fascinating organisms that a psychologist can study. It is only after birth that psychological processes can begin; only after can success and failure, reward and punishment, begin to affect the development of the child. Before that point function and practice—for many theorists the motor forces in development—have no opportunity to modify the processes of growth that produce the neural structures in the brain that must underpin any capacities that are present at birth. The newborn infant is thus the natural focus of the age-old and continuing controversy between nativists and empiricists: that is, the argument over whether human knowledge is a natural endowment, like the structure of our hand, with differences in intellectual competence as genetically determined as differences in eye colour, or is rather the product of behaviour and experience in the world, with differences in intellectual capacity a function of differences in the quality of environmental exposure. An extreme proponent of the latter viewpoint would argue that the newborn with no exposure history behind him, should therefore show no capacities at all, beyond the capacity to learn. Nativists would have to predict something very different.

To the casual eye the empiricists would seem to have the argument. The newborn seems extremely helpless, capable of little save eating, sleeping and crying. But the casual eye would be in error. The human newborn is an extremely competent organism, more competent than those of us brought up in the British Empiricist tradition would ever have suspected.

The traditional starting point for an analysis of knowledge is the input that comes in through the senses (sight, sound, smell and touch, for example). That input does not seem capable of providing the information that adults are able to get out of it. Psychologists have assumed that the deficiencies in the sensory input were made up by learning and experience. But recent experiments with newborns must cast some doubt on this point of view.

Consider, for instance, the ability to localise an odour. Adults can localise odours, to right or left, with a fair degree of accuracy. This is a problem for psychology. Because there is no right or left in the nose, the right-left dimension of experience must be elaborated from other information. There are of course two sources of relevant information: the different intensities of odour at the two nostrils (an odour source on the right will stimulate the right nostril with greater intensity than it will the left); and the different times of arrival of the odour-producing molecules at the nostrils, a source on the right reaching the right nostril fractionally before it reaches the left. These time/intensity differences are used by the perpetual system to specify position to right and left. The structure that does this is present in newborns, who will turn smoothly away from "unpleasant" odour sources, indicating that they are capable of olfactory localisation, as well as sharing adults' opinions of the pleasantness of some odours.

The auditory system poses similar problems. Adults can locate sounds to right and left, with great precision, although there is no right and left within the auditory system. Perception of position of a sound source is elaborated from time of arrival and intensity differences between the two ears, as well as patterns of reflection set up the outer ear.

Michael Wertheimer demonstrated that within seconds of birth infants can use this information, turning their eyes correctly towards a sound source. This shows not only auditory localisation, but also auditory-visual coordination, an expectation that there will be something to be seen at a sound source.

My colleague Eric Aronson has confirmed the same basic point in more complicated experiments performed in Edinburgh. While an infant is in special apparatus he can see his mother through the soundproof glass screen, but can only hear her via the two speakers of a stereo system. The balance on the stereo can be adjusted to make the sound appear to come from straight ahead or any other position. If the mother speaks to her baby with the balance adjusted so that the heard voice appears to come from her seen mouth, the baby is quite happy. But if the heard voice and seen mouth do not coincide, very young infants manifest surprise and upset, indicating auditory localisation, auditory-visual coordination, and, more surprisingly, an expectation that voices will come from mouths. This is an example of competence that seems to be lost with age. In lecture theatres or cinemas, for example, where heard voice and seen mouth are often in very different places, adults do not seem to be aware of the discrepancy.

Vision itself has attracted rather more attention than the other senses, reflecting its greater importance in normal function. Although the eye is a more elaborate structure than the nose or ear, with a built-in structure to register right-left position, for example, there are many dimensions of visual experience that do not seem to be given directly in the visual input. For example, visual experience is clearly three-dimensional, and the third dimension, distance, is clearly missing from the input to the eye (Figure 1). Beginning with Bishop Berkeley in the eighteenth century, empiricists have assumed that distance could only be gauged after man had learned to interpret clues for distance. It now seems that the interpretation of these signs, if this is what occurs, need not be learned.

With colleagues in America I discovered that infants can demonstrate adjustments to the distance of objects during the newborn period. For example if one moves an object towards the face of a baby he will execute a well-coordinated defensive movement, pulling back his head and bringing his hands and arms between himself and the object. The response occurs whether or not the object used is a real object, like the one shown in the figure, or a purely visual simulation projected on a screen. The latter result indicates that the response is elicited by visual information, and not by air movement. The response is only elicited if the approaching objects come within a certain distance, which seems to be about 30 cm. Approach closer than this distance elicits defensive movements, even if the approaching object is small. Approach which stops further away than 30 cm will not elicit defensive movements, even if the approaching object is large. This indicates that the infants are not responding simply to the size of the retinal image produced by the approaching object.

The fact that infants seem to defend themselves against the approach of seen objects seems indicative, at least, of some expectation that seen objects are tangible. I have obtained more convincing evidence of such an expectation by presenting the infant with virtual objects, objects which are visible yet intangible. Two devices that will produce such objects are shown in Figure 2. One depends on the presence of a functioning binocular vision system

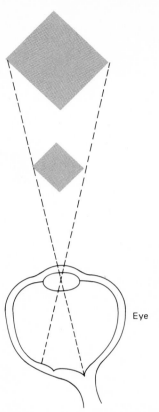

Figure 1 The retina, a two-dimensional surface, obviously cannot register three-dimensional variables such as distance, size or shape.

in the infant (Figure 2a). Two oppositely polarised beams of light cast a double shadow of an object on a rear projection screen. An infant views the double shadows through polarising goggles that made a different shadow visible to each eye. The innate processes of stereopsis fuse the two images to make the infant think he is seeing a solid object in front of the screen. The other depends on nothing more than simple optics (Figure 2b).

Newborn infants will reach out to touch seen objects. The behaviour is very crude but does result in a high proportion of contacts if a real object is presented. What happens if a virtual object is presented? When the infant's hand reaches the seen location of the object there is no tactual input, since the object is intangible. If the infant expects seen objects to be tangible, this event should surprise him, as indeed it does. Infants presented with such

(a)

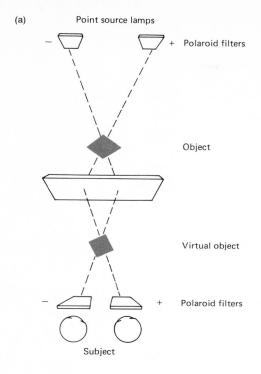

Point source lamps

Polaroid filters

Object

Virtual object

Polaroid filters

Subject

(b)

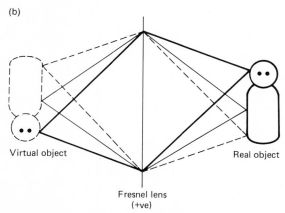

Virtual object

Real object

Fresnel lens
(+ve)

Figure 2 Two devices for producing a virtual object (a) Using shadow caster (b) Using positive fresnel lines.

objects react with extreme surprise and upset, indicating some degree of visual-tactual coordination.

None of the capacities described above would be at all obvious to a casual eye. They cannot be elicited from infants save in conditions which are somewhat special in our culture. The infant must be propped up and his head and arms must be free to move. This condition is not met if the baby is lying flat on his back, the most common position for baby observation in this culture. A newborn on his back uses head and arms to support himself in a stable position. Thus neither is free to engage in any of the indicator behaviours described above.

The experiments I have described so far indicate that newborn infants have a functioning perceptual system, with a striking degree of coordination between the senses. The last experiments on this line that I wish to mention provide the most striking instance of such coordinations: a coordination between vision and the baby's own body image. If a human adult seats himself or herself in front of a newborn infant (three weeks) and engages in any of a wide variety of face or finger movements, the infant will imitate the adult's movements. If the adult sticks his tongue out, the baby will retaliate. If the adult opens and closes his mouth repetitively, the baby will mimic the movements. Babies as young as this have no experience of mirrors, and yet they know they have a mouth and a tongue and can match the seen mouth and tongue of an adult to their own unseen mouth and tongue, a most striking demonstration of intersensory matching. The infant perceives a match, a similiarity, between himself and adults, a capacity of immense significance for all development, and particularly social development.

So far I have spoken of capacities that seem to be innate. I have not mentioned the one capacity that empiricists would maintain must be innate—the capacity to learn. The learning abilities of the newborn infant have been a major focus of research. Since new behaviours do appear at a great rate throughout infancy it is important, theoretically, to establish that learning can occur, and could, therefore, account for the emergent behaviours. Eight years ago it seemed that research had failed to demonstrate that the infant of less than six months can learn anything at all. This pessimistic conclusion has been totally overthrown since then to the extent that it has even been suggested that the newborn infant can learn better at that point in his development than he ever will again.

Psychologists assess learning with very simple paradigms involving rewards for specific activities. Increase in the rate of the rewarded activity is taken as a measure of learning. The problem is to make sure that the reward is really rewarding. If one can do this with infants they will readily demonstrate learning of a high order. Unfortunately, older infants are readily bored with most rewards. A few studies have used food, supplementary to normal diet, to elicit performance. Many more experimenters have used presentation of visual events to motivate the infant. The motivational problem seems simpler with very young babies. In the first few days of life one can demonstrate learning of a very high order. Neonate infants can learn not one but a *pair* of response-reward contingencies, requiring two different responses signalled by two different stimuli. For instance, Lew Lipsett, of Brown University, and I discovered separately that a three-day-old infant can learn to turn his head

to the left to obtain reward when a bell sounds, and to the right when a buzzer sounds. He can learn the bell-left, buzzer-right discrimination in a few minutes. Having learned it he can learn to reverse the discrimination if the experimenter reverses the contingencies, to go bell-right, buzzer-left, again very rapidly. The learning displayed here is possibly of a higher order than is ever displayed by an infra-human.

Born with a high native endowment, the human infant has the potential to acquire new knowledge, skills and competences from the very moment of birth. The newborn thus forces us to a compromise between nativism and empiricism, possessing as he does enough capacity to make rapid learning possible.

Reading 10
The Social Capacities of Young Infants
Daniel G. Freedman

As we have seen, the infant has come into the world with a substantial array of talents. Not the least of these are his socializing abilities, which, like the perceptual constancies, appear without reinforcement and as an immediate accommodation to the environment.

In systems-theory terms, the species' goal is for infant and caretaker to become socially attached, for this assures survival of the young. Each member of this partnership is equipped to contribute to this goal, and although cultural rules to some extent determine adult participation, the infant nevertheless appears to develop in all cultures according to a regular pattern.

Crying, Holding, and Caretaking The very first behavior exhibited by the newborn is the cry, a nearly universal mammalian occurrence. Detailed analyses of the behavior around human crying are only now being made (e.g., Wolff, 1969), but crying seems to share the common mammalian function of exciting the parent to caretaking activities. In dogs, for example, a puppy removed from the nest immediately starts to cry and continues until exhausted. The bitch will usually become extremely excited, seek the source of the cry until the puppy is found,

and then fetch him back. What we have here are two complementary evolved mechanisms, and neither has to be learned.

It should be added that while crying and whining exposes the young to predation, they would die in any event without parental aid; so that, like many evolutionary mechanisms, a compromise is reached between two opposing possibilities. Few mechanisms do not to some extent compromise the chances of survival, and this fact occurs with such frequency that compromise can be termed a general rule of evolution.

In the human, we have demonstrated that within hours after birth most crying infants will quiet when held and carried, and of 252 crying newborns in our study only three could not be quieted in this way. Consider how this cessation of crying coordinates beautifully with the intense anxiety felt by the parent or caretaker until the infant is quieted, for there are few sounds which humans find as unnerving as the infant's cry. Aside from caretaking and feeding, body contact is the usual outcome of crying, and the human baby does as well as the macaque in getting next to the parent without the ability to cling. There seems little doubt that such contact is a mutually edifying experience, and in the human, as in most social mammals, physical contact of one form or another remains an important means of relating throughout life.

It should be noted, however, this does not imply, as does psychoanalytic logic, that behavior occuring earlier in time is necessarily causal to related behavior appearing later in time. Within evolutionary logic, attachments between adults of a social species are as "primary" as are attachments between infant and adult.

Seeking Out the Face   As has already been mentioned, Fantz's method of measuring what an infant is looking at brought on an avalanche of similar studies (cf. Vine, 1971). Of interest to us, in the present context, is that the overall trend in these studies indicates that young infants show a general perference for looking at cards, or models, in the likeness of the human face.

A crucial question has been whether this is the result of conditioning or whether it is an unconditioned preference. The answer would seem to lie in testing very young inexperienced infants. However, newborns rarely fixate for long on a static object—and the Fantz methodology necessitates a stationary stimulus. On the other hand, newborns will readily follow a *moving* object and, in our studies, 75% of all the babies tested ($n = 272$, average age 42 hours) followed a moving object, 68% turned to a voice, 72% followed a silent moving face, while 80% followed a moving and speaking human face. [Hutt et al. (1966), Wolff, (1963), L'Allier (1961), and Eisenberg et al. (1964) have all contributed evidence that the human voice, especially the higher-pitched female voice, is the most preferred auditory stimulus in young infants.]

As a result of these observations, Jirari (1970) decided to use head-following rather than eye-fixation as the basis for a quantitative study and was consequently able to use infants of 24 hours of age and less. Four stimuli were used: a schematic face, a scrambled symmetrical face, an unsymmetrical face, and a blank card equated to the others for reflectance (Figs. 1 & 2). Using a large protractor behind the baby's head, Jirari measured how far 36 newborn infants followed each card from midline to either side, up to 90 degrees. The stimuli were randomly varied and unseen by the experimenter. A quite distinct ordering emerged, face > moderately scrambled > scrambled > blank, with all points significantly different from each other.

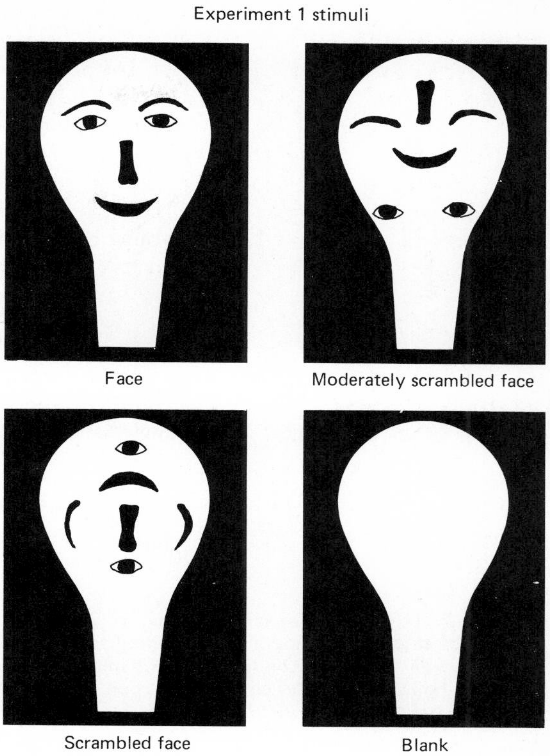

Experiment 1 stimuli

Face

Moderately scrambled face

Scrambled face

Blank

Fig. 1   Figures used in test.

She subsequently repeated this experiment with 40 infants whose average age was *10 minutes* (range 2–17 minutes)! Once again the face was followed significantly more; while there was no differentiation of moderately scrambled and scrambled, the blank again ranked significantly last.

In a second experiment, an attempt was made to ascertain which aspect of the face was salient for infants. Thus a schematic face, two normal-sized eyes, six normal-sized eyes, two large eyes, and a mouth were used as stimuli, with the same methodology as above (Figs. 3 & 4). Once again the full schematic was preferentially followed, with six eyes and two large eyes tied for second. We may then assume that, given a face, it is the eyes which are salient for the infant, a conclusion also reached by Ahrens (1954).

In yet a third experiment, however, in which a series of three checkerboards of increasing complexity were used, the checkerboard of intermediate complexity was followed about as well as the schematic face. It would appear, then, that two

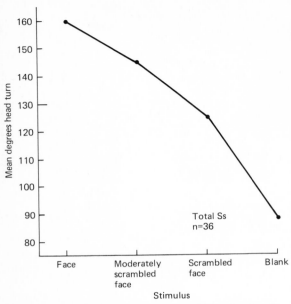

Fig. 2 Averaged head turning in newborns to stimuli varying in degree of "faceness" (maximal score is 90° to each side or 180°). On the Wilcoxin matched-pair assigned-ranks test, all the comparisons were significant (p < .005). (*From Jirari, 1970.*)

different continua may be operating in newborn preferences—"faceness" and complexity.

Finally, Jirari found that *all* stimuli were followed better when babies were propped in the lap than when propped at the same angle on an apparently comfortable little bed.

All told, then, the best following thus far obtained is to the human face-voice combination while being held in the lap, and, unsurprisingly for an evolutionist, it would appear that there is a lowered threshold for following a real-live human.

Figures 5 through 10 are a series of stills from a motion picture record of a crying 24-hour-old infant as it is picked up and cuddled for the very first time. He quiets in a matter of seconds and turns almost immediately to the caretaker's face.

Smiling   The experimental work on infant smiling appears to sustain the above data in that the most efficient visual elicitor of social smiles yet found is a full-face view of a nodding human face

Experiment 4 stimuli

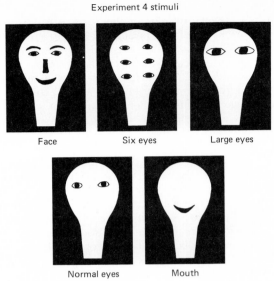

Fig. 3   Figures used in test.

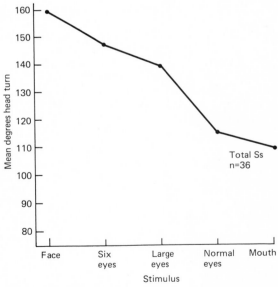

Fig. 4   Averaged head turning in newborns to schematic drawing of a face and face-parts. On the Wilcoxin test: Face > Six Eyes, p < .01; Six Eyes > Normal Eyes (as in schematic face), p < .005; Face Large Eyes, p < .03; Large Eyes > Normal Eyes, p < .01; Six Eyes = Large Eyes and Normal Eyes = Mouth. (*From Jirari, 1970.*)

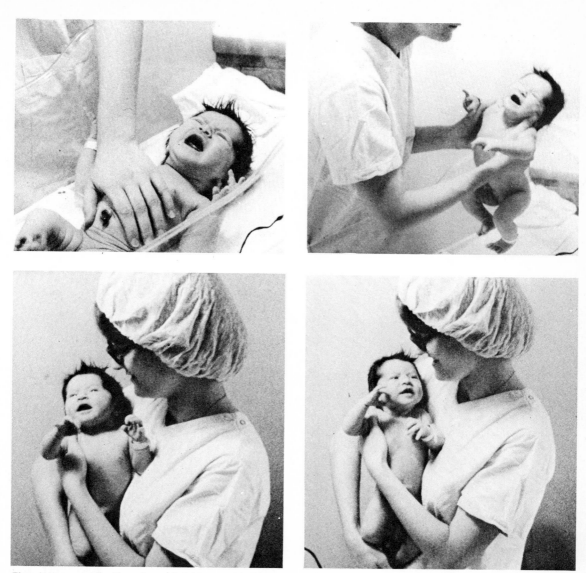

Figs. 5 through 10   One-day-old girl is consoled in arms for the first time. She ceases crying almost immediately and looks to *E*'s face. From a motion-picture film covering approximately 12 seconds of action.

or model of a face. The essential points of Ahrens' (1954) relatively crude study seem to be surviving the test of time. Using staring and/or smiling as his measure of interest, Ahrens had found a general preference for "eye"-spots in the first month, followed by a progressive preference for targets which more realistically resemble a face, until only a real face could elicit smiling. Ahrens reported, as did Kaila (1932) and Spitz and Lolf (1946) before him, that the most efficient visual elicitor of a smile, after social smiling starts, is a full-face view of a nodding model. L'Allier (1961) and Wolff (1963)

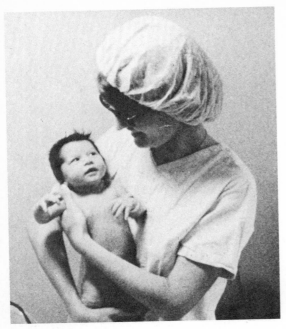

Fig. 9

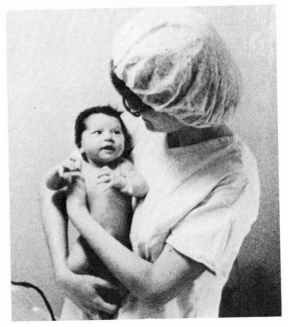

Fig. 10

found, additionally, that the human voice alone can elicit smiling, but that the best elicitor of infant smiles is a live, vocalizing human adult. This is, if the experimenter is seeking to build, element by element, an ideal model for the elicitation of smiles, the model would according to the trends in the literature, end up a human. Again, for an evolutionist this is not terribly surprising. But for a field steeped in the tradition that behavior, such as the smile, accrues through subtle reinforcement from the environment, such a conclusion finds many detractors. However, Freedman (1964) in a review of the literature on smiling, has shown that reinforcement cannot be the causal mechanism in smiling, so that we will confine ourselves here to a brief summary.

Smiling is first seen in reflexive form in newborns, including prematures, when they are dozing with eyes closed, usually after a feeding. These smiles are frequently ascribed to intestinal gas. Accordingly, we have carefully recorded facial expressions and body activities which precede gas burps and eyes-closed smiling. The former event is preceded by facial reddening, general writhing, and shifting contortions of facial muscles. The smile is invariably preceded by a distinctly different state characterized by complete relaxation of the face and body. Clearly, these are two distinctly different events, and we hope that these observations will help lay to rest the theory of gaseous smiling. Even at these early ages, smiles can also be elicited by a voice or by rocking the infant and, since it occurs in infants whose gestational age is as low as 7 months, there seems little doubt that smiling can also occur *in utero*. Visually elicited smiles usually occur considerably later than sound elicited ones, by 2 to $2^1/_2$ months, though they are occasionally seen within the first week of life. These occur most readily when the eyes of infant and adult meet, and so they are called social smiles. In the auditory mode, increased smiling to a voice over other sounds also marks such smiles as "social" (Wolff, 1963).

Regarding individual differences in smiling, some newborns never, or rarely, exhibit so-called reflexive smiling while others may become the pets of the nursery because of their constant display. From a 5-year longitudinal study, we have found consistency in the use of smiling as a social technique dating back to the reflexive eyes-closed smiles; e.g., a frequent eyes-closed smiler in the first months tends to be a frequent social smiler at 5 years.

As for the origins of smiling, the endogenous nature of the phenomena is perhaps best illustrated in the spontaneous smiling of blind infants. The following is a report on a blind infant closely observed over the first half-year of life (from Freedman, 1964):

Yvonne was an infant with Rubella induced cataracts in whom there were no other significant sequelae. According to the ophthalmologist's report (Akademiska Hospital, Uppsala), Yvonne had less than 20/200 vision in both eyes, and on our tests there was no following of the test objects, including a bright pen light. She did, however, attend to a very bright light, and although no pupillary response was noted, she furrowed her brow to light shone directly on her eyes.

As in seeing babies, Yvonne smiled frequently as she was going off to sleep but never to social contact in the first month (information from mother). Then came a period of reduced nonelicited smiling (also a normal development), followed by social smiling to voice and touch early in the second month (the time of onset for visual social smiling in precocious normals). When observed at 2 months 13 days her smiles, while beautiful, were not normal. They seemed to be a series of reflexes firing in rapid succession, so that they appeared and then faded rapidly. Of great interest was the fact that at this visit Yvonne's otherwise constant nystagmus became arrested during a smile. At this time she smiled most often to voices, but also briefly to our test bell and a familiar squeaking toy.

By 3 months 8 days her smiles were rather prolonged, especially to the human voice (Fig. 11). However, if one observed closely, the prolonged smile still consisted of a discrete series, i.e., regular twitching at the corners of her mouth. Again, nystagmus halted during the social smile. At this age it was noted that nystagmus was also arrested when she turned toward a sound or, in one series of observations, the source of a breeze caused by fanning. It was also noted that her eyes characteristically turned toward the source before her head turned, and that the eyes were always bilaterally coordinated.

We have tentatively concluded that the arrest of nystagmus and the directing of eyes towards voice and sound were manifestations of highly motivated states which enabled processes, isolated by disease, to become temporarily integrated.

In the third month, Yvonne was observed "peering" at her hands, a maturational event that

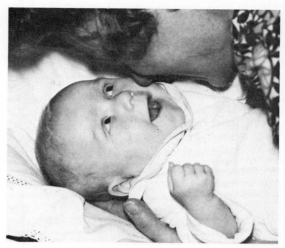

Fig. 11 Yvonne, 2-month, 20-day-old blind infant, is spoken to by her mother. Her nystagmus is momentarily arrested, she "faces" the source of the sound and smiles.

occurs regularly in seeing children, i.e., the hands are brought before the eyes and wiggled there for long periods of time. When she did this, Yvonne's eyes converted to the center and down, as if she were trying hard to see her hands. It seemed unlikely that shadows had been cast on the retina since these observations were made under dim lighting conditions. Also, she did not touch her face, so that tactile sensations were not a factor. It appears, therefore, that the motor pattern of wiggling the hands before the eyes may operate independently of peripheral stimulation. Even if one argues that forms must have been cast on the retina, it is still of singular interest that this phenomenon developed; for it is now clear that very little visual stimulation is necessary for its performance. Evolutionarily this may have come about as a "guarantee" that eye-hand coordination would occur. The hands-before-the-eyes behavior dropped out a few weeks after it appeared, and at the sixth-month visit Yvonne was still not reaching for objects introduced by sound or touch [pp. 177–178].

Since blind infants, deaf infants, deaf-blind infants, even retarded infants eventually smile fully and normally, there is no doubt as to the built-in nature of this phenomenon. The evolutionary questions then loom in importance: Are there homologs to be found in lower apes? What is the phylogeneti-cally adaptive value of human smiling?

It is pure surmise, of course, as to whether the smiling response appeared phylogenetically as an adult-adult mechanism or as an adult-infant mecha-nism. It is most akin to the "frightened grin" in other primates, a gesture that occurs quite fre-quently by a subordinate animal when passing close to a dominant one (Hall and DeVore, 1965). Human smiling may well have originated with such a ges-ture in the evolutionary "turning to the opposite," but more than this we cannot say.

With regard to adaptive value, the most obvious hypothesis is that smiling facilitates attachments between baby and caretaker, and evidence for this is readily attainable. Consider the following obser-vation:

Jock is 7 weeks old. The Experimenter and two strangers enter his room and Jock looks past them at the window. E speaks and Jock looks at E, but only briefly. E walks back and forth before Jock's crib, but Jock does not follow with his eyes.

E then bends over Jock and starts baby talk. Jock soon fixes on E's face, staring intently for a full 20 seconds, and then smiles. Several more smiles are similarly elicited.

E again walks back and forth before Jock's crib, but now Jock follows him visually every-where he goes, even craning his neck when E wanders out of sight. Jock picks E from among the strangers in the room, even when E walks back of them. This continues over the remainder of the 10-minute observation period.

For his part, E reports feeling much closer to Jock now that Jock has returned his cooing and smiling and is following him with his eyes.

If one then multiplies this event many hundred-fold between the same twosome, as in a common caretaker-baby relationship over, say, the first 6 months of life, it is not difficult to imagine how this interaction contributes to the development of strong, lasting attachments.

In later life, of course, smiling lends ease and promotes positive feelings in a wide variety of social encounters, and it plays a particularly impor-tant role in courtship behavior. It is also widely displayed between adults as a means of either overcoming or precluding dissension and angry feeling, so that one might speak of smiling as an important lubricant in one's daily encounters. It appears to have these same functions in *all* cultures in which studies have been made (Eibl-Eibesfeldt and Hass, 1967), so that it must be considered a product of hominid evolution.

Perhaps the most interesting discussion of the adaptive function of smiling is that in Goldstein (1957). Briefly, he considers man's highly devel-oped social nature as the basis for any consider-ation of this phenomenon:

Ultimately the concern for the other's existence is an intrinsic property of man's nature, and man is not to be understood without a consideration of his belonging together with the "other." This is the foundation of understanding language. It is the basis of all friendship, of all love, where with surprise and astonishment we recognize that what is taking place in the "other" is identical with what is taking place in us. This belonging of individuals to each other . . . reveals itself as a characteristic experience for human existence in the smiling of the infant in primitive form, and later conspicuously in the "encounter" of the adult with another person [p. 91].

For Goldstein, then, the smile is a means by which the biological unity of mother and child, once broken, may be reestablished, however briefly, as social unity. Thereafter smiling re-mains a major means of establishing and reestab-lishing the oneness of people who feel close to one another, while expressively, it reflects feelings of personal adequacy throughout life.

Many new mothers have reported to me that their infants did not become "real persons" until after social smiling started (although this is by no means a rule). The question then arises: What possible adaptive advantage is served by a non-smiling period from birth to 2 or 3 months of age? Visual incapacity could not be the reason since blind and seeing infants follow the same basic developmental course of smiling. Instead, the answer would ap-pear to lie in the potential advantage of a relatively loose mother-infant attachment in the first months, when a large percentage of infants die, particularly in subsistence cultures; presumably, the depression and pain caused by infant death after attachment could impair future child-bearing. The postpone-ment of deep attachments also enables infan-ticide with nonviable infants, a common eugenic practice in many cultures (cf. Carr-Saunders, 1922), as well as easing adoption when the mother cannot care for the baby. Possibly, the fact that neonates are frequently seen as "ugly" also serves the same functions.

Cooing, Babbling, and Language Soon after *en face* smiling starts, the infant begins to coo at the beholding adult who in turn feels the irresistible urge to respond, and as a result much time may be spent in such happy "conversation." Feedings and sleeping have then decreased and normally more and more time is spent in direct social interactions.

Although Lenneberg (1967) reports that the frequency of cooing in infants of deaf, silent parents is about the same as in infants of normal parents, several studies (Wolff, 1963; Rheingold et al., 1959) have found that infants of 4–8 weeks are stimulated to cooing by parental cooing (and vice versa), and that phrasing and "waiting one's turn" are present at the very inception of this behavior. Thus, there seems to be a "preprogrammed" aspect not only to the appearance and frequency of cooing, but to vocal interchange as well. That is, the infant seeks out and appears to enjoy vocal give and take. As the study by Rheingold et al. (1959) demonstrates, such behavior may be either encouraged or discouraged by parental behavior and, one consequently assumes, by cultural expectations.

At about the time of the social smile, cooing begins to give way to more complex vocalizations, usually of the consonant–vowel–consonant–vowel variety called babbling. Babbling, unlike cooing, is not so bound to a social interchange and frequently occurs when the infant is alone. However, if an adult speaks while an infant is babbling, the infant will usually stop and wait for the adult to finish before continuing; i.e., it is easy to promote a "conversation" with a babbling baby (Lewis, 1951).

Of great interest is the finding of Lenneberg (1967) that deaf infants are indistinguishable from hearing ones in their babbling, at least through 6 months of age, which strongly implies an endogenous rather than an imitative process. For the evolutionist, then, it seems reasonable to consider babbling the forerunner of linguistic use and, conversely, the sounds of a language are probably dependent to some extent on the range of vocalizations demonstrated in the infant's babbling. In this regard, Brown (1958) speaks of a human "species profile" in that the array of early occurring sounds shows considerable cross-cultural equivalence. Although this need not mean that the child can produce every possible speech sound, he does seem capable of all the rudiments. Similarly, in an experiment with infants of 1 and 4 months of age, Eimas et al. (1971) found that at both ages infants were able to discriminate different phonemic categories, as measured by rates of non-nutritive sucking. They concluded:

> The results strongly indicate that infants as young as one month of age are not only responsive to speech sounds and able to make fine discriminations but are also perceiving speech sounds along the voicing continuum in a manner approximating categorical perception, the manner in which adults perceive these same sounds. Another way of stating this effect is that infants are able to sort acoustic variations of adult phonemes into categories with relatively limited exposure to speech, as well as virtually no experience in producing these same sounds and certainly with little, if any, differential reinforcement for this form of behavior. The implication of these findings is that the means by which the categorical percept of speech, that is, perception in a linguistic mode, is accomplished may well be part of the biological makeup of the organism and moreover, that these means must be operative at an unexpectedly early age [p. 306].

A more recent study by Condon and Sander (1974), utilizing neonates as young as 12 hours of age, bears out these ideas; all sixteen newborns gave evidence of being able to perceive adult phonemic and word organization. This finding was judged from sound films and videotapes made of each infant while adult speech, both live and recorded, was emitted in his presence (English and Chinese were used). Upon microanalysis, body movements were found to correspond exceedingly well with phonemic and word boundaries, indicating that infants are "tuned-into" spoken language from the start.

In the same sense, McNeill's (1972) analysis of communication in the famous chimpanzees, Washoe and Sarah, demonstrates that although these chimpanzees were taught to communicate via symbols standing for human words and phrases, they acquired no sense of human grammatical structure.

Human infants, on the other hand, display this "knowledge" with their first words, long before an abstract understanding of grammar is possible. McNeill concludes, logically enough, that the human so easily acquires appropriate syntactical usage because of an innate disposition to do so (see also McNeill, 1970). Along with Chomsky (1965), he speaks of innately given "deep structures" which guide the acquisition of syntax and which account for the obligatory nature of a child's grammatical usage.

All this is highly reminiscent of the work of Thorpe (1963) on the development of song in the chaffinch and other birds. In the absence of the adult song, the young chaffinch develops a rudimentary song, recognizable as the species' call but very incomplete. If birdsongs of other species are heard, he will modify his singing in that direction—rarely achieving an adequate imitation. Thus the inner propulsion to sing cannot be denied, but the feedback provided by a con-specific adult is necessary for the full actualization of song. It is also clear that considerable learning occurs before the bird is himself able to do much more than peep, for the songs heard in that period usually influence the form of later singing.

In summary, then, among the ingredients leading to early language are the need to make expressive sounds and an intense social drive to "converse" with others. Further, as in the birdsong, there seems to be a "species profile" which guides the structure of the emitted sounds. Although this sounds mysterious, language acquisition is inconceivable without some such biological channeling (cf. McNeill, 1966).

Finally, consider the following hypothetical question: Would a group of children, brought up exclusively by otherwise normal deaf-dumb caretakers, and therefore without a common vocal language, proceed to invent such a language? Our answer is yes, because (a) the need to communicate vocally is great; (b) there is a shared interest in the world, and common emotions; (c) mutual imitation would serve to economize phonemic possibilities; (d) if Chomsky's (1965) notion of "deep structure" or obligatory grammar is correct, and it appears to be, the grammatical possibilities are severely limited; (e) after about 7 years of age, abstract thought (Goldstein and Sheerer, 1941) would permit the laying out of commonly agreed-upon rules.

Laughter, Playfulness, Curiosity The importance of playfulness in human behavior is heralded with the appearance of laughter at about 4 months of age. It nearly always appears as part of social interaction, as when the baby is tickled or lifted high in the air, and there seems little doubt that it is an expression of joy in social stimulation. (The objection is frequently made that such an interpretation is unscientific and "adultomorphic." This objection raises deep philosophical problems which we will not attempt to solve here. However, when I come home and my dog runs to greet me, licks me, and wags his tail, am I not justified in assuming he is happy to see me? Unless we agree to this, further argument will be pointless.)

One need not look far beyond his own experience to realize that laughter is not much transformed over the years, although it is certainly elicited by increasingly sophisticated stimulation. As for evolutionary function, whereas smiling seems in itself to be a mechanism fostering attachment, laughter has a bonding quality only insofar as mutually shared spiritedness binds people together. Laughter seems rather to be one of many emotional expressions that helps a partner evaluate one's emotional-state (cf. Bowlby, 1969). If one laughs, all is well and it is an invitation that play continue. If one cries on the other hand, the partner is signaled to stop what is going on. All this has obviously been "arranged" phylogenetically, for no baby is taught to laugh or to cry, nor do adults need previous experience with babies to read these signals expertly and immediately. Laughter and crying also have precisely the same signal value in chimpanzees (van Lawick-Goodall, 1968).

As for playfulness, its evolutionary function is apparent throughout Mammalia (cf. Ewer, 1968). Play is a means of learning about one's own capacities *vis-à-vis* the social and nonsocial environment, and it has the great adaptive value of fostering such learning anew in each generation. Naturally enough, it occurs with greatest frequency early in life, in the carefree period when needs are taken care of and protection afforded by adults.

In systems-theory terms, play may be said to operate at the level of a set-goal, with full exploitation and mastery of the living and nonliving environment as its goal. Thus play is closely related to all the other traits that aid in exploring the world, but most especially to curiosity and courage.

It is clear that curiosity, like playfulness, need not be taught nor, probably, can it be taught. As eye-hand coordination matures, at about 6 months, all objects are of interest and are exploited. Presented with wooden cubes and a cup for the first time, most 6-month-olds proceed to fill the cup with the cubes; no prior demonstration is necessary. Similarly, presented with pegs at the side of a peg-board, most 7-month-olds will spontaneously start placing pegs in the holes. Some do this deftly and complete the job on the first try. In some infants unmistakable self-praise follows successful placement, as they smile broadly and look to the examiner or to mother for such acknowledgment.

REFERENCES

Ahrens, R. Beitrag zur Entwicklung des Physiognomie und Mimikerkennes, tiel I, II. Zeitschrift fuer Experimentelle und Angewandte Psychologie. 1954, *2*, 412–454, 599–633.

Brazelton, T. B., & Freedman, D. G. The Cambridge neonatal scales. In J. J. van der Werff ten Bosch (Ed.), *Normal and abnormal development of brain and behavior.* Leiden: Leiden University Press, 1971.

Bowlby, J. *Attachment.* New York: Basic Books, 1969.

Carr-Saunders, A. *The population problem.* London and New York: Oxford University Press, (Clarendon) 1922.

Chomsky, N. A. *Aspects of the theory of syntax.* Cambridge, Mass.: M.I.T. Press, 1965.

Condon, W. S. & Sander, L. W. Neonate movement is synchronized with adult speech: Interactional participation and language acquisition. *Science,* 1974, *183*, 99–101.

Eibl-Eibesfeldt, I., & Hass, H. Film studies in human ethology. *Current Anthropology,* 1967, *8*, 477–479.

Eimas, P. D., Siqueland, E. R., Jusczyk, P., & Vigorito, J. Speech perception in infants. *Science,* 1971, *171*, 303–306.

Eisenberg, R. B., Griffin, E. J., Coursin, D. B., & Hunter, M. S. Auditory behavior in the human neonate: A preliminary report. *Journal of Speech and Hearing Research,* 1964, *7*, 245–269.

Ewer, R. F. *Ethology of mammals.* London: Logos Press, 1968.

Freedman, D. G. Hereditary control of early social behavior. In B. M. Foss (Ed.), *Determinants of infant behaviour* III. London: Methuen, 1965, 149–159.

Goldstein, K. The smiling of the infant and problem of understanding the "other." *Journal of Psychology,* 1957, *44*, 175–191.

Goldstein, K., & Sheerer, M. Abstract and concrete

behavior. *Psychological Monographs,* 1941, *53*, (No. 2, Whole No. 239).

Hall, K. R. L. & DeVore, I. Baboon social behavior. In I. DeVore (Ed.), *Primate behavior: Field studies of monkeys and apes.* New York: Holt, Rinehart and Winston, 1965, 53–110.

Hutt, S. J., Hutt, C., Lenard, H. G., Bernuth, H. V., & Muntjewerff, W. J. Auditory responsivity in the human neonate. *Nature (London),* 1966, *218*, 888–890.

Jiari, C. Form perception, innate form preferences and visually-mediated head-turning in human neonates. Unpublished doctoral dissertation, Committee on Human Development, University of Chicago, 1970.

Kaila, E. Die Reaktion des Saugling auf das menschliche Gesicht. *Annales Universitatis fennicae Aboensis, Series B,* 1932, *17,* 1–114.

L'Allier, L. Smiling as a result of aural stimuli. Unpublished doctoral dissertation, University of Montreal, 1961.

Lenneberg, E. *Biological foundations of language.* New York: Wiley, 1967.

Lewis, M. *Infant speech.* London: Routledge and Kagan Paul, 1951.

McNeill, D. Developmental psycholinguistics. In S. Smith & G. A. Miller (Eds.), *Genesis of language.* Cambridge, Mass.: M.I.T. Press, 1966, 1–92.

McNeill, D. *The acquisition of language.* New York: Harper and Row, 1970.

McNeill, D. Sentence structure in chimpanzee communication. Unpublished manuscript, Committee on Cognitive Processes, University of Chicago, 1972.

Rheingold, H. L., Gerwirtz, J. L. & Ross, A. W. Social conditioning of vocalizations in the infant. *Journal of Comparative Physiology and Psychology,* 1959, *52,* 68–73.

Spitz, R. A., & Wolf, K. M. The smiling response: A contribution to the ontogenesis of social relations. *Genetic Psychology Monographs,* 1946, *34*, 57–125.

Thorpe, W. H. *Learning and instinct in animals,* (2nd ed.) London: Methuen, 1963.

Van Lawick-Goodall, J. The behavior of free-living chimpanzees in the Gombe Stream Reserve. *Animal Behavior Monograph,* 1968, *1*, III, 161–311.

Vine, I. The significance of facial-visual signalling in human social development. In I. Vine & M. von Cranack (Eds.), *Expressive movement and nonverbal communication.* New York: Academic Press, 1971.

Wolff, P. H. Observations on the early development of smiling. In B. M. Foss (Eds.), *Determinants of infant behaviour II.* London: Methuen, 1963, 113–133.

Wolff, P. H. The natural history of crying and other vocalizations in early infancy. In B. M. Foss (Ed.), *Determinants of infant behaviour IV.* New York: Barnes and Noble, 1969.

Reading 11

Self, Other, and Fear: The Reaction of Infants to People[1]

Michael Lewis
Jeanne Brooks-Gunn

The fears of infants is an important area of inquiry, for it sits squarely on the domains of affect, cognitive and social development. The infant's reactions to other persons may be said to have an affective component: fear of strangers may be an index of attachment. Although attachment usually is defined by a positive approach to the mother, as measured by proximal and distal behaviors (Coates, Anderson & Hartup, 1972; Lewis & Ban, 1971), or by separation from the mother as measured by distress (Ainsworth & Bell, 1970; Goldberg & Lewis, 1969; Schaffer & Emerson, 1964), attachment may also be explored by examining the infant's responses to other persons, either when the mother is or is not present.

Fear of the strange may also be related to cognitive development. Indeed, the theoretical work of Hebb (1946, 1949), as well as of Piaget (1952) and others (Schaffer, 1966), has argued for a relationship between fear and novelty. Moreover, there may be a more indirect relationship, such as increased cognitive capacity leading to greater differentiation, thus producing more strange.

While the strange can include objects and events as well as people, most of the work on fear of the strange has involved people. We will only mention in passing that loud noises, in fact, intensity in general, have the possibility of frightening the infant (see Scarr & Salapatek, 1970). It is not our intention to deal with this dimension of stimulus events. As we have stated before (Lewis, 1971) this stimulus dimension adds little to our understanding of the infant's cognitive development since it acts *upon* the infant, and, as James (1895) has stated, the infant's response is an immediate passive sensorial response. Rather, we are interested in stimuli that are defined by the interaction of the organism and the stimulus event (novelty and familiarity are

examples of such interaction). We shall restrict our discussion further to include only the infant's social world, leaving out the study of nonsocial stimuli.

Fear of strangers or stranger anxiety has been studied, most of the work growing out of the ethological-attachment literature (Ainsworth & Bell, 1970; Schaffer & Emerson, 1964). Fear of strangers usually appears in the second half of the first year and extends, for some, long into the second year. While the ethological-imprinting position would argue for fear of strangers as a way of binding the infant to his caregivers, we recognize, as do Rheingold and Eckerman (1971), that not all infants exhibit fear of strangers. Some infants may show only signs of wariness or differential smiling towards unfamiliar people.

For all the current research on fear in infancy, there has been relatively little effort directed toward the social dimensions which elicit fear. Thus far, age of onset, number of infants exhibiting fear, and specific fears of animate objects have received the most attention. We are interested in the infant's fearful response to people, that is, it is the dimension of humanness that we wish to study. While humans and masks have been studied, only one study, that of Morgan and Ricciuti (1969), touches upon the dimensions that interest us. In this study a male and female stranger were used, and the data reveal that the infants were more frightened of the male. No information about the strangers was given. We do not know the sizes and shapes of each, but yet the data suggest differential fear as a function of the nature of the social event. It is to this point that our study is directed. More concretely, our current study comes from an observation of an 8-month-old female. We observed that an approach by an adult stranger produced extreme fear. The infant screamed, cried, and tried desperately to escape. How different when a stranger 3 or 4 years old approached her: smiling, cooing, and reaching behavior was then exhibited. Why should this be— they were equally strange? Would this hold for children who were generally fearful? What does this mean for the cognitive functioning of the

[1]Paper presented at Eastern Psychological Association meetings, Symposium on *Infants' Fear of the Strange*, Boston, April 1972. This research was supported in part by a Grant from the Spencer Foundation and by the National Institute of Child Health and Human Development, under Research Grant 1 PO1 HDO1762. Thanks are due to Marcia Weinraub and Gina Rhea who helped to formulate the problem and collect the data.

infant, let alone its significance for any theory of attachment? As a first step, this casual observation had to be repeated and extended.

In this study we were interested in the infants' responses to five different social events: a strange adult male and female of the same physical size, a strange female child 4 years of age, the infant's mother, and the infant itself. Twenty-four infants, 7–19 months old, were each placed in a pleasant room which was carpeted and had a few pieces of furniture and pictures on the wall. Only infants who were first-born or who had siblings over 5 years of age were included; 20 were first-born. The infant was seated in an infant tenda facing a door about 15 feet away. The mother sat next to the child. Each of the three strangers, one at a time, would first knock on the door. The mother would say "come in," and each would enter at the far end of the room. The stranger slowly walked toward the infant. Having reached the infant, the stranger would touch the infant's hand. Throughout the episode the stranger smiled but did not vocalize. Movements were deliberately slow to avoid eliciting startle responses. After touching the infant, the stranger slowly turned, walked to the door and left the room. The second and third strangers followed the same procedure. There was approximately a 2-minute wait between visits or until the infant was quiet. After the strangers, the mother went to the door and walked toward the infant in the same manner as the strangers. For the infant-itself condition it was necessary for the infant to see itself. A mirror was used, and to avoid the effect of novelty, the mirror did not approach the infant (mirrors do not walk); rather, the infant approached the mirror. To do this, the mother moved the tenda so that it was directly in front of a mirror placed at the opposite end of the room. She slowly moved the tenda toward the mirror so that the infant was able to see his reflection without observing his mother. When the tenda touched the mirror, the mother moved away. The order was balanced for the three-stranger conditions and between the mother and self conditions.

Three behavioral scales—facial expression, vocalization, and motor activity—were used to rate the infants' reactions to the stranger conditions. The checklist (see Appendix) is similar to the one developed by Morgan and Ricciuti (1969). The infants' responses were measured at four distances. Distance 1, the farthest distance, was when the stranger entered; distance 2 (middle) was when the

social event was in the middle of the room; distance 3 (close) was when the event was 3 feet from the infant; and distance 4 (touch) was when the event touched the infant. Observer reliability was measured by the proportion of agreements for two observers who were hidden behind a one-way mirror. The mean percentage of agreement across both the facial and motor scales was .90.

The vocalization scale proved worthless in that there was almost no vocalizing, crying, or fretting. The data to be presented are those for the facial and motor scales, the results of which were almost identical.

The mean data for the five social events are shown in Figures 1 & 2. A score of 3 indicates a neutral response, with 1 being the most negative and 5 being the most positive responses possible. This figure is a combination of the two scales. For the facial expression scale this varied from a broad smile to a puckering crylike expression, while for the motor scale this varied from reaching toward the social event to twisting away from the event and reaching to mother.

The data are rather obvious. Affective social differentiation increases with proximity. Thus, there are no affect differences toward the various social events at the farthest point and affect increases with approach. Social stimuli differ in their effect on the positive and negative affect of the infant. The male and female strangers elicit the most (and only) negative response, while the child stranger elicits a positive response. Moreover, the mother and self elicited the most positive responses. In an analysis of variance with social events and distance as the principal effects, stimulus distance, and stimulus $\times$ distance interaction were highly significant ($F = 11.25, p < .001, F = 16.10, p < .001, F = 18.04, p < .001$ respectively).

These findings are consonant with Morgan and Ricciuti's (1969) data and indicate that infants do not exhibit either negative or positive responses until the social event approaches or is in close proximity. This makes good sense since it is a compromise between the need to flee (something strange can hurt) and the need to experience newness in order to alter cognitive structures. The rule might be *stay and attend as long as the event does not get close; if it approaches, withdraw.* Fear and negative affects may be in the service of this escape behavior. Why, though, does the infant not show the positive affect earlier? In order to maintain a parsimonious explanation, we would need to postu-

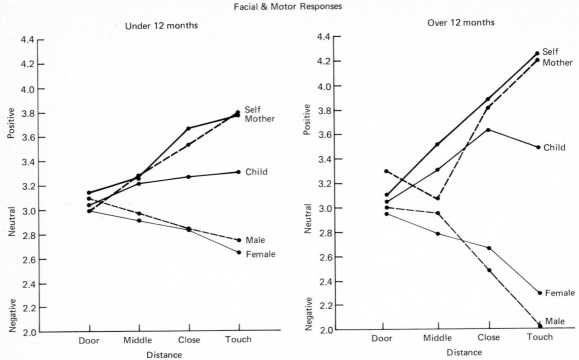

Figure 1 Mean facial and motor responses to the five social events for all infants. A score of 3 indicates a neutral response. Scores less than and more than 3 indicate negative and positive responses respectively.

late that the intensely positive affects may also interfere with cognitive processes so that they too are only elicited at approach or proximity when social interaction becomes necessary. Of course, a simpler explanation would be related to a time lag notion, wherein the expression of affect, either positive or negative, takes more time. If the social event had waited at the door, would not the same affect have occurred? Morgan and Ricciuti (1969) controlled for this time effect and found it not relevant. On the strength of their results we must reject this hypothesis.

Differentiation of responses to the various social events is also related to age as well as to distance. When the sample is divided by median age, 12 Ss are between 7 and 11.5 months of age and 12 Ss are 12–19 months old. We realize that the small sample size and the arbitrary division of the infants into two age groups limits generalization; however, interesting age differences emerge (see Figure 3). While the patterns for the two age levels are similar, older infants exhibit a greater range of

responses than do the younger ones. The older infants are more positive to the self, mother, and child, and are more negative toward the female and male strangers. It is only in amount of negative affect that the two ages are significantly different by t-test ($p < .05$ for male plus female strangers) although there is a trend indicating that they also exhibit more positive affect ($p < .10$). It is interesting to note that these age differences are only found when the social event is in close proximity. The greater age and presumably greater cognitive development of the infants more than one year old did not result in prompter affective response. Approach determines the timing, while age affects the intensity of the response.

Age differences in the intensity of fear responses have also been found by others (Morgan & Ricciuti, 1969; Scarr & Salapatek, 1970) and may be influenced by perceptual-cognitive development. However, Scarr and Salapatek (1970) and Schaffer (personal communication) found no relationship either between fear of a female stranger and object per-

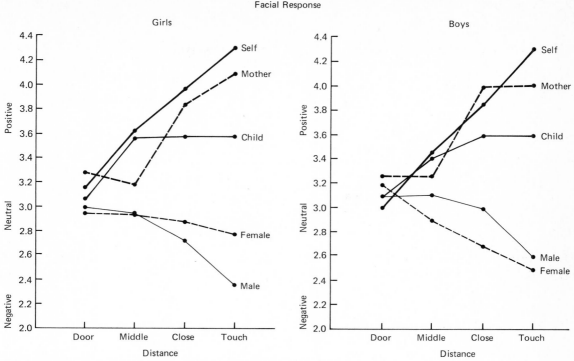

Figure 2 Mean facial responses to the five social events for all infants.

manence (when the age variance was controlled) or between fear of strangers and attention. While these may not be the relevant perceptual cognitive dimensions necessary for eliciting fear, these failures raise the question of what cognitive capacities are relevant to affective responses to social events. While discrimination between familiar and strange is essential, this may be so low a level of cognitive skill that all infants are capable of it and it is not really relevant to the study of the affective responses.

The sex of the infant may be related to the affective response to social events. The negative and positive responses of the boy and girl infants are remarkably similar except for their response to the male stranger. While the infants in general are more frightened of the male stranger, this effect is mostly produced by the girls. It is the girls who seem most frightened by the strange male. This is interesting in light of recent findings in our laboratory (Ban & Lewis, 1971). When one-year-old infants were seen in a playroom with both their mothers and fathers, the girl children appeared to be more reluctant to interact with their fathers than

the boys—especially in terms of the distal mode of looking! Although these present results are not significant, they raise the interesting questions of why infants are frightened more of a male stranger and why this is more true of females. No explanation based solely on low levels of paternal interaction as compared to mother's interaction can account for this latter sex difference.

How are we to account for the negative affect directed toward the adult strangers and the positive affect directed toward child stranger and to the mother and self? We would expect fear of the stranger; thus, the negative expression toward the adult strangers comes as no surprise. However, if it is strangeness alone that elicits fear or negative affect, why no fear (in fact, a positive affect) toward the child stranger? This brings into question the whole incongruity hypothesis. Consider the incongruity argument in relation to affect.[2] Briefly, it

[2]The effect of incongruity on attentive behavior is still being explored. It is important to note that incongruity may produce little attention not because of any cognitive reason but because it produces fear which might result in withdrawal. Gaze aversion is one type of withdrawal.

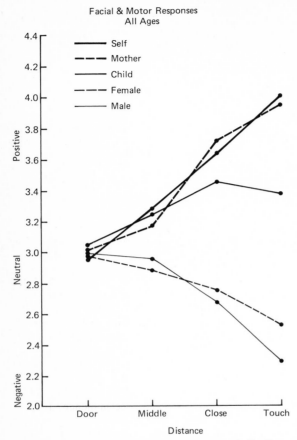

Figure 3 Mean facial and motor responses to the five social events for infants less than and more than 12 months of age.

states that events that are highly incongruent will be those which produce fear, while those that are only partially incongruous will produce little fear. For example, the head of a monkey shown to other monkeys produces extreme fear because of its incongruity (Hebb, 1946). If the judgment of congruity is made with the mother as the referent, then the strange female is least incongruent, the strange male more so, and the strange female child most. Thus, the child stranger should produce the most fear. In fact, the child stranger produces no fear but positive affect. Incongruity may not be the sole determinant of fear. On the other hand, the mother may not be the only referent for the infant in his observation of social events. Recall that infants also show positive affect to themselves. We will return to this issue of self shortly.

These data also suggest that we reconsider our

formulation about the fear of strangers in infants. It now becomes clear that we cannot state that all strange social events that approach infants will elicit the same degree of negative affect. That is, strangeness *per se* is not a sufficient dimension. The social dimensions or space that elicits fear is multi-dimensional. Strangeness is necessary, but not sufficient. What are the characteristics of the child stranger that *do not* elicit fearful responses? Two appear most likely; the first is size. Clearly, the child stranger is smaller than the adults; also, the child stranger is closer in size to the infant, especially one sitting in a baby tenda. Ethologically it makes sense to postulate that organisms should be more frightened of strange things that are bigger, than of same size or smaller strange things. Same size or smaller things are less likely or able to hurt. The second dimension is the differential facial configuration between a young child and an adult.

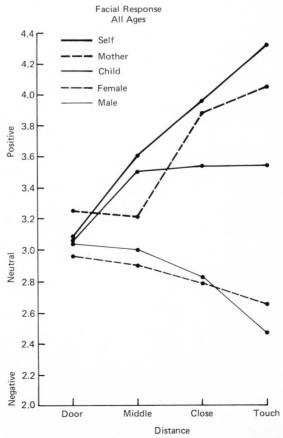

Figure 4 Mean facial responses to the five social events for male and female subjects.

Perhaps this is the cue. Observation of the verbal responses of a 12-month-old as she looks through magazines and newspapers containing pictures of adults (these pictures were, of course, miniature) reveals the widely used word "baby" as she points to the figures, suggesting that she was responding to the size of the picture rather than the facial configuration. Whatever the explanation of why the infants were not upset by the child stranger, it is clear that a simple incongruity explanation fails to satisfy the data and that the space of social strangeness is multidimensional, unfamiliar being just one dimension.

The infant's highly positive response to the mother is as we expected; however, the equally positive response to themselves in the mirror is somewhat more interesting. By using the term self we have been making an explicit assumption, one which was quite intentional. There is relatively little information on infants' responses to mirrors, but the anecdotal evidence that does exist all indicates that even at earlier ages there is an intense positive affective response to the mirror. In a recent study of 4-month-olds by Rheingold (1971), further evidence for the positive effect of seeing oneself in the mirror was reported. These infants showed more smiling to a mirror image than to either motion pictures or slides of an infant or to nonsocial stimuli.

Can one talk about the concept of the self at such early ages? Consider two aspects of the self: the first and most common is the categorical self (I am female, or I am intelligent, or I am big or small, or I am capable); the second, and by far the more primitive, is the existential statement "I am." The basic notion of self—probably as differentiated from other (either as object or person, the mother being the most likely other person)—must develop first. There is no reason not to assume that it develops from birth and that even in the early months some notion of self exists. We would argue that this nonevaluative, existential self is developed from the consistency, regularity, and contingency of the infant's action and outcome in the world. Self is differentiated by reafferent (or information) feedback; for example, each time a certain set of muscles operate (eyes close), it becomes black (cannot see). That is, the immediacy, simultaneity, and regularity of action and outcome produces differentiation and self. The action of touching the hot stove and the immediacy of the pain tells me it's my hand that is on the stove. This self is further reinforced if, when I remove my hand, the pain

ceases. The infant's world is full of such relationships and they vary from its own action on objects to its relationship with a caregiver. In these social interactions, the highly directed energy of the caregiver (touch, smile, look, etc.) is contingent and specific to infant action (smile, coo, etc.).

The relationship of self to the mirror is, likewise, related. Looking in the mirror is pleasurable because of the consistency, regularity, and contingency of the viewer's action and the viewed outcome. In no other situation is there such consistent action-outcome pairing. In other words, the mirror experience contains those elements that generally make up the fabric of the infant's growing concept of self. It is not possible for us to know if the infant is aware that the image is himself. Awareness is a difficult concept to study in nonverbal organisms, but it is clear that by the time one-word utterances emerge, such as "self" or "mine," the year-old infant has the concept of self. It is reasonable to assume that the concept existed prior to the utterance. In fact, if we consider the research on the development of object permanence (for example, Charlesworth, 1968), we find that, for the most part, object permanence has been established by 8 months of life, in many cases even earlier. If the infant has the cognition available to preserve memory of objects no longer present, how can we deny them the ability to have self-permanence? Indeed, is it reasonable to talk of object permanence capacity without self-permanence capacity? Given that this first self-other distinction is made very early, the various categorical dimensions of self may also proceed to unfold. The unfolding of the categories, whether sequential, hierarchical, etc., and the dimensions of the various categories are uncertain.

Is our understanding of the phenomenon of fear helped by evoking the concept of self? We would argue, yes. For example, Hebb's (1949, p. 243) study on the fear of monkeys could be explained by this concept. Consider the monkeys were fearful because they saw a monkey without a body and they were aware that they, too, were monkeys. Maybe they too could lose their heads to a mad professor. Would not humans placed in a similar situation show fear for *their* lives or safety?[3] In terms of our data, the notion of self also helps in explaining the data. Perhaps female infants are

---

[3]The Gardners report that in their study of sign language in the chimpanzee, the animal exhibits the concept of self. When shown a mirror Washoe responded with the signs "me Washoe." Thus, it is not unreasonable to attribute the concept of self to other primates.

more frightened than male infants of male adult strangers because, while they are equally strange, the male infant recognizes that the male adult is more like himself. The specific category of self in this case may be gender. The Money, Hampson and Hampson (1957) data on sexual identity suggest that a year-old infant may already possess this category.

That there was a positive response to the child stranger and negative responses to the adult strangers is difficult to explain in any incongruity hypothesis unless we consider that the referent for the social comparison does not always have to be the infant's mother. There could be multiple referents, one of them being the mother, another being the self. Perhaps the positive response to the child stranger is produced because infants find the child like themselves; that is, they use themselves as referent and find the child like them and are therefore not afraid. In this case the categorical dimension of self may have to do with size. I am small vis-à-vis other social events and the child is also small, therefore, like me.[4]

The present data are clear; at least for the social events used, there was significantly different affect elicited as these events approached. The dimensions on which these social events can be ordered are not at all clear. The most likely candidate for the differences between adults and child is size, but since both adults were the same size, the male-female differences cannot be accounted for by this dimension alone. We view this experiment, then, as a beginning in the study of the dimensions and consequences of social events. Clearly more work is necessary.

In this discussion of fear two major theoretical positions have been evoked, and it would help to clarify the discussion by stating them explicitly. These are the ethological and cognitive approaches. The ethological position rests less (if at all) on a cognitive and more on an imprinting, IRM, instinc-

tual approach. The argument for the present data would be as follows: infant imprinted on parents; all others, strange. Strange at a distance→observe, but do not flee. Strange approach→flee. The only caveat would be that strange has to be bigger than the organism. This model requires the use of no or little cognitive process, and following the ethological approach is rather mechanistic in nature.

The cognitive approach, on the other hand, invokes concepts such as incongruity, novelty and familiarity, and schema. These all rest on the interaction between the organism's past and its present experiences. Moreover, the cognitive approach requires the introduction of such processes as object permanence, at least in terms of remembering the mother. This approach stresses that the child's response to strange is a part of the larger emerging cognitive functions. We would extend this position by considering the concept of self and using it as an additional referent in terms of social interactions and cognitions. While the ethological approach has intrinsic appeal—especially since it evokes a biological simplicity—it is difficult for us to consider infants not responding through the use of elaborate cognitive functions which we know are already available to them.

Before concluding this paper, we should like to return to the most interesting of our findings, that of the infant's response to the child. The positive response of the infants to the child stranger is consistent with other primate evidence, all of which suggests that infant-peer interactions may have a special quality. It is well known that infants often follow and learn faster from an older sibling (peer) than from their parents. In fact, peers may serve quite well as adult substitutes in the early attachment relationships (for example, Chamove, 1966; Freud & Dann, 1951). Infants not only show little or no fear toward peers, but, in fact, can engage in a meaningful attachment behavior. We would suggest that these facts have importance for a general theory of interpersonal relationships.

The following speculations are based on these considerations. Phylogenetically, attachment relationships have changed from infant-peer to infant-adult dyads. Phylogenetically lower organisms attachment behaviors are between peers of the specie. This is especially true if we consider that at the lower end of the scale most information the organism needs for survival is prewired into the system. All that is necessary for the developing specie is to

[4]While there is no direct data to support this, there is a strong suggestion to be found in the data. A correlation matrix was obtained by comparing the children's response consistency across the five social events at the touch distance. As was to be expected, infants who were very fearful of the male stranger were also fearful of the female stranger ($r = .71$, $p < .001$); however, there was no significant relationship between the self and mother ($r = .12$). Thus, while the two strangers were treated alike, the self and mother were not. Moreover, as expected, high negative responses to the adult strangers were associated with more positive responses to both mother and the self; however, they were on the average more than twice as highly associated for the self ($r = -.47$, $p < .05$) than for mother ($r = -.22$).

practice these skills as they unfold. It would be more logical to practice these skills with someone also somewhat less proficient, for the skills of the adult would be too overwhelming. Moreover, since the adult has little or nothing to teach the infant, there needs to be little attachment to an adult. This would suggest that among birds, for example, the young could be as easily or more easily imprinted on a peer than on an adult member. Whom are the ducklings imprinted on as they swim single file on the pond? The "mother" or the young duckling in front of them? As we proceed along the phylogenetic scale, learning becomes more important for the survival of the organism. As such, peers who are good for practicing present skills are no longer sufficient, and adults who are good in teaching new skills are needed. Thus, attachment on adults rather than peers becomes increasingly important. Single births and long periods of relative helplessness facilitate the infant-adult relationship; however, the data make clear that if infant-peer relationships can be sustained (as, for example, in laboratory colo-

nies) infant-peer relationships satisfy many of the socioemotional requirements (Harlow & Harlow, 1969; Harlow, Harlow & Suomi, 1971). Its effect on learning, however, should be inhibiting.

The implication for caregiving is vast. We might argue that infant-peer relationships are not substitutes for infant-adult, but rather, are more basic, at least older in a phylogenetic sense. Small families isolated from one another may constitute a rather unique and new experience, not only for the caregivers, but for the infants themselves.

We have come a long way from the observations of the terrified 8-month-old. But we have collected information to indicate that infants of this age are not frightened of young children and often seek and are sustained by their company. In some sense they appear to be attached to all peers, familiar and strange. The social commerce with adults, however, is restricted to those that are familiar, and even then they often prefer their peers. Any theory of interpersonal relationships and fear of social events must come to grips with these facts.

APPENDIX
Scales

	Child				Mother			
	Far	Middle	Close	Touch	Far	Middle	Close	Touch
Facial								
+2 Smile broad								
+1 Smile slight								
0 Neutral express.								
−1 Slight frown								
−2 Puckering, cry								
Motor activity								
+2 { Reaches to E / Touches E								
+1 { G.B.M. to E / Looks at E								
0 { Inattention / Explores room / Att. directed away								
−1 { Neg. express. to E / Avoids E glance / Pulls hand away E								
−2 { Attempts to escape E / Reaches to M								

REFERENCES

Ainsworth, M. D. S., & Bell, S. M. Attachment, exploration, and separation: Illustrated by the behavior of one-year-olds in a strange situation. *Child Development*, 1970, *41*, 49–67.

Ban, P., & Lewis, M. Mothers and fathers, girls and boys: Attachment behavior in the one-year-old. Paper presented at Eastern Psychological Association meetings, New York City, April 1971.

Chamove, A. S. The effects of varying infant peer experiences on social behavior in the rhesus monkey. Unpublished M. A. thesis, University of Wisconsin, 1966.

Charlesworth, W. R. Cognition in infancy: Where do we stand in the mid-sixties? *Merrill-Palmer Quarterly*, 1968, *14*, 25–46.

Coates, B., Anderson, E. P., & Hartup, W. W. Interrelations in the attachment behavior of human infants. *Developmental Psychology*, 1972, *6* (2), 218–230.

Freud, A., & Dann, S. An experiment in group upbringing. In *The psychoanalytic study of the child, Vol. VI.* New York: International University Press, 1951.

Goldberg, S., & Lewis, M. Play behavior in the year-old infant: Early sex differences. *Child Development*, 1969, *40*, 21–31.

Harlow, H. F., & Harlow, M. K. Effects of various mother-infant relationships on rhesus monkey behaviors. In B. M. Foss (Eds.), *Determinants of infant behavior, Vol. IV.* London: Methuen Press, 1969.

Harlow, H. F., Harlow, M. K., & Suomi, S. J. From thought to therapy: Lessons from a primate laboratory. *American Scientist*, 1971, *59*, 538–549.

Hebb, D. O. On the nature of fear. *Psychological Review*, 1946, *53*, 259–276.

Hebb, D. O. *The organization of behavior.* New York: Wiley, 1949.

James, W. *The principles of psychology.* New York: Dover Publications, 1950 (1895).

Lewis, M. State as an infant-environment interaction: An analysis of mother-infant behavior as a function of sex. Paper presented at the Merrill-Palmer Conference on Research and Teaching of Infant Development, Detroit, February 1971. *Merrill-Palmer Quarterly,* in press.

Lewis, M., & Ban, S. Stability of attachment behavior: A transformational analysis. Paper presented at Society for Research in Child Development meetings, Symposium on *Attachment: Studies in Stability and Change,* Minneapolis, April 1971.

Money, J., Hampson, J. G., & Hampson, J. L. Imprinting and the establishment of gender role. A.M.A., *Archives of Neurology and Psychology,* 1957, *77*, 333–336.

Morgan, G. A., & Ricciuti, H. N. Infants' responses to strangers during the first year. In B. M. Foss (Ed.), *Determinants of infant behavior,* Vol. IV. London: Methuen Press, 1969.

Piaget, J. *The origins of intelligence in children.* New York: International University Press, 1952.

Rheingold, H. L. Some visual determinants of smiling in infants. Unpublished manuscript, University of North Carolina, Chapel Hill, 1971.

Rheingold, H. L., & Eckerman, C. O. Fear of the stranger: A critical examination. Paper presented at Society for Research in Child Development meetings, Minneapolis, April 1971.

Scarr, S., & Salapatek, P. Patterns of fear development during infancy. *Merrill-Palmer Quarterly,* 1970, *16*, 53–90.

Schaffer, H. R. The onset of fear of strangers and the incongruity hypothesis. *Journal of Child Psychology and Psychiatry,* 1966, *7*, 95–106.

Schaffer, H. R., & Emerson, P. E. The development of social attachments in infancy. *Monographs of the Society for Research in Child Development,* 1964, *29* (3, Serial No. 94).

Reading 12

Early Influences on Development: Fact or Fancy?

Arnold J. Sameroff

The concern of developmental psychology is directed toward understanding the changes which occur in behavior as the individual grows to maturity. Scientists with a bias for either a maturational or an environmentalist position generally make an

Preparation of this paper was supported by Grant No. 16544 from USPHS-NIMH.

implicit assumption that behaviors necessarily build on each other to produce a continuity of functioning from conception to adulthood. The continuity seen in the physical identity of each individual is generalized to the psychological identity of each individual. Just as an individual retains the same body throughout the lifespan, so must he have the same mind. The pragmatic needs of educators, clinicians, and scientists reinforce these views of long-range continuities in human behavior. The need of educators is to feel that the didactic exercises they go through are more than merely exercises and are truly affecting the prospective outcomes of their charges; the need of clinicians is to seek the roots of current deviancy retrospectively in either the experiential or constitutional history of the individual; and the pragmatic need of scientists is to feel that the small piece of the world they are studying really has a relation to the whole of life.

However, biologists have shown that physically the body does not maintain a constancy in development. At an elemental level it has long been clear that the material constituents of each organ, tissue, and cell are in constant transition. As a consequence, continuities must be sought in the organization of the body rather than in its ingredients (Bertalanffy, 1968). On a larger time scale it is also clear that the structure of the body goes through changes which produce qualitative differences in organization during development (Waddington, 1966). For humans there is an illusion of structural continuity since the major changes occur during the gestational period while the individual is hidden from view. Perhaps if human physical development consisted of the metamorphoses found in insects, a much more segmented view of biological growth would have been prevalent.

The increasing sophistication of biological theorizing combined with a series of psychological issues left unresolved by conventional wisdom influenced developmentalists, most notably Piaget (1950) and Werner (1961), to reconsider the continuous nature of mental development. Piaget focused on the logic of thought and confronted psychology with a separation between the seeming continuities in performance and dramatic discontinuities in competence. Piaget's stages of cognitive development are based on qualitatively different structural organizations at different points in life.

Werner (1957) offers a wider perspective in his concept of the multiformity of development. Recognizing the non-specificity of his orthogenetic principle that development moves in the direction of more complex differentiations and integrations, Werner allowed for reaching a particular level of functioning by means of a variety of pathways. In a material vein, modern biological research has demonstrated that the same mature organs can arise from the activities of differeing genes, cells, and

tissues (Waddington, 1966). A psychological example of "multiformity" of functioning can be found in Goldstein's (1939) explorations of the consequences of war injuries to the brain. Not only did identical lesions in different individuals produce different effects, but similar deficits in functioning could also be compensated by a variety of mechanisms.

When confronted with evidence or theorizing that continuity may not be central to development, there is a tendency to translate conceptions of discontinuity into more acceptable terms. For example, when Piagetian theory is translated by a normative and achievement-oriented Western psychology, the notion that stages are different qualitatively is expanded to include the notion that the better one is at an earlier stage of development the better one will be at the next stage. Thus, the concept of discontinuity in level of competence is reinterpreted as a concept of continuity in level of performance. From another perspective Kessen, Haith, & Salapatek (1970) note that despite the minimal evidence for continuities in development, our common-sense view that such stabilities in behavior must exist will provide sufficient basis for the continued search for these continuities. Two points threaten the potential success of this quest. First, the transition from one stage of functioning to another with a qualitatively different level of organization may make many of the adaptations and maladaptations of the earlier stage obsolete, and secondly, individuals with completely different experiential histories can not only achieve these transitions, but also after reaching the new stage show little evidence of the past diversity of functioning. However, before fully elucidating these theoretical points, it is necessary to examine empirically their premise that continuities in development are indeed more apparent than real.

The following presentation will consist of four segments. First, we shall examine the influence of a variety of factors which are thought to be related to deviant developmental outcomes in order to seek out linear chains of causality which might provide evidence for continuities in development. Secondly, we shall look at attempts to find continuities in specific classes of behavior such as intelligence and temperament. Thirdly, the suggestion will be made that difficulties in predicting outcomes result from utilizing inappropriate models of development. Finally, we will return to the issue of stages, transitions, and discontinuities with which we began.

ORIGINS OF DEVIANCY

The influence of psychoanalytic thinking, together with the increased knowledge of the complexity of behavior found in young children, has raised concerns about the effects of a variety of early trauma on functioning later in life.

Continuum of Reproductive Casualty

In recent years increasing attention has been directed toward the study and early identification of various factors which place children at a greater than average risk to later disease or disorder. Although persons of all ages are menaced by a range of life hazards, most of the available research literature has focused on a variety of trauma that are suffered early in infancy and that are expected to play a principal role in the developmental outcome of the affected individual. The seriousness of such early hazards is underscored by the fact that the death rates during the perinatal period are four times greater than those of other ages (Niswander & Gordon, 1972). Of perhaps even greater significance is a broad *continuum of reproductive casualty,* hypothesized to include congenital malformations, cerebral palsy, mental retardation, deafness, blindness, and other neurosensory defects which are thought to result from early hazards and traumas (Lilienfeld & Parkhurst, 1951; Lilienfeld, Pasamanick & Rogers, 1955). It has been estimated that approximately 10% of the population in the United States has handicaps or defects that are present at or soon after birth (Niswander & Gordon, 1972).

Of the 5–10 million conceptions occurring annually in the United States, 2–3 million result in spontaneous abortions due to genetic or chromosomal defects and pathogens, and another one million are terminated legally or illegally. Of the approximately 3.5 million fetuses that reach 20 weeks of gestational age, 1.5% die before delivery, 1.5% die in the first postnatal month, 1.5% have severe congenital malformations, and about 10% will have learning disorders that range from mild to severe retardation (Babson & Benson, 1971).

The large number of general learning disorders and specific deficits in behaviors such as reading are of great concern to clinicians. The lack of either

a clear genetic basis or anatomical damage in many children with sensory and behavioral disorders was puzzling to investigators who adhered closely to a traditional "medical model." If, according to this point of view, a disorder existed, there should have been some clear etiological factor, preferably biological, somewhere in the patient's history. If such a factor could not be located, it was presumably because diagnostic techniques were not yet sufficiently sophisticated to detect it. Gesell & Amatruda (1941), strong advocates of such a straightforward cause-effect model, proposed the concept of "minimal cerebral injury" as an explanation. The supposed reason for not being able to document the existence of such injury is because it is, by definition, minimal, i.e., undetectable. Current usage of terms like "minimal brain damage" or "special learning disabilities" are expressions of the continuing need for clinicians to be able to explain disorder on the basis of simple cause-effect relationships rather than complex developmental processes.

Pasamanick & Knobloch (1966) reviewed a series of retrospective studies which examined the delivery and birth complications of children with a variety of subsequent disorders. They found a number of such later disorders to be significantly associated with greater numbers of complications of pregnancy and prematurity. These included cerebral palsy, epilepsy, mental deficiency, behavior disorders, and reading disabilities.

Almost all studies in this area have proceeded on the general assumption that it is possible to specify particular characteristics of either the child or his parents that will permit long range predictions regarding the ultimate course of growth and development.

These retrospective studies have implicated a number of factors in early development, such as (1) anoxia, (2) prematurity, (3) delivery complications, and (4) social conditions, as being related to later disorder. After a lengthy review of studies exploring the later effects of perinatal factors Sameroff & Chandler (1975) were forced to conclude that "even if one continues to believe that a continuum of reproductive casualty exists, its importance pales in comparison to the massive influences of socioeconomic factors on both prenatal and postnatal development." Space does not permit a lengthy survey of the evidence for this conclusion to be made here, but a brief survey of some typical findings will follow. For more detail the reviews of Gottfried (1973) and Sameroff & Chandler (1975) are recommended.

Anoxia

It appears logical to assume that cerebral oxygen deprivation early in development would produce later deficits in intellectual functioning. Animal studies seemed to indicate that oxygen deprivation at birth produced brain damage and learning deficits (Windle, 1944).

Gottfried (1973) reviewed twenty studies of the effects of perinatal anoxia on later intellectual functioning. His conclusions were quite similar to those arrived at by Sameroff & Chandler (1975) in their review of the same literature. These findings can be typified by the results of a large longitudinal study carried out in St. Louis. Several hundred infants were seen in the newborn period (Graham, Matarazzo, & Caldwell, 1956), followed up at 3 years (Graham, Ernhart, Thurston, & Craft, 1962), and again at 7 years (Corah, Anthony, Painter, Stern, & Thurston, 1965). As expected, when examined during the first days of life anoxic infants were found to be "impaired" on a series of five measures which included maturation level, visual responsiveness, irritability, muscle tension, and pain threshold (Graham, Pennoyer, Caldwell, Greenman, & Hartman, 1957). When the performance on these measures was compared with scores based on the degree of prenatal anoxia, postnatal anoxia, and the clinical assessment of central nervous system disturbance, those infants with the poorest scores performed most poorly on the newborn assessments. These same infants were seen again at three years of age and tested with a battery of cognitive, perceptual-motor, personality and neurologic tests (Graham et al., 1962). The group of anoxic infants scored lower than controls on all tests of cognitive function, had more positive neurological findings, and showed some personality differences.

At seven years of age these children were again tested (Corah, et al., 1965). Surprisingly, significant IQ differences had *disappeared* between the anoxic group and the control population. Of the twenty-one cognitive and perceptual measures, only two tasks still seemed to show these children deficient. It was concluded that anoxics showed minimal impairment of functioning at seven years and that

efforts to predict current functioning on the basis of severity of anoxia were highly unreliable. To summarize, the St. Louis study showed that anoxic infants did poorly on newborn measures, still showed effects at three years of age, but by seven performed almost as well as non-anoxic controls. Gottfried (1973) concluded his review by noting that there were many methodological problems in the literature but that anoxic infants as a group do not appear to become retarded.

Prematurity

Prematurity is another of the classic perinatal hazards that has been related to later deviancy in behavior. Since prematurity is an outcome of many complications in pregnancy and represents the most prevalent abnormality of birth, it may be considered as a modal problem for assessing the effects of the continuum of reproductive casualty (Birch & Gussow, 1970).

As in the studies of anoxia, the data on long term effects of prematurity do not lead to any clear cut conclusions. Although many studies of prematurity have found small IQ deficits later in development, it is by no means clear whether these adverse consequences associated with prematurity are a function of the prematurity itself, the accompanying low birth weight, an extended period of living in an incubator, accompanying perinatal trauma, or the social climate in which the child is raised (Parmelee & Haber, in press). A gestationally premature infant who suffers no prenatal, perinatal, or postnatal traumas other than prematurity itself, and is raised in an optimal home environment may turn out to be no different from a normal full-term infant raised under the same circumstances.

It is interesting that the studies of the effects of prematurity have shown consistent, albeit small, IQ deficits, while studies of the effects of anoxia have not. A possible explanation is that the premature infant is more easily recognized and labeled by his parent than the anoxic infant. The parents may not even know if their infant had some form of asphyxia, while the premature, and especially the lower birth weight premature, is quite easily identified not only by its physical appearance but also by the initial separation from the parents, and the subsequent intense caretaking demands. It will be seen that the parents' perception of the child can play a major role in its deviant development exclusive of any actual deficit that may be present in the child.

Newborn Status

The research literature offers little evidence to suggest a relationship between specific pregnancy and delivery complications and later abnormal behavior. Another source for specific predictions of later deviancy has been aberrations in newborn behavior. Parmelee & Michaelis (1971) have provided an excellent review of the relationship between newborn neurological status and later deviancy. Although the diagnostic search for neurological signs was a successful means of identifying infants with contemporary neurological problems, there was little evidence to suggest that such signs were of any utility as predictors of later adaptational problems.

Socio-economic Influences

A recurrent theme that has run through much of the research in this area is that social status variables seem to play an important role in modulating the effects of perinatal factors. Birch & Gussow (1970) argued that high risk to infants is associated with depressed social status and ethnicity. The highest rates of infant loss were found among populations which are both poor and black. Pasamanick, Knobloch, & Lilienfeld (1956) found that the proportion of infants having some complication increased from 5% in the white upper social class stratum, to 15% in the lowest white socio-economic group, to 51% among all non-whites. These data imply that the biological outcomes of pregnancy are worse for those in poorer environments.

One of the most ambitious and revealing of the longitudinal studies of the effects of early complications has recently been completed in Hawaii. Werner, Bierman & French (1971), reported on all 670 children born on the island of Kauai in 1955. Because of the multiracial nature of Hawaii and the variety of social classes sampled when the whole population was used, Werner et al. were able to provide ample controls for both variables.

Each infant was initially scored on a four-point scale for severity of perinatal complications. At twenty months and again at ten years of age, these perinatal scores were related to assessments of physical health, psychological status, and the environmental variables of socio-economic status, family stability, and the mother's intelligence.

At 20 months of age infants who had suffered severe perinatal stress were found to have lower scores on their assessments. In addition, however, there was a clear interaction between the impairing effect of perinatal complications and environmental variables, especially socio-economic status. For infants living in a high socio-economic environment, with a stable family, or with a mother of high intelligence, the IQ differences between children with and without complication scores was only 5–7 points. For infants living in a low socio-economic environment, with low family stability, or with a mother of low intelligence, the difference in mean Cattell IQs between the high and low perinatal complications groups and between infants without perinatal complications ranged from 19 to 37 points.

The results of the Kauai study seem to indicate that perinatal complications were consistently related to later physical and psychological development only when combined with and supported by persistently poor environmental circumstances. In addition, when good prenatal care is available, socio-economic differences in the initial distribution of perinatal complications were found to disappear.

The infants of the Kauai sample were again examined when they reached 10 years of age (Werner, Honzik & Smith, 1968). There was no correlation between the perinatal-stress score and the 10-year measures. Some correlation was, however, found between the 20-month and 10-year data, especially when social-economic status and parents' educational level were taken into consideration. Stability of intellectual functioning was much higher for those children who had IQs below 80 at the 10-year testing. All of these children had 20-month Cattell scores of 100 or less, with almost half below 80. The majority of these children had parents with little education and of low socio-economic status. The Kauai study seemed to suggest that risk factors operative during the perinatal period disappear during childhood as more potent familial and social factors exert their influence.

Werner and her associates (Werner et al., 1971) noted that of every 1000 live births in Kauai, by age 10 only 660 would be adequately functioning in school with no recognized physical, intellectual, or behavior problems. Of the 34% who would have problems at the age of 10 only a minor proportion could be attributed to the effects of serious perinatal stress. The biologically vulnerable child represents only a small proportion of those children who will not function adequately. The authors concluded that in their study "ten times more children had problems related to the effects of poor early environment than to the effects of perinatal stress."

The data from these various longitudinal studies of prenatal and perinatal complications have yet to produce a single predictive variable more potent than the familial and socio-economic characteristics of the caretaking environment. The predictive efficiency of the variable of socio-economic class is especially pronounced for the low end of the IQ scale. Willerman, Broman & Fiedler (1970), compared Bayley developmental scores obtained at 8 months with Stanford-Binet IQs at age 4. For children with a high socio-economic status there was little relationship between their 8-month Bayley scores and their 4-year scores. For children with a low socio-economic status, however, those who did poorly at 8 months continued to do so at 4 years of age. In addition, there was a crossover effect, where the high socio-economic status children who were in the lowest quartile at the 8-month examination were performing better at 4 years than were the low socio-economic status children who scored in the highest quartile at 8 months. Willerman et al. (1970) see poverty as amplifying IQ deficits in poorly developed infants.

The preceding survey of early biological complications conceptualized in the continuum of reproductive casualty (Lilienfeld, Rogers & Pasamanick, 1955) has not found much support for direct long-range consequences. The hypothesized "continuity" in development from early trauma to later deviancy does not appear to hold. There is a serious question as to whether a child who has suffered perinatal trauma, but shows no obvious physical damage, is at any greater risk for later deviancy, either neurological, perceptual, or intellectual, than a child who has not suffered perinatal trauma. In the studies reviewed, the effects of social status tended to reduce or amplify intellectual deficits. In advantaged families infants who had suffered perinatal complications generally showed minor residual effects, if any, at follow-up. Many infants from lower social class homes with identical histories of complications showed significant retardations in later functioning. Socio-economic status appears to have much stronger influence on the course of development than perinatal history.

CONTINUUM OF CARETAKING CASUALTY

Sameroff & Chandler (1975) were led to propose a *continuum of caretaking casualty* to incorporate the environmental risk factors leading toward poor developmental outcomes. Although reproductive casualties may play an initiating role in the production of later problems, it is the caretaking environment that will determine the ultimate outcome. At one end of the caretaking continuum, supportive, compensatory and normalizing environments appear to be able to eliminate the effects of early complications. On the other end of the continuum, caretaking by deprived, stressed, or poorly educated parents tends to exacerbate early difficulties.

Where environmental factors have generally been ignored in research efforts aimed at finding linear chains of causality between early pregnancy and delivery complications and later deviancy, they have been the central focus for investigators exploring the role of caretaking practices in producing poor developmental outcomes. Unfortunately, environmentally-oriented researchers have generally been equally one-sided in the way they ignore the child's individuality as a major influence on the caretaking to which he is exposed. Despite these limitations, research into the developmental implications of early caretaking practices has identified many circumstances that contribute to risk. Breakdowns in the parent-child relationship may take a great variety of forms. The most heavily researched and carefully documented of these transactional failures relates to the inability of parents and their children to work out an interactional style which both guarantees the child a reasonable margin of safety and satisfies the child's basic biological and social needs. This is the issue of child abuse. Physical abuse is dramatic evidence of a disorder in the parent-child relationship.

Child Abuse

The major focus of research on the battered child has been devoted to characterizing the personality of the abusive parent. Spinetta & Rigler (1972) in a summary of this research characterized these deviant parents as of lower intelligence and with higher levels of aggressiveness, impulsivity, immaturity, self-centeredness, tenseness and self-criticism. However, knowing this constellation of personality characteristics does not greatly improve the probability of correctly predicting that child abuse will occur. Other parents with very similar characteristics do not abuse their children, while parents who are abusive will only batter one or two of their children. It appears that certain children are selected for abuse, or rather, that certain children tend to elicit abusive behavior from their parents.

Sameroff & Chandler (1975) were able to find support for the hypothesis that characteristics of the child may predispose the parents to battering or neglect. Klein & Stern (1971), for example, found an association between low birth weight and the battered-child syndrome. Whereas typically 10% of births are of low birth weights, among battered children the rate runs as high as 40%. Klaus & Kennell (1970) suggested that the birth of a premature child may function to overtax the limited resources of certain mothers and precipitate an acute emotional crisis. Many battered children whose birth weights were within normal limits had other significant medical illnesses which might also have served to deplete their mothers' emotional resources.

It has been suggested that these problems may be partly the result of separation in the newborn period (Klaus & Kennell, 1970). Because of prematurity or serious illness a high proportion of battered children had been separated earlier from their parents for prolonged periods. Early prolonged separation may permanently impair the affectional ties between parents and children and leave the children vulnerable to parental abuse and neglect.

Although it is not always possible to separate truth from rationalization, the parents of abused children frequently describe their offspring as difficult and unmanageable. In one study (Morse, Sahler & Friedman, 1970), for example, 15 of the 25 children studied were considered "difficult" by their parents. Other data collected tended to support the impressions of the parents that many battered children were problem children preceding the reported abuse or neglect.

Reciprocity in Child-Caretaker Relations

In all of the risk categories of this survey (including prenatal and perinatal pathology, parental characteristics, and other intra- or extra-familial environmental factors) it is possible to identify significant numbers of children who, although subjected to these negative influences, nevertheless develop

normally (Chess, 1971). Only some of the children subjected to these presumed psychological pathogens do in fact develop disturbances, and only small quantitative relationships have been demonstrated to exist between pathology in either the parents or the environment and pathology in the child (Beiser, 1964).

The failure to predict adequately the cases of child abuse appears to have been the result of a research strategy which has been almost exclusively concerned with environmental effects. Children labeled "at risk" have often been regarded as passive victims of external forces and as a consequence are thought to be incapable of having in any way provoked or participated in the difficulties in which they have found themselves (Galdston, 1971). As a consequence the victims have often been purposefully excluded from study because their roles have been presumed to be irrelevant. Because much of the research on child abuse has been prompted by concerns with prevention and remediation, attention has been focused on those aspects of the problem which have been thought to be more easily changed. The evident importance of the parents and their child-rearing practices pushes characteristics of the children themselves into an incidental role.

Bell (1968) took a fresh view of the literature on direction of effects in the caretaking interaction. He pointed out that while viewing infants as helpless victims fits a one-sided model of parental determination of behavior, many studies have shown that the infant is more involved in determining the nature of the interpersonal relationship than was once supposed. Many parent behaviors are not spontaneously emitted in the service of educating the child, but rather are elicited by many of the child's own characteristics and behaviors.

The infant's appearance of helplessness and dependency appears to be a strong contributor to the parents' desire to provide care (Rheingold, 1966). However, the response of all caretakers is not necessarily the same. The helplessness of a child can arouse negative as well as positive parental response. To the extent that the helplessness and dependency are accompanied by aggravating factors such as, restlessness, colic, and digestive difficulties, the chance of eliciting negative caretaking responses is increased (Bell, 1968).

The frequent assumption that the newborn is too ineffectual to carry any legitimate burden of responsiblity for the quality of his or her relationship with various caretakers is contradicted by much current research. Constitutional variability in children strongly affects the parents' attitudes and caretaking styles. The systematic investigation of such idiosyncrasies in the child's behavioral organization is, however, of fairly recent origin. In research at New York University, Thomas, Chess & Birch (1968) studied the changes that occur in the child's temperament as a function of the transactions with his family environment. These investigators have described a temperamental constellation which they have labelled "the difficult child." Difficult infants were found to have low thresholds for arousal, intense reactions when aroused, poor adaptability and irregularity in biological functioning. Although only 10% of their sample were categorized as difficult, 15% of the children who later had behavioral disturbances fell in this group. Without the benefit of longitudinal studies one could easily misinterpret these difficulties of temperament as constitutional weaknesses that predisposed the child to later emotional difficulties. Such static predictions would not, however, prove to be very accurate. In fact, when Thomas et al. examined the relationship between behavior in the first and fifth year of life few significant correlations were found. What made the difference in outcome for these children appeared to be the behavior of their parents. If the parents were able to adjust to the child's difficult temperament, a good behavioral outcome was likely. If not, the difficulties were exacerbated and behavioral disturbance often resulted.

The transaction was not simply the unidirectional influence of the parents on the child, but also the reciprocal influence of the child on his parents. The impact of these difficult children was such as to disrupt the normal caretaking abilities of their parents. The New York group reported that there were no marked differences in child-rearing attitudes expressed among the various parents in the sample. Whatever differences eventually characterized the parental attitudes of the deviant children apparently arose as a consequence of experience in the parent-child interaction.

The range of findings cited in the preceding section tends to support the hypothesis that knowing *only* the temperament of the child or knowing *only* the child-rearing attitudes and practices of the parents would not allow one to predict the developmental outcome for the child. It would appear, rather, that it is the character of the *specific transactions* that occurred between a given child and his parents which determined the course of his subsequent development. If the continuum of caretaking casualty is to be useful in elucidating developmental consequences, it must be related to the individual characteristics of the child in question. Neither the constitutionally oriented "continuum of reproductive casualty" nor the environmentally oriented "continuum of caretaking casualty" is predictive when taken alone. It is the combination of these dimensions which would make an understanding of development possible. An evaluation of alternative ways of making such an amalgam will be presented in a later section.

CONTINUITY IN INTELLIGENCE AND TEMPERAMENT

How is one to explain the general finding of the longitudinal studies reviewed above, that effects of severe early physiological trauma disappear with age? A possible explanation is that the quality of cognitive functioning changes with age, so that early aberrations may be irrelevant to later intelligence. Bayley (1949), commenting on the data from the Berkeley Growth Study of intelligence from birth to 18 years of age, noted that individual scores on the tests were unstable and that long-range predictions based on early IQ testing were not possible.

McCall, Hogarty, & Hurlbut (1972), in a review of longitudinal studies of intelligence, examined the common finding of low correlations between assessments of "intelligence" during infancy and later "intelligence." These investigators concluded that low correlations were not a consequence of unreliabilities in the test instruments, but were rather a consequence of qualitative shifts in what is defined as "intelligence" at different ages. They argued against the belief in a "pervasive and developmentally constant intelligence" on which most longitudinal comparisons have been based. From the available data it would appear that there is no basis for assuming a simple continuity in intellectual competence.

Although long-term continuities in development are not found, prediction over short periods of time should be possible (Bayley, 1949). Even this compromise appears unjustified because of the rapid transitions in early behavior. Lewis & McGurk (1972) tested infants six times at three- to six-month intervals during the first two years of life. Of the 15 intercorrelations between testings with the Bayley scales, only two were statistically significant. They found the same result in successive testings using a Piaget object conservation task. Scores on infant tests seem to have little power to predict later functioning.

Hunt & Bayley (1971) further qualify the value of infant testing by arguing that although these assessments have little predictive power for intellectual superiority, they do differentiate in a general way between normal and retarded individuals. However, this compromise too may be a culturally bound illusion created by the constancies found in Western environments. Cross-cultural studies have found that infants who would have been judged as severely retarded by Western standards grow to be competently functioning adults (Dennis & Najarian, 1957; Kagan & Klein, 1973).

These qualitative shifts in development are not restricted to intellectual functioning. Bell, Weller, & Waldrop (1971) noted a complete reversal in some behaviors between the newborn and preschool periods. Newborns who had been easy to arouse and with low thresholds to stimulation tended to be passive and quiet in the preschool period, while newborns who had been difficult to arouse and had high thresholds to stimulation tended to be active and outgoing later. McGrade (1968) found a similar transition between the newborn period and eight-months of age. Since qualitative shifts in development do occur during childhood, it might be thought to be surprising if children *did* show continuity in their intellectual performance.

DEVELOPMENTAL MODELS

The preceding review of the search for continuities in psychological functioning was not designed primarily to argue that such continuities are nonexistent, although the evidence seems to point in that direction. Rather, the discussion was aimed toward producing a conclusion that if continuities did exist we were not effectively searching for them. In order to find a more effective strategy one must "decenter," to use Piaget's terminology. Where investigators have focused on searching for developmental stabilities in either the constitution or the

environment of the child, decentering would permit placing both the child's constitution and environment into a common system. A substantial increase in the sense one can make out of the developmental process could be provided by a simultaneous integration of these two factors in development. Sameroff & Chandler (1975) outlined three models—main effect, interactional, and transactional—that have been applied with varying degrees of success to explain the data presented earlier.

Main-effect Model

The essence of the main-effect model is found in the typical nature-nurture argument as to whether constitution and environment exert influences on development which are independent of each other. A defect in the constitution of an individual will, according to this model, produce a defective adult irrespective of environmental circumstance, while a pathogenic environment will produce a defective adult independent of his constitution. Such a model is attractive to many investigators because of its parsimony and has been given strong currency in etiological research. Genetic factors as well as constitutional defects caused by pregnancy and delivery complications have often been assumed to exert such unilateral influences on development. As seen in the above review, the general findings of retrospective investigations that individuals suffering a wide range of disorders were more likely to have experienced complicated births than individuals without the disorders have not been supported by prospective studies. Although some of the effects of early trauma can be detected during infancy, by the age of seven these effects are almost completely attenuated.

While the majority of infants experiencing pregnancy and perinatal complications are not found to have later difficulties when studied prospectively, interactions have been noted between these complications and the child's environment. For infants raised in a middle-class home, with a stable family structure, and with educated parents, there was, for example, no relationship between obstetric complications and later intelligence or personality. When children with similar complications were raised in a lower SES home, or in an unstable family situation, or with uneducated parents, they were more likely to suffer mental retardation and behavioral problems. In other words, unless the environmental context is also specified, few predictions can be made about developmental outcome based on perinatal difficulties. It would appear then that the influence of constitutional characteristics on a child's development do not seem to fit a main-effect model.

Similar conclusions about the inadequacy of predictions based exclusively on environmental effects also seem warranted. The general finding of studies of deviant caretaking (Spinetta & Rigler, 1972) has been that parents who neglect or abuse their children have different personalities from those who do not. The ability to identify personality characteristics of abusing parents after-the-fact might lead one to presume that predictions can be made before-the-fact that parents having such characteristics would abuse their children. Unfortunately, however, those attributes found to characterize such parents are sufficiently common that they are of little value in attempting to predict which parents actually will abuse their children. Since abusing parents appear to be selective in the choice of the child they abuse, a missing element in the predictive equation for child abuse would seem to be characteristics specific to the child. As was the case with obstetrical complications taken alone, parental characteristics taken alone are not effective predictors of developmental outcome.

Clearly, there are extremes of constitutional disorders, such as severe brain damage, the developmental consequences of which would be deviant in any environment. Similarly, there are obvious extremes of environmental disorder which may well produce deviancy in a child of any constitution. These extreme examples are not, however, representative of the vast majority of children who evidence poor developmental outcomes. A main-effects model seems to apply neither to constitutional nor environmental components in development.

Interactional Model

The preceding discussion would suggest that, at a minimum, any prognostic equation for predicting long range developmental outcomes must include information concerning both the child's constitutional make-up and his caretaking environment. From this point of view one should be able to create a two-dimensional array of constitutions and environments (see Figure 1), with an entry describing

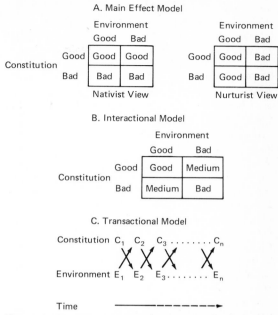

Figure 1 Models of development with outcomes predicted by main-effect and interactional models.

the child's developmental outcome for any combination of these two factors. Children with constitutional problems raised in a deviant environment would have poor outcomes. Children with constitutional problems raised in supportive environments and children without problems raised in deviant environments would have middling outcomes. The best outcomes of all would be expected for children without constitutional problems raised in a supportive environment.

While this interactive model substantially increases the statistical efficiency of developmental predictions, it is insufficient to facilitate our understanding of the actual mechanisms leading to later outcomes. The major reason behind the inadequacy of this model is that neither constitution nor environment are necessarily constant over time. At each moment, month, or year the characteristics of both the child and his environment change in important ways. Moreover, these differences are interdependent and change as a function of their mutual influence on one another. The child alters his environment and in turn is altered by the changed world he has created. In order to incorporate these progressive interactions one must move from a static interactional model to a more dynamic theory of developmental *transaction* where there is a continual and progressive interplay between the organism and its environment.

Transactional Model

Any truly transactional model must stress the plastic character of both the environment and the organism as it actively participates in its own growth. In this model the child's behavior is more than a simple reaction to his environment. Instead, he is actively engaged in attempts to organize and structure his world. The child is in a perceptual state of active re-organization and cannot properly be regarded as maintaining inborn characteristics as static qualities. In this view, the constants in development are not some set of traits but rather the *processes* by which these traits are maintained in the transactions between organism and environment.

Exceptional outcomes from this organismic or transactional point-of-view are not seen simply as a function of an inborn inability to respond appropriately, but rather as a function of some *continuous* malfunction in the organism-environment transaction across time which prevents the child from organizing his world adaptively. Forces preventing the child's normal integration with his environment act not just at one traumatic point, but must operate throughout his development.

Another major shortcoming resulting from the focus of the interactional model on product rather than process is its inability to deal with directionality found in development. Despite the great variety and range of influences on development, there are a surprisingly small number of developmental outcomes. Evolution appears to have built into the human organism regulative mechanisms to produce normal developmental outcomes under all but the most adverse of circumstances (Waddington, 1966). Any understanding of deviancies in outcome must be interpreted in the light of this self-righting and self-organizing tendency, which appears to move children toward normality in the face of pressure toward deviation.

Two possibilities that defeat the self-righting tendencies of the organism and produce deviant development can be considered. The first possibility is that an insult to the organisms' integrative mechanisms prevents the functioning of its self-righting ability, and the second possibility is that environmental forces present throughout development prevent the normal integrations that would occur in a more modal environment. The former possibility can be seen in the pregnancy and delivery complications related to the *continuum of reproductive casualty.* The latter possibility can be seen in the familial and social abnormalities related to the *continuum of caretaking casualty.* These two sources of risk appear to be closely interrelated in the production of positive or negative developmental outcomes. Where the child's vulnerability is heightened through massive or recurrent trauma only an extremely supportive environment can help to restore the normal integrative growth process. A seriously brain-damaged child requiring institutional care would be an instance of such an extreme case of reproductive casualty. On the other extreme a highly disordered caretaking setting might convert the most sturdy and integrated of children into a caretaking casualty.

Implications of the Transactional Model

Theoretical, methodological, and clinical implications can be drawn from the preceding analysis of models. Theoretically, the failure to find a linear causal chain between reproductive casualty and later deviancy raises serious questions about the frequency with which continuities occur in psychological functioning. The only continuity which is currently evident is the incapacity of certain caretaking environments to respond adaptively to infants with specialized needs (Thomas, Chess & Birch, 1968).

Methodologically, it is apparent that if developmental processes are to be understood, it will not be through continuous assessment of the child alone, but through a continuous assessment of the transactions between the child and his environment to determine how these transactions facilitate or hinder adaptive integration as both the child and his surroundings change and evolve. A statistical analog of the back and forth influences which underly the transactional model was utilized in a longitudinal study of mother-infant interactions (Clarke-Stewart, 1973). Using a cross-lagged panel correlation technique (Campbell, 1963), Clarke-Stewart was able to show a complex reciprocity between mother and infant closely resembling the transactional model in Figure 1. Between the ages of nine and 14 months maternal attention influenced the child's attachment to her, while from 14 months to

18 months the child's attachment was influencing maternal attention. Clarke-Stewart suggests that as mother and child seek a balanced interaction, first one and then the other assumes a causal role.

Clinically, the current tendency to attribute deviancy to intrinsic factors such as minimal brain damage or a schizophrenic genotype must be moderated. Attempts to treat an already ill child must be secondary to earlier attempts to help the caretaking environment adjust to the special needs of an infant who may be temperamentally deviant in order to prevent a sensorimotor abnormality from being converted into a cognitive one. Sameroff & Zax (1973) described a complex transactional sequence for the etiology of mental disorder (see Figure 2). The sequence begins when a pregnant mentally-ill mother by her anxiety influences her obstetrician to use higher levels of medication and an instrumental delivery to speed her through the childbirth experience. A consequence of the complicated delivery could be a hyperactive and fussy child who lacks responsiveness. A consequence of the unresponsive infant could be anxiety and hostility in the mother. The mother's concerns with her own poor emotional status would prevent her from adequately adapting to the temperament of the child. A vicious cycle can then be produced in which the child becomes increasingly difficult in temperament as the mother becomes increasingly maladaptive in her caretaking, resulting in emotional disturbance for the child. Using a main-effect model the child's deviant outcome would be attributed to either his complicated delivery, his constitutional hyperactivity, or his anxious mother. From the transactional view it is only the complex interweaving of all these

factors which acted to produce the abnormal outcome.

Although at first glance one might regret our inability to attribute developmental effects to single causes, once the complexities of the chain of interactions leading to deviancy are elucidated a whole variety of modal points become available, where interventions can produce better outcomes. Obstetricians can be educated to be more circumspect in their treatment of anxious women. The mother herself can undergo childbirth education in order to learn to control her anxiety during the delivery, as well as child-care education to alert her to the effects and modes of dealing with individuality in her child after delivery. Just as evolution has built in the regulating mechanism to counteract deviations in the physical development of the fetus, so too can society construct regulatory mechanisms to compensate for deviations in the behavioral development of the child.

To summarize, disorders in development have been retrospectively attributed to a variety of early constitutional or environmental factors. When these predisposing factors have been studied prospectively little support is given to their causal role or their predictive value for later deviancy. Evidence for qualitative continuities and stabilities in development appear to be artifacts of an incomplete analysis of the child in its environment. When the two are examined in combination, complex reciprocal transactions are found which reduce or amplify early problems in behavior.

Developmental outcomes must be interpreted as the products of a child's characteristics, his material environment and the cognitive levels and values

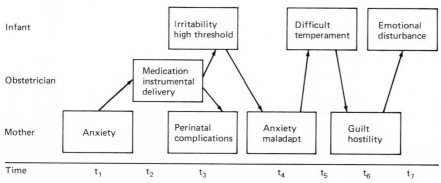

Figure 2 Hypothetical sequence of transactions in the etiology of emotional disturbance.

of his social milieu. Where the social environment fosters rigidity, stereotyping, and concreteness in thought and behavior, early deviancies can become resistant to the normal restructuring implicit in development. Where flexibility, openness, and adaptability are fundamental characteristics of the environment, early problems are dissipated as the child advances in his construction and organization of both his cognitive and social world.

REFERENCES

Babson, S. G., & Benson, R. C. *Management of high-risk pregnancy and intensive care of the neonate.* St. Louis: Mosby, 1971.

Bayley, N. Consistency and variability in the growth of intelligence from birth to eighteen years, *Journal of Genetic Psychology,* 1949, Vol. 75, 165–196.

Beiser, H. R. Discrepancies in the symptomatology of parents and children. *Journal of the American Academy of Child Psychiatry,* 1964, Vol. 3, 457–468.

Bell, R. Q. A reinterpretation of the direction of effects in studies of socialization. *Psychological Review,* 1968, Vol. 75, 81–95.

Bell, R. Q., Weller, G. M., & Waldrop, M. Newborn and preschooler: Organization of behavior and relations between periods. *Monographs of the Society for Research in Child Development,* 1971, Vol. 36, (2, Whole No. 142).

Bertalanffy, L. Von. *General system theory.* New York: Braziller, 1968.

Birch, H. & Gussow, G. D. *Disadvantaged children.* New York: Grune & Stratton, 1970.

Campbell, D. T. From description to experimentation: Interpreting trends as quasi-experiments. In C. W. Harris (Ed.), *Problems in measuring change.* Madison: University of Wisconsin Press, 1963. Pp. 212–244.

Chess, S. Genesis of behavior disorder. In J. G. Howells (Ed.), *Modern perspectives in international child psychiatry.* New York: Brunner/Mazel, 1971. Pp. 61–79.

Clarke-Stewart, K. A. Interactions between mothers and their young children: Characteristics and consequences. *Monographs of the Society for Research in Child Development,* 1973, Vol. 38 (6–7, Whole No. 153).

Cole, M., Gay, J., Glick, J. A., & Sharp, D. W. *The cultural context of learning and thinking: An exploration in experimental anthropology.* New York: Basic Books, 1971.

Corah, N. L., Anthony, E. J., Painter, P., Stern, J. A., & Thurston, D. L. Effects of perinatal anoxia after seven years. *Psychological Monographs,* 1965, Vol. 79, (3, Whole No. 596).

Dennis, W. & Najarian, P. Infant development under environmental handicap. *Psychological Monographs,* 1957, Vol. 71 (7, Whole No. 436).

Galdston, R. Dysfunction of parenting: The battered child, the neglected child, the emotional child. In J. G. Howells (Ed.), *Modern Perspectives in International Child Psychiatry.* New York: Brunner/Mazel, 1971. Pp. 571–588.

Gesell, A., & Armatruda, C. *Developmental diagnosis.* New York: Hoeber, 1941.

Goldstein, K. *The organism.* New York: American Book, 1939.

Gottfried, A. W. Intellectual consequences of perinatal anoxia. *Psychological Bulletin,* 1973, Vol. 80, 231–242.

Graham, F. K., Ernhart, C. B., Thurston, D., & Craft, M. Development three years after perinatal anoxia and other potentially damaging newborn experiences. *Psychological Monographs,* 1962, Vol. 76, (3, Whole No. 522).

Graham, F. K., Matarazzo, R. G., & Caldwell, B. M. Behavioral differences between normal and traumatized newborns: II Standardization, reliability, and validity. *Psychological Monographs,* 1956, Vol. 70 (21, Whole No. 428).

Graham, F. K., Pennoyer, M. M., Caldwell, B. M., Greenman, M., & Hartman, A. F. Relationship between clinical status and behavior test performance in a newborn group with histories suggesting anoxia. *Journal of Pediatrics,* 1957, Vol. 50, 177–189.

Hunt, J. V. & Bayley, N. Explorations into patterns of mental development and prediction from the Bayley Scales of Infant Development. In J. P. Hill (Ed.), *Minnesota Symposia on Child Psychology.* Vol. 5. Minneapolis: University of Minnesota Press, 1971. Pp. 52–71.

Kagan, J. & Klein, R. E. Cross-cultural perspectives on early development. *American Psychologist,* 1973, Vol. 28, 947–961.

Kessen, W., Haith, M. M., & Salapatek, P. H. Human infancy: A bibliography and guide. In P. H. Mussen (Ed.), *Carmichael's manual of child psychology.* (3rd ed.) Vol. 1. New York: Wiley, 1970. Pp. 287–446.

Klaus, M. H. & Kennell, J. H. Mothers separated from their newborn infants. *Pediatric Clinics of North America,* 1970, Vol. 17, 1015–1037.

Klein, M. & Stern, L. Low birth weight and the battered child syndrome. *American Journal of Diseases of Children,* 1971, Vol. 122, 15–18.

Lewis, M. & McGurk, H. Evaluation of infant intelligence. *Science,* 1972, Vol. 170, 1174–1177.

Lilienfield, A. M., & Parkhurst, E. A study of the association of factors of pregnancy and parturition with the development of cerebral palsy: A preliminary report. *American Journal of Hygiene,* 1951, Vol. 53, 262–282.

Lilienfield, A. M., Pasamanick, B. & Rogers, M. Relationships between pregnancy experience and the development of certain neuropsychiatric disorders in childhood. *American Journal of Public Health,* 1955, Vol. 45, 637–643.

McCall, R. B., Hogarty, P. S., & Hurlbut, N. Transitions in infant sensorimotor development and the prediction of childhood IQ. *American Psychologist,* 1972, Vol. 27, 728–748.

McGrade, B. J. Newborn activity and emotional response at eight months. *Child Development,* 1968, Vol. 39, 1247–1252.

Morse, C., Sahler, O., & Friedman, S. A three-year follow-up study of abused and neglected children. *American Journal of Diseases of Children,* 1970, Vol. 120, 439–446.

Niswander, K. R. & Gordon, M. (Eds.) *The collaborative perinatal study of the national institute of neurological diseases and stroke: The women and their pregnancies.* Philadelphia: Saunders, 1972.

Parmalee, A. H. & Haber, A. Who is the "risk infant"? In H. J. Osofsky (Ed.), *Clinical obstetrics and gynecology,* in press.

Parmalee, A. H. & Michaelis, R. Neurological examination of the newborn. In J. Hellmuth (Ed.), *Exceptional infant: Studies in abnormalities,* Vol. 2. New York: Brunner/Mazel, 1971. Pp. 3–21.

Pasamanick, B. & Knobloch, H. Retrospective studies on the epidemiology of reproductive casualty: old and new. *Merrill-Palmer Quarterly,* 1966, Vol. 12, 7–26.

Pasamanick, B., Knobloch, H., & Lilienfeld, A. M. Socio-economic status and some precursors of neuropsychiatric disorders. *American Journal of Orthopsychiatry,* 1956, Vol. 26, 594–601.

Piaget, J. *Psychology of Intelligence.* New York: Harcourt, Brace & World, 1950.

Rheingold, H. L. The development of social behavior in the human infant. In H. W. Stevenson (Ed.), Concept of development. *Monographs of the Society for Research in Child Development,* 1966, Vol. 31 (5, Whole No. 107).

Sameroff, A. J. Transactional models in early social relations. *Human Development,* in press.

Sameroff, A. J., & Chandler, M. J. Reproductive risk and the continuum of caretaking casualty. In F. D. Horowitz, M. Hetherington, S. Scarr-Salapatek, & G. Siegel (Eds.), *Review of Child Development Research.* Vol. 4. Chicago: University of Chicago, 1975. Pp. 187–244.

Sameroff, A. J., & Zax, M. Schizotaxia revisited: Model issues in the etiology of schizophrenia. *American Journal of Orthopsychiatry,* 1973, Vol. 43, 744–754.

Spinetta, J. J., & Rigler, D. The child-abusing parent: A psychological review. *Psychological Bulletin,* 1972, Vol. 77, 296–304.

Thomas, A., Chess, S., & Birch, H. *Temperament and behavior disorders in children.* New York: New York University, 1968.

Waddington, C. H. *Principles of development and differentiation.* New York: Macmillan, 1966.

Werner, E. E., Bierman, J. M., & French, F. E. *The children of Kauai.* Honolulu: University of Hawaii, 1971.

Werner, E., Honzik, M., & Smith, R. Prediction of intelligence and achievement at ten years from twenty months pediatric and psychologic examinations. *Child Development,* 1968, Vol. 39, 1063–1075.

Werner, H. *Comparative psychology of mental development.* New York: Science Editions, 1961.

Werner, H. The concept of development from a comparative and organismic point of view. In D. B. Harris (Ed.), *The Concept of Development.* Minneapolis: University of Minnesota Press, 1957. Pp. 125–148.

Willerman, L., Broman, S. H., & Fiedler, M. Infant development, preschool IQ, and social class. *Child Development,* 1970, Vol. 41, 69–77.

Windle, W. F. Structural and functional changes in the brain following neonatal asphyxia. *Psychosomatic Medicine,* 1944, Vol. 6, 155–156.

Reading 13

Cross-cultural Perspectives on Early Development

Jerome Kagan
Robert E. Klein

Most American psychologists believe in the hardiness of habit and the premise that experience etches an indelible mark on the mind not easily erased by time or trauma. The application of that assumption to the first era of development leads to the popular view that psychological growth during the early years is under the strong influence of the variety and patterning of external events and that the psychological structures shaped by those initial encounters have a continuity that stretches at least into early adolescence. The first part of that hypothesis, which owes much of its popularity to Freud, Harlow, and Skinner, has strong empirical support. The continuity part of the assumption, which is more equivocal, is summarized in the American adage, "Well begun is half done."

Many developmental psychologists, certain of the long-lasting effects of early experience, set out to find the form of those initial stabilities and the earliest time they might obtain a preview of the child's future. Although several decades of research have uncovered fragile lines that seem to travel both backward and forward in time, the breadth and magnitude of intraindividual continuities have not been overwhelming, and each seems to be easily lost or shattered (Kagan & Moss, 1962; Kessen, Haith, & Salapatek, 1970). A recent exhaustive review of research on human infancy led to the conclusion that "only short term stable individual variation has been demonstrated; . . . and demonstrations of continuity in process—genotype continuity—have been rare indeed [Kessen et al., 1970, p. 297]." Since that evaluation violates popular beliefs, the authors noted a few pages later:

Note: This article was presented by J. Kagan as an invited address to the annual meeting of the American Association for the Advancement of Science, Washington, D. C., December 26, 1972. The research reported in this article was supported by the Association for the Aid of Crippled Children, Carnegie Corporation of New York, Grant HD-4299 and Contract PH 43-65-640 from the National Institute of Child Health and Human Development, and Grant GS-33048, Collaborative Research on Uniform Measures of Social Competence, from the National Science Foundation.

In spite of slight evidence of stability, our inability to make predictions of later personality from observations in the first three years of life is so much against good sense and common observation, to say nothing of the implication of all developmental theories, that the pursuit of predictively effective categories of early behavior will surely continue unabated [p. 309].

The modest empirical support for long-term continuity is occasionally rationalized by arguing that although behaviors similar in manifest form might not be stable over long time periods, the underlying structures might be much firmer (Kagan, 1971). Hence, if the operational manifestations of these hidden forms were discerned, continuity of cognitive, motivational, and affective structures would be affirmed. However, we recently observed some children living in an isolated Indian village on Lake Atitlan in the highlands of northwest Guatemala. We saw listless, silent, apathetic infants; passive, quiet, timid 3-year-olds; but, active, gay, intellectually competent 11-year-olds. Since there is no reason to believe that living conditions in this village have changed during the last century, it is likely that the alert 11-year-olds were, a decade earlier, listless, vacant-staring infants. That observation has forced us to question the strong form of the continuity assumption in a serious way.

The data to be presented imply absence of a predictive relationship between level of cognitive development at 12–18 months of age and quality of intellectual functioning at 11 years. This conclusion is not seriously different from the repeated demonstrations of no relation between infant intelligence quotient (IQ) or developmental quotient (DQ) scores during the first year of life and Binet or Wechsler IQ scores obtained during later childhood (Kessen et al., 1970; Pease, Wolins, & Stockdale, 1973). The significance of the current data, however, derives from the fact that the infants seemed to be more seriously retarded than those observed in earlier studies, their environments markedly less varied, and the assessment of later cognitive functioning based on culture-fair tests of specific cognitive abilities rather than culturally biased IQ tests.

Moreover, these observations suggest that it is misleading to talk about continuity of any psychological characteristic—be it cognitive, motivational, or behavioral—without specifying simultaneously the context of development. Consider the long-term stability of passivity as an example. The vast majority or the infants in the Indian village were homogeneously passive and retained this characteristic until they were five or six years old. A preschool child rarely forced a submissive posture on another. However, by eight years of age, some of the children became dominant over others because the structure of the peer group required that role to be filled. Factors other than early infant passivity were critical in determining that differentiation, and physical size, strength, and competence at valued skills seemed to be more important than the infant's disposition. In modern American society, where there is much greater variation among young children in degree of passivity and dominance, a passive four-year-old will always encounter a large group of dominant peers who enforce a continuing role of submissiveness on him. As a result, there should be firmer stability of behavioral passivity during the early years in an American city than in the Indian village. But the stability of that behavior seems to be more dependent on the presence of dominant members in the immediate vicinity than on some inherent force within the child.

Continuity of a psychological disposition is not solely the product of an inherited or early acquired structure that transcends a variety of contexts. The small group of scientists who champion the view of stability—we have been among them—envision a small box of different-colored gems tucked deep in the brain, with names like intelligent, passive, irritable, or withdrawn engraved on them. These material entities guarantee that, despite behavioral disguises, an inherent set of psychological qualities, independent of the local neighborhood and knowable under the proper conditions, belongs to each individual. This belief in a distinct and unchanging mosaic of core traits—an identity—is fundamental to Western thought and is reflected in the psychological writings of Erik Erikson and the novels of popular Western writers. Only Herman Hesse, who

borrowed the philosophy of the East, fails to make a brief for personal identity. *Siddhartha, Magister Ludi,* and *Narcissus and Goldmund* are not trying to discover "who they are" but are seeking serenity, and each appreciates the relevance of setting in that journey.

A secondary theme concerns the interaction of maturation and environment, an issue that has seized academic conversation because of the renewed debate surrounding the inheritance of intelligence. But there is a broader issue to probe. The majority of American psychologists remain fundamentally Lockean in attitude, believing that thought and action owe primary allegiance to experience and that reinforcements and observations of models set the major course of change. Despite Piaget's extraordinary popularity, the majority of American psychologists do not believe that maturation supplies the major impetus for psychological growth during the childhood years. We have forgotten that many years ago Myrtle McGraw (1935) allowed one twin to climb some stairs and prevented his co-twin from practicing that skill. This homely experiment occurred only a few years after Carmichael (1926) anesthetized some *Amblystoma* embryos to prevent them from swimming. The twin not allowed to climb was behind his partner in learning this skill, but he eventually mastered it. Carmichael's embryos swam perfectly when the anesthetic was pumped out of the tank. In both instances, the organisms could not be prevented from displaying species-specific properties.

Our observations in these Indian villages have led us to reorder the hierarchy of complementary influences that biology and environmental forces exert on the development of intellectual functions that are natural to man. Separate maturational factors seem to set the time of emergence of those basic abilities. Experience can slow down or speed up that emergence by several months or several years, but nature will win in the end. The capacity for perceptual analysis, imitation, language, inference, deduction, symbolism, and memory will eventually appear in sturdy form in any natural environment, for each is an inherent competence in the human program. But these competences, which we assume to be universal, are to be distinguished from culturally specific talents that will not appear unless the child is exposed to or taught them directly. Reading, arithmetic, and understanding of specific words and concepts fall into this latter category.

This distinction between universal and culturally specific competences implies a parallel distinction between absolute and relative retardation. Consider physical growth as an illustration of this idea. There is sufficient cross-cultural information on age of onset of walking to warrant the statement that most children should be walking unaided before their second birthday. A three-year-old unable to walk is physically retarded in the absolute sense, for he has failed to attain a natural competence at the normative time. However, there is neither an empirical nor a logical basis for expecting that most children, no matter where they live, will develop the ability to hunt with a spear, ride a horse, or play football. Hence, it is not reasonable to speak of absolute retardation on these skills. In those cultures where these talents are taught, encouraged, or modeled, children will differ in the age at which they attain varied levels of mastery. But we can only classify a child as precocious or retarded relative to another in his community. The data to be reported suggest that absolute retardation in the attainment of specific cognitive competences during infancy has no predictive validity with respect to level of competence on a selected set of natural cognitive skills at age 11. *The data do not imply that a similar level of retardation among American infants has no future implication for relative retardation on culture-specific skills.*

THE GUATEMALAN SETTINGS

The infant observations to be reported here were made in two settings in Guatemala. One set of data came from four subsistence farming Ladino villages in eastern Guatemala. The villages are moderately isolated, Spanish speaking, and contain between 800 and 1,200 inhabitants. The families live in small thatched huts of cane or adobe with dirt floors and no sanitary facilities. Books, pencils, paper, and pictures are typically absent from the experience of children prior to school entrance, and, even in school, the average child has no more than a thin lined notebook and a stub of a pencil.

A second location was a more isolated Indian village of 850 people located on the shores of Lake Atitlan in the northwest mountainous region of the country. Unlike the Spanish-speaking villages, the Indians of San Marcos la Laguna have no easy

access to a city and are psychologically more detached. The isolation is due not only to geographical location but also to the fact that few of the women and no more than half of the men speak reasonable Spanish. Few adults and no children can engage the culture of the larger nation, and the Indians of San Marcos regard themselves as an alien and exploited group.

The Infant in San Marcos

During the first 10–12 months, the San Marcos infant spends most of his life in the small, dark interior of his windowless hut. Since women do not work in the field, the mother usually stays close to the home and spends most of her day preparing food, typically tortillas, beans, and coffee, and perhaps doing some weaving. If she travels to a market to buy or sell, she typically leaves her infant with an older child or a relative. The infant is usually close to the mother, either on her lap or enclosed on her back in a colored cloth, sitting on a mat, or sleeping in a hammock. The mother rarely allows the infant to crawl on the dirt floor of the hut and feels that the outside sun, air, and dust are harmful.

The infant is rarely spoken to or played with, and the only available objects for play, besides his own clothing or his mother's body, are oranges, ears of corn, and pieces of wood or clay. These infants are distinguished from American infants of the same age by their extreme motoric passivity, fearfulness, minimal smiling, and above all, extraordinary quietness. A few with pale cheeks and vacant stares had the quality of tiny ghosts and resembled the description of the institutionalized infants that Spitz called marasmic. Many would not orient to a taped source of speech, not smile or babble to vocal overtures, and hesitated over a minute before reaching for an attractive toy.

An American woman who lived in the village made five separate 30-minute observations in the homes of 12 infants 8–16 months of age. If a particular behavioral variable occurred during a five-second period, it was recorded once for that interval. The infants were spoken to or played with 6% of the time, with a maximum of 12%. The comparable averages for American middle-class homes are 25%, with a maximum of 40% (Lewis & Freedle, 1972). It should be noted that the infant's vocalizations, which occurred about 6% of the time, were typically grunts lasting less than a second, rather than the prolonged babbling typical of middle-class American children. The infants cried very little because the slightest irritability led the mother to nurse her child at once. Nursing was the single, universal therapeutic treatment for all infant distress, be it caused by fear, cold, hunger, or cramps. Home observations in the eastern villages are consonant with those gathered in San Marcos and reveal infrequent infant vocalization and little verbal interaction or play with adults or older siblings. The mothers in these settings seem to regard their infants the way an American parent views an expensive cashmere sweater: Keep it nearby and protect it but do not engage it reciprocally.

One reason why these mothers might behave this way is that it is abundantly clear to every parent that all children begin to walk by 18 months, to talk by age 3, and to perform some adult chores by age 10, despite the listless, silent quality of infancy. The mother's lack of active manipulation, stimulation, or interactive play with her infant is not indicative of indifference or rejection, but is a reasonable posture, given her knowledge of child development.

COMPARATIVE STUDY OF INFANT COGNITIVE DEVELOPMENT

Although it was not possible to create a formal laboratory setting for testing infants in San Marcos, it was possible to do so in the eastern Ladino villages, and we shall summarize data derived from identical procedures administered to rural Guatemalan and American infants. Although the infants in the Ladino villages were more alert than the Indian children of San Marcos, the similarities in living conditions and rearing practices are such that we shall assume that the San Marcos infants would have behaved like the Ladino children or, what is more likely, at a less mature level. In these experiments, the Guatemalan mother and child came to a special laboratory equipped with a chair and a stage that simulated the setting in the Harvard laboratories where episodes were administered to cross-sectional groups of infants, 84 American and 80 Guatemalan, at $5\frac{1}{2}$, $7\frac{1}{2}$, $9\frac{1}{2}$, and $11\frac{1}{2}$ months of age, with 10–24 infants from each culture at each age level.

Before describing the procedures and results, it will be helpful to summarize the theoretical assumptions that govern interpretation of the infant's reactions to these episodes. There appear to be two important maturationally controlled processes which emerge between 2 and 12 months that influence the child's reactions to transformations of an habituated event (Kagan, 1971, 1972). During the first six weeks of life, the duration of the child's attention to a visual event is controlled by the amount of physical change or contrast in the event. During the third month, the infant shows prolonged attention to events that are moderate discrepancies from habituated standards. Maintenance of attention is controlled by the relation of the event to the child's schema for the class to which that event belongs. The typical reactions to discrepancy include increased fixation time, increased vocalization, and either cardiac deceleration or decreased variability of heart rate during the stimulus presentation. These conclusions are based on many independent studies and we shall not document them here (Cohen, Gelber, & Lazar, 1972; Kagan, 1971; Lewis, Goldberg, & Campbell, 1970).

However, at approximately eight–nine months, a second process emerges. The infant now begins to activate cognitive structures, called hypotheses, in the service of interpreting discrepant events. A hypothesis is viewed as a representation of a relation between two schemata. Stated in different language, the infant not only notes and processes a discrepancy, he also attempts to transform it to his prior schemata for that class of event and activates hypotheses to serve this advanced cognitive function. It is not a coincidence that postulation of this new competence coincides with the time when the infant displays object permanence and separation anxiety, phenomena that require the child to activate an idea of an absent object or person.

There are two sources of support for this notion. The first is based on age changes in attention to the same set of events. Regardless of whether the stimulus is a set of human masks, a simple black and white design, or a dynamic sequence in which a moving orange rod turns on a bank of three light bulbs upon contact, there is a U-shaped relation between age and duration of attention across the period 3–36 months, with the trough typically occurring between 7 and 12 months of age (Kagan, 1972).

The curvilinear relation between age and attention to human masks has been replicated among American, rural Guatemalan, and Kahlahari desert Bushman children (Kagan, 1971; Konnor, 1973;

Sellers, Klein, Kagan, & Minton, 1972). If discrepancy were the only factor controlling fixation time, a child's attention should decrease with age, for the stimulus events become less discrepant as he grows older. The increase in attention toward the end of the first years is interpreted as a sign of a new cognitive competence, which we have called the *activation of hypotheses.*

A second source of support for this idea is that the probability of a cardiac acceleration to a particular discrepancy increases toward the end of the first year, whereas cardiac deceleration is the modal reaction during the earlier months (Kagan, 1972). Because studies of adults and young children indicate that cardiac acceleration accompanies mental work, while deceleration accompanies attention to an interesting event (Lacey, 1967; Van Hover, 1971), the appearance of acceleration toward the end of the first year implies that the infants are performing active mental work, or activating hypotheses.

Since increased attention to a particular discrepancy toward the end of the first year is one diagnostic sign of the emergence of this stage of cognitive development, cultural differences in attention to fixed discrepancies during the first year might provide information on the developmental maturity of the infants in each cultural group.

METHOD

Block Episode

Each child was shown a 2-inch wooden orange block for six or eight successive trials (six for the two older ages, and eight for the two younger ages) followed by three or five transformation trials in which a 1½-inch orange block was presented. These transformations were followed by three representations of the original 2-inch block.

Light Episode

The child was shown 8 or 10 repetitions of a sequence in which a hand moved an orange rod in a semicircle until it touched a bank of three light bulbs which were lighted upon contact between the rod and the bulbs. In the five transformation trials that followed, the hand appeared but the rod did not move and the lights lit after a four-second interval. Following the transformations, the original event was presented for three additional trials.

During each of the episodes, two observers coded (a) how long the infant attended to the event, (b) whether the infant vocalized or smiled, and (c) fretting or crying. Intercoder reliability for these variables was over .90.

RESULTS

The Guatemalan infants were significantly less attentive than the Americans on both episodes, and the cultural differences were greater at the two older than at the two younger ages. Figures 1 and 2 illustrate the mean total fixation time to four successive trial blocks for the two episodes. The four trial blocks were the first three standard trials, the last three standards, the first three transformations, and the three return trials.

The American infants of all ages had longer fixation times to the block during every trial block (F ranged from 30.8 to 67.3, $df = \frac{1}{154}$, $p < .001$). The American infants also displayed longer fixations to the light during every trial block (F ranged from 9.8 to 18.4, $df = \frac{1}{141}$, $p < .01$). However, it is important to note that at 11½ months, the American children maintained more sustained attention to the return of the standard than the Guatemalans, who showed a drop in fixation time toward the end of the episode. These data suggest that more of the American than of the Guatemalan infants had entered the stage of activation of hypotheses. Since the Ladino infants appeared more mature than the San Marcos children, it is possible that the American one-year-olds were approximately three months advanced over the San Marcos children in the cognitive function.

ADDITIONAL ASSESSMENTS OF DEVELOPMENTAL STATUS

We collected, under less formal conditions in the home, additional information on the developmental status of the San Marcos infant. Not one of the 12 infants between 8 and 16 months reached for an attractive object they watched being hidden, although many would, with considerable hesitation, reach for a visible object placed close to their hands. Furthermore, none of these 12 infants revealed facial surprise following a sequence in

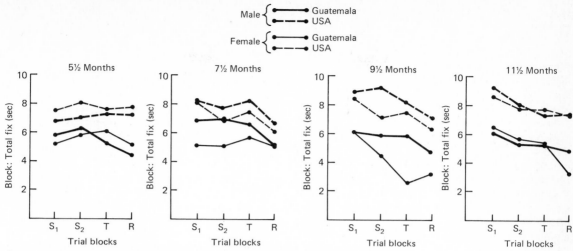

Figure 1　Average total fixation time to the block episode by age and culture.

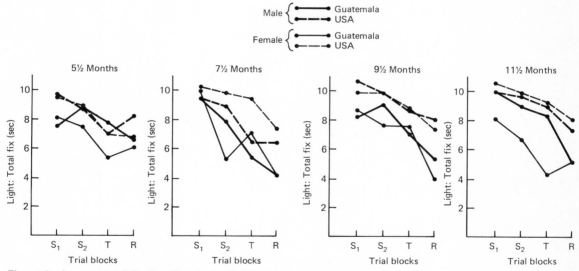

Figure 2　Average total fixation time to the light episode by age and culture.

which they watched an object being hidden under a cloth but saw no object when that cloth was removed. These observations suggest an absolute retardation of four months in the display of behavioral signs diagnostic of the attainment of object permanence.

A third source of data is based on observations of a stranger anxiety. Each of 16 infants between 8 and 20 months was observed following the first exposure to a strange male (the senior author). The first age at which obvious apprehension and/or crying occurred was 13 months, suggesting a five-month lag between San Marcos and American infants. Finally, the information on nonmorphemic babbling and the onset of meaningful speech supports a diagnosis of absolute retardation. There was no marked increase in frequency of babbling or vocalization between 8 and 16 months among the 12

San Marcos infants observed at home, while comparable observations in American homes revealed a significant increase in babbling and the appearance of morphemic vocalizations for some children. Furthermore, many parents remarked that meaningful speech typically appears first at 2½ years of age, about one year later than the average display of first words in American children.

These data, together with the extremely depressed, withdrawn appearance of the San Marcos infants, suggest retardations of three or more months for various psychological competences that typically emerge during the first two years of life. With the exception of one 16-month-old boy, whose alert appearance resembled that of an American infant, there was little variability among the remaining children. Since over 90% were homogeneously passive, nonalert, and quiet, it is unlikely that the recovery of intellectual functioning to be reported later was a result of the selective mortality of a small group of severely retarded infants.

RESILIENCE OF COGNITIVE DEVELOPMENT

The major theme of this article is the potential for recovery of cognitive functions despite early infant retardation. When the San Marcos child becomes mobile at around 15 months he leaves the dark hut, begins to play with other children, and provides himself with cognitive challenges that demand accommodations. Since all children experience this marked discontinuity in variety of experience and opportunity for exploration between the first and second birthday, it is instructive to compare the cognitive competence of older Guatemalan and American children to determine if differences in level of functioning are still present.

The tests administered were designed to assess cognitive processes that are believed to be part of the natural competence of growing children, rather than the culturally arbitrary segments of knowledge contained in a standard IQ test. We tried to create tests that were culturally fair, recognizing that this goal is, in the extreme, unattainable. Hence, the tests were not standardized instruments with psychometric profiles of test-retest reliabilities and criterion validity studies. This investigation should be viewed as a natural experiment in which the independent variable was degree of retardation in infancy and the dependent variables were performances on selected cognitive instruments during childhood. We assume, along with many psychologists, that perceptual analysis, recall and recognition memory, and inference are among the basic cognitive functions of children (even though they do not exhaust that set), and our tests were designed to evaluate those processes.

Tests of recall and recognition memory, perceptual analysis, and perceptual and conceptual inference were given to children in San Marcos, the Ladino villages, an Indian village close to Guatemala City and more modern than San Marcos, Cambridge, Massachusetts, and to two different groups of children living in Guatemala City. One of the Guatemala City settings, the "guarderia," was a day care center for very poor children. The second group, middle-class children attending nursery school, resembled a middle-class American sample in both family background and opportunity. Not all tests were administered to all children. The discussion is organized according to the cognitive function assessed, rather than the sample studied. The sample sizes ranged from 12 to 40 children at any one age.

Recall Memory for Familiar Objects

The ability to organize experience for commitment to long-term memory and to retrieve that information on demand is a basic cognitive skill. It is generally believed that the form of the organization contains diagnostic information regarding cognitive maturity for, among Western samples, both number of independent units of information and the conceptual clustering of that information increase with age.

A 12-object recall task was administered to two samples of Guatemalan children. One group lived in a Ladino village 17 kilometers from Guatemala City; the second group was composed of San Marcos children. The 80 subjects from the Ladino village were 5 and 7 years old, equally balanced for age and sex. The 55 subjects from San Marcos were between 5 and 12 years of age (26 boys and 29 girls).

The 12 miniature objects to be recalled were common to village life and belonged to three conceptual categories: animals (pig, dog, horse, cow), kitchen utensils (knife, spoon, fork, glass), and clothing (pants, dress, underpants, hat). Each child was first required to name the objects, and if the child was unable to he was given the name. The child was then told that after the objects had been randomly arranged on a board he would have 10 seconds to inspect them, after which they would be covered with a cloth, and he would be required to say all the objects he could remember.

Table 1 contains the average number of objects recalled and the number of pairs of conceptually similar words recalled—an index of clustering—for the first two trials. A pair was defined as the temporally contiguous recall of two or more items of the same category. A child received one point for reporting a pair of contiguous items, two points for three contiguous items, and three points for contiguous recall of four items. Hence, the maximum clustering score for a single trial was nine points. As Table 1 reveals, the children showed a level of clustering beyond chance expectation (which is between 1.5 and 2.0 pairs for recall scores of seven to eight words). Moreover, recall scores increased with age on both trials for children in both villages (F ranged from 11.2 to 27.7, $p < 0.5$), while clustering increased with age in the Ladino village ($F = 26.8$, $p < .001$ for Trial 1; $F = 3.48$, $p < .05$ for Trial 2).

No five- or six-year-old in either village and only 12 of the 40 seven-year-olds in the Ladino village were attending school. School for the others consisted of little more than semiorganized games. Moreover, none of the children in San Marcos had ever left the village, and the five- and six-year-olds typically spent most of the day within a 500-yard radius of their homes. Hence, school attendance and contact with books and a written language do not seem to be prerequisites for clustering in young children.

The recall and cluster scores obtained in Guatemala were remarkably comparable to those reported for middle-class American children. Appel, Cooper, McCarrell, Knight, Yussen, and Flavell (1971) presented 12 pictures to Minneapolis children in Grade 1 (approximately age 7) and 15 pictures to children in Grade 5 (approximately age 11) in a single-trial recall task similar to the one described here. The recall scores were 66% for the 7-year-olds and 80% for the 11-year-olds. These values are almost identical to those obtained in both Guatemalan villages. The cluster indices were also comparable. The American 7-year-olds had a cluster ratio of .25; the San Marcos 5- and 6-year-olds had a ratio of .39.[1]

Recognition Memory

The cultural similarity in recall also holds for recognition memory. In a separate study, 5-, 8-, and 11-year-old children from Ladino villages in the East and from Cambridge, Massachusetts, were shown 60 pictures of objects—all of which were familiar to the Americans but some of which were unfamiliar to the Guatemalans. After 0-, 24-, or 48-hours delay, each child was shown 60 pairs of pictures, one of which was old and the other new, and was asked to decide which one he had seen. Although the 5- and 8-year-old Americans performed significantly better than the Guatemalans, there was no statistically significant cultural difference for the 11-year-olds, whose scores ranged from 85% to 98% after 0-, 24-, or 48-hours delay (Kagan et al., 1973). (See Table 2.) The remarkably high scores of the American 5-year-olds have also been reported by Scott (1973).

A similar result was found on a recognition memory task for 32 photos of faces, balanced for sex, child versus adult, and Indian versus Caucasian, administered to 35 American and 38 San Marcos children 8–11 years of age. Each child

Table 1 Mean Number of Objects and Pairs Recalled

Age	Trial 1		Trial 2	
	Recall	Pairs	Recall	Pairs
Ladino village				
5	5.2	2.1	5.4	2.1
7	6.7	3.3	7.8	3.7
Indian village				
5–6	7.1	3.4	7.8	3.8
7–8	8.6	3.4	8.3	3.6
9–10	10.3	4.9	10.3	4.3
11–12	9.6	3.4	10.1	3.6

[1]The cluster index is the ratio of the number of pairs recalled to the product of the number of categories in the list times one less than the number of words in each category.

Table 2 Mean Percentage of Correct Responses

| | Americans | | | Guatemalans | | |
| | Age | | | | | |
Delay	5	8	11	5	8	11
0 hours	92.8	96.7	98.3	58.4	74.6	85.2
24 hours	86.7	95.6	96.7	55.8	71.0	87.0
48 hours	87.5	90.3	93.9	61.4	75.8	86.2

Note: Percent signs are omitted.

initially inspected 32 chromatic photographs of faces, one at a time, in a self-placed procedure. Each child's recognition memory was tested by showing him 32 pairs of photographs (each pair was of the same sex, age, and ethnicity), one of which was old and the other new. The child had to state which photograph he had seen during the inspection phase. Although the American 8- and 9-year-olds performed slightly better than the Guatemalans (82% versus 70%), there was no significant cultural difference among the 10- and 11-year-olds (91% versus 87%). Moreover, there was no cultural difference at any age for the highest performance attained by a single child.[2] The favored interpretation of the poorer performance of the younger children in both recognition memory studies is that some of them did not completely understand the task and others did not activate the proper problem-solving strategies during the registration and retrieval phases of the task.

It appears that recall and recognition memory are basic cognitive functions that seem to mature in a regular way in a natural environment. The cognitive retardation observed during the first year does not have any serious predictive validity for these two important aspects of cognitive functioning for children 10–11 years of age.

Perceptual Analysis

The Guatemalan children were also capable of solving difficult Embedded Figures Test items. The test consisted of 12 color drawings of familiar objects in which a triangle had been embedded as

part of the object. The child had to locate the hidden triangle and place a black paper triangle so that it was congruent with the design of the drawing. The test was administered to rural Indian children from San Marcos, as well as to rural Indians living close to Guatemala City (labeled Indian$_1$ in Figure 3), the Ladino villages, and two groups from Guatemala City. (See Figure 3.)

The Guatemala City middle-class children had the highest scores and, except for San Marcos, the rural children, the poorest. The surprisingly competent performance of the San Marcos children is due, we believe, to the more friendly conditions of testing. This suggestion is affirmed by an independent study in which a special attempt was made to maximize rapport and comprehension of instructions with a group of rural isolated children before administering a large battery of tests. Although all test performances were not facilitated by this rapport-raising procedure, performance on the Embedded Figures Test was improved considerably. It is important to note that no five- or six-year-old was completely incapable of solving some of these problems. The village differences in mean score reflect the fact that the rural children had difficulty with three or four of the harder items. This was the

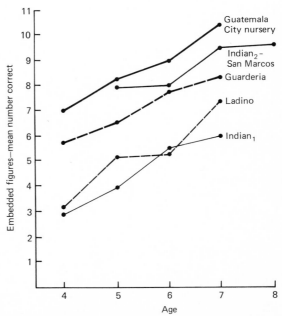

Figure 3 Mean number correct on the Embedded Figures Test.

[2]These photographs were also used in an identical procedure with 12 Kipsigis-speaking 10- and 11-year olds from a rural village in eastern Kenya. Despite the absence of any black faces in the set, the percentage of items recognized correctly was 82 for this group of African children.

first time that many rural children had ever seen a two-dimensional drawing, and most of the five-, six-, and seven-year-olds in San Marcos had had no opportunity to play with books, paper, pictures, or crayons. Nonetheless, these children solved seven or eight of the test items. Investigators who have suggested that prior experience with pictures is necessary for efficient analysis of two-dimensional information may have incorrectly misinterpreted failure to understand the requirements of the problem with a deficiency in cognitive competence. This competence seems to develop in the world of moving leaves, chickens, and water.[3] As with recall and recognition memory, the performance of the San Marcos child was comparable to that of his age peer in a modern urban setting.

Perceptual Inference

The competence of the San Marcos children on the Embedded Figures Test is affirmed by their performance on a test administered only in San Marcos and Cambridge and called Perceptual Inference. The children (60 American and 55 Guatemalan, 5–12 years of age) were shown a schematic drawing of an object and asked to guess what that object might be if the drawing were completed. The child was given a total of four clues for each 13 items, where each clue added more information. The child had to guess an object from an incomplete illustration, to make an inference from minimal information (see Figures 4 and 5).

There was no significant cultural difference for the children 7–12 years of age, although the American 5- and 6-year-olds did perform significantly better than the Indian children. In San Marcos, performance improved from 62% correct on one of the first two clues for the 5- and 6-year-olds to 77% correct for the 9–12-year-olds. The comparable changes for the American children were from 77% to 84%. (See Figure 6.)

Familiarity with the test objects was critical for success. All of the San Marcos children had seen hats, fish, and corn, and these items were rarely missed. By contrast, many American children failed these items. No San Marcos child not attending school, and therefore unfamiliar with books, correctly guessed the book item, whereas

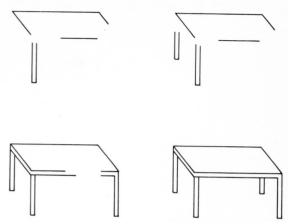

Figure 4 Sample item from the Perceptual Inference Test.

most of those in school guessed it correctly. As with memory and perceptual analysis, the retardation seen during infancy did not predict comparable retardation in the ability of the 11-year-old to make difficult perceptual inferences.

Conceptual Inference

The San Marcos child also performed well on questions requiring conceptual inference. In this test, the child was told verbally three characteristics of an object and was required to guess the object. Some of the examples included: What has wings, eats chickens, and lives in a tree? What moves trees, cannot be seen, and makes one cold? What is made of wood, is used to carry things, and allows one to make journeys? There was improved performance with age; the 5- and 6-year-olds obtained an average of 9 out of 14 correct, and the 11-

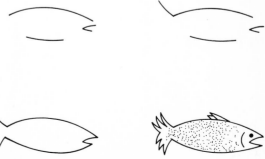

Figure 5 Sample item from the Perceptual Inference Test.

---

[3]This conclusion holds for Embedded Figures Test performance, and not necessarily for the ability to detect three-dimensional perspective in two-dimensional drawings.

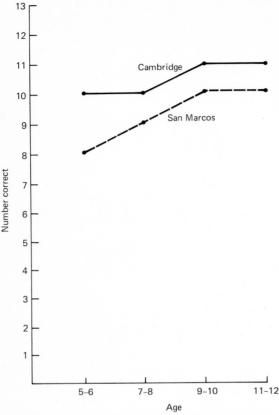

Figure 6 Number correct on the Perceptual Inference Test.

American middle-class norms. Infant retardation seems to be partially reversible and cognitive development during the early years more resilient than had been supposed.

One potential objection to this conclusion is that the tests were too easy for the Guatemalan 11-year-olds and that is why cultural differences were absent. These are two comments that can be addressed to that issue. First, it is not intuitively reasonable to argue that the ability to remember 60 photographs of objects, classify an object from a few sketchy lines, or detect the triangle hidden in a two-dimensional drawing is "easy" for children who rarely see photographs, pencils, crayons, or books. Second, we deliberately assessed cognitive functions that we believe all children should master by the time they are preadolescents. The fact that many 11-year-olds approached the ceiling on some tests is support for the basic premise of this article, namely, that infant retardation does not prevent a child from eventually developing basic cognitive competences.

This result is surprising if one believes that each child is born with a certain level of general intellectual competence that is stable from infancy through adulthood. If, on the contrary, one assumes that each stage of development is characterized by a different profile of specific competences and there is no necessary relation between early emergence of the capacities of infancy and level of attainment of the quite different abilities characteristic of childhood, then these results are more reasonable. There is no reason to assume that the caterpillar who metamorphoses a bit earlier than his kin is a better adapted or more efficient butterfly.

Consideration of why the rural Guatemalan children lagged behind the urban children on some tests during the period five through nine years of age comprises a second implication of these data. It will be recalled that on the embedded figures and recognition memory tests the performance of rural children was several years behind both the American and Guatemala City middle-class children. The differences were minimal for the object recall and perceptual inference tests. The approximately three-year lag in performance is paralleled by comparable differences between lower- and middle-class children in urban Western cities. For example, Bosco (1972) found that middle-class first and third graders were able to tolerate smaller interstimulus intervals in a backward masking procedure than

and 12-year-olds obtained 12 out of 14 correct. The San Marcos child was capable of making moderately difficult inferences from both visual and verbal information.

DISCUSSION

This corpus of data implies that absolute retardation in the time of emergence of universal cognitive competences during infancy is not predictive of comparable deficits for memory, perceptual analysis, and inference during preadolescence. Although the rural Guatemalan infants were retarded with respect to activation of hypotheses, alertness, and onset of stranger anxiety and object permanence, the preadolescents' performance on the tests of perceptual analysis, perceptual inference, and recall and recognition memory were comparable to lower-class children, but this difference had vanished among sixth-grade children. Similarly, Bakker (1971) compared good and poor readers from urban centers in Holland on a task that required operating simultaneously on two items of information in a temporal integration task. The poor readers performed less well than the good readers at ages six to eight, but were comparable to the good readers during the preadolescent years.

We interpret these results as indicating that the urban lower-class children, like the younger, rural Guatemalans, were not able to mobilize proper problem-solving strategies necessary for task solution, but achieved that level of competence by 11 years of age. Some of these strategies include focused attention, rehearsal of task information and instructions, awareness of and understanding the problem to be solved, maintenance of problem set, and the ability to remember critical information elements in the problem and to operate on that information. It is believed that these functions may emerge a little later in some groups of children than in others, but they are operative in all children by 11–12 years of age. In a recently completed study with Patricia Engle, we found that among rural Guatemalan children, 5 through 11 years of age, the rate of improvement in performance on three memory tasks (memory for numbers, memory for sentences, and auditory blending) was greatest between 9 and 11 years of age, whereas White (1970), using comparable data from American children, found that the greatest rate of improvement was between 5 and 7 years of age—a lag of about three years.

These data have implications for America's educational problems. There is a tendency to regard the poor test performances of economically impoverished, minority group 6-year-olds in the United States as indicative of a permanent and, perhaps, irreversible defect in intellectual ability—as a difference in quality of function rather than slower maturational rate. The Guatemalan data, together with those of Bosco and Bakker, suggest that children differ in the age at which basic cognitive competences emerge and that experiential factors influence the time of emergence. Economically disadvantaged American children and isolated rural Guatemalan children appear to be from one to three years behind middle-class children in demonstrating some of the problem-solving skills characteristic of Piaget's stage of concrete operations. But

these competences eventually appear in sturdy form by age 10 or 11. The common practice of arbitrarily setting 7 years—the usual time of school entrance—as the age when children are to be classified as competent or incompetent confuses differences in maturational rate with permanent, qualitative differences in intellectual ability. This practice is as logical as classifying children as reproductively fertile or sterile depending on whether or not they have reached physiological puberty by their thirteenth birthday.

When educators note correctly that poor children tend to remain permanently behind middle-class children on intellectual and academic performance, they are referring to the relative retardation on the culturally specific skills of reading, mathematics, and language achievement described earlier. That relative retardation is the product of the rank ordering of scores on achievement and IQ tests. The fact that relative retardation on these abilities is stable from age five on does not mean that the relatively retarded children are not growing intellectually (when compared with themselves), often at the same rate as economically advantaged youngsters.

The suggestion that basic cognitive competences, in contrast to culturally specific ones, emerge at different times and that the child retains the capacity for actualization of his competence until a late age is not substantially different from the earlier conclusions of Dennis and Najarian (1957). Although the 49 infants 2–12 months of age living in poorly staffed Lebanese institutions were seriously retarded on the Cattell developmental scale (mean developmental quotient of 68 compared with a quotient of 102 for a comparison group), the 4½–6-year-olds who had resided in the same institution all their lives performed at a level comparable to American norms on a memory test (Knox Cubes) as well as on Porteus mazes and the Goodenough Draw-a-Man Test.

Of more direct relevance is Dennis's (1973) recent follow-up study of 16 children who were adopted out of the same Lebanese institution between 12 and 24 months of age—the period during which the San Marcos infant leaves the unstimulating environment of the dark hut—with an average developmental quotient of 50 on the Cattell Infant Scale. Even though the assessment of later intellectual ability was based on the culturally biased Stanford-Binet IQ test, the average IQ obtained when the children were between 4 and 12 years of age, was 101, and 13 of the 16 children had IQ scores of 90 or above.

Additional support for the inherent resiliency in human development comes from longitudinal information on two sisters who spent most of their infancy in a crib in a small bedroom with no toys.[4] The mother, who felt unable to care for her fourth child, restricted her to the room soon after birth and instructed her eight-year-old daughter to care for the child. One year later, another daughter was born, and she, too, was placed in a crib with the older sister. These two children only left the room to be fed and, according to the caretaking sister who is now a married woman in her twenties, the two infants spent about 23 hours of each day together in a barren crib. When the authorities were notified of this arrangement, the children were removed from the home and taken to a hospital when the younger was 2½ and the older 3½ years old. Medical records reveal that both children were malnourished, severely retarded in weight and height, and seriously retarded psychologically. After a month in the hospital, following considerable recovery, both sisters were placed in the care of a middle-class family who had several young children. The sisters have remained with that family for the last 12 years and regard the husband and wife as their parents. One of us (J. K.) tested the sisters five times when they were between 4 and 9 years of age, and recently interviewed and tested both of them over a two-day period when they were 14½ and 15½ years old.

The younger sister has performed consistently better than the older one over the last 10 years. The IQ scores of the younger girl have risen steadily from a Stanford-Binet IQ of 74 at age 4½ (after two years in the foster home) to a Wechsler Full Scale IQ of 88 at age 14. The older girl's scores have also improved, but less dramatically, from a Stanford-Binet IQ of 59 at age 5 to a Wechsler IQ of 72 at age 15. The author also administered a lengthy battery of tests, some of which were discussed earlier. On the Perceptual Inference Test, the percentage correct was 85 for the younger sister and 61 for the older sister. On the Recognition Memory for Photographs, the percentages were 94 for both. On the Embedded Figures Test, the percentages were 92

and 100, and on the recall memory for objects, the percentages were 92 and 83 for the younger and older sister, respectively. Moreover, the interpersonal behavior of both girls was in no way different from that of the average rural Ohio adolescent—a group the author came to know well after seven years of work in the area. Although there is some ambiguity surrounding the competence of the older girl, the younger one performs at an average level on a wide range of tests of cognitive functioning, despite 2½ years of serious isolation.

These data, together with the poor predictive relation between scores on infant developmental tests and later assessments of intellectual functioning, strengthen the conclusion that environmentally produced retardation during the first year or two of life appears to be reversible. The importance of the Guatemalan data derives from the fact that the San Marcos 11-year-olds performed so well, considering the homogeneity and isolation of their childhood environment. Additionally, there is a stronger feeling now than there was in 1957 that environmentally produced retardation during the first two years may be irreversible, even though the empirical basis for that belief is no firmer in 1972 than it was in 1957.

More dramatic support for the notion that psychological development is malleable comes from recent experimental studies with animals. Several years ago Harlow's group demonstrated that although monkeys reared in isolation for the first six months displayed abnormal and often bizarre social behaviors, they could, if the experimenter were patient, solve the complex learning problems normally administered to feral-born monkeys. The prolonged isolation did not destroy their cognitive competence (Harlow, Schiltz, & Harlow, 1969). More recently, Suomi and Harlow (1972) have shown that that even the stereotyped and bizarre social behavior shown by six-month-old isolates can be altered by placing them with female monkeys three months younger than themselves over a 26-week therapeutic period. "By the end of the therapy period the behavioral levels were virtually indistinguishable from those of the socially competent therapist monkeys [Suomi & Harlow, 1972, p. 491]."

This resiliency has also been demonstrated for infant mice (Cairns & Nakelski, 1971) who experienced an initial 10 weeks of isolation from other animals. Compared with group-reared mice of the

[4]The authors thank Meinhard Robinow for information on these girls.

same strain, the isolated subjects were hyperreactive to other mice, displaying both extreme withdrawal and extreme aggressiveness. These investigators also attempted rehabilitation of the isolates by placing them with groups of mice for an additional 10 weeks, however, after which their behavior was indistinguishable from animals that had never been isolated.

By the seventieth day after interchange, the effects of group therapy were complete, and animals that had been isolated for one hundred days following weaning were indistinguishable from animals that had never been isolated [Cairns & Nakelski, 1971, p. 363.].

These dramatic alterations in molar behavior are in accord with replicated reports of recovery of visual function in monkeys and cats deprived of patterned light soon after birth (Baxter, 1966; Chow & Stewart, 1972; Wilson & Riesen, 1966). Kittens deprived of light for one year recovered basic visual functions after only 10 days in the experimenter's home (Baxter, 1966); kittens who had one or both eyes sutured for close to two years were able to learn pattern discriminations with the deprived eye only after moderate training (Chow & Stewart, 1972).

If the extreme behavioral and perceptual sequelae of isolation in monkeys, cats, and mice can be altered by such brief periods of rehabilitative experience, it is not difficult to believe that the San Marcos infant is capable of as dramatic a recovery over a period of nine years. These data do not indicate the impotence of early environments, but rather the potency of the environment in which the organism is functioning. There is no question that early experience seriously affects kittens, monkeys, and children. If the first environment does not permit the full actualization of psychological competences, the child will function below his ability as long as he remains in that context. But if he is transferred to an environment that presents greater variety and requires more accommodations, he seems more capable of exploiting that experience and repairing the damage wrought by the first environment than some theorists have implied.

These conclusions do not imply that intervention or rehabilitation efforts with poor American or minority group preschool children are of no value. Unlike San Marcos, where children are assigned adult responsibilities when they are strong and alert enough to assume them, rather than at a fixed age, American children live in a severely age graded system, in which children are continually rank ordered. Hence, if a poor four-year-old falls behind a middle-class four-year-old on a culturally significant skill, like knowledge of letters or numbers, he may never catch up with the child who was advanced and is likely to be placed in a special educational category. Hence, American parents must be concerned with the early psychological growth of their children. We live in a society in which the relative retardation of a four-year-old seriously influences his future opportunities because we have made relative retardation functionally synonymous with absolute retardation. This is not true in subsistence farming communities like San Marcos.

These data suggest that exploration of the new and the construction of objects or ideas from some prior schematic blueprint must be inherent properties of the mind. The idea that the child carries with him at all times the essential mental competence to understand the new in some terms and to make a personal contribution to each new encounter is only original in our time. Despite the current popularity of Kant and Piaget, the overwhelming prejudice of Western psychologists is that higher order cognitive competences and personality factors are molded completely by the environment. Locke's image of an unmarked tablet on which sensation played its patterned melody has a parallel in Darwin's failure to realize, until late in his life, that the organism made a contribution to his own evolution. Darwin was troubled by the fact that the same climate on different islands in the Galapagos produced different forms of the same species. Since he believed that climatic variation was the dynamic agent in evolution he was baffled. He did not appreciate that the gene was the organism's contribution to his own alteration. Western psychologists have been blocked by the same prejudice that prevented young Darwin from solving his riddle. From Locke to Skinner we have viewed the perfectibility of man as vulnerable to the vicissitudes of the objects and people who block, praise, or push him, and resisted giving the child any compass on his own. The mind, like the nucleus of a cell, has a plan for growth and can transduce a new flower, an odd pain, or a stranger's unexpected smile into a form that is comprehensible. This process is accomplished through wedding cognitive structures to selective attention, activation of hypotheses, assimilation, and accommodation. The purpose of these processes is to convert an alerting unfamiliar event, incompletely understood, to a recognized variation on an existing familiar structure. This is accomplished through the detection of the dimensions of the event that bear a relation to existing schemata and the subsequent incorporation of the total event into the older structure.

We need not speak of joy in this psychological mastery, for neither walking nor breathing is performed in order to experience happiness. These properties of the motor or autonomic systems occur because each physiological system or organ naturally exercises its primary function. The child explores the unfamiliar and attempts to match his ideas and actions to some previously acquired representations because these are basic properties of the mind. The child has no choice.

The San Marcos child knows much less than the American about planes, computers, cars, and the many hundreds of other phenomena that are familiar to the Western youngster, and he is a little slower in developing some of the basic cognitive competences of our species. But neither appreciation of these events nor the earlier cognitive maturation is necessary for a successful journey to adulthood in San Marcos. The American child knows far less about how to make canoes, rope, tortillas, or how to burn an old milpa in preparation for June planting. Each knows what is necessary, each assimilates the cognitive conflicts that are presented to him, and each seems to have the potential to display more talent than his environment demands of him. There are few dumb children in the world if one classifies them from the perspective of the community of adaptation, but millions of dumb children if one classifies them from the perspective of another society.

REFERENCES

Appel, L. F., Cooper, R. G., McCarrell, N., Knight, J. S., Yussen, S. R., & Flavell, J. H. The developmental acquisition of the distinction between perceiving and memory. Unpublished manuscript, University of Minnesota- Minneapolis, 1971.

Bakker, D. J. *Temporal order in disturbed reading.* Rotterdam: Rotterdam University Press, 1972.

Baxter, B. L. Effect of visual deprivation during postnatal maturation on the electroencephalogram of the cat. *Experimental Neurology,* 1966, 14, 224–237.

Bosco, J. The visual information processing speed of lower middle class children. *Child Development,* 1972, 43, 1418–1422.

Cairns, R. B., & Nakelski, J. S. On fighting in mice: Ontogenetic and experiential determinants. *Journal of Comparative and Physiological Psychology,* 1971, 74, 354–364.

Carmichael, L. The development of behavior in vertebrates experimentally removed from the influence of external stimulation. *Psychological Review,* 1926, 33, 51–58.

Chow, K. L., & Stewart, D. L. Reversal of structural and functional effects of longterm visual deprivation in cats. *Experimental Neurology,* 1972, 34, 409–433.

Cohen, L. B., Gelber, E. R., & Lazar, M. A. Infant habituation and generalization to differing degrees of novelty. *Journal of Experimental Child Psychology,* 1971, 11, 379–389.

Cole, M., Gay, J., Glick, J. A., & Sharp, D. W. *The cultural context of learning and thinking.* New York: Basic Books, 1971.

Dennis, W. *Children of the Crèche.* New York: Appleton-Century-Crofts, 1973.

Dennis, W., & Najarian, P. Infant development under environmental handicap. *Psychological Monographs,* 1957, 71(7, Whole No. 436).

Harlow, H. F., Schiltz, K. A., & Harlow, M. K. The effects of social isolation on the learning performance of rhesus monkeys. In C. R. Carpenter (Ed.), *Proceedings of the Second International Congress of Primatology.* Vol. 1. New York: Karger, 1969.

Kagan, J. *Change and continuity in infancy.* New York: Wiley, 1971.

Kagan, J. Do infants think? *Scientific American,* 1972, 226(3), 74–82.

Kagan, J., Klein, R. E., Haith, M. M., & Morrison, F. J. Memory and meaning in two cultures. *Child Development,* 1973, 44, 221–223.

Kagan, J., & Moss. H. A., *Birth to maturity.* New York: Wiley, 1962.

Kessen, W., Haith, M. M., & Salapatek, B. H. Human infancy: A bibliography and guide. In P. H. Mussen (Ed.), *Carmichael's manual of child psychology.* (3rd ed.) Vol. 1. New York: Wiley, 1970.

Konnor, M. J. Development among the Bushmen of Botswana. Unpublished doctoral dissertation, Harvard University, 1973.

Lacey, J. I. Somatic response patterning in stress: Some revisions of activation theory. In M. H. Appley & R. Trumbull (Eds.), *Psychological stress: Issues in research.* New York: Appleton-Century-Crofts, 1967.

Lewis, M., & Freedle, R. *Mother-infant dyad: The cradle*

of meaning. (Research bulletin RB72-22) Princeton, N. J.: Educational Testing Service, 1972.

Lewis, M., Goldberg, S., & Campbell, H. A developmental study of learning within the first three years of life: Response decrement to a redundant signal. *Monograph of the Society for Research in Child Development,* 1970, 34(No. 133).

McGraw, M. B. *Growth: A study of Johnny and Jimmy.* New York: Appleton-Century, 1935.

Pease, D., Wolins, L., & Stockdale, D. F. Relationship and prediction of infant tests. *Journal of Genetic Psychology,* 1973, 122, 31–35.

Scott, M. S. The absence of interference effects in preschool children's picture recognition. *Journal of Genetic Psychology,* 1973, 122, 121–126.

Sellers, M. J., Klein, R. E., Kagan, J., & Minton, C. Developmental determinants of attention: A cross-cultural replication. *Developmental Psychology,* 1972, 6, 185.

Suomi, S. J., & Harlow, H. F. Social rehabilitation of isolate reared monkeys. *Developmental Psychology,* 1972, 6, 487–496.

Van Hover, K. I. S. A developmental study of three components of attention. Unpublished doctoral dissertation, Harvard University, 1971.

White, S. H. Some general outlines of the matrix of developmental changes between 5 and 7 years. *Bulletin of the Orton Society,* 1970, 21, 41–57.

Wilson, P. D., & Riesen, A. H. Visual development in rhesus monkeys neonatally deprived of patterned light. *Journal of Comparative and Physiological Psychology,* 1966, 61, 87–95.

Chapter Four

Language Development

Few achievements have captured the imagination of psychologists as much as the child's acquisition of language. A vast effort has been devoted to describing the nature of language development; in other words, how does the nature of children's grammatical constructions shift as the child develops? The 1960s was characterized by an attempt to describe the rule systems that could account for the use of sentences (Bloom, 1975). One of the leaders in this effort was Roger Brown of Harvard; in his article in this section, Brown describes some of the ways in which children's grammar changes as the child develops.

However, as Brown notes, an analysis of the child's language that was limited to a description of the formal grammatical features of children's sentences was not enough. A second important direction of language research in the 1970s concerns the study of the nonlinguistic context of language. Semantics, or the study of meaning, has emerged as an important and active area of research. Children's language, in short, may be richer, more complex, and more fully understood by a consideration of the context in which the language occurs.

Another question of the 1970s has concerned the cognitive prerequisites for language learning. The relationship between language, cognition, and thought is, of course, an old recurring issue: "In its contemporary form, the issue has revolved around whether children acquire or somehow know the grammar of a language in the abstract sense proposed by Chomsky . . . or whether they learn language as a representation of their logically prior conceptual learning as proposed by Piaget" (Bloom, 1975, p. 261). To date, most evidence strongly supports the Piagetian view, namely that children first acquire conceptual notions about people, objects, events, and relationships and then learn words and structures that aid in describing their conceptual representations.

Closely related to this issue is the very difficult task of explaining the language achievements that previous investigators have described. Although few definitive theories have emerged, traditional behaviorist arguments have generally not received much support. The selective parental pressure hypothesis for example, whereby adults encourage correct grammar and punish incorrect utterances, has not been confirmed. Parents generally correct pronunciation, but typically do not correct the child's grammar. As Brown and others (Lennenberg, 1967) argue, it is conceivable that "the human species is programmed at a certain period in its life to operate in this fashion on linguistic input" (Brown, 1973, p. 519). Of course, the impressive demonstration of cross-cultural similarity presented by Slobin (1972) in this section lends some support to this possibility.

Not only are there similarities in the development of grammar across a wide range of cultures, there are striking parallels in the pattern of language acquisition of hearing children who acquire a verbal language and deaf children who learn a sign language. (Meadow, this section.) However, Meadow's (1975) review of the development of language in deaf children also underlines the difficulty that deaf children encounter in learning language. These investigations indicate that the ability to hear normal speech is an important condition for the adequate development of language. Recent research suggests that deaf children who are exposed to early sign language as well as manual-oral input seem to develop more adequate language skills than deaf children raised in a strictly verbal environment.

In the search for universals, however, we should not forget the obvious differences in the ways in which language is used in different settings and by different groups. Language as a form of communication is highly sensitive to a variety of contextual factors such as the nature of the situation (playground or classroom), the topic, (math problems vs. baseball games) or the audience (teacher vs. your best friends). As Gleason (1973) demonstrates in her article in this section, we regularly adjust our language to best suit the situational demands. In fact, a system of language that could not easily be modified to fulfill the functions of a new situation would be of very limited value in communication.

Finally, these performance and stylistic differences that vary across social class and subcultural groups are often viewed as differences in language development. Silverstein and Krate, however, persuasively argue that a deficit model, which suggests that standard English as spoken by middle class whites is superior to black dialects is mistaken. Instead, they propose a difference model, which recognizes that dialects of low-income groups represent parallel language developments. In fact, they note that the structure and syntax of the language of different racial and social class groups is very similar; what differs is style, pronunciation, and vocabulary. Finally, they explore the implications of the discontinuity between the black child's street language and the language of the school culture. As Silverstein and Krate demonstrate, language, thought, and culture interweave and interact in important and complex ways.

It is also clear that our search for the answers to the when, why, and how of language development in children is still far from complete.

REFERENCES

Bloom, L. Language Development. In F. D. Horowitz (Ed.) *Review of Child Development Research.* Volume 4, Chicago: University of Chicago Press, 1975. Pp. 245–304.

Lennenberg, E. *Biological Foundations of Language.* New York: Wiley, 1967.

Reading 14

Development of the First Language in the Human Species

Roger Brown, Ph.D.

The fact that one dares set down the above title, with considerable exaggeration but not perhaps with more than is pardonable, reflects the most interesting development in the study of child speech in the past few years. All over the world the first sentences of small children are being painstakingly taped, transcribed, and analyzed as if they were the last sayings of great sages. Which is a surprising fate for the likes of "That doggie," "No more milk," and "Hit ball." Reports already made, in progress, or projected for the near future sample development in children not only from many parts of the United States, England, Scotland, France, and Germany, but also development in children learning Luo (central East Africa), Samoan, Finnish, Hebrew, Japanese, Korean, Serbo-Croatian, Swedish, Turkish, Cakchiquel (Mayan-Guatemala), Tzeltal (Mayan-Mexico), American Sign Language in the case of a deaf child, and many other languages. The count you make of the number of studies now available for comparative analysis depends on how much you require in terms of standardized procedure, the full report of data, explicit criteria of acquisition, and so on. Brown (in press), whose methods demand a good deal, finds he can use some 33 reports of 12 languages. Slobin (1971), less interested in proving a small number of generalizations than in setting down a large number of interesting hypotheses suggested by what is known, finds he can use many more studies of some 30 languages from 10 different language families. Of course, this is still only about a 1% sample of the world's languages, but in a field like psycholinguistics, in which "universals" sometimes have been postulated on the basis of one or two languages, 30

languages represent a notable empirical advance. The credit for inspiring this extensive field work on language development belongs chiefly to Slobin at Berkeley, whose vision of a universal developmental sequence has inspired research workers everywhere. The quite surprising degree to which results to date support this vision has sustained the researcher when he gets a bit tired of writing down Luo, Samoan, or Finnish equivalents of "That doggie" and "No more milk."

It has, of course, taken some years to accumulate data on a wide variety of languages and even now, as we shall see, the variety is limited largely to just the first period of sentence construction (what is called Stage 1). However, the study of first-language development in the preschool years began to be appreciated as a central topic in psycholinguistics in the early 1960's. The initial impetus came fairly directly from Chomsky's (1957) *Syntactic Structures* and, really, from one particular emphasis in that book and in transformational, generative grammar generally. The emphasis is, to put it simply, that in acquiring a first language, one cannot possibly be said simply to acquire a repertoire of sentences, however large that repertoire is imagined to be, but must instead be said to acquire a rule system that makes it possible to generate a literally infinite variety of sentences, most of them never heard from anyone else. It is not a rare thing for a person to compose a new sentence that is understood within this community; rather, it is really a very ordinary linguistic event. Of course, *Syntactic Structure* was not the first book to picture first-language learning as a largely creative process; it may be doubted if any serious linguist has ever thought otherwise. It was the central role Chomsky gave to creativity that made the difference, plus, of course, the fact that he was able to put into explicit, unified notation a certain number of the basic rules of English.

In saying that a child acquires construction rules, one cannot of course mean that he acquires them in any explicit form; the preschool child cannot tell you any linguistic rules at all. And the chances are

The first five years of Brown's work were supported by Public Health Service Grant MH-7088 from the National Institute of Mental Health, and the second five years by Grant HD-02908 from the National Institute of Child Health and Development. The author is deeply grateful for the generosity of this support and the intelligent flexibility with which both grants have been administered.

This article was delivered as a Distinguished Scientific Contribution Award Address at the annual meeting of the American Psychological Association, Honolulu, September 1972.

that his parents cannot tell you very many either, and they obviously do not attempt to teach the mother tongue by the formulation of rules of sentence construction. One must suppose that what happens is that the preschool child is able to extract from the speech he hears a set of construction rules, many of them exceedingly abstract, which neither he nor his parents know in explicit form. This is saying more than that the child generalizes or forms analogies insofar as the generalizations he manifests conform to rules that have been made explicit in linguistic science.

That something of the sort described goes on has always been obvious to everyone for languages like Finnish or Russian which have elaborate rules of word formation, or morphology, rules that seem to cause children to make very numerous systematic errors of a kind that parents and casual observers notice. In English, morphology is fairly simple, and errors that parents notice are correspondingly less common. Nevertheless they do exist, and it is precisely in these errors that one glimpses from time to time that largely hidden but presumably general process. Most American children learning English use the form *hisself* rather than *himself* when they are about four years old. How do they come by it? It actually has been in the language since Middle English and is still in use among some adults, though called, for no good reason, a "substandard" form. It can be shown, however, that children use it when they have never heard it from anyone else, and so presumably they make it up or construct it. Why do they invent something that is, from the standard adult point of view, a mistake? To answer that we must recall the set of words most similar to the reflexive pronoun *himself*. They are other reflexive pronouns as *myself, yourself,* and *herself.* But all of these others, we see, are constructed by combining the possessive pronoun, *my, your, or her* with *self.* The masculine possessive pronoun is *his* and, if the English language were consistent at this point, the reflexive would be *hisself.* As it happens, standard English is not consistent at this point but is, rather, irregular, as all languages are at some points, and the preferred form is *himself.* Children, by inventing *hisself* and often insisting on it for quite a period, "iron out" or correct the irregularity of the language. And, incidentally, they reveal to us the fact that what they are learning are general rules of construction—not just the words and phrases they hear.

Close examination of the speech of children learning English shows that it is often replete with errors of syntax or sentence construction as well as morphology (e.g., "Where Daddy went"). But for some reason, errors of word formation are noticed regularly by parents, whereas they are commonly quite unconscious of errors of syntax. And so it happens that even casual observers of languages with a well-developed morphology are aware of the creative construction process, whereas casual observers of English find it possible seriously to believe that language learning is simply a process of memorizing what has been heard.

The extraction of a finite structure with an infinite generative potential which furthermore is accomplished in large part, though not completely, by the beginning of the school years (see Chomsky, 1969, for certain exceptions and no doubt there are others), all without explicit tuition, was not something any learning theory was prepared to explain, though some were prepared to "handle" it, whatever "handle" means. And so it appeared that first-language acquisition was a major challenge to psychology.

While the first studies of language acquisition were inspired by transformational linguistics, nevertheless, they really were not approved of by the transformational linguists. This was because the studies took the child's spontaneous speech performance, taped and transcribed at home on some regular schedule, for their basic data, and undertook to follow the changes in these data with age. At about the same time in the early 1960's, three studies of, roughly, this sort were begun independently: Martin Braine's (1963) in Maryland, Roger Brown's (Brown & Bellugi, 1964) at Harvard with his associates Ursula Bellugi (now Bellugi-Klima) and Colin Fraser (Brown & Fraser, 1963), and Susan Ervin's (now Ervin-Tripp) with Wick Miller (Miller & Ervin, 1964) at Berkeley. The attempt to discover constructional knowledge from "mere performance" seemed quite hopeless to the MIT linguists (e.g., Chomsky, 1964; Lees, 1964). It was at the opposite extreme from the linguist's own method, which was to present candidate-sentences to his own intuition for judgement as grammatical or not. In cases of extreme uncertainty, I suppose he may also have stopped next door to ask the opinion of a colleague.

In retrospect, I think they were partly right and partly wrong about our early methods. They were absolutely right in thinking that no sample of spontaneous speech, however large, would alone enable one to write a fully determinate set of construction rules. I learned that fact over a period of years in which I made the attempt 15 times, for three children at five points of development. There were always, and are always, many things the corpus alone cannot settle. The linguists were wrong, I think, in two ways. First, in supposing that because one cannot learn everything about a child's construction knowledge, one cannot learn anything. One can, in fact, learn quite a lot, and one of the discoveries of the past decade is the variety of ways in which spontaneous running discourse can be "milked" for knowledge of linguistic structure; a great deal of the best evidence lies not simply in the child's own sentences but in the exchanges with others on the level of discourse. I do not think that transformational linguists should have "pronounced" on all of this with such discouraging confidence since they had never, in fact, tried. The other way in which I think the linguists were wrong was in their gross exaggeration of the degree to which spontaneous speech is ungrammatical, a kind of hodgepodge of false starts, incomplete sentences, and so on. Except for talk at learned conferences, even adult speech, allowing for some simple rules of editing and ellipses, seems to be mostly quite grammatical (Labov, 1970). For children and for the speech of parents to children this is even more obviously the case.

The first empirical studies of the 1960's gave rise to various descriptive characterizations, of which "telegraphic speech" (Brown & Fraser, 1963) and "Pivot Grammar" (Braine, 1963) are the best known. These did not lead anywhere very interesting, but they were unchallenged long enough to get into most introductory psychology textbooks where they probably will survive for a few years even though their numerous inadequacies are now well established. Bloom (1970), Schlesinger (1971), and Bowerman (1970) made the most telling criticisms both theoretical and empirical, and Brown (in press) has put the whole, now overwhelmingly negative, case together. It seems to be clear enough to workers in this field that telegraphic speech and Pivot Grammar are false leads that we need not even bother to describe.

However, along with their attacks, especially on Pivot Grammar, Bloom (1970) and Schlesinger (1971) made a positive contribution that has turned

out to be the second major impetus to the field. For reasons which must seem very strange to the outsider not immersed in the linguistics of the 1960's, the first analyses of child sentences in this period were in terms of pure syntax, in abstraction from semantics, with no real attention paid to what the children might intend to communicate. Lois Bloom added to her transcription of child speech a systematic running account of the nonlinguistic context. And in these contexts she found evidence that the child intends to express certain meanings with even his earliest sentences, meanings that go beyond the simple naming in succession of various aspects of a complex situation, and that actually assert the existence of, or request the creation of, particular relations.

The justification for attributing relational semantic intentions to very small children comprises a complex and not fully satisfying argument. At its strongest, it involves the following sort of experimental procedure. With toys that the child can name available to him he is, on one occasion, asked to "Make the truck hit the car," and on another occasion "Make the car hit the truck." Both sentences involve the same objects and action, but the contrast of word order in English indicates which object is to be in the role of agent (hitter) and which in the role of object (the thing hit). If the child acts out the two events in ways appropriate to the contrasting word orders, he may be said to understand the differences in the semantic relations involved. Similar kinds of contrasts can be set up for possessives ("Show me the Mommy's baby" versus "Show me the baby's Mommy") and prepositions ("Put the pencil on the matches" versus "Put the matches on the pencil"). The evidence to date, of which there is a fairly considerable amount collected in America and Britain (Bever, Mehler, & Valian, in press; de Villiers & de Villiers, in press; Fraser, Bellugi, & Brown, 1963; Lovell & Dixon, 1965), indicates that, by late Stage I, children learning English can do these things correctly (experiments on the prepositions are still in a trial stage). By late Stage I, children learning English also are often producing what the nonlinguistic context suggests are intended as relations of possession, location, and agent-action-object. For noncontrastive word orders in English and for languages that do not utilize contrastive word order in these ways, the evidence for relational intentions is essentially the nonlinguistic context. Which context is also, of course, what parents use as an aid to figuring out what their children mean when they speak.

It is, I think, worth a paragraph of digression to point out that another experimental method, a method of judgment and correction of word sequence and so a method nearer that of the transformational linguist himself, yields a quite different outcome. Peter and Jill de Villiers (1972) asked children to observe a dragon puppet who sometimes spoke correctly with respect to word order (e.g., "Drive your car") and sometimes incorrectly (e.g., "Cup the fill"). A second dragon puppet responded to the first when the first spoke correctly by saying "right" and repeating the sentence. When the first puppet spoke incorrectly, the second, tutorial puppet, said "wrong," and corrected the sentence (e.g., "Fill the cup"). After observing a number of such sequences, the child was invited to play the role of the tutorial puppet, and new sentences, correct and incorrect, were supplied. In effect, this is a complicated way of asking the child to make judgments of syntactic well-formedness, supplying corrections as necessary. The instruction is not given easily in words, but by role-playing examples de Villiers and de Villiers found they could get the idea across. While there are many interesting results in their study, the most important is that the children did not make correct word-order judgments 50% of the time until after what we call Stage V, and only the most advanced child successfully corrected wrong orders over half the time. This small but important study suggests that the construction rules do not emerge all at once at the levels of spontaneous use, discriminating response, and judgment. The last of these, the linguist's favorite, is, after all, not simply a pipeline to competence but a metalinguistic performance of considerable complexity.

In spite of the fact that the justification for attributing semantic intentions of a relational nature to the child when he first begins composing sentences is not fully satisfactory, the practice, often called the method of "rich interpretation," by contrast with the "lean" behavioral interpretation that preceded it, is by now well justified simply because it has helped expose remarkable developmental universals that formerly had gone unremarked. There are now I think three reasonably well-established developmental series in which constructions and the meanings they express appear in a nearly invariant order.

The first of these, and still the only one to have been shown to have validity for many different languages, concerns Stage I. Stage I has been defined rather arbitrarily as the period when the average length of the child's utterances in morphemes (mean lengths of utterance or MLU) first rises above 1.0—in short, the time when combinations of words or morphemes first occur at all—until the MLU is 2.0, at which time utterances occasionally will attain as great a length as 7 morphemes. The most obvious superficial fact about child sentences is that they grow longer as the child grows older. Leaning on this fact, modern investigators have derived a set of standard rules for calculating MLU, rules partially well motivated and partially arbitrary. Whether the rules are exactly the right ones, and it is already clear that they are not, is almost immaterial because their only function is a temporary one: to render children in one study and in different studies initially comparable in terms of some index superior to chronological age, and this MLU does. It has been shown (Brown, in press) that while individual children vary enormously in rate of linguistic development, and so in what they know at a given chronological age, their constructional and semantic knowledge is fairly uniform at a given MLU. It is common, in the literature, to identify five stages, with those above Stage I defined by increments of .50 to the MLU.

By definition, then, Stage I children in any language are going to be producing sentences of from 1 to 7 morphemes long with the average steadily increasing across Stage I. What is not true by definition, but is true in fact for all of the languages so far studied, is that the constructions in Stage I are limited semantically to a single rather small set of relations and, furthermore, the complications that occur in the course of the Stage are also everywhere the same. Finally, in Stage I, the only syntactic or expressive devices employed are the combinations of the semantically related forms under one sentence contour and, where relevant in the model language, correct word order. It is important to recognize that there are many other things that *could* happen in Stage I, many ways of increasing MLU besides those actually used in Stage I. In Stage I, MLU goes up because simple two-term relations begin to be combined into three-term and four-term relations of the same type but occurring in one sentence. In later stages, MLU, always sensitive to increase of knowledge, rises in value for quite different reasons; for instance, originally missing obligatory function forms like inflections begin to be supplied, later on the embedding of two more simple sentences begins, and eventually the coordination of simple sentences.

What are the semantic relations that seem universally to be the subject matter of Stage I speech? In brief, it may be said that they are either relations or propositions concerning the sensory-motor intelligence which the work of the great developmental psychologist, Jean Piaget, has described as the principal acquisition of the first 18 months of life. The Stage I relations also correspond very closely with the set of "cases" which Charles Fillmore (1968) has postulated as the universal semantic deep structures of language. This is surprising since Fillmore did not set out to say anything at all about child speech but simply to provide a universal framework for adult grammar.

In actual fact, there is no absolutely fixed list of Stage I relations. A short list of 11 will account for about 75% of Stage I utterances in almost all language samples collected. A longer list of about 18 will come close to accounting for 100%. What are some of the relations? There is, in the first place, a semantic set having to do with reference. These include the nominative (e.g., "That ball"), expressions of recurrence (e.g., "More ball"), and expressions of disappearance or non-existence (e.g., "All gone ball"). Then there is the possessive (e.g., "Daddy chair"), two sorts of locative (e.g., "Book table" and "Go store") and the attributive (e.g., "Big house"). Finally, there are two-term relations comprising portions of a major sort of declarative sentence: agent-action (e.g., "Daddy hit"); action-object (e.g., "Hit ball"); and, surprisingly from the point of view of the adult language, agent-object (e.g., "Daddy ball"). Less frequent relations which do not appear in all samples but which one would want to add to a longer list include: experiencer-state (e.g., "I hear"); datives of indirect object (e.g., "Sweep broom"); datives of indirect object (e.g., "Give Mommy"); comitatives (e.g., "Walk Mommy"); instrumentals (e.g., "Sweep broom"); and just a few others. From all of these constructions, it may be noticed that in English, and in all languages, "obligatory" functional morphemes like inflections, case endings, articles, and prepositions are missing in Stage I. This is, of course, the observation that gave rise to the still roughly accurate descriptive term *telegraphic speech*. The function forms are thought to be absent because of some combination of such

variables as their slight phonetic substance and minimal stress, their varying but generally considerable grammatical complexity, and the subtlety of the semantic modulation they express (number, time, aspect, specificity of reference, exact spatial relations, etc.).

Stage I speech seems to be almost perfectly restricted to these two-term relations, expressed, at the least by subordination to a single sentence contour and often by appropriate word order, until the MLU is abouh 1.50. From here on, complications which lengthen the utterance begin, but they are, remarkably enough, complications of just the same two types in all languages studied so far. The first type involves three-term relations, like agent-action-object; agent-action-locative; and action-object-locative which, in effect, combine sequentially two of the simple relations found before an MLU of 1.50 without repeating the terms that would appear twice if the two-term relations simply were strung together. In other words, something like agent-action-object (e.g., "Adam hit ball") is made up *as if* the relations agent-action ("Adam hit") and action-object ("Hit ball") had been strung together in sequence with one redundant occurrence of the action ("hit") deleted.

The second type of complication involves the retention of the basic line of the two-term relation with one term, always a noun-phrase, "expanding" as a relation in its own right. Thus, there is development from such forms as "Sit chair" (action-locative) to "Sit Daddy chair" which is an action-locative, such that the locative itself is expanded as a possessive. The forms expanded in this kind of construction are, in all languages so far studied, the same three types: expressions of attribution, possession, and recurrence. Near the very end of Stage I, there are further complications into four-term relations of exactly the same two types described. All of this, of course, gives a very "biological" impression, almost as if semantic cells of a finite set of types were dividing and combining and then redividing and recombining in ways common to the species.

The remaining two best established invariances of order in acquisition have not been studied in a variety of languages but only for American children and, in one case, only for the three unacquainted children in Brown's longitudinal study—the children called, in the literature, Adam, Eve, and Sarah. The full results appear in Stage II of Brown (in press) and in Brown and Hanlon (1970). Stage II in

Brown (in press) focuses on 14 functional morphemes including the English noun and verb inflections, the copula *be,* the progressive auxiliary *be,* the prepositions *in* and *on,* and the articles *a* and *the.* For just these forms in English it is possible to define a criterion that is considerably superior to the simple occurrence-or-not used in Stage I and to the semiarbitrary frequency levels used in the remaining sequence to be described. In very many sentence contexts, one or another of the 14 morphemes can be said to be "obligatory" from the point of view of the adult language. Thus in a nomination sentence accompanied by pointing, such as "That book," an article is obligatory; in a sentence like "Here two book," a plural inflection of the noun is obligatory; in "I running," the auxiliary *am* inflected for person, number, and tense is obligatory. It is possible to treat each such sentence frame as a kind of test item in which the obligatory form either appears or is omitted. Brown defined as his criterion of acquisition, presence in 90% of obligatory contexts in six consecutive sampling hours.

There are in the detailed report many surprising and suggestive outcomes. For instance, "acquisition" of these forms turns out never to be a sudden all-or-none affair such as categorical linguistic rules might suggest it should be. It is rather a matter of slowly increasing probability of presence, varying in rate of morpheme to morpheme, but extending in some cases over several years. The most striking single outcome is that for these three children, with spontaneous speech scored in the fashion described, the order of acquisition of the morphemes approaches invariance, with rank-order correlations between pairs of children all at about .86. This does not say that acquisition of a morpheme is invariant with respect to chronological age: the variation of rate of development even among these children is tremendous. But the order, that is, which construction follows which, is almost constant, and Brown (in press) shows that it is not predicted by morpheme frequency in adult speech, but is well predicted by relative semantic and grammatical complexity. Of course, in languages other than English, the same universal sequence cannot possibly be found because grammatical and semantic differences are too great to yield commensurable data, as they are not with the fundamental relations of cases of Stage I. However, if the 14 particular morphemes are reconceived as particular conjunctions of perceptual salience and degrees of grammatical and semantic complexity, we may find laws of succession which have cross-linguistic validity (see Slobin, 1971).

Until the spring of 1972, Brown was the only researcher who had coded data in terms of presence in, or absence from, obligatory contexts, but then Jill and Peter de Villiers (in press) did the job on a fairly large scale. They made a cross-sectional study from speech samples of 21 English-speaking American children aged between 16 and 40 months. The de Villiers scored the 14 morphemes Brown scored; they used his coding rules to identify obligatory contexts and calculated the children's individual MLU values according to his rules.

Two different criteria of morpheme acquisition were used in the analyses of data. Both constitute well-rationalized adaptations of a cross-sectional study of the 90% correct criterion used in Brown's longitudinal study; we will refer to the two orders here simply as 1 and 2. To compare with the de Villiers' two orders there is a single rank order (3) for the three children, Adam, Eve, and Sarah, which was obtained by averaging the orders of the three children.

There are three rank orders for the same 14 morphemes scored in the same way and using closely similar criteria of acquisition. The degree of invariance is, even to one who expected a substantial similarity, amazing. The rank-order correlations are: between 1 and 2, .84; between 2 and 3, .78; between 1 and 3, .87. These relations are only very slightly below those among Adam, Eve, and Sarah themselves. Thanks to the de Villiers, it has been made clear that we have a developmental phenomenon of substantial generality.

There are numerous other interesting outcomes in the de Villiers' study. The rank-order correlation between age and Order 2 is .68, while that between MLU and the same order is .92, very close to perfect. So MLU is a better predictor than age in this study, as in ours of morpheme acquisition. In fact, with age partialed out, using a Kendall partial correlation procedure, the original figure of .92 is only reduced to .85, suggesting that age adds little or nothing to the predictive power of MLU.

The third sequence, demonstrated only for English by Brown and Hanlon (197), takes advantage of the fact that what are called tag questions are in English very complex grammatically, though semantically they are rather simple. In many other languages tags are invariant in form (e.g., *n'est-ce pas,* French; *nicht wahr,* German), and so are grammatically simple; but in English, the form of the tag, and there are hundreds of forms, varies in a completely determinate way with the structure of the declarative sentence to which it is appended and for which it asks confirmation. Thus:

"John will be late, won't he?"
"May can't drive, can she?"

And so on. The little question at the end is short enough, as far as superficial length is concerned, to be produced by the end of Stage I. We know, furthermore, that the semantic of the tag, a request for confirmation, lies within the competence of the Stage I child since he occasionally produces such invariant and simple equivalents as "right?" or "huh?" Nevertheless, Brown and Hanlon (1970) have shown that the production of a full range of well-formed tags is not to be found until after Stage V, sometimes several years after. Until that time, there are, typically, no well-formed tags at all. What accounts for the long delay? Brown and Hanlon present evidence that it is the complexity of the grammatical knowledge that tags entail.

Consider such a declarative sentence as "His wife can drive." How might one develop from this the tag "can't she?" It is, in the first place, necessary to make a pronoun of the subject. The subject is *his wife,* and so the pronoun must be feminine, third person, and since it is a subject, the nominative case—in fact, she. Another step is to make the tag negative. In English this is done by adding *not* or the contraction n't to the auxiliary verb *can;* hence *can't.* Another step is to make the tag interrogative, since it is a question, and in English that is done by a permutation of order—placing the auxiliary verb ahead of the subject. Still another step is to delete all of the predicate of the base sentence, except the first member of the auxiliary, and that at last yields *can't she?* as a derivative of *His wife can drive.* While this description reads a little bit like a program simulating the process by which tags actually are produced by human beings, it is not intended as anything of the sort. The point is simply that there seems to be no way at all by which a human could produce the right tag for each declarative without *somehow* utilizing all of the grammatical knowledge described, just how no one knows. But memorization is excluded completely

by the fact that, while tags themselves are numerous but not infinitely so, the problem is to fit the one right tag to each declarative, and declaratives are infinitely numerous.

In English all of the single constructions, and also all of the pairs, which entail the knowledge involved in tag creation, themselves exist as independent sentences in their own right, for example, interrogatives, negatives, ellipses, negative-ellipses, and so on. One can, therefore, make an ordering of construction in terms of complexity of grammatical knowledge (in precise fact, only a partial ordering) and ask whether more complex forms are always preceded in child speech by less complex forms. This is what Brown and Hanlon (1970) did for Adam, Eve, and Sarah, and the result was resoundingly affirmative. In this study, then, we have evidence that grammatical complexity as such, when it can be disentangled, as it often cannot, from semantic complexity, is itself a determinant of order of acquisition.

Of course, the question about the mother tongue that we should really like answered is, How is it possible to learn a first language at all? On that question, which ultimately motivates the whole research enterprise, I have nothing to offer that is not negative. But perhaps it is worthwhile making these negatives explicit since they are still widely supposed to be affirmatives, and indeed to provide a large part of the answer to the question. What I have to say is not primarily addressed to the question, How does the child come to talk at all? Since there seem to be fairly obvious utilities in saying a few words in order to express more exactly what he wants, does not want, wonders about, or wishes to share with others. The more exact question on which we have a little information that serves only to make the question more puzzling is, How does the child come to *improve* upon his language, moving steadily in the direction of the adult model? It probably seems surprising that there should be any mystery about the forces impelling improvement, since it is just this aspect of the process that most people imagine that they understand. Surely the improvement is a response to selective social pressures of various kinds; ill-formed or incomplete utterances must be less effective than well-formed and complete utterances in accomplishing the child's intent; parents probably approve of well-formed utterances and disapprove or correct the ill-formed. These ideas sound sensible and may be correct, but the still-scant evidence available does not support them.

At the end of Stage I, the child's constructions are characterized by, in addition to the things we have mentioned, a seemingly lawless oscillating omission of every sort of major constituent including sometimes subjects, objects, verbs, locatives, and so on. The important point about these oscillating omissions is that they seldom seem to impede communication; the other person, usually the mother, being in the same situation and familiar with the child's stock of knowledge, usually understands, so far as one can judge, even the incomplete utterance. Brown (in press) has suggested the Stage I child's speech is well adapted to his purpose, but that, as a speaker, he is very *narrowly* adapted. We may suppose that in speaking to strangers or of new experiences he will have to learn to express obligatory constituents if he wants to get his message across. And that may be the answer: the social pressures to communicate may chiefly operate outside the usual sampling situation, which is that of the child at home with family members.

In Stage II, Brown (in press) found that all of the 14 grammatical morphemes were at first missing, then occasionally present in obligatory contexts, and after varying and often long periods of time, always present in such contexts. What makes the probability of supplying the requisite morpheme rise with time? It is surprisingly difficult to find cases in which omission results in incomprehension or misunderstanding. With respect to the definite and nondefinite articles, it even looks as if listeners almost never really need them, and yet child speakers learn to operate with the exceedingly intricate rules governing their usage. Adult Japanese, speaking English as a second language, do not seem to learn how to operate with the articles as we might expect they would if listeners needed them. Perhaps it is the case that the child automatically does this kind of learning but the adults do not. Second-language learning may be responsive to familiar sorts of learning variables, and first-language learning may not. The two, often thought to be similar processes, may be profoundly and ineradicably different.

Consider the Stage I child's invariably uninflected generic verbs. In Stage II, American parents regularly gloss these verbs in one of four ways: as imperatives, past tense forms, present progressives, or imminent-intentional futures. It is an interesting fact, of course, that these are just the four modulations of the verb that the child then goes on, first, to learn to express. For years we have thought it possible that glosses or expansions of this type might be a major force impelling the child to improve his speech. However, all the evidence available, both naturalistic and experimental (it is summarized in Brown, Cazden, & Bellugi, 1969), offers no support at all for this notion. Cazden (1965), for instance, carried out an experiment testing for the effect on young children's speech of deliberately interpolated "expansions" (the supplying of obligatory functional morphemes), introduced for a period on every preschool day for three months. She obtained no significant effect whatever. It is possible, I think, that such an experiment done now, with the information Stage II makes available, and expanding only by providing morphemes of a complexity for which the child was "ready," rather than as in Cazden's original experiment expanding in all possible ways, would show an effect. But no such experiment has been done, and so no impelling effect of expansion has been demonstrated.

Suppose we look at the facts of the parental glossing of Stage I generic verbs not, as we have done above, as a possible tutorial device but rather, as Slobin (1971) has done, as evidence that the children already intended the meanings their parents attributed to them. In short, think of the parental glosses as veridical readings of the child's thought. From this point of view, the child has been understood correctly, even though his utterances are incomplete. In that case there is no selection pressure. Why does he learn to say more if what he already knows how to say works quite well?

To these observations of the seeming efficacy of the child's incomplete utterances, at least at home with the family, we should add the results of a study reported in Brown and Hanlon (1970). Here it was not primarily a question of the omission of obligatory forms but of the contrast between ill-formed primitive constructions and well-formed mature versions. For certain constructions, *yes-no* questions, tag questions, negatives, and *wh-* questions, Brown and Hanlon (1970) identified periods when Adam, Eve, and Sarah were producing both primitive and mature versions, sometimes the one, sometimes the other. The question was, Did the mature version communicate more successfully than the primitive version? They first identified all instances of primitive and mature versions, and then coded the adult responses for comprehending follow-up, calling comprehending responses "sequiturs" and uncomprehending or irrelevant responses "nonsequiturs." They found no evidence whatever of a difference in communicative efficacy, and so once again, no selection pressure. Why, one asks oneself, should the child learn the complex apparatus of tag questions when "right?" or "huh?" seems to do just the same job? Again one notes that adults learning English as a second language often do not learn tag questions, and the possibility again comes to mind that children operate on language in a way that adults do not.

Brown and Hanlon (1970) have done one other study that bears on the search for selection pressures. Once again it was syntactic well-formedness versus ill-formedness that was in question rather than completeness or incompleteness. This time Brown and Hanlon started with two kinds of adult responses to child utterances: "approval," directed at an antecedent child utterance, and "disapproval," directed at such an antecedent. The question then was, Did the two sets of antecedents differ in syntactic correctness? Approving and disapproving responses are, certainly, very reasonable candidates for the respective roles, "positive reinforcer" and "punishment." Of course, they do not necessarily qualify as such because reinforcers and punishments are defined by their effects on performance (Skinner, 1953); they have no necessary, independent, nonfunctional properties. Still, of course, they often are put forward as plausible determinants of performance and are thought, generally, to function as such. In order differentially to affect the child's syntax, approval and disapproval must, at a minimum, be governed selectively by correct and incorrect syntax. If they should be so governed, further data still would be needed to show that they affect performance. If they are not so governed, they cannot be a selective force working for correct speech. And Brown and Hanlon found that they are not. In general, the parents seemed to pay no attention to bad syntax nor did they even seem to be aware of it. They approved or disapproved an utterance usually on the grounds of the truth value of the proposition which the parents supposed the child intended to assert. This is a surprising outcome to most middle-class parents, since they are generally under the impression that they do correct the child's speech. From inquiry and observation I find that what parents generally correct is pronunciation, "naughty" words, and regularized irregular allomorphs like *digged* or *goed.* These facts of the child's speech seem to penetrate parental awareness. But syntax–the child saying, for instance, "Why the dog won't eat?" instead of "Why won't the dog eat?"—seems to be set right automatically in the parent's mind, with the mistake never registering as such.

In sum, then, we presently do not have evidence that there are selective social pressures of any kind operating on children to impel them to bring their speech into line with adult models. It is, however, entirely possible that such pressures do operate in situations unlike the situations we have sampled, for instance, away from home or with strangers. A radically different possibility is that children work out rules for the speech they hear, passing from levels of lesser to greater complexity, simply because the human species is programmed at a certain period in its life to operate in this fashion on linguistic input. Linguistic input would be defined by the universal properties of language. And the period of progressive rule extraction would correspond to Lenneberg's (1967 and elsewhere) proposed "critical period." It may be chiefly adults who learn a new, a second, language in terms of selective social pressures. Comparison of the kinds of errors made by adult second-language learners of English with the kinds made by child first-language learners of English should be enlightening.

If automatic internal programs of structure extraction provide the generally correct sort of answer to how a first language is learned, then, of course, our inquiries into external communication pressures simply are misguided. They look for the answer in the wrong place. That, of course, does not mean that we are anywhere close to having the right answer. It only remains to specify the kinds of programs that would produce the result regularly obtained.

REFERENCES

Bever, T. G., Mehler, J. R., & Valian, V. V. Linguistic capacity of very young children. In T. C. Bever & W. Weksel (Eds.), *The Acquisition of Structure.* New York: Holt, Rinehart & Winston, in press.

Bloom, L. *Language Development: Form and Function in Emerging Grammars.* Cambridge: M.I.T. Press, 1970.

Bowerman, M. Learning to talk: A cross-linguistic study

of early syntactic development with special reference to Finnish. Unpublished doctoral dissertation, Harvard University, 1970.

Braine, M. D. S. The ontology of English phrase structure: The first phase. *Language,* 39:1–14, 1963.

Brown, R. *A First Language; The Early Stages.* Cambridge: Harvard University Press, in press.

Brown, R. & Bellugi, U. Three processes in the acquisition of syntax. *Harvard Educational Review,* 34:133–151, 1964.

Brown, R., Cazden, C., & Bellugi, U. The child's grammar from from I to III. In J. P. Hill (Ed.), *Minnesota Symposium on Child Psychology.* Vol. 2. Minneapolis: University of Minnesota Press, 1969.

Brown, R. & Fraser, C. The acquisition of syntax. In C. N. Cofer & B. S. Musgrave (Eds.), *Verbal Behavior and Learning: Problems and Processes.* New York: McGraw-Hill, 1963.

Brown, R. & Hanlon, C. Derivational complexity and order of acquisition in child speech. In J. R. Hayes (Ed.), *Cognition and the Development of Language.* New York: Wiley, 1970.

Cazden, C. B. Environmental assistance to the child's acquisition of grammar. Unpublished doctoral dissertation, Harvard University, 1965.

Chomsky, N. *The Acquisition of Syntax in Children from 5 to 10.* Cambridge: M.I.T. Press, 1969.

Chomsky, N. *Syntactic Structures.* The Hague: Mouton, 1957.

Chomsky, N. Formal discussion of Wick Miller and Susan Ervin. The development of grammar in child language. In U. Bellugi & R. Brown (Eds.), The acquisition of language. *Monographs of the Society for Research in Child Development,* 29 (1):35–40, 1964.

De Villiers, J. G. & De Villiers, P. A. A cross-sectional study of the development of grammatical morphemes in child speech. *Journal of Psycholinguistic Research,* 1973, in press.

De Villiers, J. G. & De Villiers, P. A. Development of the use of order in comprehension. *Journal of Psycholinguistic Research,* 1973, in press.

De Villiers, P. A. & De Villiers, J. G. Early judgments of semantic and syntactic acceptability by children. *Journal of Psycholinguistic Research,* 1:299–310, 1972.

Fillmore, C. J. The case for case. In E. Bach & R. T. Harms (Eds.), *Universals in Linguistic Theory.* New York: Holt, Rinehart & Winston, 1968.

Fraser, C., Bellugi, U., & Brown, R. Control of grammar in imitation, comprehension, and production. *Journal of Verbal Learning and Verbal Behavior,* 2:121–135, 1963.

Labov, W. The study of language in its social context. *Stadium Generale,* 23:30–87, 1970.

Lees, R. Formal discussion of Roger Brown and Colin Fraser. The acquisition of syntax. And of Roger Brown, Colin Fraser, and Ursula Bellugi. Explorations in grammar evaluation. In U. Bellugi & R. Brown (Eds.), The acquisition of language. *Monographs of the Society for Research in Child Development,* 29 (1):92–98, 1964.

Lenneberg, E. H. *Biological Foundations of Language.* New York: Wiley, 1967.

Lovell, K. & Dixon, E. M. The growth of grammar in imitation, comprehension, and production. *Journal of Child Psychology and Psychiatry,* 5:1–9, 1965.

Miller, W. & Ervin, S. The development of grammar in child language. In U. Bellugi & R. Brown (Eds.), The acquisition of language. *Monographs of the Society for Research in Child Development,* 29 (1):9–34, 1964.

Schlesinger, I. M. Production of utterances and language acquisition. In D. I. Slobin (Ed.), *The Ontogenesis of Grammar.* New York: Academic Press, 1971.

Skinner, B. F. *Science and Human Behavior.* New York: Macmillan, 1953.

Slobin, D. I. Developmental Psycholinguistics. In W. O. Dingwall (Ed.), *A Survey of Linguistic Science.* College Park: Linguistics Program, University of Maryland, 1971.

Reading 15

Children and Language: They Learn the Same Way All around the World

Dan I. Slobin

According to the account of linguistic history set forth in the book of Genesis, all men spoke the same language until they dared to unite to build the Tower of Babel. So that men could not cooperate to build a tower that would reach into heaven, God acted to "confound the language of all the earth" to insure that groups of men "may not understand one another's speech."

What was the original universal language of mankind? This is the question that Psammetichus, ruler of Egypt in the seventh century B. C., asked in the first controlled psychological experiment in recorded history—an experiment in developmental psycholinguistics reported by Herodotus:

"Psammetichus . . . took at random, from an ordinary family, two newly born infants and gave them to a shepherd to be brought up amongst his flocks, under strict orders that no one should utter a word in their presence. They were to be kept by themselves in a lonely cottage. . . ."

Psammetichus wanted to know whether isolated children would speak Egyptian words spontaneously—thus proving, on the premise that ontogeny recapitulates phylogeny, that Egyptians were the original race of mankind.

In two years, the children spoke their first word: *becos,* which turned out to be the Phrygian word for bread. The Egyptians withdrew their claim that they were the world's most ancient people and admitted the greater antiquity of the Phrygians.

Same We no longer believe, of course, that Phrygian was the original language of all the earth (nor that it was Hebrew, as King James VII of Scotland thought). No one knows which of the thousands of languages is the oldest—perhaps we will never know. But recent work in developmental psycholinguistics indicates that the languages of the earth are not as confounded as we once believed. Children in all nations seem to learn their native languages in much the same way. Despite the diversity of tongues, there are linguistic universals that seem to rest upon the developmental universals of the human mind. Every language is learnable by children of preschool-age, and it is becoming apparent that little children have some definite ideas about how a language is structured and what it can be used for:

Mmm, I want to eat maize.
What?
Where is the maize?
There is no more maize.
Mmm.
Mmm.
[Child seizes an ear of corn]:
What's this?
It's not our maize.
Whose is it?
It belongs to grandmother.
Who harvested it?
They harvested it.

Where did they harvest it?
They harvested it down over there.
Way down over there?
Mmm. [yes]
Let's look for some too.
You look for some.
Fine.
Mmm.
[Child begins to hum]

The dialogue is between a mother and a two-and-a-half-year-old girl. Anthropologist Brian Stross of the University of Texas recorded it in a thatched hut in an isolated Mayan village in Chiapas, Mexico. Except for the fact that the topic was maize and the language was Tzeltal, the conversation could have taken place anywhere, as any parent will recognize. The child uses short, simple sentences, and her mother answers in kind. The girl expresses her needs and seeks information about such things as location, possession, past action, and so on. She does not ask about time, remote possibilities, contingencies, and the like—such things don't really occur to the two-year-old in any culture, or in any language.

Our research team at the University of California at Berkeley has been studying the way children learn languages in several countries and cultures. We have been aided by similar research at Harvard and at several other American universities, and by the work of foreign colleagues. We have gathered reasonably firm data on the acquisition of 18 languages, and have suggestive findings on 12 others. Although the data are still scanty for many of these languages, a common picture of human-language development is beginning to emerge.

In all cultures the child's first word generally is a noun or proper name, identifying some object, animal, or person he sees every day. At about two years—give or take a few months—a child begins to put two words together to form rudimentary sentences. The two-word stage seems to be universal.

To get his meaning across, a child at the two-word stage relies heavily on gesture, tone and context. Lois Bloom, professor of speech, Teachers College, Columbia University, reported a little American girl who said *Mommy sock* on two distinct occasions: on finding her mother's sock and on being dressed by her mother. Thus the same phrase expressed possession in one context (*Mommy's sock*) and an agent-object relationship in another (*Mommy is putting on the sock*).

But even with a two-word horizon, children can get a wealth of meanings across:

IDENTIFICATION: *See doggie.*
LOCATION: *Book there.*
REPETITION: *More milk.*
NONEXISTENCE: *Allgone thing.*
NEGATION: *Not wolf.*
POSSESSION: *My candy.*
ATTRIBUTION: *Big car.*
AGENT-ACTION: *Mama walk.*
AGENT-OBJECT: *Mama book* (meaning, "Mama read book").
ACTION-LOCATION: *Sit chair.*
ACTION-DIRECT OBJECT: *Hit you.*
ACTION-INDIRECT OBJECT: *Give papa.*
ACTION-INSTRUMENT: *Cut knife.*
QUESTION: *Where ball?*

The striking thing about this list is its universality. The examples are drawn from child talk in English, German, Russian, Finnish, Turkish, Samoan and Luo, but the entire list could probably be made up of examples from two-year old speech in any language.

Word A child easily figures out that the speech he hears around him contains discrete, meaningful elements, and that these elements can be combined. And children make the combinations themselves— many of their meaningful phrases would never be heard in adult speech. For example, Martin Braine studied a child who said things like *allgone outside* when he returned home and shut the door, *more page* when he didn't want a story to end, *other fix* when he wanted something repaired, and so on. These clearly are expressions created by the child, not mimicry of his parents. The matter is especially clear in the Russian language, in which noun endings vary with the role the noun plays in a sentence. As a rule, Russian children first use only the nominative ending in all combinations, even when it is grammatically incorrect. What is important to children is the *word*, not the ending; the *meaning*, not the grammar.

At first, the two-word limit is quite severe. A child may be able to say *daddy throw, throw ball,* and *daddy ball*—indicating that he understands the full proposition, *daddy throw ball*—yet be unable to produce all three words in one stretch. Again, though the data are limited, this seems to be a universal fact about children's speech.

Tools Later a child develops a rudimentary grammar within the two-word format. These first grammatical devices are the most basic formal tools of human language: intonation, word order, and inflection.

A child uses intonation to distinguish meanings even at the one-word stage, as when he indicates a request by a rising tone, or a demand with a loud, insistent tone. But at the two-word stage another device, a contrastive stress, becomes available. An English-speaking child might say BABY *chair* to indicate possession, and *baby* CHAIR to indicate location or destination.

English sentences typically follow a subject-verb-object sequence, and children learn the rules early. In the example presented earlier, *daddy throw ball,* children use some two-word combinations (*daddy throw, throw ball, daddy ball*) but not others (*ball daddy, ball throw, throw daddy*). Samoan children follow the standard order of possessed-possessor. A child may be sensitive to word order even if his native language does not stress it. Russian children will sometimes adhere strictly to one word order, even when other orders would be equally acceptable.

Some languages provide different word-endings (inflections) to express various meanings, and children who learn these languages are quick to acquire the word-endings that express direct objects, indirect objects and locations. The direct-object inflection is one of the first endings that children pick up in such languages as Russian, Serbo-Croatian, Latvian, Hungarian, Finnish and Turkish. Children learning English, an Indo-European language, usually take a long time to learn locative prepositions such as *on, in, under,* etc. But in Hungary, Finland, or Turkey, where the languages express location with case-endings on the nouns, children learn how to express locative distinctions quite early.

Place Children seem to be attuned to the ends of words. German children learn the inflection system relatively late, probably because it is attached to articles (*der, die, das,* etc.) that appear before the nouns. The Slavic, Hungarian, Finnish and Turkish inflectional systems, based on noun suffixes, seem relatively easy to learn. And it is not just a matter of articles being difficult to learn, because Bulgarian articles which are noun suffixes are learned very early. The relevant factor seems to be the position of the grammatical marker relative to a main content word.

By the time he reaches the end of the two-word stage, the child has much of the basic grammatical machinery he needs to acquire any particular native language: words that can be combined in order and modified by intonation and inflection. These rules occur, in varying degrees, in all languages, so that all languages are about equally easy for children to learn.

Gap When a child first uses three words in one phrase, the third word usually fills in the part that was implicit in his two-word statements. Again, this seems to be a universal pattern of development. It is dramatically explicit when the child expands his own communication as he repeats it: *Want that . . . Andrew want that.*

Just as the two-word structure resulted in idiosyncratic pairings, the three-word stage imposes its own limits. When an English-speaking child wishes to add an adjective to the subject-verb-object form, something must go. He can say *Mama drink coffee* or *Drink hot coffee*, but not *Mama drink hot coffee.* This developmental limitation on sentence span seems to be universal: the child's mental ability to express ideas grows faster than his ability to formulate the ideas in complete sentences. As the child learns to construct longer sentences, he uses more complex grammatical operations. He attaches new elements to old sentences (*Where I can sleep?*) before he learns how to order the elements correctly (*Where can I sleep?*). When the child learns to combine two sentences he first compresses them end-to-end (*the boy fell down that was running*) then finally he embeds one within the other (*the boy that was running fell down*).

Across These are the basic operations of grammar, and to the extent of our present knowledge, they all are acquired by about age four, regardless of native language or social setting. The underlying principles emerge so regularly and so uniformly across diverse languages that they seem to make up an essential part of the child's basic means of information processing. They seem to be comparable to the principles of object constancy and depth perception. Once the child develops these guidelines he spends most of his years of language acquisition learning the specific details and applica-

tions of these principles to his particular native language.

Lapse Inflection systems are splendid examples of the sort of linguistic detail that children must master. English-speaking children must learn the great irregularities of some of our most frequently used words. Many common verbs have irregular past tenses: *came, fell, broke.* The young child may speak these irregular forms correctly the first time—apparently by memorizing a separate past tense form for each verb—only to lapse into immature talk (*comed, falled, breaked*) once he begins to recognize regularities in the way most verbs are conjugated. These over-regularized forms persist for years, often well into elementary school. Apparently regularity heavily outranks previous practice, reinforcement, and imitation of adult forms in influence on children. The child seeks regularity and is deaf to exceptions. [See "Learning the Language," by Ursula Bellugi, PT, December 1970.]

The power of apparent regularities has been noted repeatedly in the children's speech of every language we have studied. When a Russian noun appears as the object of a sentence (*he liked the story*), the speaker must add an accusative suffix to the noun—one of several possible accusative suffixes, and the decision depends on the gender and the phonological form of the particular noun (and if the noun is masculine, he must make a further distinction on whether it refers to a human being). When the same noun appears in the possessive form (*the story's ending surprised him*) he must pick from a whole set of possessive suffixes, and so on, through six grammatical cases, for every Russian noun and adjective.

Grasp The Russian child, of course, does not learn all of this at once, and his gradual, unfolding grasp of the language is instructive. He first learns at the two-word stage that different cases are expressed with different noun-endings. His strategy is to choose one of the accusative inflections and use it in all sentences with direct objects regardless of the peculiarities of individual nouns. He does the same for each of the six grammatical cases. His choice of inflection is always correct within the broad category—that is, the prepositional is always expressed by *some* prepositional inflection, and dative by *some* dative inflection, and so on, just as an English-speaking child always expresses the past tense by a past-tense inflection, and not by some other sort of inflection.

The Russian child does not go from a single suffix for each case to full mastery of the system. Rather, he continues to reorganize his system in successive sweeps of over-regularizations. He may at first use the feminine ending with all accusative nouns, then use the masculine form exclusively for a time, and only much later sort out the appropriate inflections for all genders. These details, after all, have nothing to do with meaning, and it is meaning that children pay most attention to.

Bit   Once a child can distinguish the various semantic notions, he begins to unravel the arbitrary details, bit by bit. The process apparently goes on below the level of consciousness. A Soviet psychologist, D. N. Bogoyavlenskiy, showed five-and six-year-old Russian children a series of nonsense words equipped with Russian suffixes, each word attached to a picture of an object or animal that the words supposedly represented. The children had no difficulty realizing that words ending in augmentative suffixes were related to large objects, and that those ending in diminutives went with small objects. But they could not explain the formal differences aloud. Bogoyavlenskiy would say, "Yes, you were right about the difference between the animals—one is little and the other is big; now pay attention to the words themselves as I say them: *lar-laryonok.* What's the difference between them?" None of the children could give any sort of answer. Yet they easily understood the semantic implications of the suffixes.

Talk   When we began our cross-cultural studies at Berkeley, we wrote a manual for our field researchers so that they could record samples of mother-child interaction in other cultures with the same systematic measures we had used to study language development in middle-class American children. But most of our field workers returned to tell us that, by and large, mothers in other cultures do not speak to children very much—children hear speech mainly from other children. The isolated American middle-class home, in which a mother spends long periods alone with her children, may be a relatively rare social situation in the world. The only similar patterns we observed were in some European countries and in a Mayan village.

This raised an important question: Does it matter—for purposes of grammatical development—whether the main interlocutor for a small child is his mother?

The evidence suggests that it does not. First of all, the rate and course of grammatical development seem to be strikingly similar in all of the cultures we have studied. Further, nowhere does a mother devote great effort to correcting a child's grammar. Most of her corrections are directed at speech etiquette and communication, and, as Roger Brown has noted, reinforcement tends to focus on the truth of a child's utterance rather than on the correctness of his grammar.

Ghetto   In this country, Harvard anthropologist Claudia Mitchell-Kernan has studied language development in black children in an urban ghetto. There, as in foreign countries, children got most of their speech input from older children rather than from their mothers. These children learned English rules as quickly as did the middle-class white children that Roger Brown studied, and in the same order. Further, mother-to-child English is simple—very much like child-to-child English. I expect that our cross-cultural studies will find a similar picture in other countries.

How   A child is set to learn a language—any language—as long as it occurs in a direct and active context. In these conditions, every normal child masters his particular native tongue, and learns basic principles in a universal order common to all children, resulting in our adult Babel of linguistic diversity. And he does all this without being abel to say how. The Soviet scholar Kornei Ivanovich Chukovsky emphasized this unconscious aspect of linguistic discovery in his famous book on child language, *From Two to Five:*

"It is frightening to think what an enormous number of grammatical forms are poured over the poor head of the young child. And he, as if it were nothing at all, adjusts to all this chaos, constantly sorting out into rubrics the disorderly elements of the words he hears, without noticing as he does this, his gigantic effort. If an adult had to master so many grammatical rules within so short a time, his head would surely burst. . . . In truth, the young child is the hardest mental toiler on our planet. Fortunately, he does not even suspect this."

Reading 16

Language Development in Deaf Children

Kathryn P. Meadow

It cannot be emphasized too strongly that the basic deprivation of profound congenital deafness is the deprivation of language and not the deprivation of sound. To those who are unfamiliar with deafness and its consequences, this statement may not have full and immediate impact. It reflects the deaf child's inability to communicate in a fully meaningful way about his needs, his thoughts, his feelings, his experiences. It also means that the significant others in his environment cannot communicate their thoughts, demands, questions, reasons. Often the uninitiated social scientist or lay person believes that the worst consequence of deafness is some degree of unintelligible speech, or a need to resort to written notes in order to clarify some difficult point. We take for granted the fact that a 4-year-old hearing member of any culture has a complete working grasp and knowledge of his native language—a knowledge that he has absorbed, processed, and assimilated without formal didactic tutoring. For most deaf children, a limited grasp of oral communication is acquired at the cost of hour upon hour of intensive tutoring, investment of time, and recurring frustration. Methods of teaching language to deaf children have been the subject of bitter controversy for a period of 200 years or more (Bender 1960; Levine 1969a; Schlesinger 1969). The conflict in this area is an important part of the social and cultural context of the deaf child's development because it influences all the developmental issues related to deafness. The observation that the limits of one's language coincide with the limits of one's world has special meaning for language-deprived children and their parents.

There are several previously published reviews of language development in deaf children (Bonvillian, Charrow, & Nelson 1973; Cooper & Rosenstein 1966; Rosenstein 1961). Each of these can be useful for readers who wish to pursue the subject further. Here, research on language development and deafness is presented under four major headings: "First Language Acquisition," "Acquisition of a 'Second Language,'" "Written Language Used by Deaf Children," and "Evaluation of the Linguistic Milieus of Deaf Children."

FIRST LANGUAGE ACQUISITION

In considering the acquisition of language by deaf children, it is helpful to differentiate among three groups of children: (1) those whose deaf parents use the American Sign Language (Ameslan) as their preferred means of everyday communication, at least within the home, and whose socialization therefore takes place through manual communication; (2) those whose (hearing or deaf) parents use a simultaneous combination of signed and spoken English when they communicate with their deaf child; (3) those whose (hearing) parents use spoken English as their only means of communication with their deaf child and who hope and expect that the child's eventual sole communicative mode is oral English.

1. Linguistic Input: American Sign Language

To be considered in this section are those few studies of language acquisition in deaf children whose linguistic socialization takes place through parental use of American Sign Language, or Ameslan. Ameslan is used by approximately three-quarters of deaf American adults (Rainer et al. 1969). It is a language comprised of combinations of symbolic gestures deriving meaning from the shape of the hand, the location of the hand in relation to the body of the signer, and the movement of the hand or hands. Many of the individual signs symbolize concepts rather than individual words. The derivation of some of the signs was iconic; that is, they were apparently based on natural pantomime gestures. Ameslan has long been a stigmatized language. Many have insisted that it was not a language at all. Linguists have only recently begun to study Ameslan seriously and have found that it does have all the characteristics of language, although there are some differences deriving from crossing of modalities (Bellugi & Klima 1972, 1975; McCall 1965; Stokoe 1960; Stokoe, Casterline, & Croneberg 1965). Parents who make use of Ameslan, as "native signers," are with rare exception deaf themselves. This does not mean, however, that *all* deaf parents use Ameslan to communicate with their deaf children. Some deaf parents themselves use only or mostly spoken English as their primary mode of communication. Other deaf parents may use Ameslan with each other but use only spoken English with their deaf child (Stuckless & Birch 1966). A special characteristic of Ameslan as a "native" or "first" language is that the deaf parents of deaf children have in most cases acquired *their* Ameslan from other deaf children in a residential school after the usual and perhaps optimum age of language acquisition. Their own experiences with early language, and with early family interaction, may have been sparse and even painful. Their ideas about parent-child interaction and linguistic socialization may be quite different from those of the hearing parents whose children were the subjects of previous linguistic studies. It is only recently that the language acquisition of young deaf children has received any systematic attention and analysis. There are only three studies available of features of Ameslan acquisition. These were reported by Bellugi (1972), by Hoffmeister and Morres (1973), and by Schlesinger (Schlesinger & Meadow 1972). Schlesinger followed two children of deaf parents. Ann was observed periodically from 8 months to 22 months of age (Schlesinger & Meadow 1972, pp. 54–68). Karen was observed from age 2-6 to age 3-6 (Schlesinger & Meadow 1972, pp. 70–74). Ann's mother was also the child of deaf parents. She used English syntax in her written English and alternated between English and Ameslan syntax in her signed/spoken communications. Ann's father was more likely than her mother to utilize Ameslan syntax in all his communication.

At the age of 10 months, Ann made some first approximation of recognizable signs; at 12 months she signed "pretty" and "wrong"; at 14 months she added "cat" and "sleep" to her vocabulary and combined "bye sleep." When Ann was 17 months old, nine two-sign combinations were recorded. At age 19 months, she had a vocabulary of 117 signs and five manual letters of the alphabet. At age 19$\frac{1}{2}$ months, her recorded vocabulary was 142 signs and 14 manual alphabet letters. Thus, Ann had more than 100 signs at the age Lenneberg (1967) estimates that a normal hearing child will have acquired no more than 50 spoken words.

Numerous examples are cited in which Ann used one-word utterances in holophrastic ways just as hearing children use spoken words initially. For example, at age 15 months, she used the sign for

smell to mean "I want to go to the bathroom"; "I am soiled, please change"; and "I want the pretty smelling flower." Schlesinger observed a number of immature variations in Ann's early signs comparable with the baby talk found in the early language of hearing children. The nonstandard variations might be in hand configuration, in placement, or in movement. Thus, context plus the remaining standard features were important in deciphering the meaning of the signed utterance.

Schlesinger emphasizes that the style and feeling of the linguistic input have equal importance with the content. The enjoyment apparent in the language interaction in which Ann and her mother participated were a striking contrast with that observed for many deaf children with their mothers. She suggests that understanding of early meaning, combined with an enjoyment of mother-child communicative events, may represent a necessary feature of normal language development. This theme is elaborated in a later paper on the language development of deaf children (Schlesinger 1972).

The language of the second child in the Schlesinger study, Karen, was analyzed from a body of 200 combinations of two or more signs collected over a period of 8 months. The primary focus of this analysis was a comparison with previously published accounts of children's open and pivot word combinations. Pivot words had been defined as a small group of words used frequently by the young child presumably either first *or* last in two-word combinations. The pivot word would be combined with an unlimited number of open words. Pivot words are more like adult function words (e.g., prepositions), while open words are more like adult content words (e.g., nouns and verbs). Schlesinger's data supported those of several other investigators who were beginning to question the strict definition of the pivot in child language. Karen's pivot signs were found to occur alone as well as in combination with other open signs and in combination with other pivots. Likewise, pivot signs were found sometimes first and sometimes last in two-sign combinations (Schlesinger & Meadow 1972).

Bellugi (1967) was among the first to study the process of child language acquisition among hearing children. More recently she has looked at the (sign) language acquisition of deaf children. A report based on these studies suggests that deaf children learning sign language are systematic, regular, and productive in their language just as were the hearing children studied earlier (Bellugi & Klima 1972). One child, Pola, provided their initial data on sign language acquisition. Her sign vocabulary apparently covered the full range of concepts expressed by hearing children of a comparable age. Like hearing children, Pola appeared to overgeneralize linguistic rules initially, applying them too broadly at first, but later learning appropriate restrictions on the general linguistic rules. Before she was 3 years old, Pola used spontaneously the signs for name, stay, tomorrow, will, where, who, what, how, dead, know, understand, none, nothing, don't know, and letters of the manual alphabet. Her early sign combinations expressed the full range of semantic relations found in the expressions of hearing children. The increase in the length of her signed expression matched the increase seen in hearing children. Bellugi and Klima conclude (1972) that in spite of the difference in modality the milestones of language development may be the same in the deaf as in the hearing child.

Hoffmeister and Moores (1973) studied the initial language interaction of Alice and her deaf mother at 1-month intervals from the time she was 25 months old until she was 28 months of age. Eight 30-minute videotapes were transcribed and analyzed for the development of the use of the "pointing action" by Alice. The authors concluded that the pointing action was a separate linguistic unit, glossed as "that" or "this." As such it was used in a way very similar to the use of demonstrative pronouns by normal hearing children, but with more apparent precision of meaning. Although normal hearing children use pointing as a gesture, with Alice variations in pointing indicated differential meanings. From their observations of Alice, Hoffmeister and Moores conclude that specific reference, through the pointing action referring to "this" or "that," is an initial stage of sign language acquisition.

The differences between Alice's pointing "sign" and the pointing "gesture" used by hearing children would seem to be difficult to decipher. However, Bellugi and Klima (1975) are working on this very problem with adult signers. That is, they are attempting to develop criteria for differentiating between pantomime and sign. They have observed that certain elements must remain recognizable and constant if a gesture is to be considered to be a specific sign. While Hoffmeister and Moores seem to be observing the same phenomenon in Alice's

"this" and "that," the exact differences are nebulous and difficult to pinpoint.

2. Linguistic Input: Bimodal English

A few children who are deaf receive a simultaneous combination of signed plus spoken English as their earliest parental language input. They are the children whose (usually hearing) parents have elected to learn manual communication in some modified version of American Sign Language. Until the very recent past, the use of sign language in any form was seen as an admission of failure on the part of the deaf child, his parents, and his teachers. Since manual communication was believed to interfere with the acquisition of speech and lipreading skills, parents feared to use either nonsystematic gestures or systematic signs. In recent years, the phrase "total communication" has come to be utilized to refer to a communicative mode that combines speech, lipreading, amplification, and the simultaneous use of one of several manual sign systems. Schlesinger (1974) has suggested the term "bimodalism" as a substitute. The manual sign systems are derived from the basic signs of American Sign Language. The variations in the different systems are for the purpose of providing a means for signing a direct and precise gloss of spoken English rather than utilizing the different syntax of American Sign Language. The initial efforts in this direction began in 1962 with the work of Anthony (1966). Bornstein (1973) summarizes four major and competing sign systems currently being developed by groups in different parts of the United States: Signing Exact English, Seeing Essential English, Linguistics of Visual English, and Signed English (Gustason, Pfetzing, & Zawolkow 1972; Kannapell, Hamilton, & Bornstein 1969; O'Rourke 1970). The four systems differ in several ways, but primarily in the extent to which they incorporate traditional signs and in the method for forming the auxiliary verbs, pronouns, articles, and so forth that are not used in American Sign Language. The Rochester Method is another variant of the total communication idea. It utilizes a combination of speech and simultaneous finger spelling (Scouten 1967).

Schlesinger followed the language development of two children, Ruth and Marie, whose hearing parents were utilizing signed and spoken English as well as hearing aids and speech training. Ruth was observed and videotaped from the age of 2-8 to 3-5. Her deafness had been diagnosed at the age of 9 months, and her parents began to learn and to use total communication when she was 15 months old. At 3 years of age. Ruth's vocabulary included a total of 348 words: at 3-4 she had a vocabulary of 604 words, including one or more in each form class. On the basis of three tests of grammatical complexity administered when Ruth was 3, Schlesinger concluded that Ruth was following the same order of grammatical emergence in signed and spoken language that hearing children have previously demonstrated (Schlesinger & Meadow 1972).

Marie was adopted by a hearing family at the age of 6½ months and diagnosed as a deaf child before the age of 12 months. Her parents began to use manual communication with her when she was 3-1; she was followed by Schlesinger from the age of 3-4 to 5-3 (Schlesinger & Meadow 1972, pp. 82–86). Data on Marie's language showed that she was incorporating English syntax, using appropriately such characteristics as plurals and tense that are not part of Ameslan (e.g., "popped" and "broken" at 3-4; glasses, teachers, potatoes, shared, stabbed, working at age 3-5½. Marie's mother played many finger-spelling anagram games with her. At the age of 4-5 Marie demonstrated that she was able to transfer her finger-spelling games to reading material. Marie also gave evidence of the acquisition of negation in the same sequence as has been observed in hearing children in the past. Her lipreading score at age 3-10½ was well above the average score for a 5-year-old.

Analysis of early linguistic samples from these children demonstrated the similarities in their acquisition of bimodal language and the acquisition of spoken English by hearing children. Schlesinger's report of data collected somewhat later in the acquisition process illustrates a fascinating difference between these bimodal deaf children and previously observed hearing children. The difference is related to the perceptual salience of various morphemes in visual and auditory modalities. Hearing children typically acquire the "ing" ending for the present progressive before they learn to use the accompanying auxiliary verb (e.g., "girl running" is used for a period before "girl is running"). Apparently hearing children using oral or spoken language pay more attention to the endings of words. This principle did not apply as forcefully for some of the bimodal youngsters studied and may be related to the perceptual salience of various morphemes in the visual or the auditory mode. The

perceptual salience appears to be directly related to the amount of residual hearing and to the precision and frequency with which the child's parents use the morphemic modulations in sign language. Thus the child with the most useable residual hearing acquired the "ing" ending very much as hearing children do, although the auxiliary verb appeared more quickly in the deaf child. Another child subject who is *profoundly* deaf acquired the "ing" and the auxiliary simultaneously. The third youngster, also profoundly deaf but whose linguistic input was less precise for the use of the morphemic modulations, persisted in the use of the auxiliary alone with no trace of the "ing" form for a long period of time. Schlesinger relates these data to Brown's (1973) idea that the relatively late acquisition of the possessive form in hearing children may result from the indistinct and frequently slurred nature of the spoken form.

3. Linguistic Input: Oral English Only

By far the largest number of deaf children (practically all those with hearing parents, or approximately 90% of the total number) have had their initial exposure to language through oral or spoken English. Most parents and educators are committed to the "oral-only" approach to language acquisition for deaf children. There are several methods used. One, called acoupedics, places exclusive reliance on training the deaf child to use his residual hearing. This is also called the unisensory approach because all visual cues, including lipreading, are avoided. Mothers are counseled that they must not accept the idea that their children cannot hear because this implies resignation and will lead eventually to reliance on gestures. Proponents indicate that the program is designed for children who have an average aided hearing loss of less than 60 decibels (Pollock 1964). The Verbotonal approach, developed by Guberina in Yugoslavia, also emphasizes the use of residual hearing (Craig, Craig, & DiJohnson 1972).

Most educators, however, include lipreading within their definition of oral-only approaches to language acquisition. There is a strong commitment to the belief in an exclusively oral environment, which means the conscious elimination of any meaningful gestures from the child's linguistic input during the critical period of language development (DiCarlo 1962). For example, the deaf child would not be allowed to *wave* goodbye because the wave is a meaningful gesture (John Tracy Clinic 1954). The reasoning behind the oral-only approach is that the deaf child who is permitted to use an easier gesture communication system will not work to acquire the harder oral skills of lipreading and speech. Despite the firm convictions attached to what Furth (1966b) has called the myth of least effort, it is only recently that any attempts have been made to test the theory empirically.

Most of the many studies of various aspects of the language development and deficiencies of deaf children have as their subjects children whose early linguistic input was largely unintelligible and therefore meaningless. Much of what is written about language development of the young deaf child is based on nonsystematic observational anecdotal material. There is, it would seem, unanimous consensus that the young deaf child exposed to the difficult spoken English environment is extremely impoverished. DiCarlo comments (1964) that a 5-year-old deaf child probably has fewer than 25 words in his vocabulary unless he has had intensive language instruction. Hodgson (1953) believes that only the unusual 4- or 5-year-old deaf child knows as many as 200 words, whereas the hearing child can be expected to know about 2,000 words at that age. The normal hearing child has been estimated to produce and respond to three words at age I, 272 words at age 2, 896 words at age 3, and 1,540 words at age 4 (Vetter 1970).

Schlesinger and Meadow (1972) collected language data for 40 deaf and 20 hearing preschoolers. They found that 75% of the deaf children had a language age of 28 months or less when their mean age was 44 months. All of the hearing children scored at the expected age level.

The usual booming buzzing confusion of language is greatly increased for the deaf child. For the orally trained deaf child, reinforcement is not selective. Because his verbalizations are usually grossly distorted and often misunderstood, he often receives inappropriate and contradictory reactions from others. These inconsistent responses to his speech often produce bewilderment and may actually inhibit his future efforts to produce spoken language. He finds it more difficult to generalize, he fails to develop linguistic discrimination, he lacks both primary and secondary reinforcement for his language. It is not surprising that his vocabulary and his language are grossly retarded (DiCarlo 1964). The painfully laborious nature of language

acquisition in these circumstances may help to explain not only the impoverished nature of the deaf child's language, but also the absence of any systematic studies of deaf children whose input is spoken English. Furthermore, it has been suggested that discouraging the deaf child's attempts to communicate through the use of natural gestures may well dampen his curiosity about the world around him, thus impeding his capacity for formal cognitive development (Chess et al. 1971).

McNeill (1965) has speculated about the possible effect of the difficulty and delay experienced by deaf children in language acquisition. He suggests that the capacity to acquire language may be transitory, peaking between the ages of 2 and 4, and declining after that. McNeill also points to the greater difficulty experienced in the acquisition of a second language after puberty. These points lead him to observe that early language acquisition for the deaf child is especially crucial.

The production of speech cannot be separated from the reception of speech. Too often, in discussions of deaf children, this is forgotten. There are three aspects to speech development: the learning of motor skills, the mastery of cues for recognition, and the building of linguistic knowledge that is basic to both production and reception (Fry 1966). Available studies of the development of speech and speechreading (or lipreading) skills in deaf children have been conducted, with few exceptions, with oral-only children as subjects. These studies often equate speech development with language development.

Apparently the initial vocalizations of deaf infants have the same tonal quality as those of hearing infants. The one published study touching on early vocalization included only one deaf infant, however (Lenneberg, Rebelsky, & Nichols 1965). The researchers analyzed tape recordings of babies in deaf and in hearing homes. They concluded that crying and cooing depend upon maturational readiness rather than on environmental stimulation. Anecdotal accounts indicate that while deaf babies cry and coo normally at birth, the cooing gradually lessens and is no longer heard after the age of about 6 months. Of seven children whose speech development was followed beginning when they were between the ages of 11 and 32 months, none was judged to have normal vocal quality at the beginning of their training (Lach et al. 1970). After 12 months of training, five of the seven were judged to have normal voices. However, none of the children had produced more than 10 words during the year of training.

The interdependence of all linguistic skills is illustrated when studies of the speechreading skills of deaf children are evaluated. Speechreading has been found to correlate with both written language and with reading ability, although these correlations have not been entirely consistent from one study to another. O'Neill and Davidson (1956) found no relationship to reading but Craig (1964), Myklebust (1960), and Neyhus (1969) report significant positive correlations. Speechreading has received a great deal of attention from researchers attempting to unravel the mystery of the relative abilities of deaf persons to utilize this method. Of the many factors investigated, amount of residual hearing is the only one which continues to bear an unequivocal positive relationship to the ability to read lips (Donnelly 1969; Farwell 1975). It may well be that the contradictory nature of the results of investigations of other areas may be due to inconsistencies in the selection of research subjects in terms of some of the subtleties of the audiological variables.

Variability of reported correlations between IQ test scores and speechreading ability is great. Most researchers have reported low positive but nonsignificant correlations (Butt & Chreist 1968; Lewis 1972; O'Neill & Davidson 1956; Reid 1947; Simmons 1959). Others have considered the influence of visual synthesis, visual closure, visual memory, concept formation, and rhythm. Most studies report positive correlations between speechreading and chronological age. The fact that the correlations are generally low indicates, however, that speechreading is not a naturally developing compensatory phenomenon. The effects of training on speechreading ability are also unclear. However, training does not appear to have long-term positive effects on speechreading proficiency (Black, O'Reilly, & Peck 1963; Craig 1964; Heider & Heider 1940).

SUMMARY

1 The basic deprivation of deafness is the difficulty it produces for the process of normal language acquisition. This includes the basic inner language abilities as well as the more superficial oral language skills of speech and speechreading.

2 Language acquisition was reviewed for three categories of deaf children whose linguistic milieus and parental inputs differed. The first group includes deaf children of deaf parents who use the American Sign Language, or Ameslan, only in the home. The few existing studies illustrate some of the variations that occur when linguistic socialization takes place in a visual rather than an auditory mode, relying on some features of visual salience. Initial holophrastic usage, progress in combining two or more signs, usage of pivot and open signs, and overgeneralization of first-learned language rules were all similar to observations reported for hearing children.

3 Deaf children of deaf or hearing parents who use some simultaneous combination of signed and spoken English develop bimodal expressive language. Vocabulary growth, grammatical complexity, and syntactical structure all progress in the same way as in hearing children.

4 Deaf children whose parents use oral English only have not received systematic study in terms of the process of their language acquisition. Studies of the language proficiency of these children at various ages make it clear that acquisition is painfully slow. Linguistic retardation continues through adolescence and remains a factor among most deaf adults.

5 Analyses of the written language of deaf children have shown that the vocabulary is limited and sentence structure is simpler and more rigid than for hearing children of the same ages.

6 Analyses of studies that can be utilized for either direct or inferential evidence about the efficacy of various methods of linguistic socialization for deaf children show no reason to support continuing dedication to an oral-only approach. Children exposed to early manual or simultaneous manual-oral input appear to develop more adequate inner language with no reduction in their abilities to use speech and speechreading for communication than do children not so exposed.

REFERENCES

Anthony, C. A. Signing essential English. Unpublished master's thesis, Eastern Michigan University, 1966.

Bellugi, U. The acquisition of negation. Unpublished doctoral dissertation, Harvard University, 1967.

Bellugi, U. Studies in sign language. In T. J. O'Rourke (Ed.), *Psycholinguistics and total communication: the state of the art.* Washington, D. C.: American Annals of the Deaf, 1972.

Bellugi, U., & Klima, E. S. The roots of language in the

sign talk of the deaf. *Psychology Today,* 1972, *6,* 661–64, 76.

Bellugi, U., & Klima, E. S. *Aspects of sign language and its structure.* Cambridge, Mass.: M. I. T. Press, 1975.

Bender, R. E. *The conquest of deafness.* Cleveland: Press of Western Reserve University, 1960.

Black, J. W.; O'Reilly, P. P.; & Peck, L. Self-administered training in lipreading. *Journal of Speech and Hearing Disorders,* 1963, *28,* 183–186.

Bonvillian, J. D.; Charrow, V. R.; & Nelson, K. E. Psycholinguistic and educational implications of deafness. *Human Development,* 1973, *16,* 321–345.

Bornstein, H. A description of some current sign systems designed to represent English. *American Annals of the Deaf,* 1973, *118,* 454–463.

Brown, R. *A first language, the early stages.* Cambridge, Mass.: Harvard University Press, 1973.

Butt, D., & Chreist, F. M. A speechreading test for young children. *Volta Review,* 1968, *70,* 225–235.

Chess, S.; Korn, S. J.; & Fernandez, P. B. *Psychiatric disorders of children with congenital rubella.* New York: Brunner/Mazel, 1971.

Cooper, R. L., & Rosenstein, J. Language acquisition of deaf children. *Volta Review,* 1966, *68,* 58–67.

Craig, W. N. Effects of pre-school training on the development of reading and lipreading skills of deaf children. *American Annals of the Deaf,* 1964, *109,* 280–296.

Craig, W. N.; Craig, H. B.; & DiJohnson, A. Pre-school verbotonal instruction for deaf children. *Volta Review,* 1972, *74,* 236–246.

DiCarlo, L. M. *The deaf.* Englewood Cliffs, N. J.: Prentice-Hall, 1964.

Donnelly, K. An investigation into the determinants of lipreading of deaf adults. *International Audiology,* 1969, *8,* 501–508.

Farwell, R. M. Speechreading, a review of the research. *American Annals of the Deaf.* 1975 (in press).

Fry, D. B. The development of the phonological system in the normal and the deaf child. In F. Smith & G. A. Miller (Eds.), *The genesis of language: a psycholinguistic approach.* Cambridge, Mass.: M. I. T. Press, 1966.

Furth, H. G. *Thinking without language: psychological implications of deafness.* New York: Free Press, 1966. (b)

Gustason, G.; Pfetzing, D.; & Zawolkow, E. *Signing exact English.* Rossmoor, Calif.: Modern Signs Press, 1972.

Heider, F., & Heider, G. M. Studies in the psychology of the deaf, No. 1 Psychological Division, Clarke School for the Deaf. *Psychological Monographs,* 1940, *52,* No. 232.

Hoffmeister, R. J., & Moores, D. F. The acquisition of specific reference in the linguistic system of a deaf child of deaf parents. Research Report No. 53, Research, Development and Demonstration Center in Education of Handicapped Children, University of Minnesota, August 1973.

John Tracy Clinic. Correspondence course for parents of little deaf children. Mimeographed. Los Angeles: John Tracy Clinic, 1954.

Kannapell, B. M.; Hamilton, L. B.; & Bornstein, H. *Signs for instructional purposes.* Washington, D. C.: Gallaudet College Press, 1969.

Lach, R.; Ling, D.; Ling, A. H.; & Ship, N. Early speech development in deaf infants. *American Annals of the Deaf,* 1970, *115,* 522–526.

Lenneberg, E. H. *Biological foundations of language.* New York: Wiley, 1967.

Lenneberg, E. H.; Rebelsky, F. G.; & Nichols, I. A. The vocalization of infants born to deaf and to hearing parents. *Human Development,* 1965, *8,* 23–37.

Levine, E. S. Historical review of special education and mental health services. In J. D. Rainer, K. Z. Altshuler, & F. J. Kallmann (Eds.), *Family and mental health problems in a deaf population* (2d ed.) Springfield, Ill.: Thomas, 1969.(a)

Lewis, D. N. Lipreading skills of hearing impaired children in regular schools. *Volta Review,* 1972, *74,* 303–311.

McCall, E. A generative grammar of signs. Unpublished master's thesis, University of Iowa, 1965.

McNeill, D. The capacity for language acquisition. In Vocational Rehabilitation Administration, Research on behavioral aspects of deafness, Proceedings of a National Research Conference on behavioral aspects of deafness. New Orleans. May 1965.

Myklebust, H. R. *The psychology of deafness, sensory deprivation, learning and adjustment.* New York: Grune & Stratton, 1960.

Neyhus, A. *Speechreading failure in deaf children.* Washington, D. C.: Office of Education, Department of Health, Education, and Welfare, 1969.

O'Neill, J. J., & Davidson, J. L. Relationship between lipreading and five psychological factors. *Journal of Speech and Hearing Disorders,* 1956, 21, 478–481.

O'Rourke, T. J. *A basic course in manual communication.* Silver Spring, Md.: National Association of the Deaf, 1970.

Pollack, D. Acoupedies: a unisensory approach to auditory training. *Volta Review,* 1964, *66,* 400–409.

Rainer, J. D.; Altshuler, K. Z.; & Kallmann, F. J. (Eds.) *Family and mental health problems in a deaf population* (2d ed.) Springfield, Ill.: Thomas, 1969.

Reid, G. W. A preliminary investigation of the testing of lipreading achievement. *Journal of Speech and Hearing Disorders,* 1947, *12,* 77–82.

Rosenstein, J. Perception, cognition, and language in deaf children. *Exceptional Children,* 1961, *27,* 276–284.

Schlesinger, H. S. Beyond the range of sound. *California Medicine,* 1969, *110,* 213–217.

Schlesinger, H. S. Meaning and enjoyment: language acquisition of deaf children. In T. J. O'Rourke (Ed.), *Psycholinguistics and total communication: the state of the art*. Washington, D. C.: American Annals of the Deaf, 1972.

Schlesinger, H. S. The acquisition of sign language. Unpublished manuscript, Department of Psychiatry, University of California, San Francisco, 1974.

Schlesinger, H. S., & Meadow, K. P. *Sound and sign: childhood deafness and mental health*. Berkeley: University of California Press, 1972.

Scouten, E. L. The Rochester method, an oral multisensory approach for instructing prelingual deaf children. *American Annals of the Deaf*, 1967, *112*, 50–55.

Simmons, A. A. Factors related to lipreading. *Journal of Speech and Hearing Research*, 1959, *2*, 340–352.

Stokoe, W. C., Jr. *Sign language structure: an outline of the visual communication systems of the American deaf*. (Studies in linguistics, occasional papers, 8) Buffalo, N. Y.: Department of Anthropology and Linguistics, University of Buffalo, 1960.

Stokoe, W. C., Jr.; Casterline, D. C.; & Croneberg, C. G. *A dictionary of American Sign Language on linguistic principles*. Washington, D. C.: Gallaudet College Press, 1965.

Stuckless, E. R., & Birch, J. W. The influence of early manual communication on the linguistic development of deaf children. *American Annals of the Deaf*, 1966, *III*, 452–460, 499–504.

Vetter, H. J. *Language behavior and psychopathology*. Chicago: Rand-McNally, 1970.

Reading 17

Code Switching in Children's Language[1]

Jean Berko Gleason

Somewhere along the road to language acquisition children must gain control over not only a vast vocabulary and a complicated grammar, but a variety of styles of speaking to different people under differing circumstances. The code for addressing a policeman who has just stopped you for speeding is not the same as the code for addressing either little babies or old friends; and anyone studying adult language who restricts himself to one or another of these situations would obviously have only a part of the picture of the complexity and variety that exists in adult language. Paradoxically, until recent times, those of us who have studied child language have restricted ourselves to samples of the child's language to us, the interviewer, or to the child's mother or teacher, and we have assumed that that was it: child language. Whether children, like adults, have control of several codes, and vary their speech in accordance with the situation they are in or the person they are addressing has become an area of increasing interest to a number of researchers in the past few years. In order to investigate code switching in children's language, it is necessary to observe the same child in a number of different speech situations.

This chapter is a preliminary report on a study that Elliot Mishler and I conducted. The findings are observational, rather than quantitative; and it is my hope that experiments with hard data and statistically meaningful results will follow.

In order to investigate the child's emerging control of different styles or codes, we began with the study of the natural conversations that occur in families with several children; this enabled us to study the way that parents alter their style in speaking to children of different ages and sexes, and it put the children in a natural position to a variety of addressees: their parents, ourselves, other children, and babies.

Our basic data were collected from five similarly constituted families who have children attending a private school in Cambridge, Massachusetts. Each of these families has at least three children: a first- or second-grader; a preschool child aged 4 or 5; and an even younger child under the age of 3. All of these families are well-educated and upper middle-class. Most of the data were taped in the families' homes in two 1-hour sessions by Sara Harkness, a doctoral candidate in social anthropology at Har-

[1]This research was supported in part by Grant GS-3001 from the National Science Foundation to Elliot Mishler. The paper was written while I was a senior research associate in the Laboratory of Social Psychiatry at the Harvard Medical School. I am grateful to Dr. Mishler for many of the insights reported here.

vard, or by myself and Elliot Mishler, head of the Laboratory of Social Psychiatry at the Harvard Medical School. In addition to these tapes we have recorded one other family whose children attend public school in another community. Finally, I made extensive recordings of the 4-year-old son of one of the five families in several different settings: in his own home with his parents; outdoors with his younger and older brothers; at my home talking to me and playing with my 8-year-old daughter, Cindy; and at his nursery school with his friends and teachers. For this one 4-year-old, at least, I have captured a broad variety of speech situations and the stylistic variations that attend them.

ADULT LANGUAGE TO CHILDREN

Since we were observing families, it was inevitable that our sample contain a great deal of language to children from adults, and we examined this adult language for evidence of stylistic variation. Since this adult language is the basic input to the child, some understanding of it is prerequisite to understanding the full significance of the children's productions. It is important to know, for instance, which codes are the children's own, passed on by the peer group, and which codes are passed to the child by adults. Therefore, before discussing the children's language some description of the salient features of the adult codes is in order.

The adults use baby-talk style in talking to the babies. The features of this style have been well reported by others but, briefly, we can say they raised the fundamental frequency of their voices, used simple short sentences with concrete nouns, diminutives, and terms of endearment, expanded the children's utterances, and in general performed the linguistic operations that constitute baby-talk style. There was a lot of individual variation in the extent to which all of these features might be employed. One mother, for instance, spoke in a normal voice to her husband, a high voice to her 4-year-old, a slightly raised voice to her 8-year-old, and when she talked to her baby she fairly squeaked. Fathers and mothers did not talk in exactly the same way to the babies, and there seemed to be some sex differences, as well, in how the babies were addressed. Some of the boy babies were addressed, especially by their fathers, in a sort of hail-baby-well-met style: While turning them

upside down or engaged in similar play, the fathers said things like "Come here, you little nut!" or "Hey fruitcake!" Baby girls were dealt with more gently, both physically and verbally.

Adults used a quite different style to the children who were no longer babies, although there were some common features—the use of endearments, for instance. Both children and babies might be called "sweetie" or have their names played with—one baby was called "funny bunny," for instance, and in a different family a 5-year-old girl was called "Huffy Muffy," so this kind of rhyming play is not uncommon. Otherwise, once the little children's language was comprehensible, expansion and similar devices dropped out while other features assumed salience. Several of these features might be sketched here.

The language addressed to the children we saw who were between the ages of 4 and 8 was basically a language of socialization, and it was a very controlling language in so far as it told the child what to do, what to think, and how to feel.

Although the language was not rich in actual imperatives, the implied imperatives abounded; a mother might say to a child: "Do you want to take your own plate off the table, sweetie?" when the child really had no options in the matter. We saw a lot of dinner-table interaction because we were hoping to get samples of the father's speech as well, and this talk contained many instructions on sitting up, not throwing forks, and generally, how to behave.

The parents typically spelled out explicitly the dangers of situations: a mother might place the food in front of a child while saying, "hot, hot!" One does not give boiling hot food to a little baby, and hostesses do not say, "hot, hot!" as they serve their dinner guests, so this is a special situation. A hostess might, of course, say "Watch out for this dish—it's just out of the oven."

In their conversations with the children of this age, parents typically supplied the entire context. If they asked a question, they included with it the answer. We have, for instance, the following: a father comes to pick up his son at nursery school and says: "Where's your lunchbox? I bet it's inside," or the following conversation between a mother and her 5-year-old son:

Mother: *How was school today? Did you go to assembly?*

Son: *Yes.*

Mother: *Did the preschoolers go to assembly?*

Son: *Yes.*

Mother: *Did you stay for the whole assembly or just part of it?*

The child really does not have to do anything but say yes or no—the mother is providing the whole conversation herself, and, undoubtedly, in the process, teaching him to make a conversation and what kind of responses are expected of him.

Another feature of this adult to child language was that the adults frequently exaggerated their responses, almost beyond reason, or reacted in the way they thought the child ought to feel. For instance, the following:

A child in nursery school fills a bucket with a hose. The teacher says: "Hey, wow, that's almost full to the *top!*"

A child shows his mother some old toys that he has just been given by another child. The mother whoops with joy.

A child shows his father a simple model he has made. The father says: "Hey, that's *really* something, isn't it?"

A child tells a neighbor he has been to the circus. The neighbor says: "Boy! That must have been fun."

Since full buckets, old toys, simple models, and even the circus do not really impress adults that much, they must be telling the child how *he* ought to feel.

These are only a few of the special features of the language of socialization.

The transition from this directive socializing language to the colloquial style used by adult familiars is not easily accomplished. Quite to the contrary, parents often persist in addressing their 8-year-olds as if they were 4, much to the dismay of the children. From what we have seen, it is actually because of signals from the child, often very explicit and angry signals, that the adult ceases to address him as if he were very little. Mothers, for instance, typically spell out all the dangers of the situation to young children, as I have said. At some point the child begins to act quite disgusted with what the parents say. When the mother tells him to be careful crossing the street, he says something like, "O. K., O. K., I *know* how to cross the street." This angry negative feedback to her utterances in the

language of socialization eventually teaches her to address him in a different style, and perhaps only mention that traffic is very heavy that day. Of course some parents never do seem to understand the angry signals and continue telling their children to wear their rubbers until they are 35.

THE CHILDREN'S LANGUAGE

The children in our sample ranged in age from infancy to 8 years. By and large we were not primarily looking for evidence of baby-talk style. Some things did seem readily evident from observing the very young children and talking to their parents, however. The first is that even the tiniest children make some distinctions. The basic, earliest variation is simply between talking and not talking. Very small children will frequently talk or jabber nonsense to their own parents or siblings, but fall silent in the presence of strangers. When the parent tries to get the baby to say, "Hi," or "Bye-bye," to the interviewer, the baby stares blankly; and the mother says, "I don't know what's wrong. He really can talk. He says bye-bye all the time." The baby remains silent. After the interviewer leaves, surrounded once more by familiar faces, the baby suddenly springs to life and says a resounding "Bye-bye!" So the first variation is between speech and silence.

Another, more obviously stylistic variation we have seen in the language of the children under 4 as well as those over 4, has been the selective use of whining, by which I mean a repetitive, insistent, singsong demand or complaint, and not crying, which is very difficult for little children to inhibit. The whining basically occurs to parents and parent figures, and a child may abruptly switch to a whine at the sight of his parent, when he has previously been talking to someone else in a quite normal tone. In the nursery school I visited, for instance, one child was talking with his friends when his father arrived. At the sight of his father, he abruptly altered his tone and began to whine, "Pick me up" at him.

In listening to the tapes of the children's speech, we had in mind the generally recognized kinds of language style that linguists talk about. Baby-talk style, peer-group colloquial style, and a more formal style for talking to older people and strangers seemed to be three kinds of codes that all adults have and that we might expect to see emerging in the children as they grow older. We thought that the interviewers or other strange adults would bring out the formal style; that the other children of about the same age—close siblings and the many friends who appeared—would bring out the colloquial style; and that baby-talk style would begin to emerge in the language of these children when they talked to the babies in their families.

We did not originally count on the presence of the language of socialization, but it soon became evident that it was there in many cases where children were talking to somewhat younger children. Part of a conversation between my 8-year-old daughter, Cindy, and the 4-year-old I was studying went as follows. She wanted to give him some of her toys, and she said, "Would you like to have some for you at your house?" When he agreed, she said, "Now you just carry them home, and don't run." She then helped him across the street to his house, and when they got there said, "Ricky, you want to show your mother? You want to show your mother that you got these?"

He said, "Yeah. For me." And she replied, "You share them." We have many other instances of older children talking to younger children this way.

We have no real instances of these children using typical adult formal style, probably in part at least because we, as interviewers, were familiar to them and part of their own community. We failed to be formidable strangers, and the parents addressed us in familiar ways as well, so there was very little in the way of formal greetings and farewells, or politeness formulas. Only in one family did we get anything like formal language, and this was the one family outside our Cambridge private school sample that Elliot Mishler and I visited together. In this family, our language and the language of the family proved far more formal. The mother, for example, said to us after we had come in "Have a seat. It's the best one in the house." We had brought some small toys for the children in the family, and the first-grade boy approached Dr. Mishler somewhat later and said, "Thank you for bringing the presents" in a very formal way, with pauses between the words, careful enunciation, and a flat, affectless tone. The other families treated us in a far more colloquial way.

While it was not marked by adult formal features, the children's language to us had its own character-

istics. Ricky, the 4-year-old, who said to his father things like "I wanna be up on your shoulder" *fourteen times* in a row, gave me the following explanation of the tooth fairy:

Uh, well, you see, if your teeth come out, the teeth come back and by, uh, a fairy. And, you see, the teeth that came out you have to put under your pillow, and then the fairy comes and takes 'em, you see, and he leaves a little money or a little candy.

This language is far more narrative and far more didactic than anything he directed at either his parents or other children. This is clearly different speech.

The style the children employed in talking to one another was markedly different from their style to adults or to babies, especially in those cases where they were playing together. This peer-group style included a very rich use of expressive words like "yukk" and "blech," and of sound effects. Our tapes are full of bangs, sirens, airplane noises, animal sounds, and explosions. There are some sex differences, since the boys played more violent games and accompanied them with appropriate sounds, but the girls made a lot of noises as well.

The children playing together often launched into chants, rhymes, television commercials, theme songs of favorite shows, and animal acts. They frequently took off from what they were saying into dramatic play involving changing their voices and pretending they were other people or other creatures. This peer-group language was very different from the language directed at adults. Other features of this child-to-child language that might be mentioned are the very frequent use of first names, as in adult-child language, but no endearments, even in those cases where a somewhat older child was speaking to a somewhat younger one as if she were a parent, as I mentioned before. Finally, there was a striking amount of copying behavior in the children's utterances; many instances of one child saying just what another child has said, without any change in emphasis or structure. For instance, the following example from the nursery school:

She: *Well, don't you want to see the raspberries?*

Malcolm: *How 'bout you pick some for me and I'll eat them?*

Eric: *Yeah, and how 'bout pick some for me and I'll eat them?*

The third child adds *yeah, and* to the second child's statement and then repeats it. An adult would not have repeated *and I'll eat them* under the same circumstances, although he might have said, "How 'bout picking some for *me*?" Eric's repetition is quite flat—the intonation contours are the same as Malcolm's, and there is no shift of emphasis. He is really not varying the statement so much as echoing it. Where an adult says just what another adult has said, his intention is usually mockery, but for the children, imitation of this sort is very common, and passes unremarked.

The children's language to the babies in the families was also examined for evidence of baby-talk style. While most of the features of peer group code appeared in the language of the entire 4- to 8-year-old sample, there were age differences in the ability to use baby-talk style. The older children were in control of the basic features of baby-talk style—their sentences to the babies were short and repetitive, and uttered in a kind of singing style. In one family I asked an 8-year-old to ask his 2-year-old brother to take a glass to the kitchen. He said:

"Here, Joey, take this to the kitchen. Take it to the kitchen." (Baby-talk intonation, high voice.)

A little while later, I asked him to ask his 4-year-old brother to take a glass to the kitchen. This time he said:

"Hey, Rick, take this to the kitchen, please." (Normal intonation.) This is clear evidence of code switching in the language of this 8-year-old child.

On the other end of the spectrum, the 4-year-old, Ricky, whom I followed about, did not use baby-talk style to his 2-year-old brother. He typically did not use either a special intonation or repetition. He said to the baby: "Do you know what color your shoes are?" in just the same way he said: "What's the name of the book, Anthony?" to his brother; and "I don't think he know how to climb up" to his father.

Somewhere in between no baby-talk style and full baby-talk style lies slightly inappropriate baby-talk style, which we saw particularly in some 5- and 6-year-old girls. Unlike the 4-year-olds, 5- and 6-year-old children made clear efforts to adjust their language to suit the babies they addressed. We have the following conversation:

2-year-old: *Dead bug!*

6-year-old: *That ant!*

2-year-old: *That bug!*

6-year-old: *Hey, Susie, that's ant; that's not bug, that ant!*

The 6-year-old is here obviously trying to accommodate the baby sister by talking in what she regards as "her language," but she misses the cues when she says "That's ant." Good baby sentences would be either "That ant," as the child says, or "That a ant," but a copula without an article in "That's ant" doesn't ring true.

Listening to these children begin to use baby-talk style and then use it fluently by the time they are 7 or 8 makes it clear that knowing how to talk to babies is not something you keep with you from having been a baby; you have to learn it again. The young children in the sample who were still completing their knowledge of regular English syntax were in no position to play with it. They made their sentences the only way they knew how, grinding them out with laborious intensity at times, looking neither to the baby left nor formal right.

The observations we have made thus far are in their preliminary stages, based on only five families, all from the same socioeconomic background and geographical region. The similarities among these families were, however, so great as to make us feel confident that they are generally occurring features, at least in upper middle-class homes. From what we have seen, it seems clear that children are not faced with a vast undifferentiated body of English from which they must make some order as best they can. The parents in these families talked in a very consistent and predictable style to their babies, a style which other researchers have described; and we have found that parents and other adults use a separate style for talking to growing children. This style is different from the informal or colloquial style that teenagers or old friends use to one another, and serves special functions: It is the language of socialization. While baby-talk style is concerned with learning the language, with establishing communication, the language of socialization is filled with social rules. The mother's questions contain answers and in this way show how to make a conversation. The adult emphasizes and exaggerates his own reactions, points up relationships, names feelings, controls and directs the child, and in many ways makes explicit his own world view. The language directed at young children is a teaching language. It tells about the world, and must, because of its special features, be recognized as a separate code.

The original aim of this study was to see if, indeed, children talk in different ways to different people. The answer is yes; infants are selective about whom they talk to at all. Four-year-olds may whine at their mothers, engage in intricate verbal play with their peers, and reserve their narrative, discursive tales for their grown-up friends. By the time they are 8, children have added to the foregoing some of the politeness routines of formal adult speech, baby-talk style, and the ability to talk to younger children in the language of socialization. The details of the emergence of these codes are yet to be elaborated.

Reading 18

Cognitive-Linguistic Development

Barry Silverstein
Ronald Krate

BLACK ENGLISH VERNACULAR: DEFICIT OR DIFFERENCE?

By 1966, low-income urban black children were being described by many psychologists and educators as essentially nonverbal or so deficient in linguistic skills as to be severely inhibited in the development of intellectual abilities and academic achievement. Describing a group of four-year-olds who, they claimed, represented a "fairly unbiased selection from the lower stratum" of an urban black community, Bereiter and Englemann said:

> Language for them is unwieldy and not very useful. For some of them, speaking is clearly no fun, and they manage as far as possible to get along without it. Others enjoy social speech and use it a good deal in play and social intercourse, but seldom for purposes of learning or reasoning; their language, as they use it, is not adequate for these purposes.[1]

In addition, Bereiter and Englemann tell us, "preschool disadvantaged children are likely to show distressing tendencies to hit, bite, kick, scream, run wildly about, cling, climb into laps, steal, lie, hide, ignore directions, and defy authority." These behaviors are to be considered simply "inappropriate behaviors for the classroom"; the children's social or emotional needs are of little relevance to understanding them. "Cultural deprivation" is essentially to be understood as "language deprivation." The teacher is instructed to "see the task for what it is: *teaching naïve children how to act in a new situation.*"[2] The four-year-old child has no right to want to be held in an adult's lap, nor should he be allowed to cling to the teacher. To remedy the children's linguistic deficiencies, the teacher must restrain them from expressing strong emotions or personal concerns and drill them to behave as the controlling adults would have them behave.

In the late 1960s and early 1970s the linguistic-cognitive-deficit explanation of low school achievement among poor black children came under increasing attack. Anthropologically oriented behavioral scientists began to argue that, instead of being deficient or defective in their linguistic-conceptual systems, black children possess linguistic and cognitive systems that are structurally coherent but different from those of white children. Baratz and Baratz, for example, claim:

> The current linguistic data . . . do not support the assumption of a linguistic deficit. . . . Many lower-class Negro children speak a well-ordered, highly structured, but different dialect from that of Standard English. These children have developed a language.[3]

From the "cultural-deprivation" viewpoint, black children's linguistic-cognitive abilities are *deficient,* unable to meet the demands of the standard school curriculum without preschool remediation; from the cultural-difference viewpoint, they are *different* and require a different curriculum. The two positions have polarized. Their adherents often fail to take into account the fact that poor black children are *bicultural* and *bidialectical:* They are simultaneously inducted into the urban black community and the more inclusive mainstream, white-dominated society.[4] In socializing their children lower-class black mothers have had to take into account the demands of a widening circle of social systems: the black family, the black community, and the wider society. By the time they reached the upper elementary school grades, most of the children we knew in Central Harlem seemed to comprehend most verbal messages directed to them, whether they were framed in everyday standard English or in black dialect and idiom, although occasionally, because of pronunciation differences, *we* had difficulty understanding a word or two spoken by a child, and sometimes a child would interpret our words in a way we had not intended.

In their own verbal productions the children often used black vernacular vocabulary and syntax, but standard English was not a foreign language to them: The dialect they spoke was a variant of the English language. Just as we reject any image of these children as deficient cognitive machines, so we reject any image of the children as exotic primitives. The children were black and poor, but they were Americans—oppressed Americans, Americans with an African heritage, but Americans living in the contemporary United States.

The linguistic-cognitive-deficit theorists rely heavily on the findings of a long line of studies indicating that middle-class children, from infancy onward, generally appear to be more advanced than working-class or lower-class children in most aspects of language behavior: vocabulary acquisition, sound discrimination, articulation, and sentence structure.[5] There are some exceptions to this trend: Inner-city children, black and white, have been found to respond to verbal stimuli with free word associations at a higher rate than white suburban children (from much higher-income families) at the first-grade level; although they fall behind at the third-grade level, they become equal at the fifth-grade level.[6]

The cultural-deprivation theorists view the poorer linguistic performance of lower-class children as indicative of linguistic-cognitive deficiencies, which they trace to qualitative differences in parent-child interaction associated with social-class level. Middle-class mothers reportedly present their infants, particularly girls, with more face-to-face verbalizations unaccompanied by competing sources of stimulation than working-class mothers. Middle-class girls are reported to be the most advanced group in the rate of linguistic-cognitive development.

With specific regard to lower-class black children, deficit theorists point to research carried out in schools or school-like settings which demonstrates that black children have greater difficulty than middle-class children (black or white) in using words to classify actions or objects.[7] For example, when shown a series of four pictures, each depicting a person engaging in some activity, lower-class black children had considerable difficulty pointing to the one that showed a person "tying," "pouring," "digging," and "picking." The children were not deficient in experience with the referent actions but, rather, had difficulty applying labels to them. This difficulty in making specific connections between words and referents is related causally by deficit theorists to a relative lack of active verbal interaction between the children and adults in their homes. Deficit theorists see low-income children as less able to use words in thinking, which leads to poor performance on tasks in which words must be used to form categories or express conceptual relationships. Thus, when asked, "Why do these pictures go together?" lower-class black first-graders are more likely to answer: "Because they look the same" or "Because they have legs" than "Because they are all animals." Deficit theorists regard "They are all animals" as a more explicit statement of a concept and, hence, a developmentally more advanced reply; the alternative responses are viewed not as legitimate stylistic ways of ordering perceptions but, rather, as primitive modes of functioning.

The difference theorists argue that many of the researches in support of the conclusion that lower-class black children have linguistic-cognitive deficiencies are based on ethnocentric or racist perceptions. The deficit model is based on the assumption that only standard English as spoken by middle-class whites is acceptable and that any variant, such as the dialects of low-income populations, is a "bad" or "deficient" version. The difference theorists argue that the dialects of low-income whites and blacks as well as their differences from standard English represent parallel development, not deficits.

Cultural-difference theorists claim that no evidence has been found that low-income children have more difficulty acquiring the language of their own community than middle-class children do acquiring theirs.[8] Further, these theorists assert that careful study of the structural differences between the black English vernacular and standard English reveals no grammatical relationship that can be expressed in standard English but not in the black idiom. For example, there is an important distinction between "he workin'" and "he be workin'"—structural forms found in the black English vernacular.[9] "He workin'" means he is working right now; "he be workin'" means he works habitually. In black idiom, the word *be* is employed as an auxiliary to express the habitual tense, to express action that is of long duration. This is a tense found in West African languages but not in standard English.[10]

Children acquire language not so much through imitation as through problem-solving processes. When two-year-olds are presented with statements to imitate, what the children give back is not a verbatim repetition of what the adult said but the results of their own cognitive processing; the children reduce what was said to their current grammar.[11] Thus, "the pencil is green" is repeated as "pencil green," and "the little boy is eating some pink ice cream" is repeated as "little boy eating pink ice cream."

A similar cognitive-processing system has been revealed in studies of low-income speakers in Harlem. When asked to repeat sentences presented in standard English, Harlem boys aged eleven to fourteen demonstrated that some standard English structures were first *understood*, then *translated* to fit the speaker's own syntactic rules, whereas others were simply *repeated* as presented because they were already in a syntactical form used by the speaker. Thus, "I asked Alvin if he knows how to play basketball" became "I aks Alvin do he know how to play basketball," and "nobody ever" became "nobody never." "Money, who is eleven, can't spit as far as Boo can" was repeated as given, as was "Larry is a stupid fool."[12]

It is important to distinguish between the *production* and the *comprehension* grammars of speakers of black English vernacular. Labov and Cohen have reported variability in the grammatical rules followed by black adults in Harlem depending upon the context in which the speech is produced and the speaker's linguistic experience (e.g., his social-class level and his Northern or Southern background). In general they reported differences in the phonological rules used in careful speech and in casual speech. Middle-class black adults came much closer to the production of standard English in careful speech than did working-class black adults. Thus, in linguistic production, middle-class black adults would appear to be more bicultural than working- or lower-class black adults.

Some lower-middle-class black adults who are economically upwardly mobile have been found to display what Labov has called a "hypercorrect" linguistic pattern.[13] This phenomenon is characterized by an extensive shift from black dialect to standard English forms when changing from casual to careful speech; a sharper tendency than any other group to stigmatize the speech of others; less accurate self-reports of their own speech patterns than others—shifting their perception of their own speech toward the standard norm; the most negative overt feelings about their own speech; and the strongest reactions against their own vernacular. The "hypercorrect" pattern of the lower middle class is found more regularly and in more extreme form among black women than among men. The existence of this pattern suggests that a considerable number of upwardly mobile blacks have accepted the standard white view of black cultural characteristics. They appear to regard their own vernacular as "mistakes" in speech rather than as a second dialect or a different speech system. Such blacks are thus caught in a practical and psychological bind. If, in either-or fashion, they reject standard English, they may restrict their job opportunities in a white-dominated society. If they reject the black idiom, they may experience difficulties in relating to family and friends and, to the extent that they perceive their speech as different from a standard that they believe to be "correct" or "respectable," they may suffer damage to their self-esteem.[14]

The conflict involved in the "hypercorrect pattern" may not develop fully until late adolescence, when the youth begins to comprehend the dimensions of economic discrimination against blacks. As we have noted, low-income black children generally seem able to understand both standard English and their own dialect. However, it is not clear how early lower-class black children will make use of different rules when speaking casually and carefully, as black adults have been observed to do. One study has found some distinctions between the verbal productions of lower-class and middle-class ninth-grade black girls in Chicago depending upon whether they were aiming at "school talk" (standard English) or "everyday talk."[15] A young black field worker met with groups of three girls at a time for discussion. In some groups, the worker asked questions framed in standard English and told the girls to answer in their best "school talk" because their recorded speech would be analyzed by educators. In other groups she framed questions in a style that made use of black English forms and told the girls to use "everyday" talk in replying since their answers would be heard only by the field worker. When the lower-class black girls replied to the field worker using "school talk," their speech became a little more like standard English; however, when they replied in "everyday talk," utilizing the black English vernacular, they gave more elaborate responses. While the middle-class black girls also shifted to more standard English when speaking "school talk," they gave relatively elaborate linguistic responses whether talking "school talk" or "everyday talk." Like the middle-class girls, the lower-class girls were able to change their verbal performance somewhat to meet the performance standards of the mainstream society, but they appeared to feel inhibited in performance situations where mainstream standards would be used to judge their competence. The middle-class girls, on the other hand, gave equally complex performances whether the standard for competence was mainstream or ghetto-specific, suggesting that these girls came closer to being fully bicultural than their lower-class peers.

Although poor quality in verbal performance may seem characteristic of many low-income black children in schools that are white-middle-class-dominated, in other contexts, as we have shown, the children tend to be talkative and highly articulate. The respect accorded to the good talker, the man of words, in the black community and the extent to which verbal performance is utilized as a way to achieve status, particularly in street peer groups, suggests the survival in black America of African oral traditions.[16] Black youth may display a distinct variety of verbal skills in the streets: "Rapping," "shucking," "jiving," "running it down,"

"copping a plea," "signifying," and "sounding" are all aspects of the black idiom. Each type of talking

> . . . has it own distinguishing features of form, style, and function; each is influenced by, and influences, the speaker, setting, and audience; and each sheds light on the black perspective and the black condition . . . on those orienting values and attitudes that will cause a speaker to speak or perform in his own way within the social context of the black community.[17]

Most ghetto children learn to comprehend and communicate appropriately in these styles of talking.

Smitherman argues that the black idiom cannot be viewed apart from black culture and the black experience in America.[18] She distinguishes two perspectives in looking at black English: linguistic and stylistic. From the linguistic perspective, which emphasizes pronunciation and syntax, Smitherman argues that black English is simply one of many contemporary American dialects; it is likely that the linguistic patterns of black English differ from those of standard English only in surface structure. However, although black people use the vocabulary of the English language, some words are selected out of that lexicon and given a special black semantic slant. Smitherman suggests that the following principles apply:

1 Because of the need of blacks for a code that is unintelligible to whites, the words that are given a special black slant are discarded when they are adopted by whites; e.g., blacks no longer speak of a "hip" brother but of a "together" brother.

2 The concept of denotation *vs.* connotation is not applicable to the black idiom. The black idiom is characterized, instead, by shades of meaning along a connotative spectrum. For example, depending upon the context, "bad" may mean extraordinary, beautiful, good, versatile, or a variety of other terms of positive value. Certain words in the black lexicon may be used to indicate either approbation or denigration, depending upon context; for example, "He's my main nigger" means he is my best friend, whereas "The nigger ain't shit" may indicate a variety of negative characteristics, depending upon the context.

3 Approbation and denigration refer to the semantic level; on the grammatical level, the same word may serve two other functions: intensification and completion. Thus, in "Niggers was getting out of there left and right, them niggers was running, and so the niggers said . . . ," etc., the word "nigger" may be devoid of real meaning, serving simply to give the sentence a subject and animate the conversation rather than to indicate approbation or denigration. "Cats" or "guys" or "people" would serve as well.

Turning to the stylistic elements of black English, Smitherman enumerates the following elements that differentiate black speakers of English from white speakers:

1 *Call and response.* A speaker's solo voice alternates or is intermingled with responses from the audience. This is basic to the black oral tradition. For example, the congregation responding to the preacher—"Preach, Reverend," "That's right"—or the street audience responding to displays of repartee with laughter, palm-slapping, and such phrases as "get back, nigger," "Git down, baby."

2 *Rhythmic pattern.* This includes cadence, tone, and musical quality. Black speakers often employ a pattern that is lyrical and sonorous and generally emphasizes sound apart from sense through the repetition of certain sounds or words. For example, the preacher's rhythm, "I-I-I-I-I-Oh-I-I-Oh, yeah, Lord-I-I-heard the voice of Jesus saying . . . ," or the rhythmic, fast tempo in delivering toasts such as the signifying monkey.

3 *Spontaneity.* Generally, a speaker's performance is improvisational, including much interaction with the audience, which dictates or directs the flow and outcome of the speech event. The speaker is casual; he employs a lively conversational tone with a quality of immediacy. For example, a preacher declares, "Y'all don' want to hear dat, so I'm gon' leave it lone," and his congregation calls out, "Now, tell it, Reverend, tell it!" and he does.

4 *Concreteness.* A speaker's imagery and ideas center upon contemporary, everyday experiences, and he conveys a sense of identification with the event being described. For example, the toast teller becomes Stag-O-Lee, or the preacher declares, "I first met God in 1925."

5 *Signifying.* To signify, the speaker talks about the entire audience or one of its members, either to trigger a verbal contest or to hammer a point home, without offending the audience. "Pimp, punk, prostitute, Ph.D.—all the P's—you still in slavery," declared the Reverend Jesse Jackson. Malcolm X delivered this putdown of the nonviolent move-

ment: "In a revolution, you swinging, not singing." The rhythmic alliteration and rhyming in these examples are characteristic of black speakers.

Susan Houston, studying the speech patterns of black and white children in rural Florida, found few important syntactic differences between them.[19] There were real differences, but they were basically in style or pronunciation. In one experiment Houston worked with eighty-six pairs of first-graders from four socio-economic groups: well-to-do whites, well-to-do blacks, poor whites, and poor blacks. She sent one child in each pair out of earshot, then told the other child a story and asked him to retell it exactly to his partner. After the retelling, the partner was asked to repeat the story. All the white children and the middle-class black children tended to reproduce details correctly, according to the norms set by the adult in charge. The poor black children took the given instructions as a baseline upon which to demonstrate spontaneous verbal flair. That is, they reproduced general elements from the story but preferred to supply their own details. Thus, 26 per cent of the stories told by the poor black children contained original material, as against 12 per cent or less for the other groups. Cultural-deprivation theorists would find the poor black children linguistically deficient relative to the other groups; difference theorists would stress their creativity and closer contact with their roots in the black oral tradition.

Another finding of Houston's study is worth noting. The poor black children were the most peer-oriented; they generally interacted far more with other children than did the other groups, and this was true whether they were paired with a white child or another black child. They clearly attended to each other more than to the adult, telling their stories to their partners rather than to the adult for her approval.

To summarize, it appears to us that cultural-difference theory offers a more accurate appraisal of the linguistic-cognitive competence of low-income black children than does cultural-deprivation theory. Furthermore, contrary to those cultural-difference theorists who insist that black English must be viewed as a separate language based upon West African linguistic patterns, careful linguistic analysis reveals that it is not based primarily upon West African syntax or grammar, although West African elements are present in the black idiom. From extensive linguistic studies, Labov has concluded that, although black English shows internal cohesion,

> . . . it is best seen as a distinct subsystem within the larger grammar of English. Certain parts of the tense and aspect system are clearly separate subsystems in the sense that they are not shared or recognized by other dialects, and we can isolate other such limited areas. But the gears and axles of English grammatical machinery are available to speakers of all dialects, whether or not they use all of them in everyday speech.[20]

Although poor black children may misinterpret some words pronounced by white middle-class speakers because of differences in phonology or usage or unfamiliarity with the vocabulary there is no reason to believe that the children cannot usually comprehend the basic meaning of sentences utilizing standard English grammar and syntax. Here the distinction between competence and performance is essential. Poor black children often do not utilize certain standard English grammatical forms in their verbal productions, but this does not necessarily mean that by late childhood they are not competent to do so. Performance—what one does with one's competence—is affected by a variety of situational determinants. For example, if one is frightened or tired or in a hurry, his linguistic performance is likely to be affected, although his competence, his mastery of the basic grammar of his language, remains unchanged.[21] A college student may feel a bit anxious when speaking to a professor in a speech course and either restrict his utterances or make mistakes in performance that he is not likely to make under other circumstances. Similarly, low-income black children are likely to freeze up or make performance errors, when evaluated by middle-class adults, particularly white adults. However, their poor performance may mask considerable competence. The most significant differences between black English and white English would appear to be in the use made of selected vocabulary and in performance and communication styles.

Cultural-deprivation theorists have a valid point when they observe that middle-class children, black or white, are likely to enjoy richer verbal interaction with adults than their lower-class peers. Low-income black parents have had valid reasons, related to survival in a racist society, to quiet young children and wean them early from dependent interaction. However, these theorists grossly underestimate the linguistic-cognitive competence of low-income black children, for reasons we shall outline below. In addition, they confuse a somewhat slower rate of linguistic-cognitive maturation in lower-class black (or white) children with their own reified theoretical construct—a "cumulative deficit" in basic linguistic-cognitive capacity. They assume that low-income black children will never catch up to middle-class white children, and they employ culturally biased tests, on which low-income blacks perform poorly, to "prove" that blacks continue to be linguistically and cognitively incompetent.

Let us look more closely at the criteria employed by these theorists in judging the linguistic-cognitive competence of low-income black children. Bereiter and Engelmann, for example, report that the children respond to adult questioning, if at all, with gestures, single words, or disconnected words and phrases.[22] Such reports are based upon empirical observation. For example, here is a typical complete interview with a black boy carried out in a New York City school by a friendly white interviewer. The adult places an object on the table in front of the child and says, "Tell me everything you can about this."

12 seconds of silence
Adult: What would you say it looks like?
8 seconds of silence
Child: A spaceship.
Adult: Hmmmm.
13 seconds of silence
Child: Like a je-et.
12 seconds of silence
Child: Like a plane.
20 seconds of silence
Adult: What color is it?
Child: Orange. *(2 seconds)* An' whi-ite. *(2 seconds)* An' green.
6 seconds of silence
Adult: An' what could you use it for?
8 seconds of silence
Child: A je-et.
6 seconds of silence
Adult: If you had two of them, what would you do with them?
6 seconds of silence

Child: Give one to some-body.

Adult: Hmmm. Who do you think would like to have it?

10 seconds of silence

Child: Cla-rence.

Adult: Mm. Where do you think you could get another one of these?

Child: At the store.

Adult: Oh-ka-ay![23]

Here we have a child in a situation where anything he says may be judged "wrong" and lead to shame or punishment. He plays it safe by saying as little as possible, a survival strategy for dealing with strange adults, particularly whites. The child's defensive behavior is not necessarily a function of ineptness on the part of the adult interviewer, for, as Labov has found, a friendly, competent black male adult interviewer from the community obtained similar results when interviewing eight-year-old Harlem boys in the same manner. However, significant changes in both the volume and the style of speech of the same children occurred when the interviewer brought potato chips, making the interview more like a party; brought along one of the child's friends; reduced the height imbalance by sitting on the floor; and introduced taboo words and topics indicating that the child could say anything without fear of retaliation. These changes were striking, as is clear in this interview with eight-year-old Leon in the presence of eight-year-old Greg:

Adult: Is there anybody who says, "Your momma drink pee?"

Leon: *(rapidly and breathlessly)* Yee-ah!

Greg: *(simultaneously)* Yup.

Leon: And your father eat doo-doo for breakfas'!

Adult: Ohhh! *(laughs)*

Leon: And they say your father—your father eat doo-doo for dinner!

Greg: When they sound on me, I say "C. B. M."

Adult: What that mean?

Leon: Congo booger-snatch! *(laugh)*

Greg: *(simultaneously)* Congo booger-snatcher! *(laughs)*

Greg: And sometimes I'll curse with "B. B."

Adult: What that?

Greg: Oh, that's a "M. B. B." black boy. *(Leon crunching on potato chips)*

Greg: 'Merican black boy.

Adult: Oh.

Greg: Anyway, 'Mericans is same like white people, right?

Leon: And they talk about Allah.

Adult: Oh, yeah?

Greg: Yeah.

Adult: What they say about Allah?

Leon: Allah—Allah is God.

Greg: *(simultaneously)* Allah—

Adult: And what else?

Leon: I don't know the res'!

Greg: Allah i-Allah is God, Allah is the only God, Allah—

Leon: Allah is the son of God.

Greg: But can he make magic?

Leon: Nope.

Greg: I know who can make magic.

Adult: Who can?

Leon: The God, the real one.

Adult: Who can make magic?

Greg: The son of po'. *(Adult: Hm?)* I'm saying the po'k chop God! He only a po'k chop God! *(Leon chuckles)* [24]

Leon, a boy who barely responded to a traditional interviewer, is now competing actively for the floor. Both boys seem to have no difficulty in using the English language to express themselves. Revealing a strong peer orientation, they talk to each other as much as to the interviewer.

Cultural-deprivation theorists argue that low-income black children's careless articulation and poor auditory discrimination are signs of incompetence. Here an ethnocentric bias often affects judgment: The difficulties poor black children have in pronouncing many words in the manner of middle-class whites often is no more and no less than the problem white middle-class American children would have if asked to speak like Englishmen. All children learn to pronounce words in the manner of those in their immediate community, but cultural-deprivation theorists impose a single standard as an index of precision in articulation. Similarly, the phonology usually presented in auditory-discrimination tests are the sounds of middle-class white English. Thus, many low-income black children may perform poorly not because they have poor auditory discrimination in any absolute sense, but because some of the sounds on the test are not their sounds.[25]

Cultural-deprivation theorists argue also that low-income black children employ shorter sentences and less complex grammar than more privileged children, indicating linguistic-cognitive incompetence. However, sentence length and grammatical complexity typically are assessed by tests like the one described above, in which a strange adult asks questions such as, "Tell me all you can about the object that is on the table." As we have seen, a child who doesn't trust the adult will purposely reply as briefly as possible. Besides, the test itself may seem silly to lower-class children. Why would an adult ask such a question? Can't he see for himself? What does he really want? What trick is he trying to play? Middle-class children are less likely to see the test in this way because they have more experience in being drawn out verbally by their parents. Thus, such tests may tell us more about the manner in which children relate to adults in an evaluative context than about their basic linguistic-cognitive competence.

Further, psychologists and educators seem to have a bias in favor of long sentences and complex grammar. But sentence length and complexity sometimes hide muddled thought, and short, simple sentences may reveal clarity and precision of thought. As a reading of social-science and education journals soon reveals, involved, cumbersome sentences often do not portray reality accurately or make much sense.

Cultural-deprivation theorists and the teachers they have influenced tend to equate class and ethnic differences in grammatical forms with differences in the capacity for logical analysis, to assume that teaching children to mimic the speech patterns of their middle-class teachers is the same as teaching them to think logically, and to favor and reward children who speak the way they do. This preferred treatment may help some children to achieve in school more rapidly than others and this achievement in turn is often seen as evidence that the higher-achieving children were better equipped intellectually from the start.

CLASS AND LINGUISTIC SOCIALIZATION

Middle-class children are likely to approximate their parents' verbalizations somewhat earlier than lower-class children, perhaps because of differences in the linguistic socialization of the two groups. In one study, it was found that low-income black mothers generally relied on more restricted verbal communications in combination with status-oriented discipline in relating to their children than did middle-class black mothers.[26] When the mothers were asked to teach various tasks to their children, the low-income mothers and their children both displayed a greater tendency to act without taking time for reflection or planning. For example, after briefly demonstrating to a child what he was supposed to do, a low-income mother commonly sat silently by, watching the child try to solve a problem until he made an error, whereupon she would punish him immediately. These mothers frequently failed to structure the learning situation so that the children could learn to recognize and correct their errors. They did not stop the children before they made a mistake and ask them to think about the probable outcome of their behavior. Thus, the lower-class child often learned only that his mother wanted him to do something, although she did not specify clearly what it was; no matter what he did, he would probably be punished.

Helen Bee and her associates have also studied social-class differences in the interactions between mothers and young children.[27] Mothers were observed trying to help children carry out specific tasks and while they were in a waiting room well supplied with toys. Mothers were also interviewed concerning their ideas on taking care of children. In general, lower-class mothers appeared to be much more restrictive than middle-class mothers and more inclined to use negative reinforcements. In the helping situation, middle-class mothers tended to allow children to work at their own pace, offering many general suggestions on how to look for a solution to a problem while pointing out what the children were doing that was right. Lower-class mothers, by contrast, tended to behave in ways that did not encourage their children to attend to the basic features of the problem. They tended to tell the children to do specific things, they did not emphasize basic problem-solving strategies, and their "suggestions" were really imperative statements that did not encourage a reply from the child.

The greater verbal interaction between middle-class mothers and their children seems to be "designed" to help the children acquire learning strategies that they can generalize to future problem-solving situations. The middle-class mothers help their children to attend discriminately to various features of the situation and of their own behavior. This selective attending helps children cognitively to take situations and their behaviors apart and to put the pieces together differently in new contexts, thus increasing the range of situations within which the children can respond adaptively. Middle-class mothers tend to ask many more questions of their children when trying to help them. Thus, they help the children to perceive connections between objects and events. The children are also helped to express connections in words and to formulate general rules independent of the particular context within which they are operating. Lower-class mothers, on the other hand, by instructing children in a manner that that does not encourage verbal give-and-take, help their children somewhat to carry out specific tasks, but they do not encourage, and often discourage, a reflective and conceptual orientation to problems.

Studies such as these may be criticized on several grounds. First, the mothers and children were observed in university laboratories, a setting that may be more threatening to lower-class mothers than to their middle-class peers. Thus, the restricted quality of the low-income mothers' performance may have been in part a defense against the possibility of appearing inadequate in the eyes of middle-class observers. Second, the tasks presented by the researchers may have been more familiar to middle-class children, providing a performance advantage. Nevertheless, much of the social-class difference in performance among mothers appears to reflect significant differences in styles of socialization. The behavior of low-income mothers in the laboratory situation is basically consistent with the general socialization orientation of low-income mothers.

Low-income black children have generally not been encouraged to perform linguistically for adult approval or to strive for mastery of skills not immediately necessary for survival. The result is that many such children perform quite poorly in mainstream cultural situations, such as the psychological laboratory or school, in spite of the fact that within their peer group many of them display considerable linguistic-cognitive competence.

The typical middle-class socialization techniques, on the other hand, tend to push children to expand, as rapidly as possible, their capacities for linguistic-cognitive differentiation, categorization, and conceptualization in a widening variety of situations. The parents frequently elaborate on their children's statements, helping them to expand their categorization of experience. They encourage the children to build mental models of experience based on the use of words. By using language to help focus the children's attention on various features of their own behavior and the situations they encounter, middle-class parents provide the children with abundant experience in using the same symbols in a variety of situations. Middle-class children are encouraged to abstract the cómmon meanings of these symbols as used in various situations and to use words as referents for concepts and categories that have generalized meaning, rather than as referents for a narrow range of specific, personalized experiences. Middle-class children are pushed to move beyond the use of language in highly concrete, particularized, situation-specific orientations to the use of language for formal, rule-oriented, conceptually ordered discourse about general aspects of experience. All these skills are socialized by middle-class parents in the expectation that they will be instrumental in the children's future educational and occupational success, helping them to maintain or improve their advantaged position in the social order. These parental behaviors appear to result in accelerated linguistic-cognitive development among middle-class children relative to their lower-class peers, although the magnitude of the differences between them often seems greater than it actually is because of the tendencies of low-income children to perform poorly when tested by adults and because of class and ethnic biases in interpreting low-income children's behavior.

Earlier we discussed the importance of verbal performance in urban black children's peer groups. We also saw that the shift from adult orientation to peer orientation developed at an early age among urban blacks, stimulated by "push" factors that drive children out of the house and by "pull" factors in the lure of the street. Similarly, among black children in a Southern town, the focus of linguistic socialization has been observed to shift from adults to peers at an early age. Virginia Young, who studied childrearing practices among black residents of a medium-sized town in Georgia, found that about age three there is "an almost complete cessation of the close relationship with the mother and father and a shift in orientation to the children's gang." One of the important features of this change is that

> ... often speech becomes an indistinct children's patois in contrast to the clear enunciation used by the Knee-baby (younger child) with his parents. Children speak less to adults, and get along adequately with "Yes'm," and "No'm."[28]

We have already noted that low-income black children in the North or the South seemed inclined to direct their verbal performance toward a peer rather than an adult when both peer and adult were available. This relatively early reliance on peers for verbal socialization is likely to delay the child's development of linguistic behavior like his own parents' and to reinforce competence in the language of the streets. While such language is complex, coherent, and creative in vocabulary and style, it is not the language of the schools. Thus, by encouraging linguistic patterns associated with low-income black life-styles and often negating standard English, street peer groups contribute to the child's difficulties in coping with school and his negative attitudes toward school achievement.[29]

CLASS AND ETHNIC PATTERNING OF ABILITIES

We have noted findings that lower-class children tend much more than middle-class children to deal with concrete, emotionally significant features of situations rather than analytically abstracting common features from situations and using words to form more general categories. One interpretation of this finding is that the categorization behavior of middle-class children indicates linguistic-cognitive functioning at a relatively high level of development. Another interpretation of the same data is that young lower-class children tend not to use their abilities to form analytic, formal categories because of their class-based orientation to experience and to the use of language.[30] Both interpretations may be correct. Middle-class children may develop the capacity to utilize language to form analytic, formal categories earlier than lower-class children because the social milieu in which they live encourages and rewards this ability more than is common in lower-class homes. Lower-class children *can* use language to express complex relationships and abstract ideas, but they tend to do so largely in peer-group relationships and experiences which

have personal, affective significance rather than in relation to events, objects, categories, and concepts without subjective emotional content.

The socialization of lower-class children, particularly boys, leads to the development of individual identities that are refracted through group relationships more than through individual work and achievement and encourages an orientation toward linguistic competence in relation to expressive interpersonal experiences. For example, Ryan reports that among lower-class white ethnic adults in Boston's West End talk about relatively individualistic, impersonal experiences such as jobs and work was very uncommon in the bars, in delicatessens, and on the corner.[31] Rather, talk tended to center on issues of common concern such as the characteristics of other people and memories of places where the gang got together and events that happened there. Children socialized in this milieu learn to be highly talkative in peer-group situations in which concrete common concerns and emotionally charged experiences are shared and discussed. In such contexts, they strive to be verbally complex and creative because verbal competence leads to affirmation by peers and becomes an integral element of personal identity. Such children will bring an orientation to concretize and personalize experience to school settings, and this orientation will be revealed in their responses to concept-sorting tests.

Drake and Cayton offer a view of urban lower-class black society as they observed it during the 1940's that is reminiscent of Ryan's description of the urban world of lower-class white ethnics:

> The world of the lower class is a public world; contacts are casual and direct with a minimum of formality. ... Conversation and rumor flow continuously—about policy, "politics," sports and sex. Arguments (often on the "race problem"), while chronically short on fact, are animated and interesting. Emotional satisfactions in such situations are immediate. Physical gratifications are direct. There are status bearers within this realm, but they are not the civic leaders and intellectuals. They are, rather, the "policy kings"; sportsmen, black and white, the clever preachers and politicians; legendary "tough guys"; and the good fighters and roisterers.[32]

Some black scholars have argued that this orientation toward direct-feeling encounters with life, although characteristic of lower-class life-styles in general, is basic to the nature of black people and deeply affects their use of language:

> Knowledge in Western societies is largely derived from such propositions as "I think, therefore I am." The non-Western heritage of Afro-Americans suggests that knowledge stems from the proposition that "I feel, therefore I think, therefore I am."[33]

> The uniqueness of black culture can be explained in that it is a culture whose emphasis is on the nonverbal, i.e., the nonconceptual. . . . In black culture it is the experience that counts, not what is said.[34]

This does not mean that black people don't think or conceptualize their experience symbolically; rather, it means that many blacks (and some counter-culture whites) believe that intellectual analysis disconnected from feelings leads to incomplete knowledge of the world. Dispassionate conceptual analysis requires a fragmentation of experience and a concern with the symbols that represent the pieces of experience, preventing a subjective, empathetic encounter with the total experience. These black scholars are not rejecting intellectual knowledge but, rather, are pointing to another way of knowing, which is a necessary supplement to objective analysis and is basic to black culture. Thus, emanating from a feeling-oriented culture, black verbal expression thrives on what might appear to the analytic mind to be logical contradictions or emotional paradoxes.[35]

Julius Waiguchu maintains that, although black Americans are acculturated to a large extent to white mainstream culture, they nevertheless manifest certain "Africanisms" in their behavior.[36] He argues that the African form of communion with nature survives among black Americans, giving a unique quality to the black experience in America. In a somewhat similar vein, Joseph White illustrates the lack of compartmentalization of life in a feeling-oriented culture with the example of a black youth who goes from participation in a black nationalist rally to a storefront revival to a bar without any sense of contradiction, in spite of the seemingly different life-style each behavior represents, because for him all these activities are the same experience at the feeling level; they are all activities the youth looks forward to every Sunday because he just "dug on it."[37]

The black scholars cited above appear to be making essentially the same point concerning what they believe to be a unique quality of black culture in America. One may debate how much of this feeling orientation is a function of race (ethnicity) and how much of class, since it may be diluted, hidden, or absent among some middle-class blacks and since a similar orientation appears among other lower-class groups; nevertheless, this is an important element in the milieu in which low-income black children are socialized; it affects their orientation toward linguistic-cognitive competence. A psychologist who interprets the concrete, subjective, emotionally toned responses of black children to concept-sorting tasks as signs of linguistic-cognitive immaturity may be in error, responding ethnocentrically to a particular cultural style in experiencing reality. A study of verbal learning ability comparing the performance of 128 black female and white female college students on a paired association learning test, in which the subjects had to quickly relate various three-letter combinations to one another, demonstrates clear differences between black and white learning styles. The performance of the black students was more affected by their feelings of liking or disliking each "word," based on how it sounded to them when they spoke it, while the white students' performance depended less on the affective value of the combinations and more on the extent to which a three-letter combination looked like and sounded like a real word (association value).[38]

Charles Keil has also tried to identify ethnic influences on ways of experiencing the world brought about through socialization in urban black communities. According to Keil, "The shared sensibilities and common understandings of the Negro ghetto, its modes of perception and expression, its channels of communication are predominantly auditory and tactile rather than visual and literate."[39] Keil argues that certain modes of perception and communication are more characteristic of urban black communities than white communities; thus the prominence of aural perception, oral expression, and body movement—the emphasis on the shared sound and feel of experience—sharply demarcate the cultural experience of urban blacks and whites. We have already commented on the importance of verbal performance skills in black communities and some distinctive stylistic elements of the black oral tradition.

Some support for the assertion that black culture socializes particular sensitivity to kinesic cues is provided in a study conducted by Newmeyer.[40] He had preadolescent boys, black and white, act out a number of emotions in an effort to communicate them to observers nonverbally. Black boys were consistently better than white boys at enacting emotions so that others perceived them correctly and also at interpreting the emotions of various other actors. Additional evidence is provided by a study of 160 college students conducted by Gitter, Black, and Mostofsky.[41] Black and white students, each tested by a member of their own race, were shown, in random order, thirty-five specially prepared still photographs of professional actors (of both races) taken while the actors were attempting to portray each of seven emotions: anger, happiness, surprise, fear, disgust, pain, and sadness. The subjects were provided with a list of the seven designated emotions and requested to assign each photograph to one of the seven emotional categories. Black students made significantly more correct judgments of emotion.

Certain nonverbal modes of communication that are important to the life-style of urban blacks may be misinterpreted by whites. Suttles provides an example of such cultural misunderstanding based upon his observations of various ethnic groups living in an inner-city area of Chicago:

Negro boys . . . have a "cool" way of walking ("pimp's walk") in which the upper trunk and pelvis rock fore and aft while the head remains stable with the eyes looking straight ahead. The "pimp's walk" is quite slow, and the Negroes take it as a way of "strutting" or "showing off." The whites usually interpret it as a pointed lack of concern for those adjacent to the walker. Negro girls provide a parallel in a slow "sashay" that white males sometimes take as an unqualified invitation to their attentions.[42]

The studies of Gerald Lesser and his associates suggest that there is a strong ethnic influence on the organization of mental abilities among children.[43] These researchers tested first-grade boys and girls in New York City on verbal ability, reasoning, number ability, and spatial conceptualization. Equal numbers of children were drawn from four ethnic groups: Chinese, Jewish, black, and Puerto Rican. Each ethnic sample was, in turn, divided equally into middle- and lower-class groups. The performance data were analyzed to determine the effects of ethnicity, social class, and sex on the organization of mental abilities. A number of findings emerged:

1   Differences in *ethnic* group membership produce significant differences in the patterns of these mental abilities. Blacks performed best on tests of verbal ability and reasoning, followed by space conceptualization and number ability. By contrast, the order of performance for the other groups was as follows:
   Chinese: space, number, reasoning, verbal
   Jewish: verbal, number, reasoning, space
   Puerto Rican: space, number, reasoning, verbal
2   Within each ethnic group, the same patterning of abilities was found regardless of whether the children were middle- or lower-class.
3   Within each ethnic group, consistent with its patterning of mental abilities, middle-class children scored higher on each test.
4   Boys scored significantly higher than girls on space conceptualization and on the picture vocabulary subtest in all ethnic groups except one: Jewish girls were superior to Jewish boys on both verbal and space scales.

Lesser and his colleagues had each child tested by an examiner from his own ethnic group, using the child's primary language. Each tester was allowed to extend the length of the testing time to try to establish rapport and allow for fatigue. Each child was tested in a room of his public school during regular school hours. In spite of such precautions, it is difficult to determine whether the results indicate that middle-class children are genuinely more able and competent or whether lower-class children simply performed less well on the tests because they were less motivated to do so. In either event, the results do appear to indicate a genuine ethnic patterning of the mental abilities tapped by the tests, since the relative strengths and weaknesses within each ethnic group were the same across class lines even though level of performance always was higher among the middle-class children. The middle-class children, regardless of ethnic group, were more similar in their scores on each mental-ability scale than were the lower-class children compared from one ethnic group to another. It may be that distinct ethnic patterns of socialization tend to be blurred or lost as families move into the middle class and adopt mainstream standards of behavior.

A replication study with black and Chinese children in Boston revealed that each group there produced the same pattern of mental abilities as their counterparts in New York in both middle- and lower-class samples. Thus, the replication data support the hypothesis of a distinctive performance in test situations in general, but ethnicity appears to foster the development of different patterns of mental abilities.

One additional finding is worth noting. Social-class differences produced a greater difference in the mental-ability test scores of black children than was the case for any other group; that is, middle-class black children differed from lower-class black children more than middle-class Chinese, Jewish, or Puerto Rican children differed from lower-class children in their ethnic groups. One interpretation of these findings might be that the gap between middle- and lower-class black groups was larger— i.e., the poor black children came from lower-income families, than the lower-class children in any other group. Or it might be that the low-income black children were socialized more harshly than the other lower-class children and this had a greater negative effect on their motivation to perform well.

Lesser's findings that black children performed better on tests of verbal ability and reasoning than on tests of space conceptualization is basically consistent with Keil's finding concerning the prominence of aural perception and expression in the feeling-oriented urban black culture. Black ethnicity may be related to the relatively weak development of certain visual-spatial organization skills not directly related to feeling-interaction between people.

Francis H. Palmer has tested black children on a variety of perceptual and cognitive tasks in Manhattan, on Long Island, and on the Caribbean island of Antigua. He finds that in all these locations three-year-old black children performed significantly less well than white children on visual-perceptual measures.[44] At the same time, the black children did not perform significantly less well on verbal-conceptual items. In fact, three-year-old blacks in Antigua and Long Island (but not Manhattan) actually performed a little better than their white peers on forty-six conceptual items. Thus, it would appear that it is not the ability to manipulate abstract symbols that is poorly developed among the black children but processes related to visual discrimination and/or spatial organization of inanimate objects. Although black children were less proficient than whites on visual-discrimination-organization problems, they could be trained to perform effectively with relative ease.[45] This suggests that the black children's relative lack of

proficiency is a function of socialization. Even if there should be a strong genetic inheritance factor involved in visual-perceptual-information processing, this tells us nothing about how a given individual might have developed under different socialization conditions, since behavior results from gene-environment interaction, not absolute genetic determination, and the number of possible interactions is effectively unlimited.[46] Thus, high heritability for a given perceptual-cognitive ability does *not* mean that the ability cannot be improved by teaching.

Farnham-Diggory studied the ability of black and white children aged four to ten to synthesize pieces of symbolic information.[47] In general, there was little difference between the white and black children on the verbal-synthesis task, but the black children performed somewhat better at putting visual symbols, words, and actions together. On the other hand, there were significant racial differences on the maplike and mathematical tasks, which appeared to require something more like a spatial perception-integration factor. This finding is consistent with the findings of Palmer, Lesser, and a number of other studies.[48] Again, Farnham-Diggory found that training could easily lead to improved performance by black children.

Both sex and social class were significant factors in success on the maplike synthesis test. White middle-class boys scored highest, possibly owing to their greater experience and encouragement in playing with mechanical toys. Black girls performed better than black boys in working-class and middle-class areas. Farnham-Diggory suggests that the girls may have profited from homemaking responsibilities, such as setting the table following directions from mother, so as to increase maplike synthesis ability. Black boys from the lowest income groups performed better than working-class and middle-class black boys; Farnham-Diggory suggests that this may be related to their having learned to be particularly alert to visual signs that told them when to run and where to hide in a dangerous environment. It would appear that success on the maplike task resulted from strengths in somewhat different information-processing systems among each group that excelled.

We suggest that the source of the relative weakness of black children's spatial-perceptual abilities may lie in certain aspects of their socialization into a feeling, people-oriented culture. Consider the following observations on black socialization in a Georgia town:

One hears five-month-old babies spontaneously imitating single sounds of their parents, and often babies show precociousness which tends to be lost in later childhood when the stimulus falls off. Babies will be distracted by calling their attention to a person, seldom an object. . . . In contrast to this great stimulation of the baby's responsiveness to people, its explorations of the inanimate environment are limited. Few objects are given to babies or allowed them when they do get hold of them. . . . Babies reaching to feel objects or surfaces are often redirected to feeling the holder's face, or the game of rubbing faces is begun as a substitute. . . . Such a degree of inhibition of exploration is possible only because there are always eyes on the baby and idle hands take away the forbidden objects and then distract the frustrated baby. The personal is thus often substituted for the impersonal.[49]

In this milieu babies are kept from crawling on the floor by people holding them and passing them along from one to another. Babies not held by a person or placed on a bed are likely to be put in a walker, usually chaperoned by older children. Such a socialization experience continuously directs attention toward people and away from inanimate objects. With movement and exploration restricted, the child's attentiveness to inanimate objects and spatial perception-conceptualization may develop much more slowly than his attentiveness and perceptual sensitivity to people. It may be that perceptual-conceptual skills related to people develop faster than skills related to inanimate objects in all infants;[50] however, the type of early socialization described above may selectively reinforce perceptual-cognitive development related to interpersonal relations, thus favoring the people-oriented cognition that is highly valued in black communities. The basic elements of very early socialization described by Young among urban blacks in Georgia *may* be shared by low-income blacks in other urban areas and, perhaps to a lesser extent, by upwardly mobile middle-class blacks as well.

In summary, it would appear that black children tend to be stronger in verbal-conceptual intellective abilities than in visual-space-perception-organization mental abilities. The former are emphasized by a culture with a strong oral tradition, which shapes children to achieve peak linguistic performance in emotionally toned peer-group situations. Children from this milieu will perform least well linguistically-cognitively in impersonal contexts where they will be evaluated by adults. In responding to the world, black children are often highly subjective, operating at a basic feeling level that is reflected in their emotionally toned verbal conceptualizations. Thus, among black children, concreteness and subjectivity in verbal conceptualization may reflect an unfragmented feeling approach to experience more than immaturity of thought processes. This approach is likely to be manifested in heightened sensitivity to other people's moods and personal characteristics. Middle-class black children tend to be more acculturated to mainstream cultural patterns than their lower-class peers, so they perform at higher levels on verbal-conceptual tasks. A relative weakness in visual-discrimination abilities appears to cut across socio-economic-class lines among black children. This is a relative weakness, however, and it is easily affected by training.

We suggest that one factor responsible for the relatively poor performances of black children on impersonal, perceptual-discrimination-organization tasks may be related to lack of attention rather than to weakness in perceptual or information-processing abilities. The socialization experiences of black children, particularly of the lower class, may have discouraged attentiveness to spatial-organization aspects of inanimate objects. Thus, in testing situations, the children may pay less attention to certain materials or have more difficulty sustaining attention to the physical features of inanimate objects than children from some other groups. On the other hand, it may be that black children pay more attention to people around them, and this tendency may distract them from impersonal tasks and disorganize their efforts to sustain attention to the inanimate, impersonal features of the environment. We suspect that the reading difficulties some low-income black children have are related to a lack of sustained attention to reading materials.

In many elementary school classrooms we observed that black children were often more attentive to the physical mannerisms of the teacher than to anything she was saying, even when lessons were carefully prepared and of real interest to the children. The children also spent much time watching each other in the classroom. Training procedures that lead to improved perceptual-discrimination-organization performances among children may have their effect as much through directing and strengthening attentiveness to certain features of the environment as through any other route.

NOTES

1 Carl Bereiter and Siegfried Engelmann, *Teaching Disadvantaged Children in the Preschool* (Englewood Cliffs, N. J.: Prentice-Hall, 1966), pp. 39–40.

2 *Ibid.*, p. 41.

3 Stephens S. Baratz and Joan C. Baratz, "Early Childhood Intervention: The Social Science Base of Institutional Racism," *Harvard Educational Review*, 40 (1970): 35.

4 See Vernon J. Dixon and Badi G. Foster, *Beyond Black or White: An Alternate America* (Boston: Little, Brown, 1971); Albert Murray, *The Omni-Americans: New Perspectives on Black Experience and American Culture* (New York: Outerbridge & Dienstfrey, 1970); Charles A. Valentine, "Deficit, Differences, and Bicultural Methods of Afro-American Behavior," *Harvard Educational Review*, 41 (1971): 137–57; and Andrew Billingsley, *Black Families in White America* (Englewood Cliffs, N. J.: Prentice-Hall, 1968).

5 See, for example, Mildred C. Templin, *Certain Language Skills in Children* (Minneapolis: University of Minnesota Press, 1957), and Walter Loban, *The Language of Elementary School Children* (Champaign, Ill.: National Conference of Teachers of English, 1963).

6 See Doris R. Entwisle, "Developmental Sociolinguistics: Inner-City Children," *American Journal of Sociology*, 74 (1968): 37–49, and *idem*, "Semantic Systems of Children," in Frederick Williams, ed., *Language and Poverty* (Chicago: Markham, 1970), pp. 123–39.

7 E.g., see Vera P. John and L. Goldstein, "The Social Context of Language Acquisition," *Merrill-Palmer Quarterly*, 10 (1964): 265–76, and Irving E. Sigal, L. Anderson, and H. Shapiro, "Categorization Behavior of Lower- and Middle-Class Negro Preschool Children: Differences in Dealing with Representations of Familiar Objects," *Journal of Negro Education*, 35 (1966): 218–29.

8 See Paula Menyuk, "Language Theories and Educational Practice," in Williams, ed., *Language and Poverty*, pp. 190–211.

9 W. A. Stuart, "Understanding Black Language," in John F. Szwed, ed., *Black America* (New York: Basic Books, 1970), pp. 121–31.

10 See D. Z. Seymour, "Black English," *Intellectual Digest*, 2 (1972): 78–80, and J. L. Dillard, *Black English* (New York: Random House, 1972), pp. 39–72. The habitual tense is not the same as the present tense, and the difference can be important. For example, "my brother sick" indicates that the sickness is in progress but probably of short duration; "my brother be sick" indicates a long-term condition—a distinction that may be missed by a teacher who is limited to standard English (and who might therefore be labeled "culturally deprived").

11 Dan I. Slobin and C. A. Welsh, "Elicited Imitation as a Research Tool in Developmental Psycholinguistics," unpublished paper, Department of Psychology, University of California, Berkeley, 1967.

12 William Labov and P. Cohen, "Systematic Relations of Standard and Nonstandard Rules in the Grammars of Negro Speakers," *Project Literacy Reports*, No. 8, Cornell University, Ithaca, N. Y., 1967, pp. 66–84.

13 William Labov, "Psychological Conflict in Negro American Language Behavior," *American Journal of Orthopsychiatry*, 41 (1971): 636–37. Essentially the same conflict in speech patterns of upwardly mobile blacks is described in Frantz Fanon, *Black Skin, White Masks* (1952) (New York: Grove Press, 1967), pp. 17–40.

14 See John J. Hartman, "Psychological Conflicts in Negro American Language Behavior: A Case Study," *American Journal of Orthopsychiatry*, 41 (1971): 627–35.

15 B. Wood and J. Curry, " 'Everyday Talk' and 'School Talk' of the City Black Child," *The Speech Teacher*, 18 (1969): 282–96. See also Menyuk, "Language Theories" (n. 8 *supra*).

16 See Roger D. Abrahams, "Rapping and Capping: Black Talk as Art," in Szwed, ed., *Black America* (n. 9 *supra*), pp. 132–42, and *idem, Deep Down in the Jungle: Negro Narrative Folklore from the Streets of Philadelphia*, rev. ed. (Chicago: Aldine, 1970).

17 Thomas Kochman, "Rapping in the Ghetto," in Lee Rainwater, ed., *The Black Experience: Soul* (Chicago: Aldine, 1970), p. 51. See also Charles Keil, *Urban Blues* (Chicago: University of Chicago Press, 1966), and Iceberg Slim, *Pimp: The Story of My Life* (Los Angeles: Holloway House, 1967).

18 Geneva Smitherman, "White English in Blackface, or, Who Do I Be?" *The Black Scholar*, 4 (May–June, 1973): 32–39.

19 Susan H. Houston, "Black English," *Psychology Today*, 6 (March, 1973): 45–48.

20 William Labov, *Language in the Inner City: Studies in the Black English Vernacular* (Philadelphia: University of Pennsylvania Press, 1972), p. 64.

21 See Owen P. Thomas, "Competence and Performance in Language," in Roger D. Abrahams and Rudolph D. Troke, eds., *Language and Cultural Diversity in American Education* (Englewood Cliffs, N. J.: Prentice-Hall, 1972), pp. 108–11.

22 Bereiter and Engelmann, *Teaching Disadvantaged Children* (n. 1 *supra*), pp. 34–40.

23 William Labov, "Academic Ignorance and Black Intelligence," *Atlantic Monthly*, June, 1972, p. 60.

24 *Ibid.*, p. 62.

25 See R. Burling, *English in Black and White* (New York: Holt, Rinehart & Winston, 1973), pp. 29–47 and 91–110.

26 Robert D. Hess and Virginia C. Shipman, "Early Experience and the Socialization of Cognitive Modes in Children," *Child Development*, 36 (1965): 869–86.

See also *idem,* "Cognitive Elements in Maternal Behavior," in John P. Ill, ed., *Minnesota Symposia on Child Psychology* (Minneapolis: University of Minnesota Press, 1967), 1: 57–81.

27 Helen C. Bee *et al.,* "Social Class Differences in Maternal Teaching Strategies and Speech Patterns," *Developmental Psychology,* 1 (1969): 726–34. See also G. F. Brody, "Socioeconomic Differences in Stated Maternal Child-rearing Practices and in Observed Maternal Behavior," *Journal of Marriage and the Family,* 30 (1968): 656–60.

28 Virginia H. Young, "Family and Childhood in a Southern Georgia Community," *American Anthropologist,* 72 (1970): 282.

29 See William Labov and C. Robbins, "A Note on the Relation of Reading Failure to Peer-Group Status in Urban Ghettos," *Teachers College Record,* 70 (1969): 395–405.

30 See Jerome S. Bruner, *The Relevance of Education* (New York: Norton, 1971), and Michael Cole and Jerome S. Bruner, "Cultural Differences and Inferences About Psychological Processes," *American Psychologist,* 26 (1971): 867–76.

31 E. J. Ryan, "Personal Identity in an Urban Slum," in Leonard J. Duhl, ed., *The Urban Condition* (New York: Basic Books, 1963), pp. 135–50.

32 St. Clair Drake and Horace R. Cayton, *Black Metropolis: A Study of Negro Life in a Northern City* (New York: Harper Torchbooks, 1962), 2: 603–6.

33 Vernon J. Dixon and Badi G. Foster, *Beyond Black or White* (Boston: Little, Brown, 1971), p. 18.

34 Julius Lester, *Look Out Whitey! Black Power's Gon' Get Your Mama!* (New York: Grove Press, 1969), p. 87. See also Robert H. Decoy, *The Nigger Bible* (Los Angeles: Holloway House, 1967).

35 James Haskins and Hugh F. Butts, *The Psychology of Black Language* (New York: Barnes & Noble, 1973).

36 Julius M. Waiguchu, "Black Heritage: Of Genetics, Environment, and Continuity," in Rhoda L. Goldstein, ed., *Black Life and Culture in the United States* (New York: T. Y. Crowell, 1971), pp. 64–86.

37 Joseph White, "Toward a Black Psychology," in Reginald L. Jones, ed., *Black Psychology* (New York: Harper & Row, 1972), pp. 43–50.

38 Joseph F. Rychlak, C. W. Hewitt, and J. Hewitt, "Affective Evaluations, Word Quality, and the Verbal Learning Styles of Black Versus White Junior College Females," *Journal of Personality and Social Psychology,* 27 (1973): 248–55.

39 Keil, *Urban Blues* (n. 17 *supra*), p. 16.

40 J. A. Newmeyer, "Creativity and Nonverbal Communication in Preadolescent White and Black Children," unpublished doctoral dissertation, Harvard University, 1970.

41 A. George Gitter, H. Black, and David I. Mostofsky, "Race and Sex in Perception of Emotion," *Journal of Social Issues,* 28 (1972): 63–78.

42 Gerald D. Suttles, *The Social Order of the Slum: Ethnicity and Territory in the Inner City* (Chicago: University of Chicago Press, 1968), p. 66.

43 Gerald S. Lesser, G. Fifer, and Donald H. Clark, "Mental Abilities of Children from Different Social Class and Cultural Groups," *Monographs of the Society for Research in Child Development,* vol. 30, no. 4 (1964). See also S. S. Stodolsky and Gerald S. Lesser, "Learning Patterns in the Disadvantaged," *Harvard Educational Review,* 37 (1967): 546–93.

44 Personal communication from Francis H. Palmer, State University of New York at Stony Brook, January, 1973.

45 Francis H. Palmer, "Minimal Intervention at Age Two and Three and Subsequent Intellective Changes," in Ronald K. Parker, ed., *The Preschool in Action: Exploring Early Childhood Programs* (Boston: Allyn & Bacon, 1972), pp. 437–64. Palmer's studies at the Harlem Research Center in New York showed that the area of development most affected by educational intervention at age two and three is the perceptual domain, even though the curriculum used was not specifically designed for that purpose.

46 See Jay Hirsch, "Behavior-Genetic Analysis and Its Biosocial Consequences," in Kent S. Miller and Ralph Mason Dreger, eds., *Comparative Studies of Blacks and Whites in the United States* (New York: Seminar Press, 1973), pp. 34–51.

47 Sylvia Farnham-Diggory, "Cognitive Synthesis in Negro and White Children," *Monographs of the Society for Research in Child Development,* 35 (1970):2.

48 These are summarized in Thomas Pettigrew, *A Profile of the Negro American* (Princeton, N. J.: Van Nostrand, 1964), pp. 113–14. Pollack suggests that the relative lack of proficiency of black children on visual information-processing tasks may be related to their more darkly pigmented retinas. However, in the Farnham-Diggory study, white boys were far superior to white girls on the maplike synthesis task, and it is unlikely that the white girls had more pigmented retinas. See Robert H. Pollack, "Some Implications of Ontogenetic Changes in Perception," in David Elkind and John H. Flavell, eds., *Studies in Cognitive Development: Essays in Honor of Jean Piaget* (New York: Oxford University Press, 1969), pp. 365–407.

49 Young, "Southern Georgia Community" (n. 28 *supra*), pp. 279–80.

50 See Silvia M. Bell, "The Development of the Concept of Object as Related to Infant-Mother Attachment," *Child Development,* 41 (1970): 291–311.

Chapter Five

Cognition and Learning

It is not inadvertent that this section on cognition and learning begins with David Elkind's paper presenting the work and theory of Jean Piaget. Piaget has created a revolution in our thinking about cognitive development.

Although Piaget has been writing about human development for over fifty years and has been an extremely prolific author with over 30 books and 200 papers, his major impact on American psychology was not felt until the last two decades. This was in part because he presented a theory of cognitive development alien to the behavioristic approaches to learning which dominated child psychology in the United States.

Although there are many variations among behavioristic theories certain common principles, which are not congruent with Piaget's thinking, run through many of them. Most behaviorists are interested in the way in which a child's response becomes linked to a stimulus. How does a child learn to fear some objects and not others? How does a child associate verbal symbols with written symbols in learning to read? How does a child learn to be aggressive with peers but not with teachers? In answering such questions, behaviorists study the role of rewards and punishment, modeling, contiguity, discrimination, and generalization in forming and maintaining links between stimuli and responses. It is assumed that even complex problem solving and social responses can be understood in terms of such variables and in terms of overt observable behaviors.

Behavioristic approaches to the study of child development have been criticized for many reasons. First, it is argued that such theories are not developmental theories. The same principles are used to explain learning at all ages and consideration is not given for qualitative changes in cognitive processes with age. Second, a view of development in which the child's behavior is shaped by externally administered rewards and punishments is one in which the child has little control over his experiences, in which he is a relatively passive recipient rather than an active agent in the learning process. Finally it is argued that principles derived from experiments run under restricted laboratory conditions using simple learning tasks may have little relevance to the process involved in complex learning in naturalistic situations in the neighborhood, the family, the school, or with peers.

The student will see that Piaget's work stands in marked contrast to the behavioristic approach to development. It is a truly developmental theory of cognitive development. Piaget maintains that in different stages of development children's thinking is qualitatively different than that in other stages. Cognitive development must proceed through a fixed developmental sequence. Stages cannot be missed or passed through in different orders since cognitive changes in one period are dependent on the attainments and competencies developed in earlier stages. Piaget regards the child as an active participant in his cognitive development. The child is acting on his environment, modifying and interpreting his experience, seeking stimulation, as the environment is acting upon the child. It is this adaptive interaction that leads to changes in mental structures in the child. Finally Piaget's methods differ from those of most behaviorists. Rather than relying on experiments run in a controlled laboratory setting to gain understanding of cognitive development, Piaget used observations in naturalistic settings and interviews to build his theory. In recent years, however, Piaget and his followers have been supplementing these methods with experimental studies of hypotheses derived from Piagetian theory.

One of the Piagetian concepts which has generated the most research is that of conservation, or the understanding that matter remains constant in spite of irrelevant changes in such things as height, width, or shape. In a classic conservation of mass task, the child views two round pieces of clay of the same size and then sees one of them rolled out into a sausage shape. If a preoperational child (age about two to seven) is then asked if the pieces contain equal amounts of clay he is likely to respond that the long one is bigger because of its shape. In contrast the child in the concrete operations stage (about age seven to twelve) will respond correctly that they are the same size. The child in the more advanced stage is using different logical operations than the younger child in responding to the problem. These operations include such things as identity, that if nothing has been added or taken away they must be the same size, and reversibility, that clay that can be rolled out into a sausage can be rerolled back into a round ball again. Piaget believes it is the use of such logical operations that distinguishes the thinking of the concrete operational child from that of the preoperational child.

Many recent studies of conservation involved the use of various training procedures to accelerate conservation. In the paper by Miller and Brownell the role of peer interaction in changes in responses to conservation tasks is investigated. In addition investigators have been interested in the relationship between performance on various conceptual tasks. Bernstein and Cowan in an ingenious study ask if the same Piagetian cognitive developmental sequence is found in tasks involving physical or social conservation and identity.

In the next article, Bandura notes that children's learning is not restricted to direct experience, but can occur through observation of other's actions. This is an important way in which children learn not only new social behaviors, but also acquire new conceptual and language patterns as well. Bandura offers an important analysis of the processes that underlie observational learning. One of the main messages of this paper is the highly cognitive nature of this form of learning. Memory, perceptual, and attentional processes play important roles in learning by imitation.

In the process of socialization, some behaviors often need to be suppressed or inhibited. In the article by Parke, some of the factors that alter the impact of punishment as a control technique are outlined. In this area as well as in other areas of child development, the child's cognitive capacities are receiving recognition; specifically, reasoning techniques are found to become increasingly effective inhibitory tactics as the child develops. Moreover, in light of the ethical problems involved in the use of punishment, for both parents and researchers, this reorientation to cognitive forms of control is a welcome change. Finally, these studies remind us of a recurring theme: the child plays an active role in determining the type or intensity of disciplinary techniques that adults will select. The child, in short, plays an active role in the learning process.

The final paper in this section by Schaefer surveys an issue which is not directly related to Piagetian psychology and reflects much more the historical mainstream of American psychology. Developmental psychologists in the United States have always been concerned with factors that improve the intellectual or academic functioning of children. Psychologists working on learning have been interested in the conditions under which learning is facilitated or impeded. Educational psychologists have studied the types of school programs that optimize academic achievement. More recently, developmental psychologists have begun to investigate the role of the home and parents in the intellectual development of children. This is in part attributable to the finding that most compensatory education programs which have focused on changing the child's extra-familial environment, through such things as special training in language or concept formation in the preschool period, have had few lasting effects if the parents, or at least the mother, were not involved. Effective educational programs need to be extended to the child's total milieu, to the home as well as the school. Watson's famous quotation (Watson, 1959), which was cited in the introduction to the first section in this book, stated that if he was given a dozen healthy infants he could transform them into anything he desired. On the basis of current research evidence he would be more successful if he were given the infants and their parents.

In understanding intellectual development in children some convergence between the cognitive approach of Piaget and the behaviorist tradition seems essential. Although Piaget has emphasized the role of the child in cognitive development he paid relatively little attention to the role of environmental factors. A comprehensive theory of intellectual development must take into account the cognitive processes involved in the learning of children of different ages and in addition should consider the effects of experiential factors in modifying intellectual performance in a wide range of settings.

Giant in the Nursery—Jean Piaget

David Elkind

In February, 1967, Jean Piaget, the Swiss psychologist, arrived at Clark University in Worcester, Mass., to deliver the Heinz Werner Memorial Lectures. The lectures were to be given in the evening, and before the first one a small dinner party was arranged in honor of Piaget and was attended by colleagues, former students and friends. I was invited because of my long advocacy of Piaget's work and because I spent a year (1964–1965) at his Institute for Educational Science in Geneva. Piaget had changed very little since I had last seen him, but he did appear tired and mildly apprehensive.

Although Piaget has lectured all over the world, this particular occasion had special significance. Almost 60 years before, in 1909, another famous European, Sigmund Freud, also lectured at Clark University. Piaget was certainly aware of the historical parallel. He was, moreover, going to speak to a huge American audience in French and, despite the offices of his remarkable translator, Eleanor Duckworth, he must have had some reservations about how it would go.

Piaget's apprehension was apparent during the dinner. For one who is usually a lively and charming dinner companion, he was surprisingly quiet and unresponsive. About half way through the meal there was a small disturbance. The room in which the dinner was held was at a garden level and two boys suddenly appeared at the windows and began tapping at them. The inclination of most of us, I think, was to shoo them away. Before we had a chance to do that, however, Piaget had turned to face the children. He smiled up at the lads, hunched his shoulders and gave them a slight wave with his hand. They hunched their shoulders and smiled in return, gave a slight wave and disappeared. After a moment, Piaget turned back to the table and began telling stories and entering into animated conversation.

Although I am sure his lecture would have been a success in any case and that the standing ovation he received would have occurred without the little incident, I nonetheless like to think that the encounter with the boys did much to restore his vigor and good humor.

It is Piaget's genius for empathy with children, together with true intellectual genius, that has made him the outstanding child psychologist in the world today and one destined to stand beside Freud with respect to his contributions to psychology, education and related disciplines. Just as Freud's discoveries of unconscious motivation, infantile sexuality and the stages of psychosexual growth changed our ways of thinking about human personality, so Piaget's discoveries of children's implicit philosophies, the construction of reality by the infant and the stages of mental development have altered our ways of thinking about human intelligence.

The man behind these discoveries is an arresting figure. He is tall and somewhat portly, and his stooped walk, bulky suits and crown of long white hair give him the appearance of a thrice-magnified Einstein. (When he was at the Institute for Advanced Study at Princeton in 1953, a friend of his wife rushed to a window one day and exclaimed, "Look, Einstein!" Madame Piaget looked and replied, "No, just my Piaget.") Piaget's personal trademarks are his meerschaum pipes (now burned deep amber), his navy blue beret and his bicycle.

Meeting Piaget is a memorable experience. Although Piaget has an abundance of Old-World charm and graciousness, he seems to emanate an aura of intellectual presence not unlike the aura of personality presence conveyed by a great actor. While as a psychologist I am unable to explain how this sense of presence is communicated, I am nevertheless convinced that everyone who meets Piaget experiences it. While talking to me, for example, he was able to divine in my remarks and questions a significance and depth of which I was entirely unaware and certainly hadn't intended. Evidently one characteristic of genius is to search for relevance in the apparently commonplace and frivolous.

Piaget's is a superbly disciplined life. He arises early each morning, sometimes as early as 4 A.M., and writes four or more publishable pages on square sheets of white paper in an even, small hand. Later in the morning he may teach classes and attend meetings. His afternoons include long walks during which he thinks about the problems he is currently confronting. He says, "I always like to think on a problem before reading about it." In the evenings, he reads and retires early. Even on his international trips, Piaget keeps to this schedule.

Each summer, as soon as classes are over, Piaget gathers up the research findings that have been collected by his assistants during the year and departs for the Alps, where he takes up solitary residence in a room in an abandoned farmhouse. The whereabouts of this retreat is as closely guarded as the names of depositors in numbered Swiss bank accounts; only Piaget's family, his long-time colleague Bärbel Inhelder and a trusted secretary know where he is. During the summer Piaget takes walks, meditates, writes *and* writes. Then, when the leaves begin to turn, he descends from the mountains with the several books and articles he has written on his "vacation."

Although Piaget, now in his 72d year, has been carrying his works down from the mountains for almost 50 summers (he has published more than 30 books and hundreds of articles), it is only within the past decade that his writings have come to be fully appreciated in America. This was due, in part, to the fact that until fairly recently only a few of his books had been translated into English. In addition, American psychology and education were simply not ready for Piaget until the fifties. Now the ideas that Piaget has been advocating for more than 30 years are regarded as exceedingly innovative and even as avant-garde.

His work falls into three more or less distinct periods within each of which he covered an enormous amount of psychological territory and developed a multitude of insights. (Like more creative men, Piaget is hard put to it to say when a particular idea came to him. If he ever came suddenly upon an idea which sent him shouting through the halls, he has never admitted to it.)

During the first period (roughly 1922–1929), Piaget explored the extent and depth of children's spontaneous ideas about the physical world and about their own mental processes. He happened upon this line of inquiry while working in Alfred Binet's laboratory school in Paris where he arrived, still seeking a direction for his talents, a year after receiving his doctorate in biological science at the University of Lausanne. It was in the course of

some routine intelligence testing that Piaget became interested in what lay behind children's correct, and particularly the incorrect, answers. To clarify the origins of these answers he began to interview the children in the open-ended manner he had learned when serving a brief interneship at Bleler's psychiatric clinic in Zurich. This semiclinical interview procedure, aimed at revealing the processes by which a child arrives at a particular reply to a test question, has become a trademark of Piagetian research investigation.

What Piaget found with this method of inquiry was that children not only reasoned differently from adults but also that they had quite different world-views, literally different philosophies. This led Piaget to attend to those childish remarks and questions which most adults find amusing or nonsensical. Just as Freud used seemingly accidental slips of the tongue and pen as evidence for unconscious motivations, so Piaget has employed the "cute" sayings of children to demonstrate the existence of ideas quite foreign to the adult mind.

Piaget had read in the recollections of a deaf mute (recorded by William James) that as a child he had regarded the sun and moon as gods and believed they followed him about. Piaget sought to verify his recollection by interviewing children on the subject, and he found that many youngsters do believe that the sun and moon follow them when they are out for a walk. Similar remarks Piaget either overheard or was told about led to a large number of investigations which revealed, among many similar findings, that young children believe that anything which moves is alive, that the names of objects reside in the objects themselves and that dreams come in through the window at night.

Such beliefs, Piaget pointed out in an early article entitled "Children's Philosophies," are not unrelated to but rather derive from an implicit animism and artificialism with many parallels to primitive and Greek philosophies. In the child's view, objects like stones and clouds are imbued with motives, intentions and feelings, while mental events such as dreams and thoughts are endowed with corporality and force.

Children also believe that everything has a purpose and that everything in the world is made by and for man. (My 5-year-old son asked me why we have snow and answered his own question by saying, "It is for children to play in.")

The child's animism and artificialism help to explain his famous and often unanswerable "why" questions. It is because children believe that everything has a purpose that they ask, "Why is grass green?" and "Why do the stars shine?" The parent who attempts to answer such questions with a physical explanation has missed the point.

In addition to disclosing the existence of children's philosophies during this first period, Piaget also found the clue to the egocentrism of childhood. In observing young children at play at the *Maison des Petits*, the modified Montessori school associated with the Institute of Educational Science in Geneva, Piaget noted a peculiar lack of social orientation which was also present in their conversation and in their approaches to certain intellectual tasks. A child would make up a new word ("stocks" for socks and stockings) and just assume that everyone knew what he was talking about as if this were the conventional name for the objects he had in mind. Likewise, Piaget noted that when two nursery school children were at play they often spoke *at* rather than *to* one another and were frequently chattering on about two quite different and unrelated topics. Piaget observed, moreover, that when he stood a child of 5 years opposite him, the child who could tell his own right and left nevertheless insisted that Piaget's right and left hands were directly opposite his own.

In Piaget's view, all of these behaviors can be explained by the young child's inability to put himself in another person's position and to take that person's point of view. Unlike the egocentric adult, who can take another person's point of view but does not, the egocentric child does not take another person's viewpoint because he cannot. This conception of childish egocentrism has produced a fundamental alteration in our evaluation of the preschool child's behavior. We now appreciate that it is intellectual immaturity and not moral perversity which makes, for example, a young child continue to pester his mother after she has told him she has a headache and wishes to be left alone. The preschool child is simply unable to put himself in his mother's position and see things from her point of view.

The second period of Piaget's investigations began when, in 1929, he sought to trace the origins of the child's spontaneous mental growth to the behavior of infants; in this case, his own three children, Jaqueline, Lucienne and Laurent. Piaget kept very detailed records of their behavior and of their performance on a series of ingenious tasks which he invented and presented to them. The books resulting from these investigations, "The Origins of Intelligence in Children," "Play, Dreams and Imitation in Children" and "The Construction of Reality in the Child" are now generally regarded as classics in the field and have been one of the major forces behind the scurry of research activity in the area of infant behavior now current both in America and abroad. The publication of these books in the middle and late nineteen-thirties marked the end of the second phase of Piaget's work.

Some of the most telling observations Piaget made during this period had to do with what he called the *conservation of the object* (using the word conservation to convey the idea of permanence). To the older child and to the adult, the existence of objects and persons who are not immediately present is taken as self-evident. The child at school knows that while he is working at his desk his mother is simultaneously at home and his father is at work. This is not the case for the infant playing in his crib, for whom out of sight is literally out of mind. Piaget observed that when an infant 4 or 5 months old is playing with a toy which subsequently rolls out of sight (behind another toy) but is still within reach, the infant ceases to look for it. The infant behaves as if the toy had not only disappeared but as if it had gone entirely out of existence.

This helps to explain the pleasure infants take in the game of peek-a-boo. If the infant believed that the object existed when it was not seen, he would not be surprised and delighted at its re-emergence and there would be no point of the game. It is only during the second year of life, when children begin to represent objects mentally, that they seek after toys that have disappeared from view. Only then do they attribute an independent existence to objects which are not present to their senses.

The third and major phase of Piaget's endeavors began about 1940 and continues until the present day. During this period Piaget has studied the development in children and adolescents of those mental abilities which gradually enable the child to construct a world-view which is in conformance with reality as seen by adults. He has, at the same time, been concerned with how children acquire the adult versions of various concepts such as number, quantity and speed. Piaget and his colleagues have amassed, in the last 28 years, an astounding amount of information about the thinking of children and adolescents which is only now beginning to be used by psychologists and educators.

Two discoveries made during this last period are of particular importance both because they were so unexpected and because of their relevance for education. It is perhaps fair to say that education tends to focus upon the static aspects of reality rather than upon its dynamic transformations. The child is taught how and what things are but not the conditions under which they change or remain the same. And yet the child is constantly confronted with change and alteration. His view of the world alters as he grows in height and perceptual acuity. And the world changes. Seasons come and go, trees gain and lose their foliage, snow falls and melts. People change, too. They may change over brief time periods in mood and over long periods in weight and hair coloration or fullness. The child receives a static education while living amidst a world in transition.

Piaget's investigations since 1940 have focused upon how the child copes with change, how he comes to distinguish between the permanent and the transient and between appearance and reality. An incident that probably played a part in initiating this line of investigation occurred during Piaget's short-lived flirtation with the automobile. (When his children were young, Piaget learned to drive and bought a car, but he gave it up for his beloved bicycle after a couple of years.) He took his son for a drive and Laurent asked the name of the mountain they were passing. The mountain was the Saleve, the crocodile-shaped mass that dominates the city of Geneva. Laurent was in fact familiar with the mountain and its name because he could see it from his garden, although from a different perspective. Laurent's question brought home to Piaget the fact that a child has difficulty in dealing with the results of transformations whether they are brought about by an alteration in the object itself or by the child's movement with respect to the object.

The methods Piaget used to study how the child comes to deal with transformations are ingenuously simple and can be used by any interested parent or teacher. These methods all have to do with testing the child's abilities to discover that a quantity

remains the same across a change in its appearance. In other words, that the quantity is conserved.

To give just one illustration from among hundreds, a child is shown two identical drinking glasses filled equally full with orangeade and he is asked to say whether there is the "same to drink" in the two glasses. After the child says that this is the case, the orangeade from one glass is poured into another which is taller and thinner so that the orangeade now reaches a higher level. Then the child is asked to say whether there is the same amount to drink in the two differently shaped glasses. Before the age of 6 or 7, most children say that the tall, narrow glass has more orangeade. The young child cannot deal with the transformation and bases his judgment on the static features of the orangeade, namely the levels.

How does the older child arrive at the notion that the amounts of orangeade in the two differently shaped glasses is the same? The answer, according to Piaget, is that he discovers the equality with the aid of reason. If the child judges only on the basis of appearances he cannot solve the problem. When he compares the two glasses with respect to width he must conclude that the wide glass has more while if he compares them with respect to the level of the orangeade he must conclude that the tall glass has more. There is then no way, on the basis of appearance, that he can solve the problem. If, on the other hand, the child reasons that there was the same in the two glasses before and that nothing was added or taken away during the pouring, he concludes that both glasses still have the same drink although this does not appear to be true.

On the basis of this and many similar findings, Piaget argues that much of our knowledge about reality comes to us not from without like the wail of a siren but rather from within by the force of our own logic.

It is hard to overemphasize the importance of this fact, because it is so often forgotten, particularly in education. For those who are not philosophically inclined, it appears that our knowledge of things comes about rather directly as if our mind simply copied the forms, colors and textures of things. From this point of view the mind acts as a sort of mirror which is limited to reflecting the reality which is presented to it. As Piaget's research has demonstrated, however, the mind operates not as a passive mirror but rather as an active artist.

The portrait painter does not merely copy what he sees, he interprets his subject. Before even commencing the portrait, the artist learns a great deal about the individual subject and does not limit himself to studying the face alone. Into the portrait goes not only what the artist sees but also what he knows about his subject. A good portrait is larger than life because it carries much more information than could ever be conveyed by a mirror image.

In forming his spontaneous conception of the world, therefore, the child does more than reflect what is presented to his senses. His image of reality is in fact a portrait or reconstruction of the world and not a simple copy of it. It is only by reasoning about the information which the child receives from the external world that he is able to overcome the transient nature of sense experience and arrive at that awareness of permanence within apparent change that is the mark of adult thought. The importance of reason in the child's spontaneous construction of his world is thus one of the major discoveries of Piaget's third period.

The second major discovery of this time has to do with the nature of the elementary school child's reasoning ability. Long before there was anything like a discipline of child psychology, the age of 6 to 7 was recognized as *the age of reason.* It was also assumed, however, that once the child attained the age of reason, there were no longer any substantial differences between his reasoning abilities and those of adolescents and adults. What Piaget discovered is that this is in fact not the case. While the elementary school child is indeed able to reason, his reasoning ability is limited in a very important respect—he can reason about things but not about verbal propositions.

If a child of 8 or 9 is shown a series of three blocks, ABC, which differ in size, then he can tell by looking at them, and without comparing them directly, that if A is greater than B and B greater than C, then A is greater than C. When the same child is given this problem, "Helen is taller than Mary and Mary is taller than Jane, who is the tallest of the three?" the result is quite different. He cannot solve it despite the fact that it repeats in words the problem with the blocks. Adolescents and adults, however, encounter no difficulty with this problem because they can reason about verbal propositions as well as about things.

This discovery that children think differently from adults even after attaining the age of reason has educational implications which are only now beginning to be applied. Robert Karplus, the physi-cist who heads the Science Curriculum Improvement Study at Berkeley has pointed out that most teachers use verbal propositions in teaching elementary school children. At least some of their instruction is thus destined to go over the heads of their pupils. Karplus and his co-workers are now attempting to train teachers to instruct children at a verbal level which is appropriate to their level of mental ability.

An example of the effects of the failure to take into account the difference between the reasoning abilities of children and adults comes from the New Math experiment. In building materials for the New Math, it was hoped that the construction of a new language would facilitate instruction of set concepts. This new language has been less than successful and the originators of the New Math are currently attempting to devise a physical model to convey the New Math concepts. It is likely that the new language created to teach the set concepts failed because it was geared to the logic of adults rather than to the reasoning of children. Attention to the research on children's thinking carried out during Piaget's third period might have helped to avoid some of the difficulties of the "New Math" program.

In the course of these many years of research into children's thinking, Piaget has elaborated a general theory of intellectual development which, in its scope and comprehensiveness, rivals Freud's theory of personality development. Piaget proposes that intelligence—adaptive thinking and action—develops in a sequence of stages that is related to age. Each stage sees the elaboration of new mental abilities which set the limits and determine the character of what can be learned during that period. (Piaget finds incomprehensible Harvard psychologist Jerome Bruner's famous hypothesis to the effect that "any subject can be taught effectively in some intellectually honest form to any child at any stage of development.") Although Piaget believes that the order in which the stages appear holds true for all children, he also believes that the ages at which the stages evolve will depend upon the native endowment of the child and upon the quality of the physical and social environment in which he is reared. In a very real sense, then, Piaget's is both a nature *and* a nurture theory.

The first stage in the development of intelligence (usually 0-2 years) Piaget calls the sensory-motor period and it is concerned with the evolution of those abilities necessary to construct and reconstruct objects. To illustrate, Piaget observed that when he held a cigarette case in front of his daughter Jaqueline (who was 8 months old at the time) and then dropped it, she did not follow the trajectory of the case but continued looking at his hand. Even at 8 months (Lucienne and Laurent succeeded in following the object at about 5 months but had been exposed to more experiments than Jaqueline) she was not able to reconstruct the path of the object which she had seen dropped in front of her.

Toward the end of this period, however, Jaqueline was even able to reconstruct the position of objects which had undergone hidden displacement. When she was 19 months old, Piaget placed a coin in his hand and then placed his hand under a coverlet where he dropped the coin before removing his hand. Jaqueline first looked in his hand and then immediately lifted the coverlet and found the coin. This reconstruction was accomplished with the aid of an elementary form of reasoning. The coin was in the hand, the hand was under the coverlet, the coin was not in the hand so the coin is under the coverlet. Such reasoning, it must be said, is accomplished without the aid of language and by means of mental images.

The second stage (usually 2-7 years), which Piaget calls the preoperational stage, bears witness to the elaboration of the symbolic function, those abilities which have to do with representing things. The presence of these new abilities is shown by the gradual acquisition of language, the first indications of dreams and night terrors, the advent of symbolic play (two sticks at right angles are an airplane) and the first attempts at drawing and graphic representation.

At the beginning of this stage the child tends to identify words and symbols with the objects they are intended to represent. He is upset if someone tramps on a stone which he has designated as a turtle. And he believes that names are as much a part of objects as their color and form. (The child at this point is like the old gentleman who when asked why noodles are called noodles, replied that "they are white like noodles, soft like noodles and taste like noodles so we call them noodles.")

By the end of this period the child can clearly distinguish between words and symbols and what they represent. He now recognizes that names are arbitrary designations. The child's discovery of the arbitrariness of names is often manifested in the "name calling" so prevalent during the early school years.

At the next stage (usually 7-11 years) the child acquires what Piaget calls concrete operations, internalized actions that permit the child to do "in his head" what before he would have had to accomplish through real actions. Concrete operations enable the child to think about things. To illustrate, on one study Piaget presented 5-, 6- and 7-year-old children with six sticks in a row and asked them to take the same number of sticks from a pile on the table. The young children solved the problem by placing their sticks beneath the sample and matching the sticks one by one. The older children merely picked up the six sticks and held them in their hands. The older children had counted the sticks mentally and hence felt no need to actually match them with the sticks in the row. It should be said that even the youngest children were able to count to six, so that this was not a factor in their performance.

Concrete operations also enable children to deal with the relations among classes of things. In another study Piaget presented 5-, 6- and 7-year-old children with a box containing 20 white and seven brown wooden beads. Each child was first asked if there were more white or more brown beads and all were able to say that there were more white than brown beads. Then Piaget asked, "Are there more white or more wooden beads?" The young children could not fathom the question and replied that "there are more white than brown beads." For such children classes are not regarded as abstractions but are thought of as concrete places. (I once asked a pre-operational child if he could be a Protestant and an American at the same time, to which he replied, "No," and then as an afterthought, "only if you move.")

When a child thought of a bead in the white "place" he could not think of it as being in the wooden "place" since objects cannot be in two places at once. He could only compare the white with the brown "places." The older children, who had attained concrete operations, encountered no difficulty with the task and readily replied that "there are more wooden than white beads because all of the beads are wooden and only some are white." By the end of the concrete operational period, children are remarkably adept at doing thought problems and at combining and dividing class concepts.

During the last stage (usually 12-15 years) there gradually emerge what Piaget calls formal operations and which, in effect, permit adolescents to think about their thoughts, to construct ideals and to reason realistically about the future. Formal operations also enable young people to reason about contrary-to-fact propositions. If, for example, a child is asked to assume that coal is white he is likely to reply, "But coal is black," whereas the adolescent can accept the contrary-to-fact assumption and reason from it.

Formal operational thought also makes possible the understanding of metaphor. It is for this reason that political and other satirical cartoons are not understood until adolescence. The child's inability to understand metaphor helps to explain why books such as "Alice in Wonderland" and "Gulliver's Travels" are enjoyed at different levels during childhood than in adolescence and adulthood, when their social significance can be understood.

No new mental systems emerge after the formal operations, which are the common coin of adult thought. After adolescence, mental growth takes the form—it is hoped—of a gradual increase in wisdom.

This capsule summary of Piaget's theory of intellectual development would not be complete without some words about Piaget's position with respect to language and thought. Piaget regards thought and language as different but closely related systems. Language, to a much greater extent than thought, is determined by particular forms of environmental stimulation. Inner-city Negro children, who tend to be retarded in language development, are much less retarded with respect to the ages at which they attain concrete operations. Indeed, not only inner-city children but children in bush Africa, Hong Kong and Appalachia all attain concrete operations at about the same age as middle-class children in Geneva and Boston.

Likewise, attempts to teach children concrete operations have been almost uniformly unsuccessful. This does not mean that these operations are independent of the environment but only that their development takes time and can be nourished by a much wider variety of environmental nutriments than is true for the growth of language, which is dependent upon much more specific forms of stimulation.

Language is, then, deceptive with respect to thought. Teachers of middle-class children are often misled, by the verbal facility of these youngsters, into believing that they understand more than they actually comprehend. (My 5-year-old asked me what my true identity was and as I tried to recover my composure he explained that Clark Kent was Superman's true identity.) At the other end, the teachers of inner-city children are often fooled by the language handicaps of these children into thinking that they have much lower mental ability than they actually possess. It is appropriate, therefore, that preschool programs for the disadvantaged should focus upon training these children in language and perception rather than upon trying to teach them concrete operations.

The impact which the foregoing Piagetian discoveries and conceptions is having upon education and child psychology has come as something of a shock to a good many educators and psychological research in America, which relies heavily upon statistics, electronics and computers. Piaget's studies of children's thinking seem hardly a step beyond the prescientific baby biographies kept by such men as Charles Darwin and Bronson Alcott. Indeed, in many of Piaget's research papers he supports his conclusions simply with illustrative examples of how children at different age levels respond to his tasks.

Many of Piaget's critics have focused upon his apparently casual methodology and have argued that while Piaget has arrived at some original ideas about children's thinking, his research lacks scientific rigor. It is likely that few, if any, of Piaget's research reports would have been accepted for publication in American psychological journals.

Other critics have taken somewhat the opposite tack. Jerome Bruner, who has done so much to bring Piaget to the attention of American social scientists, acknowledges the fruitfulness of Piaget's methods, modifications of which he has employed in his own investigations. But he argues against Piaget's theoretical interpretations. Bruner believes that Piaget has "missed the heart" of the problem of change and permanence or conservation in children's thinking. In the case of the orangeade poured into a different-sized container, Bruner argues that it is not reason, or mental operations, but some "internalized verbal formula that shields him [the child] from the overpowering appearance of the visual displays." Bruner seems to believe that the syntactical rules of language rather than logic can account for the child's discovery that a quantity remains unchanged despite alterations in its appearance.

Piaget is willing to answer his critics but only when he feels that the criticism is responsible and informed. With respect to his methods, their casualness is only apparent. Before they set out collecting data, his students are given a year of training in the art of interviewing children. They learn to ask questions without suggesting the answers and to test, by counter-suggestion, the strength of the child's conviction. Many of Piaget's studies have now been repeated with more rigorous procedures by other investigators all over the world and the results have been remarkably consistent with Piaget's findings. Attempts are currently under way to build a new intelligence scale on the basis of the Piaget tests, many of which are already in widespread use as evaluative procedures in education.

When it comes to criticisms of his theoretical views, Piaget is remarkably open and does not claim to be infallible. He frequently invites scholars who are in genuine disagreement with him to come to Geneva for a year so that the differences can be discussed and studied in depth. He has no desire to form a cult and says, in fact, "To the extent that there are Piagetians, to that extent have I failed." Piaget's lack of dogmatism is illustrated in his response to Bruner:

"Bruner does say that I 'missed the heart' of the conservation problem, a problem I have been working on for the last 30 years. He is right, of course, but that does not mean that he himself has understood it in a much shorter time . . . Adults, just like children, need time to reach the right ideas . . . This is the great mystery of development, which is irreducible to an accumulation of isolated learning acquisitions. Even psychology cannot be learned or constructed in a short time." (Despite his disclaimer, Piaget has offered a comprehensive theory of how the child arrives at conservation and this theory has received much research support.)

Piaget would probably agree with those who are critical about premature applications of his work to education. He finds particularly disturbing the efforts by some American educators to accelerate children intellectually. When he was giving his other 1967 lectures, in New York, he remarked:

"If we accept the fact that there are stages of development, another question arises which I call 'the American question,' and I am asked it every time I come here. If there are stages that children reach at given norms of ages can we accelerate the stages? Do we have to go through each one of these stages, or can't we speed it up a bit? Well, surely, the answer is yes . . . but how far can we speed them up? . . . I have a hypothesis which I am so far incapable of proving: probably the organization of operations has an optimal time . . . For example, we know that it takes 9 to 12 months before babies develop the notion that an object is still there even when a screen is placed in front of it. Now kittens go through the same sub-stages but they do it in three months—so they're six months ahead of the babies. Is this an advantage or isn't it?

"We can certainly see our answer in one sense. The kitten is not going to go much further. The child has taken longer, but he is capable of going further so it seems to me that the nine months were not for nothing . . . It is probably possible to accelerate, but maximal acceleration is not desirable. There seems to be an optimal time. What this optimal time is will surely depend upon each individual and on the subject matter. We still need a great deal of research to know what the optimal time would be."

Piaget's stance against using his findings as a justification for accelerating children intellectually recalls a remark made by Freud when he was asked whatever became of those bright, aggressive shoeshine boys one encounters in city streets. Freud's reply was, "They become cobblers." In Piaget's terms they get to a certain point earlier but they don't go as far. And the New York educator Eliot Shapiro has pointed out that one of the Negro child's problems is that he is forced to grow up and take responsibility too soon and doesn't have time to be a child.

Despite some premature and erroneous applications of his thinking to education, Piaget has had an over-all effect much more positive than negative. His findings about children's understanding of scientific and mathematical concepts are being used as guidelines for new curricula in these subjects. And his tests are being more and more widely used to evaluate educational outcomes. Perhaps the most significant and widespread positive effect that Piaget has had upon education is in the changed attitudes on the part of teachers who have been exposed to his thinking. After becoming acquainted with Piaget's work, teachers can never again see children in quite the same way as they had before.

Once teachers begin to look at children from the Piagetian perspective they can also appreciate his views with regard to the aims of education.

"The principal goal of education," he once said, "is to create men who are capable of doing new things, not simply of repeating what other generations have done—men who are creative, inventive and discoverers. The second goal of education is to form minds which can be critical, can verify, and not accept everything they are offered. The great danger today is of slogans, collective opinions, ready-made trends of thought. We have to be able to resist individually, to criticize, to distinguish between what is proven and what is not. So we need pupils who are active, who learn early to find out by themselves, partly by their own spontaneous activity and partly through materials we set up for them; who learn early to tell what is verifiable and what is simply the first idea to come to them."

At the beginning of his eighth decade, Jean Piaget is busy as ever. A new book of his on memory will be published soon and another on the mental functions in the preschool child is in preparation. The International Center for Genetic Epistemology, which Piaget founded in 1955 with a grant from the Rockefeller Foundation, continues to draw scholars from around the world who wish to explore with Piaget the origin of scientific concepts. As Professor of Experimental Psychology at the University of Geneva, Piaget also continues to teach courses and conduct seminars.

And his students still continue to collect the data which at the end of the school year Piaget will take with him up to the mountains. The methods employed by his students today are not markedly different from those which were used by their predecessors decades ago. While there are occasional statistics, there are still no electronics or computers. In an age of moon shots and automation, the remarkable discoveries of Jean Piaget are evidence that in the realm of scientific achievement, technological sophistication is still no substitute for creative genius.

Reading 20

Peers, Persuasion, and Piaget: Dyadic Interaction between Conservers and Nonconservers

Scott A. Miller
Celia A. Brownell

Two issues underlie the present study. The first concerns the certainty with which children experience Piagetian concepts. Piaget (e.g., 1971) has argued that concepts such as conservation, once fully understood, are experienced as logically necessary truths. Evidence in support of this claim has been difficult to obtain. Conservers are not particularly resistant to the extinction of their beliefs (Miller, 1971, 1973), nor do they express much surprise when conservation is apparently violated (Miller, 1973). By most measures, in fact, conservers appear no more certain about conservation than nonconservers do about nonconservation. Yet both Piaget's theory and common sense suggest that the former belief should be held with more certainty than the latter.

There are, it is true, reasons to question this apparent equivalence of nonconservation and conservation. Miller (1973) did find that verbalizations that suggested resistance to change were more frequent for conservers than for nonconservers. Furthermore, there are methodological limitations in the research conducted thus far. Most of the studies have focused on conservation of weight, making conclusions about conservation in general uncertain. And in both the extinction and the surprise paradigms, the social pressures from an adult tester may well have obscured any feelings of certainty that the child possessed.

The second issue to be examined is the role of

This research was supported by Grants No. 315660 and 360624 from the Horace H. Rackham School of Graduate Studies, University of Michigan. We are grateful to Susan Miller for her assistance with the testing, and to the staff and children of Martin Luther King Elementary School and Carpenter Elementary School, Ann Arbor, Michigan, for their generous cooperation.

peer interaction in cognitive development. Attempts to explain the child's progression through Piagetian stages typically have emphasized either adult teaching or the child's interaction with the physical world. The possibility that peers may play an important role in cognitive change has been largely ignored. This neglect has occurred despite the fact that Piaget's early writings suggested a central role for peer interaction. Specifically, Piaget (1932) argued that the conflicts that arise between peers are an important source of decentering and hence of cognitive change.

The present procedure for examining these issues is to pair conservers with nonconservers and require them to discuss the conservation problem and arrive at a common solution. Certain control problems are also included; these are an attempt to assure that any differences between conservers and nonconservers are specific to conservation and not a reflection of general differences in social influence.

The closest previous analogues to the current experiment are two studies by Silverman and associates (Silverman & Geiringer, 1973; Silverman & Stone, 1972). In both, conservers and nonconservers were paired and required to discuss their answers, and in both, conservers won the arguments significantly more often than nonconservers. In the absence of control tasks, however, it is not clear whether this outcome is specific to conservation or a reflection of the general dominance of conservers. Also, in neither report is there much information about the interaction between the children. The present report attempts to provide a fuller picture of the children's discussions prior to agreement.

METHOD

Subjects

The final sample consisted of 100 second graders (58 boys and 42 girls) from two predominantly middle-class schools in Ann Arbor, Michigan. These children were selected from an initial sample of 223 on the basis of their performance on pretests for conservation of length and weight. During the second (interaction) session, 14 pairs were tested only on length, 17 only on weight, and 19 on both concepts.

Procedure

The testing was divided into two sessions. The first session included the pretests for conservation of length and conservation of weight. The stimuli for the length trials were sticks 20.5 cm. in length. Length trials began with two sticks aligned horizontally. On the first trial the top stick was moved forward about 5 cm; on the second trial the bottom stick was made into a zigzag. The conservation question was "Are the two sticks still the same length, or is one longer than the other?" followed by "Why is that?"

The stimuli for the weight trials were clay balls. A balance scale was used to indicate the initial equality. On the first trial one ball was made into a sausage; on the second trial one ball was broken into six smaller balls. The form of the conservation question was similar to that for length.

The length and weight trials were balanced for order. The first session concluded with the two questions that were to be used as control items during the interaction session: "What is the most dangerous animal in the world?" and "What is the very best TV show?"

The pairs for the second session always included one conserver and one nonconserver. A child was considered a conserver for a given concept if he answered both questions correctly and also provided logical explanations for his answers. He was considered a nonconserver if he answered both questions incorrectly. Any other pattern was regarded as transitional. Whenever possible, children were paired on both concepts; if necessary, however, they were paired on just length or just weight. The pairs were formed randomly, subject to three constraints: children were paired only if they differed on at least one control question; members of a pair were always from the same classroom; members of a pair were always of the same sex.

It was not possible to make the interval between sessions the same for all children. The modal interval was two days; the range was one to eight days.

The second session began with the experimenter explaining that she was going to ask some of the same questions as before, but that this time she would ask both children together. She told them that she would check their answers from the first time; if the answers were different, then she would ask them to discuss the question and try to agree on an answer. The lead-in stressed several points: the children would have to give reasons for their answers; that the important thing was to work together to arrive at the best answer; and that it was all right for a child to change his mind.

The question about "most dangerous animal" was administered first, followed by "best TV show," followed by the conservation problem or problems. In the case of conservation, only the first of the two pretest trials were used. The order of the length and weight tasks were balanced for subjects receiving both. On all problems, conservation continued until the children had clearly agreed on one answer, or until the experimenter decided that they were hopelessly deadlocked.

At the conclusion of the session, the child who had changed his answer on conservation stayed behind for an individual posttest (the choice of which child stayed was made to appear random through use of a "guess the number closest to mine" game). The posttest was a repetition of both pretest trials for the conservation or conservations on which the child had given in.

Scoring

Two judges independently rated the adequacy of the conservation explanations. Explanations of the following types were considered adequate: Revers-

ibility, Compensation, Addition/Subtraction, Previous Equality, Irrelevancy of Transformation, and (for weight only) Same Amount of Clay. The percentage of agreement with respect to adequacy was 96%.

The categories that were used in scoring the discussions of conservation tasks are shown in Table 1, along with the percentages of agreement obtained by two judges who independently scored the second-session tapes.

RESULTS

Pretest

The pretest for conservation of length yielded 35% conservers, 39% nonconservers, and 26% transitional. The figures for weight were 46% conservers, 27% nonconservers, and 26% transitional. A sign test revealed that conservation of weight was significantly easier than conservation of length, $Z = 4.12$, $p < .001$ (here and throughout, all p values are based on two-tailed tests). There were no significant sex differences.

Table 1 Categories Used to Score the Discussions of Conservation Problems

Category	Description	Percentage of interrater agreement
First relevant statement	Utters the first statement relevant to the problem	94%
First explanation	Utters the first explanation in support of an answer	91%
Asserts answer	States own answer from the pretest	96%
Total number of assertions	Number of distinct statements of own answer	88%
Explains answer	Offers an explanation in support of own answer	99%
Total number of explanations	Number of distinct occurrences of explanations in support of an answer	88%
Type of explanation (conservers only)	Assignment of explanations to the various logical types (e.g., Reversibility, Compensation)	77%
Number of distinct explanations (conservers only)	Number of different types of explanation offered	86%
Counters other	Provides an argument against an explanation just advanced by the other child (must be in response to the other child's statement)	86%
Questions other	Asks a task-relevant question of the other child	97%[a]
Moves or suggests moving stimuli	Moves or suggests moving the sticks or clay balls	96%[a]
Time	Total time for trial	87%[b]

[a]Since neither of these categories was scored with much frequency, a percentage of agreement based on the total number of trials is somewhat inflated. If the agreement is calculated on the basis of the number of trials on which at least one rater scored the response, the percentages are 90% for Questions Other and 88% for Moves Stimuli.

[b]Agreement was credited if the two raters' times were within 5 seconds of each other.

Interaction

The control problems yielded 90 usable trials across the 50 pairs. Conservers won the argument on 41 of these trials, nonconservers on 38, and there were 11 stalemates. There was no evidence, therefore, that conservers and nonconservers differed in relative social influence.

The picture on the conservation trials was quite different. On conservation of length, conservers won 27 times, nonconservers 3 times, and there were 3 stalemates, $Z = 4.20$, $p < $ ej ctors in modifying t ive t .001 by the normal approximation to the binomial. On conservation of weight, conservers won 25 times, nonconservers 5 times, and there were 6 stalemates, $Z = 3.47$, $p < .001$.

The analysis of the interaction is presented in Table 2. Results for males and females have been combined, since the patterns for the two sexes were quite similar. The data are presented in two ways, conserver vs. nonconserver and winner vs. loser. These comparisons are, of course, overlapping, given the high proportion of trials on which the conservers were the winners. They are not identical, however, since there were eight trials on which nonconservers won and nine trials which ended in stalemates.

Significant differences between conservers and nonconservers emerged on several measures. (Unless otherwise noted, all comparisons are based on Fisher's exact test.) On the weight task, conservers were more likely than nonconservers to assert their answer at least once, $p < .02$; a similar comparison on the length trials approached significance, $p < .10$. This finding reflects the fact that on 17 of the 68 trials (5 on length, 12 on weight) the nonconserver gave in without even stating his original answer. Similarly, on the length problems conservers were more likely than nonconservers to offer at least one explanation in support of their answer, $p < .01$. On length, in fact, there was no trial on which the conserver did not both assert and explain his answer.

The remaining differences between conservers and nonconservers reached significance only on length. Conservers were more likely than nonconservers to produce a Counter to the other child's explanation, $p < .01$. Conservers were also more likely to move or suggest moving the stimuli, $p < .02$. The fact that the latter difference did not appear on the weight trials may reflect a difference in the meaning of the "moves stimuli" response on the two tasks. Instances of this category on the length trials consisted mainly of demonstrations of an answer (e.g., moving the stick back to show reversibility), whereas occurrences on the weight problems were often simply requests for a solution (e.g., "Could we weigh them and see?").

A comparison of winners vs. losers reveals significant differences in all of the above-mentioned cases in which conservers and nonconservers differed (all $ps < 05$ by Fisher's exact test) and in several additional cases as well. All of the addition-

Table 2 Proportion of Subjects Giving at Least One Instance of the Different Categories of Response[a]

Category	Length				Weight			
	C	NC	Winners	Losers	C	NC	Winners	Losers
First relevant statement	.45	.55	.50	.50	.56	.44	.79**	.21
First explanation	.64	.36	.67	.33	.56	.44	.78**	.22
Asserts answer	1.00	.85	1.00	.83	.91*	.66	1.00**	.48
Explains answer	1.00**	.73	1.00**	.70	.77	.63	.83**	.45
Counters other[b]	.71**	.30	.71**	.23	.36	.21	.57**	.16
Questions other	.33	.27	.33	.23	.23	.20	.24	.07
Moves or suggests moving stimuli	.48*	.18	.47*	.13	.29	.40	.24	.34

Note. C=Conservers NC=Nonconservers

[a]One pair tested on weight was omitted from this analysis because the tape recorder failed. This pair is included, however, in the analyses of yielding and of posttest performance.

[b]Percentages for this category are based on the number of trials on which the other child offered an explanation.
*p of the difference between groups $< .05$.
**p of the difference between groups $< .01$.

al differences appeared on the weight trials. On these trials, the child who eventually won the argument was significantly more likely than the other child to utter the first task-relevant statement, $Z = 2.83$, $p < .01$ by the normal approximation to the binomial, as well as the first explanation in support of his answer, $p = .01$, binomial test. The eventual winner was also more likely to offer an explanation for his answer, $p < .01$, as well as to attempt a Counter of the other child's explanation, $p < .05$. These latter differences parallel similar differences on the length trials.

Part of the information provided by an analysis of the interactions is descriptive rather than comparative in nature. The degree of discussion can best be described as moderate. This conclusion is suggested not only by the proportions reported in Table 2 but by certain other results as well. Thus, the average number of times a subject asserted his answer was 7.1 on length and 4.7 on weight. The average number of explanations offered was 4.0 for length and 2.3 for weight. The average time per trial was 178 seconds (median = 114 seconds) for length and 131 seconds (median = 47 seconds) for weight. It should be noted, however, that the distribution of times was decidedly bimodal. While 31 of the 68 trials were resolved in less than 50 seconds, 28 of the remaining trials lasted 3 minutes or more.

A final analysis concerns the variety of explanations offered. The great majority of the nonconservers' explanations were simple variants of a perceptual theme (e.g., "It's skinnier now."). The great majority of the conservers' explanations were logically adequate justifications. The most common type of explanation was Irrelevancy of Transformation, which was used on 62% of the trials (an example would be "You just pushed it up."). All of the arguments appeared with some frequency, however, and it was quite common for a conserver to resort to several distinct explanations. Thus, on 20 of the 68 trials the conserver produced three or more distinct explanations; on 10 trials he produced four or more different explanations. Of the 28 trials which lasted for more than 3 minutes, 17 contained at least three distinct explanations by the conserver.

Posttest

The proportion of conservation judgments by nonconservers on the posttest was 50% for length and 54% for weight. In both cases, 93% of the judg-ments were accompanied by adequate explanations. And in both cases, performance was better on the first trial (the problem discussed during the interaction) than on the second. With both concepts combined, there were 73% conservation judgments on trial 1 and 31% on trial 2.

Since the nonconserver prevailed on only eight trials, data concerning the posttest performance of conservers are limited. What data there are, however, seem similar to those for nonconservers. Conservers gave 44% nonconservation answers on the posttest—75% on trial 1 and 13% on trial 2. All of the nonconservation judgments were accompanied by perceptual explanations.

DISCUSSION

The results from the analysis of yielding confirm and extend those of Silverman and Stone (1972) and Silverman and Geiringer (1973). As in their studies, the conserver's answer prevailed on the great majority of conservation trials. The inclusion of control tasks permits an important clarification, however: The superiority of conservers is specific to conservation, and not a reflection of general social dominance. In contrast to data from extinction and surprise studies, the interaction paradigm indicates that a belief in conservation is in fact more firmly held than a belief in nonconservation.

It should be noted that the certainty that can be identified in such a paradigm is largely a relative certainty. The fact that conservers are more certain than nonconservers does not indicate the absolute level of the conservers' confidence; in particular, it does not indicate that conservers experience conservation as logically necessary. Statements that might have reflected feelings of necessity (e.g., "They *have* to weigh the same.") were almost nonexistent. This finding is similar to the results of extinction research, in which explicit statements of necessity are also rare.

The measurement of certainty is relative in a second sense as well. The extent to which conservers or nonconservers win the argument must surely depend on the developmental level of the sample. Specifically, the more advanced the sample, the greater should be the dominance of conservers: Not only should the conservers' concepts become more solid with increasing age, but the nonconservers should become more willing to abandon their belief in nonconservation. Conversely, a very young sample might show a higher proportion of nonconservation solutions than that obtained here. There is clearly no single "correct" point in development at which to sample, and further studies might profitably examine a range of ages.

The analysis of the interactions suggests two general conclusions about processes of peer persuasion in the context of conservation problems. First, many children (mostly nonconservers) were apparently so uncertain of their original answer that mere exposure to an opposing answer was sufficient to produce giving in. Thus, on 25 trials the loser never offered an explanation, and on 20 of these trials he never even asserted his original answer. Silverman also found (personal communication) that the mere presentation of a contradiction seemed to be a major element in the efficacy of peer interaction.

The second conclusion concerns the children who engaged in a more prolonged discussion. In such pairs, the qualities that seemed to distinguish the conservers were the variety and adaptability of their approach. Conservers and nonconservers did not differ in tendency to initiate the discussion, nor in the total number of times that they asserted their answers, nor in the total number of times that they offered explanations. The conservers, however, were more likely to attempt to rebut the other child's explanation, more likely (on length trials) to manipulate the stimuli, and more likely to generate a variety of explanations in support of their answer. The nonconservers, in contrast, seemed to be limited largely to restatements of their original perceptual response, with little ability to supplement their reasoning or to counter the other child's reasons.

Performance on the posttest suggests that the degree of genuine training or extinction was modest at best. Similar studies which have included more interaction trials (Murray, 1972; Silverman & Geiringer, 1973; Silverman & Stone, 1972) have reported more impressive training effects. The interest of the present research, however, was not in posttest performance per se. A consideration of conservation training studies suggests two conclusions: A great variety of training procedures can induce gains in conservation, and none of these procedures (including peer interaction) has much direct resemblance to the way in which children acquire conservation outside the laboratory. The obvious implication is that research should focus less exclusively on posttest gain and more on identifying the potentially generalizable aspects of the processes by which change comes about.

REFERENCES

Miller, S. A. Extinction of conservation: A methodological and theoretical analysis. *Merrill-Palmer Quarterly*, 1971, *17*, 310–334.

Miller, S. A. Contradiction, surprise, and cognitive change: The effects of disconfirmation of belief on conservers and nonconservers. *Journal of Experimental Child Psychology*, 1973, *15*, 47–62.

Murray, F. B. Acquisition of conservation through social interaction. *Developmental Psychology*, 1972, *6*, 1–6.

Piaget, J. *The moral judgment of the child.* London: Routledge & Kegan Paul, 1932.

Piaget, J. *Biology and knowledge.* Chicago: University of Chicago Press, 1971.

Silverman, I. W., & Geiringer, E. Dyadic interaction and conservation induction: A test of Piaget's equilibration model. *Child Development*, 1973, *44*, 815–820.

Silverman, I. W., & Stone, J. M. Modifying cognitive functioning through participation in a problem-solving group. *Journal of Educational Psychology*, 1972, *63*, 603–608.

Children's Concepts of How People Get Babies

Anne C. Bernstein
Philip A. Cowan

What do children think about how babies come to be? Almost 5 decades ago, Piaget (1929) suggested that children's ideas about the cause of babies should follow the same sequence of cognitive developmental stages as their concepts of physical causality. Despite the testability of the hypothesis and the importance of the topic, only three subsequent studies have provided an empirical developmental assessment of what children think about the origin of babies.

A study by Conn (1947) used doll play as an interviewing technique with 100 4–11-year-old children. Analysis of the data was confined to summary descriptions of the child's response content. Conn concluded that "it is inconceivable to the child of preschool age that the baby may be in the mother." He also concluded that sex information is beyond the grasp of the intelligent child of 7 or 8 and that not until 9 or 10 do children first notice and discuss the mother's distended abdomen during pregnancy. It is possible that these results were biased in part by the doll-play method or the particular sample chosen; it is certainly our impression, 25 years later, that younger children are more knowledgeable than Conn suggested.

Two more recent studies directly examined Piaget's hypothesis (Kreitler & Kreitler 1966; Moore & Kendall 1971). Both studies question Piaget's conclusion, but the age range of the subjects was narrow (4–5$\frac{1}{2}$, 3–5$\frac{1}{2}$), and the interviewers used a standardized format rather than Piaget's more flexible clinical method.

Both practical and theoretical considerations make further studies absolutely necessary. Sex educators and the general public are locked in bitter dispute concerning what children should be taught and what they already know (Breasted 1971). Per-

sonality theorists, beginning with Freud ([1908] 1963), have based important conclusions on data obtained from patients' or college students' reconstructions of childhood. Child analysts now obtain data from their patients (A. Freud 1965), but the literature contains only anecdotal reports filtered through theorists' eyes. There appears to be no shortage of adult opinions on the subject. The present study, within a cognitive developmental framework, represents a new attempt to gather systematic normative data directly from children. In part, it shifts the emphasis away from the prevailing views which assume that changes in children's concepts of procreation are a function of what they themselves observe, of peer and adult (mis)information, and of physiological growth related to libidinal or sexual functioning.

It seems to us that the cognitive concepts most relevant to the origin of babies are those concerning causality and identity. It is only when the child begins to perceive that events and phenomena have causes that he can attempt to investigate what they are; it is only when the child recognizes that he himself and other persons are continuous beings, conserving identity despite the transformations in appearance due to maturation, that he can think about his own origins or those of his siblings.

In the present study children from the ages of 3 to 12 were presented with four tasks. A newly constructed social causality questionnaire examined their concepts of the origin of babies. An analogous questionnaire about the origin of night developed by Laurendeau and Pinard (1962) represented an index of physical causality. The development of social identity was investigated with an as-yet unpublished task (Lemke 1973), and the development of physical identity was inferred from children's performance in the traditional conservation interview. If children's concepts concerning how people get babies are embedded in a cognitive developmental matrix, then scores on the four tasks should be correlated within and between age levels. There should also be instances of systematic developmental ordering in which performance on some tasks is more advanced than on others (i.e., décalages), but previous theoretical and empirical evi-

This paper was based upon a dissertation by Anne Bernstein, submitted in partial fulfillment of the requirement for a doctoral degree in psychology at the University of California, Berkeley. The authors wish to thank Professors Ken Craik, Joseph Kuypers, and Margaret Singer for their guidance. Thanks also to Sonne Lemke for making available her social identity task, and to Carolyn Cowan for her constructive comments on the manuscript. We extend our gratitude to the Children's Community Center of Berkeley, and to the children and parents who cooperated in this study.

dence was not conclusive enough to make specific predictions. Finally, this study provides a qualitative analysis of children's concepts of how people get babies, in part to provide more information about what children think and in part to provide data for speculation about the cognitive processes involved.

METHOD

Subjects

Sixty children participated in this study, 10 boys and 10 girls at each of three age levels (3–4, 7–8, 11–12). It was expected that performance would range from preoperational to a level transitional between concrete and formal operations in Piaget's system.

Given the hesitance of many parents to have their children questioned about sexual matters, random sampling was not attempted in this study. The final sample, referred by our acquaintances, consisted primarily of upper-middle-class Caucasian children who had at least one younger sibling and thus would have had to comprehend the entrance of a younger child into their families. Since most of the children were from two-child families, there was no confounding of age of subject and number of siblings. Because the study focused on establishing invariant sequences of performance and within-individual developmental cohesion, the lack of random sampling was not considered a serious drawback at this stage of our knowledge.

Measures

Social and physical causality and identity concepts were measured by four different tasks. Each task adopted a clinical interview format in which standardized questions were followed up with interviewer probes designed to clarify the meaning of the child's response and to locate the response more precisely at a particular developmental level. All tasks were scored on a seven-point scale; an attempt was made to establish the same score for the same developmental stage level on each task. Interrater reliability was established at 75%–90% on a random selection of half the protocols for each task.

1. Physical Conservation-Identity: Manipulation with Clay and Water The children's ability to conserve nonsocial objects was assessed by the familiar tasks involving transformations of clay. They were asked to judge the equality or inequality of amount in two clay balls, one of which was

changed in shape and then divided in two. Those who succeeded in conserving amount with these initial tasks were given two volume-conservation problems. In the first the experimeter placed one clay ball in a glass of water and asked the child to estimate the height of water if an identical clay ball were placed in a second glass. In the next volume task the experimenter transformed the shape of the second clay ball and then repeated the question.

Level 0: No answer of all incorrect answers.
Level 1: Preoperational. Incorrect answers with perceptual explanations ("It looks bigger or it's larger"), or correct answers with no explanations.
Level 2: Transitional. Satisfactory explanations on one but not both conservation-of-amount tasks (e.g., "It's longer but it's thinner").
Level 3: Concrete operations. Conservation of amount in both tasks with adequate explanation. No conservation of volume.
Level 4: Transitional. Correct predictions of water height but explanations on a concrete level (e.g., "It will rise to the same height because it's the same amount").
Level 5: Transitional. Correct predictions and adequate explanation in only one of two volume tasks.
Level 6: Formal operations. Successful conservation of amount and volume with explanations reflecting the fact that volume is conserved despite transformations in appearance.

Initially the physical conservation task had been chosen as an index of children's concepts of physical identity. We subsequently found that Piaget (Piaget & Voyat 1968) had clarified the two concepts, showing that physical identity is concerned with transformations in which one of two objects remains unchanged. It appears that physical identity concepts slightly precede conservation and are necessary for conservations to occur. We will, therefore, refer to the task as "physical conservation-identity" in order to emphasize potential parallels with the social identity task.

2. Social Identity Lemke (1973) has developed a measure of the child's sense that an individual's identity continues through time despite changes in physical appeaance. It also assesses the child's ability to identify individuals on the basis of their relationship to others. In the present study, Lemke's measure was interpreted as an index of the child's ability to "conserve" social objects.

Each subject was presented with two photographs of an eight-member family taken several years apart. After discussion established that the pictures came from the same family, the child was presented with six photos of that family, from both earlier and later periods, asked to identify the individuals in each picture, to provide his rationale for making the identifications, and to arrange the photos in their proper time sequence. The subject was then asked to explain why a younger female child was not in the earliest picture. If the subjects did not volunteer the information that she was not yet born, they were asked a series of questions concerning her whereabouts (e.g., "Do you think she was taking a nap?"), ending with the direct question, "Do you think she was born yet?"

Because Lemke had not administered this measure to children over the age of 9, it was not anticipated that successful completion of this task would occur as late as 11–12 years. Two additional transition stages were added to Lemke's original rating schedule. The rating schedule as amended includes the following stages:

Level 0: An initial stage in which any individual may be any other individual without clear distinctions based upon sex or race or general physical characteristics.
Level 1: Identity of a person in the different photos is denied except where all qualities are the same. Attention to alterations in appearance due to clothing, etc., interfere with judgments of identity.
Level 2: Static identifications based on same size, hair style, hat. Fewer errors. Beginning to grasp principle of ordering and to realize younger children in late photos could not yet have been in the first one.
Level 3: Transitional stage. Fewer errors than above. All grasp that youngest siblings not yet born in early photos.
Level 4: Correct identifications but the relationships of individuals within the family are not firmly grasped and identity is based solely on appearance. Principle of ordering established.
Level 5: Transitional stage, distinguished from the preceding in that the use of context, or the relations of individuals within the family, is becoming more established in the child's reasoning, but is still not firmly held or consistently applied.
Level 6: Systematic operational thinking. Implications for individual identity include identification by relation of unit to other units and to the whole.

3. Physical Causality: The Origin of Night Laurendeau and Pinard's (1962) standardized version of Piaget's questions concerning the origin of night was chosen to represent a physical causality task. All children were asked to tell the interviewer what night is, why it is dark, where the dark comes from, and what makes it night. Children usually attribute the origin of night to sleep, to clouds, or to the disappearance of the sun. A further set of standardized questions followed up whatever answers the child gave. All children were asked if "we can make the night in this room," and if pulling blinds down would make it dark. Finally, they were asked where the dark in the room comes from and to explain what makes it day.

Laurendeau and Pinard developed a scale to rate the child's level of reasoning about the origin of night and, by inference, about problems of physical causality.

Level 0: No understanding of question; refusal to answer.
Level 1: Absolute finalism (e.g., it becomes dark so we may go to sleep).
Level 2: Explicit artificialism mixed with finalism (e.g., it becomes dark because God calls the dark, or Mother puts the light out).
Level 3: Artificialism desguised as physicalism; fabricating agent necessary but uses natural, physical elements. Animistic elements (e.g., the moon opens his eyes, he blows the sun away and he blows the night in).
Level 4: Additional stage not delineated by Laurendeau and Pinard. Physical explanations mixed with strong animistic and finalistic elements (e.g., when the sun turns the other way, it's real dark, when the moon comes).
Level 5: Physicalism with taints of finalism or animism (e.g., it becomes dark because we need rest and the sun goes to the other side of the world).
Level 6: Absolute physicalism (e.g., it becomes dark because the sun is shining on the other side of the world).

4. Social Causality: The Origin of Babies The clinical method provided the experimenter the opportunity to assess the child's understanding of her questions as well as an opportunity to go beyond mere rote-learned, parroted answers. All concepts and terms describing reproduction were introduced by the child himself; only after the child indicated the trend of his thinking was the line of questioning by the interviewer determined. Each answer was probed until the child's thinking became as explicit and as detailed as he or she was able to make it, following through on the implications of the initial explanation. It was not assumed that the child's use of any given word necessarily meant that he comprehended its common usage definition.

Each interview included the following questions: "How do people get babies?" "What does the word 'born' mean?" "What does it mean to say someone [e.g., you] was born?" "How do mothers get to be mothers?" "How did your mother get to be your mother?" "When did she start being your mother?" "How do fathers get to be fathers?" "How did he start being your father?" "How was it that [name of younger sibling] came to live in your family and be your sister/brother?"

In addition, younger children were asked: "What if some people who lived in a cave in the desert, where there weren't any other people, wanted to have a baby. Because they had never known any other people, they didn't know how people get babies. What if they asked you for help? If they asked you what they should do if they wanted a baby, what would you tell them?"

Older children were asked: "What did you think about how people get babies before you understood it as well as you do now? What did you think when you were little?"

Pilot protocols were used to create a scale which, while following the structural outline of the Laurendeau and Pinard scale, dealt specifically with the application of similar levels of cognitive development to the problem of the origin of babies.

Level 0: Lack of comprehension of questions.

Level 1: Spatial causality. Question is perceived as spatial, not causal, i.e., "Where do people get babies?" Child assumes that babies have always existed; the problem is to discover where the baby was before it was present in the family, no need to explain how.

Example: MIKE (3-8). You go to a baby store and buy one. JACK (3-2). From tummies.

Level 2: Artificialism, including finalism and animism. Child answers the "how" questions as such. Egocentric interpretation of body parts and processes involved, which are limited to those they themselves have experience with, e.g., the "digestive fallacy," whereby the baby gets into the tummy by being ingested and exits as in elimination. Artificialism, the origin of natural phenomena described as if produced by a process of manufacture, here entails only natural materials. Emphasis on purpose rather than process, although need for explanation is assumed.

Example: JANE (3-7). [How does the baby get in the tummy?] Just make it first. [How?] Well, you just make it. You put some eyes on it. . . . Put the head on, and hair, some hair all curls. [With?] You make it with head stuff. [How?] ance " rs in modifyiYou find it at a store that makes it. . . . Well, they get it and then they put it in the tummy and then it goes quickly out.

Level 3: Transitional. Explanations are semi-physical, semipsychological, semiartificialistic, but only technically feasible operations are given credence; e.g., "agricultural fallacy," or concretization of the metaphor of "planting a seed." Animistic distortions: anthropocentric and zoocentric, i.e., subautonomous organic units are endowed with the will and the physical motility of people and animals. Moral causality: social convention treated as an immutable given.

Example: JANE (4-6). The sperm goes into the Mommy to each egg and puts it, makes the egg safe. So if something bump comes along it won't crack the egg. [Where does the egg come from?] From the Daddy. [Then what happens?] It swims in, into the penis and then it . . . I think it makes a little hole and then it swims into the vagina. [How?] It has a little mouth and it bites a hole.

Level 4: Explanations are primarily physical, although still tinged with finalism and egocentrism. The attributes of the fabricating agent, heretofore either God or man, are now given over to nature or social convention. This level is distinguished from 5 and 6 in that the child, while aware of the physical processes involved in procreation, cannot explain why these processes must occur, i.e., he knows the "facts of life" but does not understand what about these processes causes the new life to begin.

Example: LARA (7-9). The man and the woman get together, and they they put a speck, then the man has his seed and the woman has an egg, and then I guess, that's all I know really. [Why do the seed and the egg have to come together?] Or else the baby, the egg won't really get hatched very well. [How does the baby come from the seed and the egg?] The seed makes the egg grow. [How?] It's just like plants. If you plant a seed a flower will grow.

Level 5: Preformation. This level is distinguished from the preceding in that the child explains what there is about the seed and the egg coming together that produces the child. It is distinguished from Level 6 in that the child still does not conceive of any stage before the baby's existence; it is a latent form that can be transferred (e.g., from one person's body to another). But its original substance is invariable. There is no perceived need for a final cause.

Example: PATRICK (12-9). The lady has an egg and the man has a sperm, and they, sort of he fertilizes the egg, and then the egg slowly grows, the sperm grows into a baby inside the egg. . . . [Fertilize?] It means it gets inside the egg, the sperm. It just sort of goes in. The egg before the sperm goes in is sort of like, well, I guess, it doesn't have anything in it to grow, it just has food and I guess a shell on the outside. . . . It's sort of the beginning of the baby. It has to happen, because otherwise the sperm would just die because it has no shelter on the outside to keep it alive, no food, nothing. And then the egg, there's nothing in it to grow, I guess. It has no . . . no . . . no . . . living animal in there.

Level 6: Physicalism freed from precausality. Physical explanations of this physiological process. Psychological and moral connotations, while taken into account, are not given determinist status. Distinguished from Level 5 in that the exchange of genetic materials during fertilization is seen as the point of origin of the new being.

Example: TINA (11-11). [Fertilize?] Well, it just starts it off I guess. . . . Mixes the genes or, well, puts particles or something into the egg. [Genes?] Genes are the things from the father and the mother, you know, and they put a little bit of each into the baby so the baby turns out to be a little bit like the mother or father or something.

Developmental Scoring

Each task was scored on a seven-point (0–6) scale, in which higher scores were assumed to represent higher developmental levels. In physical conservation-identity and in physical causality tasks it has been traditional to assume that scores correspond to Piaget's developmental stages: preoperational concrete, and formal operations, and the transitions between them. Table 1 presents a summary of the scoring criteria for all four tasks. It indicates our best estimate of the comparable structural-stage level represented by each score. It reflects our intentions to compare task performance rating not only in terms of relative rank (correlation) but also in terms of absolute levels (χ^2).

Procedure

Children were tested individually in their homes. The Origin of Babies interview was given first, and the following three tasks were administered in random order. The testing period lasted between 30 and 60 minutes.

In sum, four tasks assessing concepts of physical conservation-identity (Clay), social identity (Family Pictures), physical causality (Origin of Night), and social causality (Origin of Babies) were administered to 20 boys and girls at each of three age levels (3–4, 7–8, 11–12). The study attempted to establish a Piagetian sequence of children's con-

cepts of procreation; it examined the place of this sequence within a matrix of physical and social concepts.

RESULTS AND DISCUSSION

In the first part of this section we will present a quantitative analysis of the four tasks and their interrelationships. In the second part we include a selection of qualitative data in order to convey a more concrete sense of children's concepts of procreation.

Quantitative Analysis

Developmental Data A frequency distribution of children's responses to the Origin of Babies interview is presented in table 2. Responses scored were in fact more often given by the younger children, while the oldest children were consistently rated near the top of the stage hierarchy. A slight deviation from this pattern in the 7–8-year-olds will be discussed below. Except for this 7–8-year-old deviation, frequency distributions for the other three tasks were virtually identical to table 2. The consistent increase in stage scores with increasing age supports the hypothesis that the concepts are ordered in a developmental sequence.

Separate two-way analyses of variance (age × sex) were performed for each of the four measures (the results are summarized in table 3). In all tasks F ratios for age were statistically significant ($p <$ .01) while those for sex differences or interactions were not. Again, age increases are accompanied by regular increases in cognitive performance.

An additional analysis of variance was made for the social causality Origin of Babies measure, since it appeared from examination of the raw data that a real difference between boys and girls in the 7–8-year-old group was being masked by combining the 2-year levels. This second analysis of variance, which treated each age year as a separate group, produced an F ratio significant at $p <$ .05 for variance attributed to difference in sex, with girls showing higher scores, especially in the 7-year-old group. Despite the larger difference at one age level, the interaction between age and sex was statistically insignificant. It is the sex difference in the 7–8-year-old group that is responsible for the deviation from gradually ascending gradations on the frequency distribution measure (table 2).

Between each pair of tasks correlations were calculated in order to determine whether age in-

Table 1   A Developmental Comparison of Scoring Systems

Piagetian stage	Physical conservation-identity (volume of clay)	Social identity (family pictures)	Physical causality (origin of night)	Social causality (origin of babies)
	Task			
Preoperational	0: No answer or all wrong 1: Preoperational	0: Arbitrary identifications 1: Insistence on sameness 2: Static identifications	0: No answer or incomprehension 1: Finalistic interpretations 2: Artificialistic beliefs	0: Lack of comprehension 1: Spatial answers, absolute precausality 2: Artificialism, including finalism and animism
Transitional	2: Transitional	3: Transitional	3: Semiartificialistic and semiphysical interpretations	3: Transitional between artificialism and physicalism
Concrete	3: Conservation of clay but not when displacing water	4: Intuitive personal identity reversibility but little use of context	4: Physicalism with no artificialism but some finalistic or animistic constructions	4: Physicalism with lacunae
Transitional	4, 5: Conservation of clay in water, reasoning inadequate	5: Inconsistent use of context in making identifications	5: Physicalism with taints of finalism	5: Physicalism with preformation
Formal?	6: Conservation with reference to volume consistently made in explanations	6: Systematic operational thinking; individual identity linked to relation of unit to other units and the whole	6: Physicalism freed from all precausality	6: Physicalism freed from precausality, insistence on a final cause

Table 2   Distribution of Subjects by Age and Developmental Stage Scores: Social Causality Task

Age	N	0	1	2	3	4	5	6
		Stage						
11–12	20	0	0	0	0	10	50	40
7–8	20	0	30	0	40	20	5	5
3–4	20	5	60	30	0	5	0	0
Total	60	5	90	30	40	35	55	45
Mean age		3–6	5–1	4–7	7–10	8–9	11–8	11–7

Table 3   Analyses of Variance of Four Tasks: Age × Sex

Source	df	Physical conservation-identity	Social identity	Physical causality	Social causality
Age	1,54	97.70*	92.65*	49.00*	75.98*
Sex	2,54	1.15	3.92	2.61	3.92
Interaction	2,54	2.30	0.49	0.87	1.47

*$p < .01$.

creases in one task were accompanied by age increases in another. Table 4 shows the value of Pearson correlation coefficients for each pair of measures, both for the sample as a whole and for each age group. All six whole-sample correlations were statistically significant ($p < .01$, $df = 58$) and ranged between .73 and .83. Four of the six correlations between pairs of tasks in the 3–4-year-old group were statistically significant, two of six were significant in the 7–8-year-olds, and only one in the oldest group. Thus, the whole-sample trend is supported best within the youngest sample. The scores of the 3–4-year-olds showed most variance. With older subjects the lower variance and a ceiling

effect probably combined to reduce the statistical association among tasks.

The data indicate that task scores were consistently related to age (table 2, analyses of variance) and that the relative rate of development in each task was similar (correlations). The results are consistent with the hypothesis that there is an invariant necessary sequence of development in the four tasks, but they do not provide conclusive evidence. Only longitudinal studies can determine definitively whether each child must progress through each level in the given order.

Décalage   Piaget's concept of the décalage (Piaget & Inhelder 1969) is an elusive one. It posits

Table 4   Correlations between Tasks: Within-Age and Total Sample

	Physical-conservation-identity (clay)	Social identity (family pictures)	Physical causality (night)	Social causality (babies)
Physical conservation:				
3–4[a]		.36	.62*	.68*
7–8[a]		.18	−.19	.21
11–12[a]		.53*	.13	.08
Total[b]		.83**	.80**	.73**
Social identity:				
3–4			.49*	.23
7–8			.26	.38*
11–12			.02	−.01
Total			.79**	.76**
Physical causality:				
3–4				.50*
7–8				.70**
11–12				.03
Total				.74**

[a]$df = 18$.
[b]$df = 58$.
*$p < .05$.
**$p < .01$.

developmental lags in the application of a child's cognitive structure to particular content areas in order to account for the fact that children do not arrive simultaneously at the same stage in all concepts or tasks. A first step in examining the issue of décalage was to find out whether children performed at the same absolute level on each task. Table 5 presents the χ^2 tables constructed for each pair of measures. Subjects' performance was categorized as preoperational (p) or at least concrete operational (o) on each task.[1] Fisher Exact Tests for each 2 × 2 table produced values of χ^2 that were all statistically significant ($p < .001$). From 68% to 93% of the subjects were at exactly the same developmental level in both tasks. It is evident that there is an absolute as well as a relative association among the tasks.

An examination of the χ^2 tables indicates that the relatively low number of exceptions to perfect agreement appear to follow a pattern. For example (top left), four subjects were operational in physical causality but not in the physical conservation task, while none was at a high level on conservation but not causality. And (top middle) 11 subjects were operational on physical causality but not social identity, while one showed the reverse trends. These results suggest that in addition to a strong correlation between tasks there is also a develop-

[1] The dividing line occurred between scores of 2 and 3 for physical conservation-identity and between 3 and 4 for the other three tasks (see table 1).

mental ordering which could be conceptualized as a rough Guttman scaling. Of the total of 60 subjects, 46 were at or beyond concrete operations in physical causality (Origin of Night), 42 in physical conservation-identity (Clay), 36 in social identity (Family Pictures), and 27 in social causality (Origin of Babies).

This rough ordering was further explored in analysis of variance comparisons among tasks as a function of age and sex; these comparisons incorporated the total range of scores rather then the two-step χ^2 division of levels. No statistically significant main effects or interactions with sex were found. In addition to the significant age effect, F $(2,54) = 149.5$, $p < .001$, there was a significant task effect, $F (3,162) = 24.4$, $p < .001$, and a significant age × task interaction, $F (6,162) = 9.7$, $p < .001$. The relevant means are presented in table 6. Again, the Origin of Night task was the easiest (4.40), followed by the Clay task (3.87), the Family Pictures (3.48), and the Origin of Babies task (3.18). All differences were statistically significant (t tests, $p <$ .01). Subjects performed at a higher level on both physical form (Night) and most difficult in its social form (Babies), so no generalizations concerning the relative difficulty of causality and identity concepts could be made.

In general, the trends were similar but not as marked within each age group. The clearest physical-social concept difference occurred in the 7–8-year-old sample. We have noted before that at

Table 5 Chi-Square Tables for Pairs of Tasks: Performance either Preoperational (p) or Concrete Operational (o)

		Physical causality					Physical causality					Physical causality	
		p	o				p	o				p	o
Physical conser- vation	p	14	4		Social identity	p	13	11		Social causality	p	14	19
	o	0	42			o	1	35			o	0	27

		Physical conservation					Physical conservation					Social identity	
		p	o				p	o				p	o
Social identity	p	17	7		Social conser- vation	p	18	15		Social causality	p	22	11
	o	1	35			o	0	27			o	2	25

Table 6   Average Development Scores (0–6) on Four Tasks: Within-Age and Total Sample

	Physical causality	Physical conservation-identity	Social identity	Social causality
3–4	2.50	1.25	1.10	1.40
7–8	5.00	5.00	4.00	2.85
11–12	5.70	5.25	5.35	5.30
Total	4.40	3.87	3.48	3.18

this age in the Origin of Babies task the 7-year-old boys produce particularly low scores.

The evidence from both χ^2 and analysis of variance clearly indicates that the logical structures underlying concrete operations are applied to the four tasks in a consistent order, that is, there is clear evidence of a décalage. While Piaget has found it theoretically and empirically necessary to acknowledge the existence of décalages, explanations of the phenomenon are far from clear.

Generally, three types of variables have been suggested by Piaget to account for a décalage: the child's experience, the role of affect, and the nature of the task itself. All three may be operative in the present case.

1 Experience. Among the four tasks under consideration, the social causality Origin of Babies questionnaire produced the lowest developmental level of performance. In our culture it is likely that experience in the form of verbal discussion would be least in this area. In addition, experience in the form of direct physical-sensorimotor contact with the phenomenon is least possible. Finally, in terms of Piaget's concept of logicomathematical experience—experience with operating upon and transforming things and ideas—again, the origin of babies is least accessible to children of the four concepts under discussion.

2 Affect. Piaget's writings in the area of affect are often sketchy (see Piaget 1967). He views the affective and cognitive aspects of development as inseparable and irreducible, with affectivity constituting the "energetics of behavior patterns whose cognitive aspect refers to the structures alone" (Piaget & Inhelder 1969). Usually, Piaget notes affect as an intrusion factor which promotes lower levels of performance in a particular area.

In the present study, 7-year-old boys were at a significantly lower level of reasoning about human reproduction. This was the only task and the only

age at which clear sex differences emerged. Perhaps the affective intrusion was simply the embarrassment of 7-year-old boys talking to a female interviewer "about sex." Perhaps, though, more complex factors were involved. The Freudian concept of latency should be considered at this point.

Latency is described as a time of decreased sexual interest but increased interest in the development of masculine and feminine sex roles. In the present sample many of the 7–8-year-old boys were occupied with stereotypically "boyish" things, while many of the girls had rooms replete with doll babies and playhouse furnishings. Thus a combination of affective-libidinal and experiential factors may have led to the girls' higher scores in this age range.

3 The nature of the task. Piaget often comments that some tasks more than others seem to "resist" assimilation to a particular structural level. The tasks were obviously different in method of presentation, for example, two were verbal, while two were presented with concrete stimuli. This particular variable does not appear to account for performance differences, since the verbal tasks (Night and Babies) showed the highest and lowest levels of performance, but it is certainly possible that other aspects of what has been called "method variance" may have led to developmental discrepancies in performance.

What may have been centrally important in producing a décalage was the nature of the transformations involved in each task. The tasks with physical referents (Clay, Night) were clearly easier than tasks with social referents (Family, Babies). Both physical tasks involved transformations of the physical world which were reversible, while the social tasks both involved irreversible transformations. Piaget and Voyat (1968) in a study of identity found that an irreversible transformation, even in a physical object, makes the problem of conservation-identity more difficult.

It appears, then, that experience, affect, and task variables may all interact to produce the obtained décalage. Exactly how this occurs must be the subject of future research.

Summary of Quantitative Findings The quantitative data indicate that children's concepts of how people get babies show a Piagetian developmental sequence. They are highly correlated with conservation, causality, and identity measures, but all the tasks show some important absolute differences. Children attain concrete operations first on physical causality, then physical conservation, then social identity, and finally social causality. Physical concepts appear to develop before social concepts.

Concepts of physical causality appear to develop before conservation or identity concepts, but social causality, at least on the topic of how babies are born, comes relatively later. Before discussing these trends in more detail, we will present some descriptive data concerned with children's concepts of procreation.

Qualitative Analysis

We wish to convey to the reader a concrete sense of what and how children think about the origin of babies. To meet obvious needs for abbreviation, we focus on children's answers to only one of the questions in the interview. "How does the baby happen to be inside the mother's body?" generated the most comprehensive answers and was the single most important question in terms of differentiating between cognitive levels.

Level 1 Most 3–4-year-olds believe that a baby has always existed, but they have several different notions concerning how it comes to be in the mother's body. Some believe it was always there, others assume it was located somewhere else in the same form and then somehow came into the mother, and still others speculate about a series of transformations.

[How did the baby happen to be in your Mommy's tummy?] It just grows inside. [How did it get there?] It's there all the time. Mommy doesn't have to do anything. She waits until she feels it. [You said that the baby wasn't in there when you were there.] Yeah, then he was in the other place in . . . in America. [In America?] Yeah, in somebody else's tummy. [In somebody else's tummy?] Yeah, and then he went through somebody's vagina, then he went in, um, in my Mommy's tummy. [In whose tummy was he before?] Um, the, I don't know, who his, her name is. It's a her.

At Level 1, children appear to be assimilating directly from their own experience. There is no "first cause." If something comes out, it can go back in.

Level 2 Children at this level begin to attribute babies to some cause, primarily a person or persons who function as manufacturers. Laura described how people get babies.

Maybe they just paint the right bones. . . . Maybe they just paint the bones and paint the blood, and paint the blue blood. . . .

Similarly Tom, a 4-year-old boy, suggested that a woman who wants a baby to grow in her stomach should "maybe get a body" at a store, she could then "put it all together" with "tools" to "produce a baby." This child, described by his mother as having received no religious training, was one of two children, both Level 2 boys, to mention God in his account of how people get babies. According to Tom, God makes Mommies and Daddies "with the little seed":

He puts it down . . . on the table . . . then, it grows bigger. The people grow together. . . . He makes them eat [the seed], then they grow . . . to be people . . . then they stand up and go someplace else, where they could live . . . [the seed] makes them into people [from] skeletons [which were at] God's place.

Note that 4-year-old Tom assumes that a baby is bought at the store, but that his Mommy and Daddy were made by God from seeds. It is as if the remoteness of his parents' childhood requires a more remote cause. Especially for young children it may be necessary to explore differences and similarities in their concepts of parent origin, self origin, and their own future role in producing offspring. Note also that despite differences in content the manufacturing analogy was present in both explanations. Tom was the only child who attributed the role of manufacturer to God, a startling contrast to Conn's study in which half of the children in the entire sample and the great majority of the preschoolers attributed a decisive role to the Deity.

A few children at Level 2 connect a father with the birth process, but assimilate what they have been told to a mechanical process. A girl responds:

[If the seed is in the Daddy, how does it get on the egg?] I don't know. Cause he can't really open up all his tummies. [Then how?] It rolls out. [How does it get to the egg?] Well, I think that the Daddy gets it. [How?] Puts his hand in the tummy. [Whose?] His tummy. [Then?] He puts it on the bottom of the Mommy and the Mommy gets the, gets the egg out of her tummy, and puts the egg on top of the seed. And then they close their tummies . . . and the baby is born. . . .

For her the seed and the egg can only come together by manual means. She expressed some doubts that her version of the story could be accurate, but her experience provided her with no real alternatives and she very conscientiously tried to confine her description to physical processes and causes.

Two Level 2 children had an apparently oblique approach to questions about procreation:

[How would the lady get a baby to grow in her tummy?] Um, get a rabbit. 'Cause one day I saw a book about them, and . . . they just get a duck or a goose and they get a little more growned . . . and then they, turn into a baby. [A rabbit will turn into a baby?] They give them some food, people food, and they grow like a baby. [If I asked you to tell me just one way that people get babies, what would you say?] I would say, a store, buy a duck, and a duck. [A duck?] Yeah. [Who told you that? How'd you find out about the duck?] I saw it in a book, and my Mommy told me it. [Your Mommy told you that ducks turn into babies?] No, I just saw, find out from this book.

This story of the duck transformed into a baby highlights one of the difficulties children have with books that attempt to teach them about human reproduction by analogy with other animals. Often such books will start out with how other animals mate and give birth, working up the animal kingdom until they reach human beings. When unable to account for a given aspect of human reproduction, the child assimilates details from other sections of the book, details which for him are no more fantastic in their adopted contexts than they were as originally stated.

This example, and others we will cite, begins to illustrate a general point: "knowledge" about babies and sex is not simply a matter of information and misinformation. It is difficult to believe that children have somehow been told the answers they give. Rather, it appears that children who wonder about, or are asked about, the origin of babies, *make up* answers. These answers represent assimilations both from the context of experience and from the structure of thought.

Level 3 Children giving Level 3 responses appeared to have isolated three major ingredients in the creation of babies: social relationship (some affective and/or marital bond between man and woman), the external mechanics of sexual intercourse, and the fusion of biological-genetic materials. They conceptualize these ingredients in a more sophisticated way than Level 2. However, consis-

tent with the general description of children in transition between preoperations and concrete operations, they are unable to coordinate any of the variables in a coherent system.

Sometimes, children attempting to relate two areas may themselves be aware of the hazy link between them.

[How does the father give "the stuff" for the baby?] Well, he puts his penis right in the place where the baby comes out, and somehow it comes out of there. It seems like magic sort of, 'cause it just comes out. Sometimes, I think the father pushes maybe.

There is no preformation in either sperm or egg; this child clearly stated that the egg is not a baby until the father gives his part, but she was somewhat vague and rather concretistic in describing why his contribution is necessary:

If he didn't then a baby wouldn't come. [Why?] Because it would need the stuff that the father gives. [Why?] I don't know. [What does it do?] Helps it grow. . . . I think that stuff has the food part, maybe, and maybe it helps protect it. . . . I think he gives the shell part, and the shell part, I think, is the skin.

Another example of how one variable becomes assimilated to the other can be seen in Frank's responses. His mother reports that he was taught "sperm/egg physiology" and about "intercourse as a function of procreation and a love relationship." It would seem that 8-year-old Frank has absorbed more about the "love relationship" than about the physiology.

It's like when people are naked, and they're together, and they're together, and they just lie together, I guess. Like they're hugging. Some men give hickies, except my Dad don't. They're just . . . together. [What does that have to do with getting babies?] I don't know. I guess it's like mothers and fathers are related, and their loving each other forms a baby, I guess. [How?] I don't know. It's just there's love and I guess it just forms a baby, like I said before. . . .

Thus, he described love as a relationship quality that substantively forms the developing baby.

Some children at Level 3 seem as if they are beginning to keep the variables separate, but the variables still run together. For example, one girl was becoming aware that intercourse and "baby making" are not synonymous. However, her method of birth control was still tied to the mechanics of intercourse:

Well, I think when you get married, you go on your honeymoon . . . and you fuck on your honeymoon, you know, then that makes it so you've got each other's germs, and then when you do it again you've got a baby. But sometimes you don't do it like for long enough or something like that; although I'm not sure, and then it doesn't, you don't get a baby.

Level 4 Table 1 noted our assumption that Level 4 represented a qualitatively new stage: concrete operations. Thus, there should be a different kind of reasoning as well as a different content of response. In fact, Level 4 is the first of three levels which rely completely on physical causes of conception. All artificialism and mechanical manufacturing theories of Levels 1 and 2 are rejected. Variables are coordinated in a biological system. Level 4 is distinguished from Levels 5 and 6 because at this stage the child cannot provide an explanation of the *necessity* of uniting genetic materials. Karen, when asked why the seed and the egg have to come together replied:

Or else the baby, the egg won't really get hatched very well. [How does the baby come from the egg and the seed?] The seed makes the egg grow. [?] It's just like plants; if you plant a seed a flower will grow. [There's no egg with plants.] No, it's just a special kind of seed, that makes an egg hatch. . . . [Why must seed touch egg for the baby to grow?] The egg won't hatch. [What about its coming together makes a baby?] I don't know. Well, I don't think. . . . I don't know. [Can the egg grow into a baby without the seed?] I don't think so. [Can the seed grow into a baby without the egg?] I don't know.

She had absorbed the information that seed and egg are necessary to create a new life and that they must come together to begin the process of development, but she had no clear idea of why this was so. She had, however, in another part of the interview, integrated the sperm and egg system in the notion of intercourse.

Level 5 The protocols at this level included a concept of the baby as inherent in either the sperm or the egg; thus, the embryo is preformed in one

germ cell and sexual intercourse merely provides necessary and sufficient conditions for development to occur. In the history of embryology, preformation is used to refer to growth without differentiation, that is, the preexistence in miniature of all living creatures in the germ cells of animals and the seeds of plants. In this section it will be used to refer to both ovism—the preexistence of the embryo in the egg—and animalculism—the preexistence of the embryo in the sperm.

Four of the 11 Level 5 children might be called ovists. These children described the sperm as the catalyst, energizing or giving life to the latent embryo in the egg. They all referred in some manner to sexual intercourse. When asked what that had to do with getting babies, most replied that the egg was fertilized during sexual intercourse. Asked to define fertilization, they revealed their "ovist" tendencies:

[Then, what does "fertilize" mean?] Kind of give it food and things like that. . . . [How is it that the baby starts growing when the sperm goes into the egg?] by es:
   r er ant modifying t ive t t,III guess when it gets in there it just does something to the egg, and it makes it start growing. . . . [Can egg grow if no sperm goes into it?] I don't think so. [Can sperm grow with no egg?] No, that doesn't have the baby; it's the egg that would have the baby in it.

In contrast to ovism, animalculism consisted of the belief that genetic parenthood was exclusively a paternal matter. This belief was an ancient one. Four of the Level 5 children were explicit animalculists; the protocols of two others were laden with implications of the preformation of the embryo in the sperm, although there were no explicit statements about how preformation works. For these children, the sperm is "real tiny and has to go into the lady" where it "grows into a baby." Sexual intercourse is necessary in order to transfer the sperm from its point of origin in the father to an environment more conducive to development in the mother. Responding to the question "How do fathers get to be fathers?" Kathy said:

Well, if they're the man that made love to your mother, then they're your father because you really originally came out of him, and then went into your mother. [More?] Well, you were a sperm inside of him, there. So that you're the, you're really his daughter or son. 'Cause he was the one that really had you first. [Why must the egg be there for the sperm to develop into a baby?]'Cause otherwise the sperm will have, uh, nothing to nourish it, or sort of keep it warm or, you know, able to move or something. Just has, it's not, just has to have the egg to be able to do something, develop. It just dies if it doesn't have the egg.

Thus, the egg is described as having the female cultural role of providing warmth and nourishment for the developing fetus.

These explicit explanations of ovism and animalculism demonstrate two important points. First, the 11–12-year-olds have a preformist notion of conception. But, in contrast with 3- and 4-year-olds, this notion is embedded in a much more complex causal theory. Like other aspects of Piaget's theory, development seems to occur in a spiral rather than a straight line. Children "circle back" to the same issues, but deal with them on a more differentiated and integrated structural level. Second, these explanations suggest that children may recapitulate part of the history of the science of embryology in trying to make sense of human reproduction. The next step after Level 5, historically and ontogenetically, is the realization that the genetic material for the embryo is furnished by *both* parents and that the system is interactive rather than additive. Contrary to popular usage, the child is not a simple composite of "his mother's eyes," "his grandfather's ears," and "his father's temper." It is possible that formal operations may be necessary for Level 6 explanations of the origin of babies.

Level 6 Children rated at Level 6 had to include in their physiological explanations of reproduction the ideas that the embryo begins its biological existence at the moment of conception and that it is a product of genetic materials from both parents.

The most scientifically accurate description of conception was provided by Michael:

The sperm encounter one ovum, and one sperm breaks into the ovum which produces, the sperm makes like a cell, and the cell separates and divides. And so it's dividing, and the ovum goes through a tube and embeds itself in the wall of the, I think it's the fetus of the woman.

Vera referred to the role of genes in the inheritance of parental traits. She explained the function of fertilization in embryonic development:

Well, it just, it starts it off, I guess. You know, well . . . mixes something or, you know. [?] Mixes the genes or, well, puts particles or something into the egg, to make it, you know, fertilized. And so it will, you know, have genes and different kind of blood and stuff like that I guess. Because if it didn't it would be more like the mother, I guess. [What do genes have to do with it?] Well, genes are the things from the father and the mother, you know, and they put a little bit of each into the baby so the baby turns out to be a little bit like the mother or father or something. Not always, but a little bit.

Other explanations of the necessity for the union of the reproductive cell were not as extensive. Children in this group offered such statements as "The two cells meet and start growing," and "The fluids have to be together to make the baby." The highly complex scientific technical knowledge of some children at Level 6 caps a trend evident in all of the qualitative examples we have cited and the many others that were collected. We have described the Origin of Babies interview as focusing on an aspect of social causality. But the children's explanations rely heavily on notions of physical causality (especially biochemical-genetic) and social and physical identity (through transformations). Explanations concerning the origin of babies clearly involve, at the very least, all four of the conceptual dimensions we have been considering. The qualitative data from the Origin of Babies task alone indicate clearly that the observed quantitative intercorrelations among the four tasks were not accidental.

Summary of Qualitative Results Children's concepts concerning the origin of babies follow a developmental sequence and are embedded in a matrix of cognitive-structural variables. At Level 1, children are preformist and, in essence, do not see the need for a "cause" of babies. In Level 2 the causes are assimilated from notions of people as manufacturers. Children at Level 3 isolate two or three main factors: social, sexual, and biological—but do not coordinate them in a true system. With the advent of concrete operations, children at Level 4 do coordinate the variables in a system of physical causes but fail to come to grips with genetic transmission. Level 5 children are quite familiar with genetic transmission but conceptualize it as additive rather than interactive. Thus, they enter a new level of preformism, becoming ovists or animalculists. Finally, at Level 6, children provide a reasonably sophisticated scientific theory of how people get babies. We should note, at the close of this section, that not all questions on this topic have been answered. Most notably, in its ultimate form, the question of how babies come to be raises the issue of the origins of life itself. At this time, we can only wonder whether an answer will ever be attained.

Implications This study is an example of what will likely become a common research strategy in the area of cognitive development. It is an attempt to take some known developmental task "anchors" (Night, Clay) as indices to locate a previously unexplored area of children's thought. Presumably the Piagetian sequence will be found in many such content areas important to both children and adults. Each study, like this one, will raise more questions concerning the necessary "components" of thought in a particular area, and also concerning the explanations of particular developmental lags or décalages.

The findings of this investigation support the hypothesis that children's understanding of human reproduction proceeds through a Piagetain developmental sequence, embedded in a matrix of physical and social causality and identity concepts. Qualitative data illustrating the content of the concepts concerning how people get babies also demonstrate their interdependence with the matrix of causality and identity concepts. The qualitative data also provide illustrations supporting an interactive theory of development. Specifically, "sex information" is both taken in (accommodated) and radically transformed (assimilated) on the basis of the child's experience, affect, and cognitive structural level.

This last conclusion indicates that the study has important practical implications. Sex education of children is an increasingly controversial area. Our results suggest strongly that children actively construct their notions about babies; they don't wait to be told about procreation before they have an idea of how it occurs. What is often taken as misinformation may largely be a product of their own assimilative processes at work on materials with too complex a structure for them to understand. This account of children's six levels of understanding may provide a beginning guideline in the assessment of their present level.

Further study is obviously needed before it is possible to guide children along the path from their present level to a more differentiated picture of human conception. Studies of moral development by Turiel (1969) provide a model for assessing the effects of educational materials on children at different levels of cognitive functioning. He suggests that concepts one level beyond the child's original stage of functioning will be assimilated, while prior stages will be rejected and later stages distorted or not comprehended. We expect that similar findings will be obtained in assessing the impact of educational materials about procreation. The highly politicized and controversial nature of this topic makes it plain that not all of the issues can be resolved by empirical research.

REFERENCES

Breasted, M. *Oh, sex education.* New York: New American Library, 1971.

Conn, J. M. Children's awareness of the origins of babies. *Journal of Child Psychiatry,* 1947, **1**, 140–176.

Freud, A. *Normality and pathology in childhood: assessments of development.* New York: International Universities Press, 1965.

Freud, S. On the sexual theories of children. 1908. In P. Rieff (Ed.), *The collected papers of Sigmund Freud.* New York: Collier, 1963.

Kreitler, H., & Kreitler, S. Children's concepts of sexuality and birth. *Child Development,* 1966, **37**, 363–378.

Laurendeau, M., & Pinard, A. *Causal thinking in the child.* New York: International Universities Press, 1962.

Lemke, S. Children's identity concepts. Unpublished doctoral dissertation, University of California, Berkeley, 1973.

Moore, J. E., & Kendall, D. C. Children's concepts of reproduction. *Journal of Sex Research,* 1971, **7**, 42–61.

Piaget, J. *The child's conception of the world.* New York: Harcourt, Brace, 1929.

Piaget, J. *Six psychological studies.* D. Elkind (Ed.). New York: Random House, 1967.

Piaget, J., & Inhelder, B. *The psychology of the child.* New York: Basic, 1969.

Piaget, J., & Voyat, G. Recherche sur l'identité d'un corps en développement et sur celle du mouvement transitif. In *Epistémolgie et psychologie de l'identité.* Paris: Presses Universitaires de France, 1968.

Turiel, E. Developmental processes in the child's moral thinking. In P. Mussen, J. Langer, & M. Covington (Eds.), *New directions in developmental psychology.* New York: Holt, Rinehart & Winston, 1969

Reading 22

Analysis of Modeling Processes

Albert Bandura

Among the numerous topics that have attracted the interest of psychologists over the years, the phenomenon of learning has occupied a central position. Most of the research in this area examines the process of learning as a consequence of direct experience: This volume is principally concerned with learning by example.

It is evident from informal observation that human behavior is transmitted, whether deliberately or inadvertently, largely through exposure to social models. Indeed, as Reichard (1938) noted some years ago, in many languages "the word for 'teach' is the same as the word for 'show'." It is difficult to imagine a culture in which language, mores, vocational activities, familial customs, and educational, religious, and political practices are gradually shaped in each new member by direct consequences of their trial-and-error performances without benefit of models who display the cultural patterns in their behavior.

Although much social learning is fostered through observation of real-life models, advances in communication have increased reliance upon symbolic models. In many instances people pattern their behavior after models presented in verbal or pictorial form. Without the guidance of handbooks that describe in detail how to behave in particular situations, members of technologically advanced societies would spend much of their time groping for effective ways of handling situations that arise repeatedly. Pictorially presented models, provided in television and other filmed displays, also serve as influential sources of social behavior.

Considering the prevailing influence of example in the development and regulation of human behavior, it is surprising that traditional accounts of learning contain little or no mention of modeling processes. If the peripatetic Martian were to scrutinize earth man's authoritative texts on learning he

The preparation of this paper and research by the author which is reported here was facilitated by grants M—5162 and 1F03MH42658 from the National Institute of Mental Health, United States Public Health Service. The author also gratefully acknowledges the generous assistance of the staff of the Center for Advanced Study in the Behavioral Sciences.

would be left with the belief that there are two basic modes of learning: People are either conditioned through reward and punishment to adopt the desired patterns, or emotional responsiveness is established by close association of neutral and evocative stimuli. If these methods alone were applied on the distant planet, the life span of Martians would not only be drastically shortened, but their brief period of survival would be expended in prolonged and laborious efforts to master simple skills.

The marked discrepancy between textbook and social reality is largely attributable to the fact that certain critical conditions present in natural situations are rarely, if ever, reproduced in laboratory studies of learning. In laboratory investigations experimenters arrange comparatively benign environments in which errors do not create fatal consequences for the organism. By contrast, natural environments are loaded with potentially lethal consequences for those unfortunate enough to perform hazardous errors. For this reason it would be exceedingly injudicious to rely on differential reinforcement of trial-and-error performances in teaching children to swim, adolescents to drive automobiles, medical students to conduct surgical operations, or adults to develop complex occupational and social competencies. Had experimental situations been made more realistic so that animals toiling in Skinner boxes and various mazes were drowned, electrocuted, dismembered, or extensively bruised for the errors that invariably occur during early phases of unguided learning, the limitations of instrumental conditioning would have been forcefully revealed.

There are several reasons why modeling influences are heavily favored in promoting everyday learning. Under circumstances in which mistakes are costly or dangerous, skillful performances can be established without needless errors by providing competent models who demonstrate the required activities. Some complex behaviors can be produced solely through the influence of models. If children had no opportunity to hear speech it would be virtually impossible to teach them the linguistic skills that constitute a language. It is doubtful whether one could ever shape individual words by selective reinforcement of random vocalizations, let alone grammatical utterances. Where desired forms of behavior can be conveyed only by social cues, modeling is an indispensable aspect of learning. Even in instances where it is possible to establish new response patterns through other means, the process of acquisition can be considerably shortened by providing appropriate models (Bandura & McDonald, 1963; John, Chesler, Bartlett, & Victor, 1968; Luchins & Luchins, 1966).

DIFFERENTIATION OF MODELING PHENOMENA

Modeling phenomena have been differentiated, and much time has been spent in conflict over the criteria used in these arbitrary classifications. Among the diverse terms applied to matching behavior are "imitation," "modeling," "observational learning," "identification," "internalization," "introjection," "incorporation," "copying," "social facilitation," "contagion," and "role-taking."

In theoretical discussions imitation is most frequently differentiated from identification on the basis of the content of the changes resulting from exposure to modeling influences. Imitation is generally defined as the reproduction of discrete responses, but there is little agreement concerning the use of the term identification. Different writers have ascribed to identification the adoption of either diverse patterns of behavior (Kohlberg, 1963; Parsons, 1955; Stoke, 1950), symbolic representation of the model (Emmerich, 1959), similar meaning systems (Lazowick, 1955), or motives, values, ideals, and conscience (Gewirtz & Stingle, 1968).

Distinctions are sometimes made in terms of the conditions assumed to produce and maintain matching behavior, as illustrated by Parsons's (1951) view that "a generalized cathectic attachment" is required for identification, but is unnecessary in imitation. Kohlberg (1963) differs in reserving the term identification for matching behavior that is presumed to be maintained by intrinsic satisfactions derived from perceived similarity, and applying the label imitation to instrumental matching responses supported by extrinsic rewards. Others define imitation as matching behavior occurring in the presence of the model, and identification as performance of the model's behavior in his absence (Kohlberg, 1963; Mowrer, 1950). Not only is there little consensus with respect to differentiating criteria, but some theorists assume that imitation produces identification, while others contend with equally strong conviction that identification results in imitation.

Unless it can be shown that modeling of different forms of behavior is governed by separate determinants, distinctions proposed in terms of the content of what is emulated not only are gratuitous, but may cause needless confusion. Limited progress would be made in understanding learning processes if fundamentally different mechanisms were invoked, without empirical justification, to account for the acquisition of one social response versus ten social responses that are arbitrarily designated as elements of a role. Results of numerous studies reviewed in detail elsewhere (Bandura, 1969a) reveal that the same determinants influence acquisition of isolated matching responses and of entire behavioral repertoires in identical ways. Moreover, retention and delayed reproduction of even discrete matching responses require symbolic representation of previously modeled events, especially in early stages of learning. There is also little reason to suppose on empirical or on theoretical grounds that the principles and processes involved in the acquisition of modeled behaviors later performed in the presence of models are different from those performed in their absence.

Several experiments (Bandura, Blanchard & Ritter, 1969; Blanchard, 1970; Perloff, 1970) have demonstrated that exposure to the same modeling influence simultaneously produces in observers analogous changes in specific behavior, emotional responsiveness, valuation of objects involved in the modeled activities, and in self-evaluation. It may be questioned whether any conceptual benefits accrue from arbitrarily designating some of these changes as identification and others as imitation. Indeed, if the diverse criteria enumerated above were seriously applied either singly or in various combinations in categorizing modeling outcomes, most instances of matching behavior that have been traditionally labeled imitation would also qualify as identification, and much of the behavior cited as identificatory learning would be reclassified as imitation.

In social learning theory (Bandura, 1969a) the phenomena ordinarily subsumed under the labels imitation and identification are designated as *modeling*. The latter term was adopted because modeling influences have much broader psychological effects than the simple response mimicry implied by the term imitation, and the distinguishing properties of identification are too diffuse, arbitrary, and empirically questionable either to clarify issues or to aid scientific inquiry. Research conducted within this framework has shown that modeling influences can produce three separable types of effects depending on the different processes involved. First, observers can acquire new patterns of behavior by watching the performances of others. This *observational learning effect* is demonstrated most clearly when models exhibit novel responses which observers have not yet learned to make and which they later reproduce in substantially identical form.

A second major function of modeling influences is to strengthen or to weaken inhibition of previously learned responses. The effects that modeled activities have on behavioral restraints are largely determined by observation of rewarding and punishing consequences accompanying the actions. *Inhibitory effects* are indicated when observers show either decrements in the modeled class of behavior or a general reduction of responsiveness as a result of seeing the model's behavior produce punishing consequences. Observed punishment has been shown to reduce exploratory behavior (Crooks, 1967), aggression (Bandura, 1965b; Wheeler, 1966), and transgressive behavior (Walters & Parke, 1964; Walters, Parke & Cane, 1965). Comparable reductions in performance are obtained in observers when models respond self-punitively to their own behavior (Bandura, 1971a; Benton, 1967).

Disinhibitory effects are evident when observers increase performance of formerly inhibited behavior after observing models engage in threatening or prohibited activities without adverse consequences. This type of change is most strikingly illustrated in the treatment of phobic conditions through modeling procedures (Bandura, 1971b). People who strongly inhibit even attenuated approach responses toward objects they fear are able to interact closely with them after observing bold performers engaging in threatening activities without experiencing any untoward consequences.

The behavior of others can also serve as cues in facilitating performance of existing responses in the same general class. People applaud when others clap; they look up when they see others gazing skyward; they adopt fads that others display; and in countless other situations their behavior is prompted and channeled by the actions of others. *Response facilitation effects* are distinguished from observational learning and disinhibition because no new responses are acquired, and disinhibitory processes are not involved because the behavior in question is socially sanctioned and hence is unencumbered by restraints.

EXPLANATORY THEORIES

Some of the major controversies in the explanation of modeling phenomena can best be illustrated by tracing the evolution of theories of imitation. Disputes between theoretical positions often arise from failure to distinguish the diverse effects that modeling influences can have. Since different conditions are required to produce observational learning, modification of behavioral restraints, and social facilitation, a theory proposed to explain learning by observation will necessarily differ from one that is principally concerned with social facilitation. A number of other important issues that are raised by current theorizing and research will be discussed later.

Instinctual Interpretations

The earliest explanations of imitation (Morgan, 1896; Tarde, 1903; and McDougall, 1908) regarded modeling as instinctual: People reproduce the behavior of others because they have an innate propensity to do so. As the practice of attributing human behavior to instinctual forces gained widespread acceptance, psychologists became increasingly critical of the explanatory value of the instinct concept. Subsequent theories assumed that imitativeness is acquired through some type of learning mechanism, though they differed as to what is learned and the factors considered essential for imitation to occur.

Associative Theories

After the instinct doctrine fell into disrepute, a number of psychologists, notably Humphrey (1921), Allport (1924), Holt (1931), and Guthrie (1952), portrayed modeling in terms of associative principles. As Guthrie succinctly states, "If we have performed an act, the stimuli associated with that act tend to become cues for its performance (p. 287)." Associative learning was believed to be achieved most rapidly through initial reverse imitation. According to Holt's conceptualization, when an adult copies the response of a child, the latter tends to repeat the reiterated behavior. As this circular associative sequence continues, the adult's behavior becomes an increasingly effective stimu-

lus for the child's responses. If during this spontaneous mutual imitation the adult performs a response that is novel for the child, he will copy it.
Piaget (1952) likewise cited imitations at early stages of development in which the child's spontaneous
behaviors serve initially as stimulu for matching
responses by the model in alternating imitative
sequences. Allport believed that imitativeness develops through classical conditioning of verbalizations, motor responses, or emotions to similar
classes of social stimuli with which they have been
contiguously associated.

The associative theories explained how previously learned behavior might be elicited by the actions
of others. But the principle of association does not
adequately account for the fact that behavior is
controlled by some social stimuli, but not by others
that have been associated with equal frequency. A
more serious limitation is the failure of these for-
mulations to explain how novel responses are
learned to begin with. Observational learning in
humans and animals does not ordinarily commence
by having a model reproduce irrelevant responses
of the learner. In using modeling procedures to
teach a myna bird to talk, for example, the trainer
does not engage initially in circular crowing behavior; he begins by uttering words he wishes to teach
that clearly do not exist in integrated form in the
bird's vocal repertoire.

Reinforcement Theories

With the advent of reinforcement principles, the
emphasis in learning theory shifted from classical
conditioning to instrumental conditioning based on
reinforcing consequences. Theories of modeling
similarly assumed that observational learning occurred through reinforcement of imitative behavior. Learning was still conceptualized in terms of
the formation of associations between social stimuli and matching responses, but reinforcement was
added as the selective factor determining which of
the many responses displayed by others will be
imitated.

The foremost proponents of behaviorism, Watson (1908) and Thorndike (1898), dismissed the
existence of observational learning on the basis of
disappointing results from a few animals tested
under conditions in which observation of the demonstrator's performance was not adequately controlled. Since the theories in vogue at the time
assumed that learning required performance of

responses, the notion of learning by observation
alone was perhaps too divergent to be given serious
consideration.

There was no research to speak of on modeling
processes until the publication of the classic *Social
Learning and Imitation* by Miller and Dollard in
1941. They advanced the view that in order for
imitative learning to occur, observers must be
motivated to act, modeling cues for the requisite
behavior must be provided, observers must perform matching responses, and they must be positively reinforced. It was further assumed that if
imitative behavior is repeatedly rewarded, imitation
itself becomes a secondary drive presumably reduced by acting like the model.

The experiments conducted by Miller and Dollard demonstrated that when subjects are consistently rewarded for imitating the choice responses
of a model in two-choice discrimination problems,
they show a marked increase in imitativeness, but
cease imitating the model if they are never rewarded for making the same choices. Moreover, subjects generalize copying responses to new models
and to different motivational states. No attempt
was made, however, to test whether imitation functions as a drive, which presumably should be
altered in strength by deprivation or satiation of
matching behavior.

These experiments have been widely accepted as
demonstrations of imitative learning although they
actually represent only a special form of discrimination place-learning in which social rather than
environmental cues serve as stimuli for choice
responses that already exist in the subject's behavioral repertoire. Indeed, had a light or some other
distinctive cue been used to signify the outcomes of
choices, the behavior of models would have been
irrelevant, perhaps even a hindrance, to efficient
performance. By contrast, most forms of imitation
involve *response* rather than *place-learning,* in
which observers organize behavioral elements into
new compound responses solely by observing
modeled performances. Since Miller and Dollard's
theory requires a person to perform imitative responses before he can learn them, it accounts
more adequately for the expression of previously
established matching responses than for their
acquisition. It is perhaps for this reason that the
publication of *Social Learning and Imitation,* which
contained many provocative ideas, stimulated little
new research, and modeling processes continued to

be treated in a cursory fashion or ignored entirely in accounts of learning.

The operant conditioning analysis of modeling phenomena (Baer & Sherman, 1964; Skinner, 1953), which also specifies reinforcement as a necessary condition, relies entirely upon the standard three-component paradigm $S^d \rightarrow R \rightarrow R^r$, where S^d denotes the modeled stimulus, R represents an overt matching response, and S^r designates the reinforcing stimulus. Except for deletion of the motivational requirement, the Skinnerian interpretation contains the same necessary conditions for imitation (that is, cue, response, reinforcement) originally proposed by Miller and Dollard. Observational learning is presumed to be achieved through a process of differential reinforcement. When imitative behavior has been positively reinforced and divergent responses either not rewarded or punished, the behavior of others comes to function as discriminative stimuli for matching responses.

It is difficult to see how this scheme applies to the observational learning that takes place without overt performance of the model's responses during the acquisition phase, without reinforcers administered to the model or to the observer, and in which the first appearance of the acquired response may be delayed for days, weeks, or even months. In the latter case, which represents one of the most prevalent forms of social learning, two of the events $(R \rightarrow S^r)$ in the three-term paradigm are absent during acquisition, and the third element (S^d, or modeling stimulus) is typically absent from the situation in which the observationally learned response is performed. Like the Miller and Dollard theory, the Skinnerian interpretation explains how performance of established matching responses is facilitated by social stimuli and reinforcing consequences. It does not adequately explain how a new matching response is acquired observationally in the first place. This occurs through symbolic processes during the period of exposure to modeling stimuli, prior to overt responding or the appearance of any reinforcing events.

In a recent operant conditioning analysis of generalized imitation, Gewirtz and Stingle (1968) conceptualized observational learning as analogous to the matching-to-sample paradigm used to study discrimination learning. In this procedure a subject chooses from among a number of comparison stimuli one that shares a common property with the sample stimulus. Although modeling and matching-to-sample performances both involve a matching process, they can hardly be equated. A person can achieve errorless choices in matching comparison Italian and Wagnerian operatic arias with a sample Wagnerian recital, but remain totally unable to perform the vocal behavior contained in the sample. Accurate stimulus discrimination is merely a precondition for observational response learning.

In reducing observational learning to operant conditioning, Gewirtz usually cites examples in which models simply facilitate previously learned responses. However, the purpose of a theory of observational learning is not to account for social facilitation of established responses, but to explain how observers can acquire a novel response that they have never made before as a result of observing a model. Gewirtz argues that since the entire past learning history of an observer is not known, one cannot prove the negative: that a given response had not been learned prior to the modeling experience. That people can learn by observation can be readily demonstrated without controlling or cataloguing the entire life history of the observer. One need only model an original response, such as the word *zoonick*—never before encountered because it was just created—and test whether observers acquire it. Other forms of learning, including operant conditioning, also are studied by using novel responses rather than by assessing past performances which would require monitoring every action that an organism has ever made both within and outside the experimental situation. Gewirtz's position with regard to observational learning is somewhat indeterminate because he alternately questions whether the phenomenon exists, reduces it to social facilitation of learned responses, and offers new descriptive labels (for example, "generalized imitation," "learn-to-learn," and "discriminated-operant") as explanations. To say that people learn by observation because they have "learned-to-learn," or because they have acquired a "complex discriminated-operant" in no way explains how responses are organized to form new observed patterns without reinforced performance.

Affective-Feedback Theories

Mowrer (1960) developed a sensory-feedback theory of imitation that emphasizes classical conditioning of positive and negative emotions evoked by reinforcement to stimuli arising from matching behavior. He distinguishes two forms of imitative learning in terms of whether the observer is reinforced directly or vicariously. In the first case, the model performs a response and at the same time rewards the observer. Through repeated contiguous association of the model's behavior with rewarding experiences, his responses eventually take on positive value for the observer. Through stimulus generalization, the observer can later produce self-rewarding experiences simply by performing the model's positively valenced behavior.

In the second "empathetic" form of imitative learning, the model not only exhibits the response, but also experiences the reinforcing consequences. It is assumed that the observer experiences the sensory concomitants of the model's behavior empathetically and intuits his satisfactions or discomforts. As a result of this empathetic conditioning, the observer is predisposed to reproduce the matching responses for the attendant positive sensory feedback.

There is substantial evidence (Bandura & Huston, 1961; Grusec, 1966; Henker, 1964; Mischel & Grusec, 1966; Mussen & Parker, 1965) that modeling can be augmented by increasing the positive qualities of a model or by having the observer witness the model being rewarded. These same studies, however, contain some contradictory findings with regard to the affective conditioning theory. Even though a model's rewarding qualities are equally associated with the different types of behaviors he performs, modeling affects tend to be specific rather than general. That is, model nurturance enhances imitation of some responses, has no effect upon others, and may actually diminish the adoption of still others (Bandura, Grusec, & Menlove, 1967a). A preliminary study by Foss (1964), in which mynas were taught unusual whistles played on a tape recorder, also failed to confirm the proposition that modeling is enhanced through positive conditioning. Sounds were imitated to the same extent regardless of whether they were presented alone or played only when the birds are being fed.

Mowrer's analysis of imitation is principally concerned with how modeled responses can be invested with positive or negative emotional qualities. Modeling theory, on the other hand, is more often called upon to explain the mechanics of acquisition of patterned behavior observationally rather than

its emotional concomitants. A comprehensive theory must therefore elucidate how new patterns of behavior are constructed and the processes governing their execution.

In an elaboration of the affective-feedback theory of imitation, Aronfreed (1969) advanced the view that pleasurable and aversive affective states become conditioned to both response-produced stimuli and cognitive templates of modeled actions. Imitative performances are presumed to be controlled by affective feedback from intentions as well as from proprioceptive cues generated during an overt act. This conceptualization of imitation is difficult to verify empirically because it does not specify in sufficient detail the characteristics of templates, the process whereby cognitive templates are acquired, the manner in which affective valences become coupled to templates, and how the emotion-arousing properties of templates are transferred to intentions and to proprioceptive cues intrinsic to overt responses. There is some experimental evidence, however, that has important implications for the basic assumptions contained in the notion of feedback.

Feedback theories, particularly those that attribute controlling functions to proprioceptive cues, are seriously challenged by the findings of curare-conditioning experiments in which animals are skeletally immobilized by the drug during aversive conditioning or extinction. These studies (Black, 1958; Black, Carlson, & Solomon, 1962; Solomon & Turner, 1962) demonstrate that learning can occur in the absence of skeletal responding and its correlated proprioceptive feedback. Results of deafferentation studies (Taub, Bacon, & Berman, 1965; Taub et al., 1966) also show that responses can be acquired, performed discriminatively, and extinguished with sensory somatic feedback surgically abolished by limb deafferentation. It would seem from these findings that the acquisition, integration, facilitation and inhibition of responses can be achieved through central mechanisms independent of peripheral sensory feedback.

It is also evident that rapid selection of responses from among a varied array of alternatives cannot be governed by sensory feedback since relatively few responses could be activated even incipiently during the brief time that people usually have to decide how to respond to the situations confronting them (Miller, 1964). Recognizing this problem, Mowrer (1960) has conjectured that the initial scanning and selection of responses occurs primarily at the cognitive rather than at the action level. Consistent with this view, in the social learning analysis of self-regulatory systems (Bandura, 1971a; 1971c) human behavior is largely controlled by anticipated consequences of prospective actions.

Human functioning would be exceedingly inflexible and unadaptive if responsiveness were controlled by affectivity in the behavior itself. Considering the highly discriminative character of social responsiveness, it is extremely doubtful that actions are regulated by affective qualities implanted in behavior. Aggression will serve as an example.

Hitting responses directed toward parents, peers, and inanimate objects differ little, if at all. Nevertheless, hitting parents is generally strongly inhibited, whereas physical aggression toward peers is freely expressed (Bandura, 1960; Bandura & Walters, 1959). Moreover, in certain well-defined contexts, particularly in competitive physical contact sports such as boxing, people will readily display vigorous physical aggression. One can more accurately predict the expression or inhibition of identical aggressive responses from knowledge of the social context (church or athletic gymnasium), the target (parent, priest, policeman, or peer), and other cues that reliably signify potential consequences, than from assessment of the affective value of aggressive behavior per se. It has been amply demonstrated (Bandura, 1971a) that selection and performance of matching responses is mainly governed by anticipated outcomes based on previous consequences that were either directly encountered, vicariously experienced, or self-administered. In other words, responses are chosen from available alternatives more often on the basis of their functional than their emotional value.

Affective feedback conceptions of modeling also fail to account for matching behavior when neither the model nor the observer is reinforced. In these instances, the theory can be preserved only by attributing inherent emotional properties to the behavior that may not always be warranted. In fact, a vast majority of the responses that are acquired observationally are not affectively valenced. This is exemplified by studies of observational learning of mechanical assembly tasks from filmed demonstrations that do not contain stimuli that would arouse the emotion essential for affective conditioning (Sheffield & Maccoby, 1961). Mowrer has, of course, pointed out that sensory experiences can also produce conditioned sensations or images. In most cases of observational learning imaginal or other symbolic representations of modeling stimuli may be the only important mediating processes. Sensory-feedback theories of imitation may therefore be primarily applicable to instances in which modeled responses incur relatively potent consequences so that observers come to anticipate similar emotional consequences if they were to imitate the behavior. Affective conditioning should therefore be regarded as a facilitative rather than a necessary condition for modeling.

Social Learning Theory

Most contemporary interpretations of learning assign a more prominent role to cognitive functioning in the acquisition and regulation of human behavior than did previous explanatory systems. Social learning theory (Bandura, 1969a; 1971c) assumes that modeling influences operate principally through their informative function, and that observers acquire mainly symbolic representations of modeled events rather than specific stimulus-response associations. In this formulation, modeling phenomena are governed by four interrelated subprocesses. These four subsystems are briefly discussed in the sections that follow.

Attentional Processes

One of the main component functions in observational learning involves attentional processes. Simply exposing persons to modeled responses does not in itself guarantee that they will attend closely to them, select from the total stimulus complex the most relevant events, and perceive accurately the cues to which their attention has been directed. An observer will fail to acquire matching behavior at the sensory registration level if he does not attend to, recognize, and differentiate the distinctive features of the model's responses. Discriminative observation is therefore one of the requisite conditions for observational learning.

A number of attention-controlling variables can be influential in determining which models are closely observed and which are ignored. The incentives provided for learning modeled behavior, the motivational and psychological characteristics of the observer, and the physical and acquired distinctiveness of the model as well as his power and interpersonal attractiveness are some of the many factors that exert selective control over the attention people pay to the variety of modeled activities they encounter in their everyday life. The people with whom one regularly associates delimit the types of behavior that one will repeatedly observe and hence learn most thoroughly.

Retention Processes

A second basic component function in observational learning that has been virtually ignored in theories of imitation is the retention of modeled events. When a person observes a model's behavior without performing the responses, he can acquire the modeled responses while they are occurring only in representational form. In order to reproduce this behavior without the continued presence of external modeling cues, he must retain the original observational inputs in some symbolic form. This is a particularly interesting problem in the instance of observationally acquired response patterns that are retained over extended periods, though rarely, if ever, activated into overt performance until attainment of an age or social status at which the activity is considered appropriate.

Observational learning involves two representational systems, the imaginal and the verbal. During exposure, modeling stimuli produce through a process of sensory conditioning relatively enduring, retrievable images of modeled sequences of behavior. Indeed, when stimulus events are highly correlated, as when a name is consistently associated with a given person, it is virtually impossible to hear the name without experiencing imagery of the person's physical characteristics. Similarly, reference to activities (for example, golfing or surfing), places (San Francisco, New York, Paris), and things (the Washington Monument, an airliner) that one has previously observed immediately elicits vivid imaginal representations of the absent physical stimuli.

The second representational system, which probably accounts for the notable speed of observational learning and long-term retention of modeled contents by humans, involves verbal coding of observed events. Most of the cognitive processes that regulate behavior are primarily verbal rather than visual. To take a simple example, the route traversed by a model can be acquired, retained, and later reproduced more accurately by verbal coding of the visual information into a sequence of right-left turns (RRLRR) than by reliance upon visual imagery of the itinerary. Observational learning and retention are facilitated by such codes because they carry a great deal of information in an easily stored form. After modeled responses have been transformed into images and readily utilizable verbal symbols, these memory codes serve as guides for subsequent reproduction of matching responses.

The influential role of symbolic representation in observational learning is supported in several studies differing in age of subjects and in content of modeled activities. In one experiment (Bandura, Grusec, & Menlove, 1966) children observed several complex sequences of behavior modeled on film. During exposure the children either watched attentively, coded the novel responses into their verbal equivalents as they were performed by the model, or counted rapidly while watching the film to prevent implicit verbal coding of modeling stimuli. A subsequent test of observational learning disclosed that children who verbally coded the modeled patterns reproduced significantly more matching responses than those in the viewing-along condition, who in turn showed a higher level of acquisition than children who engaged in competing symbolization. Children within the verbalizing condition reproduced a high proportion (60%) of the modeled responses that they had coded into words, whereas they retrieved a low proportion (25%) of the responses they failed to code.

Coates and Hartup (1969) investigated developmental changes in the role of verbal coding of modeling stimuli in observational learning within the context of the production deficiency hypothesis. According to this hypothesis, which was originally proposed by Keeney, Cannizzo and Flavell (1967), young children are capable of but do not utilize symbolic activities that would facilitate performance, whereas older children spontaneously produce and employ verbal mediators, and therefore do not benefit from further prompts to engage in symbolic activities. Consistent with this view, Coates and Hartup found that induced verbal labeling of modeling stimuli enhanced observational learning in young children but had no effect on older subjects. The issue required further study in view of further evidence that induced verbal coding can facilitate observational learning in both older children (Bandura, Grusec & Menlove, 1966) and adults (Bandura & Jeffery, 1971; Gerst, 1971). Moreover, van Hekken (1969) found that it was the older children who spontaneously used symbolic skills in other learning tasks rather than the "nonmediators" who achieved increases in observational learning through induced verbal coding of modeling stimuli.

Additional evidence for the influence of symbolic coding operations in the acquisition and retention of modeled responses is furnished by Gerst (1971). College students observed a filmed model perform complex motor responses composed of intricate movements taken from the alphabet of the deaf. Immediately after observing each modeled response, subjects engaged in one of four symbolic activities for a period of one minute. One group reinstated the response through vivid imagery; a second group coded the modeling stimuli into concrete verbal terms by describing the specific response elements and their movements; the third group generated concise labels that incorporated the essential ingredients of the responses. (For example, a pretzel-shaped response might be labeled as an orchestra conductor moving his baton in a symphonic finale.) Subjects assigned to the control group performed mental calculations to impede symbolic coding of the depicted events. The subjects reproduced the modeled responses immediately after coding, and following a 15-minute period during which they performed a distracting task designed to prevent symbolic rehearsal of modeled responses.

All three coding operations enhanced observational learning. Concise labeling and imaginal codes were equally effective in aiding immediate reproduction of modeled responses, both being superior to the concrete verbal form. The delayed test for retention of matching responses showed concise labeling to be the best coding system for memory representation. Subjects in this condition retained significantly more matching responses than those who relied upon imagery and concrete verbalizations.

The relative superiority of the summary labeling code is shown even more clearly when matching performances are scored according to a stringent criterion requiring that all response elements be reproduced in the exact sequence in which they were originally modeled. Subjects who coded the modeling stimuli with concise labels were able to reproduce approximately twice as many well-integrated responses in the retention test as the other groups. Moreover, modeled responses for which subjects retained the summary codes were reproduced at a higher level of accuracy (52%), than those for which the code was lost (7%).

In a recent paper, Gewirtz and Stingle (1968)

questioned the value of theories of modeling that include symbolic processes on the grounds that the symbolic events are inferred from the matching behavior they are designed to explain. This type of criticism might apply to theories that attribute behavior to hypothetical internal agencies having only a tenuous relationship to antecedent events and to the behavior that they supposedly explain. In the experiments cited here, symbolic events are independently manipulated and not simply inferred from matching behavior.

Before discussing other factors that facilitate retention of symbolically modeled contents, the structural characteristics of representation should be clarified. Internal representations are not necessarily exact replicas of external modeling stimuli. Indeed, the changes that could be produced through modeling influences would be limited if coded representations were always structurally isomorphic to individual responses performed by others. Relevant evidence will be cited later to show that observers often abstract common features from a variety of modeled responses and construct higher-order codes that have wide generality. Moreover, results reported by Gerst (1971) indicate that modeled behavior is most effectively acquired and retained when modeled configurations are likened to events that are familiar and meaningful to the observer. These findings accord with the common observation that learning through modeling is often enhanced when required performances are represented as resembling familiar activities. The members of a ski class that could not learn to transfer their weight to the downhill ski despite several demonstrations by the instructor were observed to promptly master the maneuver when asked to ski as though they were pointing a serving tray downhill throughout the turns and traverses.

In social learning theory observers function as active agents who transform, classify, and organize modeling stimuli into easily remembered schemes rather than as quiescent cameras or tape recorders that simply store isomorphic representations of modeled events.

Another means of stabilizing and strengthening acquired responses is rehearsal operations. The level of observational learning can be considerably enhanced through practice or overt rehearsal of modeled response sequences, particularly if the rehearsal is interposed after natural segments of a larger modeled pattern. Of greater import is evidence that covert rehearsal, which can be readily engaged in when overt participation is either impeded or impracticable, may likewise increase retention of acquired matching behavior (Bandura & Jeffery, 1971; Michael & Maccoby, 1961). Like coding, rehearsal involves active processes. There is reason to believe that the benefits accruing from rehearsal result from an individual's reorganization and recoding of input events rather than from sheer repetition.

Motoric Reproduction Processes

The third major component of modeling phenomena is concerned with motoric reproduction processes. This involves the utilization of symbolic representations of modeled patterns to guide overt performances. The process of representational guidance is similar to response execution under conditions in which a person follows an externally depicted pattern, or is directed through a series of instructions to enact novel response sequences. The only difference is that a directed performance is guided by external cues, whereas in delayed modeling, behavioral reproduction is monitored by symbolic counterparts of absent stimuli.

The rate and level of observational learning will be partly governed, at the motoric level, by the availability of essential component responses. Complex modes of behavior are produced by combinations of previously learned components which may in themselves be relatively complicated compounds. In instances where observers lack some of the necessary components, the constituent elements may be modeled first; then in stepwise fashion, increasingly intricate compounds can be developed imitatively.

Reinforcement and Motivational Processes

The final component function concerns motivational or reinforcement processes. A person may acquire and retain the capability of skillful execution of modeled behavior, but the learning will rarely be activated into overt performance if negative sanctions or unfavorable incentive conditions obtain. In such circumstances, the introduction of positive incentives promptly translates observational learning into action (Bandura, 1965b). Reinforcement variables not only regulate the overt expression of matching behavior, but they can also affect observational learning by exerting selective control over the types of modeled events to which people are most likely to attend. Further, they facilitate selective retention by activating deliberate coding and rehearsal of modeled behaviors that have functional value. These and other issues bearing on the role of reinforcement in modeling are discussed more fully in subsequent sections.

If one is merely interested in producing imitative behavior, some of the subprocesses outlined above can be disregarded. A model who repeatedly demonstrates desired responses, instructs others to reproduce them, manually prompts the behavior when it fails to occur, and offers valued rewards for correct imitations, will eventually elicit matching responses in most people. It may require 1, 10, or 100 demonstration trials, but if one persists, the desired behavior will eventually be evoked. If, on the other hand, one wishes to explain the conditions governing modeling phenomena, a diverse set of controlling variables must be considered. The critical subprocesses and their determinants are summarized in the following chart.

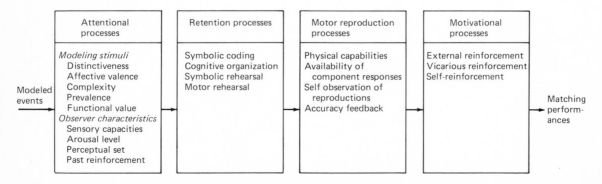

Subprocesses in the social learning view of observational learning.

Theories of imitation that disregard cognitive functioning cannot adequately account for variations in matching performances that result from symbolic activities (Bandura & Jeffery, 1971; Gerst, 1971) when modeling stimuli and reinforcement contingencies remain the same for all subjects. Nor can such differences be attributed to prior history of reinforcement since there is no reason to believe that subjects randomly assigned to a symbolic coding condition have been more often rewarded for imitation than those not induced to code modeled events into words or images. The limitations of conceptual schemes that depict matching behavior as controlled solely by external stimuli and reinforcing consequences are also readily apparent in instances of repeated presentation of modeling stimuli under favorable reinforcement conditions that fail to produce matching responses. The difficulties encountered by Lovaas in creating imitative behavior in some autistic children have stimulated research on attentional deficits (Lovaas, Rehm & Schreibman, 1969). Preliminary findings indicate that autistic children have difficulty in processing information conveyed through different sensory modalities. However, their rate of learning is greatly facilitated by various attention-enhancing procedures (Wasserman, 1969) that would undoubtedly improve observational learning. Given evidence that observers often fail to remember what they have learned, nonmediational theories will eventually be forced to consider retention processes as well.

In any given instance, absence of appropriate matching behavior following exposure to modeling stimuli may result from failures in sensory registration of modeled events, inadequate coding of modeling stimuli for memory representation, retention decrements, motoric deficiencies, or unwillingness to perform matching behavior because of inadequate reinforcement. For these reasons theories which contend that people imitate because they have been intermittently reinforced for imitating in the past may have limited explanatory power.

Other theorists have proposed interpretations of imitation in which representational processes, in one form or another, figure prominently. In Sheffield's view (1961), matching performances are mediated by perceptual representations of modeled events, mainly in the form of visual imagery. These perceptual responses, or "blueprints," which serve as cues for overt action, are assumed to be conditioned solely through contiguous association with stimulus events.

This conceptualization and social learning have some points of similarity. Both positions postulate a representational guidance system for matching behavior which can be established without overt responding. But they differ in several important respects. In the social learning view, modeling stimuli serve more as sources of information than as automatic conditioners; observers often perform operations on modeling inputs so that transformational and organizational processes are involved as well as associational ones; less structural correspondence is assumed between memory codes and the original modeled patterns; verbal representation is assigned a greater response guidance function; and reinforcement, which receives no mention in Sheffield's formulation, is treated in social learning as a factor that can facilitate observational learning.

Piaget's Theory

Piaget (1951) presents a developmental account of imitation in which symbolic representation assumes an important function, especially in higher forms of modeling. At the earlier sensorimotor stages of development, imitative responding can be evoked only by having the model repeat the child's immediately preceding responses in alternating imitative sequences. During this period, according to Piaget, the child is unable to imitate responses that he has not previously performed spontaneously because actions cannot be assimilated unless they correspond to already existing schemas. Piaget reports that when models introduce new behavioral elements or even familiar responses that children have acquired but are not exhibiting at the moment, they do not respond imitatively. Imitation is thus restricted to reproduction of activities that children have already developed, that they can see themselves make, and that they have performed immediately before the model's reiteration.

If the above observations based on Piaget's longitudinal study of his own three children are replicable, then young children have weaker capabilities for observational learning than subhuman species. Animals (Adler & Adler, 1968) and birds (Foss, 1964) can learn new patterns of behavior observationally, and modeling stimuli can acquire the capacity to evoke existing matching responses even though the organism was not performing them beforehand. It is assumed by Piaget that during initial stages children do not distinguish between self-imitation and imitation of the actions of others. If this is the case, then the theory must explain why a child's own behavior can originally induce matching responses but identical actions initiated by others cannot.

In Piaget's view, schemas, which refer to schematic outlines of activities, determine what behaviors can or cannot be imitated. Unfortunately, the descriptive account does not specify in any detail the extent to which schemas are learned or furnished innately and, if learned, the process whereby general features of an activity are abstracted from otherwise different instances. From the perspective of the multiprocess theory of modeling, deficiencies in imitative performance, which are typically attributed by Piaget to insufficiently differentiated schemas, may likewise result from inadequate observation of modeling stimuli, from motoric difficulties in executing learned patterns, or from faulty reinforcement. The latter factor deserves further comment because of its important bearing on evaluation of findings from naturalistic studies of modeling.

Observational data must be accepted with reservation when the model's reactions to the child's performances are not reported. Lovaas (1967) has shown that young children imitate precisely when they are rewarded only for exact matches, but if they are positively reinforced without regard to the quality of the reproduction, the imitations deteriorate rapidly. When only the child's responses are observed and recorded, imitative deficiencies arising from faulty reinforcement are likely to be erroneously attributed to his shortcomings. Since observational studies of the type conducted by Piaget involve a two-way influence process, imitative performances reflect not only the competency of the child but the reactions of the participating model to accurate and inadequate matches. If models respond alike to performances that differ widely in quality, children will tend to disregard modeling stimuli, whereas they reproduce accurately any activities within their capacity if models respond discriminately.

The discussion thus far has been concerned with early stages in the development of imitation as depicted by Piaget. As a child's intellectual development progresses, he becomes capable of delayed imitation of modeled events which he cannot see himself make. These changes presumably come about through coordination of visual and sensorimotor schemas, and differentiation of the child's own actions from those of others. He now begins systematic trial-and-error performance of responses until he achieves good matches to new modeled patterns.

At the final stages of development, which generally begin in the second year of life, children attain representative imitation. Schemas are coordinated internally to form new and complex patterns of modeled behavior without requiring overt provisional trials of actions. This covert imitation occurs through imaginal representation of modeled performances, which also serves as the basis for reproducing matching behavior when models are no longer present. Had Piaget extended his studies of imitation into later childhood years, it is likely that verbal representation would also have emerged as an important functional mediator in delayed modeling.

A comprehensive theory of modeling must explain not only how patterned behavior is acquired observationally, but also when and how frequently imitative behavior will be performed, the persons toward whom it will be expressed, and the social settings in which it is most likely to be exhibited. Piaget's account of imitation contains only a few passing remarks about the motivational factors regulating performance of matching behavior. Imitation is variously attributed to an intrinsic need for acting and knowing, to a desire to reproduce actions that differ partially from existing schemas, and to the esteem in which the model is held. Most researchers in the field of modeling would regard these factors as much too general to account satisfactorily for the highly discriminative character of imitative responding. In view of the abundant evidence that imitative performances can be strongly controlled by their external consequences, the influence of reinforcement variables must be considered in explanatory schemes, whatever their orientation may be.

Scope of Modeling Influences

It is widely assumed that imitation can produce at best mimicry of specific responses exhibited by others. There are several reasons why such limited learning effects are ascribed to imitation. The term carries a strong connotation that the process is confined to literal copying of particular modeled responses. Formal definitions of imitation do not specify which properties of the model's behavior are adopted. Some investigators have therefore concluded that the phenomenon applies only to matching of simple physical characteristics. The behavior displayed by others ordinarily varies on a number of stimulus dimensions which differ in content, complexity, and discriminability. It is arbitrary which modeled attributes are selected as relevant in any given experiment. Although the matching process frequently involves reproduction of concrete patterns of behavior, in many instances observers must match subtle features common to a variety of modeled responses that differ on several other attributes.

Another factor that contributed to underestimation of the scope of modeling influences was the widespread use of a restricted experimental paradigm. In these studies a model performs a few responses designated by a single prominent feature and observers are subsequently tested for precise reproduction of the modeled behavior in identical or similar situations. Under these circumscribed conditions, experiments could yield only mimicry of specific responses. This led many researchers to place severe limitations on the behavioral changes that can be attributed to modeling influences.

In order to demonstrate that limitations ascribed to modeling were inherent in the methodology rather than in the phenomenon itself, several experiments were conducted (Bandura & Harris, 1966; Bandura & McDonald, 1963; Bandura & Mischel, 1965) requiring a more complex form of modeling. These studies utilized a paradigm in which persons observed models responding consistently to diverse stimuli in accordance with a pre-selected rule. Tests for generalized imitation were later conducted by different experimenters, in different social contexts with the models absent, and with different stimulus items. The results disclosed that observers respond to new situations in a style that is consistent with the models' dispositions without ever having observed the models responding to these particular stimuli.

In this higher-order form of modeling the performer's behavior conveys information to observers about the characteristics of appropriate responses. Observers must abstract common attributes exemplified in diverse modeled responses and formulate a rule for generating similar patterns of behavior. Responses performed by subjects that embody the observationally derived rule are likely to resemble the behavior that the model would be inclined to exhibit under similar circumstances,

even though subjects had never witnessed the model's behavior in these new situations.

Evidence that response-generative rules can be acquired observationally has interesting implications for controversies regarding language learning. Because of the highly generative character of linguistic behavior it has commonly been assumed by psycholinguists (Brown & Bellugi, 1964; Ervin, 1964; Menyuk, 1964) that imitation cannot play much part in language development and production. This conclusion is largely based on the mistaken assumption that one can learn through observation only the concrete features of behavior, not its abstract properties. Obviously children are able to construct an almost infinite variety of sentences that they have never heard. Therefore, rather than acquiring specific utterances through imitation, children must learn sets of rules on the basis of which they can generate an unlimited number of novel grammatical sentences. The importance of imitative learning in language development was further discounted on the grounds that children often display only crude approximations of adult verbalizations (Brown & Bellugi, 1964), and they can acquire linguistic rules without engaging in any motor speech (Lenneberg, 1967).

The above criticisms have validity when applied to theories of imitation that emphasize verbatim repetition of modeled responses and that assume matching responses must be performed and reinforced in order to be learned. It is evident from the material already discussed at length that the social learning interpretation of modeling processes is compatible with rule-learning theories advanced by psycholinguists. Both points of view assign special importance to the abstraction of productive rules from diverse modeled examples. The differentiation made by psycholinguists between language competence and language performance corresponds to the distinction made between learning and performance in social learning theory. Another point of similarity is that neither approach assumes that observational learning necessitates performance. Finally, the basic rules, or prototypes, that guide production of grammatical utterances are presumed to be extracted from individual modeled instances rather than innately programmed. People are innately equipped with information-processing capacities, not with response-productive rules.

Rules about grammatical relations between words cannot be learned unless they are exemplified in the verbal behavior of models. A number of experiments have been conducted to discover conditions that facilitate abstraction of rules from verbal modeling cues. The principle underlying a model's varied responses can be most readily discerned if its identifying characteristics are distinctly repeated in responses which differ in other aspects. If, for example, one were to place a series of objects first on tables, then on chairs, boxes, and other things, simultaneously verbalizing the common prepositional relationship between these different objects, a child would eventually discern the grammatical principle. He could then easily generate a novel grammatical sentence if a toy hippopotamus were placed on a xylophone and the child were asked to describe the stimulus event enacted.

Changes in linguistic behavior are difficult to achieve because sentences represent complex stimulus patterns in which the identifying features of syntactic structure cannot be easily discerned. The influential role of both modeling and discrimination processes in language development is revealed in an experiment designed to alter the syntactic style of young children who had no formal grammatical knowledge of the linguistic features selected for modification (Bandura & Harris, 1966). Children increased grammatical constructions in accord with the rules guiding the modeled utterances when verbal modeling influences were combined with attention-directing and reinforcement procedures designed to increase syntactic discriminability. This finding was replicated by Odom, Liebert, and Hill (1968) and extended by Rosenthal and his associates (Carroll, Rosenthal, & Brysh, 1969; Rosenthal & Whitebook, 1970), who demonstrated that exposure to verbal modeling altered structural and tense components of children's linguistic behavior congruent with the model's sentence rules.

The studies cited above were principally devoted to the modification of linguistic features with which the children had some familiarity. A recent study by Liebert, Odom, Hill, and Huff (1969) has shown that children can acquire through modeling an arbitrary ungrammatical rule, which they use to generate peculiar sentences.

Further evidence for the influential role of modeling processes in language acquisition is provided by naturalistic studies employing sequential analyses of children's verbalizations and the immediately following parental responses. Such studies disclose that young children's speech is at best semi-grammatical; in approximately 30 percent of instances adults repeat children's verbalizations in a grammatically more complex form, accenting the elements that may have been omitted and inaccurately employed (Brown & Bellugi, 1964); and children often reproduce the more complicated grammatical reconstructions modeled by adults (Slobin, 1968). Of special interest is evidence (Lovaas, 1967) that the accuracy of children's imitations is subject to reinforcement control. That is, when rewards are contingent on correct reproduction of modeled responses, children display precise imitativeness. On the other hand, when children can gain rewards irrespective of the accuracy with which they reproduce modeled utterances, the fidelity of their matching responses deteriorates.

Additional illustrations of how behavior-guiding principles can be transmitted through modeling are provided in experiments designed to modify moral judgmental orientations (Bandura & McDonald, 1963; Cowan, Langer, Heavenrich, & Nathanson, 1969; Le Furgy & Woloshin, 1969); delay of gratification patterns (Bandura & Mischel, 1965; Stumphauzer, 1969); and styles of information-seeking (Rosenthal, Zimmerman, & Durning, 1970). Researchers have also begun to study how modeling influences alter cognitive functioning of the type described by Piaget and his followers. Some of these studies are concerned with the principle of conservation, which reflects a child's ability to recognize that a given property remains invariant despite external changes that make it look different (as when the same amount of liquid is poured into different shaped containers.) Young children who do not conserve are able to do so consistently as a result of observing a model's conservation judgments and supporting explanations (Rosenthal & Zimmerman, 1970). Moreover, conservation judgments induced through modeling generalize to new characteristics; they endure over time; and they do not differ from conservation concepts acquired by children in the course of their everyday experiences (Sullivan, 1967).

The broader effects of modeling influences are further revealed in experimental paradigms employing multiple models who display diverse patterns of behavior. Contrary to common belief, it is possible to create novel modes of response solely through imitation (Bandura, Ross, & Ross, 1963a). When individuals are exposed to a variety of models, they may select one or more of them as primary sources of behavior; but rarely do they confine their imitation to a single source, nor do they reproduce all of the characteristics of the preferred model. Rather, observers generally exhibit relatively novel responses representing amalgams of the behavior of different models. The particular admixtures of behavioral elements vary from person to person. Within a given family even same-sex siblings may thus develop unlike personality characters as a result of imitating different combinations of parental and sibling attributes. A succession of modeling influences in which observers later became sources of behavior for new members would most likely produce a gradual imitative evolution of novel patterns bearing little resemblance to those exhibited by the original models.

The degree of behavioral innovation that can be achieved through imitation will depend on the diversity of modeled patterns. In homogeneous cultures in which all models display similar modes of response, imitative behavior may undergo little or no change across successive models, but model dissimilarity is apt to foster new divergent patterns. The evidence accumulated to date suggests that, depending on their complexity and diversity, modeling influences can produce, in addition to mimicry of specific responses, behavior that is generative and innovative in character.

REFERENCES

Adler, L. L., & Adler, H. E. 1968. Age as a factor in observational learning in puppies. *American Dachshund*, 13–14.

Allport, F. H. 1924. *Social psychology.* Cambridge, Mass.: Riverside Press.

Aronfreed, J. 1969. The problem of imitation. In L. P. Lipsitt & H. W. Reese (Eds.), *Advances in child development and behavior.* Vol. IV. New York: Academic Press. Pp. 210–319.

Baer, D. M., & Sherman, J. A. 1964. Reinforcement control of generalized imitation in young children. *Journal of Experimental Child Psychology,* **1**, 37–49.

Bandura, A. 1960. Relationship of family patterns to child behavior disorders. Progress Report, Stanford University, Project No. M–1734, United States Public Health Service.

Bandura, A. 1956b. Behavioral modifications through modeling procedures. In L. Krasner & L. P. Ullmann (Eds.), *Research in behavior modification.* New York: Holt, Rinehart & Winston. Pp. 310–340.

Bandura, A. 1969a. *Principles of behavior modification.* New York: Holt, Rinehart & Winston.

Bandura, A. 1969b. Social-learning theory of identificato-

ry processes. In D. A. Goslin (Ed.), *Handbook of socialization theory and research.* Chicago: Rand McNally. Pp. 213–262.

Bandura, A. 1971a. Vicarious and self-reinforcement processes. In R. Glaser (Ed.), *The nature of reinforcement.* Columbus, Ohio: Merrill.

Bandura, A. 1971c. *Social learning theory.* New York: General Learning Press.

Bandura, A., Blanchard, E. B., & Ribber, B. 1969. The relative efficacy of desensitization and modeling approaches for inducing behavioral,

Bandura, A., Grusec, J. E., & Menlove, F. L. 1966. Observational learning as a function of symbolization and incentive set. *Child Development,* **37**, 499–506.

Bandura, A., Grusec, J. E., & Menlove, F. L. 1967b. Vicarious extinction of avoidance behavior. *Journal of Personality and Social Psychology,* **5**, 16–23.

Bandura, A., & Harris, M. B. 1966. Modification of syntactic style. *Journal of Experimental Child Psychology,* **4**, 341–352.

Bandura, A., & Huston, A. C. 1961. Identification as a process of incidental learning. *Journal of Abnormal and Social Psychology,* **63**, 311–318.

Bandura, A., & Jeffery, R. 1971. The role of symbolic coding, cognitive organization, and rehearsal in observational learning. Unpublished manuscript, Stanford University.

Bandura, A., & McDonald, F. J. 1963. The influence of social reinforcement and the behavior of models in shaping children's moral judgments. *Journal of Abnormal and Social Psychology,* **67**, 274–281.

Bandura, A., & Mischel, W. 1965. Modification of self-imposed delay of reward through exposure to live and symbolic models. *Journal of Personality and Social Psychology,* **2**, 698–705.

Bandura, A., Ross, D., & Ross, S. A. 1963b. A comparative test of the status envy, social power, and secondary reinforcement theories of identificatory learning. *Journal of Abnormal and Social Psychology,* **67**, 527–534.

Bandura, A., & Walters, R. H. 1959. *Adolescent aggression.* New York: Ronald.

Bandura, A., & Walters, R. H. 1963. *Social learning and personality development.* New York: Holt, Rinehart & Winston.

Benton, A. A. 1967. Effect of the timing of negative response consequences on the observational learning of resistance to temptation in children. *Dissertation Abstracts,* **27**, 2153–2154.

Black, A. H. 1958. The extinction of avoidance responses under curare. *Journal of Comparative and Physiological Psychology,* **51**, 519–524.

Black, A. H., Carlson, N. J., & Solomon, R. L. 1962. Exploratory studies of the conditioning of autonomic responses in curarized dogs. *Psychological Monographs,* **76**, No. 29 (Whole No. 548).

Brown, R., & Bellugi, U. 1964. Three processes in the child's acquisition of syntax. *Harvard Educational Review,* **34,** 133–151.

Carroll, W. R., Rosenthal, T. L., & Brysh, C. G. 1969. The social transmission of grammatical parameters. Unpublished manuscript, University of Arizona.

Coates, B., & Hartup, W. W. 1969. Age and verbalization in observational learning. *Developmental Psychology,* **1,** 556–562.

Cowan, P. A., Langer, J., Heavenrich, J., & Nathanson, M. 1969. Social learning and Piaget's cognitive theory of moral development. *Journal of Personality and Social Psychology,* **11,** 261–274.

Crooks, J. L. 1967. Observational learning of fear in monkeys. Unpublished manuscript, University of Pennsylvania.

Emmerich, W. 1959. Parental identification in young children. *Genetic Psychology Monographs,* **60,** 257–308.

Ervin, S. M. 1964. Imitation and structural change in children's language. In E. H. Lenneberg (Ed.), *New directions in the study of language.* Cambridge, Mass.: M.I.T. Press. Pp. 163–189.

Flanders, J. P. 1968. A review of research on imitative behavior. *Psychological Bulletin,* **69,** 316–337.

Foss, B. M. 1964. Mimicry in mynas (*Gracula religiosa*): A test of Mowrer's theory. *British Journal of Psychology,* **55,** 85–88.

Gerst, M. S. 1971. Symbolic coding processes in observational learning. *Journal of Personality and Social Psychology,* **19,** 9–17.

Gewirtz, J. L., & Stingle, K. G. 1968. Learning of generalized imitation as the basis for identification. *Psychological Review,* **75,** 374–397.

Grusec, J. E. 1966. Some antecedents of self-criticism. *Journal of Personality and Social Psychology,* **4,** 244–252.

Guthrie, E. R. 1952. *The psychology of learning.* New York: Harper.

Henker, B. A. 1964. The effect of adult model relationships on children's play and task imitation. *Dissertation Abstracts,* **24,** 4797.

Holt, E. B. 1931. Animal drive and the learning process, Vol. 1. New York: Holt, Rinehart, and Winston.

Humphrey, G. 1921. Imitation and the conditioned reflex. *Pedadogical Seminary,* **28,** 1–21.

John, E. R., Chesler, P., Bartlett, F., & Victor, I. 1968. Observation learning in cats. *Science,* **159,** 1489–1491.

Keeney, T. J., Cannizzo, S. R., & Flavell, J. H. 1967. Spontaneous and induced verbal rehearsal in a recall task. *Child Development,* **38,** 953–966.

Kohlberg, L. 1963. Moral development and identification. In H. W. Stevenson (Ed.), *Child psychology: The sixty-second yearbook of the National Society for the Study of Education.* Part I. Chicago: National Society for the Study of Education. Pp. 277–332.

Lazowick, L. 1955. On the nature of identification. *Journal of Abnormal and Social Psychology,* **51,** 175–183.

Le Furgy, W. G., & Woloshin, G. W. 1969. Immediate and long-term effects of experimentally induced social influences in the modification of adolescents' moral judgments. *Journal of Personality and Social Psychology,* **12,** 104–110.

Lenneberg, E. H. 1962. Understanding language without ability to speak. *Journal of Abnormal and Social Psychology,* **65,** 419–415.

Liebert, R. M., Odom, R. D., Hill, J. H., & Huff, R. L. 1969. Effects of age and rule familiarity on the production of modeled language constructions. *Developmental Psychology,* **1,** 108–112.

Lovaas, O. I. 1967. A behavior therapy approach to the treatment of childhood schizophrenia. In J. P. Hill (Ed.), *Minnesota symposia on child psychology.* Vol. 1. Minneapolis: University of Minnesota Press. Pp. 108–159.

Lovaas, O. I., Rehm, R., & Schreibman, L. 1969. Attentional deficits in autistic children to multiple stimulus inputs. Unpublished manuscript, University of California, Los Angeles.

Luchins, A. S., & Luchins, E. H. 1966. Learning a complex ritualized social role. *Psychological Record,* **16,** 177–187.

McDougall, W. 1908. *An introduction to social psychology.* London: Methuen.

Menyuk, P. 1964. Alteration of rules in children's grammar. *Journal of Verbal Learning and Verbal Behavior,* **3,** 480–488.

Michael, D. N., & Maccoby, N. 1961. Factors influencing the effects of student participation on verbal learning from films: Motivating versus practice effects, "feedback," and overt versus covert responding. In A. A. Lumsdaine (Ed.), *Student response in programmed instruction.* Washington, D. C.: National Academy of Sciences—National Research Council, 1961. Pp. 271–293.

Miller, N. E. 1964. Some implications of modern behavior theory for personality change and psychotherapy. In P. Worchel & D. Byrne (Eds.), *Personality change.* New York: Wiley. Pp. 149–175.

Miller, N. E., & Dollard, J. 1941. *Social learning and imitation.* New Haven: Yale University Press.

Mischel, W., & Grusec, J. 1966. Determinants of the rehearsal and transmission of neutral and aversive behaviors. *Journal of Personality and Social Psychology,* **3,** 197–205.

Morgan, C. L. 1896. *Habit and instinct.* London: Arnold.

Mowrer, O. H. 1950. Identification: A link between learning theory and psychotherapy. In *Learning theory and personality dynamics.* New York: Ronald, Pp. 573–615.

Mowrer, O. H. 1960. *Learning theory and behavior.* New York: Wiley.

Mussen, P. H., & Parker, A. L. 1965. Mother nurturance

and girls' incidental imitative learning. *Journal of Personality and Social Psychology, 2*, 94–97.

Odom, R. D., Liebert, R. M., & Hill, J. H. 1968. The effects of modeling cues, reward, and attentional set on the production of grammatical and ungrammatical syntactic constructions. *Journal of Experimental Child Psychology, 6*, 131–140.

Parsons, T. 1951. *The social system.* New York: The Free Press of Glencoe.

Parsons, T. 1955. Family structure and the socialization of the child. In T. Parsons & R. F. Bales, *Family, socialization and interaction process.* Glencoe, Ill.: Free Press. Pp. 35–131.

Perloff, B. 1970. Influence of muscular relaxation and positive imagery on extinction of avoidance behavior through systematic desensitization. Unpublished doctoral dissertation, Stanford University.

Piaget, J. 1951. *Play, dreams, and imitation in childhood.* New York: Norton.

Rosenthal, T. L., & Whitebook, J. S. 1970. Incentives versus instructions in transmitting grammatical parameters with experimenter as model. *Behaviour Research and Therapy, 8*, 189–196.

Rosenthal, T. L., & Zimmerman, B. J. 1970. Modeling by exemplification and instruction in training conservation. Unpublished manuscript, University of Arizona.

Rosenthal, T. L., Zimmerman, B. J., & Durning, K. 1970. Observationally induced changes in children's interrogative classes. *Journal of Personality and Social Psychology, 16*, 681–688.

Sheffield, F. D. 1961. Theoretical considerations in the learning of complex sequential tasks from demonstration and practice. In A. A. Lumsdaine (Ed.), *Student response in programmed instruction.* Washington, D. C.: National Academy of Sciences—National Research Council, 1961. Pp. 13–32.

Sheffield, F. D., & Maccoby, N. 1961. Summary and interpretation of research on organizational principles in constructing filmed demonstrations. In A. A. Lumsdaine (Ed.), *Student response in programmed instruction.* Washington, D. C.: National Academy of Sciences—National Research Council, 1961. Pp. 117–313.

Skinner, B. F. 1953. *Science and human behavior.* New York: Macmillan.

Slobin, D. I. 1968. Imitation and grammatical development in children. In N. S. Endler, L. R. Boulter, & H. Osser (Eds.), *Contemporary issues in developmental psychology.* New York: Holt, Rinehart & Winston. Pp. 437–443.

Solomon, R. L., & Turner, L. H. 1962. Discriminative classical conditioning in dogs paralyzed by curare can later control discriminative avoidance responses in the normal state. *Psychological Review, 69*, 202–219.

Stoke, S. M. 1950. An inquiry into the concept of identification. *Journal of Genetic Psychology, 76*, 163–189.

Stumphauzer, J. S. 1969. Increased delay of gratification in young prison inmates through imitation of high-delay peer-models. Unpublished doctoral dissertation, Florida State University.

Sullivan, E. V. 1967. The acquisition of conservation of substance through film-mediated models. In D. W. Brison & E. V. Sullivan (Eds.), *Recent research on the acquisition of conservation of substance. Education Monograph.* Toronto: Ontario Institute for Studies in Education.

Tarde, G. 1903. *The laws of imitation.* New York: Holt, Rinehart, & Winston.

Taub, E., Bacon, R. C., & Berman, A. J. 1965. Acquisition of a trace-conditioned avoidance response after deafferentation of the responding limb. *Journal of Comparative and Physiological Psychology, 59*, 275–279.

Taub, E., Teodoru, D., Ellman, S. J., Bloom, R. F., & Berman, A. J. 1966. Deafferentation in monkeys: Extinction of avoidance responses, discrimination and discrimination reversal. *Psychonomic Science, 4*, 323–324.

Thorndike, E. L. 1898. Animal intelligence: An experimental study of the associative processes in animals. *Psychological Review Monograph Supplements, 2*, No. 4 (Whole No. 8).

van Hekken, S. M. J. 1969. The influence of verbalization on observational learning in a group of mediating and a group of non-mediating children. *Human Development, 12*, 204–213.

Walters, R. H., & Parke, R. D. 1964. Influence of response consequences to a social model on resistance to deviation. *Journal of Experimental Child Psychology, 1*, 269–280.

Walters, R. H., Parke, R. D., & Cane, V. A. 1965. Timing of punishment and the observation of consequences to others as determinants of response inhibition. *Journal of Experimental Child Psychology, 2*, 10–30.

Wasserman, L. Discrimination learning and development of learning sets in autistic children. Unpublished doctoral dissertation, University of California, Los Angeles, 1968.

Watson, J. B. 1908. Imitation in monkeys. *Psychological Bulletin, 5*, 169–178.

Wheeler, L. 1966. Toward a theory of behavioral contagion. *Psychological Review, 73*, 179–192.

Reading 23

Some Effects of Punishment on Children's Behavior—Revisited[1]

Ross D. Parke

A casual review of magazines, advice to parent columns, or (until recently) the psychological journals quickly reveals that there is considerable controversy concerning the usefulness of punishment as a technique for controlling the behavior of young children. For many years, the study of the impact of punishment on human behavior was restricted to armchair speculation and theorizing. In part, this paucity of information was due to the belief that punishment produced only a temporary suppression of behavior and that many undesirable side-effects were associated with its use. Moreover, ethical and practical considerations prohibited the employment of intense punishment in research with human subjects—especially children—thus contributing to this information gap.

Through both studies of child rearing and laboratory investigations, however, some of the effects of punishment on children's social behavior are being determined. It is the main aim of this paper to review these findings and assess the current status of our knowledge concerning the effects of punishment.

TIMING OF PUNISHMENT

A number of years ago at Harvard's Laboratory of Human Development, Black, Solomon and Whiting (1960) undertook a study of the effectiveness of punishment for producing "resistance to temptation" in a group of young puppies. Two training conditions were used. In one case, the dogs were swatted with a rolled-up newspaper just *before* they touched a bowl of forbidden horsemeat. The remaining pups were punished only *after* eating a small amount of the taboo food. On subsequent tests—even though deprived of food—the animals punished as they approached the food showed greater avoidance of the prohibited meat than did animals punished after committing the taboo act. This study is the prototype of a number of studies recently carried out with children, and it illustrates

the importance of the *timing* of the punishment for producing effective control over children's behavior.

In recent studies of the effects of timing of punishment on children's behavior, the rolled-up newspaper has been replaced by a verbal rebuke or a loud noise, and an attractive toy stands in place of the horsemeat. For example, Walters, Parke and Cane (1965) presented subjects with pairs of toys—one attractive and one unattractive—on a series of nine trials. The six- to eight-year-old boys were punished by a verbal rebuke, "No, that's for the other boy," when they chose the attractive toy. As in the dog study, one group of children was punished as they approached the attractive toy, but before they actually touched it. For the remaining boys, punishment was delivered only after they had picked up the critical toy and held it for two seconds. Following the punishment training session, the subjects were seated before a display of three rows of toys similar to those used in the training period and were reminded not to touch the toys. The resistance-to-deviation test consisted of a 15-minute period during which the boy was left alone with an unattractive German-English dictionary and, of course, the prohibited toys. The extent to which the subject touched the toys in the absence of the external agent was recorded by an observer located behind a one-way screen. The children's data paralleled the puppy results: the early punished children touched the taboo toys less than did the boys punished late in the response sequence. This timing of punishment effect has been replicated by a number of investigators (Aronfreed & Reber, 1965; Parke & Walters, 1967; Cheyne & Walters, 1969).

Extensions of this experimental model indicate that this finding is merely one aspect of a general relation: *the longer the delay between the initiation of the act and the onset of punishment, the less effective the punishment for producing response inhibition.* This proposition is based on a study in which the effects of four delay of punishment positions were examined (Aronfreed, 1965). Using a design similar to Walters, Parke and Cane (1965),

[1]The preparation of this paper and some of the studies that are reported here were supported in part by Research Grant GS 1847, National Science Foundation.

Aronfreed punished one group of children as they reached for the attractive toy. Under a second condition, the subject was permitted to pick up the attractive toy and was punished at the apex of the lifting movement. Under a third condition, six seconds elapsed after the child picked up the toy before punishment was delivered. In the final group, six seconds after the child picked up the toy he was asked to describe the toy and only then was punishment administered. The time elapsing between the experimenter's departure until the child made the first deviation steadily decreased as the time between the initiation of the act and the delivery of punishment increased.

Punishment may be less effective in facilitating learning as well as less effective in facilitating resistance to temptation if the punishment is delayed. Using a learning task in which errors were punished by the presentation of a loud noise combined with the loss of a token, Walters (1964) found that punishment delivered immediately after the error speeded learning more than did punishment which was delayed 10 seconds or 30 seconds.

Since it is often difficult to detect and punish a response in the approach phase of a transgression sequence, the practical implications of these studies may be questioned. However, Aronfreed (1968) has noted one feature of naturalistic socialization that may dilute the importance of punishing the act in the execution phase. "Parents frequently punish a child when he is about to repeat an act which they dislike" (p. 180). In this case, punishment may be delivered in the early stages of the next execution of the act, even though it is delayed in relation to the previously completed commission of the same deviant behavior.

In addition, the importance of timing of punishment may be contingent on a variety of other features of punishment administration, such as the intensity of the punishment, the nature of the agent-child relationship, and the kind of verbal rationale accompanying the punishment. The effects of these variables will be examined in the following sections.

INTENSITY OF PUNISHMENT

It is generally assumed that as the intensity of punishment increases the amount of inhibition will similarly increase. It is difficult to study severity of punishment in the laboratory due to the obvious ethical limitations upon using potentially harmful stimuli in experimentation with children. Until recently most of the evidence concerning the relative effectiveness of different intensities of punishment derived either from animal studies or from child-rearing interview studies.

The animal studies (e.g., Church, 1963), in which electric shock is most often used as the punishing stimulus, have supported the conclusion that more complete suppression of the punished response results as the intensity of the punishment increases. On the other hand, the child-rearing data relation to the effects of intensity on children's behavior have not yielded clear cut conclusions. It is difficult, however, to assess the operation of specific punishment variables using rating scales of parent behavior because most of these scales confound several aspects of punishment, such as frequency, intensity, and consistency (Walters & Parke, 1967). Differences between scale points may, therefore, be due to the impact of any of these variables, either alone or in combination.

Recent laboratory studies have avoided some of these short-comings and have yielded less equivocal conclusions concerning the effects of punishment intensity on children's behavior. Using the resistance-to-deviation approach already described, Parke and Walters (1967) punished one group of boys with a soft tone (65 decibels) when they chose an attractive but prohibited toy. A second group heard a loud tone (96 decibels) when they chose the attractive toy. In the subsequent temptation test, children who were exposed to the loud punisher were less likely to touch the prohibited toys in the experimenter's absence than were boys exposed to a less intense version of the tone. This finding has been confirmed using a noxious buzzer as the punishing stimulus (Cheyne & Walters, 1969; Parke, 1969).

This research has also yielded some suggestive evidence concerning the impact of intensity variations on other aspects of punishment such as timing (Parke, 1969). Under conditions of high intensity punishment, the degree of inhibition produced by early and late punishment was similar. Under low intensity conditions, however, the early punished subjects showed significantly greater inhibition than did subjects punished late in the response sequence. Thus, timing of punishment may be less important under conditions of high intensity punishment. However, the generality of this conclusion is limited by the narrow range of delay of punishment intervals that have been investigated. Perhaps when punishment is delayed over a number of hours, for example, this relationship would not hold. Further research is clearly required.

Other research has indicated, however, that high intensity punishment may not always lead to better inhibition or be more effective in controlling children's behavior than low intensity punishment. A study by Aronfreed and Leff (1963), who investigated the effects of intensity of punishment on response inhibition in a temptation situation, illustrates this possibility. Six- and seven-year-old boys were given a series of choice trials involving two toys roughly comparable in attractiveness, but which differed along certain stimulus dimensions that the child could use to distinguish between punished and nonpunished choices. For two groups, a simple discrimination between red and yellow toys was required; the other groups of subjects were exposed to a complex discrimination between toys which represented passive containers and toys with active internal mechanisms. The punishment consisted of verbal disapproval (no), deprivation of candy, and a noise. The intensity and quality of the noise were varied in order to control the noxiousness of the punishment. Following training, each child was left alone with a pair of toys of which the more attractive one was similar in some respects to the toys that had been associated with punishment during the training procedure. Provided that the discrimination task was relatively simple, response inhibition was more frequently observed among children who received high intensity punishment. When the discrimination task was difficult, however, "transgression" was more frequent among children under the high intensity punishment than among children who received the milder punishment. Thus, the complex discrimination task combined with high intensity punishment probably created a level of anxiety too high for adaptive learning to occur. When subtle discriminations are involved, or when the child is uncertain as to the appropriate response, high intensity punishment may create emotional levels that clearly interfere with learning and therefore retard inhibition of undesirable behaviors.

NATURE OF THE RELATIONSHIP BETWEEN THE AGENT AND RECIPIENT OF PUNISHMENT

The nature of the relationship between the socializing agent and the child is a significant determinant of the effectiveness of punishment. It is generally assumed that punishment will be a more effective means of controlling behavior when this relationship is close and affectional than when it is relatively impersonal. This argument assumes that any disciplinary act may involve in varying degrees at least two operations—the presentation of a negative reinforcer and the withdrawal or withholding of a positive one (Bandura & Walters, 1963). Physical punishment may, in fact, achieve its effect partly because it symbolizes the withdrawal of approval or affection. Hence, punishment should be a more potent controlling technique when used by a nurturant parent or teacher.

Sears, Maccoby and Levin (1957) provided some evidence in favor of this proposition. Mothers who were rated as warm and affectionate and who made relatively frequent use of physical punishment were more likely to report that they found spanking to be an effective means of discipline. In contrast, cold, hostile mothers who made frequent use of physical punishment were more likely to report that spanking was ineffective. Moreover, according to the mothers' reports, spanking was more effective when it was administered by the warmer of the two parents.

A study by Parke and Walters (1967) confirmed these child-rearing findings in a controlled laboratory situation. In this investigation, the nature of the experimenter-child relationship was varied in two interaction sessions prior to the administration of punishment. One group of boys experienced a 10-minute period of positive interaction with a female experimenter on two successive days. Attractive constructional materials were provided for the children and, as they played with them, the female experimenter provided encouragement and help and warmly expressed approval of their efforts. A second group of boys played with relatively unattractive materials in two 10-minute sessions while the experimenter sat in the room without interacting with the children. Following these interaction sessions, the children underwent punishment training involving verbal rebuke and a noxious noise for choosing incorrect toys. In the subsequent test for response inhibition, children who had experienced positive interaction with the agent of punishment showed significantly greater resistance to deviation than boys who had only impersonal contact.

It is difficult to determine whether this effect is due to an increase in the perceived noxiousness of the noise when delivered by a previously friendly agent or whether the result derives from the withdrawal of affection implied in the punitive operation. Probably it was a combination of these two sources of anxiety which contributes to our findings. A study by Parke (1967), while not directly concerned with the relative importance of these two components, shows that nurturance-withdrawal alone, unaccompanied by noxious stimulation, can effectively increase resistance to deviation in young children. Two experimental treatments were employed. In one condition—the continuous nurturance group—the subjects, six- to eight-year-old boys and girls, experienced 10 minutes of friendly and nurturant interaction with either a male or female experimenter. Subjects in the nurturance-withdrawal group experienced five minutes of nurturant interaction, followed by five minutes of nurturance-withdrawal during which the experimenter turned away from the child, appeared busy, and refused to respond to any bid for attention. Following these manipulations, all subjects were placed in a resistance-to-deviation situation, involving a display of attractive, but forbidden, toys. In the instructions to the subject, it was made clear that if the subject conformed to the prohibition, the experimenter would play with him upon returning. In this way the link between resistance-to-deviation and nurturance was established. As in previous experiments, a hidden observer recorded the child's deviant activity during the 15-minute period that the adult was absent from the room. The results provided support for the hypothesis, with subjects in the nurturance-withdrawal group deviating significantly less often than subjects in the continuous-nurturance condition. However, it was also found that nurturance-withdrawal influenced girls to a greater degree than boys, and that the effect was most marked with girls experiencing withdrawal of a female agent's nurturance.

These data are consistent with previous studies of nurturance-withdrawal, which have indicated that withdrawal of affection may motivate the previously nurtured child to engage in behavior that is likely to reinstate the affectional relationship (e.g., Hartup, 1958; Rosenblith, 1959, 1961). . . .

REASONING AND PUNISHMENT

In all of the studies discussed, punishment was presented in a relatively barren cognitive context. Very often, however, parents and teachers provide the child with a rationale for the punishment they administer. Is punishment more effective when accompanied by a set of reasons for nondeviation? Field studies of child rearing suggest that the answer is positive. For example, Sears, Maccoby and Levin (1957), in their interview investigation of child-rearing practices, found that mothers who combine physical punishment with extensive use of reasoning reported that punishment was more effective than mothers who tended to use punishment alone. Field investigations, however, have yielded little information concerning the relative effectiveness of different aspects of reasoning. In the child-training literature, reasoning may include not only descriptions of untoward consequences that the child's behavior may have for others, but also the provision of examples of incompatible socially acceptable behaviors, explicit instructions on how to behave in specific situations, and explanations of motives for placing restraints on the child's behavior. Moreover, these child-training studies do not indicate the manner in which the provision of reasons in combination with punishment can alter the operation of specific punishment parameters such as those already discussed—timing, intensity, and the nature of the agent-child relationship.

It is necessary to turn again to experimental studies for answers to these questions. First, laboratory investigations have confirmed the field results in that punishment is more effective when accompanied by a rationale. Parke (1969), for example, found that when children, in addition to being punished, were told that a toy was "fragile and may break," greater inhibition occurred than when children were punished without an accompanying rationale. In a later experiment, Parke and Murray (1971) found that a rationale alone is more effective than punishment alone. However, comparison of the results of the two studies indicates that the combination of punishment and a rationale is the most thoroughly effective procedure.

To understand the impact of reasoning on the timing of punishment effect, let us examine a pioneering set of studies by Aronfreed (1965). In the earlier timing experiments, cognitive structure was minimized and no verbal rationale was given for the constraints placed on the child's behavior. In contrast, children in a second group of experiments were provided, in the initial instructions, with a brief explanation for not handling some of the toys. In one variation, for example, the cognitive structuring focused on the child's intentions.

When punished, the child was told: "No, you should not have *wanted* to pick up that thing." The important finding here was that the addition of reasoning to a *late*-timed punishment markedly increased its effectiveness. In fact, when a verbal rationale accompanied the punishment the usual timing of punishment effect was absent; early- and late-timed punishments were equally effective inhibitors of the child's behavior. Other investigators have reported a similar relation between reasoning operations and timing of punishment (Cheyne & Walters, 1969; Parke, 1969). In these latter studies, the reasoning procedures presented in conjunction with punishment did not stress intentions, but focused on the consequences of violation of the experimenter's prohibition.

The delay periods used in all of these studies were relatively short. In everyday life, detection of a deviant act is often delayed many hours or the punishment may be postponed, for example, until the father returns home. An experiment reported by Walters and Andres (1967) addressed itself directly to this issue. Their aim was to determine the conditions under which a punishment delivered four hours after the commission of a deviant act could be made an effective inhibitor. By verbally describing the earlier deviation at the time that the punishment was administered, the effectiveness of the punishment was considerably increased in comparison to a punishment that was delivered without an accompanying restatement. An equally effective procedure involved exposing the children to a videotape recording of themselves committing the deviant act just prior to the long-delayed punishment. A partially analogous situation, not studied by these investigators, involves parental demonstration of the deviant behavior just before delivering the punishing blow. In any case, symbolic reinstatement of the deviant act, according to these data, seems to be a potent way of increasing the effectiveness of delayed punishment.

A question remains. Do reasoning manipulations alter the operation of any other parameters besides the timing of the punishment? Parke (1969) examined the modifying impact of reasoning on the intensity and nurturance variables. When no rationale was provided, the expected intensity of punishment effect was present: high intensity punishment produced significantly greater inhibition than low intensity punishment. However, when a rationale accompanied the punishment, the difference between high and low intensity of punishment was not present.

As noted earlier, children who experience nurturant interaction with the punishing agent prior to punishment training deviate less often than subjects in the low nurturance. However, this effect was present in the Parke (1969) study only when no rationale accompanied the noxious buzzer. When the children were provided with a rationale for not touching certain toys, the children who had experienced the friendly interaction and the children who had only impersonal contact with the agent were equally inhibited during the resistance-to-deviation test period. Taken together, these experiments constitute impressive evidence of the important role played by cognitive variables in modifying the operation of punishment.

A common yardstick employed to gauge the success of a disciplinary procedure is the permanence of the inhibition produced. It is somewhat surprising, therefore, that little attention has been paid to the stability of inhibition over time as a consequence of various punishment training operations. One approach to this issue involves calculating changes in deviant activity occurring during the resistance-to-deviation test session in experimental studies. Does the amount of deviant behavior increase at different rates, for example, in response to different training procedures? As a first step in answering this question, Parke (1969) divided the 15-minute resistance-to-deviation test session into three five-minute periods. As Figure 1 indicates, the low cognitive structure subjects (no rationale) increased their degree of illicit toy touching over the three time periods while the degree of deviation

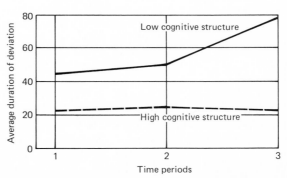

Figure 1 Stability of duration of deviation over three five-minute periods for high-cognitive and low-cognitive structure conditions.

over the three intervals did not significantly change for the high cognitive structure (rationale provided) subjects. Cheyne and Walters (1969) have reported a similar finding. These data clearly indicate that the stability of inhibition over time was affected by the reasoning or cognitive structuring procedures. The most interesting implication of this finding is that inhibition—or internalization—may *require* the use of cognitively-oriented training procedures. Punishment techniques that rely solely on anxiety induction, such as the noxious noises employed in many of the experiments discussed or the more extreme forms of physical punishment sometimes used by parents, may be effective mainly in securing only short-term inhibition.

However, children often forget a rationale or may not remember that a prohibition is still in force after a lengthy time lapse. A brief reminder or re-instatement of the original punisher or rationale may be necessary to insure continued inhibition. To investigate the impact of such re-instatement on the stability of inhibition was the aim of an experiment by Parke and Murray (1971). In this study, following the typical punishment training procedure, the seven- to nine-year-old boys were tested immediately for resistance-to-deviation and then re-tested in the same situation one week later. Half of the children were "reminded" of the earlier training by the experimenter. For example, in the case of the boys who were punished by a buzzer during the training session, the experimenter sounded the buzzer a single time and reminded the children that it signalled that they should not touch the toys ("You shouldn't touch the toys"). For children who received rationales unaccompanied by any punishment, the experimenter merely re-stated the rationale ("Remember, those toys belong to another boy" or "They are fragile and may break") before leaving the children alone with the toys. For the remaining children, no reminder or re-instatement of the earlier training was provided. As Figure 2 indicates, re-instatement of the original training clearly increased the permanence of the response inhibition.

However, the effectiveness of different types of reasoning procedures for producing inhibition varies with the developmental level of the child. Cheyne (1972) for example, found that third grade children increased their resistance to deviation in response to a prohibitory rationale stressing the norm of ownership, while first graders responded equally to both a rationale and a simple verbal prohibition.

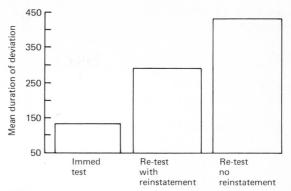

Figure 2 Stability of inhibition over one week with and without reinstatement.

However, as Parke and Murray (1971) have demonstrated, the type of rationale is important for achieving optimal inhibition with children of different ages. It is necessary to match the type and complexity of the rationale with the level of the child's cognitive development. Only if children can readily comprehend the bases of the rationale will it be an effective inhibitor. To test this proposition, Parke and Murray exposed 4-year- and 7-year-old children to two types of rationales that varied in degree of abstractness. The first—an object-oriented appeal—was relatively concrete and focused on the physical consequences of handling the toy ("the toy is fragile and might break"). This emphasis on the physical consequences of an action is similar to the types of justificatory rationales that young children use in their moral judgments (Kohlberg, 1964). The second rationale was a property rule which stressed the ethical norm of ownership. This person-oriented rationale was more abstract and assumed that children understand the rights of other individuals. In Kohlberg's moral judgment system this understanding represents a more sophisticated level of moral development. It was predicted that the property rationale would be most effective with the older children and that the concrete rationale would be more effective with the younger children. The results were consistent with this prediction. The concrete rationale was significantly more effective than was the property rationale in producing response inhibition in the younger children. At the older age level the effectiveness of the two rationales was approximately equal, the property rule being slightly more effective.

Rationales do not vary only in terms of their

object *vs.* person-oriented qualities. As a number of writers (Aronfreed, 1968; Hoffman, 1970; LaVoie, 1974) have stressed, rationales vary in terms of their focus on either (A) the consequences or outcomes of the rule violation or (B) the motivation or intention underlying the deviation. Since children utilize consequences as the basis for judging rule infractions at an earlier age than they utilize the actors' intentions, it is likely that appeals which focus on the consequences of misbehavior would be more effective for producing response inhibition than appeals which focus on the child's intentions. In fact, LaVoie (1974) recently evaluated this proposition; seven-, nine-, and eleven-year-old children heard either a consequence focused rationale ("That toy might get broken or worn out from you playing with it") or an intention focused rationale (It is wrong for you to *want* to play with that toy or think about playing with that toy"). As expected the consequence rationale was equally effective at all ages, but the intention-focused rationale increased in effectiveness across age. For younger children, focusing on the consequences of the act yields more effective control than focusing on intentions.

Other types of rationales have been investigated as well. For example, Parke and Sawin (1975a) examined the relative effectiveness of different types of emotional appeals on response inhibition in children at different ages. Children at two age levels (3-4 and 6-7 years of age) were exposed to either a fear-based rationale or an empathy-based rationale. The fear rationale focused on expressions of adult anger directed toward the child (i.e. "I will be angry if you touch the toys") while the empathy rationale focused on the negative affect that rule violation would generate in the adult ("I will be sad if you touch the toys"). The effectiveness of these two types of rationales in producing resistance to deviation in the toy touching situation varied with the age of the child. The provision of the fear invoking (angry) rationale increased the effectiveness of the prohibition for children at both age levels. However, the empathy-invoking consequences were less effective for the young children than the older children. These findings suggest that empathetic appeals are relatively ineffective with young children.

Another factor to be considered is the length of the explanation; since young children have shorter attention spans than older children, lengthy explanations may simply not be very effective with

young children. Hetherington (1975), in fact, found that parents who used brief explanations gained better control over their children than parents who used long and involved explanations.

Together the findings emphasize the importance of considering developmental factors in studies of different types of control tactics. Finally, by using cognitively based control tactics, age changes in behavioral aspects of moral development are clearly demonstrated. The task of charting in more detail age changes in relation to specific types of prohibitory rationales would appear to be worthwhile.

CONSISTENCY OF PUNISHMENT

In naturalistic contexts, punishment is often intermittently and erratically employed. Consequently, achieving an understanding of the effects of inconsistent punishment is a potentially important task. Data from field studies of delinquency have yielded a few clues concerning the consequences of inconsistency of discipline. Glueck and Glueck (1950) found that parents of delinquent boys were more "erratic" in their disciplinary practices than were parents of nondelinquent boys. Similarly, the McCords (e.g., McCord, McCord, & Howard, 1961) have found that erratic disciplinary procedures were correlated with high degrees of criminality. Inconsistent patterns involving a combination of love, laxity, and punitiveness, or a mixture of punitiveness and laxity alone were particularly likely to be found in the background of their delinquent sample. However, the definition of inconsistency has shifted from study to study in delinquency research, making evaluation and meaningful conclusions difficult (Walters & Parke, 1967).

To clarify the effects of inconsistent punishment on children's aggressive behavior, Parke and Deur (Parke & Deur, 1970; Deur & Parke, 1970) conducted a series of laboratory studies. Aggression was selected as the response measure in order to relate the findings to previous studies of inconsistent discipline and aggressive delinquency. An automated Bobo doll was used to measure aggression. The child punched the large, padded stomach of the clown-shaped doll and the frequency of hitting was automatically recorded. In principle, the apparatus is similar to the inflated punch toys commonly found in children's homes. To familiarize themselves with the doll, the boys participating in the first study (Parke & Deur, 1970) punched freely for two minutes. Then the children were rewarded with marbles each time they punched the Bobo doll for a total of 10 trials. Following this baseline session, the subjects experienced one of three different outcomes for punching: termination of reward (no outcome), receipt of marbles on half the trials and a noxious buzzer following the other half, or consistent punishment by the buzzer. Half the children were also told that the buzzer indicated that they were playing the game "badly," while the remaining boys were informed that the buzzer was a "bad noise." All the boys had been informed that they could terminate the punching game whenever they wished. The main index of persistence was the number of hitting responses that the child delivered before voluntarily ending the game. The results were clear: subjects in the no outcome group made the greatest number of punches, while the continuously punished children delivered the fewest punches; the inconsistently punished children were in the intermediate position. The results were not affected by the labeling of the buzzer; whether the buzzer meant "playing the game badly" or a "bad noise" made no difference. This laboratory demonstration confirms the common child-rearing dictum that intermittent punishment is less effective than continuous punishment.

Parents and other disciplinary agents often use consistent punishment only after inconsistent punishment has failed to change the child's behavior. To investigate the effectiveness of consistent punishment *after* the child has been treated in an inconsistent fashion was the aim of the next study (Deur & Parke, 1970). Following the baseline period, subjects underwent one of three different training conditions. One group of boys was rewarded for 18 trials, while a second group of children received marbles on nine trials and no outcome on the remaining trials. A final group of boys was rewarded on half of the trials but heard a noxious buzzer on the other nine trials. The children were informed that the buzzer indicated that they were playing the game "badly."

To determine the effects of these training schedules on resistance to extinction (where both rewards and punishers were discontinued) and on resistance to continuous punishment (where every punch was punished) was the purpose of the next phase of the study. Therefore, half of the children in each of the three groups were neither rewarded

nor punished for hitting the Bobo doll and the remaining subjects heard the noxious buzzer each time they punched. The number of hitting responses that the child made before voluntarily quitting was, again, the principal measure.

The results are shown in Figure 3. The punished subjects made fewer hitting responses than did subjects in the extinction condition, which suggests that the punishment was effective in inhibiting the aggressive behavior. The training schedules produced particularly interesting results. The inconsistently punished subjects showed the greatest resistance to extinction. Moreover, these previously punished children tended to persist longer in the face of consistent punishment than the boys in the other training groups. The effects were most marked in comparison to the consistently rewarded subjects. The implication is clear: the socializing agent using inconsistent punishment builds up resistance to future attempts to either extinguish deviant behavior or suppress it by consistently administered punishment.

The particular form of inconsistency employed in this study represents only one of the variety of forms of inconsistency which occurs in naturalistic socialization. Consistency, as used in the present research, refers to the extent to which a single agent treats violations in the same manner each time such violations occur.

What are the effects of inter-agent inconsistent

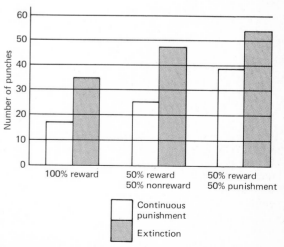

Figure 3 Mean number of punches in post-training period as a function of consistency of reward and punishment.

punishment? Parke and Sawin (1975b) recently investigated this issue. Employing the Bobo doll paradigm, 8-year-old boys were exposed to two female socializing agents who reacted in one of the following ways to the boys punching behavior: (1) the two agents were both rewarding, (2) the two agents were both punishing, or (3) one agent was rewarding, while the other agent was punishing. The results revealed that the boys persisted longer in punching when the agents were inconsistent than when the two agents were consistently punitive. Nor are the effects of inter-agent inconsistency restricted to aggression. In an earlier study, Stouwie (1972) demonstrated that inconsistent instructions between two agents in a resistance to deviation situation lessened the amount of subject control. Unfortunately, little is known concerning the impact of inter-agent inconsistency on the persistence of the behavior under extinction or consistent punishment. Nor do we know about the generalizability of these effects. Do inconsistent parents make it more difficult for teachers to gain control over children's behavior?

THE CHILD'S ROLE IN SPARING THE ROD

Research and theories of childhood socialization have traditionally been based on an undirectional model of effects; it was assumed that the rewarding and punishing activities of socializing agents serve to shape the behavior patterns of children. In fact, the research that we have discussed so far in this chapter reflects this orientation. The child, it implies, is acted upon by adults; the child is a passive recipient of adult-controlled input. However, this model is inadequate and a bi-directional model is necessary, in which the child is explicitly recognized as an active participant and modifier of adult behavior. As Bell (1968) has so persuasively argued, children shape adults just as adults shape children. Moreover, this general principle has recently been shown to operate in important ways in disciplinary contexts (Parke, 1974). Specifically, the child can modify the degree and amount of adult punitiveness by their reactions after violation of a rule or by their behavior following the administration of discipline by an adult. The following studies by Sawin and Parke (1975) will illustrate the role of the child in modifying adult disciplinary tactics.

In their study, adult females were given the opportunity to administer rewards and punishments to a 7-year-old boy. They were first shown a video-tape of two boys sitting at desks in a school-like context. They were asked to assist in assessing "how adults and children can interact by means of a remote closed circuit television monitoring and control system that might be used in understaffed day care facilities to supplement regular person to person contacts." The adult was asked to evaluate the boys' behavior by delivering or removing points that could be later traded in for varying amounts of free play time. In fact, the children's behavior on the video-tapes was pre-recorded and the adult's feedback to the child was surreptitiously recorded by the experimenter. To evaluate the impact of children's behavior on adult disciplinary actions, adults saw one of four video-taped sequences, which were similar except for one section of the tape. All tapes showed one boy pushing a second child's workbook off his desk. Prior to the adult's opportunity to discipline or reward the child, the deviant child gave one of four reactions: (1) reparation—offered to pick up the book, (2) plead—pleaded for leniency, (3) ignore—turned his back to the adult, (4) defiance—acted in a defiant fashion by saying "It was a dumb book anyway." Although all of the children were punished, the amount of punishment varied. The adults who saw the reparative child, who offered to correct his misbehavior, delivered the least amount of punishment while the adults who saw the child ignore the adult or behave in a defiant fashion delivered the harshest punishment. The way that a child reacts after misbehaving but before the adult administers punishment can significantly modify the severity of the adult's disciplinary behavior.

In a related study, the impact of the child's reaction *after* being disciplined on the adults' later disciplinary actions was examined. As in the earlier study, an adult monitored children on a video-tape. Again one of the children misbehaved but this time the adult was allowed to finish punishing the child before viewing the child's reaction to being punished. One of four reactions followed: (1) reparation, (2) plead, (3) ignore, or (4) defiance. Immediately following the target child's reaction to being punished the adult was signalled to respond again; this was the crucial test trial since it followed immediately on the child's reaction to the prior discipline. As Figure 4 illustrates, the subsequent discipline was significantly affected by the child's reaction to the earlier adult discipline. In fact, the

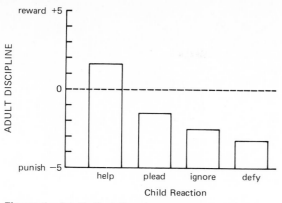

Figure 4 Adult discipline in response to children's reactions to prior punishment.

adults who witnessed the child make reparation were *not* even punitive, but were mildly rewarding. As in the earlier study, the defiance and ignore reactions elicited the most severe punitive reactions from the adults. The study clearly demonstrates that children's reactions to discipline serve as determinants of how severely they will be dealt with on future occasions. Children can play a role in sparing the rod!

UNDESIRABLE CONSEQUENCES OF PUNISHMENT

The foregoing paragraphs indicate that punishment is effective in producing response suppression. Nevertheless, punishment may have undesirable side-effects which limit its usefulness as a socializing technique. In the first place, the teacher or parent who employs physical punishment to inhibit undesirable behaviors may also serve as an aggressive model. Bandura (1967) has summarized this viewpoint as follows: "When a parent punishes his child physically for having aggressed toward peers, for example, the intended outcome of this training is that the child should refrain from hitting others. The child, however, is also learning from parental demonstration how to aggress physically. And the imitative learning may provide the direction for the child's behavior when he is similarly frustrated in subsequent social interactions" (1967, p. 43).

Evidence supporting this position is, at best, indirect. There is a sizable body of data indicating a relation between the frequent use of physical punishment by parents and aggressive behavior in their children (Becker, 1964). However, the increases in

aggression could possibly be due to the *direct* encouragement that punitive parents often provide for behaving aggressively outside the home situation. Alternatively, highly aggressive children may require strong, physically punitive techniques to control them. Thus, even if it is assumed that the punitive parent acts as an aggressive model there is no evidence demonstrating that children imitate the aggressive behaviors the disciplinarian displays while punishing the child. It is recognized that exposure to aggressive models increases aggressive behavior in young children (Bandura, 1967). It is of questionable legitimacy, however, to generalize from Bobo doll studies to children imitating a physically punitive adult who is often carrying out a justified spanking in line with his role as parent or teacher.

Fortunately, a direct test of the modeling hypothesis has recently been reported. (Gelfand, Hartmann, Lamb, Smith, Mahan, and Paul, 1974) These investigators exposed 6-to-8-year-old children to rewarding, punishing or unresponsive adults in a marble drop game. When each child was later given the opportunity to train another child to play the game, he employed techniques strikingly similar to those he had previously experienced himself. Of particular importance was the finding that children who themselves had been punished by the adult used punitive techniques in interactions with another child.

Another negative side effect is the avoidance of the punishing agent. This is illustrated in a recent study by Redd, Morris, and Martin (1975) in which five-year-old children interacted with three different adults who employed various strategies. One adult behaved in a positive manner and smiled and made positive comments ("Good," "Nice boy," "Tremendous") while the child performed a color-sorting task. A second adult dispensed mild verbal reprimands whenever the child deviated from the sorting task (for example, "Stop throwing the tokens around," "Don't play with the chair"). A third adult was present but didn't comment on the child's behavior. While the results indicated that the punitive adult was most effective in keeping the child working on the task, the children tended to prefer the positive and neutral agents more than the punitive adult. When asked to indicate which adult they wished to work with a little longer, the children always chose the positive adult. Similarly, the children always avoided the punitive adult as their partner on other tasks or as a playmate. The implication is clear: punishment may be an effective modification technique, but the use of punishment by adults may lead the child to avoid that socializing agent and therefore undermine the adult's effectiveness as a future influence on the child's behavior.

Conditions such as the classroom often prevent the child from physically escaping the presence of the agent. Continued use of punishment in an inescapable context, however, may lead to passivity and withdrawal (Seligman, Maier & Solomon, 1969) or adaptation to the punishing stimuli themselves. In any case, whether escape is possible or not, the quality of the agent-child relationship may deteriorate if punishment is used with high frequency; punishment administered by such an agent will, therefore, be less effective in inhibiting the child.

The undesirable effects of punishment mentioned here probably occur mainly in situations where the disciplinary agents are indiscriminately punitive. In child-training contexts where the agent rewards and encourages a large proportion of the child's behavior, even though selectively and occasionally punishing certain kinds of behavior, these side-effects are less likely to be found (Walters & Parke, 1967).

REINFORCEMENT OF INCOMPATIBLE RESPONSES: AN ALTERNATIVE TO PUNISHMENT

In light of these undesirable consequences, it may be worthwhile to consider other ways in which deviant behavior can be controlled. Reinforcement of incompatible responses is one such technique. Brown and Elliot (1965) asked several nursery school teachers to ignore aggressive acts and only encourage behaviors that were inconsistent with aggression, such as cooperation and helpfulness. Encouraging these alternative behaviors resulted in a marked decrease in classroom aggression. More recently, Parke, Ewall and Slaby (1972) have found that encouraging college subjects for speaking helpful words also led to a decrease in subsequent aggression. In an extension of this work, Slaby (1970) found a similar effect for eight- to 12-year-old children. The lesson is clear: speaking in a manner that is incompatible with aggression may actually inhibit hostile actions. Words, as well as deeds, can alter our physical behaviors. The advantage of the incompatible response technique

for controlling behavior is that the unwanted side-effects associated with punishment can be avoided.

CONCLUSION

This review leaves little doubt that punishment can be an effective means of controlling children's behavior. The operation of punishment, however, is a complex process and its effects are quite varied and highly dependent on such parameters as timing, intensity, consistency, the affectional and/or status relationship between the agent and recipient of punishment, and the kind of cognitive structuring accompanying the punishing stimulus.

The decision to employ punishment in child-rearing, however, cannot be evaluated simply in terms of its effectiveness as a suppressor of undesirable behavior. The decision to use a particular disciplinary tactic is inevitably intertwined with the wider socio-political and moral issue of children's rights. A number of writers are beginning to question whether or not children's rights to humane treatment are not being violated by adult use of physically punitive control tactics (Parke, 1976). As the research reviewed here indicates, children *can* both understand and effectively utilize cognitively based rationales to govern their behavior; in short, continued reliance on physical punishment as a control tactic is probably unjustified. By focusing on the task of promoting acceptable and pro-social behaviors, our need to rely on punishment to socialize our children will diminish.

REFERENCES

Aronfreed, J. Punishment learning and internalization: Some parameters of reinforcement and cognition. Paper read at biennial meeting of Society for Research in Child Development, Minneapolis, 1965.

———. *Conduct and Conscience.* New York: Academic Press, 1968.

Aronfreed, J. & Leff, R. The effects of intensity of punishment and complexity of discrimination upon the learning of an internalized inhibition. Unpubl. mss., Univ. of Pennsylvania, 1963.

Aronfreed, J. & Reber, A. Internalized behavioral suppression and the timing of social punishment. *J. pers. soc. Psychol.,* 1965, 1, 3–16.

Bandura, A. The role of modeling processes in personality development. In W. W. Hartup & Nancy L. Smothergill (eds.), *The Young Child: Reviews of Research.*

Washington: National Association for the Education of Young Children, 1967. pp. 42–58.

Bandura, A. & Walters, R. H. *Social Learning and Personality Development.* New York: Holt, Rinehart & Winston, 1963.

Becker, W. C. Consequences of different kinds of parental discipline. In M. L. Hoffman & L. W. Hoffman (Eds.), *Review of Child Development Research,* Vol. 1. New York: Russell Sage Foundation, 1964. Pp. 169–208.

Bell, R. Q. A reinterpretation of the direction of effects of socialization. *Psychological Review,* 1968, 75, 81–95.

Black, A. H., Solomon, R. L. & Whiting, J. W. M. Resistance to temptation in dogs. Cited by Mowrer, O. H. *Learning Theory and the Symbolic Processes.* New York: John Wiley, 1960.

Brown, P. & Elliot, R. Control of aggression in a nursery school class. *J. exp. child Psychol.,* 1965, 2, 103–107.

Cheyne, A. Punishment and reasoning in the development of self-control. In R. D. Parke (ed.), *Recent Trends in Social Learning Theory.* New York: Academic Press, 1972.

Cheyne, J. A. & Walters, R. H. Intensity of punishment, timing of punishment, and cognitive structure as determinants of response inhibition. *J. exp. child Psychol.,* 1969, 7, 231–244.

Church, R. M. The varied effects of punishment on behavior. *Psychol. Rev.,* 1963, 70, 369–402.

Cowan, P. A. & Walters, R. H. Studies of reinforcement of aggression: I Effects of scheduling. *Child Develpm.,* 1963, 34, 543–551.

Deur, J. L. & Parke, R. D. The effects of inconsistent punishment on aggression in children. *Develpm. Psychol.,* 1970, 2, 403–411.

Gelfand, D. F., Hartmann, D. P., Lanb, A. K., Smith, C. L., Mahan, M. A., and Paul, S. C. The effects of adult models and described alternatives on children's choice of behavior management techniques. *Child Develpm.,* 1974, 45, 585–593.

Glueck, S. & Glueck, E. *Unraveling Juvenile Delinquency.* Cambridge: Harvard Univ. Press, 1950.

Hetherington, E. M. Children of Divorce. Paper presented at Biennial meeting of Society for Research in Child Development, Denver, 1975.

Hoffman, M. L. Moral development. In P. Mussen (Ed.), *Manual of Child Psychology,* New York: Wiley, 1970.

Hartup, W. W. Nurturance and nurturance-withdrawal in relation to the dependency behavior of preschool children. *Child Develpm.,* 1958, 29, 191–201.

Kohlberg, L. Development of moral character and moral ideology. In M. L. Hoffman and Lois W. Hoffman (Eds.), *Review of Child Development Research,* Vol. 1. New York: Russell Sage Foundation, 1964, Pp. 383–431.

LaVoie, J. C. Cognitive determinants of resistance to deviation in seven, nine and eleven year old children of

low and high maturity of moral judgement. *Developm. Psychol.,* 1974, 10, 393–403. (b).

McCord, W., McCord, J. & Howard, A. Familial correlates of aggression in non-delinquent male children. *J. abnorm. soc Psychol.,* 1961, 62, 79–93.

Parke, R. D. Nurturance, nurturance-withdrawal and resistance to deviation. *Child Develpm.,* 1967, 38, 1101–1110.

———. The role of punishment in the socialization process. In R. A. Hoppe, G. A. Milton, & E. C. Simmel (eds.), *Early Experiences and the Processes of Socialization.* New York: Academic Press, 1970. Pp. 81–108.

———. Effectiveness of punishment as an interaction of intensity, timing, agent nurturance and cognitive structuring. *Child Develpm.,* 1969, 40, 213–236.

Parke, R. d. Rules, roles and resistance to deviation in children: Explorations in punishment, discipline and self control. In a. Pick (ed.), *Minnesota symposia on child psychology,* Vol. 8. Minneapolis: University of Minnesota Press, 1974.

Parke, R. D. and Sawin, D. B. The impact of fear and empathy-based rationales on children's inhibition. Unpublished manuscript, Fels Research Institute, 1975a.

Parke, R. D. and Sawin, D. B. The effects of inter-agent inconsistent discipline on aggression in children. Unpublished manuscript, Fels Research Institute, 1975b.

Parke, R. D. Socialization into child abuse: A social interactional perspective. In J. L. Tapp and F. J. Levine (Eds.), *Law, justice and the individual in society: Psychological and legal issues.* New York: Holt, Rinehart and Winston, 1976, in press.

Parke, R. D. & Deur, J. The inhibitory effects of inconsistent and consistent punishment on children's aggression. Unpubl. mss., Univ. of Wisconsin, 1970.

Parke, R. D., Ewall, W. & Slaby, R. G. Hostile and helpful verbalizations as regulators of nonverbal aggression. *J. pers. soc. Psychol.,* 1972, 23, 243–248.

Parke, R. D. & Murray, S. Re-instatement: A technique for increasing stability of ingibition in children. Unpubl. mss., Univ of Wisconsin, 1971.

Parke, R. D. & Walters, R. H. Some factors determining the efficacy of punishment for inducing response inhibition. *Monogr. Soc. Res. Child Develpm.,* 1967, 32 (Serial No. 109).

Redd, W. H., Morris, E. K., and Martin, J. A. Effects of positive and negative adult-child interactions on children's social preferences. *J. exp. child Psychol.,* 1975, 19, 153–164.

Rosenblith, J. F. Learning by imitation in kindergarten children. *Child Develpm.,* 1959, 30, 69–80.

———. Imitative color choices in kindergarten children. *Child Develpm.,* 1961, 32, 211–223.

Sawin, D. D. and Parke, R. D. The child's role in sparing the rod. Paper presented at the American Psychological Association, Chicago, September, 1975.

Sears, R. R., Maccoby, E. E. & Levin, H. *Patterns of Child Rearing.* Evanston, Ill.: Row, Peterson, 1957.

Seligman, M. E. P., Maier, S. F. & Solomon, R. L. Unpredictable and uncontrollable aversive events. In F. R. Brush (Ed.), *Aversive Conditioning and Learning.* New York: Academic Press, 1969.

Slaby, R. G. Aggressive and helpful verbalizations as regulators of behavioral aggression and altruism in children. Unpubl. doctoral dissertation, Univ. of Wisconsin, 1970.

Stouwie, R. J. An experimental study of adult dominance and warmth, conflicting verbal instructions, and children's moral behavior. *Child Developm.,* 1972, 43, 959–972.

Walters, R. H. Delay-of-reinforcement effects in children's learning. *Psychonom. Sci.,* 1964, 1, 307–308.

Walters, R. H. & Andres, D. Punishment procedures and self-control. Paper read at Annual Meeting of the American Psychological Association, Washington, D. C., Sept., 1967.

Walters, R. H. & Parke, R. D. The influence of punishment and related disciplinary techniques on the social behavior of children: Theory and empirical findings. In B. A. Maher (Ed.), *Progress in Experimental Personality Research,* Vol. 4. New York: Academic Press, 1967. Pp. 179–228.

Walters, R. H., Parke, R. D. & Cane, V. A. Timing of punishment and the observation of consequences to others as determinants of response inhibition. *J. exp. child Psychol.,* 1965, 2, 10–30.

Reading 24

Parents as Educators: Evidence from Cross-sectional, Longitudinal, and Intervention Research

Earl S. Schaefer

An awareness of the major role of the parent as educator is emerging from child development research. Research findings now suggest the need to return to a traditional comprehensive definition of education as opposed to a restricted, professional, and institutional one. Definitions of education such as "the act or process of rearing or bringing up . . ." and "the process of providing with knowledge, skill, competence or usually desirable qualities of behavior and character . . ." *(Webster's Third New International Dictionary of the English Language,* Unabridged, G. & C. Merriam Co., Springfield, Mass., 1965) apply to the activities of parents as well as professional teachers. However, the classroom model of education has focused on the shcool-age child in the classroom in company with a professional educator, learning academic subjects through formal instruction in order to earn academic credentials. Webster's definitions of educator, "one skilled in teaching" and "a student of the theory and practice of teaching," are currently applied primarily, if not exclusively, to the professional educator. Accumulating research on parent behavior and child development now suggests the need to develop a life time and life space perspec-

tive on education which recognizes the major educational role of parents.

A review of recent trends in early childhood and early education research may explain the increasing interest in the educational role of parents. From research findings, a rationale for early education can be developed emphasizing provision of experience that contributes to intellectual development. One response, from a classroom perspective, is to speed the development of preschool education. Other responses are to develop enriched day care programs and child-centered home tutoring programs. Although these programs have led to immediate gains in mental test scores, evaluations after termination of the intensive child-centered enrichment programs show significant declines in IQ. Such findings have led to recognition of the need for continued education in order to foster continued development (Klaus & Gray, 1968; Schaefer, 1970).

The development of programs to train parents to foster the intellectual development of their children has been yet another major response to the need for early and continuing education of the child. Whether brief parent training programs will be sufficient to have long-term effects upon parents' education of their children is as yet undetermined. Perhaps a comprehensive system of education that integrates the collaborative efforts of the family, the community, the mass media, and the schools must be developed to provide a continuing educational impact upon the child.

The history of education also suggests a need to develop a more comprehensive view that recognizes the role of parents in the educational process. The initial *thesis* of education through life experience in the family and community was followed by the *antithesis* of academic education in the schools. As a result, the educational professions and institutions often assume a restricted classroom perspective rather than the more comprehensive life time and life space perspective on education. Child development research now suggests that academic education in the schools will not solve the problems of low academic achievement of disadvantaged groups, again suggesting the need to support the child's education in the family and community.

Increasing recognition of the impact of the mass media, particularly television, and of their potential effectiveness in education, also suggests the need for the development of a *synthesis* that will strengthen and integrate the educational contributions of various social units.

Increasing awareness of the role of the parent in the child's education is shown by an analysis of parental involvement in early education (Hess et al., 1971). Parental roles in the classroom education of children—parents as supporters, service givers, and facilitators; parents as teacher aides and volunteers in the classroom; and parents as policy makers and partners in the operation of the school— were differentiated from more independent roles of parents as learners and parents as teachers of their own children. The research reviewed here strongly supports the need to view parents as students of educational methods and as teachers in their own right. An analysis of major characteristics of children's interactions with parents also supports the view that parents are teachers and increases the

Table 1

Major characteristics of the parent's interaction with the child	
Priority	Parents influence the early development of relationships, language, interests, task-oriented behaviors, etc.
Duration	The parent's interactions with the child usually extend from birth to maturity.
Continuity	The parent-child interaction is usually not interrupted, particularly in early childhood, apart from brief separations. Concern about such interruptions has led to research on maternal separation and deprivation.
Amount	The total amount of time spent in parent-child interaction, particularly one-to-one interaction, is usually greater than with other adults.
Extensity	The parent shares more different situations and experiences with the child than do other adults.
Intensity	The degree of involvement between parent and child, whether that involvement is hostile or loving, is usually greater than between the child and other adults.
Pervasiveness	Parents potentially influence the child's use of the mass media, his social relationships, his exposure to social institutions and professions, and much of the child's total experience, both inside and outside the home.
Consistency	Parents develop consistent patterns of behavior with their children.
Responsibility	Both society and parents recognize the parent's primary responsibility for the child.
Variability	Great variability exists in parental care of children, varying from extremes of parental neglect and abuse to extremes of parental acceptance, involvement, and stimulation.

credibility of findings concerning parental influences on child development. The combination of these different characteristics of parent-child interaction suggests that their cumulative impact upon the child's development would be substantial. Contrasting these characteristics of parent-child interactions with characteristics of the children's interactions with the child care and education professions and institutions suggests that strengthening and supporting family care and education of the child should be a major focus in child development programs.

CONCEPTUALIZATION OF PARENT BEHAVIOR

Reviews of the extensive literature on maternal deprivation by Bowlby (1951), Yarrow (1961), and Ainsworth (1962) have contributed substantially to understanding deprivation and its effects. Ainsworth's review suggests distinction of: "(a) insufficiency of interaction implicit in deprivation; (b) distortion of the character of the interaction, without respect to its quantity; and (c) the discontinuity of relations brought about through separation." Ainsworth recognized that various combinations of these types of deprivation occur. Converging conceptual models for parent behavior derived from ratings support Ainsworth's categories for they clearly distinguish hostile detachment (including neglect and ignoring) from hostile involvement (including nagging and irritability) (Schaefer, 1971). Recent studies suggest a further distinction between the amount of emotional support and the amount of educational stimulation provided by parents. Lack of educational stimulation seems to be related to school achievement problems while lack of emotional support is more closely related to emotional problems (Werner, Bierman & French, 1971).

Hess (1969), based on an extensive review, has developed a list of parent behaviors that have been found to be related to intellectual development and academic achievement. Similar lists of parental variables can be found in studies by Rupp (1969) and Wolf (1964) and in others summarized elsewhere in this review. The Hess list is as follows:

A. *Intellectual Relationship*
   1. Demand for high achievement
   2. Maximization of verbal interaction
   3. Engagement with and attentiveness to the child
   4. Maternal teaching behavior

   5. Diffuse intellectual stimulation
B. *Affective Relationship*
   1. Warm affective relationship with child
   2. Feelings of high regard for child and self
C. *Interaction Patterns*
   1. Pressure for independence and self-reliance.
   2. Clarity and severity of disciplinary rules
   3. Use of conceptual rather than arbitrary regulatory strategies.

INTRA-FAMILY RESEMBLANCE

Roff's (1950) review of intra-family resemblances in personality characteristics has provided a great deal of evidence that parents influence the development of attitudes, opinions, and interests in their children. Hartshorne et al. (1930) found relatively high correlations between parents and children in a test of moral knowledge and opinion, and Newcomb and Svehla (1937) found substantial correlations between parents and children in attitudes toward the church, war, and communism. Somewhat lower correlations have been found between fathers and sons in vocational interests and even lower, but usually positive correlations, in personality inventory scores. Reports by high school children about their own use and their parent's use of psychoactive drugs suggest that patterns of heavy drug use are heavily influenced by parental example (Smart & Fijer, 1970). Children who reported that their mothers used tranquilizers nearly every day were eight times as likely to report their own use of tranquilizers as were children who reported that their mothers never used tranquilizers. Use of one psychoactive drug by parents, both mothers and fathers, was found to influence use of many other psychoactive drugs by their children. Thus, Smart and Fijer (1970) suggested that "A likely hypothesis is that students are modeling their drug use after parents' use. . . ."

EARLY EMERGENCE OF LEVELS OF INTELLIGENCE

In the area of intellectual and language development, relatively stable differences in mean mental

---

[1]The literature that was interpreted as "clarity and severity of disciplinary rules" could be interpreted instead as setting of high standards and enforcement of rules, rather than severity, which may imply hostility or rejection.

test scores between socioeconomic groups emerge in the second and third year of life (Terman & Merrill, 1937; Hindley, 1965). This may be interpreted as evidence of the early and continuing influence of parental stimulation. Studies show that the mean IQs of different groups tend to remain stable during the school years (Terman & Merrill, 1937; Kennedy, 1969), or the mean IQs of disadvantaged groups may even decline in regions of relative deprivation (Coleman, 1966). Apparently, the typical school does not improve the level of intellectual functioning that is established and maintained by the family and community under these circumstances. Schaefer (1970), from a summary of findings on early language development and intellectual development, concluded, "The evidence of the coincidence of the emergence of early language skills with the emergence of mental test differences between social groups, of the relationship of verbal skills with socioeconomic status, ethnic groups, IQ scores, reading achievement, and academic and occupational success, supports a conclusion that the education of the child should begin prior to or at the beginning of early language development." Relations between maternal behavior and child language behavior at five months (Rubenstein, 1967) and 10 months of age (Tulkin, 1971) can be interpreted as evidence of influence of parent behavior upon early language development and, perhaps, later cognitive development.

STUDIES OF CHILDREN IN INSTITUTIONS AND ADOPTIVE HOMES

Another source of evidence showing the educational influence of parents is the study of language development of children reared in institutions (Skeels et al., 1938; Pringle & Bossio, 1958). Skeels et al. reported: "At most ages the orphanage children had a vocabulary only one-fourth to one-half that of Iowa City children of average intelligence and the same age. Explanations of this extreme retardation were advanced; namely, that the orphanage situation was characteristically deficient in the factors known to be associated with good language development—such factors as adult-child ratio, parent goals for child achievement, standard of acceptibility of verbal expression, number of hours being read to and being told stories, breadth of experiences, and extensions of environment." Skeels et al. pointed out that study of the orphanage group "demonstrates to some extent what average

homes operating in an average social milieu accomplish in the way of mental stimulation, by showing what may happen when children are bereft of such influences."

Other studies by Skeels (1940) and his coworkers at the University of Iowa provided additional data on the role of the environment in intellectual development. A study of infants in an institution for mentally retarded girls (Skeels & Dye, 1939) who received relatively high stimulation from patients and staff, as contrasted to infants who received relatively little stimulation in an orphanage, showed substantial IQ increases in the stimulated group and substantial decreases in the unstimulated group. Subsequently, most of the stimulated group were adopted while the unstimulated group remained in the orphanage. A follow-up showed very large differences in the social competence of the two groups at maturity (Skeels, 1966). Not only the early stimulation in the institution, but also the continued stimulation in the adoptive homes, contributed to the intellectual functioning and social competence of the experimental group.

A study by Skeels and Harms (1948) of children in good adoptive homes whose natural parents were either mentally retarded or of very low socioeconomic status yielded surprising results. The adopted children of mentally retarded natural mothers achieved a mean IQ of 105.5, children whose natural fathers were laborers had a mean IQ of 110.3, and children with both laborer fathers and mentally retarded mothers had a mean IQ of 104.1. Mental retardation in the children "with known inferior histories" who were placed in adoptive homes in infancy was no greater than that of a random sample of the population and the frequency of superior intelligence was somewhat greater than would be expected. Skodak and Skeels (1949) also reported a 20-point IQ difference between adopted children and their natural mothers, with a maternal mean of 86 and a child mean of 106. These data suggest that a radical change in environment can produce a major change in intellectual functioning between generations.

Despite the substantial differences between mean IQs of the adopted children and their natural mothers, Skodak and Skeels reported higher correlations between the IQs of the adopted children and those of their natural mothers than with characteristics of the adoptive parents. Thus, the data indicate that genetics may determine the potential for intellectual development but the quality of the environment may determine the level of intellectual functioning that is achieved.

CROSS-SECTIONAL STUDIES

A number of cross-sectional studies have provided detailed analyses of parent variables that are related to children's mental test scores. Milner (1951) interviewed both mothers and children to determine family variables that were related to high and low language scores on the *California Test of Mental Maturity*. High scoring children had more books, were read to more often, had more meal time conversation with parents, and received less harsh physical punishment. Interpretation of the findings is obscured by the great differences in socioeconomic status between low and high scoring groups. Milner recognized the problem in her statement, "The findings listed above may be restated, substituting for the words *mothers of low scorers and high scorers,* the words *lower-class mothers and middle-class mothers* respectively." Milner's study suggests that different socioeconomic groups have different patterns of parent behavior that are partially determined by their adaptation to their life situation but also are related to their children's intellectual development.

Kent and Davis (1957) interviewed parents of samples of school children, juvenile offenders, and psychiatric outpatient clinic referrals and classified the type of discipline used as normal, demanding, overanxious, and unconcerned. The parents of the school children showed the highest percentage of normal discipline, the parents of the juvenile offenders showed the highest percentage of unconcerned discipline, and the parents of the psychiatric outpatient clinic referrals showed the highest percentages of demanding and over-anxious discipline. Among the school sample, children of demanding parents had the highest IQ scores and had higher verbal than performance scores; children of unconcerned parents had the lowest IQ scores and reading scores. This study suggests that insufficiency of emotional support and intellectual stimulation results in lower intelligence and academic achievement than moderate degrees of distortion—demanding and overanxious discipline—but both insufficiency and distortion may be related to different types of maladjustment.

Interviews and mailed questionnaires focusing upon parental rejection and punitiveness have been correlated with *California Test of Mental Maturity* scores (Hurley, 1965, 1967). An association between parent rejection and low mental test scores was found for different measures and for different samples, with higher correlations between the mothers' education and the daughters' IQ and low correlations for the higher educational groups of parents. Although a number of studies support the conclusion that rejection tends to be negatively related to intellectual development (Baldwin, Kalhorn & Breese, 1945; Bayley & Schaefer, 1964; Kagan & Freeman, 1963; Kagan, 1964; Honzig, 1967) different findings for different socioeconomic groups and for boys and girls in different studies suggest a possible interaction between socioeconomic group, sex of child, and parent behavior as these influence the intellectual development and academic achievement of children. Perhaps different socioeconomic groups have different expectations for boys and girls that are related to parent behavior and child development.

Interviews with parents of fifth grade children about family educational processes (Dave, 1963; Wolf, 1964) have isolated a number of parental variables that are related to academic achievement and intellectual development. Family process was found to be more highly related to intelligence and achievement than was socioeconomic status. Rupp (1969) tested hypotheses about the relation of parent practices to reading success through a questionnaire study of a range of socioeconomic groups. Cultural-pedagogical patterns of child rearing were related to socioeconomic status within the lower socioeconomic groups, but not within the higher socioeconomic groups, in which the fathers had at least high school educations. A second study of children from very low socioeconomic groups from the first grade of the primary school also showed significant relations between parent behavior and attitudes and the children's reading achievement.

Although the cross-sectional studies of parent behavior and child development yield consistent findings, their interpretation is unclear. The results may reflect the parent's response to the child's behavior rather than parental influence upon the child's development. Further, the methods that have been used in these studies—interviews, questionnaires, and inventories—may not yield valid information on the parents' behavior. The longitudinal studies that have used repeated observations of a parent's actual behavior as observed in familiar situations, provide more valid data upon which to interpret parent influences on child development.

LONGITUDINAL STUDIES

Analyses of data collected in several early longitudinal studies show significant correlations between observations of maternal behavior in early childhood and the child's subsequent mental test scores (Baldwin, Kalhorn & Breese, 1945; Bayley & Schaefer, 1964; Honzig, 1967; Kagan & Freeman, 1963; Kagan, 1964). Since the maternal behavior was often observed prior to the appearance of the correlations with the children's intelligence, it is less likely that the parent behavior is a response to the child's intelligence. Small sample sizes, inconsistent results for boys and girls, difficulties in controlling for social class in these small samples, and the utilization of the data for purposes not foreseen at the time they were collected, have limited the usefulness of these early studies. However, the major trends in the significant relations found between parent behavior and the child's intellectual growth have been replicated in several major studies.

A longitudinal study of ability and educational attainment of approximately 5,000 children born in 1946 in England, Scotland, and Wales documents at length the influence of the home and of the school (Douglas, 1964). Significant differences between social classes were found in standards of infant care and management, use of medical services, interest in the child's school progress, age at which the parents wished the child to leave school, and the desire for the child to enter grammar school— higher standard, academic education. Children of manual working-class parents showed a relative decline in tests of mental ability and school achievement between eight and 11 years of age. They also had a lower chance of going to grammar school even when measured ability was controlled. The parents' interest in their children's school progress was measured by frequency of mothers' visits to the school, requests to speak to the principal as well as the teacher, and by fathers' visits. These showed striking differences between social classes. The author concluded that "The influence of level of parents' interest on test performance is greater than that of any of the three other factors—size of family, standard of home (housing), and academic record of the school—which are included in this analysis, and it becomes increasingly important as the children grow older." After controlling for socioeconomic level of the family, variations in the children's test scores were much more related to variations in degree of parent interest than to variations in the quality of the schools.

Another English longitudinal study, reported by Moore (1968), concerned material gathered from home visits. Toys, books, and experiences available to the child were rated, as were example and encouragement in the home for the development of language, emotional atmosphere of the home, and general adjustment of the child at two and a half years of age. Although these qualities of home influences were only slightly related to the child's early intelligence test scores, the relations with reading quotient at seven years and IQ at eight years were substantial. The family variables gave better predictions of IQ and reading, even after controlling for social class, than did maternal vocabulary or education. The control for social class and the early data on family variables increase the credibility of the interpretation that parent practices influence the child's development.

Werner, Bierman and French (1971) presented a longitudinal study of the effects of perinatal complications and of socioeconomic status, educational stimulation, and emotional support upon achievement problems, learning problems, and emotional difficulties of children. Socioeconomic status, educational stimulation, and emotional support showed moderate intercorrelations ranging from .37 to .57. These were all significantly related to school achievement and learning problems (IQ, perceptual, and language problems) at 10 years of age with the highest relations for educational stimulation. Emotional problems were most highly related to lack of emotional support. The findings that the child's learning, achievement, and emotional problems were more related to indices of family environment than with socioeconomic status are similar to Douglas' (1964) and Moore's (1968) findings. The authors also concluded that "Ten times more children had problems attributed to the effects of a poor environment than to the effects of serious perinatal stress." Relations between perinatal stress and the child's competence decreased with age but relations of environmental factors and competence increased with age. At 20 months of age only a four-point difference in IQ was found between children from the least and most favored environments but at 10 years of age a 20-point difference was found between children who received the least and most educational stimulation in the home.

Hess (1969) has summarized some of the significant findings from a short-term longitudinal study that correlated measures on 160 middle-class and lower-class mothers collected at the child's age of four years with the child's school performance two to four years later. Among the variables that were related significantly to reading readiness, reading achievement, and grades given by teachers were availability and use of home educational resources, the mother's personal optimism, and number of out-of-home activities. Maternal behaviors in teaching the child use of an *Etch-A-Sketch* that were related to later achievement included number of models shown the child, number of specific turning directions, orientation to the task, praise and encouragement, and specificity of maternal feedback. Maternal language scores and indices of affection—support toward the child, warmth in block-sorting task, and affectionateness in teaching tasks—also predicted later school achievement. Apparently the mother's teaching behavior, the experiences she provides, and the model she sets for the child are important influences.

Evidence that low intelligence test scores are not only developed but maintained by adverse environments of neglect and cruelty has been reported by Clarke and Clarke (1959). Their studies of mentally retarded adolescents and young adults show an average IQ increase of 16 points during the six-year period after they left their adverse home environments with 33 percent showing IQ increments of 20 points or more. The Clarkes interpret their results as showing recovery from deprivation and state that "the amount of measured recovery can be taken as a minimal estate of original damage" with the probability that the data are an underestimate of damage. The Clarkes' data are valuable not only for showing the extent to which adverse environments can influence intellectual development but also for showing the possibility of at least partial recovery, even in early maturity.

INTERVENTION RESEARCH

An increasing number of researchers are turning from descriptive and correlational studies of parent behavior and child development to research on programs that, through varied methods, teach parents methods for fostering the intellectual development and academic achievement of their children. Klaus and Gray (1968) utilized visitors actively to engage parents in the education of their own children as a supplement for a preschool program. Significant differences were found in mental test scores between the control children and those who had been involved in both the preschool and home visitor programs. Although the amount of difference between experimental and control groups decreased after termination of the special program, differences between groups persisted during the first years of elementary education. Evidence of vertical diffusion, i.e., that the younger children in the experimental group families also showed more rapid development, was found. The authors expressed guarded optimism about the long-range effects of two or three years work with the mothers, stating that the disadvantaged mother may be unable to provide a home situation that would maintain the development of the child and that the schools are, in general, unable to provide (alone) for the education of the child. Their concluding statement is an excellent summary of the evidence from intervention research:

> . . . the evidence is overwhelming in indicating that . . . performance results from the continual interaction of the organism with its environment. Intervention programs, well conceived and executed, may be expected to make some relatively lasting changes. Such programs, however, cannot be expected to carry the whole burden of providing adequate schooling for children from deprived circumstances; they can provide only a basis for future progress in schools and homes that can build upon that early intervention.

More recently, Gray (1970) has contrasted a preschool program with a program that taught mothers to foster the development of their children. The home program showed equal effectiveness at far lower cost as well as allowing vertical diffusion to younger children in the family and horizontal diffusion through the neighborhood. Gray's results suggest that a home program that teaches a mother to teach her child might either be an alternative or a supplement for a preschool program.

Weikart and Lambie (1969) have utilized trained educators to teach parents how to support their child's education in conjunction with half day preschool programs. The combined programs, after successive refinement over a period of years, have resulted in mean IQ gains of up to 30 points in low IQ disadvantaged children. Weikart and his colleagues are currently working with parents of infants in the first year of life to determine the effectiveness of very early parent-centered intervention but have not yet reported the results.

Gordon (1968) has used paraprofessional parent educators to teach parents specific infant education exercises during the first year of life. The *Griffith Mental Development Scales* at 12 months of age showed significant differences between the experimental group and a control group, with significant differences in eye-hand, personal-social, and hearing-speech skills and little difference in locomotor and performance skills. The design of this project will evaluate the effects of intervention during the first, second, and third years of life and will evalute the effects of brief early intervention as contrasted to continuing intervention.

Levenstein (1970) conceptualized books and toys as "Verbal Interaction Stimulus Materials," had toy demonstrators use the carefully selected materials in home visits with mothers, had mothers use them under the supervision of the demonstrator, and encouraged mothers to use the materials that were left in the home. With approximately 32 visits over a seven-month period her two- and three-year-old subjects showed a mean IQ gain of approximately 17 points—from an IQ of 85 to 102. Levenstein also found that the child's IQ level can be maintained or increased by a reduced number of visits the following year. In Levenstein's initial studies, professional social workers were used as toy demonstrators but in more recent studies paraprofessionals have been trained for that role. Karnes, Teska, Hodgins and Badger (1970) worked with small groups of mothers of infants in the first and second year of life on child-centered educational activities and materials. Cooperation and attendance was lower for working mothers and only 15 of the initial group of 20 mothers completed the second year of the program. Highly significant differences in IQ were found between the experimental group of children and matched controls and the experimental group and their sibling controls. The authors expressed caution about the long-term effects as contrasted to the long-term effects of preschool programs at later ages but concluded ". . . the results of the study suggest that a program of mother training can do

much to prevent the inadequate cognitive and linguistic development characteristic of the disadvantaged child."

The promising results of these parent-centered intervention programs show that working with mothers is an effective method for producing gains in intellectual functioning. Parent-centered, as contrasted to child-centered, early intervention programs have equal immediate effectiveness, greater long-term effectiveness, are less expensive, and produce vertical and horizontal diffusion through the family and community. However, the longer the time interval between the intervention and the evaluation, the less significant the effects of the program. These results suggest not only the need for early and continuing education of the child but also early and continuing support for parents in their roles as educators of their own children and as students of the theory and practice of education in the home.

A major question about the future of intervention programs designed to increase parental effectiveness in the education of their children is whether these programs would have significant effects in upper socioeconomic groups as well as in disadvantaged groups and whether intensive parental stimulation contributes substantially to superior levels of functioning as well as fostering average levels of functioning. Evidence by Moore (1968) that early parent behaviors are related to intelligence and reading achievement even after controlling for socioeconomic status and by Douglas (1964) that degree of parental involvement in the child's education is related to mental test scores at 10 years in all socioeconomic groups suggests that intervention to improve parent education would have significant effects in all socioeconomic groups. Fowler (1962) reviewed records of "25 superior IQ children, all of whom learned to read by the age of three . . . Of these, 72 percent had definitely enjoyed a great deal of unusually early and intensive cognitive stimulation. For the other 28 percent evidence regarding the quality and quantity of stimulation was lacking in the records." Current intervention research on disadvantaged groups should be extended to other socioeconomic groups to obtain evidence of the degree to which intellectual functioning can be changed in more varied populations. The result of that study would suggest whether programs to improve parental education should be offered to all or only to disadvantaged groups.

SUMMARY

The accumulating evidence suggests that parents have great influence upon the behavior of their children, particularly their intellectual and academic achievement, and that programs which teach parents skills in educating their children are effective supplements or alternatives for preschool education. These data should influence future education policies and programs. A critical decision will be whether to devote manpower and money to child-centered extensions of academic education or to develop a comprehensive system of education that strengthens and supports parental education in the home, effective use of the mass media, and collaboration between the school, the home, and the mass media. This review suggests that an exclusive focus upon academic education will not solve the major educational problems. A major task for our child care and educational institutions and professions will be the development of a support system for family care and education. Major changes in professional roles and responsibilities, in training, and in educational policies and programs will be required to achieve a goal of equal education in the home as well as in the school.

REFERENCES

Ainsworth, M. D. The effects of maternal deprivation: A review of findings and controversy in the context of research strategy. In Deprivation of Maternal Care: A Reassessment of its Effects. *Public Health Papers, 14,* Geneva: World Health Organization, 1962.

Baldwin, A. L., Kalhorn, J. & Breese, F. H. Patterns of parent behavior. *Psychol. Monogr.,* 1945, 58 (3).

Bayley, N. & Schaefer, E. S. Correlations of maternal and child behaviors with the development of mental abilities: Data from the Berkeley Growth Study. *Monogr. Soc. Res. Child Developm.,* 1964, 29 (6).

Bowlby, J. Maternal care and mental health. 2nd ed. Geneva: World Health Organization: Monograph Series, No. 2, 1951.

Clarke, A. D. B. & Clarke, A. M. Recovery from the effects of deprivation. *Acta Psychologica,* 1959, 16, 137-144.

Coleman, J. S. *Equality of Educational Opportunity.* Washington, D.C.: U.S. Government Printing Office, 1966.

Dave, R. T. The identification and measurement of environmental process variables that are related to educational achievement. Unpubl. doctoral dissertation. Univ. of Chicago, 1963.

Douglas, J. W. *The Home and the School: A Study of Ability and Attainment in the Primary School.* London: MacGibbon & Kee, 1964.

Fowler, W. Cognitive learning in infancy and early childhood. *Psychol. Bull.,* 1962, 59, 116-152.

Gordon, I. J. Early child stimulation through parent educators. A progress report of the Children's Bureau. U.S. Dept. of H.E.W., Gainesville, Fla., 1968.

Gray, S. W. Home visiting programs for parents of young children. Paper presented at the meeting of the National Association for the Education of Young Children. Boston, 1970.

Gray, S. W. & Klaus, R. The early training project: A seventh year report. John F. Kennedy Center for Research on Education and Human Development. George Peabody College, 1969.

Hartshorne, H., May, M. & Shuttleworth, F. K. *Studies in the Organization of Character.* New York: MacMillan, 1930.

Hess, R. D. Parental behavior and children's school achievement; implications for Head Start. In E. H. Grotberg (Ed.), *Critical Issues in Research Related to Disadvantaged Children.* Princeton: Educational Testing Service, 1969.

Hess, R. D., Block, M., Costello, D., Knowles, R. T. & Largan, D. Parent involvement in early education. In Edith H. Grotberg (Ed.), *Day Care: Resource for Decisions.* Washington: Office of Economic Opportunity, 1971.

Hess, R. D., Shipman, V. C., Brophy, J. & Baer, R. M. (In collaboration with A. Adelberger). The cognitive environment of urban preschool children: Follow-up phase. Report to Children's Bureau. Social Security Administration. U.S. Dept. of H.E.W., 1969.

Hindley, C. B. Stability and change in abilities up to five years: Group trends. *J. child Psychol. Psychiat.,* 1965, 6, 85-99.

Honzig, M. P. Environmental correlates of mental growth: Prediction from the family setting at 21 months. *Child Developm.,* 1967, 38, 337-364, 1967.

Hurley, J. R. Parental acceptance-rejection and children's intelligence. *Merrill-Palmer Qtrly.,* 1965, 11, 19-31.

————. Parental malevolence and children's intelligence. *J. consult. Psychol.,* 1967, 31, 199-204.

Kagan, J. Erratum. *Child Developm.,* 1964, 35, 1397.

Kagan, J. & Freeman, M. Relation of childhood intelligence and social class to behavior during adolescence. *Child Developm.,* 1963, 34, 899-901.

Karnes, M. B. & Badger, E. Training mothers to instruct their infants at home. In M. B. Karnes (Ed.), *Research and Development Program on Preschool Disadvantaged Children.* Project Report to the U.S. Dept. of H.E.W., 1969.

Karnes, M. B., Teska, I. A., Hodgins, A. S. & Badger, E. D. Educational intervention at home by mothers of disadvantaged infants. *Child Developm.,* 1970, 41, 925-935.

Kennedy, W. A. A follow-up normative study of Negro intelligence and achievement. *Monog. Soc. Res. Child Developm.*, 1969, 34 (2).

Kent, N. & Davis, D. R. Discipline in the home and intellectual development. *Brit J. med. Psychol.*, 1957, 30, 27-34.

Klaus, R. A. & Gray, S. W. The educational training program for disadvantaged children: A report after five years. *Monogr. Soc. Res. Child Developm.*, 1968, 33 (4).

Levenstein, P. Cognitive growth in preschoolers through verbal interaction with mothers. *Am. J. Orthopsychiat.*, 1970, 40, 426-32.

Milner, E. A. A study of the relationship between reading readiness in grade one school children and patterns of parent-child interaction. *Child Developm.*, 1951, 22, 95-112.

Moore, T. Language and intelligence: A longitudinal study of the first eight years. Part II: Environmental correlates of mental growth. *Human Developm.*, 1968, 11, 1-24.

Newcomb, T. & Svehla, G. Intra-family relationships in attitude. *Sociometry*, 1937, 1, 271-283.

Pringle, M. L. & Bossio, V. A study of deprived children. *Vita Humana*, 1958, 1, 65-92.

Roff, M. Intra-family resemblance in personality characteristics. *J. Psychol.*, 1950, 30, 199–227.

Rubenstein, J. Maternal attentiveness and subsequent exploratory behavior of the infant. *Child Developm.*, 1967, 38, 1089-1100.

Rupp, J. C. C. *Helping the Child to Cope with the School: A Study of the Importance of Parent-Child Relationships with Regard to Elementary School Success.* Groningen: Walters-Noordhoff, 1969.

Schaefer, E. S. Development of hierarchical configurational models for parent behavior and child behavior. In J. P. Hill (Ed.), *Minnesota Symposia on Child Psychology*, Vol. 5, Minneapolis: Univ. of Minnesota Press, 1971.

———. Need for early and continuing education. In V. H. Denenberg (Ed.), *Education of the Infant and Young Child.* New York: Academic Press, 1970.

Skeels, H. M. & Dye, H. B. A study of the effects of differential stimulation on mentally retarded children. *Proceedings of the American Association on Mental Deficiency*, 1939, 44, 114-136.

Skeels, H. M. & Harms, I. Children with inferior social histories: Their mental development in adoptive homes. *J. genet. Psychol.*, 1948, 72, 283-294.

Skeels, H. M., Updegraff, R., Wellman, B. L. & Williams, H. M. A study of environmental stimulation: An orphanage preschool project. *Univ. of Iowa Studies in Child Welfare*, 1938, 15, No. 4.

Skodak, M. & Skeels, H. M. A final follow-up of one hundred adopted children. *J. genet. Psychol.*, 1949, 75, 85-125.

Smart, R. G. & Fejer, D. Drug use among adolescents and their parents: Closing the generation gap in mood modification. Paper presented at the meeting of the Eastern Psychiatric Research Association. Nov., 1970.

Terman, L. M. & Merrill, M. A. *Measuring Intelligence: A Guide to the Administration of the New Revised Stanford-Binet Tests of Intelligence.* New York: Houghton Mifflin, 1937.

Tulkin, S. R. Infant's reactions to mother's voice and stranger's voice. Social class differences in the first year of life. Paper presented at the meeting of the Society for Research in Child Development. Minneapolis, Apr., 1971.

Weikart, D. P. & Lambie, D. Z. Ypsilanti-Carnegie Infant Education Project Progress Report. Dept. of Research and Development. Ypsilanti Public Schools, Ypsilanti, Mich., 1969.

Werner, E. E., Bierman, J. M. & French, F. E. *The Children of Kauai. A Longitudinal Study from the Prenatal Period to Age Ten.* Honolulu: Univ. of Hawaii Press, 1971.

Wolf, R. M. The identification and measurement of environmental process variables related to intelligence. Unpubl. doctoral dissertation. Univ. of Chicago, 1964.

Yarrow, L. J. Maternal deprivation: Toward an empirical and conceptual re-evaluation. *Psych. Bull.*, 1961, 58, 459.

Chapter Six

Targets of Socialization: Sex Typing, Aggression, Achievement, and Moral Development

The beliefs, values, and attitudes which guide socialization, and the means of inculcating standards and developing desired behavior in children vary among cultures. The social norms and skills regarded as appropriate differ for members of an isolated Eskimo village, for nomadic desert Berber families, or for the recently discovered people of the primitive Tasaday tribe living in the jungles of the Philippines. Even within a culture such as that of the United States there are wide subcultural variations in social standards and socialization practices. Behavior, regarded as desirable in Appalachian mountain hollows, in a black rural Southern village, in a New York Puerto Rican ghetto, or in a Midwest farming community differ.

In spite of these disparities in social standards there are certain classes of behaviors that are targets of socialization in almost every culture. In every society children are expected to become increasingly independent and able to care for themselves. They are encouraged to set and attain some achievement goals whether it is learning to read and write, to be a skilled hunter with a bow and arrow, to be a nuclear physicist, or to brew fine fermented beer. In each society members are expected to develop some degree of self-control, to inhibit or express aggression in a socially acceptable manner, to delay gratification of needs until an appropriate situation arises, and to restrain themselves from performing grossly antisocial behaviors. In addition, not only are individuals expected to exhibit self-control but they are socialized to perform prosocial behaviors such as sharing, helping, cooperation, and expressions of sympathy.

In many, but not all cultures, the norms and modes of expression of social standards vary for men and women. There may be different expectations and goals for the training of independence, achievement, self-control, and prosocial behavior in the socialization of boys and girls. Across a broad range of cultures including that of the dominant American culture these sex-role standards take the form of what Parsons has called an "expressive" role for females and an "instrumental" role for males (Parsons, 1970). Women are expected to be more sensitive and skilled in interpersonal relations, more dependent and nurturant and freer to express tender emotions than are men. Men should be more aggressive, competitive, independent, able to solve problems, and to inhibit expression of affect that might be interpreted as weakness. It can well be asked if either of these stereotypes is descriptive of a fully competent, well-adjusted individual. Aggressiveness may have had some adaptive evolutionary value for primitive man and nurturance for females but in contemporary society surely a well-functioning individual of either sex should be able to feel and express affection and care for others, be able to solve problems, and be moderately assertive and self-sufficient. This has led to the position that rather than being socialized in accord with sex-role standards children should be socialized in an androgenous fashion which aims for the same goals of competence in men and women.

In selecting papers for this section we attempted to include articles that covered behaviors that are the major targets of socialization: achievement and independence in the article by Dweck, aggression in the Hartup investigation, delinquency in the Chandler study and prosocial behavior in Yarrow's presentation. However, because of contemporary social and political implications many of the studies are focused on identifying sex differences in development, and on socialization processes and practices that may contribute to such differences. Corrine Hutt reviews the literature on sex differences in development. Willard Hartup replicates the frequently reported finding that boys are more aggressive than girls, but extends our knowledge in this area by pointing out that this is attributable to the greater incidence of hostile aggression in males, and that there are no sex differences in instrumental aggression. Carol Dweck proposes that differential reinforcement contingencies in boys and girls may lead to learned helplessness in females which may contribute to sex differences in achievement and the decline in intellectual performance in women often obtained in studies of cognitive development.

Finally Miriam Johnson presents a provocative theoretical paper discussing the role of family structure and particularly the salient role of the father in shaping sex-typed behavior in his sons and daughters. Research studies in sex-role development have fairly consistently demonstrated that fathers are more concerned than are mothers with maintaining stereotypical sex-typed behaviors in their children, especially in their sons. Johnson examines the sex-differentiating principles introduced by fathers and their role in enhancing sex differences in development.

REFERENCES

Parsons, T. *Social structure and personality.* New York: Free Press, 1970.

Reading 25

Sex Differences in Human Development[1]

Corinne Hutt

During the past two decades there has been a regrettable silence on the subject of sex differences in human development in the psychological literature. What reports there were, clearly influenced by the 'Psychosexual-neutrality-at-birth' theory [DIAMOND, 1965], dealt mainly with questions of sex-role identification, sex-role adoption, learning of appropriate sex-role behaviours, and so on.

Two timely rebukes were administered recently by GARAI and SCHEINFELD [1968] and CARLSON and CARLSON [1960]. Each pair of authors was lamenting the lack of attention paid to sex differences in their own field—the former in developmental psychology and the latter in social psychology. They noted that in each area a large number of studies failed to look for sex differences; others used single-sex samples, and some were even unaware of the sex of their subjects. Since these two areas account for a substantial proportion of psychological research undertaken, the neglect of sex differences seems to have been particularly regrettable.

A turning-point in this trend was the publication in 1966 of the book 'The development of sex differences' edited by ELEANOR MACCOBY. Although still reflecting a predominantly 'psycho-sexual-neutrality-at-birth' orientation, it nevertheless brought to light a large amount of incriminating evidence. Then followed the third edition of 'The psychology of human differences' [TYLER, 1965] which contained a cogent review of cognitive sex differences, and more recently, the impressive monograph by GARAI and SCHEINFELD [1968]. Since then, and given an ironic fillip by the Women's Liberation Movement no doubt, many reports acknowledging the presence of sex differences, have once again appeared in the literature. It is notable that, since its inception two years ago, the journal 'Developmental Psychology' has contained one or more reports on sex differences in nearly every issue.

In many ways, however, psychological sex differences are the tip of the iceberg. By the time differences in behaviour and performance manifest themselves, so much differentiation has already taken place. As contributors to the symposium on 'The biological bases of psychological sex differences' made only too clear, many of these differences are determined from the moment an ovum is fertilised by a sperm carrying an X or a Y chromosome. Possession of a Y chromosome, for example, confers a particular flavour on the development of the male zygote and embryo—an effect more pervasive than would result from simply the determination of masculinity [OUNSTED and TAYLOR, 1972]. Subsequently, the gonadal hormones exert their organisational influence on reproductive structures and, more significantly, on the central nervous system [HARRIS, 1964, 1970; LEVINE, 1966; WHALEN, 1968; HUTT, 1972a; MICHAEL, 1971].

In this paper, therefore, I would like to discuss some empirical results of behavioural and intellectual sex differences in early human development in the context of what is known about the biological determination of such differences.

EMBRYOLOGICAL DEVELOPMENT

As GARAI and SCHEINFELD [1968] point out, from the moment of conception males and females exhibit radically different patterns of development. The neuroendocrinological processes and their influence on early development are essentially the same in all placental mammals and these have been adequately described elsewhere [HARRIS, 1964, 1970; GORSKI and WAGNER, 1965; WHALEN, 1968; HUTT, 1972a].

The most notable feature of mammalian development is that there is no *neuter* sex. In the presence of a Y chromosome, the male gonad differentiates and then produces the androgenic evocator substance which exerts its action upon hypothalamic centres to produce the acyclic pattern of gonadotrophic hormone release characteristic of the male. In the absence of a Y chromosome, or more specifically, early androgenic influence, the natural

[1]Based, in part, on a paper read to the Annual Conference of the British Psychological Society, Exeter, 1971, in a symposium on 'The biological bases of psychological sex differences' convened by the author.

propensity of mammalian creatures is to differenti-ate as *females*. This is so even in the case of a genetic male in whom, due to early castration or some disorder, the testicular hormone is absent or ineffective. Such an instance occurs in humans in the syndrome of testicular feminisation, where, due to a recessive disorder, the testes of the genetic male often develop in an inguinal hernia and the gonadal hormone, if produced at all, is without effect [FEDERMAN, 1967]. This individual differen-tiates as a female. Conversely, in the presence of androgens during the critical period, even the ge-netic female will differentiate as a male, as happens in the case of the adrenogenital syndrome [WIL-KINS, 1962; BONGIOVANNI and ROOT, 1963; FED-ERMAN, 1967]. Curiously, in the absence of *any* gonadal hormone, the development might be de-scribed as excessively 'feminine': this happens in the case of Turner's syndrome, where one sex chromosome is lacking, the karyotype being XO, and there is gonadal dysgenesis. The comparison of behavioural and psychological features in androge-nised females and in cases of Turner's syndrome made by MONEY and ERHARDT [1968] is most instructive.

The particular interest of the processes and de-terminants of sexual differentiation to psycholo-gists lies in the fact that it is not merely the reproductive structures which are organised in a typically male or female pattern, but higher neural centres as well. Characteristic differences appear, therefore, in patterns of sexual behaviour as well as in non-sexual behaviour. The behavioural differ-ences are particularly striking in the higher mam-mals, namely, the primates [see HAMBURG and LUNDE, 1966; GOY, 1966, 1968, for informative reviews].

PHYSICAL GROWTH, MATURATION AND SUSCEPTIBILITY

From very early in uterine life males show their characteristic vulnerability: on average 120 males are conceived for every 100 females and by term this ratio has decreased to 110:100 [GLENISTER, 1956]. The majority of spontaneous abortions (mis-carriages), therefore, are of male foetuses [STE-VENSON and McCLARIN, 1957]. In terms of live births the ratio is only 106:100, which indicates a greater male susceptibility to perinatal complica-tions such as anoxia [STEVENSON, 1966; STEVEN-

SON and BOBROW, 1967]. Throughout life males remain more vulnerable to a variety of disorders, e.g., cerebral palsy, viral infections, ulcers, coro-nary thrombosis and some forms of mental illness [TAYLOR and OUNSTED, 1972; GARAI, 1970]. In fact the male's longevity is so curtailed that by the 6th and 7th decades of life the sex ratio is reversed in favour of the females. The sex-linked recessive disorders like haemophilia and colour-blindness predominantly affect the males; the recessive genes being carried on the X chromosome, males mani-fest the disorder even in the heterozygotic condi-tion, whereas females are protected, other than in the homozygous condition, by the normal allele on the other X chromosome. The adage of the male being the stronger sex requires a very literal inter-pretation indeed.

At birth, males are heavier and longer than females [OUNSTED, 1972]. From infancy on boys have a consistently higher basal metabolism and greater vital capacity, develop proportionately larg-er hearts and lungs, and have a higher concentra-tion of haemoglobin, notably after puberty [HUTT, 1972]. Moreover, the male hormone facilitates pro-tein synthesis whereas the female hormones have no such direct action. All these features character-ise the male for a more active and strenuous life.

In sharp contrast to his physical advantages, however, is the male's developmental retardation: growth velocity lags nearly 2 years behind the female's [TANNER, 1970], bone ossification is com-pleted much later [HUTT, 1972b] and puberty is attained about $2^{1}/_{2}$ years after the girl [NICHOLSON and HANLEY, 1953]. The onset of walking and talking, as well as aspects of dentition occur earlier in girls than in boys. In terms of maturity the newborn girl is equivalent to a 4- to 6-week-old boy [GARAI and SCHEINFELD, 1968].

BEHAVIOUR DIFFERENCES IN INFANCY

Motor Activity and Sensory Capacities   In gener-al, male newborn infants exhibit more spontaneous motor activity and this consists predominantly of gross movements, whereas the activity of the fe-male infants consists typically of finer movements, largely of the facial area, e.g., mouthing, smiling or sucking [KORNER, 1969]. Female neonates have lower tactual and pain thresholds [LIPSITT and LEVY, 1959] and this sex difference very probably obtains throughout the lifespan since GALTON observed it in adults and specifically commented upon it as early as 1894. Female infants also react more irritably to tactual stimulation [BELL and COSTELLO, 1964].

There is now substantial evidence that the visual acuity of males is superior to that of females, at least from adolescence on [BURG and HULBERT, 1961], whereas females have better auditory discrimination and localisation [CORSO, 1959; SCHAIE *et al.*, 1964]. The results obtained by LEWIS suggest that such sensory proficiency and preferences may be evident even in early infancy: he found that male infants showed greater interest in visual patterns generally, while female infants attended more to auditory sequences [KAGAN and LEWIS, 1965]; of visual patterns female infants found *facial* configurations most interesting and at 3, 6 and 9 months of age they were able to differentiate between such patterns more effectively than the males [LEWIS, 1969].

On the basis of results obtained from 3-month-old infants, MOSS and ROBSON [1970] concluded that, whereas social experience and learning appeared to have a strong influence upon the visual behaviour of females, that of the males was more a function of endogenous attributes like state. These several results illustrate not merely the sex-dependent sensory capacities but also the differences in those influences to which they are amenable. Such differences, however, are not peculiar to the human species—very similar behaviour is shown by monkeys [MITCHELL and BRANDT, 1970].

The early dependence on particular sensory modalities has the consequence that auditory and visual stimuli have different reinforcing properties, depending on the sex of the subject. For instance, WATSON [1969] found that visual fixation on a target could be operantly conditioned in 14-week-old infants, the effective reinforcers being visual for males and auditory for females. Moreover, the boys failed to learn under conditions of auditory reinforcement. This reliance of males and females on visual and auditory channels, respectively, is observable throughout childhood and adolescence [STEVENSON *et al.*, 1963] and persists in adulthood [MILLER, 1963; PISHKIN and SHURLEY, 1965].

Mother-infant Interaction The earliest social behaviour displayed by the human infant is in the context of the mother-infant interaction. Many studies reporting differences in the way mothers

handle their male and female infants, or for that matter, any sex differences in human behaviour, tend to account for such differences in terms of the mothers' expectations of a son or a daughter, of her greater affinity for the same-sex infant, or else in terms of the reinforcement of sex-appropriate behaviours. A study by MOSS [1967] is notable, therefore, for the demonstration that considerable differences in the behaviour of male and female infants exist at the age of 3 weeks. The differential reactions of the mother are very probably contingent upon these behaviours and not contrariwise, as commonly supposed. Two of MOSS' findings seem particularly significant, especially since they were also apparent at the age of 3 months: mothers stimulated their infant sons more, and imitated the vocalisations of their daughters more. The first of these raises the interesting possibility that we may have here the human analogue of the 'early-handled' animals described by LEVINE [1960], DENENBERG [1964] and others. If such findings are replicated, we may seriously have to inquire whether the early experience of male infants in any way contributes to their subsequent lower emotionality [GRAY, 1971a; GRAY and BUFFERY, 1971; BUFFERY and GRAY, 1972]. Secondly, the fact that mothers imitated, and thereby very probably reinforced, their daughters' vocalisations is surprising, since the actual amounts of vocalisation by boys and by girls were almost identical. Since a similar finding was also reported by GOLDBERG and LEWIS [1969], it immediately raises the question as to what parameters of infants vocal behaviour the mothers were responding. May this fact also explain, in part, the earlier acquisition of speech in girls?

GOLDBERG and LEWIS [1969] were able to demonstrate striking sex differences in infants of 13 months, both in their behaviour towards their mothers as well as in the character of their play. Girls were more reluctant than boys to leave their mothers, tended to stay near them when playing and sought physical reassurance more frequently.

Fear Analysing data from the Berkeley Growth Study, BRONSON [1969] found sex-differences in the onset of the fear-of-stranger reaction: fear at 10–15 months was positively correlated with fear and shyness at a later age in *boys* but not in girls. This was chiefly due to a sub-group of boys who showed a precocious onset of fear (4–6 months) and remained so throughout childhood. Thus, an early onset of fear-of-novelty in male infants was predictive of fearfulness during the entire pre-school period.

BEHAVIOURAL DIFFERENCES IN CHILDHOOD

Social Interactions In an investigation of the types of activity boys and girls generally engaged in [BRINDLEY et al., 1972], it was found that girls engaged in social interactions much more frequently than boys—a dramatic illustration of the early differentiation of masculine and feminine interests, boys being interested in objects or 'things' and girls in people [LITTLE, 1968]. HONZIK [1951] and HATTWICK [1937] observed very similar differences in older children, as did FARRELL [1957].

More specifically, *aggression* is an aspect of social behaviour that has interested many students of child behaviour and a number of studies have shown boys to be more aggressive than girls [GREEN, 1933; DAWE, 1934; JERSILD and MARKEY, 1935; HATTWICK, 1937; WALTERS et al., 1957; JEGARD and WALTERS, 1960; BANDURA et al., 1963; DIGMAN, 1963; PEDERSON and BELL, 1970]. Many of these results, however, were interpreted in terms of sex-role expectations and conventions, with no reference made to the fact that the males of most mammalian species are more aggressive than the females, nor was surprise expressed at the apparent universality of male aggression—despite differences in culture-patterns, conventions and social norms. In our own study of nursery school children [BRINDLEY et al, 1972], we found that two thirds of all aggressive acts were initiated by boys. Moreover, not only did boys *display* more aggression, but they also *elicited* aggression. Many of such disputes arose over the possession of toys, equipment or territory. Girls, whose aggression generally found verbal expression, were equally aggressive to other girls, boys, teachers or objects. Boys retaliated more and hence prolonged such encounters whereas the girls usually submitted or else employed more devious strategies to secure their objectives [McCANDLESS et al., 1961]. These sex-dependent features of aggression are observable in older children as well as in adults. In experiments which allowed subjects to mete out punishment to a mock opponent, adult males gave bigger shocks when they thought their opponent was a male than when they thought it was a female [BUSS, 1963: TAYLOR and EPSTEIN, 1967]. In a similar experi-

ment 10- and 11-year olds, using noise as punishment, behaved exactly as the adults had done [SHORTELL and BILLER, 1970].

Male monkeys engage in threat displays while the females show fear grimaces, and in a male monkey group the dominance hierarchy is established by the aggressive behaviour and threat displays of the ascendant male while in female groups the hierarchy is established and maintained by the submissive behaviours of the non-dominant females [ANGERMEIER et al., 1968]. Thus, when the human results are considered in the general context of primate social behaviour, any purely cultural or environmental sex-role theory of sexual differentiation becomes difficult to countenance. Elsewhere, [HUTT, 1972a, b] I have also presented the experimental evidence for regarding aggressive behaviour as primarily a function of the early sexual differentiation of the brain, and secondarily as an effect of circulating hormone levels.

Another aspect of early social behaviour that we studied was cooperative or mutual behaviour [BRINDLEY et al., 1972], where children joined each other, either spontaneously or at the request of one of them, to engage in some mutual activity. Girls initiated such acts much more than boys, and directed their attention in this respect predominantly towards *younger* children (chiefly girls), thus manifesting their proclivities for fulfilling a nurturant and protective role [MISCHEL, 1970]. This is evident in many ways: readiness to help younger ones carry things, to button pinafores or tie aprons, and to comfort a hurt or distressed child. The boys appear to show a remarkable indifference to a peer's discomfort or distress. McGREW [1972] has also described the characteristic tendency of the girls to shepherd and care for a new entrant to the nursery group, whereas boys manifest their customary indifference to such a newcomer. The boys in our study tended to direct their cooperative acts primarily towards other *older* boys, usually attempting to join a game or excursion already in progress. Similar sex-typical behaviours have been described in many infra-human primate groups too [DeVORE and JAY, 1963; HARLOW, 1962; GOODALL, 1968].

In general, there is a marked tendency in humans—children and adults alike [HUTT, 1972; TIGER, 1969]—to interact with others of their own sex. The men's club, the officers' mess, the women's institute, all clearly have their ontogenetic origins in the kindergartens and their phylogenetic origins in diverse primate groups.

Exploration and Play   In the study of 13-month-old infants by GOLDBERG and LEWIS [1969], boys were active, frequently banged toys, and showed an interest in manipulating the fixtures; girls were more sedentary, interested in combining toys and showed a preference for the toys with faces. Results essentially similar were obtained in our study of nursery school children in Reading [BRINDLEY *et al.*, 1972]: girls chiefly engaged in sedentary activities like crayonning, cutting-out or plasticene work; boys were much more active—running, jumping and showing a marked preference for push/pull toys. Many of these sex-dependent differences were also observed by CLARK *et al.* [1969] in Cambridge nursery schools.

In studies of the exploratory behaviour of nearly 200 nursery school children, a striking finding that emerged was that boys and girls, after investigating a new toy, went on to use it in very different ways [HUTT, 1970a, b]. Boys more frequently engaged in inventive or creative play with this toy, whereas more girls than boys failed to explore at all. Objections regarding the neutrality of the toy were shown to be invalid on several grounds [HUTT, 1970b, 1972]. To a certain extent these differences are comprehensible in the context of early sexual differentiation in psychological and cognitive faculties. Girls, being advanced developmentally in many respects, at the age of 3 and 4 years are becoming increasingly proficient in verbal and social skills while boys are still actively manipulating and exploring their environment. Nevertheless, there was one other question that concerned us: were we witnessing in this situation some characteristic expression of the originality of the future creative artist or scientist? A follow-up study of these children with tests of creativity was thus indicated. Prior to this study, however, a pilot investigation was carried out, with a view to seeing how children of 7–9 years of age in British primary schools performed on such tests.

Creativity and Divergent Thinking   On creativity tests like those described by WALLACH and KOGAN [1965], two measures can be derived: (1) the *total* number of responses given to any item, i.e. fluency; and (2) the number of *unique* responses offered for any item, i.e. originality. On testing 60 boys and 60

girls between the ages of 7 and 10 years, girls were found to score unequivocally higher than boys on the fluency measure [BHAVNANI and HUTT, 1972; HUTT, 1972a]. When, however, the unique responses alone were considered there were no differences between the sexes. This was surprising in view of the fact that the number of unique responses is dependent to some extent on the total number of responses, since the former tend to be given when the more conventional responses have been exhausted [WALLACH and KOGAN, 1965]. WALLACH and KOGAN themselves make no mention of sex differences despite the fact that they obtained a significant difference in favour of the boys on one of the uniqueness measures. HUDSON [1968], on the other hand, found that sixth form boys (16 years) were more fluent than girls, but he omits any mention of the results on the originality measure. Thus, the evidence for sex-typical performances on both the fluency and originality measures is equivocal. But certainly no study has demonstrated greater originality or uniqueness in the responses of girls.

This conclusion, moreover, is concordant with other evidence, both empirical and circumstantial, which shows adult males to be considerably more divergent and creative than females. SHOUKSMITH [1970] for instance, carried out an extensive factorial study of intelligence, reasoning, problem solving and creativity, and on the basis of his results concluded that:

'. . . males and females do not think alike. Factorially the female group is more complex than the male. . . . For females a much greater range of behaviour patterns appear to be mutually exclusive categories . . . for example, we see that "creative associating" is opposed to "deductive reasoning" in women, whereas it is not so clearly opposed in men . . . true creativity depends on an ability to switch from the one to the other of these as and when necessary. On this argument, one would expect to find fewer women among the ranks of truly inventive geniuses or scientific discoverers.' (pp. 188, 189.)

Again, MACCOBY [1966] reported a study of Radcliffe College academics who, though of equal professional status with their male colleagues, were nevertheless considerably less productive. More circumstantially, HUDSON [1966] noted that the proportion of men to women in the Royal Society

(Britain's select and august scientific body) was 40 to 1. KLEIN [1966] found that in the physical and applied sciences the male:female ratio was considerably in excess of 50 to 1. In the aesthetic fields too, despite several decades of relative feminine liberation, it is a lamentable fact that women have not figured more prominently among the creative artists. The domestic bondage of women cannot eternally be proffered as an excuse—after all, even in less auspicious times women contributed to the literary fields.

Intellectual Functions The performance of the 8- and 9-year-olds on the tests of creativity also indicated that, despite their greater verbal fluency, girls were not necessarily more original than boys. Other studies suggest that verbal fluency is an aspect of language function that is dissociated from other more conceptual aspects like reasoning and comprehension. GARAI and SCHEINFELD [1968] for instance, provocatively concluded that though girls may acquire language earlier than boys—chiefly due to their maturational advancement—and are superior in terms of verbal fluency as well as in reading, writing and spelling, they are certainly inferior in matters of verbal comprehension, verbal reasoning, and even vocabulary. In general agreement with this conclusion, the relevant evidence was documented in an earlier review [HUTT, 1972a]. Thus, although girls are indubitably superior in the *executive* aspects of language, they seem to be less adequate in manipulating and relating verbal concepts. Very striking evidence for such a conclusion is readily obtained from the norms for verbal reasoning, spelling, and sentence length, on the differential aptitude test [BENNET *et al.*, 1959] given in table I.

Although the position is rather more ambiguous with respect to intellectual capacities, once again

Table 1 Norms for 3 Sub-tests of the Differential Aptitude Test for Boys and Girls of 2 Age-groups

Age	Sex	Verbal reasoning	Language usage I, spelling	Language usage II, sentences
13	Boys	15.8	25.9	20.2
	Girls	14.6	37.9	28.6
17	Boys	29.3	59.1	40.9
	Girls	25.2	72.1	45.8

the available evidence suggests that males achieve a higher verbal IQ on the WAIS and WISC than females, whereas females obtain a higher performance IQ than males. TYLER's [1965] summary statement is even more affirmative:

'Most of the available evidence seems to indicate . . . that it is in the verbal *fluency* (what THURSTONE has called W) rather than in the grasp of verbal meanings (V) that females are superior. . . . Comparisons of various groups of males and females on various tests, however, has also made it fairly clear that girls and women do *not* have larger vocabularies than boys and men do.' (p. 244.)

Results very similar to those noted above were also observed in younger children [HEILMAN, 1933; HOBSON, 1947]. Even WECHSLER [1941] who originally maintained that there were no sex differences, having discarded those items which differentiated between the sexes, eventually [WECHSLER, 1958] conceded that:

'Our findings do confirm what poets and novelists have often asserted, and the average layman long believed, that men not only behave but *think* differently from women.'

The similarity of SHOUKSMITH's [1970] conclusion, almost 13 years later and based on very different performances, to WECHSLER's is indeed striking.

Determinants of IQ On the basis of data obtained from 26 boys and 27 girls in the Berkeley Growth Study, BAYLEY and SCHAEFER [1964] concluded that, whereas the intellectual capacities of boys were susceptible to environmental influences, those of girls were more genetically determined. This conclusion was based on the finding that the IQ of girls showed a higher correlation with those of their parents than boys with their parents, as well as a correlation between early maternal behaviour and child's IQ for boys but not for girls. BAYLEY [1966] subsequently reported other studies which had also demonstrated higher parent-daughter than parent-son correlations in intellectual capacities. MACCOBY [1966] regarded the BAYLEY and SCHAEFER [1964] conclusion circumspectly in the absence of other supportive evidence. From a follow-up study of 231 boys and 254 girls born in Hawaii,

WERNER [1969] concluded that her data did not support the Bayler-Schaefer hypothesis, but indicated a sex difference in rate of maturation in favour of the girls as well as 'a greater responsiveness of the girls to achievement demands and educational stimulation in the home in middle childhood'.

It seems to me, however, that the emphases of both BAYLEY and SCHAEFER [1964], and WERNER [1969] are misplaced for the following reasons. First, the earlier maturation of the girls would determine that a polygenic ability as IQ will be fully manifested earlier in girls than in boys, thereby yielding a higher daughter-parent correlation at any age prior to adolescence. Secondly, much evidence indicates that girls lateralise many cerebral functions earlier and more effectively than males [TAYLOR, 1969; BUFFERY, 1971] and hence acquire greater proficiency in them initially. WERNER's [1969] data, in fact, corroborates both these points: the discrepancy in parent-child correlations at 20 months and at 10 years was far greater for boys than for girls. Moreover, at 10 years girls showed a significant correlation on all 11 of the parental and environmental variables and boys on 10 of the 11 variables. Thirdly, evidence from longitudinal studies like those of MOORE [1967] have demonstrated that in the first 8 years girls are more constrained and more predictable in their intellectual development, which takes place primarily through linguistic channels. Since the principal environmental factor associated with the IQ of the girls in WERNER's [1969] study was educational stimulation, a characteristic property of which was 'enlargement of vocabulary', the higher parent-daughter correlation is predictable. The boys in MOORE's study, on the other hand, showed an almost haphazard course of development—no earlier score reliably predicted any later one. There was evidence too that non-verbal experiences and skills contributed more to the IQ of boys than to that of girls. In view of all these considerations there seems little need to postulate a different genetic contribution to the IQ of girls and boys, or a differential responsiveness of boys and girls to environmental influences. It is sufficent to state the empirical observations that: (1) the IQ of girls and boys are differently constituted; (2) that the girls' IQ is manifested largely in terms of verbal skills and is, therefore, sensitive to linguistic influences; (3) that since girls mature earlier, the several genes contributing to intelligence are all

expressed by an earlier age—this being evident in a more stable IQ—thus yielding a higher parent-daughter correlation during childhood than the comparable parent-son correlation.

There are many other respects in which males and females are characteristically different, but since these have been adequately outlined or discussed elsewhere [TYLER, 1965; MACCOBY, 1966; GARAI and SCHEINFELD, 1968; HUTT, 1972a, b], enumeration of them here seems superfluous.

CONCLUDING DISCUSSION

The foregoing discussion of the process of sexual differentiation and the phenomena of sex differences has been an attempt to reiterate the many biological and psychological differences that characteristically differentiate males and females in our species. These particular properties have clearly been selected in accordance with, on the one hand, certain morphological features, and on the other, with the particular roles human males and females fulfil. That these morphological and functional requirements are not unique to a particular society, nor even to the human species is evident in the fact that very similar differences are demonstrable in infra-human primate species. This fact alone makes an exclusively environmental theory of sex differences difficult to countenance. Moreover, as BUFFERY and GRAY [1972] point out, such similarities behove us to seek a more appropriately biological explanation for the phenomena. GRAY himself has discussed the endocrinological, neural and adaptive bases for sex differences in mammals generally [GRAY, 1971a, b; GRAY and BUFFERY, 1971; BUFFERY and GRAY, 1972]. The evidence reviewed by both GRAY and myself [HUTT, 1972] shows that not only is behaviour affected by circulating hormones, but that these hormones have an important formative and organisational influence on brain function and structure.

It is a common, but nonetheless fallacious, assumption that the recognition of individual differences, be they sex- or personality-dependent, is to commit oneself to a psychological or behavioural determinism. On the contrary, the recognition of such differences and their possible determinants enables individuals to modify and/or exploit environmental circumstances to profitable advantage.

The conformity and consistency of the female's behaviour in fulfilling a predominantly nurturant role, makes her a stable and reliable support for the dependent infant. Even her distractability [GARAI and SCHEINFELD, 1968] appears to be adaptive. In her intellectual faculties too the human female seems to have exploited those facets that ensure the optimal execution of her primary role—the maternal role. For more effective communication increasing reliance is placed on linguistic skills, and it is noteworthy that in verbal functions as in non-verbal ones, it is in *execution* that the female excels. The male on the other hand, and necessarily, excels in spatial and numerical abilities, is divergent in thought and action, and is generally superior in *conceptualisation*. The fact that such functional dimorphism exists may be unacceptable to many, but it is a dimorphism that has been uniquely successful.

REFERENCES

Angermeier, W. F.; Phelps, J. B.; Murray, S. and Howanstine, J.: Dominance in monkeys: sex differences. Psychon. Sci. *12:*344 (1968).

Bandura, A.; Ross, D. and Ross, S. A.: Transmission of aggression through imitation of aggressive models. J. abnorm. soc. Psychol. *63:*575–582 (1961).

Bayley, N.: Developmental problems of the mentally retarded child; in PHILIPS Prevention and treatment of mental retardation (Basic Books, New York 1966).

Bayley, N. and Schaefer, E. S.: Correlations of maternal and child behaviours with the development of mental abilities: data from the Berkeley Growth Study. Monogr. Soc. Res. Child Develop. *29:*1–80 (1964).

Bell, R. Q. and Costello, N. S.: Three tests for sex differences in tactile sensitivity in the newborn. Biol. Neonat. *7:*335–347 (1964).

Bennett, G. K.; Seashore, H. G. and Wesman, A. G.: Differential aptitude tests. Manual, 3rd ed. (Psychological Corporation, New York 1959).

Bhavnani, R. and Hutt, C.: Divergent thinking in boys and girls. J. child Psychol. Psychiat. (1972, in press).

Bongiovanni, A. M. and Root, A. W.: The adrenogenital syndrome. New Engl. J. Med. *268:*1283 (1963).

Brindley, C.; Clarke, P.; Hutt, C.; Robinson, I. and Wethli, E.: Sex differences in the activities and social interactions of nursery school children; in MICHAEL and CROOK Comparative ecology and behaviour of primates (Academic Press, London 1972, in press).

Bronson, G. W.: Fear of visual novelty: developmental patterns in males and females. Develop. Psychol. *1:*33–40 (1969).

Buffery, A. W. H.: Sex differences in cognitive skills. Paper Ann. Conf. Brit. Psychol. Soc., Exeter; in Symp. on Biological bases of psychological sex differences (1971).

Buffery, A. W. H. and Gray, J. A.: Sex differences in the development of perceptual and linguistic skills; in OUNSTED and TAYLOR Gender differences—their ontogeny and significance (Churchill, London 1972).

Burg, A. and Hulbert, S.: Dynamic visual acuity as related to age, sex and static acuity. J. appl. Psychol. *45:*111–116 (1961).

Buss, A. H.: Physical aggression in relation to different frustrations. J. abnorm. soc. Psychol. *67:*1–7 (1963).

Carlson, E. R. and Carlson, R.: Male and female subjects in personality research. J. abnorm. soc. Psychol. *61:*482–483 (1960).

Clark, A. H.; Wyon, S. M. and Richards, M. P.: Free-play in nursery school children. J. child Psychol. Psychiat. *10:*205–216 (1969).

Corso, J. F.: Age and sex differences in pure-tone thresholds. J. acoust. Soc. Amer. *31:*489–507 (1959).

Dawe, H. C.: An analysis of 200 quarrels of preschool children. Child Develop. *5:*139–156 (1934).

Denenberg, V. H.: Animal studies on developmental determinants of behavioural adaptability; in HARVEY Experience, structure and adaptability, pp. 123–147 (Springer, New York 1966).

DeVore, I. and Jay, P.: Mother-infant relations in baboons and langurs; in RHEINGOLD Maternal behaviour in mammals (Wiley & Sons, 1963).

Diamond, M.: A critical evaluation of the ontogeny of human sexual behaviour. Quart. Rev. Biol. *40:*147–175 (1965).

Digman, J. M.: Principal dimensions of child personality as inferred from teachers' judgments. Child Develop. *34:*43–60 (1963).

Farrell, M.: Sex differences in block play in early childhood education. J. educ. Res. *51:*279–284 (1957).

Federman, M. D.: Abnormal sexual development (Saunders, Philadelphia 1967).

Galton, F.: The relative sensitivity of men and women at the nape of the neck by Webster's test. Nature, Lond. *50:*40–42 (1894).

Garai, J. E.: Sex differences in mental health. Genet. Psychol. Monogr. *81:*123–142 (1970).

Garai, J. E. and Scheinfeld, A.: Sex differences in mental and behavioural traits. Genet. Psychol. Monogr. *77:*169–299 (1968).

Glenister, T. W.: Determination of sex in early human embryos. Nature, Lond. *177:*1135 (1956).

Goldberg, S. and Lewis, M.: Play behaviour in the year-old infant: early sex differences. Child Develop. *40:*21–31 (1969).

Goodall, J. L. van: The behaviour of free-living chimpanzees in the Gombi Stream Reserve. Anim. Behav. Monogr. *1:*161–311 (1968).

Gorski, R. A. and Wagner, J. W.: Gonadal activity and sexual differentiation of the hypothalamus. Endocrinology *76:*226–239 (1965).

Goy, R. W.: Role of androgens in the establishment and regulation of behavioural sex differences in mammals. J. anim. Sci. *25:*suppl., pp. 21–35 (1966).

Goy, R. W.: Organising effects of androgen on the behaviour of rhesus monkeys; in MICHAEL Endrocrinology and human behaviour (Oxford University Press, London 1968).

Gray, J. A.: Sex differences in emotional behaviour in mammals including man: endocrine bases. Acta psychol., Amst. *35:*29–46 (1971a).

Gray, J. A.: The psychology of fear and stress (Weidenfeld and Nicolson, London 1971b).

Gray, J. A. and Buffery, A. W. H.: Sex differences in emotional and cognitive behaviour in mammals including man: adaptive and neural bases. Acta psychol. Amst. *35:*89–111 (1971).

Green, E. H.: Friendships and quarrels among preschool children. Child Develop. *4:*236–252 (1933).

Hamburg, D. A. and Lunde, D. T.: Sex hormones in the development of sex differences in human behaviour; in MACCOBY The development of sex differences (Tavistock, London 1966).

Harlow, H. F.: Development of affection in primates; in BLISS Roots of behaviour (Harper, New York 1962).

Harris, G. W.: Sex hormones, brain development and brain function. Endocrinology *75:*627–648 (1964).

Harris, G. W.: Hormonal differentiation of the developing central nervous system with respect to patterns of endocrine function. Philos. Trans. B *259:*165–177 (1970).

Hattwick, L. A.: Sex differences in behaviour of nursery school children. Child Develop. *8:*343–355 (1937).

Heilman, J. D.: Sex differences in intellectual abilities. J. educ. Psychol. *24:*47–62 (1933).

Hobson, J. R.: Sex differences in primary mental abilities. J. educ. Res. *41:*126–132 (1947).

Honzik, M. P.: Sex differences in the occurrence of materials in the play constructions of pre-adolescents. Child Develop. *22:*15–35 (1951).

Hudson, L.: Contrary imaginations (Methuen, London 1966).

Hudson, L.: Frames of mind (Methuen, London 1968).

Hutt, C.: Specific and diversive exploration; in REESE and LIPSITT Advances in child development and behaviour, vol. 5 (Academic Press, London 1970a).

Hutt, C.: Curiosity in young children. Sci. J. *6:*68–72 (1970b).

Hutt, C.: Neuroendocrinological, behavioural and intellectual aspects of sexual differentiation in human development; in OUNSTED and TAYLOR Gender differences—their ontogeny and significance (Churchill, London 1972a).

Hutt, C.: Males and females. Penguin Books (1972b, in press).

Jegard, S. and Walters, R. H.: A study of some determinants of aggression in young children. Child Develop. *31:*739–747 (1960).

Jersild, A. T. and Markey, F. V.: Conflicts between preschool children. Child Develop. Monogr. 21 (1935).

Kagan, J. and Lewis, M.: Studies of attention in the human infant. Behav. Develop. *11:*95–127 (1965).

Klein, V.: The demand for professional Woman I power. Brit. J. Sociol. *17:*183 (1966).

Korner, A. F.: Neonatal startles, smiles, erections, and reflex sucks as related to state, sex and individuality. Child Develop. *40:*1039–1053 (1969).

Levine, S.: Stimulation in infancy. Sci. Amer. *202:*80–86 (1960).

Levine, S.: Sex differences in the brain. Sci. Amer. *214:*84–90 (1966).

Lewis, M.: Infants' responses to facial stimuli during the first year of life. Dev. Psychol. *1:*75–86 (1969).

Lipsitt, L. P. and Levy, N.: Electrotactual threshold in the neonate. Child Develop. *30:*547–554 (1959).

Little, B.: Psychospecialisation: functions of differential interest in persons and things. Bull. Brit. psychol. Soc. *21:*113A (1968).

Maccoby, E. E. (ed.): The development of sex differences (Tavistock, London 1966).

McCandless, B. R.; Bilous, B. and Bennett, H. L.: Peer popularity and dependence on adults in preschool age socialisation. Child Develop. *32:*511–518 (1961).

McGrew, W. C.: Aspects of social development in nursery school children with emphasis on introduction to the group; in BLURTON-JONES Ethological studies of child behaviour (Cambridge University Press, London 1972).

Michael, R. P.: The endocrinological bases of sex differences. Paper Ann. Conf. Brit. Psychol. Soc., Exeter, in Symp. Biological bases of psychological sex differences (1971).

Miller, A.: Sex differences related to the effect of auditory stimulation on the stability of visually fixed forms. Percept. Mot. Skills *16:*589–594 (1963).

Mischel, W.: Sex-typing and socialisation; in MUSSEN Carmichael's manual of child psychology, vol. 2 (Wiley, London 1970).

Mitchell, G. and Brandt, E. M.: Behavioural differences related to experience of mother and sex of infant in the rhesus monkey. Develop. Psychol. *3:*149 (1970).

Money, J. and Ehrhardt, A. A.: Prenatal hormonal exposure: possible effects on behaviour in man; in MICHAEL Endocrinology and human behaviour (Oxford University Press, London 1968).

Moore, T.: Language and intelligence: a longitudinal study of the first 8 years. I. Patterns of development in boys and girls. Human Develop. *10:*88–106 (1967).

Moss, H.: Sex, age and state as determinants of mother

infant interaction. Merrill-Palmer Quart. *13:*19–36 (1967).

Moss, H. A. and Robson, K. S.: The relation between the amount of time infants spend at various states and the development of visual behaviour. Child Develop. *41:*509–517 (1970).

Nicolson, A. B. and Hanley, C.: Indices of physiological maturity: derivation and interrelationships. Child Develop. *24:*3–38 (1953).

Ounsted, C. and Taylor, D. C.: The Y chromosome message: a point of view; in Ounsted and Taylor Gender differences—their ontogeny and significance (Churchill, London 1972).

Ounsted, M.: Sex differences in intrauterine growth; in Ounsted and Taylor Gender differences—their ontogeny and significance (Churchill, London 1972).

Pedersen, F. A. and Bell, R. Q.: Sex differences in preschool children without histories of complications of pregnancy and delinquency. Develop. Psychol. *3:*10–15 (1970).

Pishkin, V. and Shurley, J. T.: Auditory dimensions and irrelevant information in concept identification of males and females. Percept. Mot. Skills *20:*673–683 (1965).

Schaie, K. W.; Baltes, P. and Strother, C. R.: A study of auditory sensitivity in advanced age. J. Geront. *19:*453–457 (1964).

Shortell, J. R. and Biller, H. B.: Aggression in children as a function of sex of subject and sex of opponent. Develop. Psychol. *3:*143–144 (1970).

Shouksmith, G.: Intelligence, creativity and cognitive style (Batsford, London 1970).

Stevenson, A. C.: Sex chromatin and the sex ratio in man; in Moore The sex chromatin (Saunders, Philadelphia 1966).

Stevenson, A. C. and Bobrow, M.: Determinants of sex proportions in man, with consideration of the evidence concerning a contribution from x-linked mutations to intrauterine death. J. med. Genet. *4:*190–221 (1967).

Stevenson, A. C. and McClarin, R. H.: Determination of the sex of human abortions by nuclear sexing the cells of the chorionic. Nature, Lond. *180:*198 (1957).

Stevenson, H. W.; Keen, R. and Knights, R. W.: Parents and strangers as reinforcing agents for children's performance. J. abnorm. Soc. Psychol. *67:*183–186 (1963).

Tanner, J. M.: Physical growth; in Mussen Carmichael's manual of child psychology, 3rd ed. (Wiley, New York 1970).

Taylor, D. C.: Differential rates of cerebral maturation between sexes and between hemispheres. Lancet *iii:*140–142 (1969).

Taylor, D. C. and Ounsted, C.: The nature of gender differences explored through ontogenetic analyses of sex ratios in disease; in Ounsted and Taylor Gender differences—their ontogeny and significance (Churchill, London 1972).

Taylor, S. P. and Epstein, S.: Aggression as a function of the interaction of the sex of the aggressor and sex of the victim. J. Personality *35:*474–486 (1967).

Tiger, L.: Men in groups (Nelson, London 1969).

Tyler, L.: The psychology of human differences, 3rd ed. (Appleton-Century-Crofts, New York 1965).

Wallach, M. A. and Kogan, N.: Modes of thinking in young children (Holt, Rinehart & Winston, New York 1965).

Walters, J.; Pearce, D. and Dahms, L.: Affectional and aggressive behaviour of pre-school children. Child Develop. *28:*15–26 (1957).

Watson, T. S.: Operant conditioning of visual fixation in infants under visual and auditory reinforcement. Develop. Psychol. *1:*508–516 (1969).

Wechsler, D.: The measurement of adult intelligence (Williams & Wilkins, Baltimore 1941).

Wechsler, D.: The measurement and appraisal of adult intelligence, 4th ed. (Williams & Wilkins, Baltimore 1958).

Werner, E. E.: Sex differences in correlations between children's IQ and measures of parental ability, and environmental ratings. Develop. Psychol. *1:*280–285 (1969).

Whalen, R. E.: Differentiation of the neural mechanisms which control gonadotropin secretion and sexual behaviour; in Diamond Reproduction and sexual behaviour (Indiana University Press, Bloomington 1968).

Wilkins, L.: Adrenal disorders. II. Congenital virilizing adrenal hyperplasia. Arch. Dis. Childh. *37:*231 (1962).

Reading 26

Aggression in Childhood: Developmental Perspectives[1]

Willard W. Hartup

Although the literature dealing with aggressive behavior in children is extensive (Feshbach, 1970), little actually concerns ontogenetic issues, and very little derives from developmental theory. Among the more significant lacunae in research on aggression development are the following:

1. *For no species do we know from which early motor patterns the components of later aggression are shaped.* From time to time there have been suggestions that the rage reaction (tantrums) may be the wellspring of early aggressive behavior (Hamburg & Van Lawick-Goodall, in press; Munroe, 1955). Tantrums occur early in ontogenesis, they have great capacity for eliciting reaction from the environment (they are noxious), and both the occurrence of tantrums and their behavioral components are sensitive to feedback contingencies (Etzel & Gewirtz, 1967; Goodenough, 1931). Because tantrums produce both positive and negative feedback (parents capitulate to tantrum behavior as well as punish it), these behaviours probably serve as opportunities for the young child to learn the efficacy of aggressive action as well as the efficacy of aggressive inhibition. As yet, however, the contributions of such patterns to aggressive ontogenesis are unknown.

2. *The contexts which serve as origins for aggressive development have not been specified for most species.* Both field research and laboratory studies (Harlow & Harlow, 1965; Jay, 1968) suggest that the context which accounts for most of the variance in the development of nonhuman primate aggression is rough-and-tumble contact with peers. Conditions allowing for rough play to escalate into aggression and, in turn, to deescalate into playful interaction appear to facilitate the acquisition of two repertoires: (*a*) an armamentarium of aggressive behaviors and (*b*) mechanisms for coping with the affect and other outcomes of aggressive interaction. Although Patterson and Cobb (1971) have suggested that peer interaction is also the primary context for aggression development in human children, we can only conjecture that rough-and-tumble play during the preschool years serves the same functions for *homo sapiens* as it appears to serve for the common langur and the other nonhuman primates.

3. *Age changes in the aggressive activity of human children have been documented in an astonishingly small number of studies* (Feshbach, 1970).

(*a*) *The form of the behavior.* About all that can be said about age changes in the morphology of human aggression is that, from two through six years of age, there is an increase in the utilization of language in aggressive outbursts. Verbal aggression remains the preferred mode of attacking other humans among elementary-school-aged girls, but the evidence is inconsistent about changes in types of physical attack after the age of six. Again and again, social psychologists come back to Florence Goodenough's (1931) data about age differences in children's angry behavior. She found that

> With advancing age, the forms of behavior displayed during anger become more definitely directed toward a given end, while the primitive bodily responses of the infant and young child are gradually replaced by substitute reactions commonly of a somewhat less violent and more symbolic character [p. 69].

Then she added that frequency and duration of "after reactions," including sulking, whining, and brooding, showed a marked increase after the age of four even though the duration of the violent phases of angry outbursts changed but little during the preschool and the early elementary school years.

Surely it is time to recognize, within a developmental perspective, the functional differences ex-

[1]This article is based on an invited address presented at the meeting of the American Psychological Association, Montreal, Canada, August, 1973. The paper was completed with financial support provided by Grant 5-P0105027 from the National Institute of Child Health and Human Development. Brendan Gail Rule, Melynda Mason, Jacques Lempers, Douglas Sawin, and the staff of the Amherst H. Wilder Day Care Centers contributed in various important ways to the research described in this article.

isting among verbal aggressive episodes such as the following: (*a*) "Don't talk to Rachel. She is the most dumb in the world." (*b*) "I'm gonna pull that fucking Moira's hair out." (*c*) "Sucker, get out of here." Similarly, there would appear to be no reason to assume that all acts of physical aggression have common functions. Thus, it is inconceivable that, with increasingly sophisticated social-cognitive functioning, qualitative age changes would not be found in children's aggression in addition to the amount of language used.

(*b*)   *The instigators of aggressive behavior.* The earlier studies (Dawe, 1934; Goodenough, 1931) also contain the only differentiated information in the literature concerning age changes in the elicitors of aggression. Goodenough found that, in infancy, angry outbursts are principally keyed to physical discomforts and needs for attention. During the second and third years, however, such episodes are triggered increasingly by "habit training." Social difficulties with peers emerge at about this time as instigators of angry outbursts, and predominate in the years that follow. Dawe's (1934) study of 200 quarrels occurring in a nursery school also tells us about age changes in the events that elicit aggression: (*a*) Although possession-instigated quarrels predominated at every age level from 18 months of age through 65 months, 78% of the youngest children's quarrels were instigated in this manner while only 38% of the oldest children's quarrels began in this way. (*b*) Physical violence increased as an instigator of quarreling from 8% to 27%, and "social adjustment" increased as an instigator of quarreling from 3% to 15% during the period covered. These data hint at two concomitant developmental changes in the functional character of young children's aggression: (*a*) a relative decrease during the preschool period in straightforward instrumental aggression; and (*b*) an increase in person-directed, retaliatory, and hostile outbursts. More about these trends later.

4.   *Longitudinal studies of individual differences in aggression are few in number.* The famous studies by Kagan and Moss (1962), Bayley and Schaeffer (1964), and Emmerich (1964) stand nearly alone in elucidating sex-related differences in the stability of aggressive traits. Stabilizing of individual differences in aggressiveness appears earlier in males than in females and seems to be independent of the discontinuities in aggression development mentioned above. Evidence for developmental trans-

formations in the area of aggression is much more tenuous, although the findings reported by Kagan and Moss (1962) are intriguing: Early aggression in girls was predictive of later competitiveness and rejection of feminine sex-typing rather than later aggressiveness. All that needs to be noted here, however, is the general paucity of data on individual differences in aggression development.

Overall, then, data concerning the developmental course of aggression are in short supply. The shortage extends to information about changes in the form of the aggressive acts themselves, the contexts in which aggression originates, the circumstances that trigger aggressive episodes, and stability in individual propensities to respond aggressively across time and circumstance.

A NEW STUDY

Three developmental hypotheses concerning children's aggression formed the basis of a new study completed at the University of Minnesota: (1) There is a greater proportion of hostile, "person-directed" aggression relative to "object-oriented," instrumental aggression in the interactions of grade school children than in the interactions of preschool children. (2) Threats to self-esteem lead more frequently to hostile attempts to injure the agent of frustration than to object-oriented aggression, particularly for older children. (3) Blocking is associated primarily with aggression which has instrumental value in gaining or preserving objects, territory, or privileges and in which injury to the other person appears to be a secondary goal. This latter relation, however, should be more consistent for younger than for older subjects.

The conceptual ancestry of these hypotheses should be apparent to anyone familiar with the literature on aggression—it lies in the distinction originating with Feshbach (1964), Buss (1966), Rule (in press), and others between "hostile" and "instrumental" aggression. Basically, this distinction has been used as a means of refining the frustration-aggression hypothesis. According to this line of theorizing, the prerequisites of hostile aggression (i.e., person-oriented aggression) include (*a*) frustration-produced stimuli which have ego-threatening properties and (*b*) an inference by the subject that the agent of frustration has behaved intentionally. Other attributions may also be involved in eliciting this form of aggression, but the literature particularly emphasizes the linkage between hostile outbursts and frustrations which involve ego threats or threats to one's self-esteem. In contrast, instrumental aggression, (i.e., aggression which is aimed at the retrieval of an object, territory, or privilege) should be linked to simple goal blocking.

The distinction between hostile and instrumental aggression is far from clean. First, as Feshbach (1970) has pointed out, both instrumental and hostile elements are often involved in the same social interchange. Additionally, this distinction suggests that there is no "instrumental" value to be found in hostile aggression. Clearly, the attempt to restore one's self-esteem by making someone else feel bad is instrumental behavior. Thus, the terminology is imprecise, to say the least. Additionally, Rule and Percival (1971) have raised questions as to whether the psychological processes operating during outbursts of instrumental and hostile aggression are really very different. They found, with adult subjects, that both goal blocking and insult raised their subjects' level of aggression, but these manipulations produced perceptions and attitudes toward the agent of frustration which were virtually indistinguishable. Regardless of whether the aggressor was insulted or frustrated, he reported himself to be more annoyed with the frustrating agent, and indulged in derogation and devaluation of the agent of frustration in similar degree.

On such grounds one may question the ultimate usefulness of the instrumental-hostile dichotomy. Nevertheless, these rubrics serve reasonably well for an attempt to examine the functional properties of children's aggression. First, these concepts may be easily integrated with the existing data. Second, known facts about children's social-cognitive development also suggest that hostile aggression should not be as strongly characteristic of the aggressive activity of younger as of older children. Under the age of six, for example, children have limited capacities for role taking and the generation of inferences and attributions about other people (Flavell, 1968). To the extent that hostile aggression is dependent on attributions about the agent of frustration (especially his intentions), this type of aggression should be less evident in younger than in older children. Furthermore, self-esteem valuations of self-competence, and notions about one's status are relatively rudimentary in young children. Just as the young child's conceptions of morality are heteronomous, his conceptions of the dimensions of self-competence and self-worth are unstable. Since reference to self-esteem is a prerequisite to hostile aggression, a lesser proportion of such aggression for younger than for older children would also be expected on these grounds.

Prediction of developmental changes in instrumental aggression is a bit more difficult. Dawe (1934) reported a declining percentage of such aggression in association with increased age. But, should there be a change in the functional quality of the aggression which is elicited by goal blocking as children grow older? Feshbach (1964), Rule (in press), and others have suggested that goal blocking should elicit object-oriented aggression (rather than person-oriented aggression), whatever the individual's age. The data of Rule and Percival (1971), however, suggest that, among adults, blocking produces attitudes and perceptions which are very similar to those produced by insult and derogation. Such an admixture of instrumental and hostile aggression in response to goal blocking should occur, however, only if the individual possesses those cognitive-inferential skills which are prerequisite to the hostile components of the activity. In other words, there is the strong possibility that children's responses to goal blocking are more purely instrumental during the preschool years than during the elementary school years because of the lesser sociocognitive maturity of the younger children. By seven and eight years of age, we would expect considerable inconsistency in the way children respond to blocking (i.e., hostile activity on some occasions and instrumental activity at other times, as well as activity which is "mixed" with respect to its components).

Method

The strategy chosen for studying the functional relations outlined above was naturalistic observation. The functions of children's aggression are extremely difficult to study with experimental techniques, and some aspects of children's aggressive functioning are simply not open to experimental attack (e.g., the manner in which children respond to insult).

The study was centered in six groups of children, all in one children's program in St. Paul, Minnesota. All groups, including both preschool children and first- and second-graders, operated under a common program philosophy. The six groups were located in three different buildings, with one younger and one older group in each building; all of the subjects came from the lower socioeconomic strata of the city. It is important to note that the staff was supervised through a single administrative organization and that the structure of the groups was similar in the case of both older and younger children. All groups were "open" groups in the sense that the schedule permitted the children to have a range of choice among activities and minimal constraints on peer contact. Program activities were not identical—older children simply do not engage in the same play activities as younger children—but gross ecological differences between settings for older and younger children were minimal. One hundred and two children, 56 boys and 46 girls, were enrolled in these groups. Sixty-four were 4–6 years of age; 38 were 6–7 years of age.

Observations were conducted over a 10-week period, using a combination of time and event sampling procedures. Aggressive events were defined as *intentional physical and verbal responses that are directed toward an object or another person and that have the capacity to damage or injure.* Instructions to the observers were to record as much information about each aggressive act as he or she could reconstruct. A sample of one episode is given below:

> Marian [a seven-year-old] . . . is complaining to all that David [who is also present] had squirted her on the pants she has to wear tonight. She says "I'm gonna do it to him to see how he likes it." She fills a can with water and David runs to the teacher and tells of her threat. The teacher takes the can from Marian. Marian attacks David and pulls his hair very hard. He cries and swings at Marian as the teacher tries to restrain him; then she takes him upstairs. . . . Later, Marian and Elaine go upstairs and into the room where David is seated with a teacher. He throws a book at Marian. The teacher asks Marian to leave. Marian kicks David, then leaves. David cries and screams, "Get out of here, they're just gonna tease me."

This incident included an initial aggressive outburst followed by counteraggression and continued fighting. Other outbursts, however, were less protracted. Observers were encouraged to use clear language that would not telescope the event and to avoid inferences about the particular intentions,

motivations, or feelings of the subjects (Wright, 1960).

The specimen records were then rated on three different occasions by three pairs of coders. The first rating identified all interactions which conformed to the definition of aggression, and the coders isolated the words which described the instigating (antecedent) event and the aggressive act. Agreement for this first rating was 83% for aggressive acts and 92% for antecedent events. A second pair of coders rated the nature of each aggressive act as either hostile (person oriented) or instrumental (object oriented). Their overall agreement was 92%. The third set of coders rated the particular function of the antecedent events and aggressive acts. Nine categories ranging from *bodily injury* and *destruction of property* to *rejection, derogation,* and *defiant noncompliance* were used to classify the aggression. Eighteen categories were used to classify antecedent events, but for this report these have been collapsed into three: (*a*) *blocking* (involving possessions, space, and activity); (*b*) *bodily contact;* and (*c*) *derogations* (negative social comparisons, tattling, ridicule, criticism). To preserve independence in assessing the function of the aggressive act and the function of the antecedent event, the coders used two sets of records with either the antecedent event or the aggressive act blacked out. Thus, if the coder was rating an aggressive act, he had no information about the antecedent event, and vice versa. The functional classification of aggressive episodes and their antecedents was accomplished with an overall percentage of agreement that reached 94%.

Results

For purposes of this presentation, the results will be couched in terms of initial units of aggression, that is, those outbursts which occurred first in an aggressive sequence. Supplemental information will be provided which is based on the entire group of 758 units of aggression observed, even though the interdependence among these units prevents statistical analysis in any depth.

Age. The older children were less aggressive per unit time, overall, than the younger children ($p = .03$). This is the clearest indication in the observational literature that aggression declines in the period immediately after early childhood. The difference was comparable for both sexes. There was a significant Race × Age interaction ($p = .04$)—among younger children the rate of aggression for black and for white children did not differ, but the older black children were significantly more aggressive than the older white subjects.

The age difference in total aggression derives primarily from an age difference in the rate of occurrence of instrumental aggression. As expected, this type of outburst occurred significantly more frequently among the younger children ($p = .004$). The significant Race × Age interaction also derives from instrumental aggression ($p = .007$). That is, there was no race difference in instrumental aggressive activity among the younger children, but the older black children showed more aggression of this type than did the older white children.

The age difference which bears most directly on the hypotheses of the study concerns the proportion of aggressive units which is hostile. Indeed, for those 84 children who initiated aggressive activity, a significantly higher percentage of the aggression was classified as hostile among the older subjects than among the younger subjects ($p = .003$).

Units of aggression were next separated according to two criteria: those elicited by blocking and those elicited by bodily contact. The percentage of each child's aggression which was instrumental was then computed, along with the percentage which was hostile. Blocking produced a significantly higher percentage of instrumental aggression among the younger children than among the older children ($p = .005$), in line with expectations and supporting the notion that there is a greater admixture of instrumental and hostile reactions to this type of frustration for older children. For aggression produced by bodily contact, there was no significant difference between younger and older children in percentage rated as hostile or instrumental.

Examining the data from another viewpoint (and utilizing all of the units of aggression recorded), a functional pattern emerges which is generally consistent with the preceding pattern of results. A clear age difference was found, for example, in the types of hostile behavior which derogation elicits. For younger children, when such antecedents elicit hostile outbursts, half (48%) take the form of bodily injury (hitting) and half consist of reciprocated derogation, threats, and tattling (52%). Among the older children, however, derogation shows a decided tendency to produce reciprocal derogation: only 22% of hostile responses to derogation involved

hitting while 78% involved some type of insult or reciprocated threat to self-esteem. A parallel age difference in types of hostile aggression was not found in the aggression elicited by blocking: about 25% of blocking-produced hostility involved derogation, rejection, tattling, and threats for each age group. Thus, when elementary school children are insulted and the insult leads to aggression, the likelihood of insulting retaliation is very great; not so for preschool children. On the other hand, when either older or younger children are blocked, the proportion of insulting hostile reactions does not vary with age.

Sex. Earlier, it was noted that age was not involved in any interactions with the gender variable insofar as the sheer incidence of aggression was concerned. It will come as no surprise, however, that male subjects were more aggressive totally than the females ($p = .01$). This difference was primarily due to a sex difference in the incidence of hostile aggression ($p = .03$); no significant sex difference was obtained in the rate of occurrence of instrumental aggression. Most important of all, none of the functional analyses, that is, those relating the nature of the aggressive outburst to the nature of the antecedent, have revealed significant sex differences. Thus, there is no evidence that boys and girls are differently "wired" with respect to the operation of hostile and instrumental aggression. Such differences were not expected, and the data confirm those expectations.

Race. A similar situation prevails with respect to race. As noted, more frequent total aggression was observed among older black children than among older whites, owing primarily to the higher incidence of instrumental aggression in the former group. The validity of this finding cannot easily be questioned: There was no reference to race differences in the instructions to observers. Moreover, such differences were in no way related to the purpose of the research; the analyses were conducted only because of their obvious necessity. Indeed, the only way in which these findings could have been produced by observer bias is through more subtle racist stereotypes (the observers were white). But here, too, the more critical race differences would be those relating to the functional properties of the aggression in the interactions of the children. As with sex, no significant differences were found. The patterning of antecedents for hostile aggression and the elicitors of instrumental aggression were not different for our white and black samples.

Conclusion

These results lend support to two hypotheses: (1) The developmental course of human aggression may be best understood by means of a differentiated "functional analysis" of the problem. (2) The distinction between instrumental and hostile aggression is heuristically valuable for studying the functions of aggression in early childhood even though it may have more limited usefulness in studies of adolescent or adult aggression.

What is meant by the word *function* in the context of this article? Simply put, the word implies the question, How does it [aggression] work? Answers to this question may be sought from many different vantage points, using many different levels of analysis. One type of analysis might involve the generation of mathematical relational statements between levels of brain stimulation and differentiated aggressive outbursts; other analyses may concern the long-term biological consequences of aggression—that is, whether it serves to maintain an individual's genes in the population. Still other types of functional analysis might concern relations between specific instigating stimuli and the qualities of aggression in particular individuals or groups and how these vary in accordance with the maturation of those response capabilities necessary for a specific type of aggressive display. Each of these functional perspectives is based on the assumption that understanding how aggression "works" requires knowledge of how the specific aggressive outburst fits into the complicated nexus of events that precede and follow it (Hinde, in press). To this end, the ontogenetic history of the individual and the biological–evolutionary outcomes of the activity must be taken into consideration, as well as stimuli which function as "instigators," "goals," or "reinforcers" in individual behavioral sequences. To specify aggressive functions at only one level of analysis is to risk a myopic conception of the problem like that of the elephant produced by the blind man who only touches the beast's trunk.

Research such as that reported here points the way toward a more complete functional analysis of aggression in children's social interaction. The data, however, are descriptive and do not directly elucidate the relation between social–cognitive processes and age changes in aggression. Do changes in the child's use of attributions about intent and the developmental events mirrored in the observational data emerge in parallel sequence? If so, is there a systematic functional relation between advances in social cognition and changes in aggressive morphology and elicitation? These are the questions to which this work brings us.

REFERENCES

Bayley, N., & Schaefer, E. S. Correlations of maternal and child behaviors with the development of mental abilities: Data from the Berkeley growth study. *Monographs of the Society for Research in Child Development*, 1964, **29**(6, Whole No. 97).

Buss, A. H. Instrumentality of aggression, feedback, and frustration as determinants of physical aggression. *Journal of Personality and Social Psychology*, 1966, **3**, 153–162.

Dawe, H. C. An analysis of two hundred quarrels of preschool children. *Child Development*, 1934, **5**, 139–157.

Emmerich, W. Continuity and stability in early social development. *Child Development*, 1964, **35**, 311–332.

Etzel, B. C., & Gewirtz, J. L. Experimental modification of a caretaker-maintained high-rate operant crying in a 6- and a 20-week-old infant (Infans tyrannotearus): Extinction of crying with reinforcement of eye contact and smiling. *Journal of Experimental Child Psychology*, 1967, **5**, 303–317.

Feshbach, S. The function of aggression and the regulation of aggressive drive. *Psychological Review*, 1964, **71**, 257–272.

Feshbach, S. Aggression. In P. H. Mussen (Ed.), *Carmichael's manual of child psychology*. Vol. 2. New York: Wiley, 1970.

Flavell, J. H. *The development of role-taking and communication skills in children*. New York: Wiley, 1968.

Goodenough, F. L. *Anger in young children*. Minneapolis: University of Minnesota Press, 1931.

Hamburg, D. A., & Van Lawick-Goodall, J. Factors facilitating development of aggressive behavior in chimpanzees and humans. In W. W. Hartup & J. de Wit (Eds.), *Determinants and origins of aggressive behaviors*. The Hague: Mouton, 1974, in press.

Harlow, H. F., & Harlow, M. K. The affectional systems. In A. M. Schrier, H. F. Harlow, & F. Stollnitz (Eds.), *Behavior of nonhuman primates*. Vol. 2. New York: Academic Press, 1965.

Hinde, R. A. The study of aggression: Determinants, consequences, goals, and functions. In W. W. Hartup & J. de Wit (Eds.), *Determinants and origins of aggressive behaviors*. The Hague: Mouton, 1974, in press.

Jay, P. C. (Ed.) *Primates: Studies in adaptation and variability.* New York: Holt, Rinehart & Winston, 1968.

Kagan, J., & Moss, H. A. *Birth to maturity: A study in psychological development.* New York: Wiley, 1962.

Munroe, R. L. *Schools of psychoanalytic thought.* New York: Dryden Press, 1955.

Patterson, G. R., & Cobb, J. A. A dyadic analysis of "aggressive" behaviors. In J. P. Hill (Ed.), *Minnesota symposia on child psychology.* Vol. 5. Minneapolis: University of Minnesota Press, 1971.

Rule, B. G. The hostile and instrumental functions of human aggression. In W. W. Hartup & J. de Wit (Eds.), *Determinants and origins of aggressive behaviors.* The Hague: Mouton, 1974, in press.

Rule, B. G., & Percival, E. The effect of frustration and attack on physical aggression. *Journal of Experimental Research in Personality,* 1971, **5**, 111–118.

Wright, H. F. Observational child study. In P. H. Mussen (Ed.), *Handbook of research methods in child development.* New York: Wiley, 1960.

Reading 27

Egocentrism and Antisocial Behavior: The Assessment and Training of Social Perspective-Taking Skills[1]

Michael J. Chandler[2]

This study was undertaken in an effort to explore the possible role of persistent social egocentrism in the development and maintenance of patterns of chronic antisocial behavior. Egocentric thought, defined here as the relative inability to recognize or take into account the privileged character of one's own private thoughts and feelings, has been shown by Piaget and others (Looft, 1972; Piaget & Inhelder, 1956) to regularly characterize and prejudice the social judgments of young children. In the absence of any real working knowledge of the differences which divide people, young children are typically unable to assess accurately the informational needs of others and have been routinely shown to fail at tasks which require genuine empathy or cooperation (Chandler & Greenspan, 1972). Under normal developmental circumstances, this initial egocentric orientation has been shown to give way gradually to a more relativistic or perspectivistic style of thought which makes possible new levels of social cooperation and competence (Looft, 1972).

Because of the central role assigned to such perspective-taking skills in the normal socialization process, a number of investigators (Anthony, 1959; Chandler, 1972; Feffer, 1970; Gough, 1948; Martin, 1968; Sarbin, 1954; Thompson, 1968) have been prompted to explore the possible relationship between delays in the acquisition of these skills and the development of various forms of social deviation. As a group, these studies have provided considerable support for the view that prosocial behavior is linked to the development of age-appropriate role-taking or perspective-taking skills and have demonstrated that a variety of forms of social deviancy are associated with persistent egocentric thought. Persons demonstrating developmental delays in the acquisition of these skills have been shown to systematically misread societal expectations, to misinterpret the actions and intentions of others, and to act in ways which were judged to be callous and disrespectful of the rights of others.

Drawing upon these findings linking antisocial behavior to developmental delays in the acquisition of role-taking or perspective-taking skills, a relationship was hypothesized between persistent social egocentrism and chronic delinquent behavior, and an attempt was made (*a*) to compare the developmental course of role-taking or perspective-taking skills in groups of delinquent and nondelinquent youth, (*b*) to develop and evaluate a program of remedial training in deficient

[1]This research was supported by grants from the Rochester-Monroe County Youth Board and the Wegman Foundation.

[2]The author wishes to thank the Monroe County Department of Probation for its cooperation in this study. Thanks are also due to Pat Cavanagh, Anne Filer, Beth Kaprove, Carol Markovics and Douglas Stern who served as experimenters.

role-taking skills, and (c) to determine the effectiveness of this training on subsequent delinquent behavior.

METHOD

Subjects

The subjects of this comparative study were 45 delinquent and 45 nondelinquent boys between the ages of 11 and 13. Fifteen delinquents and 15 nondelinquents were chosen at each of the three ages studied. The delinquent subjects were located through a search of the files of a metropolitan police registry and were chosen on the basis of their lengthy police and court records. All had multiple contacts with the police, had committed one or more crimes which would have constituted felonies if committed by an adult, and were characterized by court officials as serious and chronic delinquents. Almost all were members of economically marginal families, and all lived in high crime and delinquency areas within a deteriorating center city core. The racial and ethnic background of the group mirrored that of the neighborhoods from which they were drawn. Twenty-four of the 45 subjects were black, 6 were from families recently immigrated from Puerto Rico, and the remainder were distributed among a variety of ethnic groups of largely Western European origin.

The 45 subjects who made up the two nondelinquent comparison groups were drawn from two different populations. Fifteen subjects—5 from each of the three age groups studied—lived in the same high crime rate areas as did the delinquent subjects, were from families of comparable socioeconomic standing, and were of similar racial and ethnic backgrounds. The second of the nondelinquent comparison groups consisted of 30 boys drawn from a predominantly white, middle-class and upper-middle-class suburban school system. None of these subjects had known delinquent histories, and they were all characterized by their teachers as essentially free of any serious antisocial involvements.

Assessment Procedures

The subjects of this research were seen individually and administered both the Peabody Picture Vocabulary Test (PPVT) and a measure of social egocentrism based on an assessment procedure originally introduced by Flavell, Botkin, Fry, Wright, and Jarvis (1968). In its original form, this procedure consisted of a single cartoon sequence which subjects were asked to describe first from their own point of view and then from the perspective of a coexperimenter who was shown only an abbreviated version of the same stimulus materials. In this way Flavell and his colleagues were able to put their subjects in possession of relevant, but highly privileged, information which was explicitly unavailable to the less well informed bystander whose perspective they sought to occupy. Any intrusion of this privileged information into the account intended as descriptive of the perspective of the only partially informed coexperimenter was taken as evidence of an egocentric failure in social role taking.

The assessment procedure employed in this study closely paralleled that of Flavell et al. (1968) and differed only in the identity of the partially informed witness or bystander, whose point of view the subjects were asked to assume. Whereas Flavell and his colleagues had employed a coexperimenter for this purpose, the present study incorporated the witness or bystander as a cartoon character in the stimulus materials themselves.

Ten cartoon sequences following this general format were developed. Each of these depicted a central character caught up in a chain of psychological cause and effect such that his subsequent behavior was shaped by, and fully comprehensible only in terms of, the events which prefixed them. In one of these sequences, for example, a boy, who had been saddened by seeing his father off at the airport, began to cry when he later received as a gift a toy airplane similar to the one which had carried his father away. In a second sequence a boy, who had run home after accidently breaking a window with a baseball, was shown to react with fear when he heard a knock at the door.

Midway into each of these sequences some second character was introduced who, in the role of a late-arriving bystander, witnessed the resultant behaviors of the principal character but was not privy to the antecedent events which brought them about. In the cartoon involving the broken window, for example, the boy's father observed his son's alarm when someone knocked at the door but had no basis for knowing of the earlier events which prompted this reaction. Similarly, in the story dealing with the toy airplane, the gift was delivered by a postman who clearly saw the boy's distress but had no knowledge of the antecedent events which made the receipt of an airplane a legitimate occasion for sadness. Through this process of information engineering, the subject was placed in a privileged position relative to the story character whose role he was later asked to assume. By knowing what information was available to whom, it was possible to specify the degree to which each subject was able to set aside effectively facts known only to himself and adopt a perspective measurably different from his own.

A 5-point scoring system reflecting different levels of potential egocentric intrusion was developed. A score of 4 was assigned to those accounts in which the subjects explicitly attributed to the uninformed witness or bystander knowledge legitimately available only to themselves. A score of 3 was assigned to similar accounts, which were qualified by being couched in conditional or probabilistic terms (e.g., "The father would *probably* think that he broke the window"). A score of 2 was assigned whenever a subject attributed privileged information to the uninformed bystander but embedded this attribution in a series of nonegocentric alternatives (e.g., "The father would think that somebody was chasing him, or that he broke a window, or something"). A score of 1 was employed whenever a subject made an egocentric attribution which he later spontaneously corrected, and zeros were assigned to accounts which clearly distinguished between privileged information known only to the subjects and facts equally available to the story characters whose role he was asked to assume.

The conduct of this study fell into four distinct subphases. The first of these involved the individual assessment of the 90 delinquent and nondelinquent subjects. The second, or intervention phase, involved only the delinquent subjects and lasted for a period of 10 weeks. This training program was followed by a third, postintervention assessment phase. Finally, 18 months after the completion of the intervention program, a second record search was undertaken in an effort to determine the possible effects of the training on subsequent delinquent behavior. The specific assessment and training procedures employed in each of these program phases are described separately below.

Preintervention Assessment. On the basis of a previous standardization study using 75 normal school children (Chandler, 1971), the original series of 10 cartoon sequences was subdivided into two equivalent subsets of five stories each. The Spearman-Brown split-half reliability coefficient between these alternate forms was .92. The PPVT and one or the other of these alternate egocentrism measures was individually administered to each of the 90 delinquent and nondelinquent subjects. Half of the subjects were tested on each of the alternate egocentrism measures, and the order of presentation of the individual cartoon sequences was randomized in an effort to guard against possible order effects. The subjects were first asked to describe the entire cartoon sequence and were then instructed to retell the story as they thought it would be told by the late-arriving witness or bystander. Subjects were prompted in this second version of the story by the use of a standard probe which consisted of saying, "Now I want you to tell me the story that this person would tell. He (she) would say . . ." Although many failed to offer stories on the second telling that were substantially different from their own, all of the subjects seemed to appreciate what was being asked of them and most identified spontaneously from whose point of view they were attempting to speak. All probes were carefully worded to insure that it was clear that the witnesses' rather than the subjects' point of view was being inquired into. All subjects were tested by one of three trained graduate assistants, and verbatim recordings were made of the subjects' responses. These transcripts were read and scored by two independent raters who were uninformed as to the social histories of the subjects. Interrater reliabilities computed on a sample of 15 test protocols indicated a high level ($r = .94$) of interrater agreement.

Intervention. Following the initial assessment phase, the 45 delinquent subjects were randomly assigned to one of three treatment conditions. One third of the subjects were placed in a nontreatment control group and, with the exception of the postintervention assessment program to be described below, had no further contact with the research staff. The remaining 30 subjects were invited to participate in a film workshop that was to meet in a neighborhood storefront ½ day a week for a 10-week period. All participants were provided transportation to and from the storefront center and were paid $1 an hour for their participation. All 30 of the subjects agreed to participate and attended regularly throughout this summer period. Absenteeism was extremely low, and the average participant was present for 9.5 of the 10 training sessions.

Fifteen of these subjects were enrolled in a experimental training program which employed drama and the making of video films as vehicles for helping them to see themselves from the perspectives of others and for providing remedial training in deficient role-taking skills. It was reasoned that these two training experiences might aid the subjects in stepping outside of their own egocentric vantages and in assuming roles or perspectives different from their own. These subjects met together, in groups of five. During these 3-hour training sessions the subjects were encouraged to develop, portray, and record brief skits dealing with events involving persons of their own age. A staff of three graduate assistants worked with each of the three training groups and attempted to facilitate their dramatic and film-making efforts. While the content and development of these film productions was determined by the program participants, the training staff did attempt to enforce four general ground rules. These included the stipulations that (a) the skits developed by the participants be about persons their own age and depict real-life situations (i.e., not episodes involving TV or movie characters), (b) there be a part for every participant, (c) each skit be rerun until each participant had occupied every role in the plot, and (d) that the video recordings be reviewed at the end of each set or take in an effort to determine ways of improving them. Although every effort was made to maximize the opportunities of these subjects to improve their role-taking and perspective-taking skills, special efforts were made to avoid any procedures which might be directly related to the posttest items or procedures.

The remaining 15 experimental subjects were enrolled in a kind of placebo group organized in order to provide a method of disentangling the potential effects of specific training in role-taking skills from the possible impact of other more extraneous and nonspecific treatment influences. Like the members of the experimental training group, these subjects attended the same storefront, interacted with the same research staff, and occupied themselves with the making of films. In contrast to the members of the experimental group, however, these subjects did not make use of closed-circuit TV recording equipment, and consequently were not providing any special opportunities to see themselves from the perspectives of others, and did not receive special training in role-taking skills. Instead, the group was provided with 8-millimeter color film equipment and helped to produce animated cartoons and documentary style films about their neighborhood. The only restriction placed on these activities was that the participants not be the subjects of their own film-making efforts. These activities were intended to mirror, as closely as possible, the program of the experimental training group, with the important distinction that the opportunities for feedback and role-taking practice provided in the film and actors workshop were not present.

Postintervention Assessment. Following the completion of the 10-week summer program, the subjects of the experimental, placebo, and nontreatment control groups were reevaluated using a second series of five cartoon sequences, the equivalency of which had been established in a previous standardization study (Chandler, 1971). The persons administering and scoring these post-program tests did not know the treatment status of the subjects whom they evaluated.

Follow-up. One and a half years after the completion of the intervention phase described above, the police and court records of all the delinquent subjects were reexamined. The total number of recorded delinquent offenses committed during this 18-month period was tallied for each subject and compared with the results of the initial review covering the 18-month period preceding the intervention program.

RESULTS

The results of the preintervention assessment of social egocentrism in delinquent and nondelinquent subjects, the postintervention comparison of the various treatment groups, and the results of the 18-month follow-up study are reported separately below.

Preintervention Assessment

Despite the racial, ethnic, and socioeconomic differences which characterized the nondelinquent subjects drawn from high and low crime rate areas, these groups were not measurably different in the level of their social egocentrism. As a consequence, these two groups were combined into a single, nondelinquent sample for the purposes of subsequent analysis.

By contrast, the delinquent and nondelinquent subjects demonstrated marked and statistically significant differences ($F = 80.4$, $df = 1/88$, $p < .001$) in the level of their role-taking skills (see Table 1). The nondelinquent subjects appeared to have little difficulty in adopting the role or perspectives of others, and few marked egocentric intrusions were present in their records.

The delinquent subjects, by contrast, typically demonstrated marked deficits in their ability to differentiate their own point of view from that of others and regularly attributed to others information available only to themselves. There was in fact little overlap between the egocentrism scores of the nondelinquent subjects and their delinquent counterparts, whose scores more closely resembled those of a previously reported sample of nondelinquent children almost half their chronological age (Chandler, 1971).

Although the nondelinquent subjects showed a slight, but regular reduction in egocentric errors with increasing age not apparent in the scores of the delinquent subjects, these age differences were not statistically significant.

The delinquent and nondelinquent subjects were known to have different histories of school attendance and achievement, and it was anticipated that their levels of measured intelligence might also differ. These expectations were substantiated by a comparison of mean PPVT scores for the delinquent and nondelinquent samples, which were 91 and 112, respectively ($t = 1.73$, $df = 88$, $p < .05$). Within each of these groups, level of egocentricity was significantly related to IQ ($r = -.34$ and $-.30$, $p < .05$, for the delinquent groups, respectively).

Because of these uncontrolled group differences

Table 1 Mean Egocentrism Scores for the Age and Delinquency-Status Groups

Age (in years)	Delinquents	Nondelinquents
11	13.8	3.9
12	10.2	3.6
13	10.6	1.7
Combined	11.6	3.1

Table 2 Mean Preintervention and Postintervention—Social Egocentrism Scores

Treatment group	Preintervention	Postintervention
Experimental	12.4	5.5
Placebo	12.2	8.6
Control	10.2	8.0

in measured intelligence and because of the observed relationship between IQ and level of egocentricity, an additional test of the differences in social egocentrism between the two groups was required. To this end the variance in observed social egocentrism scores contributed by differences in IQ was controlled by means of co-variance techniques. The delinquent and nondelinquent groups continued to differ sharply in their levels of social egocentrism ($F = 41.4$, $df = 1/87$, $p < .001$).

Postintervention Assessment

Differences between preintervention and postintervention scores on the role-taking tests were taken as an index of change in role-taking ability and are reported in Table 2. Following Hays (1963), a series of planned comparisons were made on these data, the most important of which were (a) whether the subjects of the experimental group changed more than did the members of the placebo and nontreatment control groups and (b) whether the change scores of the subjects of the placebo and control groups were significantly different from one another.

The first of these analyses demonstrated that as a group the subjects of the experimental training program improved significantly more in their role-taking ability ($F = 9.46$, $df = 1/42$, $p < .01$) than did the subjects of the combined placebo and control groups. Although not statistically independent from this comparison, the differences between the experimental group and either the placebo or the control group taken separately were also statistically significant. The placebo and control groups did not, however, differ significantly from one another ($F = 1.49$, $df = 1/42$, $p < .05$).

Follow-up

As a result of the high level of mobility which characterized the families of these delinquents, complete data were available on only 33 of the original 45 subjects at the time of the 18-month follow-up. The attrition rate was, however, similar in all three of the treatment groups, and the subjects for whom complete data were not available were not significantly different from the remaining sample on any of the measures of role-taking, IQ, or preintervention delinquency previously collected.

The police and court records of the 33 subjects for whom complete data were available were reviewed and the number of known delinquencies committed during the 18-month period following the intervention program was tallied and compared with the results of a comparable record review for the 18-month period preceding the intervention program (see Table 3). As can be seen from this table, the subjects of all three treatment groups committed somewhat fewer offenses during the second 18-month period. This difference was, however, most striking for the subjects of the experimental training program who, as a group, committed approximately half as many known delinquencies during the postintervention period. A Kruskal-Wallis one-way analysis of variance by ranks was performed on the difference between the number of preintervention and postintervention delinquencies for the subjects of each of the three treatment groups. These group differences were highly significant ($H = 17.9$, $df = 2$, $p < .001$), indicating a relationship between the type of intervention received and the number of subsequent delinquencies committed. In order to specify further the source of this overall treatment effect, a series of multiple comparisons was carried out between the various treatment conditions utilizing a rank-sum method (Dunn, 1964). Although the differences between the experimental training group and either of the other two treatment groups taken separately did not reach statistical significance, the subjects of the experimental training program in role taking did commit significantly fewer postintervention delinquencies ($Z = 2.4$, $p < .05$) than did

subjects of the combined placebo and control group.

DISCUSSION

The results of this study support three general conclusions concerning the role of social egocentrism in antisocial behavior. First, in contrast to their better socialized counterparts, a substantial proportion of the chronically delinquent subjects tested demonstrated a marked developmental lag in their ability to successfully adopt the roles or perspectives of others. These discrepancies persisted despite controls for the differences in socioeconomic and intellectual levels which characterized these groups. Second, intervention efforts focused on specific training in role-taking skills did substantially reduce the high level of social egocentrism which had previously characterized these subjects. The measurable impact of this remedial training program outweighed changes resulting from other nonspecific intervention efforts and from changes ascribable simply to the passage of time. The fact that the subjects of both the experimental and placebo groups met voluntarily on a regular basis and appeared equally involved and committed to their respective projects further strengthens the assumption that the test and behavioral changes observed were directly related to the specific content of the experimental training program. Finally, these observed changes in role-taking skills were associated with a measurable reduction in the amount of reported delinquent behavior among the experimental subjects.

While these findings may provide some new insights into the nature of antisocial behavior, a number of important cautions and qualifications are required. First, it must be stressed that demonstrating a relationship between persistent social egocentrism and antisocial behavior does not, in itself, provide a sufficient basis for inferring a causal relationship between these variables. The fact that experimentally induced improvements in role-taking and perspective-taking skills were associated with reductions in postintervention delinquency does provide somewhat more compelling evidence for such a causal connection. The possibility remains, however, that the experimental training program differed from the training received by the placebo group along dimensions other than the

Table 3 Mean Number of Delinquent Offenses in Preintervention and Postintervention Periods

Treatment group	Preintervention	Postintervention
Experimental	1.9	1.0
Placebo	2.5	2.1
Control	2.0	1.8

role-taking and perspective-taking training specified and that the observed differences in test performance and delinquent behavior are traceable to these effects. Second, any attempt to generalize these findings to other populations of antisocial youths should reflect an appreciation of the special character of the sample employed in this study. The method of subject selection employed insured that the persons chosen were not only delinquent, but unsuccessfully so. All of the subjects had multiple police and court contacts and are almost necessarily different from other delinquent or antisocial youth who have successfully avoided detection. The possibility exists that the persistent egocentrism which characterized this group was an index of their ineptitude rather than their antisocial orientation. If such were the case, the apparent reduction in delinquent behavior which characterized the subjects of the experimental treatment group might only reflect an improved ability to avoid detection and what looked like a promising intervention technique might prove only to be a "school for scoundrels." Finally, the present research offers no guarantee that the persistent social egocentrism demonstrated by these delinquent subjects is in any way unique to persons whose adaptational failures are of an antisocial sort. To the contrary, the research of Anthony (1956), Looft (1972), and Feffer (1970) would suggest that persistent modes of age-inappropriate egocentric thought frequently characterize persons showing a great variety of adaptational failures ranging from autism to senility.

Despite these qualifications the results of this study do suggest the utility of attempting to understand delinquent youth in terms of their developmental progress in the acquisition of certain formal, sociocognitive operations necessary for the effective solution of important human interaction problems. This approach not only suggests certain promising diagnostic and intervention strategies but provides a theoretical framework which recognizes the important developmental tasks which confront youthful offenders and permits them to be viewed as other than diminutive adult criminals.

REFERENCES

Anthony, E. J. An experimental approach to the psychopathology of childhood autism. *British Journal of Medical Psychology*, 1959, **32**, 18–37.

Chandler, M. J. Egocentrism and childhood psychopathology: The development and application of measurement techniques. Paper presented at the biennial meeting of the Society for Research in Child Development, Minneapolis, March 1971.

Chandler, M. J. Egocentrism in normal and pathological child development. In F. Monks, W. Hartup, & J. DeWitt (Eds.), *Determinants of behavioral development*. New York: Academic Press, 1972.

Chandler, M. J., & Greenspan, S. Ersatz egocentrism: A reply to H. Borke. *Developmental Psychology*, 1972, **7**, 104–106.

Dunn, O. J. Multiple comparisons using rank sums. *Technometrics*, 1964, **6**, 241–252.

Feffer, M. H. A developmental analysis of interpersonal behavior. *Psychological Review*, 1970, **77**, 197–214.

Flavell, J. H., Botkin, P. T., Fry, C. L., Wright, J. W., & Jarvis, P. E. *The development of role-taking and communication skills in children*. New York: Wiley, 1968.

Gough, H. G. A sociological theory of psychopathy. *American Journal of Sociology*, 1948, **53**, 359–366.

Hays, W. L. *Statistics*. New York: Holt, Rinehart & Winston, 1963.

Looft, W. R. Egocentrism and social interaction across the life span. *Psychological Bulletin*, 1972, **78**, 73–92.

Martin, M. *A role-taking theory of psychopathy*. (Doctoral dissertation, University of Oregon) Ann Arbor, Mich.: University Microfilms, 1968. No. 68-11, 957.

Piaget, J., & Inhelder, B. *The child's conception of space*. London: Routledge & Kegan Paul, 1956.

Sarbin, T. R. Role theory. In G. Lindzey (Ed.), *Handbook of social psychology*. Cambridge, Mass.: Addison-Wesley, 1954.

Thompson, L. A. *Role playing ability and social adjustment in children*. (Doctoral dissertation, University of Southern California) Ann Arbor, Mich.: University Microfilms, 1968. No. 69-4547.

Reading 28

Children's Interpretation of Evaluative Feedback: The Effect of Social Cues on Learned Helplessness

Carol S. Dweck

Many alternative interpretations may be given for any event, and it is likely that the interpretation the child provides will affect the way in which he reacts to that event. As my colleagues have demonstrated, when one attempts to specify the determinants of children's behavior, it is often insufficient, or even misleading, to look only at the events that the experimenter has explicitly programmed or to view them only in the way that the experimenter views them. Rather, it is necessary also to consider such things as contextual social variables to which the child might be sensitive, along with the child's individual history and how it might interact with the experimental manipulations. The purpose of this paper is to examine some of the ways in which social cues, in conjunction with the child's history, influence the child's interpretation of and reaction to failure feedback in evaluative settings.

This interest grows out of our previous research on learned helplessness in achievement situations. Learned helplessness refers to the perception of independence between one's responses and the occurrence or termination of an aversive event (Maier, Seligman, & Solomon, 1969); that is, independence between what you do and what happens to you. Our work in this area (Dweck, 1975; Dweck & Reppucci, 1973) has yielded three findings that are of interest here: (1) Children's reactions to failure are related to the way in which they interpret failure, i.e., whether they attribute it to factors within their control or beyond their control (see also Weiner & Kukla, 1970); (2) Children's expectancy for control of reinforcement can be brought under the stimulus control of a particular agent; (3) Attributions for and reactions to failure can be altered by training. I would like to describe some of this work and then go on to propose a model which suggests how these findings can be employed to understand certain individual differences in children's achievement behavior—specifically sex differences in responses to failure feedback—in terms

of the nature of the evaluating agent. It will be argued that the characteristics of the agent, such as age and sex, are important determinants of helplessness; that these characteristics serve as cues for what outcome is most likely (whether failure will occur) and, after the fact, why it occurred (to what the outcome may be attributed).

Basically, our past work on learned helplessness focused on the tendency of children to attribute failure to controllable variables and on the extent to which these tendencies could be manipulated. In one study (Dweck & Reppucci, 1973) children were given soluble problems by one experimenter (Success E) interspersed with insoluble problems from another experimenter (Failure E). Thus, one experimenter came to signal success and the other failure. After a number of trials, the Failure E administered some soluble problems. They were identical to ones the children had previously solved from the Success E, yet a number of the children did not solve them. Those children who failed to solve the problems the second time around or who showed marked decrements in performance were those who tended to attribute failure to external factors, such as the inequity of other people or the unfairness of the task, or to a specific fixed internal factor—their own lack of ability. Both of these interpretations of failure reflect the child's belief in his inability to change the situation and attain success. It should be noted that these "helpless" children continued to improve on the problems administered by the Success E and that they were no less proficient at the task than the persistent children. Those children who showed improved performance or no deterioration were the ones who tended to take responsibility for failure and to attribute it to insufficient effort, a variable very much under their control. In this study, then, different children given "identical" experiences differed in their reactions, presumably as a function of how they had learned to interpret similar experiences in the past. In addition, the deterioration of performance on the part of the helpless children was specific to one of the agents.

The question then became whether attributions for failure could be changed and, if so, whether this would result in more adaptive responses to failure. In a subsequent study (Dweck, 1975), a number of children were identified who displayed the attributional and behavioral pattern indicative of helplessness to an extreme degree. The performance of these children underwent severe deterioration in both speed and accuracy following any sort of failure. Here, through the use of a training procedure, administered over a period of several months, children were taught to take responsibility for failure and to attribute it to insufficient effort. To evaluate the effects of the training, reactions to failure we assessed in a different situation at the beginning, middle, and end of training. This procedure was compared to one in which children were given an abundance of success experiences during the training phases. The latter treatment is commonly advocated by those who adhere to a "deprivation" model of helpless reactions; that is, the notion that these children simply need success experiences to bolster their confidence and inoculate them against the effects of failure. We found that success was not enough. The majority of children in this condition continued to display marked decrements in both speed and accuracy of performance whenever failure was introduced. In a few cases, the post-training decrements following failure were larger than those prior to training. Apparently failure retained its properties as a cue for an uncontrollable situation and had not been appreciably altered in its meaning or effect as a result of prolonged success. Only the children who received attribution retraining began to respond more adaptively to failure. In fact, by the end of training, most of these children actually showed *improved* performance following failure in the test situation in striking contrast to the dramatic impairment they had shown initially.

These findings suggest a framework within which one can view some consistent yet puzzling sex differences in children's achievement behavior that have emerged from the research of numerous investigators. For example, girls are reported to display less confidence in their abilities (lower expectations of success), regardless of their past accomplishments (Crandall, 1969). Girls have been found to place less emphasis on the role of motivation vs. ability in determining failure in intellectual- and achievement-related areas (Dweck & Reppucci, 1973). Girls' performance appears to be more disrupted by failure (Maccoby, 1966). In fact, girls who perform best seem to be disrupted most (Dweck & Reppucci, 1973).

Traditionally, these sex differences have been understood by proposing that girls are more dependent on external feedback and social approval for assessing their performance and defining their competence. Boys, it is said, rely more on "internal standards of excellence" and are therefore less affected by evaluative feedback (V. J. Crandall, 1963). While this may be so, before it can be accepted one must ask: Who are the agents of evaluation in the situations in which these results have been obtained and what is the child's history with these agents?

Who are the agents? In virtually every case, the agent or experimenter is an adult. Yet there is evidence that by the middle to late elementary school years peers become major agents of evaluation for boys (Bronfenbrenner, 1970; Hollander & Marcia, 1970). It would appear, therefore, that at least part of the observed sex difference in sensitivity to failure may be due to the fact that the more effective agent for boys is the peer as opposed to the adult. If this is the case, and boys look to peers to assess their competence, then we would expect boys to display the "helpless" pattern of failure attributions to lack of ability and performance decrements in the face of failure when the agent of evaluation is a male peer, just as girls have been found to do when the agent is an adult.

What is the child's history with the various agents? For illustrative purposes, let us examine the typical histories that boys vs. girls have with one of the most important evaluative agents—the teacher. The evidence indicates that the two sexes differ considerably in their pattern of interaction with teachers. Research in the area of school behavior problems (e.g., Sarason, 1959; Ullman, 1957), academic achievement (Asher & Markel, 1973; Gates, 1961; Gowan, 1955), and motivation to succeed in school shows boys to be way ahead in the first of these, but behind in the others. Boys are criticized and scolded more (Meyer & Thompson, 1963), are evaluated more negatively on a variety of personal characteristics (Stevenson, Hill, Hale & Moely, 1966), and are consistently rated by teachers as less hardworking (Stevenson, Hale, Klein & Miller, 1968). Thus the relationship of the typical boy with the woman in his life is often less than optimal.

We would expect, then, that boys in comparison to girls generally receive more criticism, but that it is less often directed at the quality of their intellectual performance and more often at their conduct on- and off-task, as well as such nonintellectual aspects of performance as neatness, instruction-following, lack of effort or attention, and the like. Research suggests that when feedback is used in this nonspecific manner, its information value for assessing the intellectual quality of performance is considerably reduced and the feedback comes to lose its validity as an evaluation of competence (Paris & Cairns, 1972). On the other hand, *praise* given to boys may be more explicitly addressed to their intellectual successes. For girls, praise may often be given for a vast variety of behaviors, particularly the non-intellectual aspects of academic performance. However, since girls evidence few behavior problems, usually follow directions, and are generally conscientious, criticism may be more specifically directed at intellectual-academic failures. Thus it is likely that while boys and girls both receive positive and negative evaluations from teachers, the feedback is contingent to different degrees upon the intellectual quality of their work vs. conduct or some intellectually irrelevant aspect of the task. It is also likely that boys' failures are more often explicitly attributed by the teacher to lack of effort, possibly because they do in fact exert less effort, but girls' failures, because of their greater diligence, to their lack of ability.

When we view the situation in this way, boys are able to maintain confidence in their abilities despite failure delivered by a teacher-like evaluator. They can attribute it either to lack of effort or to the external agent who criticizes them a great deal. In fact, it has been reported that women teachers scold misbehaving boys far more often and more severely than they scold girls for the same behavior (Sears & Feldman, 1966). It should be noted, however, that the external attribution, while "face-saving" in comparison to an attribution to lack of ability, is not without its negative implications for performance. Indeed, attributing failure to external

factors over which one perceives one has no control is a form of helplessness.

Many girls, on the other hand, who are generally praised by these agents and are usually trying their best, have little choice but to blame their abilities. We actually found in one of our studies (Dweck & Reppucci, 1973) that the girls who showed the greatest deterioration of performance following failure were the ones who expended the greatest amount of effort initially. You will also recall that in the attribution retraining study (Dweck, 1974) the ability to cope with failure was not enhanced by providing a greater number of success experiences if the child continued to attribute failure to lack of ability. In the same way, girls' prior successes may not be used by them to buffer the effects of failure if the failure is interpreted in this manner.

This analysis suggests that certain modes of interaction with social agents promote particular patterns of attributions and that these agents can come to serve as cues for these attributions in achievement situations. We are presently conducting a series of studies to test these hypotheses. Utilizing a combination of experimental and observational techniques, we are attempting to link the effects of evaluative feedback from different agents to the differing interactions boys and girls have with these agents. One study explores sex differences in reactions to and attributions for failure as a function of the agent of evaluation (male and female peers and adults). A second examines interaction patterns, particularly within the classroom, that might constitute the basis of the sex differences, and a third attempts to establish the presence of a causal relationship between interaction patterns and sex differences by isolating the critical features of the differing interactions and manipulating them in an experimental situation.

In summary, we hope to demonstrate that the way in which the child reacts to the behavior of another person, is, in large part, dependent upon the subtle, but powerful, social cues which operate in the situation. These cues, such as the characteristics of the evaluating agent, may be viewed as providing the child with information about what the agent's behavior signifies and, therefore, what responses on his part are appropriate. In addition, this line of research emphasizes the necessity of considering how the effects of social cues on the child's interpretation of and reaction to events may vary as a function of his individual history. In an achievement situation, for example, the import of a given cue will change according to the child's prior experience with similar agents in comparable situations. To the extent that we can specify these histories and determine the manner in which social cues interact with them, we can begin to predict children's behavior with increasingly greater accuracy and perhaps to devise ways to facilitate adaptive behavior.

REFERENCES

Asher, S. R., & Markel, R. A. Effect of interest on sex-differences in reading comprehension. Paper presented at the annual meeting of the American Educational Research Association, 1973.

Bronfenbrenner, U. Reactions to social pressure from adults versus peers among Soviet day school and boarding school pupils in the perspective of an American sample. *Journal of Personality and Social Psychology*, 1970, *15*, 179–189.

Crandall, V. C. Sex differences in expectancy of intellectual and academic reinforcement. In C. P. Smith (Ed.), *Achievement-related motives in children*. New York: Russell Sage, 1969.

Crandall, V. J. Achievement. In H. W. Stevenson (Ed.), *Child Psychology. Yearbook of the National Society for the Study of Education*, 1963, *62*, 416–459.

Dweck, C. S. The role of expectations and attributions in the alleviation of learned helplessness. *Journal of Personality and Social Psychology*, 1975 (in press).

Dweck, C. S., & Reppucci, N. D. Learned helplessness and reinforcement responsibility in children. *Journal of Personality and Social Psychology*, 1973, *25*, 109–116.

Gates, A. I. Sex differences in reading ability. *Elementary School Journal*, 1961, *61*, 431–434.

Gowan, J. C. The underachieving gifted child, a problem for everyone. *Exceptional Child*, 1955, *21*, 247–249; 270–271.

Hollander, E. P. & Marcia, J. E. Parental determinants of peer-orientation and self-orientation among preadolescents. *Developmental Psychology*, 1970, *2*, 292–302.

Maccoby, E. E. *The development of sex differences.* Stanford University Press, 1966.

Maier, S. F., Seligmen, M. E. P., & Solomon, R. L. Pavlovian fear conditioning and learned helplessness. In B. A. Campbell and R. M. Church (Eds.), *Punishment and Aversive Behavior.* New York: Appleton-Century-Crofts, 1969.

Meyer, W. J., & Thompson, G. G. Teacher interactions with boys as contrasted with girls. In R. G. Kuhlen and G. G. Thompson (Eds.), *Psychological Studies of Human Development.* New York: Appleton-Century-Crofts, 1963.

Paris, S. G., & Cairns, R. B. An experimental and ethological analysis of social reinforcement with retarded children. *Child Development*, 1972, *43*, 717–729.

Sarason, S. B. *Psychological Problems in Mental Deficiency.* New York: Harper, 1959.

Sears, P. S., & Feldman, D. H. Teacher interactions with boys and with girls. *National Elementary Principal*, Nov. 1966, 30–35.

Stevenson, H. W., Hale, G. A., Klein, R. E., & Miller, L. K. Interrelations and correlates in children's learning and problem solving. *Monographs of the Society for Research in Child Development*, 1968, *33*, (7, Serial No. 123).

Stevenson, H. W., Hill, K. T., Hale, G. A., & Moely, B. E. Adult ratings of children's behavior. *Child Development*, 1966, *37*, 929–941.

Ullman, C. A. Identification of maladjusted school children. *Public Health Monograph*, No. 7. Washington, D.C.: U.S. Government Printing Office, 1957.

Weiner, B., & Kukla, A. An attributional analysis of achievement motivation. *Journal of Personality and Social Psychology*, 1970, *15*, 1–20.

Reading 29

The Emergence and Functions of Prosocial Behaviors in Young Children

Marian Radke Yarrow
Carolyn Zahn Waxler

The study of children's compassionate feelings and behaviors comprises a complex package for research. Compassion, altruism, prosocial behavior (the label is a problem) involve cognitions, principles, and judgments; they involve feelings and motives. We are well aware that not all of helping, sharing, and sympathizing arise out of identification with the feelings of or concern for the welfare of others, and aware that the phenomena of empathy, compassion, etc. are murky areas—philosophically and empirically. Despite this state of affairs, our research interest is in how compassion (concern for others) is born and bred. Our earlier research used experimental designs with nursery school children. We demonstrated differential changes in prosocial responding as a consequence of different types of modeling and reinforcement. Although these techniques increased the frequency of helping and sympathy (though increase was by no means assured), the helping response was expressed in such a variety of ways as to suggest very different meanings and feelings underlying the response.

The direction of our research program, therefore, shifted to the exploration of the phenomena of compassionate feelings and behaviors more generally. What are the precursors of prosocial inclinations and the very early capabilities of the child in this regard? To get a better grasp of these issues, it seemed important to explore more general questions about the inferential capabilities of young children, of very, very young children, inferences with regard to the affect and thoughts of others. With this kind of knowledge we could more readily ask, how does sensitivity and responsiveness to the needs of others develop? Where and how do they fit into a more general schema of the developing child, both with respect to his cognitive skills and his social behavior?

From three interrelated studies we are attempting to obtain a picture of the emergence and progression of prosocial behaviors, to investigate the cognitions, feelings, and motives involved. The subjects were 128 children, ranging in age from 10 *months* to 7 *years*.

In the first study, with the youngest children, the focus is on the child's emerging sensitivities to affective events in his environment, e.g., a parent's or child's anger or pain or fear or joy or anxiety. Our data are the child's responses to these events and, in turn, responses of others to the child. Three cohorts, of eight children each, were followed for 9 months; the youngest began at 10 months of age, the next cohort at 15 months, and the third cohort at 20 months. Mothers were trained to dictate detailed descriptions of day to day affective events. At three week intervals, investigators visited the home and simulated affective episodes (e.g., pain, anger, joy). Additional data were obtained on the child's development and the home environment.

The second and third studies began at age 3 with children in nursery school or coming back to the school setting for research purposes. Our purposes were (a) to investigate the development and relations of perspective-taking skills and prosocial behavior; and (b) to investigate the prosocial behavior in the life space of the child: the frequency, circumstances, and generality with which it occurs and its relation to its "opposite," "anti-social" behavior.

Through a battery of standard situations, we assessed the child's perspective-taking skills: That is, was the child able to recognize and identify correctly the perspective of the person in circumstances in which an object or event was encountered or experienced differently by the two of them? One set of tasks dealt with literal perspectives in a visual or tactile perceptual sense; a second set dealt with what we will call cognitive perspectives in the sense of comprehending self-

Presented at the Biennial Meeting of the Society for Research in Child Development, Denver, Colorado, April 11, 1975.

These projects have been carried out with the collaboration of Robert A. King, Judith Smith, and David Barrett, and research assistants C. Jean Darby, Frances L. Polen, Claire Horowitz, David Eaton, and Marilyn Pickett.

other perspectives deriving from long-term differences in life experiences; and a third set dealt with affective perspective-taking. An example of each follows. Some of the tasks are adapted from Flavell; others are new. An example of literal perceptions is one with a child and another person seated on opposite sides of a table. Can the child indicate that a picture or object appearing upside-down to him would be viewed as right side up to the Other, and vice versa? A cognitive perspective-taking task is illustrated by requesting the child to choose gifts for parents and opposite sex peer and for himself. Does his own preference pervade his choices? Emotional perspective-taking was tapped by the child's inability to differentiate between his own and another's immediate affective experiences in situations in which S experienced success and O, failure; S experienced pleasure with one object, but O experienced pleasure with a different object.

Prosocial behaviors (a child's potential helping, sharing, and comforting) were assessed in a series of six standard situations. On two occasions an adult accidentally spilled some materials in the context of play activities. In two other circumstances, there were limited supplies of snack or toys which might be shared. The child also had occasion to witness someone expressing pain (slamming her finger in a drawer) and to see and hear someone crying, ostensibly about a sad story. All of the experimental tasks were interwoven in meaningful contexts of play and interaction. In natural indoor and outdoor play settings, prosocial and aggressive interchanges were recorded. A measure of level of social activity was also obtained.

Our infant subjects supplied very provocative data on sensitivity to affective states of others. Responses were by no means universal. However, very young children were often finely discriminative and responsive to others' need states. Children in the youngest cohort showed distress to parental arguments and anger with each other. Responses were sometimes marked: crying, holding hands over ears, comforting a distraught parent, or (punitively) hitting the parent perceived as the guilty one. Parental affection toward each other was equally arousing: Children of 1 to $2\frac{1}{2}$ years tried to join in or to separate the parents—even kicking the mother's leg. One child, from 15 months to 2 years, showed consistently different responses depending on whether mother or father initiated the affectionate hug or kiss. Initiation by the mother aroused no affect in the child, whereas with the father's (or grandfather's) initiation toward the mother, the child would "fall apart" (hitting, glaring, sucking her thumb).

While in the youngest children others' crying tended to elicit contagious crying as well as amusement, crying began to decrease, and as it waned, it was replaced by serious or worried attending. Around one year most of the youngest cohort first showed comfort to a person crying or in pain by patting, hugging, or presenting an object. Among $1\frac{1}{2}$- and 2-year-olds comforting was sometimes sophisticated and elaborate, e.g., fixing the hurt by trying to put a band-aid on, covering mother with a blanket when she was resting, trying to locate the source of the difficulty. Children also began to express concern verbally, and sometimes gave suggestions about how to deal with the problem. Such precocity on the part of the very young gives one pause. The capabilities for compassion, for various kinds of reaching out to others in a giving sense are viable and effective responses early in life. How such behaviors develop and change in the process of socialization in various cultures and sub-cultures are issues to which science has addressed little investigation.

Lest one assume that we are ready to reformulate a theory about the innate goodness of man, it should be emphasized too that there were also many, many occasions on which benevolence was *not* forthcoming, and that early aggressions are equally impressive.

If by egocentric one means the translation of the environment in terms of one's own needs and body state in the face of different existing states of others, the data provide such evidence—namely, the child who tries to protect his own possessions when another child is being "robbed" or hit, or the child who examines his own old injuries, hurts, etc., when someone else is injured, or verbal self-references—"look at my boo-boo"—as mother ministers to the real needs of an injured child. But the interesting point is that such self-references and self-considerations which have characteristically been conceptualized as the child's inability to take the point of view of the other, or preoccupation with one's own need state, may at times have a quite different function. They may also represent active attempts to *comprehend* (to form hypotheses about) others' affects by "trying them on," in this way trying to master (act positively on) the feelings in themselves which are aroused by others' affects. Support for such an idea is found in our data where it is not uncommon to observe self-referential responses followed by compassionate responses.

In our studies of 3- to 7-year-olds, as described earlier, we explored children's perspective-taking (lateral physical and psychological) in relation to their helping, sharing, and comforting behaviors. The children's abilities to successfully deal with another's perspective on the perceptual and cognitive tasks increased with age, the most substantial jumps occurring between 4$\frac{1}{2}$ and 5 years of age. The prosocial behaviors by the same children showed no systematic developmental changes. Not surprisingly, then, there was no overall relation between perspective-taking abilities and prosocial interventions. This was true also at each given age level.

We expected the two kinds of responding to be related, since both (we assume) involve the capacity to make an inference about someone's differential experience. Prosocial responding involves also the motivation to act on someone else's behalf. The lack of correspondence was of two kinds: children who succeeded on perspective-taking tests but did not respond prosocially, and children who helped, shared, or comforted, but failed on the perspective-taking tasks. This lack of correspondence raises a number of unsettling questions: Is the conceptualization of a common underlying process of perspective-taking incorrect or simplistic? Are the test-tasks that are presumed to measure self-other perspectives really not measuring these abilities well? Perhaps, especially in young children, the language components in the instructions may have an all-determining influence. In designing perspective-taking tasks for this study and in examining tasks that other investigators have used, we have become very aware of the difficulties in good task-construction. We have the strong impression that the child's capabilities are seriously underestimated by many experimental tasks assessing self-other perspectives.

Our third study extended our information to the functioning of these same children in their peer groups. With what frequency and consistency do they help, share, and comfort? How do these prosocial behaviors relate to aggressive peer interaction?

Prosocial behaviors occurred in almost every child. There was some consistency in relative frequency across natural and experimental settings in sharing and comforting responses. Sharing and comforting were significantly related to each other; neither was reliably associated with helping. Such data provide evidence of limited consistency in behaviors that involve sensitivity to others' feeling states. The relatively impersonal utilitarian "helping" of an inconvenienced person (as measured in our study) seems to tap a different kind of behavior from that involved in responding to the emotional needs, as in reacting to hurt or sadness. The data suggest that prosociality is not a unitary concept. Observations of responding to emotional states of others (here to sadness) documented the complexity in prosocial interventions. Our data indicate that merely tabbing a child as having (or not) shared or comforted another ignores significant variants in these responses: inhibitions, approach-avoidance conflicts, anxieties, sympathy, feelings of relief, success or satisfaction.

Compassion and aggression have long been positively linked in some psychological theories, but data are few. In the present study there were no simple relations between aggressive and prosocial behaviors. There was a single significant positive association (out of 8) only for girls. When level of social interaction is controlled, the significance disappears.

Associations between aggression and prosociality were re-examined, taking into account the absolute *level* of aggression. We reasoned that children with high frequencies of aggressive acts might be expressing qualitative as well as quantitative differences in aggression, e.g., hostile vs. assertive aggression. The sample was divided, therefore, at the mean on frequency of aggression and correlations were computed for each subsample, and data for boys and girls examined separately.

For boys *below* the mean on aggression, there was a significant positive association between aggression and sharing-comforting in peer interaction. In contrast, for boys *above* the mean on aggression the relation was negative. For girls, there was no such pattern. However, since the absolute level of aggression of girls is significantly lower than that of boys, the correlation between aggression and comforting-sharing for girls across the entire range of aggression is consistent with the findings for boys at the lower range of aggression. Controlling on level of social interaction did not materially alter the findings. One might hypothesize that moderately aggressive children are assertive more than hostile and that they are secure and competent in their peer groups. Assertiveness is a quality that might reasonably be expected to go along with the ability to intervene on behalf of another person.

These analyses have emphasized the aggressive behavior *expressed by* the child. There is another element of aggression, that expressed *to* the child. Among the boys and girls who were low to moderate in exhibited aggression, frequency of being the target of aggression and frequency of sharing-comforting behaviors were significantly positively related. In other words, among the relatively non-aggressive children, sensitivity to others' feeling states increased as the frequency of experiences of aggression from others increased. There was no such relation among children high on exhibited aggression. We will hazard a hypothesis: namely, aggressions experienced may contribute to the development of sensitivity to feelings when the child is himself not highly vulnerable and is secure in his relations with others. He may be able to learn from experiencing aggression from others and better understand the feelings and be better able to act empathically.

There is still a very modest accumulation of scientific knowledge regarding the human behaviors that qualify as prosocial. They are not a simple phenomenon. As scientists, we tend to give too little thought to cultural influences on the choice and definition of our research problems. It seems to us that research on prosocial behavior carries many overtones of these influences. In our society, the study of prosocial endeavors has been rather late in coming, compared with studies of aggression (and problems in our society), and compared with individual achievement and intellectual capacities, valued commodities by the society. Theories of prosociality, too, have frequently been formulated with materialistic or economic parallels, for example, cost-accounting theory, which represents a balancing of credit-debit ledgers of human relations. We are suggesting that it might be well to reflect more on our research emphases and theories of child development as products of the cultures and subcultures from which we come.

Reading 30

Fathers, Mothers and Sex Typing

Miriam M. Johnson

In this paper the hypothesis that the father plays a more crucial and direct role than the mother in reinforcing sex typed behavior (Johnson, 1963) will be reexamined and somewhat recast in the light of further evidence. Many research findings have continued to support the conclusion that the father is important in encouraging "femininity" in females as well as "masculinity" in males. These data, many of which have been reviewed by Biller (1971) and Biller and Weiss (1970), clearly challenge the view that the degree of "femininity" in women is related to sustaining and intensifying the mother-daughter relationship and suggest instead that the father relationship is of great importance for both sexes. On the other hand, other findings indicate that mothers can by no means be discounted altogether in the sex typing process. For example, there is abundant evidence that mothers do treat male and female children differently (Kagan, 1971; Lewis, 1972) and that although "feminine" women do identify with their fathers, they do not fail to identify with their mothers (Heilbrun, 1968). Still other data seem to contradict directly the "feminizing" influence of the father on girls and suggest instead that fathers have a "masculinizing" effect (Sears, 1965; Kammeyer, 1967).

It is the purpose of this paper to specify more precisely the nature of the father's impact on sex typing. The most important specification to be made is that there are two aspects of the feminine role—the maternal and the heterosexual. If this distinction is maintained it can be argued that while the nurturant mother role is internalized by children of both sexes, it is the paternal role that reinforces the heterosexual aspects of femininity in the girl as well as the paternal *and* heterosexual aspects of masculinity in the boy. The paternal role is being thought of here as distinctly different from the maternal role. It is not simply a male acting in the mother role.

Two hypotheses concerning the role of the father presented in the earlier paper (Johnson, 1963) will be discussed. The first hypothesis was that the father differentiates his role toward opposite sexed children more than the mother. This will be further specified along the lines that the father responds more directly to his daughter's *sexuality* than the mother does to her son's. The mother, it will be argued does differentiate her role (especially outside the middle class) toward the sexes but this differentiation is of a different sort than the sexual differentiation of the father. The second hypothesis, that the father fosters independence in both sexes, will be retained while it will be argued that this should not be equated with "masculinization." Finally, data relevant to the modified hypothesis that the father does play the pivotal role with respect to *heterosexual* behaviors in both sexes will be presented. At the end of the paper the implications of this revised theoretical model for understanding the relations between the sexes will be discussed.

The essential features of the basic model to be discussed and revised are as follows: The earliest mother relationship is primarily significant not as a focus of sex typing but rather as the basis for the establishment of "socialized" behavior in general. It is by virtue of the mother attachment that infants become "hooked into" the social system in the first place and are motivated to respond to attitudinal sanctions. The paternal role by contrast, comes into play later (in the early stages the father acts only as a substitute for the nurturant mother), is less fundamental and more specialized than that of the maternal role. It is the father who, *by differentiating his paternal role* toward opposite sexed children more than the mother, reinforces "femininity" in the girl and "masculinity" in the boy. The father promotes independence and autonomy (from the mother) in both sexes while at the same time he reinforces sex differentiated behaviors within this context. The basic elements of this model will be retained while a more precise meaning for the concepts of "masculinity," "femininity" and "differentiating behavior" will be specified.

DEFINING FEMININITY

The Significance of the Maternal Role. Essentially it has been the failure to take into account systematically the early primacy of the mother for both sexes that has made interpretation of findings regarding the father's influence on sex typing so precarious. This "primacy" derives both from the fact that she is the first object of identification[1] for both sexes and also from her being the main socializer of both sexes during childhood. The mother's primacy can affect sex typing in several concrete respects: 1) failure to transcend the mother attachment can prevent the child from having a significant relationship with the father, 2) the mother's definition of the father and/or men would affect the child's willingness to form a solidary relationship with the father. Most importantly, however, the child's earliest relationship with the mother involves internalizing the nurturant maternal role by both sexes. In this sense it would be accurate to say that it is the maternal, not the paternal, principle which is generic and which symbolizes the common humanity of both sexes.[2]

For males, then, becoming "masculine" necessarily involves (in part at least) a rejection of the "femininity" in themselves. This view fits with the idea, most recently stressed by Chodorow (1972) in her discussion of child rearing cross-culturally, that much of learning to be "masculine" for boys involves learning *not* to be "feminine." This theory has also been an underlying theme in the work of David Lynn (1969).

1) The Maternal vs. the Heterosexual Aspects of Femininity. The concept of "femininity" itself, in one sense, will be used to indicate qualities of sensitivity and responsiveness to the needs and

---

[1] Parsons' (1958) definition of identification as the internalization of a reciprocal role relationship that is functional at a particular period in the child's development is being used in this paper. If one takes this view of identification, it becomes possible to postulate, as Parsons does, that the development of personality in the child involves her/his making a series of successive identifications with increasingly specialized and differentiated social roles. In this usage "being like" or "feeling like" a person and being attached to a person can both be taken as rough indices of a solidary relationship in which a system of reciprocal role expectations has been established. On the other hand, there is evidence that although felt similarity and the quality of the relationship to the parent are correlated with each other, there are considerable differences in the direction and the magnitude of their associations with measures of sex typing (Stockard, 1974).

[2] Fathers, of course, may and do participate in early child care but in so doing they are assuming the nurturant or maternal role, not what has been traditionally defined as the paternal role.

reactions of others. Johnson, Stockard and their associates (1975) have argued that this "expressiveness"[3] need not be considered undesirable, but rather that it is a *human* characteristic par excellence which women manifest to a greater degree than men.

In order to understand the impact of the father on "femininity," however, the concept itself must be broken down into at least two components: the nurturant or maternal component and the heterosexual component. By "heterosexual" is meant those aspects of femininity that are oriented to interaction with males in terms of their "masculinity." This would include "heterosexuality" in the specifically sexual sense but would also include general interactions with men in so far as their being "masculine" is relevant. While both the maternal and the heterosexual roles involve expressiveness the two roles are quite different with respect to power. The maternal role involves high power while the feminine heterosexual role does not. In addition the mother role is asexual while the heterosexual role is not. It is this heterosexual aspect of femininity then that the father seems to affect most.

To say that the feminine role may be broken down into maternal and heterosexual aspects is not to say, however, that "maternity" and "seduction" exhaust the possibilities of femininity. This would be as incorrect as saying that *only* mothers and fathers affect sex typing. Rather the use of these two fundamental categories reflects the basic status categories defining femininity as it develops within the family of orientation and is recapitulated in the family of procreation. Thus to make this distinction does not imply that innumerable other roles cannot be held by women.

2) Dependence vs. "Femininity." In addition to

distinguishing between maternal and heterosexual aspects of "femininity" it will prove vital to avoid equating "dependency" with "femininity." Certainly it is not at all clear from the available studies on dependency that it is "normal" for women. For example, in Oetzel's summary of research on sex differences (1966) virtually all of the studies reported find girls more nurturant and affiliative than boys (pp. 330–332). On the other hand, in the summary of studies on dependency there is no consistent evidence that girls are more dependent than boys (pp. 326–327). On the basis of these and other findings, Maccoby and Masters (1970) have explicitly objected to some theorists' tendency to equate dependency with the feeling that people as people are satisfying and rewarding. In the college student study mentioned previously, Johnson, Stockard and associates (1975) were able to show that "expressive" traits in women were associated with feelings of "independence" not dependence. In fact, *among women* traits connoting "dependence" correlate more highly with "instrumental" traits than with "expressive" traits.

Certainly much confusion in the interpretation of findings can be avoided if it is assumed that there is no inevitable connection between being psychologically self directing (autonomous) and "masculinity." If this distinction is maintained it may be seen how the father can foster *both* independence *and* sex typing in his children.

3) Non-achievement vs. "Femininity." Achievement sometimes appears to be motivated by a desire to please that may or may not arise from dependence. On the other hand, some types of achievement require high levels of independence and/or an ability to ignore what others think (Bardwick and Douvan 1971). Because of the considerations in (2) above and because of the difficulties in assessing motivation, "achievement" cannot readily be equated with "masculinity" or "femininity" *per se.*

Neither can competence be considered the prerogative of only one sex. In spite of the tendency for some men to equate incompetence with "femininity," women see themselves as being both positively expressive *and* instrumentally competent (Johnson, Stockard, *et al.,* 1975).

Especially now that women are being admitted to more and more occupational fields, the use of "choice of a 'usually masculine' job" is becoming an unreliable index of "masculinity." For all the

[3]In the previous paper Parsons' instrumental-expressive distinction was employed as summary terms for the social orientational differences between the sexes. In retrospect, this seems to have obscured more than it clarified because using a single dichotomy necessitated using "expressiveness" to characterize both the earliest mother-child relationship and the quite different father-daughter relationship. Further confusion was introduced because Parsons had called the mother role vis-à-vis the child "instrumental." In addition, in common sense parlance the term "instrumental orientation" is often used synonymously with "achievement orientation" or competence—a connection definitely to be avoided. Although the instrumental-expressive distinction is useful for certain purposes, especially when treated as two separate dimensions rather than as polar opposites (Johnson, Stockard, *et al.,* 1975) it needs to be carefully specified in this paper in terms of other variables.

above reasons then, the findings concerning parental antecedents of competence, ambition, career-
ism, etc., are at best only indirectly relevant to sex
typing and therefore will not be dealt with in this
paper.

4) Non-aggression vs. Femininity. While positive
expressive behaviors are non-aggressive, it does
not follow that "aggression" can be equated with
"masculinity." Rather from the present standpoint,
aggression is best conceptualized as negative expressive behavior rather than as indicative of masculinity *per se*.

All of these distinctions will be utilized both
implicitly and explicitly in the discussion to follow.

"THE FATHER DIFFERENTIATES MORE" HYPOTHESIS

A Middle Class Phenomenon? It was argued
previously (Johnson, 1963) that the crucial influence of the father with respect to sex typing results
from his "differentiating his role" toward opposite
sexed children more than the mother. The most
recent findings supporting this have been reported
by Block (1974). In each of four separate studies
representing parents of children of four different
age groups, greater paternal differentiation in child
rearing orientations was found consistently. Block
interprets this as indicating "the critical role of the
father in encouraging sex typing and enforcing sex
differences" (p. 298). On the other hand, findings
which show that middle class mothers differentiate
their behavior toward opposite sexed children less
than working class mothers (Kagan, 1971) suggest
that the mother's relative lack of differentiation
may be specific to the middle class, and hence the
proposition that fathers differentiate more may
hold only in the middle class.

It was also argued in the earlier paper (Johnson,
1963) in connection with the proposition that the
father differentiated more that there was less difference in girls' and boys' ratings of maternal
behavior than in girls' and boys' ratings of paternal
behavior on the nurturance-control dimension. In
other words, it appeared that fathers were more
nurturant toward girls and more controlling toward
boys, while mothers' behavior was in the opposite
direction (more nurturance for boys and control for
girls) but was *much less marked*. Here too further
evidence suggests that this may be more characteristic of the middle class than of the working class

(Droppleman and Schaefer, 1963). It is probable
that the nurturance-control dimension is too general a distinction to be related directly to sex typing.
In terms of the heterosexual aspects of "femininity" the father's "nurturance" of the middle class
girl may mean the same thing as the father's
"control" of the lower class girl. This point will be
discussed later.

Women as Objects to Men but Not Vice Versa.
Although the particular findings discussed above
may turn out to be specific to the middle class, there
is nevertheless a precise sense in which it can be
maintained that the father role does involve sex
differentiating behavior more than the mother role.
Furthermore this difference between the mother
and the father role is very fundamental and should
hold across class lines and even between cultures.
In essence, the difference is that the father's role
toward the girl is more directly related to control
over her sexuality or is in direct response to her
sexuality than is the mother's role toward the boy.
Thus the complementary role of the father to
daughter is not the mirror image of that of the
mother to the son. The theoretical basis for expecting this to be true derives from both psychological
and social structural considerations which will be
discussed in turn.

Psychological Considerations. From a psychological standpoint it may be argued that a sexual
relationship between mother and child is more
regressive than a sexual relationship between father and child. Precisely because of her earliest
nurturing role a "seductive" mother would be a
greater psychological danger to a child than a
seductive father would be. Parsons (1970b) in particular has stressed the regressive implications
from a psychological standpoint of mother-son
incest. While the mother may want her son to be
"masculine" and may "appreciate" his "manli-
ness," even common sense observation reveals that
somehow it is pathological for a mother to attempt
to reinforce this by playing wife to her young son.
On the other hand, it is more acceptable for a father
to mildly court his daughter.

The reason a father can play "husband" to a
daughter in a way that a mother cannot play "wife"
to a son lies in the association of the mother
relationship with dependency. The mother is the
real and symbolic focus of infantile dependency

needs in all cultures and a "seductive" mother would pose a threat to a child's "growing up." The "seductive" father on the other hand is not quite the same order of threat since he is "once removed" as it were from associations with infantile dependency. These considerations relate to why the taboo on mother-son incest is the strongest of the incest prohibitions in all cultures and why mother-son incest is in fact much less common than father-daughter incest. All this is not to say that father-daughter incest is unpathological for the daughter, but rather to say that it is less deeply regressive than incest between son and mother is for the son.

Structural Considerations. At the structural level a basic function of the incest taboo is to force consanguineal kin groups to establish solidary relations with other kin groups by virtue of marriages between their members (Levi-Strauss, 1969; Mitchell, 1974). The rules of exchange and the acts of exchange which tie kin groups to each other are, according to Levi-Strauss, the very basis of human social organization. The important point here, however, is that it is women who are the symbolic counters in this exchange and it is men who exchange women in marriage and not vice versa. This is symbolized, for instance, in Anglo Saxon Christian marriages by the fact that it is the father who gives the bride away. It is also symbolic that white prejudice against blacks is usually phrased, "Would you want your sister to marry one?", not "Would you want your brother to marry one?" In this sense women are sexual objects or sexual property to males in the kin group in a way that men are not sexual objects or sexual property to females. In the matrilineal case it is the mother's *brother* who more often assumes the formal aspects of the father role and the mother's husband who plays the informal affective aspects. This bifunction, while introducing complexity, does not negate the basic fact, however, that it is men who exchange women.

Levi-Strauss himself was not concerned with why it was women, not men, who were exchanged, but rather assumes it is because of male dominance or male authority which prevails in all cultures regardless of the particular roles assigned each sex. Ultimately this masculine dominance may rest on the linkage of women, through motherhood, with domesticity in all cultures. It is men, not women, who handle "external relations" and therefore "place" the children in the wider social structure. It is perhaps because of this linkage of the female with domesticity and males with *external* relations that women universally are "the second sex" at least in terms of formal power and prestige (Rosaldo, 1974).

An Illustration. The following description by Anne Parsons (1967) of the position of the daughter in a Southern Italian family reflects both the psychological and structural aspects described above. The father's (and brother's) role as defenders of "their" sexual property (to be exchanged and not consumed) as well as their own sexual responsiveness to the daughter may be seen:

> . . . The most fully institutionalized masculine role in Southern Italy, one which is defined positively and not by rebellion, is that of the protection of the honor of the women who are tabooed (p. 386). . . . Thus, the South Italian girl does not appear as inhibited or naive for precisely the reasons that even though carefully kept away from outside men, she has in a great many indirect ways been treated as a sexual object by her father (and brothers or other male relatives) both at puberty and during the oedipal crisis (p. 387) . . . at both these points the father is highly sensitive to the daughter's femininity and the daughter is given considerable scope for exploiting this sensitivity in a very active way (p. 385).

The above described situation is generally typical of traditional societies and may be more characteristic of the working class than the middle class in the United States. As a case in point, findings in this country about the denial of freedom and punitiveness to the working class girl by her father (Droppleman and Schaefer, 1965; Elder and Bowerman, 1963) may be taken as an indication of his more traditional view of his role as protector of his daughter's sexual virtue. The lenience and nurturance toward girls found to be characteristic of the middle class father may reflect the "courtship" aspect of the same basic response to the daughter's sexuality. Thus in both cases, the paternal role affirms heterosexuality in the girl in a way that the maternal role does *not* affirm heterosexuality for the boy. The mother's *power* over the son as her child conflicts with her less powerful role as heterosexual partner.

The "Father Differentiating" Hypothesis Specified. In summary then, it appears that the hypothesis that "the father differentiates his role toward opposite sexed children more than the mother" should be amended to read that the father's role toward the girl is more directly oriented to her sexuality than is the mother's role toward the boy. The father in his relationship with the daughter both rewards and reinforces the heterosexual aspects of her "femininity"—directly by interacting with her as an "interested" male and indirectly by protecting her from "outside" males. The mother, on the other hand, does *not* play a role complementary to her son's "masculinity" in the same way the father can play to his daughter's "femininity." Her greater association with infantile dependency makes her seductiveness a psychological danger. Also her power over the son as mother conflicts with her lesser power as "wife."

The question may be raised whether the foregoing analysis would hold if fathers participated equally with mothers in infant and child care activities and mothers participated equally with fathers in non-domestic activities. Likely it would *not* hold if there literally were no sex role ascription in terms of internal and external functions. Certainly the presumption is not being made here that it would be impossible to eliminate sex role ascription. American society is moving in this direction. However, the involvement of males in early child care is proceeding considerably more slowly than the involvement of women in the labor force. So far women have remained the primary nurturers while adding external functions.

How Mothers Differentiate. Clearly it is not tenable to maintain that mothers do not behave differently toward opposite sexed children while fathers do. On the other hand, it can be maintained that even though the mother differentiates, there is a lack of symmetry between her differentiation and that made by the father. Cross-cultural and cross-class findings amply document the differential expectations and demands which mothers make on opposite sexed children (Barry, Bacon and Child, 1957; Kagan, 1971). In fact, since the mother has more to do with very early socialization in general than the father she may actually make and implement more differential demands than the father. But all this shows is that mothers and fathers share to some degree common cultural values about desirable characteristics for males and females and that mothers as primary socializers attempt to implement these values. These differential expectations held by mothers (and fathers) would essentially be irrelevant to the "father differentiating more" hypothesis as restated since it is in specific response to his children's sexuality as opposed to sex role training that he would be expected to make the distinction.

Lately too, a number of studies have appeared regarding mothers' differential treatment of male and female infants (Lewis, 1972). Here again it appears that mothers are directly reinforcing female socio-emotional orientations and masculine instrumentalness. For example, Lewis (1972) in summarizing these studies notes that one widely used method of socializing boys is to turn the infant from a face-to-face proximal position to a face-to-back position—the infant facing away from and not touching the mother. While this certainly is training for the masculine instrumental role the significant fact from our standpoint is that the mother is not treating the male as "sex object" in a way comparable to the situation that prevails (at least potentially) between father and daughter. When the mother faces the son away from her on her lap she is not only training for instrumentalness but is symbolizing the asexual nature of the relationship. Thus although the mother is very definitely involved in sex differentiated training at a time when the father plays only a minor role, the above facts do not contradict the proposition that the mother-son relationship is a less specifically sexual one than the father-daughter relationship.

What the behavioral implications of the father's role are for the female will be discussed at a latter point. First another aspect of the father role will be considered—his connection with independence from the mother for both sexes.

THE FATHER AND INDEPENDENCE FOR BOTH SEXES

In this paper the regressive consequences for the *son* of a "seductive" mother have been emphasized. Rothbart (in press) and Chodorow (1974) have stressed the regressive consequences for the daughter of the mother's favoring her as a like sexed person. To the extent that mothers tend to "identify" with their daughters more than their sons, the process of separation and individuation might be expected to be more difficult for girls than for boys. Thus from the standpoint of both males and females, the father might be expected to have an important function as a symbol of independence.

It was argued earlier (Johnson, 1963) that growing up for both sexes involves becoming emancipated from the love-dependency relationship with the mother and that the father as mother's partner, yet an outsider to the mother-child bond was in a particularly strategic position to help bring this about. In this sense, the father is seen as affecting males and females similarly—as a link with the non-domestic world. Parsons (1970a) has tended to see the father's position in a somewhat negative way, i.e. as a threat from the point of view of the child. As he puts it, the father

> constitutes the symbolic focus of the pressure from the outside world which is responsible for breaking up the 'paradise' of the child's state of blissful security with his mother (p. 40).

Firestone (1970: 53) by contrast, interprets the turn toward the father as a positive search for power on the part of both sexes. Both would agree, however, that the breaking of the tie to the mother is equally necessary for girls as well as for boys. Forrest (1966) has also stressed the importance for the woman of breaking her symbiotic ties to the mother and learning to relate to men in a non-maternal way.

There is now considerable empirical evidence that father "identification" involving both imitation and attachment does increase with age and intelligence for children of both sexes (Kohlberg and Zigler, 1967). The Kohlberg and Zigler studies appear to be yet another confirmation of the results of the numerous studies concerned with the relationship between sex of parent with whom the child is most "identified" and the child's "psychological adjustment." The most common operational definitions of "identification" in these studies are "attachment" and/or perceived or actual similarity of attitudes or traits between a child and each of his or her parents. From the present standpoint, these measures of "identification" are best understood as a rough index of the degree to which a solidary relationship exists or has existed between the identifying individual and the person identified with (see footnote 1). These studies of "identification" then have generally found that while father "identification" in males does seem to be related to psycho-

logical adjustment, mother "identification" in females does not relate at all clearly to adjustment (Johnson, 1963; Heilbrun, 1965). It would seem that the lack of correlation between adjustment and mother identification in girls may result at least in part from the dependency implications of an exclusive mother tie. Some identification in the sense of sharing a solidary relationship with the father would be expected to facilitate "growing up" which is presumably related to adjustment in both sexes.

Do Fathers "Masculinize" Women? It is difficult to find clear cut evidence concerning the father's role in fostering feminine independence because of the general failure of most studies to distinguish "dependence" from "femininity" and within "femininity," to distinguish the maternal from the heterosexual aspects. Most empirically derived M-F tests do confound dependency with "femininity" (Johnson, Stockard et al., 1974; Lansky and McKay, 1969) and therefore findings based on them are difficult to interpret.

Much of the data purporting to show the "masculinizing" influence of the father on the daughter may actually reflect the father's encouragement of the daughter's independence from the mother and concomitantly his response to her as a male. For example, Sears (1965) states that a family fearing and restricting sensual and aggressive gratification has a "feminizing" effect on both sexes. He then concludes that the intrusion of an affectionate father into the girl's rearing tends to "masculinize" her. This illustrates rather well the problem the present conceptualization would clarify. Sears is equating mothers and "morality" with "femininity" and is hence speaking of the maternal rather than the heterosexual aspect of femininity. From our standpoint the intrusion of the affectionate father certainly does not "masculinize" the girl in the sense of making her "mannish" but it may make her more independent, less emotionally restricted and at the same time more adept at interacting with males.

Other data which has been employed to argue for the masculinizing effect of males on females has come from studies of the differential effects of older male siblings on girls (Sutton-Smith et al., 1964; Kammeyer, 1967). Certainly older brothers might very well be expected to cut down on their sisters' being "little lady" types. On the other hand, overcoming emotional dependence and maternalism as well as aspiring to certain male activities should not be equated with "masculinization" in the heterosexual sense. In other words studies showing the "masculinizing" influence of the father on females might alternatively be interpreted as showing his influence in fostering independence (as well as broader interests) rather than masculinity.

The Father and Autonomy for Both Sexes—the Data. Perhaps the most clearcut evidence that father identification is related to autonomy in both males and females comes from Heilbrun (1965). He found in a study of college students that the "instrumental father" identified females were more "self-confident" than "expressive mother" identified females. The latter were more "considerate," "fearful," "gentle," "obliging," "silent," "submissive" and "trusting." As Heilbrun himself notes these traits seem clearly to be more related to passivity and dependence than to more autonomous femininity while "self-confident" is a trait suggesting "autonomy" but not necessarily "masculinity." The traits of "expressive mother" identified males also had a dependent, inhibited quality (table 3, p. 796).

Studies of father absence in which "dependence" is treated as a separate variable from "femininity" also generally support the hypothesis that father absence is related to an increase in dependency in both sexes. Tiller (1971) reports the well-known Norwegian study (see also Lynn and Sawrey, 1959) that absent ships' officers' children, both boys and girls, were "in general less mature emotionally and socially and more dependent on their mothers than the children of the control group" (p. 86). Tiller also reported a study of the effects of paternal absence during puberty in which the daughters of absent whalers adopted aggressive and authoritarian attitudes and had an exaggerated idealization of the male role. He interprets these behaviors as compensatory expressions of the need for independence and freedom (p. 102).

While Santrock (1970) and Wohlford, Santrock and others (1971) in studies of black pre-schoolers found no differences in dependency among father absent and father present females, they did find that the presence of older male siblings in the home decreased dependency in female as well as male children. Hetherington (1972) in a study of father absent and father present adolescent females found that the father absent girls showed more dependen-

cy on adult females and manifested a greater feeling of anxiety and powerlessness than did the father present girls.

Although these studies do not isolate the specific mechanisms by which this greater dependency comes about (it may be maternal over-protection), they do indicate that the presence of a father or older males (as opposed to females) seems to facilitate the process of achieving independence for both sexes.

CONTRIBUTIONS OF THE FATHER RELATIONSHIP VS. CONTRIBUTIONS OF THE MOTHER RELATIONSHIP TO SEX TYPING

Much of the data relevant to parental roles and sex typing bears on the question of the relative influence of each parent on each sex. The hypothesis that the father is crucial in sex typing for both sexes has been considered by some (e.g., Sherman, 1971) to have been disconfirmed by some of these data. In this section it will be argued that if the distinction between the maternal and the heterosexual aspects of femininity is maintained the data do support the crucial role of the father for *heterosexual* behaviors.

There are a number of studies (reviewed by Johnson, 1963; Biller and Weiss, 1970; Biller, 1971) suggesting in one way or another the salience of the father in "feminizing" women. On the other hand, in many of these same studies the mother is also found to be of importance, especially for girls. For example, Mussen and Rutherford (1963) found that feminine preferences in girls were related less to the "femininity" of their mothers than to the "masculinity" of their fathers *and* the extent to which he encouraged sex typed play. (This latter has been reported more recently by Fling and Manosevitz, 1972.) On the other hand this same study found that while the daughter's feminine preferences are not related to the mother's "femininity" they are related to her "self-acceptance" and to her nurturance.

Again, in order to make sense of these findings it is necessary to distinguish within femininity between its maternal aspects and its heterosexual aspects. The complete findings of the Mussen and Rutherford study make sense if it is argued that liking one's mother is important to a girl's own self acceptance as a woman and to maternalism but that the mother's nurturance is not the source of "femininity" in interacting with males (the heterosexual aspect). Any test of this is difficult in this specific study since the IT Scale, which does not get at mode of interacting, was used as the measure of sex typing in the children.

This distinction between nurturance and heterosexuality must be kept in mind in interpreting studies such as that of Wright and Tuska (1966). These authors report with respect to their findings on college women's self concepts that:

> It would seem as though the 'feminine' women have experienced more nurturant, rewarding relationships with their mothers than the 'masculine' women and that through this sympathetic, influential relationship, they have been encouraged to emulate the 'feminine' role. (p. 147.)

One cannot conclude from this study that the father does *not* reinforce "feeling feminine." It simply reflects the general salience of the mother as the nurturer, and after all this *is* an important aspect of femininity. Significantly enough, almost the only and by far the largest difference with respect to the father (as opposed to the mother) that occurs between the "masculine" and "feminine" groups is that the more "feminine" feeling women (*not* the more "masculine" women) think their father has been "more successful in life" than the mother.

Father Absence and Sex Typing. The findings from father absence studies are always problematic. In the first place most children without fathers, especially in the lower class, where the nuclear unit is neither so prominent nor isolated from other kin as it is in the middle class (Schneider and Smith, 1973), often have other male relatives who play the father role. It is also possible that an "image" of a father can be as "present" and operant as the actual father's presence. Certainly too, some fathers who are present may be more psychologically absent than some physically absent fathers. In spite of these drawbacks, some of the findings from the better controlled studies of the effects of father absence, especially on females, can be useful in clarifying the argument of this paper.

The key point is that if girls (and boys) identify first with the nurturant mother then father absence would not be related to anything like a sex role reversal in girls. Rather it would leave girls (and boys) with only their primary mother identification.

Father absence then would make boys seem feminine because there has been no interference with the mother identification[4] and girls appear less feminine in the sense that they have no specific heterosexual addition to the basic mother identification. In the case of girls then, father absence could be expected to affect their social interactions with peers and most especially their interactions with males. Thus studies of the effect of father absence on female sex typing should be examined in terms of which aspect of the feminine role is being tapped in the study, the maternal aspect or the heterosexual aspect.

When studies investigate more than cognitive understanding and/or sex typed preferences and get at actual social interactions, it becomes clear how father absence affects "femininity." The several studies of this type show that father absence does affect the *peer group* interactions of both males and females. For example, Thomes (1968) in a study of lower class elementary school aged children reports that the only difference she found between father absent and father present children in terms of family interaction was that girls from father present homes perceived mildly affectionate feelings coming from the father. Although she has no observational data she does ask about interactions with peers and reports:

> In response to 'How do you usually act when you get mad at your friends?' girls from father absent homes expressed a tendency to react aggressively by 'hitting' and 'throwing things,' while most of the girls from mother-father homes said they would walk away. Mothers of the girls in the father absent homes reported that their daughters belonged to significantly fewer groups than did mothers of girls from mother-father homes. (p. 94.)

These findings suggest that the father's affectionate interaction with females does cut down on aggressive hostile behavior in girls and is related to their being more sociable than father absent girls. It would be misleading to equate "hitting" and "throwing things" with "masculinity." From the present standpoint this kind of behavior is best understood as negative "expressive" rather than "masculine" behavior and may relate both to striv-

---

[4]For a summary of studies of the effects of father absence on boys, see Biller (1971).

ings against dependency and a lack of self confidence in the father absent females.

The clearest empirical case for the present formulation concerning the effects of father absence on females comes from a study by Hetherington (1972) mentioned earlier in connection with the discussion of dependency. She found that adolescent daughters from father absent homes had not only feelings of helplessness but were socially uncomfortable and not adept in dealing with males. Girls whose fathers had died early were shy with males while girls whose fathers were absent because of divorce appeared to be overly anxious for masculine attention. In both types of cases father absence is reflected in difficulties in relating to males and dependency on females. On the other hand, Hetherington reports little deviation of father absent girls in sex typing in the sense that they did not act like men or pursue masculine activities in the recreation center where the study took place. These latter findings reflect the underlying mother identification. It is the absence of heterosexual interaction skills that characterize the father absent girls.

These studies reflect more than the fact that girls learn how to relate to men by relating to fathers. While this may indeed be true, it must be reiterated that the present theory predicts that the opposite does not seem to be as true for boys. For boys, father absence, emotional unavailability, especially in the early years, are related to *low* scores on "masculine orientation" (Biller, 1971). The present view suggests that mothers can and do influence a boy's masculinity by the way they define the father, by the way they act toward the father, etc., but they do not mediate heterosexuality for either sex.

As Hetherington (1973) has suggested, research may expect to see the effect of the father more clearly in older girls and women than in young children. This observation is borne out in the following section.

Fathers and Sexuality. While the data on father absence are at the very least consonant with the hypothesis that it is the father relationship which most affects cross-sex interactions and attitudes in both sexes, there is research indicating even more directly the pivotal role of the father with respect to heterosexual behaviors. Recently the study of the etiology of homosexuality has been criticized by many on the grounds that to study homosexuality

implies that it is an "illness" to be "cured." Here a more basic question is being considered—how do parental roles foster heterosexuality?

Two studies by Eva Bené (1965a and b) are especially relevant. In one study Bené compared male homosexuals with a matched control group of married males and in a later study she compared lesbians with a matched control group of married females. All the subjects were given the Bené-Anthony Family Relations Test. With regard to males she reports that:

> the findings are consistent in suggesting that the reason why homosexuals are relatively much more attached to their mothers than to their fathers is not that they have much stronger relationships with their mothers than have heterosexuals, but that they have much poorer relationships with their fathers. (Bené, 1965 (b) p. 812.)

She found that the female homosexuals were also characterized by unrewarding father relationships. Of the 68 items which can be used to express recollected childhood feelings, 24 show significant difference between the experimental and control groups in connection with the father and only four in connection with the mother. Bené reports that the lesbians were often more hostile towards and afraid of their fathers than were the married women and they felt more often that their fathers were weak and incompetent.

Both the male and female homosexuals investigated were living "normal" productive lives and were in no sense "mental patients." Bené speculates that those investigators who found an over-strong mother attachment in male homosexuals were studying severely disturbed patients who were unlike the normal homosexuals in her sample. Bené's research then would support an important implication of the present position, namely that a disturbed maternal relationship poses a more serious threat to an individual's total personality than a disturbed paternal relationship.[5] Bené's data also support another implication of the present position, namely that sexual object choice and sex "appropriate" heterosexual behaviors are secondary and not primary human phenomena.

Obviously many factors are involved in an indi-

---

[5] It is also significant in this connection that while father absent homes are relatively common, mother absent homes are very rare.

vidual's choice of sex objects. Any simple determinism in this matter is to be avoided. But in so far as parental relationships are influential, the evidence suggests that the father relationship is of more importance in this than the mother relationship.

Another study directly concerned with sexual behavior of women using a different measure, i.e., sexual responsiveness in marital coitus, also provides support for the greater influence of the father relationship than the mother relationship. S. Fischer (1973) in a five year study using the verbal reports of 300 middle class housewives as to orgasmic frequency found that virtually the only factor which differentiated between the "low orgasm" and the "high orgasm" women was the reported quality of the woman's early relationship with her father. He found that if a woman perceives her father as not having invested serious or dependable interest in her she tends to experience orgasmic difficulties. On the other hand, he finds no correlations between orgasm consistency in marital intercourse and attitudes toward the mother.

The above studies on homosexuality and orgasmic frequency in marital coitus then seem to support the critical impact of the father relationship as opposed to the mother relationship in heterosexual behaviors. Finally, the desire as an adult to get married and have a family appears to be related to the quality of the woman's relationship to her father, not her mother.

Jean Stockard (1974) in a dissertation study based on a large sample of female undergraduates used path analysis to clarify the relationship of a number of antecedent variables, both familial and non-familial, to several different measures of adult sex role related attitudes. One of her dependent measures was the degree to which the young woman was committed to getting married and having children (regardless of her desire to work outside the home). Separate questions were asked concerning desire for marriage and desire for children but the responses were so highly correlated that they were combined into a measure of "familism." Using this measure, she found the highest path coefficient (.2144) obtained among all the variables was that between the quality of the woman's relationship with her father and "familism." Women who described their fathers as affectionate, sympathetic, interested in their activities and non-ignoring were most likely to definitely expect to get

married and have a family. The woman's assessment of her relationship with her mother, however, in terms of these same variables was *not* related to "familism."

On the other hand, the next strongest path coefficient to "familism" was the degree to which the daughter felt similar to her mother (.1823). Daughters who said their habits, goals and reactions were similar to their mothers' tended to think marriage and having children were important for them. Certainly women who opt for marriage and motherhood might be expected to say they feel similar to their mothers, but from the present standpoint the striking finding is that it is the quality of the father-daughter relationship, not the quality of the mother-daughter relationship that effects "familism," the respective path coefficients being .2144 and −.0100. It is also significant that the father relationship effect operates independently of the "similarity to mother" variable.

Stockard's findings with respect to the influence of mothers and fathers on the degree to which women want to have a career (regardless of marriage and motherhood) and on the type of career (traditional or non-traditional) they want, show a *less* strong influence of the father relationship. This fits with the argument of this paper that occupational achievement and the lack of it should not be equated with sex typing. Specific occupational roles considered "appropriate" for women and men vary considerably from culture to culture and time to time. More or less invariant sex typing, including heterosexuality and familism seem to be what the father relationship most affects.

SUMMARY AND DISCUSSION

In this paper a theoretical argument made earlier (Johnson, 1963) for the crucial role of the father in promoting sex typed behavior has been specified more precisely and data examined in terms of these specifications. Although the findings used come largely from the United States, from a theoretical standpoint the ultimate concern is to determine how certain universal features of parental roles, i.e. the early primacy of the mother and the external focus of the father, may be related to the latter's being the focus of sex typing in both sexes. Precisely because of the primacy of the maternal role the mother cannot be the focus of "masculinity" in men or of non-maternal "femininity" in women. It is the father or paternal surrogate who as the focus of non-domestic relations symbolizes and promotes the adult heterosexual aspect of both male and female personalities. This suggests a specific and very basic sense in which it can be claimed that "patriarchy" (control by the father or male relative) is at the basis of the secondary status of women.

Ultimately the father's role in sex typing, heterosexuality, and the "object" status of females (but *not* in their maternal role) derives from the cultural imperative to relate kin groups to one another. This is done through the exchange of women by men from one kin group with men from other kin groups (necessitated by the incest taboo). The reason the exchange of men *by women* has never been institutionalized rests in large part on the "external" focus of the father role. This in turn seems to rest on the domestic focus of the mother role. The most parsimonious explanation for the association of the female with domesticity is simply that it is the woman who bears children and lactates. Thus the presumption would be to associate females with early child care and hence males with external functions (Rosaldo, 1974). Ultimately then it is being contended that the father controls sexuality and makes women "objects" not directly because of his own qualities but because of the association of women with the maternal role.

The foregoing speculations reflect essentially a structuralist approach represented by Kohlberg in psychology, Parsons in sociology and Levi-Strauss in anthropology. The reader will have noted that the words "reinforce," "enhance," "facilitate" and "symbolize" rather than "cause" have been used throughout the paper. This usage is deliberate and reflects the view that the actual events of a child's life impede or facilitate cognitive structuring capacities interacting with the socially defined structure of the outside world. The specific concern of this paper has been with delineating the common cultural features of the structuring of parental roles. The actual experiences of children affect them in terms of these role concepts which define expectations about what each parent "should" be like.

Feminists have had very mixed feelings concerning motherhood. Some have seen it as a burden that prevents women from participating fully as human beings in the public sphere. Others have glorified motherhood as the source of women's power par excellence, and have treated men's achievements as attempts to reproduce this power for themselves (e.g., Mead, 1955: 117). In this paper too it has been

said that the maternal role is primary, generic, a focus of people's most human traits. To be "masculine" then involves a kind of "deviation" from the more androgynous maternal base line. On the other hand it has also been asserted that it is motherhood which has associated women with "domesticity" and men with "external" or "public" affairs. This in turn has made women "sex objects" to men as counters in marital exchange. In a sense then, it is the linking of motherhood with marriage, the linking of maternal role with an externally oriented paternal role, that makes women "objects."

The implications of the foregoing analysis for understanding the traditional structuring of relations between the sexes then appears to be as follows: It is incorrect to see "masculinity" and "femininity" as separate but equal principles or in any simple way as masculine first, feminine second, or vice versa. The matter is more complicated, but only slightly so. Because of the initial identification of children of both sexes with the mother[6] and because it is in connection with the mother that both sexes are inducted into "socialized" behavior, the maternal aspect of the feminine principle is seen as generic and as symbolizing the common humanity of both sexes. The sex differentiating principle is introduced by the father. The woman's status as a sex object is related symbolically and ultimately to the father as is the male's "masculinity" (including its paternal aspects) related to the father. In this sense it can be claimed that "patriarchy" (father dominance) is at the basis of the secondary status of women. On the other hand, this secondary status of femininity in its heterosexual aspects *is* secondary to the primary status of the maternal aspect.

REFERENCES

Bardwick, J.M. and Douvan, E. 1971. "Ambivalence: The socialization of women," pp. 225–241 in V. Gornick and

---

[6]Recently, Stoller (1974), on the basis of his work with transsexuals has come to a similar conclusion regarding the primacy of the maternal. For Stoller, the male transsexual who feels that he is a female trapped in a male body is a kind of experimental confirmation of the initial mother identity in both sexes.

"Only if the boy . . . can comfortably separate himself from his mother's femaleness and femininity, can he then begin to develop that later, non-core gender identity we call masculinity" (p. 358).

Females on the other hand are not so threatened by gender identification problems as males precisely because they have the initial mother identification.

B. K. Moran (eds.), *Woman in Sexist Society*. N.Y.: Basic Books.

Barry, Bacon, M.K. and Child, I.L. 1957. "A cross-cultural survey of some sex differences in socialization," *Journal of Abnormal Psychology*, 55: 327, 332.

Bené, E. 1965. "On the genesis of female homosexuality," *British Journal of Psychiatry*, 3: 815–821; 1965. "On the genesis of male homosexuality," *British Journal of Psychiatry*, 3: 803–813.

Biller, H. B. 1971. *Father, Child, and Sex Role*. Lexington, Mass.: Heath Lexington Books.

Biller, H. B. and Weiss, S. 1970. "The father-daughter relationship and the personality development of the female," *Journal of Genetic Psychology*, 114: 79–93.

Block, J. H. 1974. "Conceptions of sex role: Some cross-cultural and longitudinal perspectives," in R. F. Winch and B. B. Spanier (eds.), *Selected Studies in Marriage and the Family* (4th edition). N.Y.: Holt, Rinehart and Winston.

Droppleman, L. F. and Schaefer, E. S. 1963. "Boys' and girls' reports of maternal and paternal behavior," *Journal of Abnormal and Social Psychology*, 67: 648–654.

Elder, G. and Bowerman, C. 1963. "Family structure and child-rearing patterns: the effect of family size and sex composition," *American Sociological Review*, 28: 891–905.

Firestone, S. 1971. *The Dialectic of Sex*. N.Y.: Bantam.

Fisher, S. 1973. *The Female Orgasm: Psychology, Physiology, Fantasy*. N.Y.: Basic Books.

Fling, S. and Manosevitz, M. 1972. "Sex typing in nursery school children's play interests," *Developmental Psychology*, 7: 146–152.

Forrest, T. 1966. "Paternal roots of female character development," *Contemporary Psychoanalysis*, 3: 21–38.

Heilbrun, A. B., Jr. 1968. "Sex role, instrumental-expressive behavior, and psychopathology in females," *Journal of Abnormal Psychology*, 74: 131–136.

Hetherington, E. M. 1972. "Effects of father absence on personality development in adolescent daughters," *Developmental Psychology*, 7: 313–326; 1973. "Girls without fathers," *Psychology Today*, 6: 46–52.

Johnson, M. M. 1963. "Sex role learning in the nuclear family," *Child Development*, 34: 319–333.

Johnson, M. M., Stockard, J., Acker, J. and Naffziger, C. 1975. "Expressiveness re-evaluated," *School Review*, in press.

Kagan, J. 1971. *Change and Continuity in Infancy*. N.Y.: Wiley; 1972. "The emergence of sex differences," *School Review*, 80: 217–227.

Kammeyer, K. 1967. "Sibling position and the feminine role," *Journal of Marriage and the Family*, 29: 494–499.

Kohlberg, L. 1966. "A cognitive-developmental analysis of children's sex-role concepts and attitudes," in E. E. Maccoby (ed.), *The Development of Sex Differences*. Stanford: Stanford University Press.

Kohlberg, L. and Zigler, E. 1967. "The impact of cognitive maturity on the development of sex role attitudes in the years 4 to 8." *Genetic Psychology Monographs*, 75: 89–165.

Lansky, L. M. and McKay, G. 1969. "Independence, dependence, manifest and latent masculinity-femininity: Some complex relationships among four complex variables," *Psychological Reports*, 24: 263–268.

Levi-Strauss, C. 1969. *The Elementary Structures of Kinship*. Boston: Beacon.

Lewis, M. 1972. "Parents and children: Sex role development," *School Review*, 80: 229–239.

Lynn, D. B. 1969. *Parental and Sex-role Identification*. Berkeley, Calif.: McCutchan.

Lynn, D. B. and Sawrey, W. L. 1959. "The effects of father-absence on Norwegian boys and girls," *Journal of Abnormal and Social Psychology*, 59: 258–262.

Maccoby, E. E. 1966. "Sex differences in intellectual functioning," pp. 25–55 in E. E. Maccoby (ed.), *The Development of Sex Differences*. Stanford, Calif.: Stanford University Press.

Maccoby, E. E. and Masters, J. C. 1970. "Attachment and dependency," in P. H. Mussen (ed.), *Carmichael's Manual of Child Psychology*, Vol. 2. N.Y.: Wiley.

Mead, M. 1955. *Male and Female*. N.Y.: Mentor.

Mitchell, J. 1974. "Patriarchy, kinship and women as exchange objects," *Psychoanalysis and Feminism*. N.Y.: Random House.

Mussen, P. and Rutherford, E. 1963. "Parent-child relations and parental personality in relation to young children's sex-role preferences," *Child Development*, 34: 589–607.

Parsons, A. 1967. "Is the oedipus complex universal?" In R. Hunt (ed.), *Personalities and Cultures*. Garden City, N.Y.: Natural History Press.

Parsons, T. 1970a. "The father symbol: An appraisal in the light of psycho-analytic and sociological theory," in Parsons, *Social Structure and Personality*. N.Y.: Free Press; 1970b. "The incest taboo in relation to social structure and the socialization of the child," in Parsons, *Social Structure and Personality*. N.Y.: Free Press; 1970c. "Social structure and the development of personality: Freud's contribution to the integration of psychology and sociology," *Social Structure and Personality*, N.Y.: Free Press.

Rothbart, M. K. In press. "Sibling position and maternal involvement," in K. Reigel and J. Meacham (eds.), *The Developing Individual in a Changing World*. Vol. II. The Hague: Mouton.

Santrock, J. W. 1970. "Paternal absence, sex typing, and identification," *Developmental Psychology*, 2: 264–272.

Schneider, D. M. and Smith, R. T. 1973. *Class Differences and Sex-roles in American Kinship and Family Structure*. Englewood Cliffs, N.J.: Prentice-Hall.

Sherman, J. A. 1971. *On the Psychology of Women*. Springfield, Ill.: Chas. Thomas.

Chapter Seven

The Family as a Primary Agent of Socialization

The family has traditionally been viewed as the primary and most powerful agent of socialization of children. Parents are the initial and most enduring social contacts the child encounters. These early contacts with parents are likely to be critical in shaping children's self-concepts, their expectations in interpersonal relations, and their competence in social situations. In addition the actions, attitudes, and values of the parents which are communicated to the child will serve as a cognitive framework around which the child will organize his or her subsequent perceptions of social standards and appropriate social behavior.

In the United States the nuclear family, consisting of a mother and father and one or more children, has been regarded as the most desirable child-rearing unit. Although shifts in family roles and structure are occurring, the majority of American children and adults still view parental roles in a stereotypical fashion with the father being seen as the powerful, coping decision maker, disciplinarian, and provider, and the mother as the sensitive, nurturant caretaker. In addition, until the past decade the child has been regarded as a passive object of socialization. The use of terms like "child rearing" and "child training" reflects the dominant American behavioristic orientation in which parents are seen to shape the development of children in a unilateral fashion.

Recent changes in theorizing and conceptualizations about family processes and their role in socialization have been some of the most dramatic to occur in the history of child psychology. The family is viewed as an interactive system with the behavior of each family member modifying those of other members in the system. Children are shaping and socializing their parents and siblings as the parents are socializing them. In the paper by Richard Bell, a discussion of the impact of infants in modifying the behavior of their caregivers is presented. The same author in other papers has reinterpreted the direction of effects in frequently reported findings in the family literature. Must the often noted correlation between parental punitiveness and aggressiveness in children be interpreted as a highly punitive parent acting as a frustrating agent and aggressive model for children, which facilitates the development of the children's aggressive behavior? Might not the explanation be that highly resistant, difficult, acting-out children lead parents to impose increasingly harsh sanctions in their desperate efforts to control their recalcitrant offspring? Could aggression in children be causing punishment in parents? Similarly, could the correlation between warmth of fathers and masculinity in sons. be interpreted as fathers enjoying and loving masculine sons more than feminine sons because of their concern about sex-typed behaviors, rather than that warmth in the father facilitates the son's imitation of paternal masculine characteristics? Obviously a unidirectional model of family functioning is incomplete and inaccurate whether it is one of the child shaping the parents or the parents shaping the child. The family can be understood only as a multidirectional interactive system.

A second way in which theorizing and research on the family system has changed is in the increasing emphasis on the role of the father. Until recently psychological research on the family was focused on such topics as mother-child relations, mother love, disrupted or deviant mothering, or maternal deprivation. Somehow fathers remained shadowy figures in the background who were seldom mentioned and rarely studied. In reading the papers in this section the student will become aware that this is no longer true. Psychologists are talking about parenting and fathering rather than just mothering. This can be regarded as another reflection of the emphasis on the family as an interactive system. Parke and Sawin in their paper expose some of the fallacies in our beliefs about fathers based on their careful analyses of parent-infant interaction. Diana Baumrind discusses the role of both mothers and fathers in the development of competence in children. Even in her study of divorce, Hetherington is concerned with the impact of divorce on the entire family system.

Finally, our theorizing and research on the family is changing because the structure and functioning of the American family is changing. Many of these changes are associated with intentional or unintentional shifts in sex roles, particularly in maternal and paternal roles in the family. In his paper, Bronfenbrenner reviews many of these changes and their effects on children. How has the rising divorce rate and increase in unwed mothers, and maternal employment, or the breakdown in the intended family and other family support systems contributed to the welfare or lack of well-being of our children? What will be the impact of the women's liberation movement, or of greater accessibility of day care and other child-care innovations, on the family?

The family system is changing and alternate life-styles emerging so rapidly that viewing the nuclear family as the only acceptable social unit in which to facilitate the development of competence in children seems naïve. In a country in which one out of every six children is growing up in a single-parent home, it is necessary to study these families and alternative life-styles to discover what aspects of their functioning interfere with or enhance the well-being of children. In situations where social or political experiments in restructuring the family and child-rearing unit have occurred, such as those reported in David Lynn's article, what are the effects on family members?

Neither the nuclear family nor the alternatives to it provide an ideal milieu for the fulfillment of its members. Social institutions cannot remain stable. They must change and evolve in the search for satisfaction of the needs of their members. Alternative life-styles and alterations in family structure can be regarded as a positive step in the quest for an improved society. However, as Bronfenbrenner cautions, transitions often have unfortunate concomitants. Society needs to provide a variety of support systems to parents and children in their exploration of new social contexts in which to grow and develop.

Reading 31

Contributions of Human Infants to Caregiving and Social Interaction

Richard Q. Bell

There are several indications that we need a way of thinking about how the young affect parent behavior. In the last decade there has been increasing advocacy of greater attention to this area (Bell, 1971); it has been pointed out that the behavior of the young represents its own integrations and patterning, and exerts a very important effect on parents in one period, even if it has developed out of interactions with parents in a prior period. New findings are emerging from a variety of research strategies which make it possible to isolate child and parent effects (Berberich, 1971; Hilton, 1967; Osofsky & O'Connell, 1972; Siegel, 1963). While in the past the effect of the young on parents has even been underestimated in research literature on other mammals, Harper (1970) has now drawn our attention to the fact that the young of many species affect parents to the extent of determining patterns of utilizing food resources and territory.

It has been contended that it is no more parsimonious to interpret a correlation found between parent and child characteristics at a single point in time as due to the effects of parents on children, than it is to offer the opposite interpretation (Bell, 1968). Recent reviews of research on the effect of parent practices or techniques (Mussen, 1970) now uniformly recommend caution in interpreting correlations between parent and child characteristics in a unidirectional fashion, and some even go further, offering substantive interpretations of the correlations in terms of the effects of children on parents. Clearly, some steps toward the development of a theory of the effects of the young on their parents and caregivers is in order, and the present chapter undertakes the first step toward such a theory. The present chapter is one-sided in treating only the effects of the young, but this is necessary to work toward a balance in our perspectives. It is hardly likely that another imbalance will be created, considering that such an occurrence would necessitate offsetting over three decades of socialization research committed almost entirely to studying the effects of parents on their children.

This is a review of the many ways in which it appears likely that the effects of the young may be shown in early development, particularly with reference to physical caregiving and social interaction. The chapter is frankly speculative. While interest in this area is rising, there is not sufficient research at present to provide an empirical basis for a theoretical structure. The conceptual elements have been drawn together in more of an expositional than a theoretical structure. The next logical step is to introduce general propositions which will align and organize the elements. Only a start is made in this direction.

In drawing together these guidelines toward a theory, it is clearly appreciated that meaningful and useful application of the guidelines must be found in the minute-to-minute and day-to-day ongoing interactions of parents and children. The concepts are of value only if they draw our attention to aspects of these interactions that might otherwise be overlooked, or help us focus on the task of teasing apart determinants of these interactions.

CONTRIBUTION OF THE YOUNG TO PARENT LIFE-SUPPORT AND PROTECTION ACTIVITIES

For purposes of discussion the effects of the young are detailed in terms of two very different aspects of the parent-child interaction. One aspect concerns the provision of life support and protection. In this case the parent primarily behaves so as to avoid undesirable immediate or long-range outcomes. From the parent standpoint this is an aversive system. At the other extreme is a kind of interaction which involves mutual, reciprocal, social interactions. This may be referred to as an appetitive system, in that both parent and offspring behave so as to produce or maintain the behavior of the other. There are many other kinds of interactions which this chapter does not attempt to treat, since the strategy is to develop guidelines out of a contrast between different systems, rather than to provide a comprehensive review of all kinds of parent-child exchanges.

Launching Parental Behavior

First, we present some speculations on how pregnancy and the neonate's characteristics set in motion the support and protection activities of the parent, which are subsumed under the term caregiving for brevity in most discussions for the remainder of the chapter. Harper (1972) has pointed out that pregnancy itself, with its physiological effects, and the signaling of a new role for the mother, lays the groundwork for these parental activities, which are then set in motion by the delivery of the infant. The behavior of the newborn further stimulates parental behavior. The thrashing and uncoordinated limb movements create an appearance of helplessness. The human infant's appearance alone could also have some effect on parental responsiveness in this early period, since the shape of the head (a short face relative to a large forehead and protruding cheeks) shows characteristics in line with several other species (Tinbergen, 1951). It is well known in comparative studies that the distinctive appearance of the young produces differential response from the members of a colony. Brooks and Hochberg (1960) have reported data more specifically applicable at the human level, namely, that variations in line abstractions of the human infant's face are responded to discriminatively and positively by adults—the concavity of the face, the height of the eyes, and other characteristics.

Postpartum hormonal effects could be operating at the human level, since we know from Rosenblatt's (1969) studies of rats that maternal behavior is enhanced by a pregnancy termination effect involving hormone changes. It is well to keep in mind that the human mother is not static physiologically but is maturing physiologically in the course of the process set in motion by the pregnancy.

The arrival of the infant is also capable of altering role relationships in the marriage. Ryder (1973) has reported that there is a decline in marital satisfaction reported by wives in young couples after having their first baby, in contrast to comparable couples without a baby. The decline in marital satisfaction seems to be due to less attention from the husband.

Sensory-Motor Matching   It is evident in cross-fostering animals that the sensory and motor system of the young is set up so that it matches that of the parent and not that of other species. An amusing example is described by Hersher, Richmond, and Moore (1963). When lambs and kids were cross-fostered, they retained their species typical tendencies to follow (in the case of the lambs), or to leave the mother and lie down when sated (in the case of the kids) during the first few days postpartum. This resulted in the ewes rearing kids becoming highly disturbed, since they were constantly required to leave the flock to locate their foster charges, while the goats rearing lambs were incessantly "shadowed."

It is easy to overlook the importance of sensory-motor matching at the human level, because there are few opportunities to see the effects of cross-fostering. A mother rearing a chimpanzee infant commented on the oppressive effect of the infant's clinging (Hayes, 1951). There are other kinds of data that are suggestive. Eisenberg (1970) reports that human tonal patterns and speechlike signals are remarkably effective with newborns. Richards (1971) has remarked on the fact that an endogenous patterning of neonatal sucking has an effect on the feeding interaction. There are short and long intervals between the bursts of sucking. The mother moves between short bursts, and talks to and smiles at the infant during the long intervals between bursts.

Launching the Caregiving Bout

To bring the discussion down to the level of actual interaction, it is helpful to think about how the infant initiates bouts of interaction (meaning in this context simply that both mother and infant are interacting following a period during which they were not). During the first few weeks, many bouts are started by the fussing or crying of the infant. The young mother is recovering from the birth process, and is in most cases quite willing to let the infant sleep and rest as much as possible.

The cry brings the caregiver to a position where the visual, olfactory, and tactile stimuli provided by the infant can be effective. Later in the first year, the type of cry produced by the infant will have communication functions, but it is sufficient at first that it simply brings the caregiven into the vicinity.

As a predictable pattern of infant behavior develops, the mother's response to the early items in a sequence averts a later item. For example, Wolff (1966, p. 86) has described how infants move from quiescence to highly aroused crying. First, a soft whispering was detected, then gentle movements, rhythmic kicking, uncoordinated thrashing, and then fussing or spasmodic crying. If the thrashing is overheard, it may provide discriminative stimuli for maternal behavior which averts the rest of the sequence.

After the infant can recognize and discriminate the mother, and has developed some minimal time concepts, one other way of starting bouts can be seen. Anticipatory protests occur when behaviors are shown by the mother that have been associated in the past with separation.

In placing emphasis on the contribution of the infant's cry, I nonetheless recognize that its role should not be overestimated. Bernal (1972) has reported diary data indicating that few mothers respond to what they feel is the nature of the cry as such during first 10 days of life. Their knowledge of how long it has been since the last feeding, and how adequate the feeding was, are important determinants of their response. In other words, the infant's cry is important, but mothers are in no sense puppets on a string, responding without a second thought, and cued in only by the cry qualities.

In short, it seems a reasonable proposition that the pregnancy, the infant's appearance, and the infant's behavior all interact with the mother's role proscription to create the mother-infant subsystem of the family. It might be well to add that these infant characteristics at times only interact with the mother's existence as an adult. She may simply be trying to maintain her life, without any intention of socializing anyone.

Maintaining the Caregiving System

Maintaining Behavior within Tolerance Limits of the Parent Here again the cry is used for illustrative purposes, simply because we have so much data on infant crying. During the first year, according to Bell and Ainsworth (1972), the duration of crying drops from 7.7 minutes/hour (range, 21 minutes/hour to none) in the first 3 months, to 4.4 minutes/hour in the last 3 months. Parmelee's (1972) data indicate a substantial reduction in crying between 1½ and 4 months.

The tolerance of parents probably shows a great range, but we do not have any quantitative data at present. However, from three different studies there are indications that parent tolerances are exceeded. Occasionally, crying is so excessive that it reaches the level of threatening and even breaking down the caregiving system. Robson and Moss

(1970) traced changes in subjective feelings of attachment from retrospective interviews conducted with mothers in the third postnatal month. They concluded that attachment decreases in some mothers after the first month if crying, fussing, and other demands for physiological caregiving do not decrease as they do in most infants. In one case from their study, the mother was enthusiastic during pregnancy, but her positive feelings ebbed during the first month. Her infant fussed a great deal, was not responsive to holding, and was late in exhibiting smiling and eye-to-eye contact. The mother reacted violently, wanting nothing to do with the infant. She felt estranged and unloved. The infant was later found to have suffered relatively serious brain damage.

From the normative studies of crying I have discussed, we have some idea that in the first month or so there is a period during which the mother is in essence at the mercy of the crying of her infant. Whether or not her efforts are the determining factor, by the third month crying is well within what seems to be the tolerance limits of most parents. However, the question of the effectiveness of the mother, and of the baby's testing her limits, is not settled by the third month for all cases, according to Bell and Ainsworth's (1972) analysis of sequential relations between infant crying and maternal ignoring of crying episodes in the four quarters of the first year. These investigators interpret the correlations between quarters as indicating that infants in their sample cried more in any given quarter that was preceded by a 3-month period during which their mothers ignored their crying. However, there was an increasing tendency, toward the last half of the year, indicating that the more the infant cried in any given quarter, the more the mother ignored the cry in the subsequent quarter. Of course, correlational data of this kind cannot identify causal factors, but if these interpretations are correct, for some pairs there was evidence of a breakdown in the caregiving system as such, and something of a vicious cycle developed. Apparently, some infants exceeded their mother's limits. The mother's efforts to cope with the crying were inadequate. The infant responded by crying even more, and the mother withdrew even more.

Gil (1970) has summarized several clinical and epidemiological studies of "battered children." From the early clinical studies of parents who battered their children, it was concluded that the attack on the child was an outlet for frustrations.

Parents, however, saw the *child* as the cause of the problem. Many of the parents thought they were being abused by the child. This could readily be dismissed as a parental defense mechanism, except that it is quite typical to find that other children in the family of an abused child are not abused. This fact raises questions about the stimulus qualities of the child. Constant fussing, strange and highly irritating crying, or other exasperating behaviors, were often reported for the one child subject to abuse in the family. Some children were abused in successive foster homes in which they were placed after the initial abuse. No other child had been abused previously in these foster homes. Gil's survey indicated that deviance in the child was at least as substantial a factor in explaining the incidents as was deviance in the parent, and the stressful circumstances under which they lived. Obviously, the stimulus characteristics of the child do not operate by themselves to induce mistreatment.

Most of the examples I have given involve testing the upper limits of parents. It is less obvious that extreme lethargy in infants can impair the caregiving relation. At first the young mother may feel relieved that she has a quiet baby. After the first month or two, however, she may become uneasy. She then stimulates her baby in various ways. She seeks the advice of friends or professional help if such measures, carried out over a long enough period of time, do not arouse the infant sufficiently.

Infants Define Their Own Limits   In the neonatal period the infant defines what it will or will not incorporate by swallowing or spitting out what is given to it. It turns its head away from aversive odors. Some infants reject solids and force their mothers to return to bottle or breast feedings. Others fall asleep during rigidly scheduled feedings, and this effectively limits the mother's behavior.

But what about the great volume of caregiving that is not in response to specific stimuli? Here the infant may make an unseen contribution. Startles or sustained distress reactions have sufficient impact on a mother that she is likely thereafter to prevent exposure of her baby to sudden noises, to too much noise, or to play that goes on overly long. If the mother has formed some concept of fragility and helplessness from the smallness and the thrashing, uncoordinated behavior of her newborn, she is quite likely to have this concept strengthened in later instances by the infant's startles or distress reactions. These reactions inform the parent when sensory and fatigue limits have been exceeded.

Readability of the Infant   There is a possibility that an empirical approach may be opened up to throw light on the problem of what it is that makes it difficult or easy to take care of some infants. Korner, in another chapter in this volume, has raised the possibility that the "readability" of an infant may be a function of the clarity of cues to its state. In studies of observer agreement, all of us who have studied very young infants have encountered those whose states are unclear. Mothers must have the same problem. This possibility is readily accessible to research.

Inducing a Singular Caregiving Relationship   A sequence of developmental changes in the infant contributes to the mother's concept that she has a singular and essential role to carry out. The sequence starts with discrimination of human from inanimate forms, discrimination of the mother from others, reactions to strangers, and, finally, protest at separation. Considered as a whole, these infant behaviors indicate to the mother that she has been selected for an intense one-to-one relationship, even if there were no cultural sanctions or role proscriptions to convey the same message. Of course a singular relationship is not always possible, as in some institutional settings, and yet caregiving goes on. The point here is that, where a singular relation is possible, the infant's behavior can be counted on to promote its emergence.

CONTRIBUTION OF THE YOUNG TO THE SOCIAL INTERACTION SYSTEM

In a social interaction system, the responses of each participant serve as stimuli for the other. Kohlberg (1969) amplifies this definition in the context of socialization:

"In general, even simple social play and games have the character of either complementarity, reciprocity, (I do this, then you do that, then I do this), or of imitation (I do this, you do this too). In either case there is a shared pattern of behavior, since reciprocal play is a sort of reciprocal imitation (you follow me, then I follow you) [p. 463]."

Watson (1966) has offered an explanation of how "contingency games" involving complementarity and reciprocity may develop between parent and infant increasingly after the first 3 months. Applying his line of thinking in the present context, responses of the infant that follow quickly parent behaviors could by that contingency acquire reward value, just as those of the parent could for the infant, leading to a social interchange system in which the responses of each are rewarding for the other—an appetitive system, in contrast to the aversive system in operation relative to provision of life support and protection.

In placing emphasis on the infant's contribution to noncaregiving interactions, I am assuming, as do Walters and Parke (1965), that socialization does not develop exclusively out of primary drive reduction. In the same vein, Escalona (1968) has challenged the classical psychoanalytic formulation that psychological development occurs in states of displeasure incident to delay of gratification. She feels that development from interaction is best favored by moderate levels of arousal. However, caregiving may lead to a state from which the infant starts the type of social interaction in which we expect socialization to be maximized. For example, the infant may quiet down after a diaper has been changed, or smile, and thus launch a social interaction.

Initiating the Social Interaction

Reduction in Demand for Caregiving   It is possible for social interaction to develop gradually out of early caregiving as the infant shows a decrease in the duration of crying and fussing and an increase in the time it is awake and attentive. Thus the infant provides an increased opportunity for noncaregiving activities to occur. It can be readily understood that a mother is less likely to start a playful interaction with her infant if she is stressed by inconsolable crying, or by her infant's short periods of sleep that do not come at a time permitting her to rest. When the caregiving demand has been reduced by changes that occur in normal development, the infant's changing condition can release one of the most powerful parental contributions to early social interaction—spontaneous play. Possibly even before, certainly increasingly after the third month, the mother's effort to reduce unpleasant excitation has reduced sufficiently, and the occasions on which positive affective responses

have been elicited have increased, to an extent that we would say that the social interaction system is well on its way.

Manipulability of States in the Infant   The ability of infants to show alterations in state in response to the efforts of parents is a more active contribution to the initiation of the social interaction system than the conditions just mentioned. Escalona (1968) has described how a mother stimulates a drowsy infant to bring it back to a state in which they can interact. Then the mother may have to calm the infant down and soothe it as it becomes too agitated. During visual attention the mother adjusts the level of stimulation to the infant's interest and arousal. The infant behavior that supports these parental efforts is state manipulability. Bridger and Birns (1963) have reported quantitative data indicating that infants vary greatly in response to identical efforts to manipulate states.

Approximately 18% of infants have what is termed "colic," a condition in which there is nearly a complete breakdown in state manipulability. Colic maximizes caregiving interactions and minimizes social interactions. Turning to conditions still farther from the normal range, Brazelton (1962) has described in detail a case in which an infant's inflexibility of states, as well as limited range, had a severe effect on the mother.

Responsive Behavior   The mere fact that an infant does something, literally anything other than fussing or crying, as a response to a mother's stimulation, is another and still more active contributor to the launching of the social interaction. A mass movement or a babble are responses, and again the mother learns that what she does matters. Watson (1966) was impressed with the excitement he saw developing in his infant as a response to contingency games.

Initiating Social Interactions at the Level of Bouts

Jones and Moss in our laboratory (1971) have reported that infants in the awake-active state tend to babble much more when they are by themselves than when the mother is present. The mother who hears these episodes of noncrying vocalizations, even though busy, often cannot resist the appeal, and comes to the infant to enter into the game. The infant's babbling thus may come to serve as a discriminative stimulus for a reciprocal "game." In such instances the infant often discontinues the babbling and shifts into a reciprocal relation in which the mother vocalizes or touches, and the infant responds by smiling and vocalizing.

Often, a sitting infant gurgles and smiles when a mother passes on her way to do a household chore, thus inveigling her into interaction. One of the infants in our studies could emit a special noncrying vocalization which was quite effective in bringing the mother in from the kitchen to start an interaction. One other way in which bouts of interaction are started during these early months is by the infant remaining quiet for a longer time than the mother would ordinarily expect, after awakening. The infant may simply be quiet and attentive, and not even moving. This brings the mother, and the interaction bout ensues.

Maintaining the Social Interaction System

The Role of Attachment Both the difficulties and the advantages of attempting a distinction between caregiving and social interaction are illustrated by application of Bowlby's (1969) theory of attachment in the present context. The signal aspects of the infant's repertoire (crying, smiling, babbling, and vocalization) and the executive aspects of behavior (clinging, approach, and following) create and maintain the proximity that is essential to caregiving. Also, without proximity, one cannot have a social interaction system. The shortcoming of the theory of attachment that Bowlby has developed is that it does not speak sufficiently to the social interaction that is the key to socialization. Proximity is necessary but not sufficient.

Smiling and vocalization are not only signals for promoting and maintaining attachment but are also responses that maintain mothers in the social interaction. In that they are partial equivalents of what the mother herself is doing, they are precursors of what will prove to be very engaging for the mother in later development—observational learning. The young child reproduces parts of what the model is doing, and then puts the components together in fascinating new combinations. The young are able to play with these components, as Bruner (1972) has pointed out. The mother can be maintained in the social interaction by watching this play, as well as by being played with.

Bruner (1972) also adds that a special quality in the responsiveness of the young is a positive reac-

tion to novelty when in a secure setting. This facilitates the mother's play. She can try very ridiculous things and is often rewarded with a laugh or smile.

If we follow Cairns' (1967) position, behavior that has saliency (and the infant's behavior certainly seems to have saliency for parents) can maintain social interaction systems. Gewirtz (1961) has made room in his theories for the possibility that maternal behaviors may be unlearned reinforcers. By the same token, some infant behaviors could be reasonably considered unlearned reinforcers for maternal behavior.

Successive Production of Novel Responses Each of the infant's responses may have an inherent value in triggering specific parental behavior. Cutting across all this specificity is the feature of novelty. The infant continually shows new behaviors which excite and interest the parent, as Gewirtz, (1961) pointed out long ago. If the mother is attentive to the infant during the first 3 weeks, she may notice a strange little smile appearing in some phases of sleep and she may see that some noises she makes while the infant is asleep produce this smile. Later this smile appears when the infant is open-eyed, immediately after a feeding period. Toward the end of the third week, the smile may appear in response to her voice more than to the other sounds. During this same 3-week period, she sees changes in attentive behavior. She sees that the infant quiets and looks bright-eyed when attending. She sees an increase in general activity and thrashing about in connection with attentive behavior.

In the fourth and fifth weeks she is treated to a continuing kaleidoscope of novelty. She is suddenly aware that her baby focuses on her face, that they have eye-to-eye contact, that her face is beginning to register more than some other stimuli, and that some smiles appear when she moves her head. Between the fifth and seventh weeks, she sees fewer mouth and head movements, sees much more smiling, and is delighted to hear soft cooing vocalizations accompanying the infant's periods of attention. The rapid succession of these novel behaviors makes more than a contribution to attachment. The novelty could very well contribute to the positive quality of the interaction and thus play a role in maintaining a social system.

Changes during the first few weeks have been described in detail. It is easy to imagine the impact of many other changes manifested by the infant, such as the beginning of capability for manipulating objects, the replacement of indiscriminate reaching with reaching toward the most salient object, sitting up, inhibition of reaching toward unfamiliar objects, crawling, and then standing. The toddler finally moves beyond a "stilt" walk, and then begins to emit words. The early preschooler utters sentences.

Again we need not be concerned in the present context about the earliest origins of these behaviors. The important point is that at certain points in time new behaviors emerge, and these have an impact, however maturational processes may interact with the mother's caregiving and stimulation. The average mother cannot help but be affected by these changes. The mother who essentially maintains a caregiving system may not know much about the infant, and what has been shown during the last week or so, when one asks her to report. The mother who functions both as a caregiver and as a partner in social interaction is likely to be more aware of the novel behaviors showing up in each period.

Behaviors Showing Developmental Progress That novelty itself is not enough can be clearly seen in the fact that periods of reorganization and regression in young children are very disturbing to parents. To understand why temporary setbacks are upsetting to parents, it is well to keep in mind that most of the novel changes that have been mentioned above are changes in the direction of increasingly adultlike behavior. There are oddities along the way, but generally the infant or young child continually moves in the general direction of being more like the adult and less like the strange and enigmatic physiological being with whom the parents were first confronted in the neonatal period.

Behaviors Showing Modifiability It seems likely that the kaleidoscopic movement toward more and more adultlike behaviors would in itself have a considerable supportive function, even if there were no indication that the infant's behavior is responsive to maternal behavior. However, it is clear that the infant has some basic ways of telling the mother that what she does matters. It has been mentioned earlier that responsiveness itself has a supportive role to play in the interaction. Then there is the next level of modifiability—learning. To

achieve a satisfactory criterion of conditioning, Papousek (1967 a, b) found it necessary to use 177 trials when conditioning was started within the newborn period, but used only 42 when starting in the third month and 28 when starting in the fifth month. Thus if a mother behaved in such a way as to incorporate the basic elements of Papousek's procedure, she might feel by the fourth month that she could have some effect on the infant beyond mere responsiveness or distraction. If the mother persisted as long as scientists who have conditioned social responses (Brackbill, 1958; Rheingold, Gewirtz, & Ross, 1959; Weisberg, 1963), she might see that the infant's smiling or vocalization was coming under her control. In the months and early years to follow, she would see observational learning in motor behavior, and then reproduction of partial speech forms. Finally, she would see a stage when her own verbal description of consequences could alter a child's behavior so that a trial and error process was not necessary for the child. All in all, under this heading the infant's contribution to maintaining the social interaction lies in the fact that responsiveness and modifiability are shown.

Altering the Basis for Social Interaction Birch and Lefford (1967, p. 110) have described the shift from response to tactile stimuli to visual stimuli in the first year. Studies of evoked potential on both human infants and lower animals (Ellingson, 1964) have shown that cortical response to tactile stimuli is relatively mature in earliest infancy, whereas response to auditory and visual stimuli becomes mature in form sometime later. During this same developmental period, several investigators who attended primarily to the nature of the mother-infant interaction (Lewis & Ban, 1971; Lusk & Lewis, 1972; Moss, 1967) noted a proximal-distal shift in infant behaviors, and recorded differences in maternal behavior that paralleled this shift. For both sexes, touching, a proximal behavior, decreases over age, and looking, the most distal behavior, increases. There are some sex differences which make this more complicated, but for the present purpose it is enough to note that the proximal-distal shift, whatever the origins, changes the basis for the social interaction process. In a sense the change in the infant's behavior places the relationship more on an adult basis. Interactions can occur at close range as well as at a distance.

The young child's behavior often makes a contribution to some further changes in development. To quote Maccoby and Masters (1970):

"The scraps of information that we do have point to a decline in proximity seeking, with attention seeking and approval seeking maintained at a constant level or increasing. There appears to be a shift in target from the mother and other adults to age-mates. With respect to these changes one is struck by the parallel with human primates, in whom infant play and other social contacts with age-mates take more and more of the infant's time, while occasions where the infant flees to the mother for comfort and protection decline in frequency, and the amount of time simply spent staying near the mother becomes progressively less [p. 145]."

Terminating Social Interaction Bouts

The supine and sitting infant can terminate a bout by fussing, becoming irritable, and turning its head away, or by simply falling asleep. In Papousek's studies (1967a,b) which have already been mentioned, infants subject to the conditioning procedure before the third month often showed distress. This distress was sufficiently effective to even terminate an experimental procedure (let alone a mother-infant interaction). The crawling infant can show any of the termination behaviors of the younger infants, as well as crawling away from the parent. The toddler and preschooler can also show any of the preceding but, in addition, has still more effective motor behaviors for terminating the interactions.

GENERAL PRINCIPLES

Emergent Child Behavior It is necessary to realize that each period of interaction is capable of altering the status of a child, so that during the subsequent period of interaction the child stimulates the parent in a different fashion, or reacts differently to parent behavior. This principle may be operative in the findings of Hartup (1958) and Baer (1962) that withholding positive reinforcement only increased dependency in children who were already highly dependent. Whatever conditions led to high dependency prior to the child's participation in the study altered the responsivity of the child to withdrawal of positive reinforcement. To pursue the implications of this principle, we should study parent-child interactions during one period, assess child behavior at some point when it appears stable toward the end of this phase, and then, during the next period, assess the effects on the parent of the child's way of functioning. I have not found any examples of research that have done this.

Homeostatic Model One very general principle about the behavior of the young is that they contribute too much or too little in the way of some behaviors, or show some behaviors too early or too late in terms of parent expectations (Bell, 1971). Briefly, it is assumed that each participant in a social or caregiving interaction has upper and lower limits relative to the intensity, frequency, or situational appropriateness of behavior shown by the other. When the upper limit for one participant is reached, that participant is likely to react in such a way as to redirect or reduce the excessive or inappropriate behavior (upper-limit control reaction). When the lower limit is reached, the reaction is to stimulate, prime, or in other ways to increase the insufficient or nonexistent behavior (lower-limit control reaction).

This homeostatic concept needs implementing propositions before it can lead to testable hypotheses. However, it has proved helpful in thinking about findings that have already been uncovered. For example, one of Beckwith's (1971) findings, from an observational study of mother-infant interaction in 7-month-old adopted infants, becomes meaningful when looked at from the homeostatic standpoint. Verbal discouragement was correlated .49 with infant Gesell scores, the only significant correlation found between measures of maternal speech and the Gesell. The explanation offered was that infants showing more locomotion and reaching out for objects, and thus scoring high on the Gesell, were more difficult to manage in a property-conscious home. Verbal discouragement was presumably one of the mother's upper-limit control techniques.

Maccoby and Masters (1970) have used a homeostatic concept in explaining data from Emmerich's (1964) longitudinal study in which it was found that an interesting developmental transformation occurred over a 2-year time in the preschool period. Previously interpersonally negative children became poised, while their previously interpersonally positive counterparts manifested social insecurity.

The explanation offered by Maccoby and Masters (1970) was

"Perhaps in anticipation of the child's entry into the more formal kindergarten setting, socializing agents at this time were putting pressure on the outgoing child to modulate his aggressiveness, while a simultaneous attempt is being made to influence a self-contained child to become more outgoing [p. 99]."

The Nature of Control It is evident that one of the individuals in the parent-child socialization system is much more mature than the other, and more closely approximates the adult patterns of the culture. This feature of course led to the first oversimplification of socialization research, namely, the model of an agent of socialization acting upon a malleable and unformed infant. In counteracting this earlier simplification in the history of our research, it is easy to become attracted to another simplification, that the infant and young child socialize the parents. The controls involved are far too complicated to make it likely that this other oversimplification will lead to any better understanding of the interaction system.

First of all, what are the implications of the inequality of maturity for control exerted by the infant or child on the parent? The inequality does not preclude the existence of a reciprocal relation. As Skinner (1971) has pointed out, there is even a reciprocal relation between the physicist and the subatomic particles whose behavior the experiment is designed to control. The experimenter's behavior is shaped and controlled by the nature of the particles.

It should also be considered that an individual who starts an interaction by that very fact is exercising control over the other. The other has to react on the initiator's behavioral "home ground," so to speak. Thus, when we realize that an infant or young child starts approximately 50% of the interactions (Bell, 1971), we must consider that a substantial degree of control is exerted thereby over the parent, even if it is not exerted in any other way. In this respect there is a type of balance in the relationship, which fits neither the notion of the parents socializing the young in a unidirectional fashion, or the opposite, that the young socialize adults so that they become parents.

There is also a type of balance in control due to the fact that the infant selectively reinforces parent behavior, thus modifying socialization efforts. Also, the fact that the infant or young child is more competent in one sense than the young, inexperienced parent, offsets the greater maturity of parent. The neonate is very competent in bringing the parent to the general area, and in producing desired behavior. It has a set of behaviors which are highly effective in bringing about support, protection, and maintenance of optimal states. In other words, competence in controlling the behavior of another so as to produce a certain outcome is different from maturity, which is the stage of movement toward adult forms of behavior in a culture.

At first, Skinner (1971) notes that the infant controls the parent without adjusting its own behavior to achieve certain consequences. Initially, only the parent's behavior is intentional. The parent acts so as to achieve certain consequences. (In many instances, however, as I have mentioned, the parent is simply functioning as an adult.) Parents in the socialization role are presumably guided by the norms and values of the culture in which they were reared, including the subculture defined by their own families. Even though there is increasing evidence of intentional behavior in the child by the second year of life, it is obvious that the intentional behavior of the parent covers a much longer span of time and involves much more general objectives.

In summary, then, the parent-child system is a reciprocal relation involving two or more individuals who differ greatly in maturity although not in competence, in terms of ability to affect each other. The relationship involves much more and longer-range intention on the part of one participant than on the part of the other. There is a certain balance of controls, in that the greater intentional behavior of the parent is offset by two features of the offspring's behavior: (1) the active short-range initiation of interactions, and (2) the organization of the behavior so that it is compelling and selectively reinforcing. Much of the modification of child behavior toward cultural norms occurs in the context of parental adjustments and accommodations to the initiations of the young.

SUMMARY

Pregnancy, the infant's physical appearance, the helpless thrashing movements, as well as the fact that the infant's sensory and motor system matches that of the mother, all contribute to launching caregiving, defined as the provision of life support and protection. As the behavior of the infant becomes increasingly organized, early items in a sequence become discriminative stimuli for maternal avoidance behavior, so that much of caregiving consists of preventing undesirable and unpleasant outcomes (an aversive system). Caregiving is maintained in part because infants provide interpretable cues to their conditions, define their own sensory and fatigue limits, and maintain their protest behavior within the limits of a caregiver's tolerance. Their progressively discriminating attention to the caregiver, and their proximity-maintaining behaviors, tend to induce a singular, one-to-one relationship with the caregiver, where this is possible.

Social interactions between the young and the parents involve the reciprocal exchange of behaviors with positive value, so that the contribution of the young lies not in providing signals to parents of aversive consequences that may develop. Infant behavior in this case generates appetitive parental behavior. The young contribute to social interactions by reducing the demand for caregiving (by being in states that favor mutual exchange), by being susceptible to manipulations of states, by being responsive in a very general sense, and by actively initiating social interactions.

Although the signal and executive behaviors of the young that maintain proximity are important to both caregiving and social interaction, they are not sufficient to maintain the latter. The infant's responses that have positive values for the parent, rather than those that are cues to avoid unpleasant outcomes, are the contribution of the young to social interaction. Examples are smiling and vocalization, partial reproduction of adult behaviors, playing at combinations and recombinations of these partials, successive and kaleidoscopic production of novel responses, showing developmental progress, and general modifiability of behavior. While playing their part in maintaining social interaction, the young also alter its basis, as seen in the shift from response to proximal versus distal stimuli in the first year. Increasing activity, and behaviors directed to the production of variety in stimulation, also alter the basis for social interaction. Peers can provide more activity and variety in stimulation than parents, as the young child's motor and communication capabilities make peer interaction possible.

Three general principles emerge from a consideration of the above contributions made by the young. In both caregiving and social interaction, the young change the general status of their behavior in one period of development so that their effects on parents in a subsequent period are different. Research strategies are needed that can detect these changing effects of emergent behavior. The origins of the emergent behavior are no more important than the changing effects. Another very general principle is that the behavior of the young falls between the extremes of quantitative excess or deficiency, or inappropriate timing relative to parent expectations. Excessive or premature behavior induces what is termed upper-limit parent controls that are intended to redirect or reduce behavior. Lower-limit parent controls occur in response to insufficient or delayed onset of behavior in the young. Extensions of this homeostatic model have proved helpful in explaining findings in the literature on socialization. Finally, reflection on the nature of controls exerted over parent behavior by the young leads to the thought that there may be a balance in controls due to the fact that the greater maturity and long-term intentional behavior of parents is offset by the sheer volume of interactions started by the young, by the compelling nature of these behaviors, and by the way they selectively reinforce parental behavior.

REFERENCES

Baer, D. M. A technique of social reinforcement for the study of child behavior: Behavior avoiding reinforcement withdrawal. *Child Development*, 1962, **33**, 847–858.

Beckwith, L. Relationships between attributes of mothers and their infants' I.Q. scores. *Child Development*, 1971, **42**, 1083–1097.

Bell, R. Q. A reinterpretation of the direction of effects in studies of socialization. *Psychological Review*, 1968, **75**, 81–95.

Bell, R. Q. Stimulus control of parent or caretaker behavior by offspring. *Developmental Psychology*, 1971, **4**, 63–72.

Bell, S. M., & Ainsworth, M. D. Infant crying and maternal responsiveness. *Child Development*, 1972, **43**, 1171–1190.

Bernal, J. Crying during the first ten days of life, and maternal responses. *Developmental Medicine and Child Neurology*, 1972, **14**, 362–372.

Berberich, J. P. Do the child's responses shape the

teaching behavior of adults? *Journal of Experimental Research in Personality,* 1971, **5,** 92–97.

Birch, H. E., & Lefford, A. Visual differentiation, intersensory integration, and voluntary motor control. *Monographs of the Society for Research in Child Development,* 1967, **32,** (2, Serial No. 110).

Bowlby, J. *Attachment and loss.* Vol. 1. New York: Basic Books, 1969.

Brackbill, Y. Extinction of the smiling response in infants as a function of reinforcement schedule. *Child Development,* 1958, **29,** 115–124.

Brazelton, T. Observations of the neonate. *Journal of the American Academy of Child Psychiatry,* 1962, **1,** 38–58.

Bridger, W., & Birns, B. Neonates' behavior and autonomic responses to stress during soothing. *Recent Advances in Biological Psychiatry,* 1963, **5,** 1–6.

Brooks, V., & Hochberg, J. A psychophysical study of "cuteness." *Perceptual and Motor Skills,* 1960, **11,** 205.

Bruner, J. S. Nature and uses of immaturity. *American Psychologist,* 1972, **27,** 687–708.

Cairns, R. B. The attachment behavior of mammals. *Psychological Review,* 1967, **73,** 406–426.

Eisenberg, R. B. The development of hearing in man: An assessment of current status. *Asha,* 1970, **12** (3), 119–123.

Ellingson, R. J. Cerebral electrical responses to auditory and visual stimuli in the infant (human and subhuman studies). In P. Kellaway and I. Petersen (Eds.), *Neurological and electroencephalographic correlative studies in infancy.* New York: Grune and Stratton, 1964. Pp. 78–116.

Emmerich, W. Continuity and stability in early social development. *Child Development,* 1964, **35,** 311–332.

Escalona, S. *The roots of individuality.* Chicago: Aldine, 1968.

Gewirtz, J. L. A learning analysis of the effects of normal stimulation, privation and deprivation on the acquisition of social motivation and attachment. In B. M. Foss (Ed.), *Determinants of infant behavior.* New York: Wiley, 1961. Pp. 213–290.

Gil, D. G. *Violence against children.* Cambridge, Mass.: Harvard University Press, 1970.

Harper, L. V. Ontogenetic and phylogenetic functions of the parent-offspring relationship in mammals. *Advances in the Study of Behavior,* 1970, **3,** 75–117.

Harper, L. V. Effects of the parent-offspring relationship upon the parent. Unpublished manuscript, 1972, Department of Applied Behavioral Sciences, University of California, Davis.

Hartup, W. W. Nurturance and nurturance-withdrawal in relation to the dependency behavior of preschool children. *Child Development,* 1958, **29,** 191–201.

Hayes, C. *The ape in our house.* New York: Harper, 1951.

Hersher, L., Richmond, J. B. & Moore, A. U. Modifiability of the critical period for the development of mater-

nal behavior in sheep and goats. *Behaviour,* Leiden, 1963, **20,** 311–320.

Hilton, I. Differences in the behavior of mothers toward first- and later-born children. *Journal of Personality and Social Psychology,* 1967, **7**(3), 282–290.

Jones, S. J., & Moss, H. A. Age, state, and maternal behavior associated with infant vocalizations. *Child Development,* 1971, **42,** 1039–1051.

Kohlberg, L. Stage and sequence: The cognitive-developmental approach to socialization. In D. A. Goslin (Ed.), *Handbook of socialization theory and research.* Chicago: Rand McNally, 1969. Pp. 347–480.

Lewis, M., & Ban, P. Stability of attachment behavior: A transformational analysis. Paper presented at the meeting of the Society for Research in Child Development, Minneapolis, Minnesota, 1971.

Lusk, D., & Lewis, M. Mother-infant interaction and infant development among the Wolof of Senegal. *Human Development,* 1972, **15,** 58–69.

Maccoby, E., & Masters, J. C. Attachment and dependency. In P. H. Mussen (Ed.), *Carmichael's manual of child psychology.* (3rd ed.) New York: Wiley, 1970, Pp. 73–158.

Moss, H. A. Sex, age, and state as determinants of mother-infant interaction. *Merrill-Palmer Quarterly,* 1967, **13,** 19–36.

Mussen, P. H. (Ed.) *Carmichael's manual of child psychology.* (3rd ed.) New York: Wiley, 1970.

Osofsky, J. D., & O'Connell, E. J. Parent-child interaction: Daughters' effects upon mothers' and fathers' behaviors. *Developmental Psychology,* 1972, **7,** 157–168.

Papousek, H. Experimental studies of appetitional behavior in human newborns and infants. In H. W. Stevenson, E. H. Hess, & H. L. Rheingold (Eds.), *Early behavior: Comparative and developmental approaches.* New York: Wiley, 1967. (a)

Papousek, H. Conditioning during early postnatal development. In Y. Brackbill & G. G. Thompson (Eds.), *Behavior in infancy and early childhood.* New York: Free Press, 1967. Pp. 259–274. (b)

Parmelee, A. H. Jr. Development of states in infants. In C. Clemente, D. Purpura, & F. Mayer (Eds.), *Maturation of brain mechanisms related to sleep behavior.* New York: Academic Press, 1972. Pp. 199–228.

Rheingold, H. L., Gewirtz, J. L., & Ross, H. W. Social conditioning of vocalizations in the infant. *Journal of Comparative and Physiological Psychology,* 1959, **52,** 68–73.

Richards, M. P. Social interaction in the first weeks of human life. *Psychiatria, Neurologia, Neurochirurgia,* 1971, **74,** 35–42.

Robson, K. S., & Moss, H. A. Patterns and determinants of maternal attachment. *Journal of Pediatrics,* 1970, **77,** 976–985.

Rosenblatt, J. S. The development of maternal responsiveness in the rat. *American Journal of Orthopsychiatry,* 1969, **39,** 36–56.

Ryder, R. G. The relationship between having a child and changes in reported "marriage satisfaction." *Journal of Marriage and the Family,* 1973, in press.

Siegel, G. M. Adult verbal behavior with retarded children labeled as "high" or "low" in verbal ability. *American Journal of Mental Deficiency,* 1963, **68** (3), 417–424.

Skinner, B. F. *Beyond freedom and dignity.* New York: Knopf, 1971.

Tinbergen, N. *The study of instinct.* London: Oxford, 1951.

Walters, R. H., & Parke, R. D. *The role of the distance receptors in the development of social responsiveness.* In L. P. Lipsitt and C. C. Spiker (Eds.), *Advances in Child Development and Behavior,* Vol. 2. New York: Academic Press, 1965. Pp. 59–96.

Watson, J. S. The development and generalization of "contingency awareness" in early infancy: Some hypotheses. *Merrill-Palmer Quarterly of Behavior and Development,* 1966, **12,** 123–135.

Weisberg, P. Social and nonsocial conditioning of infant vocalizations. *Child Development,* 1963, **34,** 377–388.

Wolff, P. H. *The causes, controls, and organization of behavior in the neonate.* New York: International Universities Press, 1966.

Reading 32

Father-Infant Interaction in the Newborn Period: A Re-evaluation of Some Current Myths

Ross D. Parke
Douglas B. Sawin

In spite of the theoretical interest and research activity in the area of mother-infant interaction, the role of the father in infancy remains relatively unexplored. Although the father is often recognized in theoretical discussions as playing an important role in the child's development, it is generally assumed that his role begins to take on importance only in late infancy and early childhood. This theoretical assumption is combined with the fact that fathers are also assigned a secondary position by both the culture as well as by psychology theorists. There are a number of strands of evidence that have maintained this view.

1 Cultural
2 Historical
3 Animal evidence
4 Hormonal evidence

CULTURAL

In Western, industrialized society there has been a clear set of roles prescribed for males and females, with child care being assigned almost exclusively to

*Paper presented as part of a symposium, "Fathers and Infants," at the American Psychological Association, Chicago, September 1, 1975.

the mother. In fact, as Josselyn (1956) has noted, it is even considered inappropriate in our culture for fathers to be nurturant toward their infants. Nor is the attitude restricted to our own culture: an examination of other cultures suggests a similar demarcation of roles with the mother nearly always being the primary caretaker. In part, this was due to the assumption that the feeding context was critical for adequate development of social responsiveness.

HISTORICAL

In addition to cross-cultural comparisons, historical roles have been examined with the same result. Over a wide span of history and across a large variety of economies, the father has played a minor role in the care of infants and children.

ANIMAL COMPARISONS

In addition to cultural and historical sources, evidence from the organization and behavior of animals has been examined, in part, to determine the extent to which these role allocations are prevalent among animals. Typically cited are studies of non-human primates either in captivity or in the wild. For example, DeVore (1963) found that the cynocephalus baboons take little interest in infants and play a protective role for the troupe as a whole. Few instances of either play or caretaking were observed.

Lab studies often present a similar picture. In a study from Harlow's lab, a 20–40 day old infant was introduced to male-female pairs of preadolescent monkeys. Again, the males played a lesser role: females were 4 times as likely to express nurturant behavior to an infant while the male was 10 times as hostile.

HORMONAL BASES OF "CARETAKING BEHAVIOR"

Although there is little information at the human level, there is considerable evidence that "caretaking behavior" is to some extent under hormonal control. Studies with rats (Rosenblatt & Moltz) have demonstrated that virgin females treated with female hormones show maternal behavior more rapidly. In short, the hormones associated with pregnancy and parturition "prime" the female to engage in caretaking activities.

On the basis of this kind of evidence a series of "myths" about fathers and their role in relation to the young infant has emerged. Let me list a few of the "father myths."

MYTHS

1 Fathers are uninterested in and uninvolved with newborn infants.
2 Fathers are less nurturant toward infants than mothers.
3 Fathers prefer non-caretaking roles and leave the caretaking up to mother.
4 Fathers are less competent than mothers to care for newborn infants.

To examine the validity of the propositions, let us take two approaches. First, let us point out the exceptions and qualifications surrounding the cultural, historical, animal and hormonal arguments. Secondly, and more importantly, let me briefly review some of the recent research evidence from our laboratory concerning the father's role in the newborn period.

First, there are cultures in which males and females play a more equal role in the care of young children. For example, among the Trobrianders of Melanesia the father has considerable share in the care of young children—feeding them, carrying them, and caretaking them.

Second, the historical argument is usually misused, because it implies an inevitability that role relations are biased by prior arrangements. Moreover, the argument ignores secular trends that reflect shifts in technological and economic spheres which are supporting the possibilities of new roles for males and females. As students of socialization it is important to consistently monitor shifts in the larger social and economic structure may, in turn, affect the definition and allocation of sex roles. In our preoccupation with the research for general laws, too often we have ignored the tenuousness of our findings in light of shifts in social, economic and possibly medical practices.

To cite a single example, consider the impact of bottle feeding; by a single stroke, fathers were able to overcome a biological difference which limited their participation in caretaking of young infants.

In a similar vein, research evidence can often affect historical trends. For example, Harlow—a notorious advocate of traditional sex typed roles—is, in part, responsible for the recent interest in fathers by his demonstrations that "contact comfort" was probably more important than the feeding situation for social development. Even without the invention of bottle feeding, fathers were suddenly put in a position where they were just as capable as mothers of providing the important ingredients for proper early development. Harlow, to date, has not commented on his apparently inadvertent contribution to the women's liberation movement.

Closely related to this issue is the old distinction within psychology that needs to be brought to bear on the present context, namely the competence/performance distinction. Too often the fact of low father involvement throughout history in the caretaking of children has been extended to the conclusion that the low involvement indicated low competence. However, the fact that historical, social and economic arrangements meant that fathers were allocated to other roles *need not necessarily imply that they are incapable of assuming a caretaking function.*

In fact, recent animal evidence has demonstrated that males can assume a parental role vis-à-vis infants. As Mitchell, Redican & Gomber (1974) point out: "While adult male rhesus monkeys rarely display parental behavior in the wild, they are certainly capable of doing so when given the opportunity in the laboratory" (pg. 8).

Nor can the hormonal evidence remain unqualified. As Maccoby & Jacklin (1974) recently concluded, "the hormones associated with pregnancy, childbirth and lactation are not necessary for the appearance of parental behavior. With sufficient exposure to newborns, virgin females and males will show parental behavior—although the behavior is not so readily aroused as it is in a female that has been hormonally primed" (p. 219). In short, hormones help, but are not necessary for the arousal or maintenance of parental responsivity.

In light of this evidence, it will come as little surprise that most of the "myths" are just that. Let us take each myth in turn.

Myth 1 Fathers are uninterested and uninvolved with newborn infants. *Evidence:* To evaluate this proposition, an observational study was conducted involving the mother-father-infant triad. Observations took place in the mother's hospital room between 6 and 48 hours after delivery. The sample was white, middle-class and well educated. All fathers but one were present at labor and delivery. About half of the couples attended Lamaze classes. All were first born. The procedure was as follows: the child was brought to the mother's room and the parents were asked, "Whom shall I give the baby to?" This permitted an evaluation of who held the baby first and for how long. The family was observed for 10 minutes and a time sampling observational procedure was used. The 10-minute period was divided into 40 15-second intervals and for each interval, the observer recorded the occurrence of the following infant or parent behaviors. For the infant: cry, vocalize, move, mouth movements with or without object, look at mother, father, around. For the parents: looks, smiles, vocalizes, hold, kiss, touch, imitate, explore, feed, hand over to other parent.

First, the results indicated that fathers were just as involved as mothers and the mothers and fathers did not differ on the majority of measures. In fact, fathers tended to hold the infant more than mothers and rock the infant in their arms more than mothers. Fathers, in short, in a context where it is *unnecessary* to participate are just as involved as the mother in interaction with their infants.

However, there is a variety of questions that could be raised about this study. First, the context is unique since the mother and father were together and possibly the high degree of father-infant interaction observed in the initial study was due to the supporting presence of the mother. Therefore, in the next study, the father was observed alone with the newborn as well as with the mother.

Moreover, the sample of fathers in the original study were unique in other ways that may have contributed to their high degree of interaction with their infant. Over half of the fathers had attended Lamaze childbirth classes and with one exception, all fathers were present during the delivery of the child. Both of these factors are likely to have increased the fathers' later involvement with their infants.

Finally, these fathers were well educated and middle class, and their high degree of involvement may be unique to middle-class groups; parental involvement may be less in lower-class samples due to a more rigid definition of parental roles among lower-class parents. To overcome the sample limitations of the original study, a group of lower-class fathers who neither participated in childbirth classes nor were present during delivery were observed. This study permitted a much more stringent test of father-infant involvement and permitted wider generalization of the previous findings. Little support is available for Myth #1.

But possibly fathers are less nurturant than mothers—Myth 2. A close look at the types of activities that mothers and fathers engaged in provides little support for this argument. Fathers were just as nurturant as mothers. In a first study, they touched, looked, vocalized, and kissed their newborn offspring just as often as did mothers. In a second study, an even more striking picture emerged—with the father exhibiting more nurturant behavior in the triadic context than the mother and an equal amont when alone with the baby.

There was a single nurturant behavior—smiling—in which the mother surpassed the father—in both studies.

The triadic context, however, did affect the rate of smiling: both mothers and fathers smiled more at the baby when a spouse was present than absent.

Two myths down, two to go. Myth #3 states that fathers play a less active role in caretaking activities than mothers. In both studies, the parents were free to feed the baby, but were not requested to do so. In the first study, mothers did feed more than fathers—but with 13 of 19 families breast feeding, this is no great surprise. A more legitimate comparison comes from our second study in which all babies were bottle fed. While fathers were more likely to feed than mother when both parents were present, fathers fed significantly *less* than mothers when they were alone with the baby.

Additional evidence comes from a more recent study, which provides a more detailed examination of early parent-infant interaction in a specific context—feeding. Instead of a time-sampling procedure, behaviors were recorded in sequence along a continuous time line. For this purpose, a Datamyte keyboard was used, which is a 10-key device permitting behaviors which have been assigned numerical values to be punched into the system. The keys are tone-related and record the auditory pattern on a cassette tape; in turn, this produces a printout of numerical values (*i.e.,* behaviors) in their order of occurrence and their time of occurrence.

This permits the following types of data: (1) frequency of occurrence of each parent and infant behavior; (2) duration of each parent and infant behavior; (3) the average duration of each parent and infant behavior; (4) a set of rules have been developed which define contingent sequences of interaction between the infant and his caretaker. Two sets of sequences are derived from the interaction data: (a) infant-elicited parent behavior, whereby the probability of occurrence of various parental behaviors are determined in response to an infant-signal (*e.g.,* crying, moving, sucking, etc.); (b) parent-elicited infant behavior whereby the probability of occurrence of various infant behavior is determined in response to a parental stimulus input (touch, rock, vocalize, etc.).

Again, mothers spend more time engaged in caretaking activities, such as burping, wiping the babies face, checking and changing diapers and grooming activities than fathers.

In summary, Myth 3 is not completely invalid; mothers do spend more time engaged in feeding and related caretaking activities than fathers in the newborn period.

The correlated Myth #4, however, needs to be explored as well. This myth states that fathers are less competent than mothers to care for newborn infants. How do we measure "competence?" A variety of approaches is possible, but one approach is to measure the parent's sensitivity to infant cues in the feeding context. Success in caretaking, to a large degree, is dependent on the parent's ability to

correctly "read" or interpret the infant's behavior so that their own behavior can be regulated in order to achieve some interaction goal. To illustrate, in the feeding context, the aim of the parent is to facilitate the food intake of the infant; the infant, in turn, by a variety of behaviors, such as sucking, burping, coughing, provides the caretaker with feedback concerning the effectiveness and ineffectiveness of their current behavior in maintaining the food intake process. In this context, one approach to the competence issue involves an examination of the degree to which the caretaker modifies his/her behavior in response to a set of infant cues.

Let me briefly describe how this was measured. We asked what changes in probability of a particular parental behavior occurred in the 10-second interval following an infant behavior. In other words, if an infant emits behavior, what happens in the next 10-second interval in terms of the parent's behavior.

A brief methodological note is in order. Since behaviors occur with different frequencies throughout an interaction session it is necessary to determine the unconditional or baseline probabilities of the occurrence of the target parent behavior. To do this, the probability that a parent behavior occurred in each of the sixty 10-second intervals of the interaction session was calculated. If there are no sequential dependencies of any behavior with the infant trigger variable, we would expect the behaviors to follow the infant trigger in proportion to their unconditional occurrence in the total data set.

To illustrate how this system works, consider the following example. A powerful infant signal in the feeding context is an auditory distress signal, such as a cough, spit up, or sneeze. The main reaction of parents to this signal is, quite sensibly, to stop feeding and the parent does this with a conditional probability .33. However the unconditional probability of this parent behavior—stop feed—occuring is quite low (.05). Similarly, parents vocalize with an unconditional probability of .27, but vocalize with a probability of .45 when the infant sneezes, spits up, or coughs. In addition, the parent unconditional probability of looking closely is .12, which doubles to .25 whenever the infant spits or coughs. Touching, on the other hand, is inhibited slightly by this type of infant signal. Mothers and fathers differ but only slightly: mothers have a probability of stopping their feeding activity of (.27) while fathers cease feeding with a high probability (.35). Similarly, mothers look more closely (.28) than do fathers (.21) in this feeding context. Finally, touching is dramatically reduced for fathers, (.03) from a baseline probability of .12 while mothers increase their touching slightly to .14.

There are sex of parent × sex of infant interactions as well. Mothers are more likely to stop feeding a boy (.40) than a girl (.23) when the infant spits up or coughs. Second, mothers touch a boy (.23) to a much greater extent than girls (.02) in response to this type of signal. Similarly, she is more likely to vocalize to a girl (.48 for conditional probability *vs.* baseline probability of .23) than a boy (.40 for conditional *vs.* .27 for baseline). The importance of this approach becomes clear by comparing these results with the previously noted patterns yielded by both the frequency and duration of lesser involvement of the father in the feeding context—either in terms of time spent in this task or in terms of the extent to which paternal behavior was significantly related to feeding related infant cues. However, these conditional probability results suggest a corrective to this earlier pattern. Although he may spend less time overall, *he is as sensitive as the mother to infant cues in the feeding context.* Moreover, the amount of milk consumed by the infants with their mothers and fathers was very similar (1.3 oz. *vs.* 1.2 of mothers and fathers respectively). By further adjusting, for the difference in amount of time engaged in feeding the mothers and fathers amount is nearly identical. In short, fathers and mothers are not only similar in their sensitivity, but also strikingly similar in the amount of milk that they succeed in feeding the baby.

In terms of our fourth myth, then, our data indicate that fathers are competent in caretaking as indexed by our sensitivity and feeding induces.

Overall, our data indicate that:

a fathers are interested in newborns and if provided with the opportunity, do become involved;

b are just as nurturant in their interactions with newborns as mothers;

c apparently do engage in less caretaking, but;

d are capable and competent to execute at least some caretaking activities.

Before leaving our data, however, let me point out that there are qualitative differences between mothers and fathers that emerge from an examination of the sex and ordinal position of the infant. Moreover, some of the differences are clearly consistent with cultural stereotypes concerning parent preferences and especially father preferences. Let me cite one example to illustrate the necessity for qualification of these general patterns. In one of our studies (Parke & O'Leary, 1975), we found that fathers touched first born boys more than either later born boys or girls of either ordinal position. Fathers vocalized more to first born boys than first born girls, while they vocalized equally to later born infants irrespective of their sex. A similar finding has emerged from our sequential analyses of the impact of infant vocalizations on parent behavior. Fathers are particularly likely to react to this infant cue by vocalizing—but especially in the case of the male infant. Clearly there may be some bases to the claim that fathers really do prefer boys—especially first born boys. These data are consistent with Pedersen's (1975) recent finding that variations in father behavior were related to the behavior of male three-month-old infants—but there was no relationship for fathering and female infants. Caution must be exercised in generalizing from these data since all observations were made in the newborn period. Moreover, there is little doubt that father's role and involvement shifts with age of the infant. However, in view of the assumption that involvement typically comes later in the infant's development, our data take on increased corrective significane. Observational data on the father-infant interaction in the home is currently being collected in order to determine whether or not the amount and/or patterns of father-infant interaction during the newborn period are of predictive value for later behavior.

However, the newborn period need not be viewed as simply a starting point for observation, but as a potentially important intervention point as well. For fathers, in spite of their interest and competence, clearly need support—just as mothers need support. Moreover, it is assumed that paternal behavior can be modified, both quantitatively and qualitatively by early intervention. As Klaus, Leiderman, and others have shown, mothers who are given extended contact with their infants over the first three post-delivery days were more stimulating later at one month and even one year. In light of this demonstration, it is probably important to provide this opportunity for fathers as well, if their nurturant and caretaking capacities are to be fully actualized in post-hospital contexts.

In fact, there is recent evidence from Sweden (Lind, 1974) that fathers who were provided the opportunity to learn and practice basic caretaking skills during the post-partum hospital period were more involved with their infants at six months.

The next task is to provide cultural supports for these potential activities—by modifying hospital visiting arrangements, providing paternity leaves, making available training classes so that fathers will have the opportunity to both learn and practice caretaking skills which in turn will not only make it more likely that he will share these responsibilities, but that he will execute these tasks effectively and view these behaviors as role consistent.

The slaying of myths should be viewed as only a first step; the important task of specifying the changes in father-infant interaction and involvement and indicating how these shifts will affect both the mother and the infant remains to be undertaken. In conclusion, it seems that Margaret Mead's famous dictum that "fathers are a biological necessity, but a social accident" is no longer valid.

REFERENCES

Biller, H. B. *Father, child and sex role.* Lexington, Mass.: D. C. Heath, 1971.

Chamove, A., Harlow, H. F., & Mitchell, G. D. Sex differences in the infant-directed behavior of preadolescent rhesus monkeys. *Child Development,* 1967, *38,* 329–335.

DeVore, I. Mother-infant relations in free ranging baboons. In H. L. Rheingold (Ed.), *Maternal behavior in mammals.* New York: Wiley, 1963.

Harlow, H. F. The nature of love. *American Psychologist,* 1958, *13,* 673–685.

Josselyn, I. M. Cultural forces, motherliness, and fatherliness. *American Journal of Orthopsychiatry,* 1956, *26,* 264–271.

Lind, R. Observations after delivery of communications between mother-infant-father. Paper presented at the International Congress of Pediatrics. Buenos Aires, October, 1974.

Lynn, D. B. *The father: His role in child development.* Monterey: Brooks Cole, 1974.

Maccoby, E. E., & Jacklin, C. N. *The psychology of sex differences.* Stanford: Stanford University Press, 1974.

Mitchell, G. D. Paternalistic behavior in primates. *Psychological Bulletin,* 1969, *71,* 399–417.

Mitchell, G. D., Redican, W. K., & Gomber, J. Males can raise babies. *Psychology Today,* 1974, *7,* 63–67.

Moltz, H., Lubin, M., Leon, M., & Numan, M. Hormonal induction of maternal behavior in the overiectomized rat. *Physiology and Behavior,* 1970, *5,* 1373–1377.

Parke, R. D., & O'Leary, S. E. Father-mother-infant interaction in the newborn period: Some findings, some observations and some unresolved issues. In K. Riegel & J. Meacham (Eds.), *The developing individual in a changing world, Vol. II, Social and environmental issues.* The Hague: Mouton, 1975.

Parke, R. D., O'Leary, S. E., & West, S. Mother-father-newborn interaction: Effects of maternal medication, labor and sex of infant. *Proceedings of the American Psychological Association,* 1972, 85–86.

Parke, R. D., & Sawin, D. B. Infant characteristics and behavior as elicitors of maternal and paternal responsibility in the newborn period. Paper presented at the Biannual meeting of the Society for Research in Child Development, Denver, April, 1975.

Pedersen, F. A. Mother, father and infant as an interactive system. Paper presented at the Annual Convention of the American Psychological Association, Chicago, September, 1975.

Rosenblatt, J. S. The development of maternal responsiveness in the rat. *American Journal of Orthopsychiatry,* 1969, *39,* 36–56.

Stephens, H. N. *The family in cross-cultural perspective.* New York: Holt, Rinehart, & Winston, 1963.

Reading 33

Socialization and Instrumental Competence in Young Children

Diana Baumrind

For the past 10 years I have been studying parent-child relations, focusing upon the effects of parental authority on the behavior of preschool children. In three separate but related studies, data on children were obtained from three months of observation in the nursery school and in a special testing situation; data on parents were obtained during two home observations, followed by an interview with each parent.

In the first study, three groups of nursery school children were identified in order that the child-rearing practices of their parents could be contrasted. The findings of that study (Baumrind, 1967) can be summarized as follows:

1 Parents of the children who were the most self-reliant, self-controlled, explorative, and content were themselves controlling and demanding; but they were also warm, rational, and receptive to the child's communication. This unique combination of high control and positive encouragement of the child's autonomous and independent strivings can be called *authoritative* parental behavior.

2 Parents of children who, relative to the others, were discontent, withdrawn, and distrustful, were themselves detached and controlling, and somewhat less warm than other parents. These may be called *authoritarian* parents.

3 Parents, of the least self-reliant, explorative, and self-controlled children were themselves non-controlling, nondemanding, and relatively warm. These can be called *permissive* parents.

A second study, of an additional 95 nursery school children and their parents, also supported the position that "authoritative control can achieve responsible conformity with group standards without loss of individual autonomy or self-assertiveness" (Baumrind, 1966, p. 905). In a third investigation (Baumrind, 1971), patterns of parental authority were defined so that they would differ from each other as did the authoritarian, authoritative, and permissive combinations which emerged from the first study.

PATTERNS OF PARENTAL AUTHORITY

Each of these three authority patterns is described in detail below, followed by the subpatterns that have emerged empirically from the most recent study. The capitalized items refer to specific clusters obtained in the analysis of the parent behavior ratings.

The *authoritarian* parent[1] attempts:

to shape, control and evaluate the behavior and attitudes of the child in accordance with a set of standard of conduct, usually an absolute standard, theologically motivated and formulated by a higher authority. She values obedience as a virtue and favors punitive, forceful measures to curb self-will at points where the child's actions or beliefs conflict with what she thinks is right conduct. She believes in inculcating such instrumental values as respect for authority, respect for work, and respect for the preservation of order and traditional structure. She does not encourage verbal give and take, believing that the child should accept her word for what is right (Baumrind, 1968, p. 261).

Two subpatterns in our newest study correspond to this description; they differ only in the degree of acceptance shown the child. One subpattern identifies families who were Authoritarian but Not Rejecting. They were high in Firm Enforcement, low in Encourages Independence and Individuality, low in Passive-Acceptance, and low in Promotes Nonconformity. The second subpattern contained families who met all the criteria for the first subpattern except that they scored high on the cluster called Rejecting.

The *authoritative* parent, by contrast with the above, attempts:

---

[1] In order to avoid confusion, when I speak of the parent I will use the pronoun "she," and when I speak of the child, I will use the pronoun "he," although, unless otherwise specified, the statement applies to both sexes equally.

to direct the child's activities but in a rational issue-oriented manner. She encourages verbal give and take, and shares with the child the reasoning behind her policy. She values both expressive and instrumental attributes, both autonomous self-will and disciplined conformity. Therefore, she exerts firm control at points of parent-child divergence, but does not hem the child in with restrictions. She recognizes her own special rights as an adult, but also the child's individual interests and special ways. The authoritative parent affirms the child's present qualities, but also sets standards for future conduct. She uses reason as well as power to achieve her objectives. She does not base her decisions on group consensus or the individual child's desires; but also, does not regard herself as infallible, or divinely inspired (Baumrind, 1968, p. 261).

Two subpatterns corresponded to this description, differing only in the parents' attitudes towards normative values. One subpattern contained families who were Authoritative and Conforming. Like the Authoritarian parents described above, these parents had high scores in Passive-Acceptance. However, they also had high scores in Encouraging Independence and Individuality. The second subpattern contained parents who met the criteria for the first subpattern, but who also scored high in Promotes Nonconformity.

The *permissive* parent attempts:

to behave in a nonpunitive, acceptant and affirmative manner towards the child's impulses, desires, and actions. She consults with him about policy decisions and gives explanations for family rules. She makes few demands for household responsibility and orderly behavior. She presents herself to the child as a resource for him to use as he wishes, not as an active agent responsible for shaping or altering his ongoing or future behavior. She allows the child to regulate his own activities as much as possible, avoids the exercise of control, and does not encourage him to obey externally-defined standards. She attempts to use reason but not overt power to accomplish her ends (Baumrind, 1968, p. 256).

We were able to locate three subpatterns reflecting different facets of this prototypic permissiveness. One subpattern, called Nonconforming, typified families who were noncomforming but who were not extremely lax in discipline and who did

demand high performance in some areas. The second subpattern, called Permissive, contained families who were characterized by lax discipline and few demands, but who did not stress nonconformity. The third subpattern contained families who were both conforming and lax in their discipline and demands; hence, they are referred to as Permissive-Nonconforming.

INSTRUMENTAL COMPETENCE

Instrumental Competence refers to behavior which is socially responsible and independent. Behavior which is friendly rather than hostile to peers, cooperative rather than resistive with adults, achievement rather than nonachievement-oriented, dominant rather than submissive, and purposive rather than aimless, is here defined as instrumentally competent. Middle-class parents clearly value instrumentally competent behavior. When such parents were asked to rank those attributes that they valued and devalued in children, the most valued ones were assertiveness, friendliness, independence, and obedience, and those least valued were aggression, avoidance, and dependency (Emmerich & Smoller, 1964). Note that the positively valued attributes promote successful achievement in United States society and, in fact, probably have survival value for the individual in any subculture or society.

There are people who feel that, even in the United States, those qualities which define instrumental competence are losing their survival value in favor of qualities which may be called *Expressive Competence*. The author does not agree. Proponents of competence defined in terms of expressive, rather than instrumental, attributes, value feelings more than reason, good thoughts more than effective actions, "being" more than "doing" or "becoming," spontaneity more than planfulness, and relating intimately to others more than working effectively with others. At present, however, there is no evidence that emphasis on expressive competence, at the expense of instrumental competence, fits people to function effectively over the long run as members of any community. This is not to say that expressive competence is not essential for effective functioning in work as well as in love, and for both men and women. Man, like other animals, experiences and gains valid information about reality by means of both noncognitive and cognitive processes. Affectivity deepens man's knowledge of his environment; tenderness and receptivity enhance the character and effectiveness of any human being. But instrumental competence is and will continue to be an essential component of self-esteem and self-fulfillment.

One subdimension of instrumental competence, here designated *Responsible vs. Irresponsible,* pertains to the following three facets of behavior, each of which is related to the others:

(a) *Achievement-oriented vs. Nonachievement-oriented.* This attribute refers to the willingness to persevere when frustration is encountered, to set one's own goals high, and to meet the demands of others in a cognitive situation as opposed to withdrawal when faced with frustration and unwillingness to comply with the teaching or testing instructions of an examiner or teacher. Among older children, achievement-orientation becomes subject to autogenic motivation and is more closely related to measures of independence than to measures of social responsibility. But in the young child, measures of cognitive motivation are highly correlated with willingness to cooperate with adults, especially for boys. Thus, in my study, resistiveness towards adults was highly negatively correlated with achievement-oriented behavior in boys, but not for girls. Other investigators (Crandall, Orleans, Preston & Rabson, 1958; Haggard, 1969) have also found that compliance with adult values and demands characterizes young children who display high achievement efforts.

(b) *Friendly vs. Hostile Behavior Towards Peers.* This refers to nurturant, kind, altruistic behavior displayed toward agemates as opposed to bullying, insulting, selfish behavior.

(c) *Cooperative vs. Resistive Behavior Towards Adults.* This refers to trustworthy, responsible, facilitative behavior as opposed to devious, impetuous, obstructive actions.

A second dimension of child social behavior can be designated *Independent vs. Suggestible.* It pertains to the following three related facets of behavior:

(a) *Domineering vs. Tractable Behavior.* This attribute consists of bold, aggressive, demanding behavior as opposed to timid, nonintrusive, undemanding behavior.

(b) *Dominant vs. Submissive Behavior.* This category refers to individual initiative and leadership in contrast to suggestible, following behavior.

(c) *Purposive vs. Aimless Behavior.* This refers to confident, charismatic, self-propelled activity vs. disoriented, normative, goalless behavior.

The present review is limited to a discussion of instrumental competence and associated antecedent parental practices and is most applicable to the behavior of young children rather than adolescents. Several ancillary topics will be mentioned, but not discussed in depth, including:

The Relation of IQ to Instrumental Competence. My own work and that of others indicate that, in our present society, children with high IQs are most likely to be achievement-oriented and self-motivated. The correlations between IQ and measures of purposiveness, dominance, achievement-orientation, and independence are very high even by ages three and four. In my study Stanford-Binet IQ tests were administered to 122 preschool boys and girls as part of an investigation of current patterns of parental authority and their effects on the behavior of preschool children. White children with IQs of at least 96 were grouped within sex on the basis of IQ to form five continuous groups for both boys and girls. Groups were compared on child behavior and parent socialization practices. Higher and lower IQ groups differed significantly from each other on measures of social responsibility and independence, notably with regard to clusters designated Achievement Oriented and Independence.[2]

The Relation of Moral Development and Conscience to Instrumental Competence. This area of research, exemplified by some of the work of Aronfreed, Kohlberg, Mussen, and Piaget, is of spe-

[2]A paper entitled "The relationship of cognitive ability as measured by IQ tests to interpersonal competence: educational implications" (1971, in preparation) discusses this area in full. In that paper social implications of IQ as a predictor of adult achievement, interpersonal competence, and level of moral development, are discussed. The possible effects of different types of educational environment on achievement, in particular "discovery" vs. direct training methods, and ability groups vs. integrated classrooms, are explored. The importance of evaluating current programs in which the classroom is integrated (e.g, Berkeley) is emphasized.

cial importance with older age groups and will be covered tangentially when the antecedents of social responsibility are explored.

The Relation of Will to Instrumental Competence.
This topic, which overlaps with the previous one, has received very little direct attention during the past 30 years. In the present review, this area is discussed to some extent along with antecedents of independence.

The Antecedents of Creative or Scientific Genius.
Socialization practices which lead to competence are not the same as those associated with the development of high creativity or scientific genius. Most studies, such as those by Roe (1952) and Eiduson (1962), suggest that men of genius are frequently reared differently from other superior individuals. It has been found, for example, that as children men of genius often had little contact with their·fathers, or their fathers died when they were young; they often led lonely, although cognitively enriched, existences. Such rearing cannot be recommended, however, since it is unlikely that the effects on most children, even those with superior ability, will be to produce genius or highly effective functioning.

The Development of Instrumental Competence in Disadvantaged Families.
The assumption cannot be made that the same factors relate to competence in disadvantaged families as in advantaged families. The effect of a single parental characteristic is altered substantially by the pattern of variables of which it is a part. Similarly, the effect of a given pattern of parental variables may be altered by the larger social context in which the family operates. The relations discussed here are most relevant for white middle-class families and may not always hold for disadvantaged families. In my study of current patterns of parental authority and their effects on the behavior of preschool children, the data for the 16 black children and their families were analyzed separately, since it was assumed that the effect of a given pattern of parental variables would be altered by the larger social context in which the family operates. The major conclusion from this exploratory analysis was that if black families are viewed by white norms they appear deviant, and yet, judged by the same norms, their

so-called authoritarian methods seem to produce self-assertive, independent girls.[3]

DEVELOPMENT OF INSTRUMENTAL INCOMPETENCE IN GIRLS

Rapid social changes are taking place in the United States which are providing equal opportunity for socially disadvantaged groups. If a socially disadvantaged group is one whose members are discouraged from fully developing their potentialities for achieving status and leadership in economic, academic, and political affairs, women qualify as such a group.

There is little evidence that women are biologically inferior to men in intellectual endowment, academic potential, social responsibility, or capacity for independence. Constitutional differences in certain areas may exist, but they do not directly generate differences in areas such as those mentioned. The only cognitive functions in which females have been shown consistently to perform less well than males are spatial relations and visualization. We really do not know to what extent the clearly inferior position women occupy in United States society today should be attributed to constitutional factors. The evidence, however, is overwhelming that socialization experiences contribute greatly to a condition of instrumental *incompetence* among women. It follows that if these conditions were altered, women could more nearly fulfill their occupational and intellectual potential. The interested reader should refer to Maccoby's excellent "Classified Summary of Research in Sex Differences" (1966, pp. 323–351).

Few Women Enter Scientific Fields and Very Few of These Achieve Eminence.
According to the President's Commission on the Status of Women in 1963, the proportion of women to men obtaining advanced degrees is actually dropping. Yet there is little convincing evidence that females are constitutionally incapable of contributing significantly to science. Girls obtain better grades in elementary school than boys, and perform equally to boys on standard achievement tests, including tests of mathematical reasoning. By the high school years,

---

[3]A paper reporting these results, entitled "An exploratory study of socialization effects on black children: some black-white comparisons" (1972b) is in press.

however, boys score considerably higher than girls on the mathematical portion of the *Scholastic Aptitude Test* (Rossi, 1969). It is interesting to note that a high positive relation between IQ and later occupational levels holds for males, but does not hold for females (Terman & Oden, 1947). According to one study of high school physics students, girls scored higher on understanding scientific processes, while boys scored higher on a test of physics achievement (Walberg, 1969). As Rossi has argued:

> If we want more women to enter science, not only as teachers of science but as scientists, some quite basic changes must take place in the way girls are reared. If girls are to develop the analytic and mathematical abilities science requires, parents and teachers must encourage them in independence and self-reliance instead of pleasing feminine submission; stimulate and reward girls' efforts to satisfy their curiosity about the world as they do those of boys; encourage in girls not unthinking conformity but alert intelligence that asks why and rejects the easy answer (Rossi, 1969, p. 483).

Femininity and Being Female Is Socially Devalued. Both sexes rate men as more worthwhile than women (e.g., McKee & Sherriffs, 1957). While boys of all ages show a strong preference for masculine roles, girls do not show a similar preference for feminine roles, and indeed, at certain ages, many girls as well as boys show a strong preference for masculine roles (Brown, 1958). In general, both men and women express a preference for having male children (Dinitz, Dynes & Clarke, 1954). Masculine status is so to be preferred to feminine status that girls may adopt tomboy attributes and be admired for doing so, but boys who adopt feminine attributes are despised as sissies. Feminine identification in males (excluding feminine qualities such as tenderness, expressiveness, and playfulness) is clearly related to maladjustment. But even in females, intense feminine identification may more strongly characterize maladjusted than adjusted women (Heilbrun, 1965). Concern about population control will only further accelerate the devaluation of household activities performed by women and decrease the self-esteem of women solely engaged in such activities.

Intellectual Achievement and Self-assertive Independent Strivings in Women Are Equated with Loss of Femininity by Men and Women Alike. Women, as well as men, oppose the idea of placing women in high-status jobs (Keniston & Keniston, 1964). One researcher (Horner, 1968) thinks that women's higher test anxiety reflects the conflict between women's motivation to achieve and their motivation to fail. She feels that women and girls who are motivated to fail feel ambivalent about success because intellectual achievement is equated with loss of femininity by socializing agents and eventually by the female herself.

Generally, Parents Have Higher Achievement Expectations for Boys than They Do for Girls. Boys are more frequently expected to go to college and to have careers (Aberle & Naegele, 1952). The pressure towards responsibility, obedience, and nurturance for girls, and towards achievement and independence for boys which characterizes United States society also characterizes other societies, thus further reinforcing the effect of differential expectations for boys and girls (Barry, Bacon & Child, 1957). In the United States, girls of nursery school age are not less achievement-oriented or independent than boys. By adolescence, however, most girls are highly aware of, and concerned about, social disapproval for so-called masculine pursuits. They move toward conformity with societal expectations that, relative to males, they should be nonachievement-oriented and dependent.

Girls and Women Consistently Show a Greater Need for Affiliation than Do Boys and Men. The greater nurturance toward peers and cooperation with adults shown by girls is demonstrable as early as the preschool years. In general, females are more suggestible, conforming, and likely to rely on others for guidance and support. Thus, females are particularly susceptible to social influences, and these influences generally define femininity to include such attributes as social responsibility, supportivenesss, submissiveness, and low achievement striving.

There are complex and subtle differences in the behavior of boys and girls from birth onward, and in the treatment of boys and girls by their caretaking adults. These differential treatments are sometimes difficult to identify because, when the observer knows the sex of the parent or child, an automatic adjustment is made which tends to standardize judgments about the two sexes. By the time boys enter nursery school, they are more resistant to adult authority and aggressive with peers. Thus, a major socialization task for preschool boys consists of developing social responsibility. While preschool girls (in my investigations) are neither lacking in achievement-orientation nor in independence, the focal socialization task for them seems to consist of maintaining purposive, dominant, and independent behavior. Without active intervention by socializing agents, the cultural stereotype is likely to augment girls' already well-developed sense of cooperation with authority and eventually discourage their independent strivings towards achievement and eminence. As will be noted later, there is reason to believe that the socialization practices which facilitate the development of instrumental competence in *both* girls and boys have the following attributes: (a) they place a premium on self-assertiveness but not on anticonformity; (b) they emphasize high achievement and self-control but not social conformity; (c) they occur within a context of firm discipline and rationality with neither excessive restrictiveness nor overacceptance. For a more complete discussion of changes in socialization practices which might produce greater competence in girls, see the author's paper entitled "From each woman in accord with her ability" (Baumrind, 1972a).

SOCIALIZATION PRACTICES RELATED TO RESPONSIBLE VS. IRRESPONSIBLE BEHAVIOR

The reader will recall that I defined Responsible vs. Irresponsible Behavior in terms of Friendliness vs. Hostility Towards Peers, Cooperation vs. Resistance Towards Adults, and High vs. Low Achievement Orientation. Socialization seems to have a clearer impact upon the development of social responsibility in boys than in girls, probably because girls vary less in this particular attribute. In my own work, parents who were authoritative and relatively conforming, as compared with parents who were permissive or authoritarian, tended to have children who were more friendly, cooperative, and achievement-oriented. This was especially true for boys. Nonconformity in parents was not necessarily associated with resistant and hostile behavior in children. Neither did firm control and high matu-

rity demands produce rebelliousness. In fact, it has generally been found that close supervision, high demands for obedience and personal neatness, and pressure upon the child to share in household responsibilities are associated with responsible behavior rather than with chronic rebelliousness. The condition most conducive to antisocial aggression, because it most effectively rewards such behavior, is probably one in which the parent is punitive and arbitrary in his demands, but inconsistent in responding to the child's disobedience.

Findings from several studies suggest that parental demands provoke rebelliousness only when the parent both restricts autonomy of action and does not use rational methods of control. For example, Pikas (1961), in a survey of 656 Swedish adolescents, showed that differences in the child's acceptance of parental authority depended upon the reason for the parental directive. Authority based on rational concern for the child's welfare was accepted well by the child, but arbitrary, domineering, or exploitative authority was rejected. Pikas' results are supported by Middleton and Snell (1963) who found that discipline regarded by the child as either very strict or very permissive was associated with rebellion against the parents' political views. Finally, Elder (1963), working with adolescents' reports concerning their parents, found that conformity to parental rules typified subjects who saw their parents as having ultimate control (but who gave the child leeway in making decisions) and who also provided explanations for rules.

Several generalizations and hypotheses can be drawn from this literature and from the results of my own work concerning the relations of specific parental practices to the development of social responsibility in young children. The following list is based on the assumption that it is more meaningful to talk about the effects of *patterns* of parental authority than to talk about the effects of single parental variables.

1. *The modeling of socially responsible behavior facilitates the development of social responsibility in young children, and more so if the model is seen by the child as having control over desired resources and as being concerned with the child's welfare.*

The adult who subordinates his impulses enough to conform with social regulations and is himself charitable and generous will have his example followed by the child. The adult who is self-indulgent and lacking in charity will have his example followed even if he should preach generous, cooperative behavior. Studies by Mischel and Liebert (1966) and by Rosenhan, Frederick and Burrowes (1968) suggest that models who behave self-indulgently produce similar behavior in children and these effects are even more extensive than direct reward for self-indulgent behavior. Further, when the adult preaches what he does not practice, the child is more likely to do what the adult practices. This is true even when the model preaches unfriendly or uncooperative behavior but behaves toward the child in an opposite manner. To the extent that the model for socially responsible behavior is perceived as having high social status (Bandura, Ross & Ross, 1963), the model will be most effective in inducing responsible behavior.

In our studies, both authoritative and authoritarian parents demanded socially responsible behavior and also differentially rewarded it. As compared to authoritative parents, however, authoritarian parents permitted their own needs to take precedence over those of the child, became inaccessible when displeased, assumed a stance of personal infallibility, and in other ways showed themselves often to be more concerned with their own ideas than with the child's welfare. Thus, they did not exemplify prosocial behavior, although they did preach it. Authoritative parents, on the other hand, both preached and practiced prosocial behavior and their children were significantly more responsible than the children of authoritarian parents. In this regard, it is interesting that nonconforming parents who were highly individualistic and professed anticonforming ideas had children who were more socially responsible than otherwise. The boys were achievement-oriented and the girls were notably cooperative. These parents were themselves rather pacific, gentle people who were highly responsive to the child's needs even at the cost of their own; thus, they modeled but did not preach prosocial behavior.

2. *Firm enforcement policies, in which desired behavior is positively reinforced and deviant behavior is negatively reinforced, facilitate the development of socially responsible behavior, provided that the parent desires that the child behave in a responsible manner.*

The use of reinforcement techniques serves to establish the potency of the reinforcing agent and, in the mind of the young child, to legitimate his authority. The use of negative sanctions can be a clear statement to the child that rules are there to be followed and that to disobey is to break a known rule. Among other things, punishment provides the child with information. As Spence (1966) found, nonreaction by adults is sometimes interpreted by children as signifying a correct response. Siegel and Kohn (1959) found that nonreaction by an adult when the child was behaving aggressively resulted in an increased incidence of such acts. By virtue of his or her role as an authority, the sheer presence of parents when the child misbehaves cannot help but affect the future occurrence of such behavior. Disapproval should reduce such actions, while approval or nonreaction to such behavior should increase them.

In our studies, permissive parents avoided the use of negative sanctions, did not demand mannerly behavior or reward self-help, did not enforce their directives by exerting force or influence, avoided confrontation when the child disobeyed, and did not choose or did not know how to use reinforcement techniques. Their sons, by comparison with the sons of authoritative parents, were clearly lacking in prosocial and achievement-oriented behavior.

3. *Nonrejecting parents are more potent models and reinforcing agents than rejecting parents; thus, nonrejection should be associated with socially responsible behavior in children provided that the parents value and reinforce such behavior.*

It should be noted that this hypothesis refers to nonrejecting parents and is not stated in terms of passive-acceptance. Thus, it is expected that nonrejecting parental behavior, but not unconditionally acceptant behavior, is associated with socially responsible behavior in children. As Bronfenbrenner pointed out about adolescents, "It is the presence of rejection rather than the lack of a high degree of warmth which is inimical to the development of responsibility in both sexes" (1961, p. 254). As already indicated, in our study authoritarian parents were more rejecting and punitive, and less devoted to the child's welfare than were authoritative parents; their sons were also less socially responsible.

4. *Parents who are fair, and who use reason to legitimate their directives, are more potent models and reinforcing agents than parents who do not encourage independence or verbal exchange.*

Let us consider the interacting effects of punishment and the use of reasoning on the behavior of children. From research it appears that an accompanying verbal rationale nullifies the special effectiveness of immediate punishment, and also of relatively intense punishment (Parke, 1969). Thus, by symbolically reinstating the deviant act, explaining the reason for punishment, and telling the child exactly what he should do, the parent obviates the need for intense or instantaneous punishment. Immediate, intense punishment may have undesirable side effects, in that the child is conditioned through fear to avoid deviant behavior, and is not helped to control himself consciously and willfully. Also, instantaneous, intense punishment produces high anxiety which may interfere with performance, and in addition may increase the likelihood that the child will avoid the noxious agent. This reduces that agent's future effectiveness as a model or reinforcing agent. Finally, achieving behavioral conformity by conditioning fails to provide the child with information about cause and effect relations which he can then transfer to similar situations. This is not to say that use of reasoning alone, without negative sanctions, is as effective as the use of both. Negative sanctions give operational meaning to the consequences signified by reasons and to rules themselves.

Authoritarian parents, as compared to authoritative parents, are relatively unsuccessful in producing socially responsible behavior. According to this hypothesis, the reason is that authoritarian parents fail to encourage verbal exchange and infrequently accompany punishment with reasons rather than that they use negative sanctions and are firm disciplinarians.

SOCIALIZATION PRACTICES RELATED TO INDEPENDENT VS. SUGGESTIBLE BEHAVIOR

The reader will recall that Independent vs. Suggestible Behavior was defined with reference to: (a) Domineering vs. Tractable Behavior, (b) Dominance vs. Submission, (c) Purposive vs. Aimless Activity, and (d) Independence vs. Suggestibility. Parent behavior seems to have a clearer effect upon the development of independence in girls than in boys, probably because preschool boys vary less in independence.

In my own work, independence in girls was clearly associated with authoritative upbringing (whether conforming or nonconforming). For boys, nonconforming parent behavior and, to a lesser extent, authoritative upbringing were associated with independence. By independence we do not mean anticonformity. "Pure anticonformity, like pure conformity, is pure dependence behavior" (Willis, 1968, p. 263). Anticonforming behavior, like negativistic behavior, consists of doing anything but what is prescribed by social norms. Independence is the ability to disregard known standards of conduct or normative expectations in making decisions. Nonconformity in parents may not be associated in my study with independence in girls (although it was in boys) because females are especially susceptible to normative expectations. One can hypothesize that girls must be trained to act independently of these expectations, rather than to conform or to anticonform to them.

It was once assumed that firm control and high maturity demands lead to passivity and dependence in young children. The preponderance of evidence contradicts this. Rather, it would appear that many children react to parental power by resisting, rather than by being cowed. The same parent variables which increase the probability that the child will use the parent as a model should increase the likelihood that firm control will result in assertive behavior. For example, the controlling parent who is warm, understanding, and supportive of autonomy should generate less passivity (as well as less rebelliousness) than the controlling parent who is cold and restrictive. This should be the case because of the kinds of behavior reinforced, the traits modeled, and the relative effectiveness of the parent as a model.

Several generalizations and hypotheses can be offered concerning the relations between parental practices and the development of independence in young children:

1. *Early environmental stimulation facilitates the development of independence in young children.*

It took the knowledge gained from compensatory programs for culturally disadvantaged children to counteract the erroneous counsel from some experts to avoid too much cognitive stimulation of the young child. Those Head Start programs which succeed best (Hunt, 1968) are those characterized by stress on the development of cognitive skills, linguistic ability, motivational concern for achievement, and rudimentary numerical skills. There is reason to believe that middle-class children also profit from such early stimulation and enrichment of the environment. Fowler (1962) pointed out, even prior to the development of compensatory programs, that concern about the dangers of premature cognitive training and an overemphasis on personality development had delayed inordinately the recognition that the ability to talk, read, and compute increase the child's self-respect and independent functioning.

Avoidance of anxiety and self-assertion are reciprocally inhibiting responses to threat or frustration. Girls, in particular, are shielded from stress and overstimulation, which probably serves to increase preferences for avoidant rather than offensive responses to aggression or threat. By exposing a child to stress or to physical, social, and intellectual demands, he or she becomes more resistant to stress and learns that offensive reactions to aggression and frustration are frequently rewarding. In our studies, as the hypothesis would predict, parents who provided the most enriched environment, namely the nonconforming and the authoritative parents, had the most dominant and purposive children. These parents, by comparison with the others studied, set high standards of excellence, invoked cognitive insight, provided an intellectually stimulating atmosphere, were themselves rated as being differentiated and individualistic, and made high educational demands upon the child.

2. *Parental passive-acceptance and overprotection inhibits the development of independence.*

Passive-acceptant and overprotective parents shield children from stress and, for the reasons discussed above, inhibit the development of assertiveness and frustration tolerance. Also, parental anxiety about stress to which the child is exposed may serve to increase the child's anxiety. Further, willingness to rescue the child offers him an easy alternative to self-mastery. Demanding and nonprotective parents, by contrast, permit the child to extricate himself from stressful situations and place

a high value on tolerance of frustration and courage.

According to many investigators (e.g., McClelland, Atkinson, Clark & Lowell, 1953), healthy infants are by inclination explorative, curious, and stress-seeking. Infantile feelings of pleasure, originally experienced after mild changes in sensory stimulation, become associated with these early efforts at independent mastery. The child anticipates pleasure upon achieving a higher level of skill, and the pleasure derived from successfully performing a somewhat risky task encourages him to seek out such tasks.

Rosen and D'Andrade (1959) found that high achievement motivation, a motivation akin to stress-seeking, was facilitated both by high maternal warmth when the child pleased the parent and high maternal hostility and rejection when the child was displeasing. Hoffman et al. (1960), found that mothers of achieving boys were more coercive than those who performed poorly, and it has also been found (Crandall, Dewey, Katkovsky & Preston, 1964) that mothers of achieving girls were relatively nonnurturant. Kagan and Moss (1962) reported that achieving adult women had mothers who in early childhood were unaffectionate, "pushy," and not protective. Also, Baumrind and Black (1967) found paternal punitiveness to be associated positively with independence in girls. Finally, in a recent study (Baumrind, 1971), there were indications for girls that parental nonacceptance was positively related to independence. That is, the most independent girls had parents who were either not passive-acceptant or were rejecting.

Authoritarian control and permissive noncontrol both may shield the child from the opportunity to engage in vigorous interaction with people. Demands which cannot be met, refusals to help, and unrealistically high standards may curb commerce with the environment. Placing few demands on the child, suppression of conflict, and low standards may understimulate him. In either case, he fails to achieve the knowledge and experience required to desensitize him to the anxiety associated with nonconformity.

3. *Self-assertiveness and self-confidence in the parent, expressed by an individual style and by the moderate use of power-oriented techniques of discipline, will be associated with independence in the young child.*

The self-assertive, self-confident parent provides a model of similar behavior for the child. Also, the parent who uses power-oriented rather than love-oriented techniques of discipline achieves compliance through means other than guilt. Power-oriented techniques can achieve behavioral conformity without premature internalization by the child of parental standards. It may be that the child is, in fact, more free to formulate his own standards of conduct if techniques of discipline are used which stimulate resistiveness or anger rather than fear of guilt. The use of techniques which do not stimulate conformity through guilt may be especially important for girls. The belief in one's own power and the assumption of responsibility for one's own intellectual successes and failures are important predictors of independent effort and intellectual achievement (Crandall, Katkovsky & Crandall, 1965). This sense of self-responsibility in children seems to be associated with power-oriented techniques of discipline and with critical attitudes on the part of the adult towards the child, provided that the parent is also concerned with developing the child's autonomy and encourages independent and individual behavior.

In my study, both the authoritative and the nonconforming parents were self-confident, clear as well as flexible in their child-rearing attitudes, and willing to express angry feelings openly. Together with relatively firm enforcement and nonrejection, these indices signified patterns of parental authority in which guilt-producing techniques of discipline were avoided. The sons of nonconforming parents and the daughters of authoritative parents were both extremely independent.

4. *Firm control can be associated with independence in the child, provided that the control is not restrictive of the child's opportunities to experiment and to make decisions within the limits defined.*

There is no logical reason why parents' enforcing directives and demands cannot be accompanied by regard for the child's opinions, willingness to gratify his wishes, and instruction in the effective use of power. A policy of firm enforcement may be used as a means by which the child can achieve a high level of instrumental competence and eventual independence. The controlling, demanding parent can train the child to tolerate increasingly intense and prolonged frustration; to broaden his base of adult support to include neighbors, teachers, and others; to assess critically his own successes and failures and to take responsibility for both; to develop standards of moral conduct; and to relinquish the special privileges of childhood in return for the rights of adolescence.

It is important to distinguish between the effects on the child of restrictive control and of firm control. *Restrictive control* refers to the use of extensive proscriptions and prescriptions, covering many areas of the child's life; they limit his autonomy to try out his skills in these areas. By *firm control* is meant firm enforcement of rules, effective resistance against the child's demands, and guidance of the child by regime and intervention. Firm control does not imply large numbers of rules or intrusive direction of the child's activities.

Becker (1962) has summarized the effects on child behavior of restrictiveness vs. permissiveness and warmth vs. hostility. He reported that warm-*restrictive* parents tended to have passive, well-socialized children. This author (Baumrind, 1967) found, however, that warm-*controlling* (by contrast with warm-*restrictive*) parents were not paired with passive children, but rather with responsible, assertive, self-reliant children. Parents of these children enforced directives and resisted the child's demands, but were not restrictive. Early control, unlike restrictiveness, apparently does not lead to "fearful, dependent and submissive behaviors, a dulling of intellectual striving, and inhibited hostility," as Becker indicated was true of restrictive parents (1964, p. 197).

5. *Substantial reliance upon reinforcement techniques to obtain behavioral conformity, unaccompanied by use of reason, should lead to dependent behavior.*

To the extent that the parent uses verbal cues judiciously, she increases the child's ability to discriminate, differentiate, and generalize. According to Luria (1960) and Vygotsky (1962), the child's ability to "order" his own behavior is based upon verbal instruction from the adult which, when heeded and obeyed, permits eventual *cognitive* control by the child of his own behavior. Thus, when the adult legitimizes power, labels actions clearly as praiseworthy, explains rules and encourages vigorous verbal give and take, obedience is not likely to be achieved at the cost of passive dependence. Otherwise, it may well be.

It is self-defeating to attempt to shape, by extrinsic reinforcement, behavior which by its nature is autogenic. As already mentioned, the healthy infant is explorative and curious, and seems to enjoy mild stress. Although independent mastery can be accelerated if the parent broadens the child's experiences and makes certain reasonable demands upon him, the parent must take care not to substitute extrinsic reward and social approval for the intrinsic pleasure associated with mastery of the environment. Perhaps the unwillingness of the authoritative parents in my study to rely solely upon reinforcement techniques contributed substantially to the relatively purposive, dominant behavior shown by their children, especially by their daughters.

6. *Parental values which stress individuality, self-expression, initiative, divergent thinking, and aggressiveness will facilitate the development of independence in the child, provided that these qualities in the parent are not accompanied by lax and inconsistent discipline and unwillingness to make demands upon the child.*

It is important that adults use their power in a functional rather than an interpersonal context. The emphasis should be on the task to be done and the rule to be followed rather than upon the special status of the powerful adult. By focusing upon the task to be accomplished, the adult's actions can serve as an example for the child rather than as a suppressor of his independence. Firm discipline for both boys and girls must be in the service of training for achievement and independence, if such discipline is not to facilitate the development of an overconforming, passive life style.

In our study, independence was clearly a function of nonconforming but nonindulgent parental attitudes and behavior, for boys. For girls, however, nonconforming parental patterns were associated with independence only when the parents were also authoritative. The parents in these groups tended to encourage their children to ask for, even to demand, what they desired. They themselves acquiesced in the face of such demands provided that the demands were not at variance with parental policy. Thus, the children of these parents were positively reinforced for autonomous self-

expression. In contrast to these results, the authoritarian parents did not value willfulness in the child, and the permissive parents were clearly ambivalent about rewarding such behavior. Further, the permissive parents did not differentiate between mature or praiseworthy demands by the child and regressive or deviant demands. These permissive parents instead would accede to the child's demands until patience was exhausted; punishment, sometimes very harsh, would then ensue.

CONCLUSIONS

Girls in Western society are in many ways systematically socialized for instrumental incompetence. The affiliative and cooperative orientation of girls increases their receptivity to the influence of socializing agents. This influence, in turn, is often used by socializing agents to inculcate passivity, dependence, conformity, and sociability in young females at the expense of independent pursuit of success and scholarship. In my studies, parents designated as authoritative had the most achievement-oriented and independent daughters. However, permissive parents whose control was lax, who did not inhibit tomboy behavior, and who did not seek to produce sex-role conformity in girls had daughters who were nearly as achievement-oriented and independent.

The following adult practices and attitudes seem to facilitate the development of socially responsible and independent behavior in both boys and girls:

1 Modeling by the adult of behavior which is both socially responsible and self-assertive, especially if the adult is seen as powerful by the child and as eager to use the material and interpersonal resources over which he has control on the child's behalf.

2 Firm enforcement policies in which the adult makes effective use of reinforcement principles in order to reward socially responsible behavior and to punish deviant behavior, but in which demands are accompanied by explanations, and sanctions are accompanied by reasons consistent with a set of principles followed in practice as well as preached by the parent.

3 Nonrejecting but not overprotective or passive-acceptant parental attitudes in which the parent's interest in the child is abiding and, in the preschool years, intense; and where approval is conditional upon the child's behavior.

4 High demands for achievement and for conformity with parental policy, accompanied by receptivity to the child's rational demands and willingness to offer the child wide latitude for independent judgment.

5 Providing the child with a complex and stimulating environment offering challenge and excitement as well as security and rest, where divergent as well as convergent thinking is encouraged.

These practices and attitudes do not reflect a happy compromise between authoritarian and permissive practices. Rather, they reflect a synthesis and balancing of strongly opposing forces of tradition and innovation, divergence and convergence, accommodation and assimilation, cooperation and autonomous expression, tolerance and principled intractability.

REFERENCES

Aberle, D. F. & Naegele, K. D. Middle-class fathers' occupational role and attitudes toward children. *Am. J. Orthopsychiat.*, 1952, 22, 366–378.

Bandura, A., Ross, D. & Ross, S. A. A comparative test of the status envy, social power, and the secondary-reinforcement theories of identificatory learning. *J. abnorm. soc. Psychol.*, 1963, 67, 527–534.

Barry, H., Bacon, J. K. & Child, I. L. A cross-cultural survey of some sex differences in socialization. *J. abnorm. soc. Psychol.*, 1957, 327–332.

Baumrind, D. Effects of authoritative parental control on child behavior. *Child Develpm.*, 1966, 37, 887–907.

———. Child care practices anteceding three patterns of preschool behavior. *Genet. Psychol. Monogr.*, 1967, 75, 43–88.

———. Authoritarian vs. authoritative parental control. *Adolescence*, 1968, 3, 255–272.

———. Current patterns of parental authority. *Develpm. Psychol. Monogr.*, 1971, 4(1), 1–102.

———. From each woman in accord with her ability. *School Rev.*, Feb. 1972, in press. (a)

———. An exploratory study of socialization effects on black children: Some black-white comparisons. *Child Develpm.*, 1971, in press. (b)

Baumrind, D. & Black, A. E. Socialization practices associated with dimensions of competence in preschool boys and girls. *Child Develpm.*, 1967, 38, 291–327.

Becker, W. C. Consequences of different kinds of parental discipline. In M. L. Hoffman & L. W. Hoffman (Eds.), *Review of Child Development Research*, Vol. 1. New York: Russell Sage Foundation, 1964. Pp. 169–208.

Bronfenbrenner, U. Some familial antecedents of responsibility and leadership in adolescents. In L. Petrullo & B. M. Bass (Eds.), *Leadership and Interpersonal Behavior*. New York: Holt, Rinehart & Winston, 1961. Pp. 239–271.

Brown, D. Sex role development in a changing culture. *Psychol. Bull.*, 1958, 55, 232–242.

Crandall, V., Dewey, R., Katkovsky, W. & Preston, A. Parents' attitudes and behaviors and grade school children's academic achievements. *J. genet. Psychol.*, 1964, 104, 53–66.

Crandall, V., Katkovsky, W. & Crandall, V. J. Children's beliefs in their own control of reinforcements in intellectual-academic achievement situations. *Child Develpm.*, 1965, 36, 91–109.

Crandall, V., Orleans, S., Preston, A. & Rabson, A. The development of social compliance in young children. *Child Develpm.*, 1958, 29, 429–443.

Dinitz, S., Dynes, R. R. & Clarke, A. C. Preferences for male or female children: Traditional or affectional. *Marriage & Family Living*, 1954, 16, 128–130.

Eiduson, B. T. *Scientists, Their Psychological World.* New York: Basic Books, 1962.

Elder, G. H. Parental power legitimation and its effect on the adolescent. *Sociometry*, 1963, 26, 50–65.

Emmerich, W. & Smoller, F. The role patterning of parental norms. *Sociometry*, 1964, 27, 382–390.

Fowler, W. Cognitive learning in infancy and early childhood. *Psycho. Bull*, 1962, 59, 116–152.

Haggard, E. A. Socialization, personality, and academic achievement in gifted children. In B. C. Rosen, H. J. Crockett & C. Z. Nunn (Eds.), *Achievement in American Society.* Cambridge, Mass.: Schenkman Publishing, 1969. Pp. 85–94.

Heilbrun, A. B. Sex differences in identification learning. *J. genet. Psychol.*, 1965, 106, 185–193.

Hoffman, L., Rosen, S. & Lippitt, R. Parental coerciveness, child autonomy, and child's role at school. *Sociometry*, 1960, 23, 15–22.

Horner, M. S. Sex differences in achievement motivation and performance in competitive situations. Unpubl. doctoral dissertation, Univ. of Michigan, 1968.

Hunt, J. McV. Toward the prevention of incompetence. In J. W. Carter, Jr. (Ed.), *Research Contributions from Psychology to Community Mental Health.* New York: Behavioral Publications, 1968.

Kagan, J. & Moss, H. A. *Birth to Maturity: A Study in Psychological Development.* New York: John Wiley, 1962.

Keniston, E. & Keniston, K. An American anachronism: the image of women and work. *Am. Scholar*, 1964, 33, 355–375.

Luria, A. R. Experimental analysis of the development of voluntary action in children. In *The Central Nervous System and Behavior.* Bethesda, Md.: U. S. Dept. of Health, Education, & Welfare, National Institutes of Health, 1960. Pp. 529–535.

Maccoby, E. E. (Ed.). *The Development of Sex Differences.* Stanford, Calif.: Stanford Univ. Press, 1966.

McClelland, D., Atkinson, J., Clark, R. & Lowell, D. *The Achievement Motive.* New York: Appleton-Century-Crofts, 1963.

McKee, J. P. & Sherriffs, A. C. The differential evaluation of males and females. *J. Pers.,* 1957, 25, 356–371.

Middleton, R. & Snell, P. Political expression of adolescent rebellion. *Am. J. Sociol.,* 1963, 68, 527–535.

Mischel, W. & Liebert, R. M. Effects of discrepancies between observed and imposed reward criteria on their acquisition and transmission. *J. pers. soc. Psychol.,* 1966, 3, 45–53.

Parke, R. D. Some effects of punishment on children's behavior. *Young Children,* 1969, 24, 224–240.

Pikas, A. Children's attitudes toward rational versus inhibiting parental authority. *J. abnorm. soci. Psychol.,* 1961, 62, 315–321.

Roe, A. *The Making of a Scientist.* New York: Dodd, Mead, 1952.

Rosen, B. C. & D'Andrade, R. The psychological origins of achievement motivation. *Sociometry,* 1959, 22, 185–218.

Rosenhan, D. L., Frederick, F. & Burrowes, A. Preaching and practicing: Effects of channel discrepancy on norm internalization. *Child Develpm.,* 1968, 39, 291–302.

Rossi, A. Women in science: why so few? In B.C. Rosen, H. J. Crockett, C. Z. Nunn (eds.), *Achievement in American Society.* Cambridge, Mass.: Schenkman Publishing, 1969. Pp. 470–486.

Siegel, A. E. & Kohn, L. G. Permissiveness, permission, and aggression: The effects of adult presence or absence on aggression in children's play. *Child Develpm.,* 1959, 36, 131–141.

Spence, J. T. Verbal-discrimination performance as a function of instruction and verbal reinforcement combination in normal and retarded children. *Child Develpm.,* 1966, 37, 269–281.

Terman, L. M. & Oden, H. H. *The Gifted Child Grows Up.* Stanford, Calif.: Stanford Univ. Press, 1947.

Vygotsky, L. S. *Thought and Language.* Cambridge, Mass.: M. I. T. Press, 1962.

Walberg, H. J. Physics, femininity, and creativity. *Developm. Psychol.,* 1969, 1, 47–54.

Willis, R. H. Conformity, independence, and anticonformity. In L. S. Wrightsman, Jr. (Ed.), *Contemporary Issues in Social Psychology.* Belmont, Calif.: Brooks/Cole Publishing, 1968. Pp. 258–272.

Reading 34

Beyond Father Absence: Conceptualization of Effects of Divorce

E. Mavis Hetherington
Martha Cox
Roger Cox

The incidence of children raised in homes with single parents is accelerating at a dramatic rate. In 1974 it was estimated that one out of every six children was living in a home with a single parent. In 95% of the cases the single parent is the mother. This increase in single parent families is largely attributable to a rising divorce rate, particularly in families with young children (Bronfenbrenner, 1975).

The psychological research on single parent families has usually involved comparative studies of the development of children in intact homes or homes with fathers absent. Although the findings are complex and not altogether consistent they can be summarized by saying that early divorce seems to have more deleterious effects on children than later divorce, and that these effects differ for boys and girls with the most marked effects occurring in boys. Disruptions in sex role typing, cognitive development, moral development and self-control have been reported in children with absent fathers (Biller 1974; Hetherington and Deur 1971; Lynn, 1974). If you read this literature you will be struck by how little we know about factors that may mediate differences found between children in intact homes and those reared by a divorced mother. These differences are usually attributed to the lack of a father to serve as an adequate male model and as a disciplinarian with boys.

Undoubtedly the lack of a male model and the controlling influence of the father are important factors in the development of these children; however, there may be less direct but equally powerful ways in which divorce and the relative unavailability of a father effects children.

Following a divorce in which custody has been granted to the mother, the mother-child relationship may become more intense and salient. The father is infrequently to moderate or mediate in the interaction. The mother must most of the time take over parenting roles assumed by both the mother and father in intact families, and this often imposes considerable stress on the mother. There are fewer time outs in the parenting game in one-parent families. In intact families it has been demonstrated that a supportive father facilitates good mothering in their wives. (Pederson and Robson, 1969).

In addition to pressures associated with lack of paternal support in child rearing following divorce, the divorced mother has other stresses to cope with. The lack of the paternal support system is also felt in economic needs, maintaining the household, emotional support, needs for intimacy and sexual gratification, restrictions in social and recreational activities and contacts with adults. How she copes with these stresses will impact on the development of the child.

It would be just as unfortunate to view the effects of father absence solely in terms of the effects of absence of a father on mothers and their related effects on children, as it is to lean too heavily on modeling as an explanation for these effects. Divorce affects the whole family system and the functioning and interactions of the members within that system. To get a true picture of the impact of divorce, its effects on the divorced father living out of the home and on the mother and children must be examined. Because of space limitations, this presentation will be restricted to a discussion of changes in functioning of mothers and fathers following divorce. Our findings on changes in the behavior of children following divorce will not be presented although this was a main focus of our project. Many of the stresses imposed on the parents following divorce and alterations in their life style mediated how the child adapted to the divorce, and in turn the child's responses modified the parents behavior.

The findings to be reported are part of a two year longitudinal study of the impact of divorce on family functioning and the development of children. The goals of the study were first to examine the response to the family crisis of divorce, and

patterns of reorganization of the family over the two-year period following divorce. It was assumed that the family system would go through a period of disorganization immediately after the divorce, followed by recovery, reorganization and eventual attainment of a new pattern of equilibrium. The second goal was to examine the characteristics of family members that contributed to variations in family processes. The third goal was to examine the effects of variations in family interaction and structure on the development of children.

The original sample was composed of 36 white, middle class boys and 36 girls and their divorced parents from homes in which custody has been granted to the mother, and the same number of children and parents from intact homes. The final sample was 24 families in each of the groups, a total of 96 families on which complete data was available. Sample attrition was largely due to remarriage in the divorced families, to families or a parent leaving the area, to lack of cooperation by schools which made important measures on the child unavailable, and to eight families who no longer wished to participate in the study. Families with stepparents were excluded, since one of the interests in the investigation was seeing how mothers and children functioned in father absent homes and how their functioning might be related to deviant or nondeviant behavior in children. In the analyses to be presented in this paper, six families were randomly dropped from groups to maintain equal sizes in groups.

When a reduction in sample size occurs from 144 families to 96 families one immediately becomes concerned about bias in the sample. On demographic characteristics such as age, religion, education, income, occupation, family size, and maternal employment there were no differences between subjects who dropped out or were excluded from the sample and those who remained. In addition when a family was no longer included in the study a comparative analysis was done of their interaction patterns and those of the continuing families. Some differences in these groups will be noted in the course of this presentation. In general, there were few differences in parent-child interactions in families who did or did not remain in the study. However, there were some differences in the characteristics of parents who remarried and how they viewed themselves and their lives.

The study used a multimethod, multimeasure

approach to the investigation of family interaction. The measures used in the study included interviews and structured diary records of the parents, observations of the parents & child interacting in the laboratory and home, behavior checklists of parent-child interaction kept by the parents and a battery of personality scales on the parents. In addition, observations of the child were conducted in nursery schools, peer nomination and teacher ratings of the child's behavior, and measures of the child's sex role typing, cognitive performance and social development were obtained. The parents and children were administered these measures at two months, one year, and two years following divorce.

In this presentation the discussion will be restricted mainly to the findings based on parent interviews and the observations of the parent and child in an interaction situation in the laboratory, although I will occasionally refer to related findings on other measures. Therefore only these two procedures will be presented in detail.

As was found by Baumrind (1967, 1971), using some similar measures, the parent-child interaction patterns in the home observations and in the laboratory sessions and as reported in the interviews showed considerable congruency. For example, parents who were nurturant, made high use of positive or negative sanctions, or had good control over their children tended to be so across situations. Children who were compliant, oppositional, or affiliative with parents also tended to maintain these behaviors across situations. These behaviors, of course, vary when the interactions involve different people such as parents, teachers, or peers.

Parents were interviewed separately on a structured parent interview schedule designed to assess discipline practices and the relationship with the child, support systems outside the family household system, social, emotional and heterosexual relationships, quality of the relationship with the spouse, economic stress, family disorganization, satisfaction and happiness, and attitudes toward the self. The interviews were tape recorded. Each of the categories listed in Table 1 were rated on scales by two judges. In some cases the category involved the rating of only a single 5- or 7-point scale. In others it represents a composite score of several ratings on a group of subscales. Interjudge reliabilities ranged from .69 to .95 with a mean of .82. The interviews were derived and modified from those of Baumrind, (1967, 1971), Sears, Rau, and Alpert, (1965), Martin and Hetherington, (1971), and others.

Each parent was observed separately interacting with the child in the laboratory in a half hour free play situation and in a half hour structured situation involving puzzles, block building, bead stringing, and sorting tasks. The interaction sessions with the mother or father were on different days, separated by a period of about a month. Half of the children interacted with the mother first and half with the father first. Behavior was coded in the categories in Table 2. The coding procedure was similar to that used by Patterson and his colleagues where the

Table 1

Control of child	Problems in running household
Maturity demands of child	Relationship with spouse
Communication with child	Emotional support in personal matters
Nurturance of child	Immediate support system
Permissiveness-restrictiveness with child	Social life and activities
Negative sanctions with child	Contact with adults
Positive sanctions with child	Intimate relations
Reinforcement of child for sex-typed behaviors	Sexuality
Paternal availability	Number of dates
Maternal availability	Happiness and satisfaction
Paternal face-to-face interaction with child	Competence as a parent
Maternal face-to-face interaction with child	Competence as a male/female
Quality of spouse's relationship with the child	Self esteem
Agreement in treatment of the child	Satisfaction with employment
Emotional support in child rearing from spouse	Conflict preceding divorce
Economic stress	Tension in divorce
Family disorganization	

Table 2

Interaction coding	
Parent behavior	**Child behavior**
Command (positive)	Opposition
Command (negative)	Aversive opposition
Question	Compliance
Nonverbal intrusion	Dependency
Ignore	Negative demands (whining, complaining, angry tone)
Affiliate (interact)	
Positive sanctions	Aggression (tantrum, destructiveness)
Negative sanctions	
Reasoning and explanation	Requests
Encourages	Affiliate
Dependency	Self manipulation
Indulgence	Play
Opposition	Ignore
Compliance	Cry
Encourages independence	

observation period is divided into 30-second intervals and an average of about five behavior sequences of interactions between the subject and other family members were coded in the 30-second interval. However, in order to improve reliability, a tone sounded every six seconds during the recording interval. Two raters rated all sessions. Interjudge agreement on individual responses averaged .83%.

In changing to a new single life style, what kinds of stresses are likely to be experienced by members of a divorced couple? How might these be related to parent-child relations?

Greater economic stress in divorced couples was apparent in our sample. Although the average income of the divorced families was equal to that of the intact families, the economic problems associated with maintaining two households for divorced couples led to more financial concerns and limitations in purchasing practices in divorced couples. It has been suggested by Herzog and Sudia that many of the deleterious effects of father absence on children could be eliminated if economic stability was provided for mothers with no husband in the home. However, in our study the number of significant correlations was not above chance between income or reported feelings of economic stress and parents' reported or observed interactions with their children or with behavior of the child in nursery school. It may be that in our middle class sample with an average family income of about

$22,000 the range is not great enough to detect the effects of economic stress. In a lower class sample, the greater extremes of economic duress might be associated with variations in parent-child interaction or the development of the child.

A second area in which stresses are experienced by divorced couples are in social life and in meaningful, intimate interpersonal relationships. Divorced adults often complain that socializing in our culture is organized around couples and that being a single adult, particularly a single woman with children, limits recreational opportunities. Both the interview findings and the diary records kept by parents indicate that social life is more restricted in divorced couples and that this effect initially is most marked for women. Divorced mothers report having significantly less contact with adults than do the other parents and often commented on their sense of being locked into a child's world. Several described themselves as prisoners and used terms like being "Walled in" or "Trapped." This was less true of working than nonworking mothers. Many nonworking mothers complained that most of their social contacts had been made through professional associates of the husband and that with divorce these associations terminated. In contrast, the employed mothers had contact with their co-workers and these relations often extended into after hour social events. Although the employed women complained that it was difficult to get household chores done and of their concern about getting adequate care for their children, most felt the gratifications associated with employment outweighed the problems. Although social life for our total sample of divorced women increased over the two year period it always remains lower than that of married women.

Divorced men had a restricted social life two months after divorce, followed by a surge of activity at one year and a decline in activity to the wife's level by two years. Divorced men and women who had not remarried in the two years following divorce repeatedly spoke of their intense feelings of loneliness.

Heterosexual relations play a particularly important role in the happiness and attitudes toward the self of both married and divorced adults. Happiness, self esteem, and feelings of competence in heterosexual behavior increased steadily over the two year period for divorced males and females, but they are not as high even in the second year as those for married couples. It should be noted, however, that the subjects who later remarried and were shifted from this study of divorce and father absence to a stepparent study, scored as high on happiness although lower on self esteem and feelings of competence, as did parents in intact families. Frequency of sexual intercourse was lower for divorced parents than married couples at two months, higher at one year for males and about the same frequency at two years. Divorced males particularly seemed to show a peak of sexual activity and a pattern of dating a variety of women in the first year following divorce. However the stereotyped image of the happy, swinging single life was not altogether accurate. One of our sets of interview ratings attempted to measure intimacy in relationships. Intimacy referred to love in the Sullivanian sense of valuing the welfare of the other as much as one's own, of a deep concern and willingness to make sacrifices for the other, and strong attachment and desire to be near the other person. It should be understood that this use of the term intimacy is not synonomous with sexual intimacy although, of course, the two frequently occur together. Intimacy in relationships showed strong positive correlations with happiness, self esteem, and feelings of competence in heterosexual relations for both divorced and married men and women. Table 3 shows that in the divorced but not in the married sample if subjects were divided into those above and below the median in terms of intimacy in relationships, happiness correlated negatively with frequency of intercourse in the low intimacy group and positively in the high intimacy group. The same pattern held for self esteem. This was true for both divorced males and females. The only nonsignificant correlation was for low intimacy males imme-

diately following divorce. Many males but few females were pleased at the increased opportunity for sexual experiences with a variety of partners immediately following divorce. However by the end of the first year both divorced men and women were expressing a want for intimacy and a lack of satisfaction in casual sexual encounters. Women expressed particularly intense feelings about frequent casual sexual encounters, often talking of feelings of desperation, overwhelming depression, and low self esteem following such exchanges.

Thus far we have been focusing mainly on changes in the divorced partners in the two years following divorce. We will now look at differences in family functioning and in parent-child interactions as measured both in the interview and in direct observations in the laboratory situation.

One of the sets of interview scales was family disorganization, which dealt with the degree of structure in proscribed household roles, problems in coping with routine household tasks, and the regularity and scheduling of events. The fathers' scales dealt with similar problems but focused on those in his life and household. The households of the divorced mothers and fathers were always more disorganized than those of intact families, although this disorganization was most marked in the first year following divorce and had significantly decreased by the second year. Children of divorced parents were more likely to get pick-up meals at irregular times. Divorced mothers and their children were less likely to eat dinner together. Bedtimes were more erratic and the children were read to less before bedtime and were more likely to arrive at school late. These results were found both in interviews and in the structured parental diaries.

The interaction patterns between divorced par-

Table 3   Correlations between Frequency of Sexual Intercourse and Happiness in High and Low Intimacy Divorced Groups

| | High intimacy | | Low intimacy | |
	Male (N=24)	Female (N=24)	Male (N=24)	Female (N=24)
Two months	+.40*	+.43*	−.09 (n.s.)	−.42*
One year	+.49**	+.47**	−.41*	−.46*
Two years	+.54**	+.52**	−.48**	−.57**

*p < .05.
**p < .01.

ents and children differed significantly from those in intact families on almost every variable studied in the interview, and on many of the parallel measures in the structured interaction situation. On these measures the differences were greatest during the first year and a process of re-equilibration seemed to be taking place by the end of the second year, particularly in mother-child relationships. However, even at the end of the second year on many dimensions parent-child relations in divorced and intact families differed. Some of the findings for fathers must be interpreted in view of the fact that divorced fathers become increasingly less available to their children over the course of the two year period. Although at two months divorced fathers are having almost as much face-to-face interaction with their children as are fathers in intact homes who are often highly unavailable to their children (Blanchard and Biller, 1971), this interaction declines rapidly. At two months about one quarter of the divorced parents even reported that fathers in their eagerness to maximize visitation rights and maintain contact with their children were having more face-to-face contact with their children than they had before the divorce. This contact was motivated by a variety of factors in the different fathers. Sometimes it was based on a deep attachment to the child or continuing attachment to the wife, sometimes it was based on feelings of duty or attempts to assuage guilt, often it was an attempt to maintain a sense of continuity in their lives and unfortunately it was frequently at least partly motivated by a desire to annoy, compete with, or retaliate against the spouse.

The results of the interview findings and laboratory observations relating to parent-child interaction will be presented in a simplified fashion and where possible presented together.

Divorced parents make fewer maturity demands of their children, communicate less well with their children, tend to be less affectionate with their children and show marked inconsistency in discipline and lack of control over their children in comparison to parents in intact families. Poor parenting seems most marked, particularly for divorced mothers, one year after divorce which seems to be a peak of stress in parent-child relations. Two years following the divorce, mothers are demanding more autonomous mature behavior of their children, communicate better and use more explanation and reasoning, are more nurturant and consistent and are better able to control their

children than they were the year before. A similar pattern is occuring for divorced fathers in maturity demands, communication and consistency, but they are becoming less nurturant and more detached from their children with time. In the laboratory and home observations, divorced fathers were ignoring their children more and showing less affection.

The lack of control that divorced parents have over their children, particularly one year following divorce, was apparent in home and laboratory observations. When the percent of times the child complied to various types of parental demands was examined the lack of compliance especially to the divorced mother at one year with a marked increase in successful commands at two years is dramatic. These results for the laboratory situation are presented in Table 4. Some divorced mothers described their relationship with their child one year after divorce as "declared war," a "struggle for survival," "the old Chinese water torture," or "like getting bitten to death by ducks." It can also be seen in Table 4 that boys comply less to parental demands than do girls and that children are more compliant to their fathers than their mothers commands in spite of the fact that mothers usually give about twice as many commands as fathers.

The interviews and observations showed that the lack of control in the divorced parents was associated with very different patterns of relating to the child for mothers and fathers. The divorced mother tries to control the child by being more restrictive and giving more commands which the child ignores or resists. The divorced father wants his contacts with his children to be as happy as possible. He begins by initially being extremely permissive and indulgent with his children and becoming increasingly restrictive over the two-year period, although he is never as restrictive as fathers in intact homes. The divorced mother uses more negative sanctions than the divorced father does or than parents in intact families do. However by the second year her use of negative sanctions is declining as the divorced father's is increasing. In a parallel fashion, the divorced mother's use of positive sanctions increases after the first year as the divorced father's decreases. The "every day is Christmas" behavior of the divorced father declines with time. The divorced mother decreases her futile attempts at authoritarian control and becomes more effective in dealing with her child over the two year period.

Effectiveness in dealing with the child is related to support in child rearing from the spouse and

Table 4

Percentage of compliance to parental commands (positive)

| | Intact | | | | Divorced | | | |
| | Girl | | Boy | | Girl | | Boy | |
	Father	Mother	Father	Mother	Father	Mother	Father	Mother
Two months	60.2	54.6	51.3	42.6	51.3	40.6	39.9	29.3
One year	63.4	56.7	54.9	44.8	43.9	31.8	32.6	21.5
Two years	64.5	59.3	57.7	45.3	52.1	44.2	43.7	37.1

Percentage of compliance to parental commands (negative)

| | Intact | | | | Divorced | | | |
| | Girl | | Boy | | Girl | | Boy | |
	Father	Mother	Father	Mother	Father	Mother	Father	Mother
Two months	55.7	49.3	47.5	36.4	47.0	34.8	35.6	23.4
One year	59.2	51.5	50.3	38.8	39.1	27.2	28.3	17.2
Two years	60.5	54.6	53.6	39.0	49.9	39.7	39.7	31.8

Percentage of compliance to parental reasoning and explanation

| | Intact | | | | Divorced | | | |
| | Girl | | Boy | | Girl | | Boy | |
	Father	Mother	Father	Mother	Father	Mother	Father	Mother
Two months	49.1	43.3	41.0	31.1	41.3	29.2	29.6	18.4
One year	55.4	48.0	46.2	34.5	26.3	23.1	24.5	14.1
Two years	62.3	58.1	58.1	47.6	50.3	42.5	41.4	36.9

agreement with the spouse in disciplining the child in both divorced and intact families. When support and agreement occurred between divorced couples the disruption in family functioning appeared to be less extreme and the re-stabilizing of family functioning occurred earlier, by the end of the first year.

When there was agreement in child rearing, a positive attitude toward the spouse, low conflict between the divorced parents, and when the father was emotionally mature as measured by the California Personality Inventory socialization scale and the Personal Adjustment Scale of the Adjective Checklist, frequency of father's contact with the child was associated with more positive mother-child interactions. When there was disagreement and inconsistency in attitudes toward the child, and conflict and ill will between the divorced parent, or when the father was poorly adjusted, frequent visitation was associated with poor mother-child functioning and disruptions in the children's behav-

ior. Emotional maturity in the mother was also found to be related to her adequacy in coping with stresses in her new single life and relations with children.

Other support systems such as that of grandparents, brothers and sisters, close friends, or a competent housekeeper also were related to the mother's effectiveness in interacting with the child in divorced but not in intact families. However, they were not as salient as a continued positive relationship of the ex-husband with the family.

In summary, following divorce the family system is in a state of disequilibrium. Disorganization and disrupted family functioning seem to peak at one year and be re-stabilizing by two years following divorce. Stresses in family functioning following divorce are reflected not only in parent-child relations but in the changes in life style, emotional distress, and changes in attitudes toward the self of the divorced couple. These changes in the parents may be mediating factors in changes in the child's behavior. A want for intimacy seems to be a pervasive desire for both males and females and the attainment of intimate relations seems to be associated with positive adjustment and coping behavior.

Since this study only lasted two years it is impossible to state whether the re-stabilizing process in the divorced family had reached an asymptote and was largely completed at two years or whether this readjustment would continue over a longer period of time until it would ultimately more closely resemble that in intact families.

It should be remembered that the results reported in a study such as this represent averages and that there are wide variations in coping and parenting within intact and divorced families. There are many inadequate parents and children with problems in intact families. A conflict ridden intact family is more deleterious to family members than a stable home situation in which parents are divorced. Divorce is often a positive solution to destructive family functioning. However for most family members divorce is a stressful event involving adapting to new problems and different life style. Our ultimate goal in this study is not to condemn divorce but to be able to identify factors associated with constructive parenting and coping following divorce and to use these findings to develop means of modifying or eliminating the deleterious sequelae of divorce.

REFERENCES

Baumrind, D. Child care practices anteceding three patterns of preschool behavior. *Genetic Psychology Monographs,* 1967, *75,* 43–83.

Baumrind, D. Current pattern of parental authority. *Developmental Psychology Monographs,* 1971, *41* (1) part 2.

Biller, H. B. Paternal deprivation. Lexington, Massachusetts: Lexington Books, 1974.

Blanchard, R. W. & Biller, H. B. Father availability and academic performance among third grade boys. *Developmental Psychology,* 1971, *4,* 301–305.

Bronfenbrenner, U. The changing American family. Paper presented at the Meeting of the Society for Research in Child Development. Denver, 1975.

Hetherington, E. M., & Deur, J. The effects of father absence on child development. *Young Children,* 1971, *26,* 233–248.

Lynn, D. B. The father: His role in child development. Monterey, California: Brooks Cole Publishing Company, 1974.

Martin, B., & Hetherington, E. M. Family interaction and aggression, withdrawal and nondeviancy in children. Progress Report, 1971, University of Wisconsin. Project no. M. H. 12474, National Institute of Mental Health.

Pederson, F. A., & Robson, K. S. Father participation in infancy. *American Journal of Orthopsychiatry,* 1969, *39,* 466–472.

Sears, R. R., Rau, L. & Alpert, R. Identification and child rearing. Stanford: Stanford University Press, 1965.

Reading 35

The Changing American Family[1]

Urie Bronfenbrenner

I OVERALL TRENDS

The American family has been undergoing rapid and radical change. Today, in 1975, it is significantly different from what it was only a quarter of a century ago. In documenting the evidence, we begin with aspects that are already familiar, and then proceed to other developments that are less well known. We shall then show how these various trends combine and converge in an overall pattern that is far more consequential than any of its components.

Since our aim is to identify trends for American society as a whole, the primary source of almost all the data to be presented are government statistics, principally the *Current Populations Reports* published by the Bureau of the Census, the *Special Labor Force Reports* issued by the Department of Labor, and the *Vital and Health Statistics Reports* prepared by the National Center for Health Statistics. These data are typically provided on an annual basis. What we have done is to collate and graph them in order to illuminate the secular trends.

1. More Working Mothers

Our first and most familiar trend is the increase in working mothers (Figure 1). There are several points to be made about these data.

1 Once their children are old enough to go to school, the majority of American mothers now enter the labor force. As of March 1974, 51% of married women with children from 6 to 17 were engaged in or seeking work; in 1948, the rate was about half as high, 26%.

2 Since the early fifties, mothers of school-age children have been more likely to work than married women without children.

3 The most recent and most rapid increase has been occurring for mothers of young children.

One-third of all married women with children under six were in the labor force in 1974, three times as high as in 1948. Mothers of infants were not far behind; three out of ten married women with children under three were in the work force last year.

4 Whether their children were infants or teenagers, the great majority (two-thirds) of the mothers who had jobs were working full time.

5 The foregoing figures apply only to families in which the husband was present. As we shall see, for the rapidly growing numbers of single-parent families, the proportions in the labor force are much higher.

2. Fewer Adults in the Home

As more mothers have gone to work, the number of adults in the home who could care for the child has decreased. Whereas the number of children per

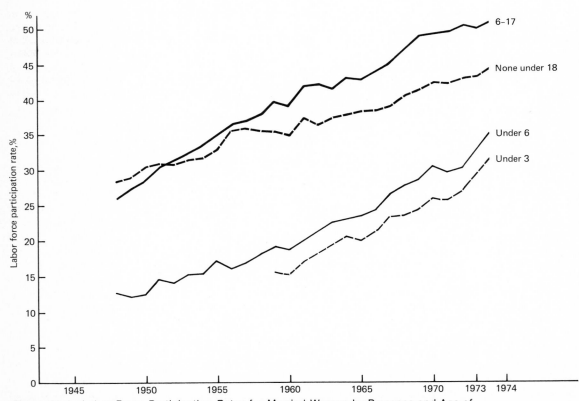

Figure 35-1 Labor Force Participation Rates for Married Women by Presence and Age of Children, 1948–1973. (*Data through 1955 from Current Population Reports 1955, P-50, No. 62, Table A, from 1956, Special Labor Force Reports 1959, No. 7, Table 1 and 1974, No. 164, Table 3.*)

family is now about the same today as it was twenty to thirty years ago, the number of adults in the American household has dropped steadily to a 1974 average of 2.2. This figure of course includes some households without children. Unfortunately, the Bureau of the Census does not publish a breakdown of the number of adults besides parents present in households containing children. A conservative approximation is obtainable, however, from the proportion of parents living with a relative as family head, usually a grandparent.[2]

Over the past quarter century the percentage of such "extended" families has decreased appreciably. Although parents with children under six are more likely to be living with a relative than parents with older children (6–17), the decline over the years has been greatest for families with young children.

3. More Single-Parent Families

The adult relatives who have been disappearing from families include parents themselves. Over a twenty-five year period, there has been a marked rise in the proportion of families with only one parent present, with the sharpest increase occurring during the past decade. According to the latest figures available, in 1974, *one out of every six children under 18 years of age was living in a single-parent family.*[3] This rate is almost double that for a quarter of a century ago.

With respect to change over time, the increase has been most rapid among families with children under six years of age. This percentage has doubled from 7% in 1948 to 15% in 1974. The proportions are almost as high for very young children; in 1974, one out of every eight infants under three (13%) was living in a single-parent family.

Further evidence of the progressive fragmentation of the American family appears when we apply our index of "extended families" to single-parent homes. The index shows a marked decline from 1948 to 1974, with the sharpest drop occurring for families with preschoolers. Today, almost 90% of all children with only one parent are living in independent families in which the single mother or father is also the family head.

The majority of such single parents are also working, 67% of mothers with school-age children, 54% of those with youngsters under six. Even among single-parent mothers with children under three, 45% are in the labor force.

The comment is frequently made that such figures about one-parent families are misleading, since single-parenthood is usually a transitional state soon terminated through remarriage. While this may be true for some selected populations, it does not appear to obtain for the nation as a whole. Figure 2 depicts the relevant data. The solid line in the middle shows the divorce rate for all marriages, the crosshatched curve indexes divorces involving children, and the broken line describes the remarriage rate. To permit comparability, all three rates were computed with the total population for the given year as a base. It is clear that the remarriage rate, while rising, lags far behind the divorce rate, especially where children are involved.

Moreover, there is good reason to believe that the remarriage rate shown on the graph is substantially higher than that which applies for divorced, widowed, or other persons who are single parents. The overwhelming majority of single parents, about 95% of them, are women. In 1971, the latest year for which the data are available, the female remarriage rate per 1000 divorced or widowed wives, was 37.3; the corresponding figure for men was 130.6, four times as high. Given this fact, it becomes obvious that the rate of remarriage for single-parent families involving children is considerably lower than the remarriage rate for both sexes, which is the statistic shown in the graph.

4. More Children of Unwed Mothers

After divorce, the most rapidly growing category of single-parenthood, especially since 1970, involved unmarried mothers. In the vital statistics of the United States, illegitimate births are indexed by two measures: the *illegitimacy ratio,* computed as the ratio of illegitimate births per 1000 live babies born; and the *illegitimacy rate,* which is the number of illegitimate births per 1000 unmarried women aged 15–44 years. The ratio has consistently been higher and risen far more rapidly than the rate. This pattern indicates not only that a growing proportion of unmarried women are having children, but that the percentage of single women among those of childbearing age is becoming ever larger. Consistent with this conclusion, recent U. S. census figures reveal an increasing trend for women to postpone the age of marriage. The rise in percent single is particularly strong for the age group under 25; and over 80% of all illegitimate children are being born to women in this age bracket.

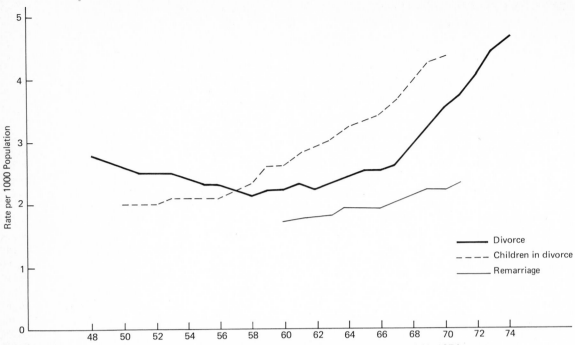

Figure 35-2   Rates of Divorce, Number of Children in Divorce, and Remarriage, 1948–1974.

Such findings suggest that the trends we have been documenting for the nation as a whole may be occurring at a faster rate in some segments of American society, and more slowly, or perhaps not at all, in others. We turn next to an examination of this issue.

II WHICH FAMILIES ARE CHANGING?

Which Mothers Work?   Upon analyzing available data for an answer to this question, we discover the following:

1 With age of child constant, it is the younger mother, particularly one under 25 years of age, who is most likely to enter the labor force. This trend has been increasing in recent years particularly for families with very young children (i.e., infants under 3).

2 One reason why younger mothers are more likely to enter the labor force is to supplement the relatively low earnings of a husband just beginning his career. In general, it is in families in which the husbands have incomes below $5,000 (which is now

close to the poverty line for a family of four) that the wives are most likely to be working. And for families in this bottom income bracket, almost half the mothers are under 25. All of these mothers, including the youngest ones with the youngest children, are working because they have to.

3 But not all the mothers whose families need the added income are working. The limiting factor is amount of schooling. It is only mothers with at least a high school education who are more likely to work when the husband has a low income. Since, below the poverty line, the overwhelming majority (68%) of family heads have not completed high school, this means that the families who need it most are least able to obtain the added income that a working mother can contribute.

4 In terms of change over time, the most rapid increase in labor force participation has occurred for mothers in middle and high income families. To state the trend in somewhat provocative terms, mothers from middle income families are now entering the work force at a higher rate than married women from low income families did in the early 1960's.

But the highest labor force participation rates of all are to be found not among mothers from intact families, on whom we have concentrated so far, but as we have already noted, among mothers who are single parents. Who are these single-parent families, and where are they most likely to be found?

Who and Where Are Single-Parent Families?   As in the case of working mothers, single-parenthood is most common and is growing most rapidly among the younger generation. By last year, almost one out of four parents under 25 heading a family was without a spouse.

The risk of parental separation is also greater for families with large numbers of small children, and this trend too has been increasing steadily over time.

The fact that family disruption is more likely to occur among younger families with large numbers of young children points to low income as an underlying factor. Single-parent families are much more likely to occur and increase over time in the lower income brackets. Among families with children under 18 and incomes under $4000 (and these contain six million children, almost a tenth of the national total), the overwhelming majority, 67%, now contain only one parent. This figure represents a marked increase from 42% only six years before. In sharp contrast, among families with incomes over $15,000, the proportion has remained consistently below 2%.

Further analysis reveals that single-parenthood is especially common for *young* families in the low income brackets. For example, among family heads under 25 with earnings under $4000, the proportion of single parents was 71% for those with all children under 6, and 86% with all children of school age. The more rapid increases over the past few years, however, tended to occur among older low income families, who are beginning to catch up. It would appear that the disruptive processes first struck the younger families among the poor, and are now affecting the older generation as well.

But a word of caution is in order. It is important to recognize what might be called a pseudo-artifact, pseudo because there is nothing spurious about the data reported, artifact because the pattern is susceptible to more than one possible interpretation. For example, though the percentage for the highest income group is very low, it would be a mistake to conclude that a well-to-do, intact family is at low risk of disruption, for there is more than one explanation for the falling fencepost we see in the figure. The interpretation that most readily comes to mind is that families with children are more likely to split up when they are under financial strain. But the causal chain could also run the other way. The breakup of the family could result in a lower income for the new, single-parent head, who, in the overwhelming majority of cases, is, of course, the mother.

Evidence on this issue is provided by the average income for 1973, the median income for all families headed by a male with wife present and at least one child under six was $12,000. The corresponding figure for a single-parent female-headed family was $3600, less than 30% of the income for an intact family, and well below the poverty line. It is important to bear in mind that these are nationwide statistics.

The nature and extent of this inequity is further underscored when we take note that the average income for the small proportion of father-headed single-parent families with preschool children was $9500. In other words, it is only the single-parent *mother* who finds herself in severely strained financial circumstances.

Economic deprivation is even more extreme for single-parent mothers under the age of 25. Such a mother, when all her children are small (i.e., under 6), must make do with a median income of only $2800. Yet there are more than a million and a half mothers in this age group, and they constitute one-third of all female-headed families with children under six.

We can now understand why the frequency and rate of increase of single parents are so low among families in the highest income brackets. There are simply few single parents who have incomes as high as $10,000. Once separation occurs, family income drops substantially, transferring the family into lower income brackets.

Does this mean that the low income is primarily a consequence rather than a cause of single-parent status? To answer this question directly we would need to know the income of the family before the split. Unfortunately this information was not obtained in the census interview. We do have data, however, that are highly correlated with the family's socio-economic status and generally precede the event of separation; namely, the mother's level of schooling. Is it the well-educated or poor-educated woman who is most likely to become a single parent?

In general, the less schooling a parent has received, the more likely is he or she to be left without a spouse. There is only one exception to the general trend. The proportion of family disruption tends to be highest, and has risen most rapidly, not for parents receiving only an elementary education, but for those who attended high school but failed to graduate. It seems likely that many of these are unwed mothers who left school because of this circumstance. Consistent with this interpretation, further analysis reveals that the foregoing pattern occurs only for women in the younger age groups, and is most marked for mothers of children from 1 to 3 years of age. In 1974, among mothers of infants in this age group, 14%, or one out of every seven, was a high school dropout.

This finding is misleading in one respect. It leaves the impression that there has been little increase recently in the percent of single-parent families among college graduates. A somewhat different picture emerges, however, when the data are broken down simultaneously by age of mother and child. When this is done, it becomes apparent that college graduates are more likely to defer family breakup until children are older. Once the child can be entered into school, or even preschool, the rates of parental separation go up from year to year, especially among the younger generation of college educated parents.

In the case of split families, we are in a position to examine not only who is likely to become an only parent, but also where, in terms of place of residence. Figure 10 shows the rise over the last six years in the percentage of single-parent families with children under six living in non-urban and suburban areas, and in American cities increasing in size from 50,000 to over 3,000,000. The graph illustrates at least three important trends. First, the percentage of single-parent families increases markedly with city size, reaching a maximum in American metropolises with a population of over 3 million. Second, the growing tendency for younger families to break up more frequently than older ones is greatest in the large urban centers and lowest in non-urban and suburban areas. Thus the proportion of single parents reaches its maximum among families with heads under 35 and living in cities with more than 3 million persons. Here one out of three to four households has a single parent as the head. Finally, the most rapid change over time is occurring not in the larger cities but those of medium size. This pattern suggests that the high levels of family fragmentation which, six years ago, were found only in major metropolitan centers, are now occurring in smaller urban areas as well.

The Ecology of a Race Difference. Up till now, we have shown breakdowns by age, income, education, and place of residence, but have not presented any data separately by race. We have deferred this separation for a reason which will become apparent in the next chart (Figure 3). It shows the rise, between 1960 and 1970, in the percentage of single-parent families by income of head within three types of residence areas: urban, suburban, and non-urban, separately for Black and White families. Unfortunately, no breakdown was available within the urban category by city size so that, as a result, the effects of this variable are considerably attenuated. Nevertheless, it is clear that both income and place of residence make an independent contribution to the frequency and increase of broken families.

Turning to the issue of race, we note that in the graph, the rising lines for Blacks and Whites are almost parallel. In other words, within each setting and income level, the percentage of single parents is increasing about as fast for Whites as it is for Blacks. To put it in more general terms, *families that live in similar circumstances, whatever their color, are affected in much the same ways.* To be sure, at the end of the decade, the Blacks within each setting and income bracket experience a higher percentage of single-parent families than do the Whites. But they entered the decade in the same relative positions. This suggests that some different experiences prior to 1960 must have contributed to the disparity we now observe between Black and White families living in similar conditions. One does not have to seek long in the historical records, especially those written by Blacks, to discover what some of these experiences may have been.

But, of course, in reality the overwhelming majority of Blacks and Whites do not live in similar conditions. It is only in our artificially selected comparison groups, especially in the context which is most homogeneous, namely suburbia, that data for the two races begin to look alike. Without statistical control for income and urbanization, the curves for the two races are rather different; they are much farther apart, and the curve for Blacks rises at a substantially faster rate. Specifically,

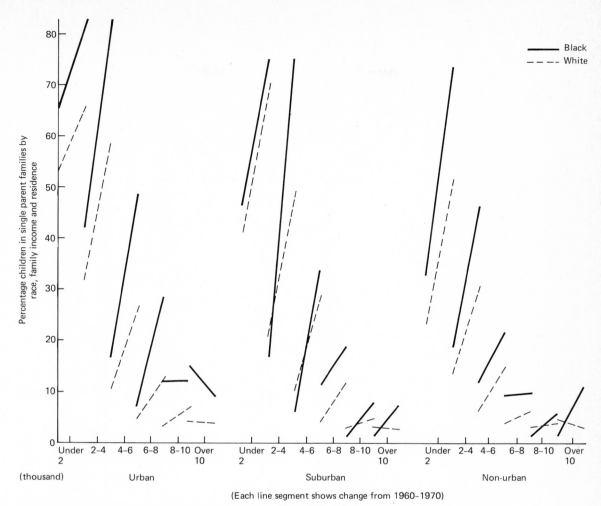

Figure 35-3 Percentage of Children in Single Parent Families by Race, Family Income in Previous Year, and Residence.

between 1960 and 1970, the percentage of single-parent families among Blacks increased at a rate five times that for Whites, and at the end of that period the percentage was over four times as high, 35% versus 8%. In the last four years, both figures have risen and the gap has widened. In 1974, the percentage of single-parent families with children under 18 was 13% for Whites and 44% for Blacks.

This dramatic disparity becomes more comprehensible, however, when we apply what we have learned about the relation of urbanization and income to family disruption. Upon inquiry, we discover that in 1974 about 6% of all White families with children under 18 were living in cities with a population of 3 million or more, compared to 21% for Blacks, over three and one-half times as high; this ratio has been rising steadily in recent years.

Turning to family income, in 1973, the latest year for which the data are available, the median income for an intact family with children under six was $12,300 when the family was White, $6700 when it was Black. Ironically, single-parenthood reduced the race difference by forcing both averages down to the poverty level—$3700 for Whites, $3400 for Blacks. Consistent with these facts, the percentage of Black families who fall below the poverty line is much higher than that for Whites. In 1973, 33%, or one-third, of all Black families with children under 18, were classified in the low income bracket, compared to 8% for Whites, a ratio of over four to one. Moreover, the advantage of Whites over Blacks in family income, which decreased during the 1960's, reversed itself at the turn of the decade and has been increasing since 1969. In the language of the latest census report:

The 1973 median income for Black families was 58 percent of the White median income and this continued a downward trend in this ratio from 61 percent, which occurred in both 1960 and 1970. In contrast to the 1970's, the ratio of Black to White median family income had increased during the 1960's.[4] (p. 5)

We can now understand why non-White mothers have gone to work in increasing numbers and at rates substantially higher than their White counterparts. In 1974, almost one-third of White married women with husbands present and children under six were in the labor force; the corresponding fraction for non-White families was over half (52%). Fifteen years ago, the gap between the racial groups was much smaller, 18% versus 28%, and it is of course the non-Whites who have increased at the faster rate.

But the more vulnerable position of Black families in American society becomes clearest when we examine the comparative exposure of both ethnic groups to the combined effects of low income and urbanization. Unfortunately, once again the data are not broken down by city size, but we can compare the distribution of Black and White families with children under 18 living in so-called "poverty areas" in urban, suburban, and rural settings, further sub-classified by family income. A poverty area is a census tract in which 20% or more of the population was below the low income level in 1969. As might be expected, in 1974 more White families with children (44% of them) resided in suburban than in central cities or rural areas, and the overwhelming majority (70%) lived outside of poverty areas and had incomes above the poverty line. In contrast, the corresponding percentages for Black families were much smaller, 17% and 32% respectively; well over half of Black families (58%) were concentrated in central cities, more than half of these lived in poverty areas within those cities, and

half of these, in turn, had incomes below the poverty line. Seventeen percent, or one out of every six Black families with children under 18, were found in the most vulnerable ecological niche (low income in a poverty area of a central city), compared to less than 1% of all Whites. Even though only 14% of all American families with children are Black, among those living in poverty areas of central cities and having incomes below the poverty level, they constitute the large majority (66%).

The grossly differential distribution of Blacks and Whites in American society by income, place of residence, and other ecological dimensions which we have not been able to examine for lack of adequate data makes even more comprehensible the difference in degree of family disruption experienced by these two major classes of American citizens. Indeed, given the extent of the disparity in conditions of life, one wonders what keeps the figures for Black families from running even higher than they do.

A possible answer is suggested by the data which measures "extended familism" separately for White and non-White families. These data are consistently and markedly higher for non-Whites. In other words, non-Whites are much more likely to be living in a household that includes more than two generations, with another relative besides the child's parent acting as the family head. To be sure, the decline since 1959 has been greater for non-Whites than for Whites, but the former curve has shown an upswing in the last four years.

But there are other less favorable developments as well. If we examine, separately by race, the extent to which single parents head their own families, we observe the same trend toward greater isolation for both Whites and non-Whites. Again, regardless of color, families in similar circumstances are affected in the same way, for better or for worse.

What this means is that the disparity in the fate of White and Black families in American society is a reflection of the way in which our society now functions and, hence, is subject to change if and when we decide to alter our policies and practices.

We have now completed our analysis of changes in the American family over the past quarter century. For the nation as a whole, the analysis reveals progressive fragmentation and isolation of the family in its child rearing role. With respect to different segments of American society, the changes have been most rapid among younger families with younger children, and increase with the degree of economic deprivation and industrialization, reaching their maximum among low income families living in the central core of our largest cities. But the general trend applies to all strata of the society. Middle class families, in cities, suburbia, and non-urban areas, are changing in similar ways. Specifically, in terms of such characteristics as the proportion of working mothers, number of adults in the home, single-parent families, or children born out of wedlock, the middle class family of today increasingly resembles the low income family of the early 1960's.

III THE CHANGING AMERICAN CHILD

Having described the changes in the structure and status of the American family, we are now ready to address our next question: What do these changes mean for the well-being and growth of children? What does it mean for the young that more and more mothers, especially mothers of preschoolers and infants, are going to work, the majority of them full-time? What does it mean that, as these mothers leave for work, there are also fewer adults in the family who might look after the child, and that, among adults who are leaving the home, the principal deserter is one or the other parent, usually the father?

Paradoxically, the most telling answer to the foregoing questions is yet another question: *Who cares for America's children? Who cares?*

At the present, substitute care for children of whatever form—nursery schools, group day care, family day care, or just a body to babysit—falls so far short of the need that it can be measured in millions of children under the age of six, not to mention the millions more of school-age youngsters, so-called "latch-key" children, who come home to empty houses, and who contribute far out of proportion to the ranks of pupils with academic and behavior problems, have difficulties in learning to read, who are dropouts, drug users, and juvenile delinquents.

But we are getting ahead of our story. Unfortunately, statistics at a national level on the state of the child are neither as comprehensive nor as complete as those on the state of the family, but the available data do suggest a pattern consistent with the evidence from our prior analysis.

We begin at the level at which all the trends of disorganization converge. For this purpose, there is an even better index than low income level—one that combines economic deprivation with every kind—health, housing, education, and welfare. Let us look first at children who are born to American citizens whose skin color is other than white.

1. Death in the First Year of Life

The first consequence we meet is that of survival itself.

In recent years, many persons have become aware of the existence of the problem to which we refer, but perhaps not of the evidence for its practical solution. America, the richest and most powerful country in the world, stands fourteenth among the nations in combating infant mortality; even East Germany does better. Moreover, our ranking has dropped steadily in recent decades. A similar situation obtains with respect to maternal and child health, day care, children's allowances, and other basic services to children and families.

But the figures for the nation as a whole, dismaying as they are, mask even greater inequities. For example, infant mortality for non-Whites in the United States is almost twice that for Whites, the maternal death rate is four times as high, and there are a number of Southern states, and Northern metropolitan areas, in which the ratios are considerably higher. Among New York City health districts, for example, the infant mortality rate in 1966–67 varied from 13 per 1000 in Haspeth, Forest Hills to 41.5 per 1000 in Central Harlem.[5] One illuminating way of describing the differences in infant mortality by race is from a time perspective. Babies born of non-White mothers are today dying at a rate which White babies have not experienced for almost a quarter of a century. The current non-White rate of 28.1 was last reported for American Whites in the late 1940's. The rate for Whites in 1950, 26.8%, was not yet achieved by non-Whites in 1974. In fact, in recent years the gap between the races, instead of narrowing, has been getting wider.

The way to the solution is suggested by the results of the two-stage analysis carried out by Dr. Harold Watts for the Advisory Committee on Child Development of the National Academy of Sciences. First, Watts demonstrated that 92% of the variation in infant death among the 30 New York

City health districts is explainable by low birth weight. Second, he showed that 97% of the variation in low birth weight can be attributed to the fraction of mothers who received no prenatal care or received care only late in their pregnancy, and the fraction unwed at the time of delivery.

Confirmatory evidence is available from an important and elegant study, published in 1973, on the relations between infant mortality, social and medical risk, and health care.[6] From an analysis of data in 140,000 births in New York City, the investigators found the following:

1 The highest rate of infant mortality was for children of Black native-born women at social and medical risk and with inadequate health care. This rate was 45 times higher than that for a group of White mothers, those who had been born and brought up outside the United States, were not at medical or social risk, and had access to adequate care. Next in line were Puerto Rican infants with a rate 22 times as high.

2 Among mothers receiving adequate medical care, there was essentially no difference in mortality among White, Black, and Puerto Rican groups, even for mothers at high medical risk.

3 For mothers at socio-economic risk, however, adequate medical care substantially reduced infant mortality rates for all races, but the figures for Black and Puerto Rican families were still substantially greater than those for Whites. In other words, other factors besides inadequate medical care contribute to producing the higher infant mortality for these non-White groups. Again these factors have to do with the social and economic conditions in which these families have to live. Thus, the results of the New York City study and other investigations point to the following characteristics as predictive of higher infant mortality: employment status of the breadwinner, mother unwed at infant's birth, married but no father in the home, number of children per room, mother under 20 or over 35, and parents' educational level.

4 Approximately 95% of those mothers at risk had medical or social conditions that could have been identified at the time of the first prenatal visit; infants born to this group of women accounted for 70% of the deaths.

What would have happened had these conditions been identified and adequate medical care provided? The answer to this question is available from an analysis of data from the Maternal and Infant Care Projects of HEW which, in the middle 1960's, were established in slum areas of fourteen cities across the nation and in Puerto Rico. In Denver, a dramatic fall in infant mortality from 34.2 per 1000 live births in 1964 to 21.5 per 1000 in 1969 was observed for the 25 census tracts that made up the target area for such a program. In Birmingham, Alabama, the rate decreased from 25.4 in 1965 to 14.3 in 1969, and in Omaha from 33.4 in 1964 to 13.4 in 1969. Significant reductions have also occurred over the populations served by these programs in prematurity, repeated teenage pregnancy, women who conceive at 35 years of age or older, and families with more than four children.

It is a reflection of our distorted priorities that these programs are currently in jeopardy, even though their proposed replacement through revenue sharing is not yet on the horizon. The phasing out of these projects will result in a return of mortality to earlier levels; more infants will die.

2. The Interplay of Biological and Environmental Factors

The decisive role that environmental factors can play in influencing the biological growth of the organism, and, thereby, its psychological development, is illustrated by a series of recent follow-up studies of babies experiencing prenatal complications at birth, but surviving and growing up in families at different socio-economic levels. As an example we may take an excellently designed and analyzed study by Richardson.[7] It is a well-established finding that mothers from low income families bear a higher proportion of premature babies, as measured either by weight at birth or gestational age, and that prematures generally tend to be somewhat retarded in mental growth. Richardson studied a group of such children in Aberdeen, Scotland from birth through seven years with special focus on intellectual development. He found, as expected, that children born prematurely to mothers in low income families showed significantly poorer performance on measures of mental growth, especially when the babies were both born before term and weighed less than five pounds. The average I. Q. for these children at seven years of age was 80. But the higher the family's socio-economic level, the weaker the tendency for birth weight to be associated with impaired intellectual function. For example, in the higher social class group, infants born before term and weighing under five pounds had a mean I. Q. of 105, higher than the average for the general population, and only five points below the mean for full term babies of normal weight born to mothers in the same socio-economic group. In other words, children starting off with similar biological deficits ended up with widely differing risks of mental retardation as a function of the conditions of life for the family in which they were born.

But low income does not require a biological base to affect profoundly the welfare and development of the child. To cite but two examples: child abuse is far more common in poor than in middle income families,[8] and the socio-economic status of the family has emerged as the most powerful predictor of school success in studies conducted at both the national and state level.[9]

Nor does income tell the whole story. In the first place, other social conditions, such as the absence of the parent, have been shown to exacerbate the impact of poverty. For example, in low income homes, child abuse is more likely to occur in single-parent than in intact families, especially when the mother is under 25 years of age.[10] It is also the young mother who is most likely to have a premature baby.

In terms of subsequent development, a state-wide study in New York State of factors affecting school performance at all grade levels[11] found that 58% of the variation in student achievement could be predicted by three factors: broken homes, over-crowded housing, and the educational level of the head of the household; when racial and ethnic variables were introduced into the analysis, they accounted for less than an additional 2% of the variation.

Finally, and perhaps most importantly, low income may not be the critical factor affecting the development and needs of children and families. The most powerful evidence for this conclusion comes from census data on trends in family income over the past quarter century. Even after adjustment for inflation, the level has been rising steadily at least through 1974, and for Black families as well as White. A reflection of this fact is a drop over the years in the percentages of children in families below the poverty line, 27% in 1959, 15% in 1968, and 14% in 1973.[12] And yet, as we have seen, the percentage of single-parent families has been grow-ing, especially in recent years. And there are analo-gous trends for indices bearing on the state and development of the child.

3. Changes over Time

Although lack of comparability between samples and measures precludes a valid assessment of change in child abuse rates, an index is available for this phenomenon in its most extreme form; homi-cide, or the deliberate killing of a child. As shown in Figure 4, the rate has been increasing over time for children of all ages. Adolescents are more likely to be the victims of homicide than younger children except in the first year of life, in which the rates again jump upward.

Children who survive face other risks. A recent study of national trends in reading achievement conducted for the Department of Health, Educa-tion, and Welfare, and based on data from several state systems of public instruction and from associ-ations of private schools found that, while there had been a steady improvement in reading achieve-ment from the 1940's to the middle 60's, there has been a negative trend since that time. The "losses are typically slight, but they appear steady and genuine."[13] The most consistent decline occurred in two states containing large urban populations, Ohio and New York. In the latter state, the proportion of children failing to perform at minimum levels was observed to increase not only in reading, but also in arithmetic: each year "more and more children are below minimum competence."[14]

One might conclude that such a decrease in competence is occurring primarily, if not exclusive-ly, among families of lower socio-economic status, with limited income, education, and cultural back-ground. The data of Figure 5 indicate that the trend is far more general. The graph shows the average score achieved each year in the verbal and mathe-matical sections of the Scholastic Aptitude Test, taken by virtually all high school juniors and sen-iors who plan to go to college. The test scores are used widely as the basis for determining admission. As is apparent from the figure, there has been a steady and substantial decrease over the past decade—35 points in the verbal section, 24 in the mathematical section. In interpreting the signifi-cance of this decline, Dr. T. Anne Clarey, Chief of the Program Services Division of the College Board, warned that it is incorrect to conclude from

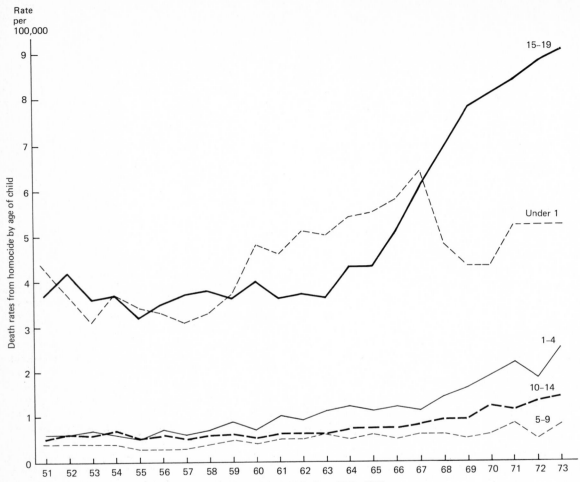

Figure 35-4   Death Rates for Homicide by Age of Child Victim: 1951–1973.

a score decline that schools have not been preparing students in verbal and mathematical skills as well as they have in former years. "The SAT measures skills developed over a youngster's lifetime—both in and out of the school setting. . . . It is evident that many factors, including family and home life, exposure to mass media, and other cultural and environmental factors are associated with students' performance."[15]

Finally we shift attention from the cognitive to the emotional and social areas. There has been an increase in suicide rates in recent years for children ages 10 to 14, and adolescents from 15 to 19. There has been an even more precipitous climb in the rate

of juvenile delinquency. Since 1963, crimes by children have been increasing at a higher rate than the juvenile population. In 1973, among children under 15,[16] almost half (47%) of all arrests involved theft, breaking and entry, and vandalism, and, with an important exception to be noted below, these categories were also the ones showing the greatest increase over the past decade. The second largest grouping, also growing rapidly, constituting almost a quarter of all offenses,[17] included loitering, disorderly conduct, and runaways. The most rapid rises, however, occurred in two other categories, drug use and violent crimes. In 1973, drug arrests accounted for 2.6% of all offenses by children under

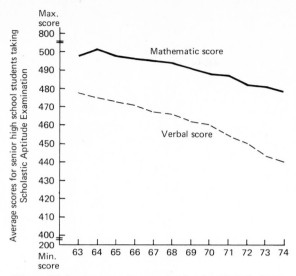

Figure 35-5 Average Scores for Senior High School Students taking the Scholastic Aptitude Examinations 1963–1974. (*Data provided courtesy Educational Testing Service.*)

15. The precise rate of increase over time is difficult to estimate because of inconsistent enforcement and reporting. In the same year, the next most rapid rise was for violent crimes (aggravated assault, armed robbery, forcible rape, and murder). These accounted for 3.3% of all arrests. While the proportion of children involved is of course very small, this figure represents at least a 200% increase over the 1964 level.[18]

It is significant that much of the juvenile violence takes place within the setting charged with major responsibility for the rearing of the young, the nation's schools. In a recent nationwide survey of 750 school districts carried out by the Senate Subcommittee to Investigate Juvenile Delinquency,[19] the investigators found that in the three years between 1970 and 1973:

1 Dropouts increased by 11.7 percent;

2 Drug and alcohol offenses on school property increased by 37.5 percent;

3 Burglaries of school buildings increased by 11.8 percent;

4 Robberies increased by 36.7 percent;

5 Assaults on students increased by 85.3 percent;

6 Assaults on teachers increased by 77.4 percent;

7 Rapes and attempted rapes increased by 40.1 percent;

8 Homicides increased by 18.5 percent.

The total number of children with a criminal record is substantial and growing. "If the present trends continue, one out of every nine youngsters will appear before a juvenile court before age 18."[20] The figures, of course, index only offenses that are detected and prosecuted. One wonders how high the numbers must climb before we acknowledge that they reflect deep and pervasive problems in the treatment of children and youth in our society.

IV THE ROOTS OF ALIENATION

What are the basic sources of these problems? The data we have examined point the accusing finger most directly at the destructive effect, both on families and children, of economic deprivation. In the light of our analysis, there can be no question that variation in income plays a critical role in accounting for the marked differences in the state of families and their children in different segments of American society.

But while income is crucial to the understanding and reduction of cross-sectional differences, our analyses indicate that the financial factor, taken by itself, cannot explain, or counteract, the profound longitudinal changes that have been taking place over the past quarter century, and that are documented in so many of our charts and figures. Other forces besides the purely economic have been operating to produce the present state of affairs, and will need to be invoked to bring about any desired improvement. These forces are reflected, but not identified, in our data on the effects of urbanization. Available research does not enable us to pin them down with any degree of precision, but some indication of their possible nature is provided from studies of child socialization and development in other cultures.[21] These investigations call attention to a distinctive feature of American child rearing: segregation, not by race or social class, but by age. Increasingly, children in America are living and growing up in relative isolation from persons older, or younger than themselves. For example, a survey of changes in child rearing practices in the

United States over a 25-year period reveals a decrease in all spheres of interaction between parent and child.[22] A similar trend is indicated by data from cross-cultural studies comparing American families with their European counterparts.[23] Thus, in a comparative study of socialization practices among German and American parents, the former emerged as significantly more involved in activities with their children including both affection and discipline. A second study, conducted several years later, showed changes over time in both cultures reflecting "a trend toward the dissolution of the family as a social system," with Germany moving closer to the American pattern of "centrifugal forces pulling the members into relationships outside the family."[24]

Although the nature and operation of these centrifugal forces have not been studied systematically, they are readily apparent to observers of the American scene. The following excerpt from the report of the President's White House Conference on Children summarizes the situation as seen by a group of experts, including both scientists and practitioners.

In today's world parents find themselves at the mercy of a society which imposes pressures and priorities that allow neither time nor place for meaningful activities and relations between children and adults, which downgrade the role of parents and the functions of parenthood, and which prevent the parent from doing things he wants to do as a guide, friend, and companion to his children . . .

The frustrations are greatest for the family of poverty where the capacity for human response is crippled by hunger, cold, filth, sickness, and despair. For families who can get along, the rats are gone, but the rat-race remains. The demands of a job, or often two jobs, that claim mealtimes, evenings, and weekends as well as days; the trips and moves necessary to get ahead or simply hold one's own; the ever increasing time spent in commuting, parties, evenings out, social and community obligations—all the things one has to do to meet so-called primary responsibilities—produce a situation in which a child often spends more time with a passive babysitter than a participating parent.[25]

Although no systematic evidence is available, there are indications that a withdrawal of adults from the lives of children is also occurring outside the home. To quote again from the report of the White House Conference:

In our modern way of life, it is not only parents of whom children are deprived, it is people in general. A host of factors conspire to isolate children from the rest of society. The fragmentation of the extended family, the separation of residential and business areas, the disappearance of neighborhoods, zoning ordinances, occupational mobility, child labor laws, the abolishment of the apprentice system, consolidated schools, television, separate patterns of social life for different age groups, the working mother, the delegation of child care to specialists—all these manifestations of progress operate to decrease opportunity and incentive for meaningful contact between children and persons older, or younger, than themselves.[26]

This erosion of the social fabric isolates not only the child but also his family. As documented in earlier sections of this report, even in intact families the centrifugal forces generated within the family by its increasingly isolated position have propelled its members in different directions. As parents, especially mothers, spend more time in work and community activities, children are placed in or gravitate to group settings, both organized and informal. For example, since 1965 the number of children enrolled in day care centers has more than doubled, and the demand today far exceeds the supply. Outside preschool or school, the child spends increasing amounts of time solely in the company of his age-mates. The vacuum created by the withdrawal of parents and other adults has been filled by the informal peer group. A recent study has found that at every age and grade level, children today show a greater dependency on their peers than they did a decade ago.[27] A parallel investigation indicates that such susceptibility to group influence is higher among children from homes in which one or both parents are frequently absent.[28] In addition, "peer oriented" youngsters describe their parents as less affectionate and less firm in discipline. Attachment to age-mates appears to be influenced more by a lack of attention and concern at home than by any positive attraction of the peer group itself. In fact, these children have a rather negative view of their friends and of themselves as well. They are pessimistic about the future, rate lower in responsibility and leadership, and are more likely to engage in such anti-social behavior as lying, teasing other children, "playing hooky," hurting others, or "doing something illegal."[29]

What we are seeing here, of course, are the roots of alienation and its milder consequences. The more serious manifestations are reflected in the rising rates of child homicide, suicide, drug use, and juvenile delinquency previously cited.

V SOME IMPLICATIONS FOR NATIONAL POLICY

How are we to reverse this delibitating trend? To the extent to which this problem has been recognized and addressed in the recent past, the principal focus of attention and programmatic effort has been the child, and in the context not of the family but of the school. At both the local and national levels, a variety of educational programs have been instituted, beginning at the preschool level through Head Start, and extending into the elementary years via Follow Through and similar compensatory efforts, all designed to enhance, or at least prevent decline in, the all-round development of children, especially from low income families.

As we now know, the results of these educational strategies have proved disappointing, at least in the narrow realm of intellectual performance as measured by standardized tests. By and large, early intervention programs were effective while they lasted, but gains tended to wash out once the children entered school.[30] The only exception to this general trend occurred with programs emphasizing the direct involvement of parents in activities with their children. But the success of this approach was qualified by the realization that the families who were willing and able to participate in these programs tended to be the least disadvantaged among those eligible.

With respect to the effects of school programs, an impressive series of investigations, notably the studies published by James Coleman in 1966,[31] and by Christopher Jencks in 1972,[32] demonstrate that the characteristics of schools, of classrooms and even of teachers predict very little of the variation in school achievement. What does predict it is family background, particularly the characteristics that define the family in relation to its social context: the world of work, neighborhood, and community.

The critical question thus becomes: Can our social institutions be changed—old ones modified and new ones introduced—so as to rebuild and revitalize the social context that families and children require for their effective function and growth? Specifically, we need to develop a variety of *support systems* for families, and for others engaged in the care of the nation's children. We have documented elsewhere some of the concrete forms that such support systems might take in American society.[33]

The primary problem, however, is not one of means but ends. We as a society have yet to follow the lead of other modern industrialized countries in making a national commitment to families and children, and implementing it through publicly supported systems of family health services, income maintenance, substitute care, and other measures necessary to sustain the integrity of the family and its capacity to function effectively in its child rearing role. Until we are willing to make this commitment, the trends documented in this report may be expected to continue. We shall be observing, and having to cope with, the consequences of increasing numbers of broken children.

REFERENCES AND NOTES

1 This paper is based on data assembled and analyzed by the author in connection with his responsibilities as a member of the Advisory Committee on Child Development of the National Academy of Sciences and the National Research Council. Appreciation is expressed to the following for their advice and assistance: Joyce Brainard, Orville Brim, David Goslin, Alfred Kahn, Mary Keyserling, Lynn Mandelbaum, Heidi Sigal, Susan Turner, Harold Watts, and Carol Williams, as well as the staff members at the Bureau of the Census and the National Center for Health Statistics, especially Howard Hayghe, Robert Heuser, Arthur Norton, and Alexander Plateris.

2 This proportion represents a minimum estimate since it does not include adult relatives present besides parents, when the parent rather than the relative is the family head. For example, a family with a mother-in-law living in would not be counted unless she was regarded as the family head, paid the rent, etc. The percentage was calculated from two sets of figures reported annually in the *Current Population Reports* (Series P-20) of the U. S. Census; (a) the number of families (defined as two or more related persons, including children, living together) and (b) the number of subfamilies (a married couple or single parent with one or more children living with a relative

who is the head of the family). Since 1968, information has been provided as to whether or not the relative was a grandparent. This was the case in a little over 80% of all instances.

3 This figure includes a small number of single-parent families headed by fathers. The proportion has remained relatively constant, around 1% since 1960.

4 U. S. Bureau of the Census, *Current Population Reports,* Series P-60, No. 97, "Money Income in 1973 of Families and Persons in the United States," U. S. Government Printing Office, Washington, D. C., 1975.

5 Kessner, D. S., *et al. Infant Death: An analysis by maternal risk and health care.* Washington, D. C.: Institute of Medicine, National Academy of Sciences, 1973.

6 Kessner, *et al., op. cit.*

7 Richardson, S. A. Ecology of malnutrition: Non-nutritional factors influencing intellectual and behavioral development. In *Nutrition, the nervous system, and behavior.* Scientific Publication #251, Pan American Health Organization, Washington, D. C., 1972, pp. 101–110.

8 Gil, D. G. *Violence against children: Physical child abuse in the United States.* Cambridge, Mass.: Harvard University Press, 1970.

9 Coleman, J. S. *Equality of educational opportunity.* Washington, D. C.: U. S. Office of Education, 1966; Jencks, C. *Inequality.* New York: Basic Books, 1972; *Report of the New York State Commission on the Quality of Cost, and Financing of Elementary and Secondary Education.* Vol. 1, 1972.

10 Gil, *ibid.*

11 *Report of the New York State Commission, ibid.*

12 Unfortunately, the curve levelled off in 1969 and has shown no decline in the 1970's.

13 Farr, R., Tuinman, J., and Rowls, M. *Reading achievement in the United States: Then and now.* Bloomington, Indiana: Reading Program Center and Institute for Child Study. Indiana University, 1975, p. 133.

14 *New York State Commission, op. cit.,* p. 33.

15 Press release, College Entrance Examination Board, New York, New York, December 20, 1973. A report in *Time* (March 31, 1975) quotes Sam McCandless, Director of Admissions Testing for the College Entrance Examination Board, as refuting arguments that the decrease in SAT scores is not "real" but a reflection of changes on the tests or in the social composition of students taking them. According to McCandless, the reason for the drop is a decline in students' "developed reasoning ability."
The same article reports another development which corroborates the downward trend:
The National Assessment of Educational Progress—a federally funded testing organization—reported last week that students knew less about

science in 1973 than they did three years earlier. The test, which covered 90,000 students in elementary and junior and senior high schools in all parts of the nation, showed the sharpest decline among 17-year-olds in large cities, although suburban students' test scores fell too.

16 The figures which follow are based on the *Uniform Crime Reports for the United States* published annually by the Federal Bureau of Investigation.

17 It is noteworthy that the highest level and most rapid rise within this grouping occurred for runaways, an increase of more than 240% since 1964 (the rate has decreased somewhat since 1970). It would appear that the trend we have observed in the progressive breakup of the family includes the departure not only of its adult members, but its older children as well.

18 We may take what comfort we can from the fact that the reported rates of drug arrests and of juvenile violence have dropped somewhat since 1970.

19 Our Nation's Schools—A report card: "A" in School Violence and Vandalism." Preliminary Report of the Subcommittee to Investigate Juvenile Delinquency. Washington, D. C.: U. S. Government Printing Office, 1975.

20 *Profiles of Children.* White House Conference on Children. Washington, D. C., 1970, p. 79.

21 Berfenstam, R. & William-Olsson, I. *Early child care in Sweden.* New York: Gordon and Breach, 1974; Bronfenbrenner, U. *Two worlds of childhood: U. S. and U. S. S.R.* New York: Russell Sage Foundation, 1970; David, M. and Lezine, I. *Early child care in France.* New York: Gordon and Breach, 1975; Devereux, E. C., Jr., *et al.* Child rearing in England and the United States: A cross-national comparison. *Journal of Marriage and the Family,* May 1969, *31,* 257–270; Hermann, A. & Komlosi, S. *Early child care in Hungary.* New York: Gordon and Breach, 1973; Kessen, W. *Childhood in China.* New Haven: Yale University Press, 1975; Liegle, L. *The family's role in Soviet education.* New York: Springer Publishing Company, 1975; Lüscher, K. L., *et al. Early child care in Switzerland.* New York: Gordon and Breach, 1973; Pringle, M. K. & Naidoo, S. *Early child care in Britain.* New York: Gordon and Breach, 1975; Robinson, H. B., *et al. Early child care in the United States of America.* New York: Gordon and Breach, 1973; Rodgers, R. R. Changes in parental behavior reported by children in West Germany and the United States. *Human Development,* 1971, *14,* 208–224.

22 Bronfenbrenner, U. Socialization and social class through time and space. In E. E. Maccoby, T. M. Newcomb, and E. Hartley (Eds.), *Readings in social psychology,* 3rd edition. New York: Holt, 1958, pp. 400–425.

23 Bronfenbrenner, 1970, *op. cit.;* Devereux, *et al.,* 1969, *op. cit.*

24 Rodgers, 1971, *op. cit.*
25 *Report to the President. White House Conference on Children.* Washington, D. C.: U. S. Government Printing Office, 1970, pp. 240–255.
26 *Report of Forum 15.* White House Conference on Children. Washington, D. C., 1970.
27 Siman, M. A. Peer group influence during adolescence: A study of 41 naturally existing friendship groups. A thesis presented to the Faculty of the Graduate School of Cornell University for the degree of Doctor of Philosophy, January 1973.
28 Condry, J. C. and Siman, M. A. An experimental study of adult vs. peer orientation. Unpublished manuscript, Cornell University, 1968.
29 Condry, J. C. and Siman, M. A. Characteristics of peer- and adult-oriented children. *Journal of Marriage and the Family,* 1974, *36,* 543–554.
30 Bronfenbrenner, U. Is early intervention effective? Department of Health, Education, and Welfare, Office of Child Development. Washington, D. C., 1974.
31 Coleman, *op. cit.*
32 Jencks, *op. cit.*
33 Bronfenbrenner, U. The origins of alienation. *Scientific American,* 1974, *231,* 53–61.

Reading 36

Cultural Experiments in Restructuring the Family

David B. Lynn

From each according to his ability.
To each according to his need.

A kibbutz principle

Many of the families in the cultures reviewed in Chapter Three are dominated by authoritarian fathers, if not traditionally patriarchal. Now we will examine some systematic efforts to eradicate patriarchy. The People's Republic of China, the U.S.S.R., and Sweden have methodically attacked patriarchy on a nationwide scale. Efforts have also been made to eliminate patriarchy among groups within the broader culture; for example, in the *kibbutz* of Israel and in communes in North America. We will discuss the father role in the Soviet Union, Sweden, the *kibbutz,* and the communes of North America.

THE SOVIET EXPERIMENT

The prerevolutionary legal code of Russia gave the husband unlimited power in his family, but following the Revolution the government and much of the urban population denounced patriarchal patterns as backward and unenlightened "remnants" of an outmoded, decadent way of life.

The chief target was the patriarchal institution of the Church and its tradition of ascribing inferior status to women. This tradition was especially strong among the peasants, who clung to the old patriarchal mores. The attitude of the Communist officials versus that of the peasants can be seen in the Party's attack on jealousy as an extension of the concept of private property. Because emancipated women could no longer be regarded as property, it became one of the worst crimes to kill a woman for jealousy. Equality of power and authority between husband and wife within the family not only was encouraged but became law. No legal distinctions remain between the sexes regarding domestic rights and duties. Husband and wife enjoy full freedom of choice concerning their individual occupation and place of residence. Each spouse is required to support the other if he or she is in need and unable to work, and husband and wife are jointly responsible for the support and upbringing of the children.

Equality of the sexes went beyond legal parity. The state's plan was that after private ownership of property was abolished, after women were engaged in production on an equal footing with men, and after the state assumed most of the functions of the family, then couples could bear children without having to assume the obligations usually involved in family life. The separation of the housewife from the kitchen was to be a more significant event than the separation of the church and state. Communal kitchens, dining halls, laundries, and children's homes and preschool centers would be established. Even the possibility of separate residences for husband and wife was proposed to assure genuine emancipation of women.

These and other measures were designed to abolish traditional parent-child ties as well. Motivation for these measures stemmed partly from the fact that parents were apt to be more resistant to the new regime than children and should therefore have less influence over their children. In addition, the measures were designed to abolish the advantages in wealth, education, and position that some parents were able to afford for their children, and instead to offer equal opportunity to all children.

The Soviets have been only partly successful with their reforms. Although the role of women in the society has improved in many respects, men still predominate in governing and managerial positions. The much-heralded predominance of women in clinical medicine in Russia is easily misinterpreted as symbolizing equality of the sexes. The fact is that clinical medicine (as opposed to medical research and teaching) is considered one of the nurturing professions, like grade-school teaching and nursing, and therefore especially suited to women. Clinical medicine is not given the prestige it receives in our society.

Most schoolteachers are women, although some men do teach especially in the secondary schools; but the greater proportion of female teachers is even more pronounced than in North America. Activities in the home are still sex-typed. The primary responsibility of the husband is to provide material security for the family, while the wife's is to care for young children, prepare food, wash clothes, and so on. Most Soviet women are both wife and mother on the one hand and full-time worker on the other, a dual role that is a strain on them and their families. Soviet men, Communists as well as others, are amused when told that American men don't mind helping women wash dishes, sweep floors, and change diapers. To them these are strictly women's tasks, and the equality of the sexes proclaimed by the revolution does not extend to sharing household chores.

Men seem more willing to work under women in public life than to relinquish dominance in the home, and this fact is a bitter pill for women. One woman wrote to the newspaper that her husband,

an important activist, had forbidden her to engage in political activity. She complained that in those very meetings that he forbids her to attend, and which she attends secretly, he makes thunderous speeches about the active role that women should play in the revolution. What he needs, she wrote, is a cook and a mistress. Although women carry their burden cheerfully, on the whole, they deeply resent the fact that life seems easier for their husbands. Even so, cooperation and good comradeship seem to prevail in Soviet marriages; indeed, everything in the couple's background and training has equipped them for cooperative living.

Although preschool centers and collective dining facilities are not as prevalent as early proponents had envisioned, over 10 percent of all Soviet children from 3 months to 2 years of age are currently enrolled in public nurseries, and about 20 percent of the children between 3 and 6 years of age attend preschool institutions. About 5 percent of all school-age children (7 years old and over) are enrolled in boarding schools or extended-day schools. In the extended-day school, pupils arrive early in the morning and leave at about six o'clock in the evening. Priority for admission to these facilities is given to children from families in which one parent is absent or away for long periods, or in which the parents work on different shifts. So although most women have not been relieved of the obligations involved in family life, as was the original plan, considerable headway has been made in providing some families with public nurseries, boarding schools, and extended-day schools.

Although most children live with their parents, primary responsibility for rearing children does not center in the family. Soviet parents are not without authority, but their authority is only the reflected power of the state. The duty of the father toward his children is a particular form of his duty toward society: to do a good job of raising its citizens. The state, in fact, expects parents to give their children love as part of that correct upbringing. Schools, camps, children's institutions, and youth programs provide the child with formalized character training aimed at the development of Communist collectivist morality (duty, honor, conscience, patience, perseverance, proper attitude toward work and public property, and so on), responsible attitudes toward learning, good conduct, esthetic appreciation, and physical culture and sports.

Most of the child's activities, including those in

the home, are taught him in the children's collective of which he is a member. Each classroom is a unit of the Communist youth organization appropriate to that grade level. The child is instructed to engage in certain activities at home: for example, in the first grade he is taught to greet parents upon arising, to thank them after meals, and to take care of his own things (including sewing on buttons). In the fifth grade, he is instructed to assist in the home garden and to help care for the elderly members of the family. These activities are rehearsed through role playing and systematically reported on in school. The schools may ask parents to submit reports on the child's behavior at home; they also recommend appropriate punishment. As the children mature, collectively and individually, they become increasingly responsible for their own behavior. First-grade children are appointed as monitors to record achievements and conduct. Older children learn public self-criticism. Occasionally an older child is disciplined by the collective through a trial conducted by his peers.

From our perspective, the Soviet state intrudes upon the domain of the family. In fact, though, the values of the state and those of the parents seem generally to coincide, so that the home and the collective reinforce each other. The child experiences continuity between home and society, and both are strong sources of security, support, and satisfaction. In both, deviance is interpreted as betrayal and elicits withdrawal of acceptance, which produces guilt (Bronfenbrenner, 1970).

Soviet parents lavish both affection and demands on their children. Babies are held more often than are American babies. Breast feeding is virtually universal, and babies are frequently held even when they are not being fed. Young Russian children receive considerably more hugging, kissing, and cuddling than American children. On the other hand, they are given little opportunity for freedom and initiative. There is concern to protect them from discomfort, illness, injury, and drafts. Children in the park are expected to stay in the immediate vicinity of their accompanying adult.

The American psychologist Urie Bronfenbrenner, who did research in Russia, reports (1970) that when his children, aged 9 and 4, would run about the park well within his view, kindly citizens of all ages would bring them back by hand, often with a reproachful word about his lack of parental concern. It is common when sitting in a crowded public conveyance to have a child placed on one's lap by strangers.

Older children of both sexes also show a lively interest in young children and are much more comfortable handling them than our society. Urie Bronfenbrenner reports that once when his 4-year-old son was walking briskly ahead of him, a group of teen-age boys coming from the opposite direction scooped him up, hugged him, kissed him resoundingly, and passed him fron one to the other. They then began a merry children's dance, caressing him with words and gestures.

What differentiates Russian parents from their American counterparts is the emotional loading of the parent-child relationship, both in its positive and negative aspects. On the one hand, the parents are more demonstrative toward the child. On the other hand, any departure from proper behavior evokes a prompt withdrawal of affection, expressed to the child by gesture, word, intonation, or eloquent silence. The child is made to feel that he has ungratefully betrayed an affectional bond with his parent.

Despite the affection, patience, and nurturance of the Soviet father toward his child, the mother still has primacy in child rearing. It is still common practice in Russia to give a man work assignments in a locality away from his family, with no apparent concern either for the consequences of separating father from child or for leaving the mother with the entire responsibility for child rearing during his absence. The popular literature on bringing up children is addressed to the mother and portrays her as the principal decision maker where the child is concerned.

Since the child is accustomed from birth to the nurturance of strangers, it is not surprising that he easily transfers his dependence from his mother to the collective as the primary source of security and incontestable authority. The evidence suggests that the combined force of the values held in common by parents and the collective does produce a child who conforms to adult standards of good conduct. A study (Bronfenbrenner, 1970) of 12-year-olds in different countries, including the U.S.S.R., tested children's readiness to engage in morally disapproved behavior, such as cheating on a test or denying responsibility for property damage. Hypothetical situations involving such behavior were presented under three different conditions: (1) no one would know their answers; (2) only parents and teachers would be informed of their answers; and (3) only classmates would be informed of their answers. Under all three conditions, Soviet children proved much less willing to engage in antisocial behavior than their age-mates in the United States, England, and East Germany. When told that their classmates would know of their actions, American children were even more inclined to take part in misconduct than if no one knew. Soviet youngsters showed just the opposite tendency; in fact, their classmates were about as effective as their parents in inhibiting misbehavior.

In another study (Bronfenbrenner, 1970), which compared Swiss and Soviet boarding-school children, the child was asked to tell what he would do if he learned that a classmate or friend had engaged in some form of misconduct. The Soviet child was much more likely than the Swiss to talk to the misbehaving comrade or to invoke the help of other children in dealing with the problem, and much *less* likely to tell an adult or simply to do nothing at all about it. Taken together, the results of these studies strongly indicate that the collective upbringing, reinforced in the home, does achieve some of its intended effects, at least at the school-age level. Not only does the child's peer group in the U.S.S.R. support behavior consistent with the values of the adult society, but it also succeeds in inducing its members to take personal initiative and responsibility for maintaining such behavior in others (Bronfenbrenner, 1970; Geiger, 1968; Mace & Mace, 1963).

THE SWEDISH EXPERIMENT

Sweden has swept away almost all traces of statutory patriarchy. Its laws make few distinctions between men and women in rights and obligations, and the few remaining distinctions are under review. But it is not satisfied with statutory sex-role egalitarianism alone; the government is also trying to alter the very structure of its institutions and the attitude of all its people to make its legal ideal a living reality.

The Swedish ideology specifies that the conditions in the society should be such that men and women have the same obligations to society and the same opportunities to participate in all cultural roles; this equality includes the opportunity for a man to stay home and mind the house and children while his wife works, if the couple so chooses. The government knows that equal opportunities are not afforded people through legislation alone, but that prejudices and preconceptions about masculine and feminine roles must be eradicated, and that facilitating institutions (such as day-care centers) must be created and the supporting economic structure established before true equality can be achieved.

Perhaps it is a sign of the future that a rugged Nordic male mannequin in a window of a large Stockholm department store was shown ironing, and that Swedish boys as well as girls are now taught to cook, sew, and care for children. In this regard, Prime Minister Olaf Palme of Sweden said, "If any responsible Swedish politician should say today that men and women should have separate life roles, he would be regarded as being from the Stone Age" (Choate, 1971). Men should no longer be mainly breadwinners and women mainly caretakers of the children; men should be educated for child care and given the same parental rights and duties as those enjoyed by women, and women should bear their share of responsibility for child support. The expression "male emancipation" has been coined to denote the right of a husband to remain at home while his children are small. There is a demand for legislation whereby the father would receive a leave of absence with pay to stay home with newborn babies, bringing the rights of men in line with those of Swedish women, who are already entitled to such a leave with pay.

In a society in which each human being can develop his own intellectual and emotional possibilities to the maximum without being hampered by preconceptions about sex roles, men should have the right to experience their children to the full. This right is thought to benefit not only the man but the child. Swedish leaders are impressed by recent research associating boys' delinquency and other disturbances with father absence and with the general lack of adult male models in the growing boy's environment. They use this research to bolster their arguments for paid leaves for fathers of newborns, shorter working hours for men with children, and for hiring males in child-care institutions.

The goal of sex-role equality is an ideal not realized even in Sweden except in a very patchy way. For example, little direct effort has been made to change the concept of what a father is, although some changes have been instituted that may later revise the definition of fatherhood. Granting men shorter working hours and leaves to be with young children would seem more practical if there were more women in the labor force. To this end, Sweden has launched a special program designed to increase the proportion of working women. Although over half of Swedish mothers with children under 17 already work full or part time, those women have frequently done so at a considerable sacrifice. Although Sweden has accomplished more toward developing low-cost day-care facilities than most other nations, there is still a lack of adequate inexpensive day care for children. To cope with this shortage, the government recently announced that it would give priority to constructing more day-care centers. It has also modified the tax laws to make it financially more attractive for women to work.

Even if many more women did join the labor force, however, a new definition of the father role in Sweden would still perhaps have to wait a more equitable occupational distribution of the sexes. Women are still found predominantly in the lowest-paid jobs; only an extremely low proportion hold managerial and high-level technical positions. This inequity is likely to continue for some time because women are not preparing for careers as thoroughly as men are. For example, not nearly as many women as men graduate from the universities; not as many girls as boys take vocational training; and women who do choose vocational training take shorter courses.

Parity between the sexes comes slowly; in Sweden, as in the rest of the world, working women still bear the brunt of the housework on top of their work outside the home. Despite definite steps toward equality in sex roles, the Swedes have a long way to go. We will simply have to wait and see how the role of the father will be defined if true equality of the sexes is in fact achieved (Anér, 1966; Linnér, 1969; *The Status of Women in Sweden,* 1968; Thorsell, 1969).

THE *KIBBUTZ* EXPERIMENT

Most family patterns throughout the world, rooted in abiding traditions, are taken for granted by the people living them; the cultural family pattern is considered to be simply "the way folks live." In societies in which the traditional family organization is breaking down, there is more awareness of the possibility of structuring family life in more than one way. Such awareness seems particularly acute in societies in which realigning family roles is a clear-cut national goal, such as in the U.S.S.R. and Sweden.

Experiments in restructuring family life occur not only on a national scale, however, but also among groups within the nation, such as the *kibbutz* collectives of Israel or the communal families within our own country. Communes are by no means new; the dream of a communal rather than a competitive order traces to Plato's *Republic,* which proposed collectivization of property under the authority of the ruling aristocracy. Religious sects, such as the Anabaptists, Separatists, and Moravians, formed communes shortly after the Reformation, seeking to live "as the early Christians did." Let's examine the role of the father first in the *kibbutz* and then in recent North American experiments in communal living.

A *kibbutz* is an agricultural collective in Israel whose main features include communal living, collective ownership of all property, and the communal rearing of children. Its guiding principle is "from each according to his ability, and to each according to his needs." Although there is a basic *kibbutz* structure, there are important differences among individual *kibbutzim* (plural of *kibbutz*); keep in mind that what is described here may not be true in every particular in all *kibbutzim* (Bettelheim, 1969). There are, in fact, about 83,000 people living in over 200 *kibbutzim* in Israel.

A *kibbutz* couple lives in a single bedroom-living room; meals are eaten in a communal dining room. Their children live separately from them and are reared in a communal children's dormitory. The children's own parents do not provide directly for their physical care. The children sleep and eat in special "children's houses," obtain their clothes from a communal store, and when ill are taken care of by the "nurses." Although the *kibbutz* as a whole is vested with the parental power to control and care for the child and plan his future, a strong parent-child relationship does exist and is characteristically more significant than one might expect.

Although their nurses and teachers are responsible for the education and socialization of *kibbutz* children, parents do spend time with their children. An infant's mother often comes to play with him and to nurse him. *Kibbutz* parents are free to visit their children any time during the day. If a father passes his child's dwelling on his way to work or on an errand, he may stop to visit for a few minutes. In general, whether a parent visits frequently or only to fetch the child in the evening depends on whether his work is located in or near the living area of the *kibbutz* or out in the fields. Since mothers are more likely to work nearby, they are apt to visit more often than fathers do. As the child grows older, he may go to his parents' room whenever he chooses during the day, although he must return to the children's house at night. Because of his schooling and his parents' work, he is usually with his parents for only an hour or two before the evening meal, but he may also spend all day Sunday with them.

The time children spend with parents within the *kibbutz* compares favorably with findings on some American families. A study of conventional families in Michigan (Thorpe, 1957) found that those families spent only about an hour a day together, most of that time during meals. In that study, farm families spent even less time together than did urban families (Thorpe, 1957).

Neither *kibbutz* parent is the primary disciplinarian; since the nurses bear that responsibility, the child-parent interaction is free of that source of tension. The child's attachment, which in non-*kibbutz* families usually focuses on parents, is, within the *kibbutz,* shared by his nurses and peers. The child grows up from the very beginning among a group of peers who are viewed virtually as siblings and with whom he is constantly encouraged to cooperate and share. Age-mates are viewed so strongly as siblings that fellow members of the same *kibbutz* typically do not marry each other, although there are no rules either discouraging or prohibiting their doing so.

The roles the father actually plays within the *kibbutz* are particularly interesting when one bears in mind both the authority characteristic of the traditional Judaic patriarch and the goals of the *kibbutzim.* The theme of emancipation from bondage to the authoritarian father pervades the literature of the *kibbutz* founders. They aimed to achieve equality in status of men and women and thus the destruction of the father's formal authority. The goal was that women, relieved of their domestic burdens by means of the various institutions of collective living, could take their place as men's equals in all activities. The communal dining room would free a woman from the burden of cooking; the communal nurseries, from the responsibilities of raising children; and the couple's small room, from excessive cleaning.

Equality of men and women has not, however, been fully realized. The original settlers did indeed divide labor equally. Women, like men, worked the fields and drove tractors; men, like women, worked in the kitchen and did laundry. Although some women were capable of performing extremely strenuous physical tasks, many of them simply could not do the arduous jobs of which the men were capable, such as tractor driving or harvesting. Moreover, a pregnant woman could not work too long, even in the vegetable garden, and a nursing mother had to work near the nursery. When these women temporarily left the "productive" branches of the economy and entered the "service" branches, their places were filled by men. Thus some women ended up without the variety of cooking *and* sewing *and* baking *and* cleaning characteristic of traditional households, but instead either cooked *or* sewed *or* took care of the children *eight hours a day.* This new housekeeping is more boring and less rewarding than the traditional type. The end result in the *kibbutz* is that men predominate in the agricultural branches of the economy and women in the service branches. Women are the teachers in the early grades, although men are found teaching at the high-school level. With such clear-cut distinctions prevailing in sex roles, it is not surprising to find that little girls play at being nurses while boys play at being truck drivers (a high-prestige job in the *kibbutz*).

Although males tend to hold the jobs with higher prestige, the father is not the specific breadwinner for his particular child, since the *kibbutz* as a whole provides for the children. A bachelor contributes just as much to a child's economic well-being as his father does. Elimination of economic dependence on the father nullifies, at least in theory, one source of paternal authority. Major decisions that shape the child's destiny are made not by his parents but by the collective, and minor daily decisions are made by his nurses. Instead, the father, along with the mother, plays a crucial role in the psychological development of the child by providing love, emotional security, and an adult model that no one else can provide.

That the *kibbutz* child is also attached to nurses and peers does not imply that he is less attached to his parents than a child in our own society. At least one observer considers the attachment of young *kibbutz* children to be stronger (Spiro, 1954). Fathers generally display an interest in their infants from the first, holding them, bouncing them, discussing their particular characteristics with their wives and other mothers, and boasting of their new accomplishments. If a mother is away from the *kibbutz*, the father may come to the nursery to give his baby a bottle or to the toddlers' house to feed him. His interest increases as the child matures. An observer's impression is that the father interacts with the child in approximately the same ways as the mother. One study of *kibbutz* children (Spiro, 1966) revealed few differences between mothers and fathers in the way children characterized their socialization roles.

Because he is male, the father may have advantages over the mother in his relationship with the child. First, he gains by holding the more prestigious job; second, he gains by *not* being a woman, as the nurses are. The younger child is with the nurses all day, and his father is virtually the only man he sees. Moreover, the nurses inevitably must sometimes punish, since they are the primary disciplinarians. The child's ambivalent feelings toward nurses may be transferred to the mother, another woman. The father, in contrast, is an exclusively permissive and nurturant figure—perhaps the nurturant figure *par excellence.* One observer (Spiro, 1966) noted that when the younger children cry for their parents during the day, they cry for their fathers more frequently than for their mothers, and when a nurse discusses the important persons in a particular child's life, the father emerges as the dominant figure. In interviews, most of the children spontaneously expressed a preference for their fathers, although they were not even asked to state a preference. The observer (Spiro, 1966) noted that this preference was expressed by males and females alike, and that it seemed most intense in two females who showed signs of deep emotional involvement with their fathers. One said that she could ask him anything because he knew everything and always made the right decisions. She left the dining room in anger when a visitor replied to her boasts that he had never heard of her father.

Despite the observation that *kibbutz* children do not perceive many differences between the socialization practices of their mothers and their fathers, there is some evidence that the children of several *kibbutzim* did feel that the parent of the same sex related to them in a very different way from the parent of the opposite sex. In this investigation, eighth-grade *kibbutz* children were asked who made decisions at home, who demanded more of them, and to whom they turned for advice. Boys generally

answered "father," and girls answered "mother." On the other hand, girls generally thought that their fathers were kinder to them than their mothers, but boys thought that their mothers were more considerate and took their side in arguments (Kugelmass & Breznitz, 1966).

It is interesting that when the same questions were asked of an urban Israeli high school, where the children were *not* from *kibbutzim,* the children did not perceive nearly so many differences in the the same sex and the opposite-sex parent related to them. This study revealed that fathers tended to make decisions at home for both boys and girls, and that girls thought that their mothers, not their fathers, were kinder to them, and agreed with the boys that their mothers were also more considerate and took their side in arguments (Breznitz & Kugelmass, 1965). This investigation concluded that, despite strong efforts to eradicate sex roles within the family, boys and girls within the *kibbutzim* had different perceptions of their relationship with their father.

Kibbutz children tend to choose their parents' occupation, but they do not necessarily choose that of the parent of the same sex. Despite the differentiation of occupations along sex lines described above, one study (Spiro, 1966) showed that half of the adult males had chosen the same branch of agriculture as their *mothers,* and half had chosen the branch of their fathers. It may be that it is difficult for boys to identify with the father as a way of learning the adult male role. With his child, the father "lets down" and acts as an affectionate, nurturant playmate, a role similar to the mother's. Since the young boy is in the charge of women during the day, he does not experience the father as the responsible person he actually is. Although in most conventional families the boy does not experience the father at work either, he *does* experience his father's discharge of responsibilities within the home, an experience that may give the boy some cues to his adult masculine role.

One investigation, which compared the fantasies of 9- and 11-year-old *kibbutz* and non-*kibbutz* boys, suggests that boys in conventional families are more likely to model themselves after the father, whereas *kibbutz* boys may be as likely to pattern themselves after the mother or their siblings. The boys were given the Blacky Pictures Test, which showed cartoonlike pictures representing various scenes in the life of a dog called Blacky, his mama, his papa, and a sibling named Tippy. The boys ascribed imaginary thoughts to the characters in each cartoon. Fewer of the *kibbutz* boys said that Blacky would prefer to be like his father; more said that he would rather be like his mother or like Tippy (Rabin, 1958).

YOUTH EXPERIMENTS IN COMMUNAL LIVING

Turning to communes in North America, let us keep in mind that today's communal movement is a reawakening of the search for Utopia that started in America as early as 1680, when religious sects first retreated to the wilderness to live as a community. The transcendental movement of the nineteenth century produced a variety of communal groups, including the Fourierists, Shakers, Zoarites, Perfectionalists, and Spiritualists. While experiments in communal living have always been part of the American landscape, only a few dozen—such as the Shakers, the Amana community, and the Hutterites—survived for more than a few years.

Within the past few years, a significant new element has appeared in America's communal movement as thousands of young people, most from middle-class homes, have rejected the life style of the prevailing culture in favor of communal living. Hundreds of "hippie" communes have appeared in the United States, particularly in California and Oregon. A belief in mysticism and nonviolence, derived, at least in part, from the use of psychedelic drugs, especially LSD, mescaline, and marijuana, seems to be common to most. A drug as powerful as LSD sometimes shatters the conventional view of the social order and allows concepts of possible new life styles to emerge; its ingestion is also commonly accompanied by mystical or spiritual experiences (Smith & Sternfield, 1970).

Present-day communes may be found in either urban or rural areas. They vary widely in structure: at one end of the continuum is the anarchistic commune seeking intimacy and involvement, characterized by little structure, no overt concern with permanence, a vague philosophical foundation, open membership, and a weak financial base; at the other end is the highly organized commune, with an integrative and explicit philosophical system, stringent entrance requirements, fixed daily routines, and a solid financial footing, usually through economic ties with the rest of society. Communes without an adequate financial base dominate. Even most agricultural communes are not self-sufficient,

and, even when some of their members work in the community, their most common sources of support are welfare, unemployment compensation, food stamps, and money from home.

Communes also vary in sexual patterns. Some encourage sexual experimentation, attempting group marriages or encouraging random and unrestricted sexual promiscuity; but the available evidence suggests that such are the minority. Although sexual mores are usually very liberal, communes also range from an emphasis on the solidarity of the traditional nuclear unit within the larger communal family to the practice of regarding the child as "belonging" to the commune as a whole, each adult member sharing responsibility for the child's welfare and upbringing.

Child rearing in many contemporary American communes, reminiscent of attitudes and practices in the *kibbutz*, is self-consciously founded on a rejection by its members of their own restrictive upbringing. Although their rebellion may well be against an authoritarian style characteristic of many fathers in our society, there is some evidence that in many cases it may, in fact, be against their mothers, not their fathers. Some young people who have adopted a hippie life style seem to be reacting against a restrictive mother who contrasts sharply with a father who encouraged independence, curiosity, and open exploration. This evidence was gathered in a study (Kendall & Pittell, 1969) of young people who had come to the Haight-Ashbury Research Project in San Francisco to participate in an intensive psychological and sociological investigation of the drug-based hippie culture. The research did not attempt to find out how many of the subjects lived in urban communes at that time or sought communal living later. It is known that many Haight-Ashbury residents did later seek refuge in rural communes.

In this study, one group, labeled "contented," often freely described themselves as "hippies" and expressed a philosophical commitment to that life style. Members of this group reported that their fathers talked things over and reasoned with them, joked with them, and encouraged them to be curious, to question, and to make decisions on their own. They generally characterized their relationship with their fathers as warm and understanding. Their mothers, on the other hand, had been authoritarian with them, worried about bad and sad things that could happen to them, and punished them by taking away privileges. The mothers, unlike the fathers, were not warm and understanding and did not encourage independence.

Another group of subjects, labeled "dysphoric," seldom described themselves as "hippies" although they lived in the Haight-Ashbury community and participated in the drug culture. Most of them had experienced adverse drug reactions; all of them found the hippie culture unsatisfactory. This group had had a generally negative relationship with a rejecting and rigid father who did not allow them to question his decisions and often felt angry with them. Their mothers, in contrast, were said to be warm and supportive and to encourage independence.

Since the hippie culture characteristically values aesthetic experience, cooperation, nonviolence, tenderness, and warmth—values typically cherished more by mothers than by fathers in our society—it may be that the "contented" group in this study was seeking and finding a substitute for a mother who lacked these matristic values herself. At the same time, this group felt supported by their fathers' attitudes. The "dysphoric" group, in contrast, might be actively rebelling against the strictness of their fathers. In rearing their own children, each group might rebel against the values of one of their parents: the "contented" group against the values of their mothers and the "dysphoric" group against the values of their fathers. In either case, both groups would be apt to value child-rearing practices of tolerance, permissiveness, little guidance and protection, much warmth and affection, and open and egalitarian communication. These were indeed found to be the child-rearing values of West Coast urban hippie adults. The single exception to highly permissive child-rearing attitudes was suppression of the child's aggression. The men held child-rearing values much more characteristic of mothers than of fathers in our society (Blois, 1971).

An investigation of families preparing for communal living found that the fathers promoted nonconformity in their preschool children and were not authoritarian with them. Like the mothers, they encouraged independence and individuality, tried to enrich the children's environment, and were very accepting of the children (Baumrind, 1971b).

The research discussed above did not differentiate between those who were living in communes and those who were not. Now let us discuss what little is known about fathers in communes. Bennett Berger and his colleagues (1971) studied child rearing in rural communes in northern California. Each commune included at least five adults and two children who had been sharing resources and facilities in a common household or domestic establishment for at least six months. Most of the communes regarded themselves as extended families, consciously using the term. In one case they actually adopted a common surname. A typical way of settling disputes among children was to appeal to kinship, even when the children were unrelated: "Mary is your sister, don't hit her." This approach is reminiscent of the way *kibbutz* children relate to peers as though they were siblings. Within the larger communal family were found a variety of nuclear units: legally married spouses and children, unmarried couples with and without children, couples in which the male partner is not the father of the child, and even one case in which the female partner was not the mother of the man's child.

In most of the communes observed in this study, sexual fidelity was approved as a general pattern; at the same time, the concept of the partner as sexual property was rejected. Although the researchers observed couples who remained together despite occasional sexual relations with others, they also observed that deep tensions sometimes resulted from infidelity. Apparently the ideology that condemns viewing another person as sexual property is often incapable of overriding the deeply entrenched motive demanding exclusive rights of the other. A vivid example of the strength of the desire for exclusive ownership of the partner was reported by Sara Davidson (1970) at the Wheeler Ranch. A group marriage between two teen-age girls, a 40-year-old man, and two married couples ended abruptly when one of the husbands saw his wife with another man in the group, pulled a knife, and dragged his wife off, yelling, "She belongs to me."

The entire commune, including the children, is frequently present at the birth of a baby. The father of the child is encouraged to assist directly in delivery, on the assumption that actual participation in the birth process encourages a profound attachment to his child. This belief is consistent with findings from animal research that early contact between adult male and infant seems to enhance paternal behavior (see Chapter 2, Question 1). In one instance, not only was childbirth ritually celebrated, but a photographic record was made of the entire process and the father composed an invocational poem in praise of life.

Even when the biological father is absent, there is usually a man present who is considered a father to the child and regarded as stable even if he and the mother have been together only a short time and have not yet settled on the degree of commitment they have to each other. Children may refer to having had many "fathers" in their young lives.

The distinction is by no means clear between the rights of parents and the rights of another commune member. One observer saw an argument between the mother of a 4-year-old girl and an adult male commune member (neither the father of the child nor the mother's "old man"). He was holding the child on his lap and feeding her at the dinner table. The man reproached the mother for interfering with him and the child while they were doing their "dinner thing" together, implying that in this instance the mother had no special rights over her child.

The dominant child rearing ideology is to let the child "do his thing," to allow maximum expression of his individuality and creativity. If forced to choose between training the next generation toward the communal life and training it to be free, most communes would choose the latter. Generally, only mild pressures toward conformity are exercised; in one instance, a father refused to take by force an adult's pipe from his 16-month-old son, who insisted upon smoking it and would not give it up, even as he was coughing on the smoke.

It remains to be seen whether children raised in these communes will follow in their parents' footsteps or whether, as has been typical in utopian communities in the history of this country, they will reject the communal values of their parents and become "uptight" businessmen and suburban housewives.

SUMMARY

This chapter has explored several experiments in uprooting traditional family roles. The Soviet Union and Sweden have not fully achieved their goal of equality between the sexes. Both, however, have gone far in eradicating the authoritarian father figure. In the Soviet Union, the parents and the collective reinforce each other in inducing the desired values and conduct in children (Bronfen-

brenner, 1970; Geiger, 1968; Mace & Mace, 1963). But in both the Soviet Union and Sweden, the mother still dominates in child rearing. In the Israeli *kibbutz,* although parental power rests with the collective, the father may become the child's favorite source of nurturance and affection. In the youth communes of America, even in cases in which the biological father is absent, there is usually some man present who is considered a father to the child. Commune fathers and mothers encourage maximum freedom and exercise minimum guidance and control.

These first four chapters have raised questions that are beyond the powers of this writer to resolve. Does human fathering have some animal base, or at least primate base? To what extent do the varieties of human fathering, brought about by cultural differences, represent a primary distinction between man and other animals? The focus of Chapters Three and Four has been on the influence of economic and cultural-historical conditions on fatherhood. Viewed from another perspective, do styles of fathering influence the economic conditions of a culture, and ultimately, its history?

REFERENCES

Bronfenbrenner, U. *Two worlds of childhood: U.S. and U.S.S.R.* New York: Russell Sage Foundation, 1970.

Geiger, K. *The family in Soviet Russia.* Cambridge, Massachusetts: Harvard University Press, 1968.

Mace, D., and Mace, V. *The Soviet family.* Garden City, New York: Doubleday, 1963.

Choate, R. Swedes iron out differences. *San Francisco Chronicle,* March 29, 1971.

Anér, K. *Swedish women today.* Stockholm, Sweden: The Swedish Institute, 1966.

Linnér, B. *Society and sex in Sweden.* Stockholm, Sweden: The Swedish Institute, 1969.

The status of women in Sweden: Report to the United Nations 1968. Stockholm, Sweden: The Swedish Institute, 1968.

Thorsell, S. *For children's minds—Not just to mind the children.* Stockholm, Sweden: The Swedish Institute, 1969.

Bettelheim, B. *Children of the dream.* New York: Macmillan, 1969.

Thorpe, A. C. Patterns of family interaction in farm and town homes. Michigan Agricultural Experiment Station, Technical Bulletin No. 260, 1957.

Spiro, M. E. Is the Family universal? *American Anthropologist,* 1954, 56, 840–46.

Spiro, M. E. *Children of the kibbutz: A study in child training and personality.* New York: Schocken Books, 1966.

Kugelmass, S., and Breznitz, S. Perception of parents by kibbutz adolescents. *Human Relations,* 1966, 19, 117–122.

Rabin, A. I. Some psychosexual differences between kibbutz and non-kibbutz Israeli boys. *Journal of Projective Techniques,* 1958, 22, 328–332.

Smith, D. E., and Sternfield, J. The hippie communal movement: Effects on child birth and development. *American Journal of Orthopsychiatry,* 1970, 40, 527–530.

Kendall, R. F., and Pihell, S. M. Life history antecedents of subjective contentment and dysporia in a hippie culture. Paper presented at the meeting of the Society for Research in Child Development, March, 1969.

Blois, M. S. Child-rearing attitudes of hippie adults. *Dissertation Abstracts,* 1971, *31* (7-A), 3329–3330.

Baumrind, D. Harmonious parents and their preschool children. *Developmental Psychology,* 1971, 4, 99–102.

Berger, B., Hackett, B., Cavan, S., Zickler, G., Miller, M., Noble, M., Theiman, S., Farrell, R., and Rosenbluth, B. Child-rearing practices of the communal family. In A. S. Skolnick and J. H. Skolnick (Eds.), *Family in transition.* Boston: Little, Brown, 1971. Pp. 509–523.

Davidson, S. Open land: Getting back to the communal garden. *Harper's,* June, 1970, 91–102.

Chapter Eight

Extrafamilial Agents of Socialization: Peers, the School, and the Mass Media

Although the family is the earliest agent of socialization, as the child grows older his or her values are influenced by other social agents and institutions. Schools, churches, law enforcement agencies, and many other social institutions are established with the inculcation and maintenance of socially desired values and behaviors as one of their main missions. Peers and the mass media, although less formally oriented toward shaping social attitudes and behavior, also remain two of the most influential forces in socialization.

Peer interactions are encouraged early by parents, and the influence of peers increases rapidly in the preschool years. Children's views of themselves, of social standards, and of other people are modified by their experience with peers. In the review by Hartup on peer interaction and development, it is suggested that peer influences are particularly marked in the development of aggression, sexuality, and self-control.

What factors are associated with friendship formation and acceptance by peers? In the paper by Asher, Oden, and Gottman the relation of personal and situational characteristics and social skills in successful or unsuccessful interactions with peers is explored. These authors also present shaping, modeling, and coaching techniques which are effective in teaching social skills to young children.

In the final paper on peers, by Freedman, the development of dominance hierarchies in both animals and children is discussed, and the differences in factors influencing social hierarchies for boys and girls noted.

Although contact with the family and peers precedes that with the school, once the child attains school age, the child spends much of his or her waking hours in the school or in school-related tasks or activities. How salutary the school experience will be depends not only on formal educational programs but on the structure of the school, on the characteristics of the teacher and the child, and on the interface between the home and the school.

The research presented by Gump indicates that the experience of children attending a large school is very different than that of children in a small school. Children in a large school identify with the school but are more likely to be passive than active participants in school activities. In contrast, in small schools more children participate in school activities, and it is perhaps because of this more active involvement that there are fewer dropouts in small schools.

It is frequently stated that schools are inhospitable places for males, minority groups, and lower-class children since our schools tend to be dominated by middle-class white female teachers. It is argued that these teachers have negative expectancies for such children and treat them in ways that are damaging to their social and cognitive development. Some evidence for this position is presented in the papers by Rubovits and Maeher and by Lee and Wolinsky. Rubovitz and Maeher note the differential effects of teacher expectations on the achievement of black and white children. Lee and Wolinsky discuss the differences in behavior of male and female teachers toward boys and girls, and the positive effects of male teachers on the attitudes and behavior of boys in their classes.

In the last paper on the school, Heber and Garber present the results of the Milwaukee Project, a highly successful intervention program to prevent mental retardation in high-risk disadvantaged children. It shares with other successful programs the training and involvement of both the mothers and the children in the intervention procedures. Programs which have focused solely on the child and school have been less successful than those in which the mothers and their children are the targets of the study.

In addition to the more personal influences of the family, peers, and teachers on child development, the impersonal mass media have great effects in modifying children's values, attitudes, and behavior. Television viewing is one of the most frequent activities of young people. Because of wide variations in the use of television it is difficult to offer a meaningful statement about the average time spent watching television, but it has been reported that by the age of eighteen a child will have spent more time watching television than doing anything else except sleeping. Some of the information and effects conveyed by television are positive, others are damaging to the development of children. Television has been effectively used as an educational tool and as a way of promoting prosocial behavior. One of the most effective and popular educational programs has been "Sesame Street." Ball and Bogatz present an analysis of the goals of "Sesame Street" and an evaluation of its outcomes on young children.

Unfortunately many of the effects of the mass media are not constructive ones. Ethnic, social class, and sex-role stereotypes are frequently maintained in an undesirable fashion. Mary Ritchie Key analyzes the content of children's readers and finds adverse sex-role stereotypes are pervasive in these texts. These stereotypes usually present males as successful, achievement-oriented, competent problem solvers and girls as helpless and inept. She argues that the presentation of these masculine and feminine images contributes to undesirable passivity, helplessness, and low achievement in women.

Finally, Liebert, Davidson, and Neale present a review of the impact of television on aggression in children. Television content is predominantly aggressive. Laboratory studies of aggression have repeatedly found that viewing aggressive models increases the incidence of aggressive behavior in children. Do these findings hold true for the frequent exposure of the child to aggressive acts by television characters? These authors argue persuasively that they do.

Reading 37

Peer Interaction and the Behavioral Development of the Individual Child

Willard W. Hartup[1]

Experience with peers is commonly assumed to make numerous contributions to child development. Such experiences are believed to provide a context for sex-role learning, the internalization of moral values, the socialization of aggression, and the development of cognitive skills. The research literature, however, contains relatively little hard data concerning the functional contributions of peer interaction to the development of the individual child. There is little evidence that the give-and-take occurring during peer interaction actually determines the moral restructuring that occurs in middle childhood, as Piaget (1932) suggested; there is no direct evidence that rough-and-tumble play contributes to the effectiveness with which the human child copes with aggressive affect (Harlow, 1969); and the contributions of peer attachments to social and intellectual development are largely unspecified.

Nevertheless, the purpose of this paper is to argue that peer interaction is an essential component of the individual child's development. Experience with peers is not a superficial luxury to be enjoyed by some children and not by others, but is a necessity in childhood socialization. And among the most sensitive indicators of difficulties in development are failure by the child to engage in the activities of the peer culture and failure to occupy a relatively comfortable place within it.

Two issues provide the basis for this discussion: a) the thesis that peer interactions are essential to the normal development of children; and b) the contention that intervention in children's peer relations can appropriately alter the general course of behavioral development.

PEER RELATIONS AND THE INDIVIDUAL CHILD'S DEVELOPMENT

Attachment and Sociability. Recent research confirms that during the third and fourth years of life there is a decrease in the frequency with which the child seeks proximity with the mother (Maccoby & Feldman, 1972), an increase in the frequency of attention-seeking and the seeking of approval relative to the frequency with which the child seeks affection (Heathers, 1955), and a change in the objects toward whom social overtures are made—specifically, there is an increase in the frequency of contact with peers (Heathers, 1955). Peer attachments become even more characteristic of the child's social life during middle childhood.

The bonds which children establish with age-mates are dissimilar to the earlier bonds which are forged between mother and child (Maccoby & Masters, 1970). First, children employ different behaviors to express affection to agemates and to adults. They follow one another around, giving attention and help to each other, but rarely express verbal affection to agemates, hug one another, or cling to each other. Moreover, children do not seem to be disturbed by the absence of a specific child even though the absence of specific adults may give rise to anxiety and distress.[2] Second, the conditions which elicit attachment activity differ according to whether the available attachment object is an adult or another child. For example, fear tends to elicit running to the teacher rather than fleeing to one's peers. Third, the behavior of adults toward children differs qualitatively from the behavior of one child toward another. Adults do not engage in sustained periods of playful behavior with children; rather, they assume roles as onlookers or supervisors of children's playful activities. In fact, play appears to emerge in the human repertoire almost completely within the context of peer interaction.[3] This fact

[1]This paper was completed with assistance from Grant No. 5-P01-05027, National Institute of Child Health and Human Development.

[2]A possible exception to this statement is the mild depression that is sometimes reported when younger children are separated from their siblings.

[3]Just why adults do not engage in long periods of play with their children is something of a mystery. From a psychological viewpoint, it is probably not possible for an adult to regress cognitively to a degree sufficient to permit sustained, child-like play. From an evolutionary viewpoint, it is probably not conducive to species survival for adult members of a troupe to spend large blocks of time playing with their offspring instead of hunting and gathering. The fact remains, however, that play occurs primarily in the context of peer interaction rather than in interaction with adults.

casts further doubt on the assumption that the parent-child and child-child social systems are manifestations of a unitary "attachment" orientation.

What developmental benefits does the child derive from peer attachments? What are the correlates and/or consequences of sociability with agemates? What attitudes and orientations typify the child who is *not* involved in easy-going social activities with peers? To my mind, the best evidence (although not the only evidence) bearing on this problem is to be found in Bronson's (1966) analysis of the data from the Berkeley Guidance Study. Among three "central" behavioral orientations emerging in her analysis, the clearest was a bi-polar dimension labeled *reserved-somber-shy/ expressive-gay-socially easy.* Across each of four age periods, covering the ages from 5 through 16 years, this orientation (social reservedness) in boys was associated with: a) an inward-looking social orientation, b) high anxiety, and c) low activity. In later childhood, the correlates of reservedness also came to include: a) vulnerability, b) lack of dominance, c) nonadventuresomeness, and d) instability. In other words, lack of sociability in boys was correlated with discomfort, anxiety, and a general unwillingness to engage the environment.

The correlates of social reservedness among girls were not substantially different. The associations between sociability and vulnerability, level of activity, and caution were significant across all four age periods, and a correlation with passivity tended to increase over time. Note that the cluster of traits which surrounds low sociability may be indicative of behavior which is in greater accord with social stereotypes among the girls than among the boys. In general, though, the findings suggest that failure to be involved with one's peers is accompanied by a lower level of instrumental competence (Baumrind, 1972) and higher anxiety than is the condition of high peer involvement. Other research provides a composite picture of the socially *rejected* child which is very much like the composite picture of the socially *inactive* child: he is neither outgoing nor friendly; he is either very high or very low in self-esteem; he is particularly dependent on adults for emotional support; he is anxious and inappropriately aggressive (Hartup, 1970).

Although the foregoing findings are relatively firm, interpretation of them is difficult. Everything we know concerning the developmental conse-

quences of peer involvement is based on correlational data. It is not clear, therefore, that peer involvement is instrumental in producing an outgoing, active, non-anxious, assertive posture toward the world, or whether a reverse interpretation is to be preferred. More than likely, some set of external influences is responsible for this whole configuration of traits, i.e., for both sociability and its correlates. But what might such external influences be? Clearly, biological factors may be operative as well as social influences. Individual differences in sociability stabilize early, such differences are not closely associated with child rearing practices (Bronson, 1966), and these characteristics possess moderate heritabilities (Scarr, 1969). Thus, the origins of the linkage between general personal-social effectiveness and the presence or absence of effective peer relations remain obscure. It is important, however, for both theoreticians and practitioners to know that this linkage exists and to know that it characterizes child behavior across a variety of samples, times, and circumstances.

Aggression.   Scattered evidence suggests that children master their aggressive impulses within the context of the peer culture rather than within the context of the family, the milieu of television, or the culture of the school. Nonhuman primate studies demonstrate rather convincingly that peer contact during late infancy and the juvenile stage produces two effects on the individual: a) he acquires a repertoire of effective aggressive behaviors, and b) he acquires mechanisms for coping with the affective outcomes of aggressive interaction (Harlow, 1969). In fact, socialization seems to require both rough-and-tumble play and experiences in which rough play escalates into aggression, and de-escalates into playful interaction (Hamburg & Van Lawick-Goodall, 1974). Field studies suggest that such experiences are readily available to the young in all primate species, including *Homo sapiens,* although opportunities are greater for males than for females (Jay, 1968; Hartup, 1974).

Whether parents can produce such a marked impact on the development of aggression is doubtful. The rough-and-tumble experiences necessary for aggressive socialization seem to be incompatible with the demands for maternal bonding because, for all primate species, some tie to the mother must be maintained after the time when socialization of aggression is begun. Fathers may contribute significantly to aggression learning, both because they provide frequent and effective displays of aggressive behavior with their children and because bonding to the father is "looser," more "secondary," and less constraining than is bonding with the mother. Selected studies support this: research on father absence shows that boys from such homes are less aggressive than boys in father present homes (Hetherington & Deur, 1972). Nevertheless, whether fathers alone could effectively socialize their children's aggression—even their male children—remains doubtful. The father's social role in Western culture requires him to spend most of his time outside the family and, even in close-knit family cultures, paternal contacts with the young child are insufficient to produce all of the learning required for the successful modulation of aggressive behavior.

Thus, nature seems to have prepared for human socialization in such a way that child-child relations are more important contributors to the successful control of aggressive motivation than parent-child relations. Patterson and his associates (Patterson, Littman, & Bricker, 1967; Patterson & Cobb, 1971) have confirmed convincingly the various ways in which reinforcement for both aggression and yielding to aggression are provided within the context of peer interactions.

According to this line of reasoning, children who show generalized hostility and unusual modes of aggressive behavior, or children who are unusually timid in the presence of aggressive attack may be lacking exposure to certain kinds of contacts with peers, i.e., rough-and-tumble play. In other words, peer contacts which never allow for aggressive display or which allow only for successful aggression (never for unsuccessful aggression) may be precursors of malfunctioning in the aggression system. Clearly, this hypothesis is plausible when applied to boys, although it is more tenuous for girls. Traditional socialization produces women who are ineffectively prepared for exposure to aggressive instigating events (except perhaps, for threats to their children). Women are notably more anxious and passive than men when exposed to aggressive instigation, and this sex difference may be greater than is good for the future of the species. In any event, if women are to assume social roles more like those of men, and men are to assume roles more like those of women, some manipulation of early peer experiences is necessary. Opportuni-

ties for early exposure to rough-and-tumble play must be as equal for males and for females as opportunities for exposure to other normative behaviors.

Sex. If parents were to be given sole responsibility for the socialization of sexuality, *Homo sapiens* would not survive. With due respect to the efforts of modern sex educators, we must recognize that the parent-child relationship is no better suited to the task of socializing sex than to the task of socializing aggression. Evolution has established the incest taboo (Lindzey, 1967), a taboo which is so pervasive that interaction with agemates is virtually the only opportunity available to the child in which he may engage in the trial and error, the modeling, and the information gathering that ultimately produce his sexual life style.

There can be little doubt that sexual attitudes and the basic sexual repertoire are shaped primarily by contacts with other children. Kinsey (1948) said: "Children are the most frequent agents for the transmission of the sexual mores. Adults serve in that capacity only to a smaller extent. This will not surprise sociologists and anthropologists, for they are aware of the great amount of imitative adult activity which enters into the play of children, the world around. In this activity, play though it may be, children are severe, highly critical, and vindicative in their punishment of a child who does not do it 'this way,' or 'that way.' Even before there has been any attempt at overt sex play, the child may have acquired a considerably schooling on matters of sex. Much of this comes so early that the adult has no memory of where his attitudes were acquired (p. 445)." These comments are repeated, nearly word for word, in the records of those many investigators who have observed the various non-human primate species in the field (Jay, 1968).

Of course, the child's earliest identification of itself as male or female and the earliest manifestations of sex-typed behavior patterns derive from interactions with its parents. Parents are known to respond differentially to boys and to girls from infancy onward (Rothbart & Maccoby, 1966), and the sex-typed outcomes of parent-child interaction have been discussed extensively in the child development literature (e.g., Lynn, 1969). Nevertheless, there is strong evidence that the peer culture supports and extends the process of sex-typing beginning in the earliest preschool years. Sex is the overriding polarizer in peer group formation in all primate species from the point of earliest contact (Hartup, 1975). Sex is a more powerful determinant of "who plays with whom" than age, race, social class, intelligence, or any other demographic factor with the possible exception of propinquity. And clearly, this sex cleavage is instrumental in transmitting normative sex-role standards to the child. How else to account for the vast number of sex differences that have been observed in the social activities of children (e.g., aggression) beginning with the preschool years?

Another vivid demonstration of the power of the peer culture in early sex-typing is contained in a series of experiments by Kobasigawa (1968). With kindergarten children, he found that: a) exposure to peer models who inhibited playing with inappropriate-sex toys enhanced the observer's self-control over inappropriate responses; b) exposure to models demonstrating alternative activities to sex-inappropriate responses also reduced inappropriate sex-typed activity; c) exposure to peer models who displayed sex-inappropriate behavior had disinhibitory effects on the observer, although the amount of the disinhibition depended on the sex of the model in relation to the sex of the child—that is, boys disinhibited inappropriate sex behavior only when the model was a boy while the sex of the model made relatively little difference in amount of disinhibition for girls. Similar results have been found in other modeling work: for example, aggressive peer models enhance aggression in young children, but more effectively if the model is a boy than if the model is a girl (Hicks, 1967).

Do these findings imply that aberrant and inadequate sexual behaviors derive from aberrant and/or inadequate contacts with the peer culture? My knowledge of life history research in sexual pathology is very limited, but my impression is that most such pathologies derive from some combination of early hangups with parents and hangups with peers. Peer modeling, in other words, seldom accounts for all of the variance in criminally violent or aberrant sexual behavior. Even so, Roff (1966) has shown that a history of poor peer relations is more characteristic of certain kinds of homosexual males than comparison groups of heterosexual males; case studies show with considerable frequency that persons committing crimes of sexual assault have histories of peer rejection and social isolation.

Moral Development.   According to Piaget (1932), both the quantity and the quality of social participation are related to the child's moral development. Moral understanding is assumed to derive partly from the amount of social interaction in which the child participates and partly from his centrality in the peer group. During early childhood, the child's behavior reflects an "objective" moral orientation (i.e., he believes that rules are immutable and the power of adults is absolute). Adoption of a "subjective" moral orientation requires some opportunity to view moral rules as changeable products of group consensus. For this purpose, social give-and-take is required. Such opportunity is not common in the child's experiences with his parents and teachers because social systems such as the family and the school are structured in authoritarian terms. Only in rare instances is there sufficient reciprocity in adult-child interaction to facilitate the disequilibration which is necessary to form a mature moral orientation. The peer group, on the other hand, is seldom organized along authoritarian dimensions and possesses the inherent characteristics for furthering moral development.

Precious little data exist to support the thesis that the *amount* of agemate contact is associated with advanced moral development. Keasey (1971) has recently published a study, however, based on 144 preadolescents, in which he found that children who belonged to relatively many clubs and social organizations had higher moral judgment scores than children belonging to few organized groups. These results, which were somewhat stronger for boys than for girls, stand alone in revealing a correlation between amount of social participation with peers and advances in moral functioning.

Evidence is more profuse concerning the association between the *quality* of a child's peer contacts and the level of his moral reasoning. Keasey (1971) also reported that self-reports of leadership functions, peer ratings of leadership and friendship nominations, and teacher ratings of leadership and popularity were all positively related to level of moral judgment as assessed by Kohlberg's (1958) techniques. Irwin (1967) was unable to demonstrate consistent relations between popularity and measures of moral understanding within several groups of nursery school children, either because the samples were too homogeneous or because the period in question is too early for the relation between acceptance and morality to be reflected in a systematic manner. Other data, though, support Keasey's findings: Gold (1962) reported that peer leaders have "more socially integrative" ideologies than non leaders; Porteus and Johnson (1955) showed that acceptance was related to good moral judgment as perceived by peers; Campbell and Yarrow (1961) found that popular children, as compared to less popular children, made more extensive use of subtle inferences concerning the causes of other children's behavior; and Klaus (1959) found that accepted children tend to emphasize being neat and tidy, being a good sport, and being able to take a joke in their descriptions of classmates. Each of these diverse findings suggests that popularity is linked with effectively internalized social norms. Studies of peer group leaders also show them to be actively and appropriately sociable.

Once again, there is difficulty in interpreting the findings. Existence of a significant correlation between the extent of social participation and level of moral functioning does not prove that the latter derives from the former. Membership in clubs may facilitate change in the structuring of moral understanding but higher levels of moral understanding may also be prerequisite to membership in large numbers of social clubs. Children may choose friends and teachers may nominate children as popular who can demonstrate advanced levels of moral understanding; on the other hand, popularity itself may enhance the child's level of moral reasoning. Another possibility is that the linkages cited here exist partly because estimates of moral understanding and estimates of popularity are both modestly related to intelligence.

Thus, the basic hypothesis that peer interaction contributes to advances in moral development remains unproven. The available evidence is consistent with this hypothesis, to be sure, but only controlled manipulation of the child's social experiences with agemates can provide adequate causal evidence. Needless to say, much manipulations are very hard to produce.

Are children who have successful peer relations more overtly honest and upright than children who are loners and/or who are rejected by their peers? Some of the previously-cited evidence is suggestive of such a state of affairs, although additional evidence is not extensive. In one early investigation, Roff (1961) found that in a sample of servicemen,

all of whom were former patients in a child guidance clinic, those receiving bad conduct discharges were significantly more likely to have been rated by their childhood counselors as having poor peer adjustment than those with successful service records. These data are important for two reasons: a) they demonstrate a linkage between peer adjustment and moral behavior; and b) the relation is a predictive one—childhood failure in peer relations was correlated with bad conduct discharge rates in adulthood. In a more recent study (Roff & Sells, 1968), a significant relation was demonstrated between peer acceptance-rejection during middle childhood and delinquency during early adolescence. Among upper lower-class and middle-class children, there was a dramatically higher delinquency rate among children who were not accepted by their peers than among those who were. Among the very lowest social class subjects, however, a different pattern held—both highly accepted and highly rejected boys had higher delinquency rates than those who were moderately accepted by their peers. Examination of individual case records indicated that the nature of the delinquency and the adequacy of the child's personality adjustment differed between the chosen and nonchosen lower class groups—in fact, there is every reason to expect that, among the subjects from the lowest social strata, ultimate adjustment of the peer accepted delinquent group will be better than the nonaccepted delinquent subjects. Thus far, path analysis techniques have not been applied to Roff's data, so that some question still remains concerning the relative primacy of delinquent activity and the poor peer relations. But the data point to peer interaction as one source of the individual's willingness to live according to accepted social standards.

Other research, dealing with the problem in a different manner, suggests that peer pressures can move child behavior both in the direction of socially accepted and socially nonaccepted norms. Such pressures are directly revealed in the studies of spontaneous peer groups published by the Sherifs (1964) and more indirectly in Kandel's (1973) study of peer influences in relation to drug use among adolescents.[4] Indirect peer influences on moral

---

[4] A significant concordance between friends in incidence of drug use does not, of course, reveal which comes first—the use of drugs or contact with drug-using friends.

behavior are also shown in a set of studies by Shelton and Hill (1969) in which it was found that children were more likely to falsify their scores in a laboratory game if they expected that their peers would be informed about their performance than if information about the subject's performance was to be kept secret.

Anxiety and emotional disturbance. Evidence can be found in at least twenty studies to show that a child's general emotional adjustment is related to his popularity (Hartup, 1970). Assessment of adjustment in these studies has been accomplished with devices as various as the TAT, on the one hand, and observations of school adjustment, on the other. The data consistently show that, in samples of children who are functioning within the normal range, degree of maladjustment is inversely related to degree of social acceptance. In addition to the studies with normal samples, work with institutionalized populations shows that popularity in disturbed groups is also inversely related to relative degree of maladjustment (Davids & Parenti, 1958). Sheer quantity of social participation has not been studied in relation to general personality adjustment, although one suspects that such a relation exists.

Some fifteen years ago, a spate of studies was published concerning the relation between a more specific affective component, anxiety, and social acceptance. In general there tends to be a low negative correlation between anxiety, as measured by the *Children's Manifest Anxiety Scale*, and sociometric status (e.g., McCandless, Castaneda, & Palermo, 1956) although, once again, we know very little about the relation between amount of social participation and anxiety.

The major predictive studies of the relation between childhood peer status and adult emotional adjustment have been completed by Roff (1963) within the context of his follow-up investigations of the adult status of boys who, as children, were seen in child guidance clinics. Within these samples, poor peer relations in childhood have been predictive of both neurotic disturbance and psychotic episodes of a variety of types.

Once again, the evidence relating affective disturbance and peer relations is correlational and invites an interpretation suggesting that rejection leads to anxiety, lowered self-esteem, and hostility which, in turn, lead to further rejection. A simple uni-directional interpretation does not seem plausible. However, in spite of the fact that explanatory hypotheses do not receive clear support from this research, there is no evidence which contradicts the basic hypothesis that peer relations are of pivotal importance in personality development (Roff, Sells, & Golden, 1972).

Intellectual Development. The contributions of peer relations to intellectual development are difficult to specify. There seems to be no evidence that sociability is related to IQ, either in younger or older children. Parten (1932) found a small positive correlation between cooperative participation and IQ ($r = .33$) but an even larger correlation was obtained between parallel play and IQ ($r = .62$). On the other hand, amount of social participation appears to be neither markedly greater or less among gifted children than among children of average IQ (Terman, 1947), and moderately retarded children are not notably less sociable than children of greater intellectual ability. Brighter children occupy more central positions in the peer culture, being of higher sociometric status than less bright children (Roff, Sells, & Golden, 1972) and of higher social effectance (Hartup, 1970), but competence in social relations does not bear a consistent relation to IQ. At least one study (Lurie, Newburger, Rosenthal, & Outcalt, 1941) shows an inverse relation between measured intelligence and social maturity. Thus, it is difficult to make a case for the hypothesis that social participation is related to mental abilities (as measured by IQ tests) in any systematic way.

The evidence is also conflicting concerning the relation between sociability and achievement; much depends on the parameters of achievement and social behavior being measured. For example, Van den Munckhof (1970) reported a correlation of .42 between sociability and performance on the *Nijmegen School Achievement Test* for a sample of 454 Dutch school children, a finding which was replicated with a second sample including 91 handicapped young girls. On the other hand, Crandall (1970) found that both men and women who spend large amounts of time in academic achievement efforts had early childhood histories of alienation from their peers.

Several studies indicate that peer affiliations can either reward or punish academic performance, depending on the values of the peer group. An inverse correlation has sometimes been found between studiousness and popularity (Coleman, 1961) but opposite findings have also been obtained (Hartup, 1970). Thus, at the moment, there is no strong evidence that either sheer amount of social participation or the centrality of the child's position in the peer group has a consistent bearing on achievement behavior.

The status of Piaget's (1926) hypothesis that peer interaction is the primary mechanism for overcoming childhood egocentrism is also uncertain. Most of the research based on this hypothesis has involved the study of correlations between measured popularity, on the one hand, and measures of role-taking ability or referential communication, on the other hand. Using this paradigm, Rubin (1972) found that popular kindergarten and second grade children had low scores on a measure of communicative egocentrism as compared to their nonpopular peers. Finley, French, and Cowan (1973), however, reported that they were unable to generate any significant relations between popularity and three different measures of egocentrism in two different samples of elementary school children. And finally, Rardin and Moan (1971) reported very, very weak relations between popularity and classification and conservation abilities among kindergarten and first grade children.

Thus, the evidence does not support the Piagetian thesis that the peer group is the primary locus of social "decentration." Of course, certain questions may be raised concerning the adequacy of the research strategies which have been used to explore the interface between peer relations and cognitive development. Co-variation of individual differences within age groups should not be expected to reveal the functional contribution of social experience to the restructuring of mental abilities. Also, popularity may not be the most appropriate index of social participation for studying this problem. Although popular children are more sociable than nonpopular children (McCandless & Marshall, 1957), the relation between amount of social experience and cognitive change should be explored more directly.

Thus, the contribution of peer relations to intellectual development is unclear. Neither general nor specific cognitive abilities appear to be consistently related to either the quanitity or quality of a child's contact with the peer culture. Whether such social experiences represent unimportant contributions to mental development or whether our research strategies have been defective remains an open question. But no claim can be made, on the basis of present data, to the effect that large portions of variance in children's intellectual competencies derive from their commerce with agemates.

IMPROVING CHILDREN'S PEER RELATIONS

Calculated attempts to improve children's peer relations have been successful since the first behavior modification experiments (Jack, 1934; Page, 1936; Chittenden, 1942). These early studies included the invention of protocols which utilized out-of-class training experiences in modifying assertive and dominance behaviors. The protocols, which made liberal use of contingent social reinforcement, modeling, and verbal instructions, represent excellent examples of efficient supplemental socialization experiences for young children. The procedures were clearly explicated, and the outcomes were documented with respect to both short-term and somewhat longer-term effects. More recent studies, such as those by Harris, Wolf, and Baer (1967), demonstrate how contingencies of adult attention can be used within the classroom itself to bring about increased peer contacts from isolated, socially-incompetent children. Although most of these studies have included follow-up checks which were conducted weeks or months later and which demonstrate the lastingness of the induced effects, long-term follow-up studies are rare. This deficit can be cited as a critical gap in this literature.

Other ways of modifying children's social competencies consist of manipulating the context in which peer interaction occurs. One contextual element which can be used to modify the individual child's behavior is feedback from the peer group itself. Thus, Wahler (1967) picked five nursery school children, established baseline rates for a number of different response classes (e.g., cooperation, social overtures, and social speech), and then instructed the peer group to behave toward the target children with different contingencies than were ordinarily used. Two outcomes of this experiment should be mentioned: a) the children's peers were able to use attention selectively, thus demonstrating the feasibility of programming peer interaction; and b) behavior change in the selected response class occurred during the experimental phase for each of the five subjects. Other studies (e.g., Patterson & Brodsky, 1966) have described instances in which the peer group has been used to modify more deviant behaviors than in the Wahler experiment.

Group leaders can manipulate the context of peer interaction in a variety of other ways. The classic studies of group atmosphere, in which social behavior was determined by leadership style, are pertinent to this discussion (e.g., Lewin, Lippitt, & White, 1938). So are the studies of the effects of superordinate goals on intergroup conflict and cooperation (Sherif, Harvey, White, Hood, & Sherif, 1961).

Simply manipulating the composition of the peer group apparently has therapeutic potential. For example, there is the possibility that interaction with nonagemates provides a more sanguine context for the development of social competence by low competent children than does interaction with children who are similar in age. Suomi and Harlow (1972) reported that the untoward effects of prolonged isolation on the social development of rhesus monkeys is effectively reversed by a carefully managed program of contact between the isolated monkey and other monkeys who are appreciably *younger* in age. The data indicate that such a program of social rehabilitation is more effective than contact with agemates. Similarly, human children who are not especially competent in social situations may be assisted by opportunities to interact with younger children. Indeed, this idea seems implicit in the strategies commonly employed by nursery school and kindergarten teachers. Two practices are typical: a) at the beginning of the school year, socially incompetent children are frequently assigned to classes of younger rather than older children, and b) subgroups are used within a classroom in which less skilled children are placed in contact with younger (but not inept) peers. These procedures undoubtedly maximize the less competent child's chances of obtaining positive feedback for prosocial activity while, at the same time, chances of social punishment are minimized.

CONCLUSION

Access to agemates, acceptance by them, and constructive interactions with them are among the necessities of child development. The sensitive student of child behavior has a variety of avenues available to maximize the input of peer relations to

the development of the individual child. Ensuring each child the opportunity for productive intercourse with peers is not an easy task, but such experiences are the child's inalienable right.

REFERENCES

Baumrind, D. Socialization and instrumental competence in young children. In. W. W. Hartup (Ed.), *The young child: Reviews of research,* Vol. 2. Washington, D. C.: National Association for the Education of Young Children, 1972. Pp. 202–224.

Bronson, W. C. Central orientations: A study of behavior organization from childhood to adolescence. *Child Development,* 1966, *37,* 125–155.

Campbell, J. D., & Yarrow, M. R. Perceptual and behavioral correlates of social effectiveness. *Sociometry,* 1961, *24,* 1–20.

Chittenden, G. E. An experimental study in measuring and modifying assertive behavior in young children. *Monographs for the Society for Research in Child Development,* 1942, 7, No. 1.

Colemen, J. S. *The adolescent society.* Glencoe, Ill.: Free Press, 1961.

Crandall, V. C., & Battle, E. S. The antecedents and adult correlates of academic and intellectual achievement effort. In J. P. Hill (Ed.), *Minnesota symposia on child psychology,* Vol 4. Minneapolis: University of Minnesota Press, 1970. Pp. 36–93.

Davids, A., & Parenti, A. N. Time orientation and interpersonal relations of emotionally disturbed and normal children. *Journal of Abnormal and Social Psychology,* 1958, *57,* 299–305.

Finley, G. F., French, D., & Cowan, P. A. Egocentrism and popularity. XIVth Interamerican Congress of Psychology. Sao Paulo, Brazil, April, 1973.

Gold, H. A. The importance of ideology in sociometric evaluation of leadership. *Group Psychotherapy,* 1962, *15,* 224–230.

Hamburg, D. A., & Van Lawick-Goodall, J. Factors facilitating development of aggressive behavior in chimpanzees and humans. In W. W. Hartup & J. de Wit (Eds.), *Determinants and Origins of Aggression.* The Hague: Mouton (1974).

Harlow, H. F. Age-mate or peer affectional system. In D. S. Lehrman, R. A. Hinde, & E. Shaw (Eds.), *Advances in the study of behavior.* Vol. 2. New York: Academic Press, 1969. Pp. 333–383.

Harris, F. R., Wolf, M. M., & Baer, D. M. Effects of adult social reinforcement on child behavior. In W. W. Hartup & N. L. Smothergill (Eds.), *The young child: Reviews of research.* Washington, D.C.: National Association for the Education of Young Children, 1967. Pp. 13–26.

Hartup, W. W. Peer interaction and social organization. In P. H. Mussen (Ed.), *Carmichael's manual of child psychology.* Vol. 2. New York: John Wiley, 1970. Pp. 361–456.

Hartup, W. W. Violence in development: The functions of aggression in childhood. *American Psychologist,* 1974, *29,* 336–341.

Hartup, W. W. Cross-age vs. same age peer interaction: Ethological and cross-cultural perspectives. In V. L. Allen (Ed.), *Interage-interaction in children: Theory and research on the helping relationship.* Madison, Wisconsin: University of Wisconsin Press, 1975.

Heathers, G. Emotional dependence and independence in nursery school play. *Journal of Genetic Psychology,* 1955, *87,* 37–57.

Hetherington, M., & Deur, J. The effects of father absence on child development. In W. W. Hartup (Ed.), *The young child: Reviews of research,* Vol. 2. Washington, D. C.: National Association for the Education of Young Children, 1972. Pp. 303–319.

Hicks, D. J. Imitation and retention of film-mediated aggressive peer and adult models. *Journal of Personality and Social Psychology,* 1965, *2,* 97–100.

Irwin, D. M. Peer acceptance related to the young child's concept of justice. Unpublished bachelor's thesis, University of Minnesota, 1967.

Jack, L. M. An experimental study of ascendant behavior in preschool children. *University of Iowa Studies in Child Welfare,* 1934, *9,* No. 3.

Jay, P. (Ed.) *Primates: Studies in adaptation and variability.* New York: Holt, Rinehart, & Winston, 1968.

Kandel, D. Adolescent marihuana use: Role of parents and peers. *Science,* 1973, *181,* 1067–1070.

Keasey, C. B. Social participation as a factor in the moral development of preadolescents. *Developmental Psychology,* 1971, *5,* 216–220.

Kinsey, A. C., Pomeroy, W. B., & Martin, C. E. *Sexual behavior in the human male.* Philadelphia: W. B. Saunders, 1948.

Klaus, R. A. Interrelationships of attributes that accepted and rejected children ascribe to their peers. Unpublished doctoral dissertation, George Peabody College for Teachers, 1959.

Kobasigawa, A. Inhibitory and disinhibitory effects of models on sex-inappropriate behavior in children. *Psychologia,* 1968, *11,* 86–96.

Kohlberg, L. The development of modes of moral thinking and choice in the years ten to sixteen. Unpublished doctoral dissertation, University of Chicago, 1958.

Lewin, K., Lippitt, R., & White, R. K. Patterns of aggressive behavior in experimentally created "social climates." *Journal of Social Psychology,* 1938, *10,* 271–299.

Lindzey, G. Some remarks concerning incest, the incest taboo, and psychoanalytic theory. *American Psychologist,* 1967, *22,* 1051–1059.

Lurie, L. A., Newburger, M., Rosenthal, F. M., & Outcalt, L. C. Intelligence quotient and social quotient. *American Journal of Orthopsychiatry,* 1941, *11,* 111–117.

Lynn, D. B. *Parental and sex role identification: A theoretical formulation.* Berkeley: McCutchan, 1969.

Maccoby, E. E., & Feldman, S. S. Mother-attachment and stranger-reactions in the third year of life. *Monographs of the Society for Research in Child Development,* 1972, *37* (No. 146).

Maccoby, E. E., & Masters, J. C. Attachment and dependency. In P. H. Mussen (Ed.), *Carmichael's manual of child psychology.* Vol. 2. New York: Wiley, 1970, Pp. 73–157.

McCandless, B. R., Castaneda, A., & Palermo, D. S. Anxiety in children and social status. *Child Development,* 1956, *27,* 385–391.

McCandless, B. R., & Marshall, H. R. A picture sociometric technique for preschool children and its relation to teacher judgments of friendship. *Child Development,* 1957, *28,* 139–148.

Page, M. L. The modification of ascendant behavior in preschool children. *University of Iowa Studies in Child Welfare,* 1936, *12,* No. 3.

Parten, M. B. Social participation among preschool children. *Journal of Abnormal and Social Psychology,* 1932–1933, *27,* 243–269.

Patterson, G. R., & Brodsky, G. A behavior modification program for a child with multiple problem behavior. *Journal of Child Psychology and Psychiatry,* 1966, *7,* 277–295.

Patterson, G. R., & Cobb, J. A. A dyadic analysis of "aggressive" behavior. In J. P. Hill (Ed.), *Minnesota symposia on child psychology.* Vol. 5. Minneapolis: University of Minnesota Press, 1971.

Patterson, G. R., Littman, R. A., & Bricker, W. Assertive behavior in children: A step toward a theory of aggression. *Monographs of the Society for Research in Child Development,* 1967, *32,* No. 113.

Piaget, J. *The language and thought of the child.* New York: Harcourt, Brace, 1926.

Piaget, J. *The moral judgment of the child.* Glencoe, Ill.: Free Press, 1932.

Porteus, B. D., & Johnson, R. C. Children's responses to two measures of conscience development and their relation to sociometric nomination. *Child Development,* 1965, *36,* 703–711.

Rardin, D. R., & Moan, C. E. Peer interaction and cognitive development. *Child Development,* 1971, *42,* 1685–1699.

Roff, M. Childhood social interactions and young adult bad conduct. *Journal of Abnormal and Social Psychology,* 1961, *63,* 333–337.

Roff, M. Childhood social interaction and young adult psychosis. *Journal of Clinical Psychology,* 1963, *19,* 152–157.

Roff, M. Some childhood and adolescent characteristics of adult homosexuals. U.S. Army Medical Research and Development Command, Report No. 66-5, May, 1966.

Roff, M., & Sells, S. B. Juvenile delinquency in relation to peer acceptance-rejection and socioeconomic status. *Psychology in the Schools,* 1968, *5,* 3–18.

Roff, M., Sells, S. B., & Golden, M. M. *Social adjustment and personality development in children.* Minneapolis: University of Minnesota Press, 1972.

Rothbart, M. K., & Maccoby, E. E. Parents' differential reactions to sons and daughters. *Journal of Personality and Social Psychology,* 1966, *4,* 237–243.

Rubin, K. H. Relationship between egocentric communication and popularity among peers. *Developmental Psychology,* 1972, *7,* 364.

Scarr, S. Social introversion-extraversion as a heritable response. *Child Development,* 1969, *40,* 823–832.

Shelton, J., & Hill, J. P. Effects on cheating of achieve- ment anxiety and knowledge of peer performance. *Developmental Psychology,* 1969, *1,* 449–455.

Sherif, M., Harvey, O. J., White, B. J., Hood, W. R., & Sherif, C. W. *Intergroup conflict and cooperation: The robbers cave experiment.* Norman: University of Okla- homa Press, 1961.

Sherif, M., & Sherif, C. W. *Reference groups.* New York: Harper & Row, 1964.

Suomi, S. J., & Harlow, H. F. Social rehabilitation of isolate-reared monkeys. *Developmental Psychology,* 1972, *6,* 487–496.

Terman, L. M., & Oden, M. H. *Genetic studies of genius, Vol. IV: The gifted child grows up: Twenty-five years' follow-up of a superior group.* Stanford, Calif.: Stan- ford University Press, 1947.

Van den Munckhof, H. C. P. Sociale interaktie en cognit- ieve ontwikkeling bij kleuters. Niet-gepubliceerde doc- toraalscriptie ontwikkelingspsychologie, Universiteit Nijmegen, 1970.

Wahler, R. G. Child-child interactions in five field set- tings: Some experimental analyses. *Journal of Experi- mental Child Psychology,* 1967, *5,* 278–293.

Reading 38

Children's Friendships in School Settings

Steven R. Asher
John M. Gottman
Sherri L. Oden

INTRODUCTION

As children grow older their social interaction typically increases and their friendships become more stable (Horrocks and Buker, 1957; Parten, 1932; Shure, 1963). Still, there are many children who go through the preschool and elementary school years without friends or with few friends. One study found that 6% of third to sixth graders had no classroom friends and an additional 12% had only one friend (Gronlund, 1959).

The consequences of low acceptance by peers has been extensively documented. Children who are socially isolated are more likely to drop out of school (Ullmann, 1957), be later identified as juve- nile delinquents (Roff, Sells and Golden, 1972), and have mental health problems in later life (Cowen, Pederson, Babijian, Izzo, and Trost, 1973). The consequences of low peer acceptance may be more severe than the consequences of low achievement.

In one study (Cowen, et al., 1973), extensive data were gathered on third grade children. Measures included absenteeism, grade point average, IQ scores, achievement test performance, teacher rat- ings, and peer ratings. Eleven years later the re- search team examined a community mental health register to learn which of these children were being seen by a mental health professional. Of all the measures taken in third grade the one that best predicted which children would later have emotion- al problems were peer ratings. Children who were less liked by their peers were more likely to be receiving treatment for mental health problems eleven years later.

This paper reviews research on children's friend- ships in nursery school and elementary school settings. Since school dominates many of the hours of a child's day, it is obviously an important setting in which to study social as well as academic events. Most of the research on children's friendships reflects this fact. While there is some research on friendships in camps, neighborhood settings, etc., the size of this literature is dwarfed in comparison to what is known about social relationships in school.

In reviewing this research, we have tried to select studies that have implications for educational practice. Most of the studies are rather well-designed and well-executed. We have not hesitated, however, to include less rigorous research if its conception or findings might stimulate further research or suggest ideas for educational practice.

The first part of the paper is concerned with the influence of enduring personal characteristics on peer relations. In this section we consider some of the stereotypes that affect children's friendships and offer a few suggestions about ways to overcome these biasing factors. Next, we review research on the influence of the school environment on friendships. Classroom and school situation variables affect social interactions and the extent to which children will make friends with one another. In the third section we examine research on the kinds of social skills that are important to achieving peer acceptance. Many children lack friends because they do not have the necessary social skills. Finally, the paper concludes with a discussion of the ways in which children who lack social skills can be taught how to make friends. A number of teaching methods can be quite effective in increasing the social interaction and peer acceptance of formerly isolated children. It *is* possible to have classrooms in which far fewer children are socially isolated!

PERSONAL CHARACTERISTICS AND FRIENDSHIP

Among the determinants of peer acceptance are personal characteristics that are rather enduring. One's name, physical appearance, race and sex are not easily changed. Yet all of these variables influence friendship selection and peer acceptance.

Names

In every generation, a few first names which are previously uncommon become popular. This is particularly true for girls' names. A recent survey of New York City hospitals (Beadle, 1973) indicated that seven of the ten most popular names given

to boys in 1972 were among the ten most popular names given to children in 1948. However, none of the girls' names appeared on both lists.

But does it make a difference what names children are given? Apparently so. Names like John, Sherri and Steven are among those common appellations that would seem to minimize social discomfort. On the other hand, names like Frances, Hugo, and Hilda seem to carry with them social risks.

McDavid and Harari (1967) asked a group of ten- to twelve-year-old children in a community center to indicate their friends while another group of children, unfamiliar with children in the first group, rated the desirability of the children's names. The correlation between desirability of names and the popularity of children with these names was significant. Children with more desirable names were better liked. In a follow-up study Harari and McDavid (1973) found that teachers were also affected by children's names. Teachers graded student essays lower when those essays were randomly paired with rare, unpopular and unattractive names.

What accounts for the relationship between names and peer acceptance? One possibility is that the simple unfamiliarity or strangeness of certain names leads people to dislike or avoid their bearers. Perhaps children initially behave differently toward a Herbert than a Bill and in so doing set up a cycle of less positive interaction. An alternative explanation is that parents who lack social skills are more likely to give their children odd names and fail to teach effective social skills. In this case, peers would be reacting more to the child's behavior than to the child's name.

If the unfamiliarity explanation is correct, then teachers could help an oddly-named child to be included by making the child's name more of an "everyday household word." Repeated classroom use may help. Associating the name with a famous person in history, science, music, etc., may also be effective. But if the issue isn't the child's name, per se, but the associated lack of social skills, then the child should be helped to learn social skills. Thus, for each child the teacher should assess whether the child's name is the real cause of his social difficulty.

One last word: It is important not to overestimate the importance of names. It is only one of the many variables that influence social acceptance. United States Presidents in the twentieth century have included a Theodore, Woodrow, Warren, Calvin,

Herbert, Franklin, Dwight, Lyndon, and Gerald. The last five Vice Presidents have included an Alben, Hubert and Spiro. It may be that many Americans will vote for a man they wouldn't want as a friend; a more plausible interpretation is that names aren't everything.

Physical Attractiveness

In American society there seems to be considerable agreement about who is or is not physically attractive. In one study (Cross and Cross, 1971), seven, twelve, and seventeen-year-olds, as well as adults, were shown twelve sets of photographs. Each set contained six faces of a particular race, sex, and age group. Respondents were asked to select from each set the most beautiful face and then were asked to rate the twelve faces that had been selected. Results showed no significant difference in the evaluations of beauty made by different age groups. Even the youngest tested shared the conception of beauty held by older people.

Not only is there consensus about physical attractiveness, but there is a strong tendency for children's friendship selection to be influenced by appearance. Young and Cooper (1944) studied factors that influence popularity among elementary school children. They correlated over 30 variables with social acceptance. The most significant was attractiveness of the child's facial appearance. The better looking children were better liked. An interesting aspect of the results was that when the ratings of attractiveness were made by children the relationship between attractiveness and popularity was stronger than when adults made the ratings. In both cases the raters did not know the children they rated and could not have been influenced by any previous associations with the children.

What accounts for the relationship between physical attractiveness and social acceptance? As with names, the cause of greater attraction is unclear. Perhaps better looking children are responded to more positively and thereby develop more effective social skills. Dion and Berscheid (1974) found that nursery school children attributed more negative social behavior to their less attractive peers.

Adults also tend to respond to physical appearance in judging children. Dion (1972) gave college students a photo of a second grade child along with a description of a behavioral episode. The photo showed either an attractive or less attractive child.

The behavioral episode consisted of some unacceptable kind of behavior. After the subjects read the episodes, they were asked, among other questions, to predict how likely the child would be to do the same thing again. The physically attractive child was judged to be less likely to repeat the unacceptable behavior. Furthermore, on a series of six personality ratings the attractive child was judged to be more honest and pleasant than the less attractive child. These findings are striking since the behavior being judged was identical; only physical appearance varied.

One group of children who tend to be considered low in physical attractiveness are the physically disabled. In one study (Richardson, Goodman, Hastorf, and Dornbusch, 1961) 10- and 11-year-old children from many different social classes, regions and ethnic backgrounds were found to rank figures of disabled children lower in desirability. Furthermore, the same rank ordering occurred in every sample. From most to least liked they were: the normal child, a child with crutches and brace, a child in a wheelchair, a child with a left hand missing, a child with a facial disfigurement, and finally, an obese child.

Many explanations have been offered to account for people's rejection of the disabled. One view is that the disabled are victimized by an excessive societal value on beauty (Wright, 1960). Undoubtedly, this at least partially explains children's feelings toward the less attractive, in general, and the disabled, in particular. Another interpretation (Wright, 1960) is that the disabled are less liked because they are presumed to be different. Asher (1975) has found that people attribute different attitudes and personality characteristics to disabled and able-bodied individuals. In another study (Asher, 1973) she found that the extent to which college students perceived a disabled person as similar did indeed influence their feelings toward the person.

It is plausible that the same trend would be found with children since children are more attracted to those who are attitudinally similar to themselves (Byrne and Griffit, 1967). If children could discover for themselves areas of similarity with a disabled person, friendships might be possible. The emphasis should be on guided discovery. In the studies mentioned, the subject was not told that he or she was similar to the person being rated. The subject discovered the similarity when reading the person's attitude profile. Adults often tell children: "He is really just like you" but it is likely that this message is believed most when children discover similarities for themselves. This line of reasoning suggests that teachers should provide situations in which children can discover their similarities of attitude, personalities, values, etc.

The variable of similarity-dissimilarity can, of course, cut both ways. If, in interactions with disabled persons, able-bodied children discover more differences than similarities, increased rejection rather than acceptance could result. Rejection might occur, for example, in an environment which stressed physical prowess above all other skills or where the disabled child was overprotected, given unnecessary preferential treatment, or prevented from developing skills and interests of value to children.

Race

Racial awareness comes quite early in life. Children three years of age and older are clearly aware of racial lables and can appropriately identify their own racial membership (Clark and Clark, 1947; Durrett and Davy, 1970; Hraba and Grant, 1970).

Children also use race as a criterion for selecting friends. Criswell (1939) asked New York City children in three schools to write down the names of classmates they would like to sit next to. Results indicated that children were significantly more likely to choose friends from among their own race. What is interesting, however, is that children did make a considerable number of cross-race selections. Forty percent of their choices would have been cross-race selections if they had been making choices without regard to race. When we averaged Criswell's results across all schools, the results indicated that approximately 25% of the selections were cross-race. Thus, although there was a tendency to prefer children of one's own race many cross-race friendships did exist.

Some recent evidence shows a similar pattern of results. Asher (1973) asked fourth and fifth grade children in a middle-sized midwestern city to write down the names of their five best friends. About 40% of the school population was black. Each month from October to April approximately fifty-five children, randomly selected, were asked to name their five best friends. The results showed that children made fewer cross-race selections than would be expected by chance. Still, approximately

18% of white children's selections and 44% of black children's selections were cross-race.

In another study Shaw (1974) asked fourth, fifth and sixth grade children in February and in June whom they most preferred to be with. Approximately 80% of the children were white and 20% black. Both blacks and whites overselected members of their own race. Nonetheless, both whites and blacks chose members of the other race. Overall, about 33% of black children's selections were white and 6% of white children's selections were black.

The studies reviewed thus far show less racial bias than one might expect given the history of poor race relations in the United States. One possibility is that children might show more racial bias if they were asked not only to name a few friends, but to describe their feelings about each classmate. A child might feel more positively about a few members of another race while feeling quite negatively about others. A recent study by Singleton (1974) is relevant to this issue. Third grade classrooms were surveyed in eleven different schools in a single moderate-sized city. These children had experienced desegregated education throughout their public school careers and school system personnel were interested in the children's race relations.

Children were asked to rate each of their classmates on two scales: how much they like to work with other children in their class and how much they like to play with other children. The scales were constructed so that "1" indicated "I don't like to" and "5" indicated "I like to a lot." The results were that both blacks and whites rated members of their own race higher than members of the other race. This result was statistically significant. As in the Criswell, Asher and Shaw studies, however, there was considerable cross-race acceptance. For example, on the play time, blacks gave blacks an average rating of 3.58 and whites an average rating of 3.17. Whites gave whites an average rating of 2.96 and blacks a rating of 2.86. Thus, children's cross-race ratings were in reality not very different from their same-race ratings.

Although the interracial picture in the preschool and elementary school years is surprisingly positive, the pattern in high school is less hopeful. In one study of high school students (Silverman and Shaw, 1973) social interaction was observed at a popular meeting place in the school. The school's population was 70% white and 30% black. Of all the interactions observed, those between white and black students averaged below 3%. It may be that the "threat" of interracial dating draws students at this age apart. If so, we need to provide children with models of positive interracial relationships so that their teenage years are not characterized by nearly complete racial separation.

What conditions promote positive or negative relations between children of different races? Asher (1973) and Shaw (1973), both of whom collected data across the school year, found little systematic change in children's acceptance of members of another race from the beginning to the end of the school year. It is clear from this that contact per se does not guarantee unbiased friendship selections. It is undoubtedly the nature of the interracial experience that influences the extent to which children make friends across ethnic and racial lines.

One critical issue is the extent to which contact leads children of different races to perceive themselves as similar versus dissimilar. There is evidence that white children more positively evaluate black children when they discover them to hold similar attitudes (Insko and Robinson, 1967). To the extent that children share the same social class, values, life style, level of educational attainment etc., it is likely that more interracial acceptance will occur. One way that a classroom teacher may be able to increase cross-race friendship is by attending to similarities of interests between black and white children. In one study (Asher, 1975), fifth grade children were asked to rate the interest value of a series of 25 pictures. The correlation between black male and white male ratings was strongly significant. The correlation between white females and black females, although lower, was also significant. So within each sex there appeared to be considerable similarity of interest between black and white children. For example, both white males and black males rated basketball and race cars highly. Commonly held interests may provide a basis for bringing together children of different races.

Another factor that contributes to interracial acceptance is parent attitude. Analysis of integration case reports suggests that the school atmosphere is far more positive when parents are supportive rather than opposed to the integration process. Authorities, whether Supreme Court justices, the President or parents, serve to legitimize certain points of view. There was, for example, a marked increase in prointegration sentiment after the 1954 Supreme Court decision. If children perceive their parents as supportive of integration they are probably far more likely to make an effort to reach out to children of another race.

Sex

Although racial factors influence friendship choice, the sex of the child is a more important factor. American social scientists, heavily committed to the elimination of racial bias, have sometimes underestimated the extent to which their sociometric data contains evidence of the existence of two separate cultures: boys' and girls'. The degree to which children chose same sex friends can be seen in three of the studies discussed in the previous section.

Criswell (1939) summarized her data with the comment that "cleavage between the sexes was greater than racial cleavage," and that "a given group of boys or girls nearly always preferred classmates of the same sex but different race to those of the same race but different sex" (p. 18). Asher (1973) found a strong preference in children for same sex friends. Approximately 95% of children's friendship choices were same sex choices and there was little variation from month to month. Singleton (1974) also discovered strong and statistically significant acceptance of same sex and rejection of opposite sex children. On her 1–5 play scale, boys rated boys 3.95 and rated girls 2.08. Girls rated girls 3.78 and boys 2.26. Comparison of these results with those presented for race in the previous section indicate the extent to which sex is an important factor in friendship selection.

A study by Challman (1932) indicates the early age at which children exclude members of the opposite sex. He observed 33 nursery school children, recording the names of children who were in the same group. Results of over 200 hours of observation indicated predominantly same-sex grouping even among children between the ages of 27 and 45 months. Only one boy and one girl showed strong preferences for opposite sex friendships. More recently, Omark and Edelman (1973) observed playground interaction and found that kindergarten, first, and second grade children interacted predominantly with members of the same sex.

One very interesting finding is that when cross-sex friendships are formed they tend to be quite unstable. Gronlund (1955) gave two sociometric surveys four months apart. Only 20% of the cross-sex friendship choices made on the first survey were also made on the second survey. In contrast, children's same-sex choices were about three times as stable.

One concomitant of restricted interaction between boys and girls is a sharp differentiation of interests. Even young children show strong sex-typing of interests. Shure (1963), for example, found that four-year-old nursery school boys spent more time in the block area while girls spent time in the art, book and doll areas. The same study that showed a high degree of cross-race similarity of interests (Asher, 1975) found that the correlation of boys' and girls' interest ratings was low. Among white children the top five interests of boys and girls were completely different. Among black children only one of the top five interests was common to boys and girls. Finally, there is evidence that children's interests are highly related to traditional sex-role conceptions. Markell and Asher (1974) had judges rate the "masculinity" and "femininity" of 25 pictures. When these ratings were correlated with children's interest in the same pictures, the results showed that boys were more interested in "masculine" pictures and girls were more interested in "feminine" pictures.

It seems likely, then, that in the long run the occurrence of many cross-sex friendships depends upon diminishing sex-role rigidity. If boys and girls were reared to have a wider range of interests and to enjoy a wider range of activities, there would probably be many more boy-and-girl friends. An interesting question is whether educational programs such as "Free to be You and Me" or "Sesame Street" will produce change in children's sex-role concepts and friendship patterns.

In the short run, one way to bring boys and girls together may be to provide common or superordinate goals (Sherif, 1958). In a study by DeVries and Edwards (1972), seventh grade math classes were organized so that children worked individually in two classes and were rewarded for individual achievement while in two other classes boys and girls were teamed together and children were rewarded according to their team's performance. After the four-week experiment was over, children were asked a number of questions; one of these requested them to list their friends. In the two "no

team" classes, the number of children's choices that crossed sex-lines was 21% and 17%. In the "team" classes, however, the number of cross-sex choices was 33% and 27%. The findings of this experiment suggest that using superordinate goals may help overcome the social distance between boys and girls.

SITUATIONAL CHARACTERISTICS AND FRIENDSHIP

One way to increase friendships among children is to structure the educational environment so that friendships are likely to develop and endure. Many children may lack friends or have few friends because the environment does not promote friendship. A variety of situational factors which influence friendship will be discussed.

Population Mobility

Although contact alone is not sufficient to create peer acceptance, children who have prolonged contact with the same peers should at least have greater opportunity to form friendships. Following this line of reasoning, researchers have investigated the effect of residential mobility of individual children and school populations in relation to peer acceptance. In a study of individual mobility (Young and Cooper, 1944), the five least and five most accepted children in each of eleven elementary school classrooms were compared on the length of time in the current school and the number of schools previously attended. The most accepted and least accepted children did not differ on either of these measures. More recently Roistacher (1974) found that the degree of an individual child's mobility had no relationship to the number of peers in school who knew him. Neither study, then, found evidence that the more mobile child is at a social disadvantage. It should be noted, however, that neither study controlled for within-school differences in socioeconomic status or social skill repertoire. If the more mobile children within schools were socioeconomically more advantaged they may have had skills which offset potential disadvantages of mobility. There is evidence, for example, that middle class children are more effective communicators than lower class children (Gottman, Gonso, and Rasmussen, 1975; Heider, 1971).

While individual mobility may not be an important factor, the mobility of an entire school population may well be important. In one study (Roistacher, 1974), four inner city and four suburban schools were compared. The inner city schools had an annual pupil turnover rate of over 35%; in contrast, the turnover rate in the suburban schools averaged below 10%. Eighth grade boys in each school were asked to indicate those students they knew well. In schools with high turnover fewer children were known by others. Furthermore, these results were obtained even when other differences between the schools such as income and racial composition were statistically controlled.

It would seem, then, that children who attend "high turnover" schools have a social disadvantage when it comes to making friends. In this type of environment, it is necessary for the school staff and community to take special steps to bring children in contact with one another. Other environments with high population turnover (e.g., universities, military bases) provide a variety of social activities for integrating new members and building cohesiveness. Perhaps schools could adopt some of their techniques. Having children eat or play with children from different classrooms might help, especially if the teacher made sure that children learned each other's names. It might also help if children could learn about each other's background, where they lived before, their interests, etc. In a high-mobility environment, children, like adults, need to identify characteristics in others that will help them to rapidly build relationships.

Opportunities for Participation

Situations vary in the extent to which they allow people to participate fully in social interaction. For example, if there is a large variety of social roles to be filled and a limited number of potential "actors," more people will get involved. This is the type of situation that exists in smaller schools. Whatever the size of the school, there are a certain number of roles that must be filled (e.g., student council member, band member, club member, football player, cheerleader, etc.). Thus, students who attend small schools should have greater opportunities for participation. Indeed, Gump and Friesen (1964) and Wicker (1969) have found that students in small high schools participated in a wider range of activities and held more positions of responsibility than students in large schools.

Size of classroom also appears to be an important influence on social participation. Dawe (1934) observed teacher-led discussions in kindergartens ranging in size from 14 to 46 children. As one might expect the average number of comments contributed by each child decreased as size increased. The average child in the 14-person class spoke nearly seven times while children in classes above 30 spoke less than two times each. There is, after all, a finite amount of "air time" which must be shared among classroom members.

The higher participation characteristic of small school settings should lead students to be better known by their peers. Interestingly, Roistacher (1974) found that junior high school students in smaller schools knew more fellow students, in absolute numbers, than did students in larger schools. These data should give pause to those who urge consolidation of smaller school districts into large ones. It may be that there are social disadvantages that offset the potential economic or academic advantages to be gained from consolidation.

If participation and responsibility are important determinants of peer acceptance, then increasing participation and responsibility should promote peer acceptance. A study by McClelland and Ratliff (1947) found this to be the case. They worked in a junior high school where a particularly large number of children seemed to have no friends. They decided to intervene in one class of 35 students. On a pretest measure, 12 students received no sociometric choices of any of four sociometric questions. (With whom would you like to go to a show? With whom would you like to study? Whom would you like to have as a guest in your home? With whom would you rather share a secret?)

One part of their intervention consisted of providing isolated children with special classroom roles (e.g., chairman of the hospitality committee who had responsibility for sending cards to sick classroom members). The class was also divided into small groups based on seating rows. Each group had a captain and various activities such as parties and charity drives were conducted by the groups so that individual member participation was increased. Sociometric choice made after this intervention indicated that only two children were still ignored on all four questions. These results, although based on only a single classroom, are promising. Creating new roles which give children a chance to participate may be a powerful way to overcome isolation.

The importance of participating in a visible and

valued classroom role is also demonstrated in a study of Chennault (1967). Two isolated children from 16 special education classes were grouped with the two most popular children from the same classes. Each group's task was to produce a skit for their classroom. They met for 15 minutes twice a week for five weeks, and then presented their skit to the class. Sociometric ratings taken after this activity indicated that the participating isolated children were more accepted than a control group of isolated children who had not been involved with the skit.

A follow-up study (Rucker and Vincenzo, 1972) shows that maintenance of this type of change is dependent on continued participation. Isolated children from special education classes met with the most popular members of their class for 45 minutes. The group met twice weekly for two weeks to produce a classroom carnival. The group planned events, decorated the room, awarded prizes, etc. A sociometric measure given three days after the carnival indicated that the participating isolated children were far more accepted than the control group of isolated children. However, a follow-up measure taken one month after the carnival showed that these children were no longer more accepted than the control group. Once their participation ceased, the level of peer acceptance they experienced also declined. The same pattern of initial gain followed by long-run decline has also been found by Lilly (1971). These results suggest that isolated children may be unable to maintain relationships which have been situationally nurtured.

Rewarding Social Interaction

One critical situational component is whether children are rewarded or reinforced by the teacher or by peers for engaging in friendship-making behavior. When the environment rewards certain behavior, the likelihood is greater that the behavior will occur again. If rewards are withheld, the behavior is less likely to occur. Children, like adults, are reinforced by approval of their conduct.

The power of reinforcement was demonstrated in a study by Blau and Rafferty (1970). They paired children together to play a game in which a light went on when the children cooperated. One group of children played the game without receiving any reward from the experimenter. In other groups, each time children cooperated they received a ticket redeemable for prizes. After playing, the same children rated how much they liked each other. These ratings indicated that the children rewarded for cooperation regarded each other more highly than children who were not rewarded.

An important point is that reinforcement has to be maintained to some degree if the desired behavior is to continue. One study (Hauserman, Walen, and Behling, 1973) examined the effect of reinforcing black and white first grade children for sitting with each other in the lunchroom. The study was carried out in a school lunchroom where children usually sat in racially separate groups. The teacher introduced a game in which children drew papers out of a hat. Each paper had the name of one black and one white child and children were told to sit with their "new friend." At the end of the lunch session, children who had carried out this instruction received tickets, redeemable for candy. In the next phase of the experiment, the name drawing was discontinued. Instead, children simply were encouraged to sit with "new friends" and were reinforced if they sat with an interracial group. In the final phase, reinforcement procedures were terminated.

Results of the study indicated an increase of interracial interaction in the lunchroom during the experimental phase. More important, this effect also generalized to a free play session held in the classroom after lunch. Here, too, children engaged in more cross-race interaction. However, once reinforcement procedures were ended, children once again sat with members of their own race. These results demonstrate the power that environmental reward has on children's social interactions.

Success and Failure

Another important situational variable is the extent to which the school helps the child to succeed academically. The cognitive and social areas of development are interrelated. Children who have difficulty with cognitive tasks are also likely to have greater problems in social relationships. This is demonstrated by the finding that low achieving children tend to have fewer friends in school (Gronlund, 1959).

Why might academic progress be related to peer acceptance? One possibility is that success leads children to "feel good" and be more concerned for other children. Isen, Horn, and Rosenhan (1973) did an experiment in which they arranged for some children to succeed at a game while others failed.

After playing the game, children were asked by an adult experimenter to contribute money to buy toys for poor children. When contributions were made without the experimenter watching, the children who had succeeded at the game were more generous than those who had failed. When the contributions were made publicly, the two groups gave similar amounts.

While success leads children to feel good, school failure probably leads many children to be aggressive and unkindly disposed toward their peers. And from available evidence, the aggressive child (Hartup, Glazer and Charlesworth, 1967), particularly the inappropriately aggressive child (Lesser, 1959), is disliked and rejected.

Such results suggest that environments which provide children with opportunities for feeling successful would simultaneously be promoting positive peer relations. This means first of all that the curriculum should provide children with a chance to succeed. Second, evaluation of student progress should emphasize the child's own rate of progress (Hill, 1972). In environments where children are compared with one another ("grading on a curve"), a certain percentage of children experience failure regardless of their level of performance and rate of progress.

Activities

Observation of classrooms indicates that the type of available activities influences the kinds of social interaction which may occur. A study by Charlesworth and Hartup (1967) was concerned with activities in which children interacted positively with each other. They observed four nursery school classrooms and counted the frequency of four categories of positive social response: giving positive attention and approval, giving affection and personal acceptance, submission (passive acceptance, imitation, allowing another child to play) and token giving (spontaneously giving physical objects such as toys or food). Sixty-five percent of the positive responses given by children occurred in what the authors termed dramatic play activities (housekeeping area, blocks, trucks, puppet play, etc.). In contrast, table activities (puzzles, manipulative table toys, art activities, stories, flannel board, etc.) were less likely to elicit positive social behaviors. Finally, when children were wandering about the room without engaging in any activity, they were also less likely to reinforce others.

Another relevant variable is the number of activity resources available. Since limited resources can lead to conflict and aggression, one way to minimize disturbance and keep children "on task" would be to provide lots of available resources. Indeed, evidence exists (Doke and Risely, 1972) that providing children with activity options, increasing the amount of materials, and dismissing children individually (rather than en masse) from one activity to another results in greater participation by children with the materials. Each of these techniques has the effect of increasing the ratio of available materials per child.

But is a high degree of participation with materials totally desirable? A second look suggests that the picture is more complicated. When the children worked with no activity options and were dismissed en masse, it appeared that ". . . children spent more time talking to each other," (Doke and Risley, 1972; p. 416). Since talking can lead to social learning, some nonparticipation with materials may be valuable. Having fewer material resources may be functional in another sense; the conflict and frustration that result provides children with opportunities to learn how to share and cooperate.

SOCIAL SKILLS AND FRIENDSHIP

Many children may lack friends not because the situation is particularly interfering or constraining but because they do not have certain important social skills. Help for these children requires that they be taught necessary social behaviors. In this section we will consider some of the behaviors associated with being liked and having friends.

Responding Positively

One important set of behaviors involves a child's ability to interact positively with others. As children grow older, they are likely to engage in more positive social responses with one another (Charlesworth and Hartup, 1967). The extent to which children behave constructively toward peers seems to be pretty consistent within a single context. Kohn (1966) observed kindergarten children throughout the school year. He found that the degree of positive interaction shown by children in the fall semester correlated with the degree of positive interaction in the spring. One reason for the stability of positive interaction is that children who give a lot of positive responses also tend to receive a lot. For example, Kohn (1966) found a high correlation between the percent of positive acts made by a child and the percent of positive acts which others made toward him or her. Charlesworth and Hartup (1967), in their study of nursery school children, found that the number of children to whom a child positively responded was correlated significantly with the number of children who responded positively to him.

From these data we can hypothesize that children who engage in a high degree of positive interaction would also be chosen as friends on a sociometric measure. Studies in which children are asked to name their friends support this hypothesis. For example, Hartup et al. (1967) observed social interaction in a nursery school and correlated the type of interaction each child displayed with the number of acceptances and rejections received on a sociometric test. Social behavior was categorized as positive or negative. The first category included giving attention and approval, giving affection and personal acceptance, submitting to another's wishes, and giving things to another. Negative behaviors included noncompliance, interference, derogation, and attack. Peer acceptance and rejection were measured by asking children to identify three children they "especially like" and three they "don't like very much." Results of this study indicated that in both classrooms the number of positive responses a child made toward peers was positively correlated with peer acceptance. Furthermore, children who gave the most negative responses to peers were the most rejected. It seems, then, that children who lack friends tend not to positively reinforce interpersonal contact.

In teaching a child to be more socially effective with peers, it is necessary to develop those behaviors that will be perceived by a child's peers as positive. These behaviors may vary across settings. Gottman, Gonso, and Rasmussen (1975) correlated social interaction patterns with peer acceptance in third and fourth grade classrooms. One-half of the classrooms were in a middle class school and one-half were in a working class school. As in the Hartup et al. (1967) study, the frequency of positive and negative social interactions was recorded. However, the observation categories were extended to include verbal and nonverbal behavior. The results indicated that the children who were liked in the middle class school were those who engaged in positive verbal interaction. In the working class

school, the most liked children were those who engaged in positive nonverbal interaction. Middle class children who engaged in positive nonverbal behavior actually tended to be more disliked. These data imply that it is important for children to learn what types of behavior are reinforcing to other children. A child must learn to "psych out" the environment to figure out what kinds of behavior will lead to acceptance or rejection.

Communicating Accurately

Another skill that appears to be important is the ability to communicate accurately with another person. In one study (Gottman et al., 1975), children played a password type communication game and also wrote down the names of their friends. Third and fourth grade children who communicated more accurately also had more friends, according to the sociometric measure. Rubin (1972) had children play a communication game in which a speaker described unusually-shaped patterns to a listener. He also collected data on children's three friendship play choices. The correlation between having friends and doing well on the patterns communication task was strongly significant in kindergarten and second grades. The correlations were nonsignificant in fourth and sixth grades.

Why might poorer communicators be less liked? One reason, perhaps, is that it is not very reinforcing or personally validating to be with someone who cannot express his ideas clearly and who may not be an especially good listener either. Another reason is that effective collaboration, whether it be in play or at work, depends on two people having a common idea of what they are about. The child who communicates poorly may also be playing or working at cross-purposes with peers.

Whatever the reason, it is important to identify possible reasons for poor communication performance. Some children may communicate poorly because they have less adequate vocabularies. Kingsley (1971) found that kindergarten children who did poorly on a communication task had more limited vocabulary. Second, some children may not recognize that effective communication often involves making fine distinctions. Asher and Parke (1975) found that young children can communicate as effectively as older children if fine distinctions aren't required but do poorly when fine distinctions are required. Third, some children may not be taking the listener's perspective when communicating to another person. In one study (Flavell, Botkin, Fry, Wright, and Jarvis, 1968) elementary school children taught a game to a listener who was either sighted or blind. Children gave rather useful information to the sighted person but far less useful information when the listener was blind. For example, they would say "Put this piece here."; or "Take the red one and put it next to the blue one." This type of behavior suggests that children weren't thinking about the listener's point of view.

Research is needed on whether teaching children to be more accurate communicators increases their acceptance by other children. There is evidence that communication skills can be improved through practice or teaching (Chandler, Greenspan, and Barenboim, 1974). One study (Gottman, Gonso, and Schuler, 1975) included sociometric measures and found that isolated children who were taught to be better communicators were more accepted by their classmates. No firm conclusion can be drawn since communication skill training was only one of a number of interventions with the children. Still, the results suggest that future exploration is warranted. If an isolated child is also a poor communicator, it could help to teach communication skills.

Being Expert

One way for a child to gain peer acceptance is to be very good at something valued by other children. For example, being a competent athlete is likely to be a social asset. McCraw and Tolbert (1953) compared the sociometric status of junior high school boys with their athletic ability. They measured sociometric status by asking boys to indicate the three children they liked best in their class, grade level, and school. From these ratings, a total status score was derived for each individual. Athletic ability was measured by an index composed of performance on the 50-yard dash, the standing broad jump, and the softball distance throw. At each grade level and in each class, the correlation between athletic ability and being liked was significant.

One group of children who are relatively lacking in expertise are the retarded. A study by Goodman, Gottlieb, and Harrison (1974) found that elementary school children expressed less liking for a sample of educably mentally retarded children from their school than for a sample of non-retarded children. Furthermore, there was evidence that increased contact through integrated classrooms led to increased *rejection* of the retarded. The retarded children in integrated classrooms were more rejected as potential friends. A follow-up study by Gottlieb and Budoff (1973) also found rejection of the retarded as friends and provided additional evidence that increased contact between retarded and non-retarded may lead to increased rejection. In a school with no interior walls, retarded children were more rejected than in a school with walls and segregated classrooms. As long as people judge others by their abilities, increased contact with those who are relatively less expert may lead to less rather than more acceptance.

How might the retarded be more successfully integrated with the non-retarded? The hypothesis that expertness is a critical determinant of peer acceptance suggests that activities should be emphasized in which the retarded have a chance to perform at or near the same level as non-retarded children. There are many areas in which EMR children are nearly indistinguishable from "normal" children. For example, they are likely to be more competent on the playground than in the classroom. Gottlieb (1971) found that children in Norway express more positive attitudes about playing with than working with retarded children. It is likely that the same is true for American children.

If expertness is an important determinant of being liked, not just for the retarded, but for all children, then it should be possible to improve the status of an isolated child by making an existing talent more visible to the class. For example, while working in a third grade class, two of the authors had an isolated child plan, with two other children, a puppet show which was presented to the class. Follow-up data indicated that the child gained one friend. If a child lacks skills valued by the group, it should be possible to increase his acceptance by teaching him a valued skill. For example, in a classroom where children emphasize athletics, teaching an isolated child to play a better game of basketball should increase his acceptance into the group. Although we know of no formal research that has evaluated the effectiveness of either of these strategies, many teachers report positive results from their own experience. It remains for researchers to catch up with effective practice.

Initiating a Relationship

It is conceivable that some children are positively responsive, effective communicators and expert in certain areas but still lack friends. One possibility is that they may not know how to go about making a friend. In one study (Gottman, et al., 1974), third and fourth grade children were asked individually to pretend that the experimenter was a new child in school and that he or she wanted to make friends. Children's responses were scored according to whether they offered a greeting, asked the "new child" for information (e.g., "Where do you live?"), attempted to include (e.g., "Wanna come over to my house sometime?"), or gave information (e.g., "My favorite sport is basketball."). In addition to participating in this role play, children were asked to name their best friends. Children who were chosen as a friend by six or more peers were found to be much more skillful on the "new friend" role play than children who received five choices or less.

TEACHING SOCIAL SKILLS

If children have few friends because they lack effective social behaviors, then teaching social skills can be helpful. In this section we will review research on teaching friendship making behavior to isolated children. Our focus is on teaching strategies that have practical value for the nursery school or elementary school classroom.

Shaping

Shaping uses positive reinforcement to change behavior gradually. The first step is to wait until the child's behavior somewhat approximates the behavior to be learned and then give the child a reinforcer. As the child's behavior further approaches the desired behavior, he or she is again reinforced. This shaping process continues until the new behavior is learned. One of the first studies to demonstrate the effects of shaping on an isolated child's behavior was done by Allen, Hart, Buell, Harris and Wolf (1964). Their subject was Ann, a four-year-old nursery school child, who, after six weeks of school, was isolated from other children and engaged in a variety of behaviors to gain the teachers' attention. The study began with a five-day baseline period in which Ann's behavior was observed but no attempts were made to change her behavior. During this baseline period, Ann was observed to interact approximately 10 percent of the time with peers and approximately 40 percent of the time with teachers.

In the next phase of the study, the teacher reinforced Ann by giving her attention as she interacted with other children. At first, she was reinforced for standing close to another child or playing beside another child. Later, she was reinforced only for direct interaction. The researchers discovered that direct comments to Ann such as "Ann, you are making dinner for the whole family" had the effect of leading Ann away from the children into interaction with the teacher. Reinforcing statements that focused on Ann as a member of a group (e.g., "You three girls have a cozy house! Here are some more cups, Ann, for your tea party.") were quite successful; interaction with adults fell below 20 percent and interaction with children increased to about 60 percent.

Then the procedure was reversed. Ann was reinforced for being alone or interacting with teachers and ignored when she interacted with peers. Her behavior returned to the baseline level. This reversal to her previously isolated situation indicates the power of the teacher's attention. Ann's behavior was strongly influenced by what she was reinforced for doing. As a final test, the teachers once again reinforced Ann only for interacting with children. As before, her time spent interacting with children increased and her time with adults decreased.

What happens to isolated children weeks after reinforcement procedures are terminated? A study by O'Connor (1972) is relevant. Eight isolated children were reinforced for making social contact. The percent of time they spent in social interaction dramatically increased. However, when reinforcement was terminated their behavior reverted back to the baseline level. The failure to produce generalization or longer lasting effects is somewhat surprising. One might think that isolated children would find it reinforcing to be with other children and that the experience of being included by others would adequately sustain the new behavior. Perhaps the isolated children were socially unskilled and other children found them unpleasant to be with.

One approach to the problem of generalization is to gradually decrease or fade out the reinforcement rather than abruptly terminate it. A case study (Coast, 1967, reported in Baer and Wolf, 1970) with a four-year-old child found that when the teacher gradually decreased the frequency of reinforcing the child's social behavior the behavior lasted. Perhaps the gradual decrease in reinforcement gave the isolated child more time to learn and practice social skills. In this case, over time peers would begin to reinforce the child for social interaction. They would take over, as it were, the reinforcing function.

The studies considered here have been primarily concerned with increasing a child's tendency to approach other children. How do you teach an isolated child what to do once he approaches peers? One method would be to shape appropriate behavior by reinforcing closer and closer approximations of the desired behavior. This approach might be inefficient for teaching complex social skills; one could wait a long time for even an approximation of the appropriate behavior to occur. The next two teaching strategies to be discussed are more direct and possibly more efficient. Modeling and coaching can provide children with rules or general strategies of social interaction. These rules can guide the child's behavior so that he is reinforcing to be with.

Modeling

One way to learn something is to watch someone do it. In every culture a tremendous amount of information is transmitted from one generation to the next. Much of this information is acquired through observation. Children watch their parents shave, hunt, get up early for work, cook, make a bed, ride a bike, read, etc. By watching they learn. There has been a growing interest in using observational methods to change the behavior of children. Just as watching an aggressive model can lead children to be more aggressive (Bandura, Ross and Ross, 1961), models may serve more positive functions. For example, children have been found to imitate models who reflect thoughtfully on a problem (Ridberg, Parke, and Hetherington, 1971), contribute to charity (Rosenhan and White, 1967), and express moral judgments characteristic of older children (Turiel, 1966).

If children learn by observing others, then an isolated child's social involvement could be increased by showing him a model of a socially effective person. O'Connor (1969) identified socially isolated children in nine nursery school classes by using a combination of teacher nominations and direct behavioral observation. Half of the isolated children saw a social interaction modeling film; the other half, the control group, saw a film about dolphins. The modeling film, 23 minutes long, consisted of eleven episodes in which a child entered a

group of other children. The situations were graduated from low threat (sharing a book or toy with two other children) to high threat (joining a group of children who were gleefully tossing play equipment around the room). The model was always well received by the children (e.g., offered a toy, talked to, smiled at, etc.). A narrator described the action as it occurred in order to call children's attention to the relevant behaviors. For example, in one sequence the narrator says "Now another child comes up close to watch. She wants to play, too. She waits for them to see her. Now she gets a chair and she sits down with them so they will play with her. She starts to do what they are doing so they will want to play with her. . . ."

After seeing the film, each child returned to the classroom where postfilm observations were immediately made. Results showed that the social interaction of children in the modeling condition greatly increased. In fact, they were interacting somewhat more frequently than a sample of non-isolated children. The control group that watched the dolphin film did not change at all. These are impressive results, particularly in light of the brief nature of the "therapy."

But does it last? A second study by O'Connor (1972) is relevant. Again, isolated children were selected from nursery school classrooms. One group of children saw the modeling film. As in the previous study, the behavior of the children following the film was as interactive as that of the non-isolated children. In addition, follow-up observations were made weeks after the film. The children who saw the modeling film continued to interact with their peers. Another study using the modeling film observed children one month after exposure to the film models and also found that social interaction continued at a high level (Evers and Schwarz, 1973).

One intriguing issue left unresolved by this research is why isolated children learn from O'Connor's film models but haven't learned from the real-life peer models who are in their classes. Nearly every class has highly popular children who are also socially quite skillful. One possible explanation is that the film narrator draws the children's attention to appropriate social details that they otherwise miss. Perhaps in the flow of events in the real world the isolated child fails to attend to significant elements of the popular child's behavior. This analysis suggests that making the peer's model's presence explicit could have positive results. A study of disruptive behavior by Csapo (1972) is suggestive. She paired six emotionally disturbed children with six peers who were exemplars of classroom decorum. The disturbed children sat next to their classmate model and were told to watch the model and do what he was doing so that he could learn how to get along better in class. Observations indicated that all six disruptive children improved their behavior dramatically. Follow-up data were collected for ten days after the intervention was concluded and the six children continued their socially appropriate behavior.

Coaching

The development of language is a significant advance in a child's educational potential. Once children comprehend language, they can acquire new social behavior through direct instruction. Teachers and peers can become coaches who verbally transmit rules of social behavior. As we are using it here, coaching has a number of components. First, the child is provided with a rule or standard of behavior. In simple terms he is told what he should do. Second, the child has opportunities to rehearse or practice the behavior. Finally, there are opportunities for feedback in which the child's performance is discussed and suggestions for improvement made. The studies we will review here use at least two of these three components.

Studies of assertiveness training with college students can be used to illustrate coaching. McFall and Twentyman (1973) were interested in teaching assertive behaviors to unassertive people. As part of the training, the trainee was confronted with a series of simulated, or role play, situations which typically pose difficulty for unassertive people (e.g., saying "no" to an illegitimate request). In each situation the trainee was given verbal instructions on how best to handle the situation. Coaching was found to be effective in improving assertive behavior in the training situation and in a real-life situation. Of particular interest was the finding that trainees who had a chance to rehearse or practice the new behavior improved more than those whose training did not include opportunities for practice.

Coaching can also be effective with young children. Using verbal reasoning techniques appears to be one of the best ways to insure that children internalize rules of social behavior. For example,

studies of child-rearing methods suggest that verbal reasoning leads to more prosocial behavior by the child than physical punishment (e.g., Hoffman and Saltzstein, 1967). More recently, Parke (1970) has found that punishment when it is administered, is more effective if accompanied by a verbal rationale. Parke suggested that rationales might include various kinds of information such as descriptions of consequences of behavior, examples of acceptable behavior, and explicit instructions on what to do in specific situations.

These types of rationales were provided in a study by Chittenden (1942). A critical situation for young children is one in which there are limited play resources (e.g., two children and one toy). Chittenden chose this situation and sought to teach children to take turns with materials, divide or share the materials where possible, or play cooperatively with the materials. She selected 19 nursery school children whose play with others included a high proportion of dominating behavior and a low proportion of cooperation. Ten of these children received training in how to play cooperatively with others; the other nine children served as the control group.

Chittenden's training situation was ingenious. Each child was introduced to two dolls named "Sandy" and "Mandy." In a series of situations, the dolls confronted the problem of how to play with a single toy. Sometimes they were unsuccessful and their interaction ended in a fight. At other times they were successful and they took turns, shared, or played cooperatively. Eleven training sessions were held. In the first session Sandy and Mandy were introduced; and in the next ten sessions the dolls faced a series of limited resource situations. Chittenden provides scripts for each of the sessions that could be used to repeat her training. Briefly, the first sessions served to teach the children to discriminate unhappy outcomes such as fighting, anger, etc., from happy outcomes such as sharing, having a good time, etc. In later sessions, the dolls sometimes played successfully, thereby modeling appropriate behavior. At other times they fought and the experimenter-teacher and child discussed possible ways of resolving conflicts the dolls faced. In still later sessions the child was asked to show the dolls what they could do to play more successfully. For example, after Sandy and Mandy fought over who was to use some toy cars the experimenter-teacher asked "What would you do?

Show them what to do." These situations provided tests of the child's understanding.

More than a week after training, the children were observed in a real-life play situation. The results showed that the trained children had significantly decreased in their amount of dominating behavior. They also increased in cooperative behavior but the increase was not statistically significant. The control group children showed little change in their behavior from pre- to post-test.

A more recent coaching study by Zahavi (1973) has also obtained impressive results. She selected eight nursery school children who had been the most aggressive during six hours of observation over a two-week period. The head teacher, who was highly regarded by the children, met individually with four of the eight children for approximately fifteen minutes. The meeting consisted of three phases. First, the teacher explained to each child that hitting others causes harm; second, the other children wouldn't like the child if he hit them and that hitting doesn't solve the problem; and third, the child was asked to think of alternative behaviors to hitting such as sharing or taking turns. At each phase, the teacher asked the child questions so that he would participate in formulating these concepts. Six hours of follow-up observation conducted during the two weeks after training indicated that two of the four children greatly decreased in amount of aggressive activity. Furthermore, the decrease in aggression was accompanied by an increase in positive behaviors. The four control group children didn't change. Next, these four children were coached by the teacher. Observations made one week later indicated that three of these four children dramatically changed their behavior. These results are quite impressive in light of the short coaching session held by the teacher. They provide testimony to the way a teacher can verbally guide the behavior of even very young children.

Neither of these studies obtained sociometric measures so there is no way of knowing in the coached condition whether children gained friends as a result of their change in behavior. Two recent coaching studies have included measures of friendship. In one, (Gottman, Gonso and Schuler, 1975), "low-friend" children from a single third grade classroom were selected. Two of the children received training and two were control subjects. The training consisted of modeling and coaching in which the child saw a video-tape of a girl entering a group of peers. The video-tape was discussed and the low-friend child role played situations in which she was a new child in class and wanted to make friends. After this role play the child was taught to be a more effective communicator. The emphasis of the training was on thinking of the listener's perspective when talking to another person.

Results of this study indicated that the two coached children were rated more highly by peers while the two control children received ratings quite similar to their earlier ones. Observation in class suggested that none of the children increased their frequency of interaction. However, the two coached children changed in the kind of children they interacted with. One girl sought out more popular children and the other interacted more with other "low-friend" children. Apparently the training affected children's selection strategies.

In another coaching and friendship study (Oden and Asher, 1975) three low-friend children in eleven different third and fourth grade classrooms were identified based on sociometric measures. One of the three was coached. This child, on five separate sessions, played a game with a classmate. Each session the child played with a different classmate. Before playing, the child was advised on how to have the most fun. The coach suggested such things as participating fully, cooperating, communicating, and showing interest in the other person. The child was asked to think of examples for each of these categories. After playing the game the coach asked the child "how it went" and the child discussed his experience in terms of issues such as participation, cooperation, communication, and validation. One of the other three low-friend children in each classroom participated in the same number of play sessions but received no coaching. The remaining child from the classroom came out of the room with a classmate, received no coaching, and played a game alone.

The experiment lasted for three weeks. About five days later children were once again asked to indicate how much they like to play with and work with the other children in the class and to name their friends. The results were encouraging. On the "play with" rating the children who played alone didn't change; the children who were paired but didn't receive coaching actually went down slightly; and most important, the coached children received significantly higher ratings. On the rating "work with" and the naming of friends the results were generally in the same direction but not significant.

In summary, it appears from a number of studies that coaching can improve children's social skills and lead to increased peer acceptance. Given the capacity of children to learn from verbal instruction and the opportunity to practice, a teacher would be wise to include coaching as a method for helping socially isolated children.

SUMMARY

We have considered some of the characteristics that are associated with having friends. It is important to keep in mind that children who lack friends may do so for different reasons. Social relationships are affected by the child's personal characteristics, varied aspects of the situation, and the child's social skills. With careful observation and informal "experimenting," it should be possible to infer the reasons for a particular child's social difficulty.

If a child's personal characteristics seem to be distracting from his or her friendship-making capability, emphasis could be placed on the child's similarity to other children such as a common interest, value or goal. If the situation seems to be constraining peer relationships, there are a number of classroom features that could be changed. Introducing opportunities for children to participate in activities, rewarding social interaction, facilitating success experiences, and providing socially conducive activities can make a difference. Research to date suggests that it is important to maintain changes in the situation if friendships are to continue. If children lack friends due to limited social skills, a variety of teaching methods can be used. Shaping, modeling, and coaching have been found to improve the social interaction of isolated children. The results are particularly encouraging in light of the short term nature of the "treatment" employed in most training research.

In terms of teaching social skills there are two areas, in particular, that we need to know more about. First, do the effects of social skill training last? To date, there have been no long term follow-up studies. Results gathered about one month after training are encouraging, but there is a need for

more longitudinal information. A formerly isolated child may need the psychological equivalent of "booster shots".

Second, we need to know which changes in social behavior lead to increased peer acceptance. For example, in shaping and modeling studies, the proportion of time children spend interacting with peers increases. Typically, however, no sociometric data is gathered, so it is impossible to say whether increased friendships result. For example, it is hard to know how the other children are perceiving the new behavior. It is possible that a formerly isolated child's classmates are thinking: "What a kid! He used to be by himself all the time; now he's always hanging around." The attention of the teacher and researcher should, therefore, be directed toward *both* changes in behavior and changes in sociometric status.

Although we need to know more about how friendships develop and how they can be facilitated, we do know enough right now to improve the social relationships of children. The best strategy may be to use multiple methods of teaching social skills. The combined effects of shaping, modeling, and coaching would probably be more effective than any single technique alone. Finally, it would probably be best to consider situational variables when teaching social skills. Children need a suitable environment in which to practice newly developing abilities.

REFERENCES

Allen, K. E., Hart, B., Buell, J. S., Harris, F. R., & Wolf, M. M. Effects of social reinforcement of isolate behavior of a nursery school child. *Child Development*, 1964, *35*, 511–518.

Asher, N. W. Manipulating attraction toward the disabled: An application of the similarity-attraction model. *Rehabilitation Psychology*, 1973, *20*, 156–164.

Asher, N. W. Social stereotyping of the physically handicapped. Submitted for publication, 1975.

Asher, S. R. The influence of race and sex on children's sociometric choices across the school year. Unpublished manuscript, University of Illinois, 1973.

Asher, S. R. The effect of interest on reading comprehension for black children and white children. Unpublished manuscript, University of Illinois, 1975.

Asher, S. R. & Parke, R. D. Influence of sampling and comparison processes on the development of communication effectiveness. *Journal of Educational Psychology*, 1975, *67*.

Baer, D. M. & Wolf, M. M. Recent examples of behavior modification in preschool settings. In C. Neuringer and J. L. Michael (Eds.) *Behavior modification in clinical psychology*. New York: Appleton-Century-Crofts, 1970.

Bandura, A., Ross, D., & Ross, S. A. Transmission of aggression through imitation of aggressive models. *Journal of Abnormal and Social Psychology*, 1961, *63*, 575–582.

Beadle, M. The game of the name. *N.Y. Times Magazine*, October 21, 1973.

Blau, B. & Rafferty, J. Changes in friendship status as a function of reinforcement. *Child Development*, 1970, *41*, 113–121.

Byrne, D. & Griffit, W. A developmental investigation of the law of attraction. *Journal of Personality and Social Psychology*, 1966, *4*, 699–702.

Challman, R. C. Factors influencing friendships among preschool children. *Child Development*, 1932, *3*, 146–158.

Chandler, M. J., Greenspan, S. & Barenboim, C. Assessment and training of roletaking and referential communication skills in institutionalized emotionally disturbed children. *Developmental Psychology*, 1974, *10*, 546–553.

Charlesworth, R. & Hartup, W. W. Positive social reinforcement in the nursery school peer group. *Child Development*, 1967, *38*, 993–1003.

Chennault, M. Improving the social acceptance of unpopular educable mentally retarded pupils in special classes. *American Journal of Mental Deficiency*, 1967, *72*, 455–458.

Chittenden, G. F. An experimental study in measuring and modifying assertive behavior in young children. *Monographs of the Society for Research in Child Development*, 1942, 7, (1).

Clark, K. B. & Clark, M. K. Racial identification and racial preference in Negro children. In T. Newcomb and E. Hartley (Eds.) *Readings in social psychology*. New York: Holt, 1947.

Cowen, E. L., Pederson, A., Babijian, H., Izzo, L. D. & Trost, M. A. Long-term follow-up of early detected vulnerable children. *Journal of Consulting and Clinical Psychology*, 1973, *41*, 438–446.

Criswell, J. H. A sociometric study of race cleavage in the classroom. *Archives of Psychology*, 1939, No. 235, 1–82.

Cross, J. F. & Cross, J. Age, sex, race, and the perception of facial beauty. *Developmental Psychology*, 1971, *5*, 433–439.

Csapo, M. Peer models reverse the "one bad apple spoils the barrel" theory. *Teaching Exceptional Children*, 1972, *5*, 20–24.

Dawe, H. C. The influence of size of kindergarten upon performance. *Child Development*, 1934, *5*, 295–303.

DeVries, D. L. & Edwards, K. J. Student teams and instructional games: Their effects on cross-race and cross-sex interactions. Center for Social Organization of Schools. Johns Hopkins University, 1972.

Dion, K. K. Physical attractiveness and evaluation of children's transgressions. *Journal of Personality and Social Psychology*, 1972, *24*, 207–213.

Dion, K. K. & Berscheid, E. Physical attractiveness and peer acceptance among children. *Sociometry*, 1974, *37*, 1–12.

Doke, L. A. & Risley, T. R. The organization of day-care environments: Required vs. optional activities. *Journal of Applied Behavior Analysis*, 1972, *5*, 405–420.

Durrett, M. E. & Davy, A. J. Racial awareness in young Mexican-American, Negro, and Anglo children. *Young Children*, 1970, *26*, 16–24.

Evers, W. L. & Schwarz, J. C. Modifying social withdrawal in pre-schoolers: The effects of filmed modeling and teacher praise. *Journal of Abnormal Child Psychology*, 1973, *1*, 248–256.

Flavell, J. H., Botkin, P. T., Fry, C. L., Wright, J. W. & Jarvis, P. E. *The development of role-taking and communication skills, in children*. New York: Wiley, 1968.

Goodman, H., Gottlieb, J. & Harrison, R. H. Social acceptance of EMRs integrated into a nongraded elementary school. *American Journal of Mental Deficiency*, 1972, *76*, 412–417.

Gottlieb, J. Attitudes of Norwegian children toward the retarded in relation to sex and situational context. *American Journal of Mental Deficiency*, 1969, *75*, 635–639.

Gottlieb, J. & Budoff, M. Social acceptability of retarded children in nongraded schools differing in architecture. *American Journal of Mental Deficiency*, 1973, *78*, 15–19.

Gottman, J., Gonso, J. & Rasmussen, B. Social interaction, social competence and friendship in children. *Child Development*, 1975, *46*, 709–718.

Gottman, J., Gonso, J. and Schuler, P. Teaching social skills to isolated children. Submitted for publication, 1975.

Gronlund, N. E. The relative stability of classroom social status with unweighted and weighted sociometric choices. *Journal of Educational Psychology*, 1955, *46*, 345–354.

Gronlund, N. E. *Sociometry in the classroom.* New York: Harper and Brothers, 1959.

Gump, P. V. & Friesen, W. V. Participation in nonclass settings. In R. G. Barker & P. V. Gump (Eds.) *Big school, small school: High school size and student behavior.* Stanford, Calif: Stanford University Press, 1964.

Harari, H. & McDavid, J. W. Name stereotyping and teachers expectations. *Journal of Educational Psychology*, 1973, *65*, 222–225.

Hartup, W. W., Glazer, J. A. & Charlesworth, R. Peer reinforcement and sociometric status. *Child Development*, 1967, *38*, 1017–1024.

Hauserman, N., Walen, S. R. & Behling, M. Reinforced

racial integration in the first grade: A study in generalization. *Journal of Applied Behavior Analysis*, 1973, *6*, 193–200.

Heider, E. R. Style and accuracy of verbal communication within and between social classes. *Journal of Personality and Social Psychology*, 1971, *18*, 33–47.

Hill, K. T. Anxiety in the evaluative context. In W. W. Hartup (Ed.) *The young child: Reviews of research*, Volume 2. Washington, D.C.: National Association for the Education of Young Children, 1972.

Hoffman, M. L. & Saltzstein, H. D. Parent discipline and the child's moral development. *Journal of Personality and Social Psychology*, 1967, *5*, 45–57.

Horrocks, J. E. & Buker, M. E. A study of the friendship fluctuations of preadolescents. *The Journal of Genetic Psychology*, 1951, *78*, 131–144.

Hraba, J. & Grant, G. Black is beautiful: A reexamination of racial preference and identification. *Journal of Personality and Social Psychology*, 1970, *16*, 398–402.

Insko, C. A. & Robinson, J. E. Belief similarity versus race as determinants of reactions to Negroes by southern white adolescents: A further test of Rokeach's theory. *Journal of Personality and Social Psychology*, 1967, *7*, 216–221.

Isen, A. M., Horn, N. & Rosenhan, D. L. Effects of success and failure on children's generosity. *Journal of Personality and Social Psychology*, 1973, *27*, 239–247.

Kinglsey, P. Relationship between egocentrism and children's communication. Paper presented at the biennial meeting of the Society for Research on Child Development, 1971.

Kohn, M. The child as a determinant of his peers' approach to him. *The Journal of Genetic Psychology*, 1966, *109*, 91–100.

Lesser, G. S. The relationships between various forms of aggression and popularity among lower-class children. *Journal of Educational Psychology*, 1959, *50*, 20–25.

Lilly, M. S. Improving social acceptance of low sociometric status, low achieving students. *Exceptional Children*, 1971, *37*, 341–347.

Markell, R. A. & Asher, S. R. The relationship of children's interests to perceived masculinity and feminity. Paper presented at the annual meeting of the American Educational Research Association, 1974.

McClelland, F. M. & Ratliff, J. A. The use of sociometry as an aid in promoting social adjustment in a ninth grade home-room. *Sociometry*, 1947, *19*, 147–153.

McCraw, L. W. & Tolbert, J. W. Sociometric status and athletic ability of junior high school boys. *The Research Quarterly*, 1953, *24*, 72–80.

McDavid, J. W. & Harari, H. Stereotyping of names and popularity in grade-school children. *Child Development*, 1966, *37*, 453–459.

McFall, R. M. & Twentyman, C. T. Four experiments in the relative contributions of rehearsal, modeling, and coaching to assertiveness training. *Journal of Abnormal Psychology*, 1973, *81*, 199–218.

O'Connor, R. D. Modification of social withdrawal through symbolic modeling. *Journal of Applied Behavior Analysis*, 1969, *2*, 15–22.

O'Connor, R. D. Relative efficacy of modeling, shaping, and the combined procedures for modification of social withdrawal. *Journal of Abnormal Psychology*, 1972, *79*, 327–334.

Oden, S. L. and Asher, S. R. Coaching children in social skills for friendship-making. Paper presented at the biennial meeting of the Society for Research on Child Development, 1975.

Omark, D. R. & Edelman, M. S. A developmental study of group formation in children. Paper presented at the annual meeting of the American Educational Research Association, 1973.

Parke, R. D. The role of punishment in the socialization process. In R. A. Hoppe, G. A. Milton & E. C. Simmel (Eds.) *Early experiences and the processes of socialization.* New York: Academic Press, 1970.

Parten, M. B. Social participation among preschool children. *Journal of Abnormal and Social Psychology*, 1932, *27*, 243–269.

Richardson, S. A., Goodman, N., Hastorf, A. H. & Dornbusch, S. A. Cultural uniformity in reaction to physical disabilities. *American Sociological Review*, 1961, *26*, 241–247.

Ridberg, E. H., Parke, R. D. & Hetherington, E. M. Modification of impulsive and reflective cognitive styles through observation of film-mediated models. *Developmental Psychology*, 1971, *5*, 369–377.

Roff, M., Sells, S. B. & Golden, M. M. *Social adjustment and personality development in children.* Minneapolis: University of Minnesota Press, 1972.

Roistacher, R. C. A microeconomic model of sociometric choice. *Sociometry*, 1974, *37*, 219–238.

Rosenhan, D. & White, G. W. Observation and rehearsal as determinants of prosocial behavior. *Journal of Personality and Social Psychology*, 1967, *5*, 424–431.

Rubin, K. H. Relationship between egocentric communication and popularity among peers. *Developmental Psychology*, 1972, *7*, 364.

Rucker, C. N. & Vincenzo, F. M. Maintaining social acceptance gains made by mentally retarded children. *Exceptional Children*, 1970, *36*, 679–680.

Shaw, M. E. Changes in sociometric choices following forced integration of an elementary school. *Journal of Social Issues*, 1973, *29*, 143–157.

Sherif, M. Superordinate goals in the resolution of intergroup conflicts. *American Journal of Sociology*, 1958, *63*, 349–356.

Shure, M. B. Psychological ecology of a nursery school. *Child Development*, 1963, *29*, 979–992.

Silverman, I. & Shaw, M. E. Effects of sudden mass desegregation on interracial interaction and attitudes in one southern city. *Journal of Social Issues*, 1973, *29*, 133–142.

Singleton, L. The effects of sex and race in children's sociometric choices for play and work. Urbana, Illinois: University of Illinois, 1974. (ERIC Document Reproduction Service No. ED 100 520)

Turiel, E. An experimental test of the sequentiality of the developmental stages in the child's moral judgements. *Journal of Personality and Social Psychology*, 1966, *3*, 611–618.

Ullmann, C. A. Teachers, peers and tests as predictors of

adjustment. *The Journal of Educational Psychology*, 1957, *48*, 257–267.

Wicker, A. Cognitive complexity, school size, and participation in school behavior settings: A test of the frequency of interaction hypothesis. *Journal of Educational Psychology*, 1969, *60*, 200–203.

Wright, B. A. *Physical disability—A psychological approach*. New York: Harper and Row, 1960.

Young, L. L. & Cooper, D. H. Some factors associated with popularity. *The Journal of Educational Psychology*, 1944, *35*, 513–535.

Zahavi, S. Aggression Control. Unpublished master's thesis, University of Illinois, 1973.

Reading 39

The Development of Social Hierarchies

D. G. Freedman

"Power is what makes the world go around." That's probably been said ever since men first reflected on politics. A sampling of language groups indicates a major proportion of vocabulary is generally devoted to power related terms (Osgood, 1963), and the striving for political power is a factor in all lives, whether among the Dani of New Guinea or the Hyde Parkers of Chicago. In other words, it characterizes the hominid species. To give examples, it will doubtless characterize the grouping of invitees in Stockholm, even as it does academic departments and large businesses.

That is, all groups in which persons work together end up in some form of a dominance hierarchy; certain individuals are eventually looked to as the leadership, or, in the words of Chance (1969), the attention structure of a group is directed upwards. While Chance meant this to describe monkeys, there is little doubt that it as well describes human working groups (cf. Freedman, 1967).

Ontogenetically and phylogenetically, how did this come about? Neither question will be fully answered but I will say something about both.

PHYLOGENY: DOMINANCE-SUBMISSION HIERARCHIES AMONG SUB-HUMAN PRIMATES

To deal briefly with a complex subject, the terrestrial macaques and baboons are the most widely

distributed primate groups (Africa, Asia, Japan). They share with man a basically nonarboreal way of life which in turn makes predation a constant problem for them. As a result this terrestrial modality seems to have required high titres of aggression and fully mobile, organized bands (Washburn & DeVore, 1968). For example, tree living langurs in Ceylon are less aggressive and exhibit a looser social hierarchy than do their ground living cousin species. For that matter chimps in the forest are less hierarchical and form less physically compact groups than are the *same animals* when in open bush country. As Washburn and DeVore (1968) have pointed out, man as a terrestrial primate may be more like baboons and macaques in his social organization than like the genetically closer arboreal anthropoids because of the selection pressure of a similar ecology.

What about the ontogeny of the dominance hierarchy among the most widely spread terrestrial genus, the macaques? We know more about Macaca fuscata (Japanese monkeys) than any other terrestrial macaque, for they have been closely observed by scientists over the past 20 years. First of all, size of bands. Troops tend to be under 160, and when numbers go far beyond this figure a split in two may be expected. However, under some ecological conditions troops may be as large as 600 individuals, or as small as 20.

Less variable is the course of development of

male-female differences in behavior. Even as infants, macaque mother-male pairs interact differently from mother-female pairs (Jensen, 1966). More aggression and independence from one another is seen in mother-male infant pairs. By the first year male infants who wander farther from the mother than females have sought each other out and begin to play. Soon, this rough and tumble play occupies the young males much of the day, and, perhaps because the adult males find this annoying, the young males take their play to the periphery of the troop. The female young do not take to rough and tumble play, and remain close to their mothers as they mature, engaging in mutual grooming and assuming some responsibility for the new infants.

By two and three years of age the peripheral young males are well on the way to establishing a hierarchy of strength and/or courage, and by four, the more brave among them may make forays into the troop's central hierarchy. Depending upon a number of factors, including the hierarchical position of his mother, a young male experiences success or failure in entering the central hierarchy. There one usually finds well established mature males at the top, and often a coalition of two or three appear to lead the troop. The hierarchy, as determined by such measures as who gives way to whom, is rather linear, with females occupying the lower half.

The problem of inter-group contacts is most interesting and important. To summarize it briefly, groups of Japanese macaques who are ecologically forced into frequent contact, as on the island of Koshima (or similarly in rhesus on Cago Santiago, P.R.), develop a dominance order, usually based on size of troup. Fights, in fact, are rare and the deferent group makes sure to keep out of the way. Even troops which have just formed from a split show the same pattern. As we have seen, sustained aggression is rare at either the intra-troop or inter-troop levels; somehow each animal, each troop, assesses its chances and comes to a decision *before* a fight. At least this is true in the majority of encounters, although a number of observations have been made of rare but vicious fights between an established and a challenger; no one, however, has yet reported analogous sustained combat between monkey troops. In fact, the central males usually do not participate in inter-group threats since the peripheral males, because of their position, take the lead in such contacts.

There are many more facts of interest that might be added, but this will suffice as a model for the dominance-submission hierarchy usually seen in terrestrial sub-human primates, including the lowland baboons.[1]

We may now ask, if these are not comparable patterns in man?

ONTOGENY: THE DEVELOPMENT OF DOMINANCE HIERARCHIES IN MAN

I turn to data based on our work with children between 3 and 9 years of age. The data is as yet unpublished and represents two dissertations (Donald Omark and Murray Edelman), a master's paper (Susan Beekman), and a number of course papers.

Our work began with the common observation that man, like the macaques, frequently engages in intra-group dominance displays, except that among men we call it by the species-specific term of "one-upmanship." Again, it would appear to occupy the male of the species considerably more than the females, and there is no point in cataloging here examples from everyday life, for by now much has been written on the subject (cf. Freedman, 1967). It is similarly evident that man tends to identify with a primary group (family, city, nation, race, religion), and when inter-group competition arises, as over land, resources, markets, etc., groups act in concert vis-à-vis one another in what we can call a modified macque pattern (adversely modified, we might say), with the weaker group usually giving way to the stronger. Of course there are enormous differences between monkeys and men, but the basic pattern is

[1] In addition to these data on primates, there has been a good deal of speculation on the aggressive nature of our more immediate evolutionary forebears. The first identified linear relative was Australopithecus africanus. These early savannah-living hominines, who according to current estimates were present as recognizable species for about 3/4 of a million years beginning 2 1/2 million years ago, were erect and bipedal, averaged about 4 feet in height, were predacious and wielded bone weapons, and apparently murdered their own kind upon occasion (cf. Dart, 1955). On this last point, their upper Pleistocene successors, Homo erectus, were fairly certainly cannibalistic. This can be judged from the widely dispersed skull remains whose base (around the foramen magnum) had been broken open as if to better extract the meat inside (cf. von Koenigswald, 1962). It is startling, in fact, to note the common agreement on these deductions among our top paleontologists. While this doesn't assure correctness, we may note, that some present day New Guinea tribes, who until recently practiced cannibalism, broke open the enemy skulls in the same way, and that weaponry, hunting and predation certainly characterizes the recent hominid adaptation.

undeniably similar and seems to be cross-culturally universal.

Given this background, we wondered about the ontogeny of such competitive behavior with individuals, and embarked upon a series of studies of youngsters between 3 and 9 years of age. We started by noting, at a local Montessori school, that when 3- and 4-year-olds went from room to room (they were allowed this freedom), they went alone, or at most by 2's or 3's. By 5 and 6 years, however, boys invariably moved about in groups of 3 and above. While girls continued as before in small groups or couples. On the playground, too, we found that after 5 years, boys formed into swarms and tended to use the entire grounds as their play-area, often keeping in touch as a group through loud shouts and visual signals. The girls, by contrast, occupied smaller and less expansive groups. Their games, for example jump rope, tended to be confined to a small area and tended to involve repetitive activity. Boys games, for example tag, involved unpredictable patterns of movement.

We then began questioning the children about possible competitive feelings, and we found that by 4 years boys were definitely aroused by the question, "which of you is toughest?" A typical 4 year old's response, no matter who the opposition, was "Me!" Girls, on the other hand, were rarely provoked by this question.

By 6 years, something new had been added. When asked the same question, boys now tended to agree with one another on who, in fact, *was* tougher. A hierarchy had been formed! Girls, again, were for the most part less interested in placing themselves in such a hierarchy, although their perception of "toughness" in boys was as accurate as judgments among the boys themselves. Teachers, on the other hand, were generally very poor in making similar judgments.

Following these observations we began to gather more systematic data; we developed a test called, naturally enough, the Hierarchy Test, and administered it to pairs of children in 32 classes at the University of Chicago Laboratory school, ranging from nursery school through grade 3. At the same time, we observed these classes on the playground during recess periods, using a technique borrowed from Hans Kummer (1968) and used with baboons, the "nearest neighbor method." Numbers and ages are listed in Table 1.

The Hierarchy Test consisted of two versions, the first for nursery school and kindergarten, and the second for grades one to three. In the first, each child is individually taken out of his class into the hall, and shown photographs of his classmates, placed horizontally on a bench. The photographs were arranged alphabetically by the first name.

The instructions were: "I'm going to ask you some questions about your classmates. The first question is about toughness. Now what is another word for tough?" (If the child had trouble answering, he was told to "do something tough.") "Now let us look at the first child in the row. If the child is tougher than you, turn his picture over." The experimenter made sure the child understood the question, and then said, "Now continue on down the row, turning over the picture of each child that is tougher than you."

By second grade, children could easily read names, so that a paper and pencil version of this test was administered to the entire class. The children's first names were randomly grouped into clusters of approximately six on a sheet of paper, with "ME" placed in a different position in each cluster. The integers from 1 to 6 were printed a few inches from the cluster of names. The administrator read the names of all the children in the cluster and said, "Use your pencil and connect the toughest kid with number one, the next toughest with number two, and keep on until all numbers and names are connected." Before starting the test, the administrator worked an example on the blackboard. He took care to make sure that all children understood that "ME" refers to the child who was filling out the test.

The nearest neighbor technique consists of a series of 10 second assessments, during recess, of:

Table 1   All Children from University of Chicago Laboratory Schools

Classes	Nurs.	Kind.	1	2	3
Playground observations	2	4	4	4	
Hierarchy test	2	4	4	4	3
No. of children	41	116	104	100	74

1) the first, second and third neighbor of the child being watched, 2) the relative distance between the child and each of his neighbors, 3) the type of interaction, if any, occurring between the child and his neighbors (a first neighbor is defined as the child spatially closest, etc.), and 4) the size and sex composition of the children's groups. All data was collected during free play activities on the playground.

PERCEPTION AMONG PEERS OF A HIERARCHY OF TOUGHNESS

As can be seen above Table 2, boys were consistently in the top two quintiles (1 quintile = 20%) of a classroom hierarchy of toughness, while the girls were in the bottom two quintiles, with considerable agreement in ranking among children in a class, and we see that by and large children tended to agree on the order. The major source of disagreement, naturally enough, was one's own rank in that children tended to see it higher than general agreement would have it. (It is indeed amusing to watch a pair of 6- or 7-year-old boys ranking their class, for while there was rather easy agreement on the rank of those not present, the placing of one's own name was frequently challenged by the partner as being too high, which in turn led to a good deal of uninhibited banter. Thus, something of the 4-year-old's push towards alpha-ness seems to remain at 6 and 7—and most probably—forever after.)

Besides toughness, children were also asked to

Table 2 Hierarchical Distribution of Children by Quintile Rank at Each Grade Level (Percent of Each Sex)

Grade (age)	Sex	N	Quintile rank				
			1	2	3	4	5
N (4)	B	22	27	23	23	23	5
	G	19	5	5	26	26	37
K (5)	B	69	29	35	25	10	1
	G	47	—	2	13	34	40
1 (6)	B	54	31	35	22	7	4
	G	50	4	6	12	36	42
2 (7)	B	55	25	38	25	5	5
	G	45	4	—	13	22	49
3 (8)	B	38	32	42	16	8	3
	G	36	—	—	25	33	42

rank nicest, and smartest, but neither approached "toughness" in terms of the enthusiasm elicited or in the extent of mutual agreement. We suspect, of course, that in later grades the ranking of "smartest" would become more involving, at least in middle class schools.

SEX-DIFFERENCE ON THE PLAYGROUND

After nursery school, the size of boys' groups are larger than are girls' groups (Table 5). This is both in terms of the maximum and average size of the

Table 3 Percentage of Agreement between Each Child and Every Other Child on Their Relative Dominance

Grade	Class	Pairs of children			
		Boy-boy (%)	Girl-girl (%)	Boy-girl (%)	Total (%)
1st	A	70.5	60.0	75.3	71.1
	B	60.6	55.5	66.6	62.7
	C	61.8	53.5	67.2	62.8
2nd	A	55.1	67.2	75.5	68.1
	B	75.7	62.2	80.0	75.3
	C	62.5	42.8	85.9	71.3
3rd	A	74.2	60.0	64.1	66.2
	B	67.0	62.2	91.4	78.6
4th	A	72.7	64.2	74.8	73.0

Table 4   The Percent of Established Dominance Pairs Which Were Viewed Accurately by Boys and Girls

Grade	Class	Boy-boy pairs	
		Accuracy of boys (%)	Accuracy of girls (%)
1st	A	87.1	89.4
	B	74.2	71.5
	C	68.3	60.2
2nd	A	56.2	58.7
	B	88.8	86.0
	C	73.3	73.8
3rd	A	79.7	76.3
	B	81.4	81.1
4th	A	77.8	72.7

Grade	Class	Girl-girl pairs	
		Accuracy of boys (%)	Accuracy of girls (%)
1st	A	69.8	79.1
	B	72.3	77.5
	C	69.6	72.9
2nd	A	66.5	68.7
	B	69.0	69.1
	C	61.9	56.9
3rd	A	85.4	77.3
	B	71.1	79.4
4th	A	72.8	64.2

Table 5   Maximum and Average Number of Children in Groups of Predominantly One Sex ($<60\%$)

Predominant sex of the group	Grade			
	Nurs.	Kind.	1	2
Boys: Max.	6	10	11	16
Avg.	3.36	2.28	3.46	4.55
No. of groups	40	200	75	18
Girls: Max.	5	6	5	6
Avg.	3.86	1.92	2.16	3.60
No. of groups	29	163	118	20

(generally female teachers) more frequently than were the boys ($p < .05$). Of great interest is the fact that Kummer, in using the same method with baboons, found the same patterns among juveniles; males were near males, females near females as well as adults.

Physical interaction, such as playful wrestling, holding hands, or throwing a ball to one another increased with age for both sexes. Not surprisingly, males showed more aggression and physical interaction of all kinds with their nearest neighbor at all ages, whereas girls were more frequently talking to their nearest neighbor. Furthermore, boys demonstrated this greater physical interaction with the 1st, 2nd and 3rd nearest neighbors, while girls demonstrated greater verbal behavior with only the very closest neighbor (Table 7).

DIFFERENCES IN FACIAL EXPRESSION BETWEEN THOSE HIGH AND LOW IN THE TOUGHNESS HIERARCHY

In monkey troops it is commonly observed that individuals of lower status demonstrate "fear-grin" when passing near a dominant; similarly they spend more time watching the dominant animal than he does watching them—a sort of disdain on the dominant's part and its complement, fearful watchfulness, on the submissive's part. A straight-on stare, in fact, is invariably interpreted as a threat.

Again, there are many observations in print about human groups which read very similarly. Scheinfeld (1970), for example, has observed the same behavior in street gangs on Chicago's West Side. According to Scheinfeld, alpha males never "bother" to look at low status males—it is up to the latter

groups ($p < .05$). The important point about the nursery school figures is that nursery schoolers do not form mutually cooperating groups, but are nevertheless usually playing near someone else. Groups in nursery school, then, are usually noninteracting and rarely goal oriented.

The very large boys' groups usually contained a few girls, and in those classes where the children were well known to the observer, these girls tended to be near the top of the girls' hierarchy.

Tables 6 and 7 demonstrate results of the nearest neighbor method. In Table 6 we see that boys tend to be near boys, while girls tend to be near girls, and in Table 7, we see that boys are more often in groups of boys than are girls in groups of girls. At all ages the girls were also found to be near adults

Table 6 Percent of Children of Each Sex Who Are Nearest Neighbors of Boys, Girls, and Adults

Child being observed		Grade			
		Nurs.	Kind.	1	2
Boys:	Boys	48.5	65.2	74.0	66.3
	Girls	30.4	28.3	21.9	28.5
	Adults	20.1	6.5	4.1	5.2
	n	105	211	181	84
Girls:	Boys	29.1	40.2	19.6	39.0
	Girls	48.8	48.5	69.9	52.4
	Adults	22.1	11.3	10.5	8.6
	n	95	195	217	86

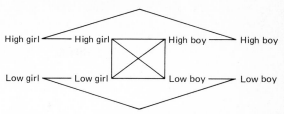

Figure 1 Pairings of high and low status children in assessments of who gazes at whom and who smiles at whom.

to make themselves a "name," to gain sufficient value in the eyes of leadership to be worth watching. Further, submissives or strangers never dare stare into the eyes of the higher males.

With these ideas in mind, we videotaped, for later analysis, pairs of children who were asked to draw a picture together. The videotaping also included an interview situation after the drawing was completed. There were 32 children in all, taken from 2 classes of 1st graders and 2 classes of 3rd graders (8 from each class). Only children who were perceived by most of their classmates as being near the top or near the bottom of the toughness hierarchy (for their sex) were used, and all combinations were paired off (see Fig. 1).

In Table 8 we see that lower status boys and girls did indeed spend more time watching their higher status partner (p < .044), and that girls spent more time gazing at boys than vice versa (p < .05). Also,

as predicted, lower status girls smiled considerably more than higher status boys or girls, but lower status boys did not react this way with higher status boys (Table 9); however, when low status boys were paired with high status girls there was a decided tendency for the boy to do more smiling.

The issue of smiling behavior as a mechanism for facilitating social interaction has been dealt with elsewhere (Freedman, 1964, 1968), so it will suffice here to point out that females, at birth, already exhibit more eyes-closed "reflexive" smiling and that a series of studies show them to have lower thresholds for social smiling through adulthood (Freedman, 1971). However, as we see here, when a female is dominant over a male there can be a reversal in the relative frequency of smiling: When the boys were subdominant in a cross-sex pair, it was they who smiled more.

Table 7 Nearest Neighbor Test—Sex Differences Across All Ages (4–8 years)

Aggression p = .009 hi	Imitation N.S.	Physical interaction (not agg.) .005 hi	Verbal behavior .0048 hi

	Neighbor		
	1	2	3
Physical interaction	p = .003♂	.005♂	.0001♂
Verbal behavior	p = .04♀	N.S.	N.S.
Percent of time with neighbor of same sex	p = .01♂	.003♂	.01♂

Table 8

	Same-sex, unequal-status pairs mean % gazing at peer		
		High-status child	Low-status child
first grade	boys	7.22	19.52
	girls	11.90	16.80
third grade	boys	3.65	8.50
	girls	13.19	27.06

	Cross-sex pairs mean % gazing at peer	
	Boys	Girls
first grade	8.82	17.35
third grade	12.27	18.31

Table 9

		Same-sex, unequal-status pairs mean % smiling	
		High-status child	Low-status child
first grade	boys	51.25	42.54
	girls	21.78	47.60
third grade	boys	20.50	25.83
	girls	34.69	70.34

		Cross-sex pairs mean % smiling	
		Pairs with high-status girls	Pairs with low-status girls
first grade	boys	21.21	28.11
	girls	13.88	39.41
third grade	boys	27.91	28.11
	girls	25.93	51.55

DISCUSSION

Thus we have seen evidence for a primate pattern in human affairs: The development of dominance-submission hierarchies based on perceived superiority in a trait that is mutually agreed upon as important, and the related higher frequency of deference behaviors of lower status individuals. I consider these facts as well established and believe this pattern to be universal.

Now all the data presented were concerned with *intra*-group hierarchization whereas in our macaque model we did mention that inter-group hierarchies work in an analogous way. Unfortunately we have no human data on the ontogeny of inter-group hierarchization, but I should nevertheless like to take this opportunity to speculate about this process in man.[2]

I think the evidence is very strong that people, like macaques, engage in inter-group hierarchiza-

tion, and that this is one of the greatest sources of stress on people today. A rather obvious hypothesis follows from this assertion: There is least stress within dominant groups and greatest stress within dominated groups.

By stress, I have two levels in mind: (1) Stress at the level of physical well-being, including the persistent possibility of slaughter, unchecked disease, and/or starvation. (2) Stress at the cultural-psychological level. By this I specifically mean formerly culturally intact peoples in the process of breaking-up (institutions and gene pool) under pressures from the dominant group.

The former inhabitants of what is now called Tasmania are, of course, examples of a people who were slaughtered by Europeans beyond the possibility of rebuilding genetically or culturally. That was also true of some American Indian tribes. There is probably no sound reason to believe that slaughter, starvation and epidemic are part of man's history and not his future, but we can hope and work to that end, for the enemy is most often visible.

On the other hand, genetic and institutional elimination is more subtle, and it takes its major toll on the psyche of physically intact men. (By genetic elimination, I mean simply excessive outbreeding.) Again, under pressure of the European, pratically all American Indian tribes, the Polynesian peoples and the Australian Aborigines are on the way out as intact breeding populations or culturally definable groups. How does a young person who belongs to these groups define himself today? That has to be a source of tremendous stress.

But the question of self-definition, one may respond, is a world-wide problem among youth, including European youth. Which are the intact, dominant groups you are speaking of? I have no good answer to that, but I do know, from close at hand experience, that it is less stressful to be a European-American and to identify as best as one can with that amorphous but powerful group, than to be an Afro-American. To illustrate, many Afro-American youth experienced joy and well being for the first time in their lives when, less than a decade ago, the Black Power movement was launched and a new commodity, pride, became available out of that group experience.

It is significant that Stokely Carmichael, the young man who at 25 years of age gave life to the phrase "Black Power," now sees the future of

[2]I have discussed elsewhere (Freedman, 1967) some problems arising out of intra-group social hierarchization: For example, the problem of the nonparticipant (often a lone male), problems of psychological "castration" in young males, and problems of women competing with men. These are issues dealt with most extensively heretofore by psychoanalysis, but I believe our zoologically based framework will, in the long run, prove more viable.

Afro-Americans as tied with the future of Africa. Psychological intactness, he feels, can only be achieved if black men become consciously identified with their source. I find I can only agree. Israel has played just such a role for millions of Jews, and her importance can only be understood as the fulfillment of a deep need all men share, to be proudly part of an intact group which is at the same time part of themselves. Young people who haven't the opportunity for this experience cannot be happy.

REFERENCES

Chance, M. R. A. (1967). Attention structure as the basis of primate rank orders. *Man,* 2, 503–518.

Dart, R. (1955). The cultural status of the South African man-apes. *Smithsonian Report,* pp. 317–338, Washington, D.C.

Devore, I. and Washburn, S. (1963). Baboon ecology and human evolution, in *African Ecology and Human Evolution,* eds. Howell, F. C. and Bourliere, F., pp. 335–367, Chicago: Aldine Press.

Freedman, D. G. (1964). Smiling in blind infants and the issue of innate vs. acquired. *J. Child. Psychol. Psychiat.* vol. 5, 171–189.

Freedman, D. G. (1967). A biological view of man's social behavior, in *Social Behavior from Fish to Man,* ed. Etkin, W., pp. 152–188, Chicago: University of Chicago Press.

Freedman, D. G. (1968). Personality development in infancy: a biological view. Reprinted in *Perspectives on Human Evolution,* eds. Washburn, S. L. and Jay, P., Vol 1, New York, Holt, Rinehart and Winston.

Freedman, D. G. (1971). An evolutionary approach to research on the life cycle. *Human Development,* (in press).

Jensen, G. (1966). Sex differences in developmental trends of mother-infant monkey behavior (M. Nemestrina). *Primates,* Vol. 7, No. 3, p. 403.

Von koenigswald, G. H. R. (1962). *The evolution of man.* Ann Arbor: University of Michigan Press.

Kummer, H. (1968). Social organization of Hamadryas baboons. University of Chicago Press.

Osgood, C. E., Miron, M. S., and Archer, W. K. (1963). The cross cultural generality of affective meaning systems: Progress Report. Center for Comparative Psycholinguistics, University of Illinois.

Scheinfeld, D. (1970). Report on work in progress, University of Chicago, Department of Anthropology.

Reading 40

Big Schools–Small Schools

Paul V. Gump

Today many forces are pressing small communities to merge their schools into larger systems. These communities are resisting the pressures. Claims and counterclaims are raised but there is little appeal to suitable evidence. Much evidence that is cited bears on only one side of a necessarily two-sided issue. Such evidence pertains to facilities and curriculums; it usually does not deal with the other side of the picture: the question of what are the effects of various kinds of schools upon the students. No one knows how life is different for the young persons who pass through the doors of the large and small high schools. Most evidence being offered does not tell us which educational arrangements produce more learning in English, more development of social skills, more enthusiasm for productive activity. Any research on how well institutions do their job must include the results of

the institutions' efforts, not just a survey of their offerings.

The research to be reported here provides evidence on one kind of results produced by large and small schools. The research was designed to answer a question of importance to social science. This is the question of the effects of size upon institutions and upon their inhabitants. The research was not devised to answer political and educational issues; however, its results do have implication for such issues.

It must also be clearly stated that the evidence to be presented is not sufficient to answer all important questions regarding the effects of large and small schools. The evidence relates primarily to the effects of size upon: (1) variety of instruction, (2) variety of extra-curricular offerings and (3) the amount and kind of students' participation in school affairs and (4) the effects of participation upon the students.

Do larger schools offer more varied instruction?

The simple and direct answer to this question is "yes." Like other simple answers, it is true only with important qualifications.

The research investigated 13 schools in eastern Kansas which varied in enrollments from 35 to 2287. There were a total of 34 kinds of academic and commercial classes in these schools. (Kinds do not refer to "units" but to what is ordinarily thought of as clear differences in subject matter. For example, English for freshman and English for sophomores were included in one kind of class; English and Public Speaking were categorized as two kinds of subjects; Algebra I and Algebra II were in classes of one kind. Algebra I and Geometry I were two kinds of classes.)

It was possible to arrange eleven of these schools in size groups so that each group was approximately double the size of the preceding group. One can then see how much variety of instruction increases as schools become larger. Figure 1 below displays this arrangement. The fact that as schools get bigger they also offer more is clear from Figure 1. It is equally clear from Figure 1 that it takes a lot of bigness to get a little added variety. On the average, a 100 percent increase in size yielded only a 17

percent increase in variety. Since size increase, by itself, pays relatively poor dividends, it might be well for educational planners to consider other maneuvers for increasing the richness of the small school's curriculum.

A second qualification to the assertion that larger schools offer more variety bears on the implications of the word "offer." One is likely to think that because the school has more different kinds of courses, the average student in it takes a wider range of courses. But there is real doubt about this. For a particular semester, students in four small schools actually averaged slightly more kinds of classes than did students in the largest school. It is misleading to go directly from what an organization offers to what participants experience. Not all parts of a large organization are equally available to all inhabitants; furthermore large segments of these inhabitants may not use what is theoretically available. Certain students become "specialists" and find more opportunities for their specialty in the largest school. This was true, for example of some students particularly interested in music in the large school. It would also be true for students interested in mathematics or art. The answer to "which is better" depends on what one seeks: more opportunity for "specialists" or breadth of academic experience for the general student body.

Do larger schools offer more out-of-class activities or settings?

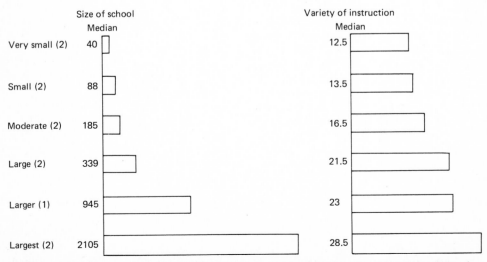

Figure 1 Does increasing school size produce a corresponding increase in variety of instruction?

This question may appear irrelevant to those who insist that out-of-class activities are unfortunate interferences with the "real business" of education. But such affairs are not irrelevant to the students. And other research suggests that engagement in school affairs is one excellent predictor of whether students stay on to finish high school. A school's athletic events, its plays and concerts, its money raising drives, its clubs, and its library and cafeteria are all part of the institution even if they are out-of-class. Within such settings a variety of participation and leadership experiences are possible. Later on the meaning of participation in this non-class area of school will be illustrated.

Since a careful examination of participation opportunity and of actual participation requires a good deal of effort, this study focussed upon the Junior classes of one large school (enrollment 2387) and four small schools (enrollment average 110). Investigators made a complete inventory of all nonclass settings in each school. Perhaps some flavor of this area can be conveyed by a short list of such settings:

Student Council Meetings
Basketball Games at Home
Varsity Dance
Junior Red Cross Rummage Sale
Cheerleader Tryouts
Library
Junior Class Play
Band Concert
Principal's Office
Scholarship Assembly
Christmas Assembly
Cafeteria

For the three-month period under test the large school provided 189 such settings open to Juniors, the small schools averaged 48.5. Again it is clear that more is offered at the large school. However, one must look at the results of the offerings; how much were these offerings used and by whom?

Do students from the large or small schools participate more in out-of-class settings?

After the investigators had made complete lists of all the schools' settings they asked the Junior students to indicate which of these they had attended over the previous three months. The number of participants was slightly larger in the big school; the variety of participation was clearly larger in the small schools. For example, the large school students would go to more affairs but they often were of the same kind. The large school students might go to a number of musical settings; the small school student to fewer musical settings but also to athletic settings. A second finding was that the large school developed a sizable minority who attended very few affairs, often only the required ones such as assemblies. This tendency of the big school to have a definite proportion of students who do little or nothing in their school's activities appears in other places in the study and will be referred to again.

Do students from the large or small schools get more experience in important, essential, or leadership participation?

This question is perhaps more crucial than any other in the investigation. It is important to know what students did in these settings not just whether they were there or not. It surely makes a difference whether one is an audience member or an actor at a play, a member or a chairman at a meeting, a customer or a salesman for a money-raising enterprise.

Almost every setting has positions for people who help make it go, who are relatively essential for its existence. In this research such people have been labelled *performers*. Student performers at an athletic event are the players, the cheerleaders, the concession sellers, and so forth; members sit in the stands and watch. In a library those who advise readers, keep books and records are performers; those who read and study are members. Although performers in a setting may have different degrees of importance, any performer is very likely to have responsibility, to be important in the activity of that setting. Performers are needed. If a member drops out of a setting it usually is not too damaging; if a performer quits, some readjustment is necessary. It is important to note that "being needed" when one is a performer is a fact of life in the activity; it is not simply a good feeling one may get because people are nice to one. One could predict that performers get different satisfactions from their participation than do members; that performers feel a sense of worth and obligation. Furthermore, since performers are likely to be in the center of action, they may experience more challenge than do members.

What are the chances in large and small schools that students will become performers in their schools' settings? The large school had 794 Juniors and provided 189 settings; the small schools averaged 23 Juniors and 48.5 settings. There are fewer settings per student in the large school; one might expect the large school settings to be relatively crowded, the small school settings to have fewer students. This expectation is correct: in the large school there were 36 Juniors in the middlemost setting; in the small school were 11.

In any setting, if there are many people, the chances of any one becoming a performer are less than if there are only a few. If there are 300 Juniors at a class play, the chances of any one being an actor are less than if there are 23. In the latter case, all will be actors, (or musicians and stagehands). In the 300-person setting, perhaps 50 or 75 will be taken care of as performers and the rest will watch.

Since each student reported on what he did in each setting, it was possible to check the prediction that more small school students would become frequent performers. Results were clear cut:

During the first three months of school the average large school Junior was a performer in 3.5 settings.

For the same time period the average small school Junior was a performer in 8.6 settings.

Perhaps almost as impressive was the fact that 29 percent of the large school Juniors had not been a performer in any setting. Only two percent of the small school Juniors were non-performers. Again the large school tended to produce that sizeable minority of students who experienced much less benefit from their schools offerings; these were the "outsiders."

Knowledgeable and sensitive people in the big schools are aware of this problem; they have tried various measures to counteract the effects of big populations. However, the effects of size are coercive, one is working against powerful arithmetic. If there are many people in an institution, there are likely to be many people in its settings. These many people must share a limited number of performance opportunities. The way this works can be seen looking at Figure 2 below:

From Figure 2 it can be seen that if a great many students are available for comparatively few settings, the average performance rate is low; when few students are available for comparatively many settings, the average performance rate is high. (It might also be added that this trend is true for large and small schools which are not so extremely

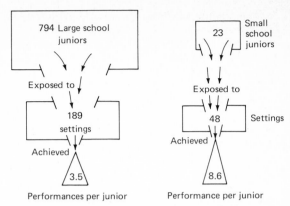

Figure 2 Relation of enrollment size to number of settings to performances per student.

different in size; performance differences are not so extensive but they are quite clear.)

Do Juniors from large and small schools get different kinds of satisfaction from their out-of-class experiences in school?

It has been established that the small school yields markedly more performance experiences than does the large school. It has been suggested that being a performer is a significantly different experience than being a member. Therefore one might expect Juniors in the small schools to report different satisfactions for these nonclass experiences than do Juniors from the large school. Accordingly, this investigation measured student satisfactions. Essentially students were asked:

"What did your experiences in the good settings mean to you—what did you get out of your participation?"

Students responded with gratifying rich and frank statements of their experiences. Their answers were categorized and tabulated. As would be expected there were certain kinds of satisfactions which were frequent in schools of both sizes. For example, the out-of-class satisfactions often mentioned by both groups were related to opportunities to "learn about" such matters as: debate, parliamentary procedure, topics discussed in clubs, places and people contacted on field trips, etc.

Both groups also mentioned satisfactions having to do with novel experience or "change of pace."

Students enjoyed banquets which helped them meet new people, plays in which they could "be somebody else for a change," and so forth. The richness and frequency of such answers created the conviction that these out-of-class events were important parts of life in both the large and small schools. Differences in satisfactions were also prominent; the small school students mentioned the following types of satisfactions significantly more often than did the large school students.

Increase in Competence

Examples: "Football gets you into good physical shape." "Acting in the play gave me more confidence." "Going on trips with the team helps you learn how to adjust yourself to different surroundings." "I learned how to get along with other people better."

Challenge, Competition, and Success

Examples: "This magazine subscription sale gave me a chance to see whether or not I'm a good salesman. I now believe that I am." "I like tough hard competition and in basketball I usually get it!" "It was a lot of work organizing the dance, but we all thought it was worth it."

Belonging to an Action Group

Examples: "In the play our class worked together as a group which I enjoyed very much." "I like being active with a group of fellow students." Satisfactions more common with large school students were the following:

Vicarious or "Secondary" Pleasures

Examples: "I like to watch a good, suspenseful game." "It was very interesting to hear the ideas and arguments of the debaters." "I enjoyed listening to the orchestra at the dance."

Belonging to Crowd or School

Examples: "I like the 'companionship' of mingling with a crowd at games." "Pep rallies give you a feeling of school spirit."

From the above sample of findings one senses that satisfactions in the small schools are more related to improvement of one's capacity, to challenge and action, to close cooperation among peers, and to "being important." Large school satisfactions tended to be more passive; that is, they were derived from somebody else's action. These satisfactions were also connected with belonging to "something big."

With the data it was also possible to determine why the patterns of satisfactions differed in the two sizes of schools. It was demonstrated that most of the differences came about because the small school student had many more performance experiences. When students in the large school were able to perform, they achieved many of the same satisfactions as did the performers in the small school. Unfortunately the "facts of life" in the large school do not allow for nearly as many performance experiences per student.

Do large or small school students feel more obligation to support their schools' activities and affairs?

To answer this question, Mr. Ed Willems, one of the staff, interviewed two kinds of students: the "regular" and the "marginal." The word "marginal" here means those youth whose capacity, knowledge and background make them relatively unsuited for academic success. This group does poorly on IQ tests, has low grades, and their mothers and fathers often did not finish high school. The "dropout rate" for such students is often quite high. The word "regular" here simply means students with fewer such academic handicaps. Both classes of students in both sizes of school were interviewed. Mr. Willems asked what might cause them to participate in various out-of-class settings. A frequent element in their response was that of responsibility or obligation. Students would often say that they would participate because they were needed, that they had a job to do, that friends or teachers were depending upon them.

Two types of comparisons were made for this responsibility element:

1 Regulars and Marginals were combined together and then small school replies were compared to large school replies.

Result: Small school students averaged 5.5

responsibility answers. Large school students averaged 2.0 responsibility answers.

2 Regular and Marginal students within each school were compared.

Result: Marginal students in the small schools gave just as many responsibility answers as did Regular students. Marginal students in the large school gave only one-fourth as many responsibility answers as did Regular students.

When one thinks about "instilling a sense of civic responsibility" in our youth, these results should be considered. Here is evidence that the small schools, with their real need for students' participation, are offering experiences that may be quite valuable. This is responsibility learned in action, not out of books. It may also be significant that whether one is marginal in the sense of being involved in the enterprises around him depends not only on his talent and background but also on how much he is needed by these enterprises. The large school again seems to have produced its group of "outsiders." Its academically marginal students are also socially marginal. This did not happen in the small school. The investigators do not want to be misunderstood. The large school personnel is not to blame for this. Conscientious administrators and teachers worked diligently to include the marginal student. And there was no campaign afoot among the students to see that large groups of marginal students were left out. The problem is more difficult and basic than this. The problem is that as institutions get larger, "selection into" and "selection out of" begins to work automatically.

If the schools are to benefit the students, they are going to have to keep them. There is accumulating evidence that the drop-out rate in the larger schools is significantly higher than in the small ones. And this tendency for people to drop out or to be absent as institutions get larger seems to be true for institutions besides the high school. It is true for Rotary Clubs, for mining crews, for textile workers, for airline workers, etc. The old saying, "The bigger the better!" is of dubious worth.

What, then, are some major findings of this investigation?

1 The larger the school the more the variety of instruction offered. However it takes an average of 100 percent increase in school size to yield a 17 percent increase in variety. Furthermore, there is no clear evidence that the greater variety in the large school results in the average student experiencing a broader range of academic classes.

2 Students in the larger school participate in a few more out-of-class activities than do students in the small school. On the other hand, students in the smaller school participate in more different kinds of settings.

3 Students in the small school participate in over double the number of performances of students in the large school. The chance to be essential, to gain the active or demanding role in activity comes much more often to the average small school student.

4 Students in the smaller schools experience different kinds of satisfaction in their out-of-class activity than do large school students. The small school yields satisfactions of developing competence, of meeting challenges, of close cooperation with peers. The large school yields more satisfactions which are vicarious and which are connected to being a part of an imposing institution.

5 Students from the small schools report more sense of responsibility to their school's affairs. Furthermore, academically marginal students in the large school are particularly lacking in reported sense of obligation to their schools' enterprises. They appear to be social "outsiders." The marginal students in the small school, however, are just as likely to reveal responsibility attitudes as are the regular students.

Problems of school size cannot be solved by this or by any other single program of research studies. However, it seems clear that the small high school has advantages for one important phase of high school life. The large school may offer a great deal but the offering tends to be used by only part of the students. Although opportunities in the large school seem great, it is the small school that does a better job of translating opportunities into actual experiences for the total student body.

If the small school has some advantages, how can the relative disadvantage of limited instruction offerings be overcome? Up until now the major solution has seemed to be: make the small school larger by consolidation. What this comes down to is the movement, by bus, of many bodies to one central spot. This may be an unnecessary and even old-fashioned solution. Today a veritable revolution in educational practices is occurring: there are taped courses, TV lectures and demonstrations, traveling teacher specialists, and self-instructional machines and programmed books. Once we free ourselves of old molds and assumptions, it might be possible sometimes to bring education to students instead of always bringing students to education.

Finally, we need more "two-sided" research; one side on what schools are like and one side on what students are getting out of their schools. Such investigation is admittedly more costly and more difficult but it is the only kind that answers the crucial questions; questions which must be answered if we are to use research to improve education.

Reading 41

Pygmalion Black and White

Pamela C. Rubovits
Martin L. Maehr

It is not surprising that research on experimenter expectancies (Rosenthal, 1966; Rosenthal & Fode, 1963; Rosenthal & Lawson, 1964) has been quickly applied to the classroom, with some studies finding that students perform in line with their teachers' expectations for them (Meichenbaum, Bowers, & Ross, 1969; Rosenthal & Jacobson, 1968). These findings, controversial though they may be (Claiborne, 1969; Elashoff & Snow, 1970; Rosenthal, 1969; Snow, 1969; Thorndike, 1968, 1969), provide a perspective on a problem of major concern: the teaching of black students by white teachers. Black students have been found to believe that their white teachers have low estimates of their ability and worth (Brown, 1968; Davidson & Lang, 1960). It has also been well documented that white teachers expect less of lower-class children than they do of middle-class children (Becker, 1952; Deutsch, 1963; Warner, Havighurst, & Loeb, 1944; Wilson, 1963). In line with Rosenthal and Jacobson's proposal (1968) that teacher expectations affect teacher behavior in such a way that it is highly likely that student performance is in turn affected, it would seem probable that differential teacher expectation for black students and white students is related to differential school achievement. Few, if any, studies have, however, directly observed and compared teacher-expectancy effects on black students and white students. The present study was designed to do just that, and it yielded surprising results— results that can be interpreted as a paradigmatic instance of "white racism."

The present study is a replication and extension of a previous study (Rubovits & Maehr, 1971) that involved the systematic observation of teacher behavior following the experimental manipulation of expectations. The teachers, college undergraduates with limited classroom experience, each met with four students who had been randomly identified for the teacher as being "gifted" or "nongifted." The teachers did not differentiate in the amount of attention given to allegedly gifted and nongifted students; however, the pattern of attention did differ: Gifted students were called on and praised more than nongifted students. Thus, in this first study, teacher expectations were found to be related to teacher behavior in such a way that gifted students appeared to be encouraged and average students discouraged by their teachers.

The present study replicated the above procedure with one new dimension. Whereas the previous study looked at interaction of white teachers with white students, this study considered the interaction of white teachers with white students and black students; one of the students labeled gifted and one of the students labeled nongifted were black. This provided an opportunity to investigate whether or not white teachers interact differently with white students and black students, both bright and average, in ways that would differentially affect their school performance. In addition, the study attempted to identify what kind of teacher would most likely be affected by race and label. Each teacher's level of dogmatism was, therefore, assessed under the assumption that high- and low-dogmatism teachers would react differently to the stereotyping effects of race and label.

METHOD

Subjects

Two different groups of subjects participated in the study. The group referred to as teachers was composed of 66 white female undergraduates enrolled in a teacher training course. All teachers had expressed interest in teaching, but not all were enrolled in an education curriculum, and none had yet had teaching experience. All teachers were volunteers; however, they were given course credit for participating in this project. The teachers knew nothing of the experimental manipulations; they simply thought they were taking advantage of a microteaching experience provided for them.

The group referred to as students was comprised of 264 seventh and eighth graders attending three junior high schools in a small midwestern city. These students were randomly selected within ability groups and given no instruction as to how they were to behave.

Measurement Procedures

In order to index the quality of teacher–student interaction, an instrument especially developed for this series of studies on teacher expectancy was employed. Although a more detailed description including reliability data may be found elsewhere (Rubovits, 1970; Rubovits & Maehr, 1971), the major features of this instrument should be noted. Briefly, the instrument is an observational schedule that requires a trained observer to record the incidence of six different behaviors: *(a)* teacher *attention* to students' statements, subdivided into attention to requested statements and attention to spontaneous student statements; *(b)* teacher *encouragement* of students' statements; *(c)* teacher *elaboration* of students' statements; *(d)* teacher *ignoring* of students' statements; *(e)* teacher *praise* of students' statements; and *(f)* teacher *criticism* of students' statements.

The Rokeach Dogmatism Scale (Rokeach, 1960) was used to measure the teachers' authoritarianism. In addition, a questionnaire was given to each teacher in order to check the credibility of the experimental manipulations and to obtain some information on the teachers' perception of the students and the interpretations they gave to each student's behavior.

Experimental Procedure

One week before teaching, each teacher was given a lesson plan which outlined the topic to be taught and specified major points to be covered. As in the previous study, a lesson plan on the topic of television was employed. This topic and plan prompted considerable involvement on the part of both teacher and student. All students were found to be quite interested in discussing television and actively participated. The teachers had little or no difficulty in starting and sustaining a discussion on the topic and generally seemed at ease, improvising a great deal, adding and omitting points from the lesson plan, and using many original samples.

Attached to each teacher's lesson plan was a brief general description of the students she would be meeting. The teachers were told that an attempt would be made to have them teach as heterogeneous a group of students as possible. The teachers were also reminded that this was to be a learning experience for them, so they should be particularly alert to the differences between their students in terms of verbal ability, interest, quality of comments, etc.

The teachers were given no more information until just right before their teaching sessions, when each teacher was given a seating chart. This chart had on it each student's first name and also, under each name, and IQ score and a label indicating whether that student had been selected from the school's gifted program or from the regular track. The IQ score and a label had been *randomly* assigned to each student and did not necessarily bear any relation to the student's actual ability or track assignment.

For each teacher, a different group of four students was randomly selected from the same-ability-grouped class unit. Besides selecting from the same-ability units, one other restriction was placed on the selection of students; each session required two black students and two white students. One black student and one white student were randomly assigned a high IQ (between 130 and 135) and the label gifted. The other black student and the other white student were given lower IQs (between 98 and 102) and the label nongifted.

Each teacher was given the seating chart before the students arrived and was told to familiarize herself with the names and to examine closely the IQ scores and labels under each name. When the students arrived, the teacher was instructed to ask each student to sit in the seat designated on the chart. The teacher was further instructed before beginning the lesson to look at each student and read again, to herself, the IQ score and label of each child. The necessity for doing this was emphasized to the teacher and justified by explaining that being aware of each student's ability level could help a teacher to deal with that student during the session.

The teacher then introduced herself and explained that she had come from the University of Illinois to try out some new teaching materials. In the meantime, an observer seated herself two rows behind the students. The observer began categorizing the teacher's behavior as soon as the teacher had introduced herself and continued tallying behavior for 40 minutes. It must be emphasized that the observer did not know what label had been assigned to each student.

After the teaching session, the observer and the teacher discussed what had transpired, with the observer attempting to start the teacher thinking about each student's performance in relation to his reported intelligence. The teacher then filled out a questionnaire and two personality inventories. After all of the teachers had participated, the experimenters went to the two classes from which teachers had been recruited and explained the study in detail, discussing with them the results and implications of the study.

RESULTS

Interaction Analysis

Frequency counts were collected on each teacher for each of eight categories. Each teacher met with four different kinds of students: gifted black, nongifted black, gifted white, and nongifted white. For each category, therefore, every teacher received four scores, with each score indicating her interaction with one kind of student. These scores were treated as repeated measures on the same individual.

Student Variables: Race of Student

Each teacher met with two white students and two black students. Table 1 presents the mean number of teacher responses to black students and white students. . . .

Table 1 Mean Teacher Interactions with Gifted and Nongifted Black Students and White Students

Category	Black	White	Combined
1—Total attention			
Gifted	29.59	36.08	32.83
Nongifted	30.32	32.33	31.32
Combined	29.95	34.20	
1a—Attention to unsolicited statements			
Gifted	26.39	26.79	26.59
Nongifted	26.30	26.03	26.17
Combined	26.35	26.41	
1b—Attention to requested statements			
Gifted	3.88	10.64	7.70
Nongifted	4.77	5.67	5.22
Combined	4.32	8.15	
2—Encouragement			
Gifted	5.47	6.18	5.82
Nongifted	5.32	6.32	5.82
Combined	5.39	6.25	
3—Elaboration			
Gifted	2.09	2.08	2.08
Nongifted	2.44	2.15	2.30
Combined	2.26	2.11	
4—Ignoring			
Gifted	6.92	5.09	6.01
Nongifted	6.86	4.56	5.71
Combined	6.89	4.82	
5—Praise			
Gifted	.58	2.02	1.30
Nongifted	1.56	1.29	1.42
Combined	1.07	1.65	
6—Criticism			
Gifted	1.86	.77	1.32
Nongifted	.86	.68	.77
Combined	1.36	.73	

The analysis of variance for Category 1 (total attention) shows a significant difference in *quantity* of attention, with white students receiving far more attention from teachers than black students. This interpretation should be qualified in light of a Race $\times$ Label interaction and subsequent comparison of gifted and nongifted black and white means (see Table 1 and Figure 1). Such a consideration would suggest that the significant main effect in this case is almost entirely attributable to the great amount of attention given the gifted whites. . . . It can be seen that treatment of black students and white students

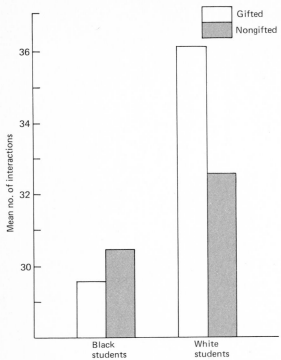

Figure 1 Teacher interaction with gifted and nongifted black and white students (Category 1: Total attention).

differed most on the dimensions of ignoring, praise, attention to requested statements, and criticism. Across all teachers and also across labels, a pattern can be seen in the way teachers treated black students and white students. The directions of this pattern can be seen from the means in Table 1. Fewer statements were requested of blacks than of whites. More statements of blacks than of whites were ignored. Possibly most interesting of all, black students were praised less and criticized more.

Three dependent variables contributed little to the difference in treatment of black and white students. For one of these (Category 1a), it had been expected that little effect would be found. This category measures the amount of student initiated interaction. Since little effect for this category was found this would allow for the inference that there was no difference in the spontaneity of the students. . . . Thus it can be assumed that black students and white students were not treated differently by teachers because of differences in their verbosity.

Student Variables: Label of Student

Two students taught by each teacher, one black and one white, had been randomly given the label "gifted," and two, one black and one white, the label "nongifted." Table 1 presents the mean number of teacher responses in each category to gifted and nongifted students. . . .

There was no significant difference in total amount of attention to gifted and nongifted students. No differences had been expected for this category, as it was hypothesized that the *amount* of interaction between the teacher and the students would be fairly similar regardless of the student's label and that the crucial variable would be the *quality* of the interaction.

. . . However, there were differences in teacher interaction with gifted and nongifted students. . . . Two variables accounted for almost all of the difference in treatment of gifted and nongifted students. These two variables are Categories 1b (attention to requested statements) and 6 (criticism). From the means in Table 1, it can be seen that the significance occurs because more statements were requested of gifted than of nongifted students and also that gifted students were criticized more than nongifted students.

Once again, Category 1a contributed little to the total difference. . . . This allows for the inference that gifted students were not called upon more often simply because they volunteered less.

Student Variables: Interaction of Race × Label

A prime consideration of this study was any difference in the effect of label depending on the race of the student. . . . Gifted white students received more attention than nongifted white students with a reverse tendency occurring in the case of black students.

A significant . . . interaction of Race × Label was found. This difference was mostly attributable to Category 5 (praise) with Category 1b (attention to requested statements) also contributing toward the difference. In addition, Categories 1a (attention to unsolicited statements), 2 (encouragement), 4 (ignoring), and 6 (criticism) all contributed to the differences in treatment of differently labeled students of different races. . . . Category 6 (criticism) contributed little to the overall interaction effect. . . .

The direction of these interactions can be ascertained from Table 1. In the case of Categories 1, 1b, and 5, the interactions are also portrayed in Figures 1, 2, and 3. Considering these interactions collectively, a pattern begins to emerge in which the expectation of giftedness is associated with a generally positive response of teachers—*if* the student is white. For black students, if anything, a reverse tendency is evident in which the expectation of giftedness is associated with *less* positive treatment.

Teacher Variables: Level of Dogmatism

It had been hypothesized that level of dogmatism might affect susceptibility to racial and labeling effects (see Table 2). Regardless of interaction with either student variable, level of dogmatism itself was found to affect overall teacher behavior. There were . . . no quantitative differences in the attention given students by teachers high and low in dogmatism. . . . However, teachers higher in dogmatism ignored many more statements than teachers lower in dogmatism. Some of the overall difference can also be attributed to Category 6 (criticism) with teachers higher in dogmatism criticizing more statements than teachers lower in dogmatism.

Interaction of Teacher and Student Variables: Dogmatism × Race

Of particular interest in this study was whether or not teachers with different levels of dogmatism would respond differently to black students and

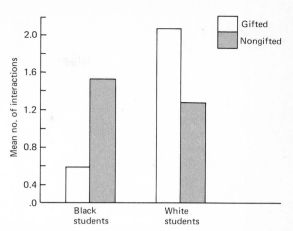

Figure 3 Teacher interaction with gifted and nongifted black and white students (Category 5: Praise).

white students. No significant interaction was found for Category 1 (total attention). . . . However . . . from Figure 4 it can be seen that dogmatism is associated with the encouraging of white rather than black students. Complementing the result is the finding that dogmatism was also associated with a tendency to ignore the statements of black students (see Figure 5). . . .

Credibility of Experimental Situation

A postexperiment questionnaire and an interview were given in order to check whether or not teachers accepted the experimental situation. No teacher expressed any suspicion of the experimental hypotheses. The teachers also showed great agreement with the assigned labels. One hundred and

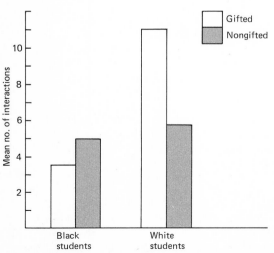

Figure 2 Teacher interaction with gifted and nongifted black and white students (Category 1*b*: Attention to requested statements).

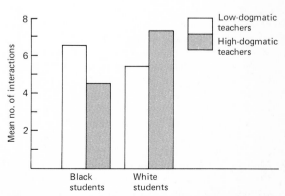

Figure 4 Interaction patterns of high- and low-dogmatic teachers (Category 2: Encourage).

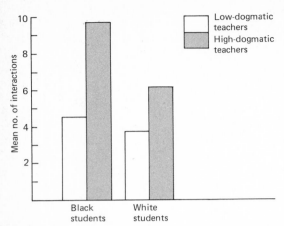

Figure 5 Interaction patterns of high- and low-dogmatic teachers (Category 4: Ignore).

thirty-two students had been labeled gifted and 132 nongifted. Only in the case of 14 gifted students and 13 of the nongifted students did teachers express any reservations about accepting these labels as true indicants of the students' ability levels. These reports of the teachers, as well as clinical observations during the postexperimental interviews, suggest that the teachers not only accepted the situation as presented to them, but they also viewed each student in terms of the label assigned him.

DISCUSSION

As in a previous study (Rubovits & Maehr, 1971), teachers were found to treat students labeled gifted different from students described as average. There was no difference in the *amount* of attention given to the supposedly different-ability groups, but there were differences in the *quality* of attention. Gifted students were called on more, thus replicating a previous finding (Rubovits & Maehr, 1971). Gifted students were also criticized more, but this difference may have been caused by the inclusion of black students in the gifted group as they were the recipients of almost all the criticism.

Considering the differences due to label for whites only, it can be seen that the gifted white student was given more attention than his nongifted counterpart, called on more, praised more, and also criticized a bit more. It is interesting, incidentally, that in the informal interviews with teachers the gifted white student was also chosen most frequently as the most liked student, the brightest student, and the certain leader of the class.

Of special interest, of course, are the comparisons of teacher interaction with black students and white students. In this regard, the present study provides what appears to be a disturbing instance of white racism. Black students were given less attention, ignored more, praised less and criticized more. More startling perhaps are the Race × Label interactions that suggest that it is the gifted black who is given the least attention, is the least praised, and the most criticized, even when comparing him to his nongifted black counterpart.

It is important to stress that these results are not easily attributable to an experimental artifact of some kind. There is no reason to suppose that the expectancy communication varied for race. Moreover, it cannot be argued that teachers were responding to any actual intellectual differences between black students and white students or to any incongruity between label and actual potential. Recall that students were specifically selected so as to be of equivalent intellectual ability regardless of race.

An obvious question, of course, is whether the expectancy resided in the observer or in the teacher. It is impossible to rule out observer expectancy effects completely. While the observer could not know which students were labeled gifted or average, it is obvious that she would know black from white. However, it is difficult to see how such knowledge might have determined the pattern of results that were obtained. First, the observational instrument is reasonably objective in nature, allowing for minimal judgment on the part of the observer (Rubovits, 1970). Second, the present authors in fact had no clear and obvious basis for postulating the results that did indeed occur. For example, it would have been equally logical to argue before the fact that young, idealistic teachers, most of whom expressed liberal beliefs, would make a special attempt to ingratiate themselves to blacks. Finally, the fact that high-dogmatic teachers were more inclined toward a prejudicial pattern than low-dogmatic teachers further suggests that the reported interactions were not just a figment of the observer's expectancy. If the observer were, in fact, the responsible agent, it would be difficult to see how, not knowing the dogmatism scores, she could have effected a generally predictable pattern

Table 2   Mean Interaction with Gifted and Nongifted Black and White Students ✕
Teachers High and Low in Dogmatism

Category	Black	White	Combined	Gifted	Nongifted
1—Total attention					
High dogmatism	29.94	35.68	32.81	34.54	31.08
Low dogmatism	29.97	32.73	31.35	31.12	31.58
1a—Attention to unsolicited					
statements					
High dogmatism	26.06	26.67	26.36	27.27	25.45
Low dogmatism	26.64	26.15	26.39	25.91	26.88
1b—Attention to requested					
statements					
High dogmatism	5.47	8.82	7.14	8.85	5.44
Low dogmatism	3.18	7.48	5.33	6.56	4.11
2—Encouragement					
High dogmatism	4.44	7.17	5.80	5.88	5.73
Low dogmatism	6.35	5.33	5.84	5.77	5.91
3—Elaboration					
High dogmatism	2.50	2.53	2.52	2.53	2.50
Low dogmatism	2.03	1.70	1.86	1.64	2.09
4—Ignoring					
High dogmatism	9.39	6.14	7.76	8.29	7.24
Low dogmatism	4.39	3.52	3.95	3.73	4.18
5—Praise					
High dogmatism	1.06	1.48	1.27	1.20	1.35
Low dogmatism	1.08	1.82	1.45	1.39	1.50
6—Criticism					
High dogmatism	1.86	1.02	1.44	1.76	1.12
Low dogmatism	.86	.44	.65	.88	.42

for high and low dogmatists as well as the overall pattern. A bias leading toward differential observation of teacher–student interaction in the case of blacks and whites would presumably operate across all teachers regardless of dogmatism, thereby making it virtually impossible to obtain any meaningful Dogmatism × Race interaction. In brief, the most logical explanation of the results is that the teachers were indeed exhibiting the negative pattern toward blacks that the reported interactions indicate.

It is important to emphasize that this prejudicial pattern was not exhibited by all teachers. Teachers higher in dogmatism seemed to differentiate more in their treatment of blacks and whites. Moreover, one may wonder about the degree to which the patterns observed are unique to young, inexperienced teachers. After all, these teachers not only had little teaching experience but, as the questionnaire data would indicate, little experience of any

kind with blacks. One might at least hope that the appropriate experience could be of benefit.

All in all, then, this study clearly suggests how teacher expectations may affect teacher behavior. Although the results must be interpreted within the limits of the study, with cautious generalization, the data do suggest answers to the question of why teachers are often able to do little to equalize the performance levels of blacks and whites.

REFERENCES

Becker, H. S. Social class variations in the teacher-pupil relationship. *Journal of Educational Sociology*, 1952, *25*, 451–465.

Brown, B. The assessment of self-concept among four-year-old Negro and white children. (Cited by H. Proshansky & P. Newton: The nature and meaning of Negro self-identity) In M. Deutsch, I. Katz, & A. R. Jensen (Eds.), *Social class, race and psychological development.* New York: Holt, Rinehart & Winston, 1968.

Claiborne, W. L. Expectancy effects in the classroom: A failure to replicate. *Journal of Educational Psychology,* 1969, *60,* 377–383.

Davidson, H. H., & Lang, G. Children's perception of teachers' feelings toward them. *Journal of Experimental Education,* 1960, *29,* 107–118.

Deutsch, M. The disadvantaged child and the learning process. In A. H. Passow (Ed.), *Education in depressed areas.* New York: Bureau of Publications, Teachers College, Columbia University, 1963.

Elashoff, J. D., & Snow, R. E. *A case study in statistical inference: Reconsideration of the Rosenthal-Jacobson data on teacher expectancy.* (Tech. Rep. No. 15) Stanford, Calif.: Stanford Center for Research and Development in Teaching, Stanford University, 1970.

Meichenbaum, D. H., Bowers, K. S., & Ross, R. R. A behavioral analysis of teacher expectancy effect. *Journal of Personality and Social Psychology,* 1969, *13,* 306–316.

Rokeach, M. *The open and closed mind.* New York: Basic Books, 1960.

Rosenthal, R. *Experimenter effects in behavioral research.* New York: Appleton-Century-Crofts, 1966.

———. Empirical vs. decreed validation of clocks and tests. *American Educational Research Journal,* 1969, *6,* 689–691.

Rosenthal, R., & Fode, K. L. The effect of experimenter bias on the performance of albino rats. *Behavioral Science,* 1963, *8,* 183–189.

Rosenthal, R., & Jacobson, L. *Pygmalion in the classroom: Teacher expectation and pupils' intellectual development.* New York: Holt, Rinehart & Winston, 1968.

Rosenthal, R., & Lawson, R. A longitudinal study of the effects of experimenter bias on the operant learning of laboratory rats. *Journal of Psychiatric Research,* 1964, *2,* 61–72.

Rubovits, P. C. Teacher interaction with students labeled gifted and nongifted in a microteaching situation. Unpublished master's thesis, University of Illinois, 1970.

Rubovits, R. C., & Maehr, M. L. Pygmalion analyzed: Toward an explanation of the Rosenthal-Jacobson findings. *Journal of Personality and Social Psychology,* 1971, *19,* 197–203.

Snow, R. E. Unfinished pygmalion. *Contemporary Psychology,* 1969, *14,* 197–199.

Tatsuoka, M. *Multivariate analysis.* New York: Wiley, 1971.

Thorndike, R. L. Review of *Pygmalion in the classroom. American Educational Research Journal,* 1968, *5,* 708–711.

———. But do you have to know how to tell time? *American Educational Research Journal,* 1969, *6,* 692.

Warner, W. L., Havighurst, R. J., & Loeb, M. B. *Who shall be educated?* New York: Harper & Row, 1944.

Wilson, A. B. Social stratification and academic achievement. In A. H. Passow (Ed.), *Education in depressed areas.* New York: Teachers College, Columbia University, 1963.

Reading 42

Male Teachers of Young Children: A Preliminary Empirical Study

Patrick C. Lee
Annie Lucas Wolinsky

In recent years there has been an increasing interest in the potential contribution which male teachers might make to the education of young children. Since 1968 at least 20 articles have appeared in the literature and several caucuses and symposia have been held at national educational conferences calling for more extensive introduction of male teachers into early childhood settings. For the most part, these commentators have been concerned with the welfare of young boys who are growing up both at home and in school, in a world which is female dominated and which fosters values and standards of behavior that are traditionally more closely associated with the female than the male sex role. There is also a secondary concern with the long range effects a relatively male-absent environment may have on the full development of young girls. As Kendall (1972) has noted, young children "are caught in a feminine world . . . one-parent homes . . . father who is frequently absent . . . primary school teachers . . . Day Care Centers . . . baby sitters" (p. 360).

Sentiments such as these have begun to strike a responsive chord in many early childhood educators for two basic reasons. First, we have become increasingly aware of a sex-role imbalance in schools for young children and of the detrimental effect this may have on the education of young boys and girls. Second, there is a growing concern with the high incidence of father absence and low father availability in the lives of young children and with the school's apparent inability to supply substitute masculine role models. It would be a mistake, of course, to expect male teachers to provide total solutions to problems which we have only begun to comprehend. It is entirely reasonable, however, to expect that competent male teachers, by their simple presence, would add an element of masculinity to the experience of young children.

THE CLASSROOM AS A SEX-TYPED ENVIRONMENT

It is no secret that the overwhelming majority of teachers at the preschool and early elementary levels are women. The NEA Research Division (1971, 1972) estimated that less than 2 percent of teachers at third grade and below during 1971-1972 were men. This means that the typical child is introduced to school by a woman, has his first experience with "official" learning mediated by a woman, and undergoes three or four years of socialization to formal schooling before he has even the slightest chance of being taught by a man.

This overrepresentation of female teachers may have differential effects on the ability of boys and girls to respond positively to their early years of schooling. In one recent study, for example, Portuges and Feshbach (1972) found that, in a role-playing situation, third and fourth grade girls imitated female teachers significantly more than boys did. Madsen (1968) checked the other side of the coin and found that nursery school boys imitated male assistant teachers significantly more than girls did. Apparently young children are inclined to imitate behaviors of same-sex teachers only, thereby placing sex-role obstacles between most teachers and their male pupils.

Two other studies by Kagan (1964) and Kellogg (1969) explored how second, third and fourth graders sex-typed school related objects. Their female subjects were much more inclined to view the objects as feminine rather than masculine, while boys had a slight tendency to see the objects as feminine. When these results are considered along with the findings of the teacher modeling studies, one might safely conclude that young girls see schools as being congruent with their sex role and that boys are in considerable conflict about this.

If, indeed, boys do see strong incongruities between their emerging sex-role identity and the sex-typed attributes of schools and teachers, then we should expect to find greater evidence of conflict between boys and schools than between girls and schools. An overview of the research literature clearly indicates that boys receive a disproportionate share of low school marks, grade retention, referral to extra-classroom specialists and informal teacher disapproval. Reviews by Arnold (1968) and Oetzel (1066), along with a more recent study by McCandless, Roberts and Starnes (1972), indicate that boys consistently receive lower grades than girls, even when they are equal on I.Q. and achievement test scores. These studies have been done on the later elementary grades, so we do not have any direct evidence of grade bias at the early childhood levels, where school marks are not always used anyway.

There is, however, some direct evidence that young boys are forced to repeat grades more frequently than young girls. In 1958 there was a nationwide survey of 504 schools on the promotion rates of boys and girls from first to second grade. Of the 402 responding schools, 73.2 percent reported higher rates for girls, while 23.6 percent reported no difference and only 3.2 percent had higher promotion rates for boys (AASA, 1958).

As regards referrals for school related problems, Bentzen (1966) found that young boys were referred much more frequently than young girls. In a large-scale study of learning problems among elementary school children, she noted that the highest number of referrals was in the *first* grade: of 147 referrals, 110 were boys and 37 were girls, a ratio of 3:1. For every girl referred for reading problems, there were two boys. Of 36 first graders referred solely for "social and emotional immaturity," 33 were boys, and three were girls, a ratio of 11:1. Bentzen commented that boys are at a distinct disadvantage when competing with girls because, while they are developmentally less mature, they are expected to meet the same standards of performance.

Aside from the official actions of grading, promoting and referring, life in the classroom involves a great deal of "off the record" disapproval on the part of teachers, and most of this seems to be directed at boys. In two studies done on older elementary school children, Meyer & Thompson (1956) and Davidson & Lang (1960) found that teachers, 12 women and one man, disapproved of boys more frequently than girls, gave girls higher behavior ratings and tended to view girls as higher academic achievers. Moreover, the children perceived boys as receiving more disapproval than girls, and saw teachers as feeling more favorable toward girls than toward boys. In a study done on first graders, McNeil (1964) found that teachers assessed boys more negatively than girls on readiness and motivation for reading, and that the children perceived boys as receiving more negative comments than girls and as having less opportunity to read.

As might be expected (c.f. Minuchin, 1966), boys are inclined to respond to all this with negative feelings and counter-aggression. Jackson (1968, pp. 47–57), for example, in his review of children's feelings about school, found that boys were consistently more negative than girls in their response to schooling. And Lippitt and Gold (1959) found that elementary school girls made friendly approaches to teachers about twice as often as boys did, while boys made almost three times as many unfriendly approaches as girls did.

Clearly then, something has gone wrong between young boys and their schools. From the earliest elementary grades, boys are left back more frequently than girls, are referred more often and receive more than their fair share of disapproval. Moreover, the children themselves, both boys and girls, are aware that school is a more punishing experience for boys, and the research indicates that their awareness corresponds to reality. None of this is to say that school is a totally benign experience for young girls. There is good reason to suspect that it is not. We are only trying to say that, in terms of measurable outcomes, and during the early years in school, boys manifestly have more problems than girls.

It would be presumptuous, of course, to conclude that male teachers would automatically eliminate these inequities. Some impressionistic reports seem to indicate that male teachers alter the tone of classroom life in more "masculine" directions, but we have no hard evidence that they change the

pattern of official and unofficial disapproval of boys' behavior, or that they encourage children to view school as a more masculine experience (see Johnston, 1970; Kendall, 1972; Murgatroyd, 1955). What seems clear at this point is that female teachers are relatively unsuccessful in socializing young boys to "acceptable" standards of classroom behavior and, perhaps, too efficient in socializing young girls to these standards, and that male teachers *might* provide classroom conditions more congenial to young boys and more liberating for young girls.

FATHER ABSENCE AND LOW FATHER AVAILABILITY

As mentioned earlier, a second concern of early childhood specialists is with the increasingly pervasive phenomenon of father absence and low father availability. Herzog & Sudia (1972) estimated that over 7 million American children and adolescents now live in "one-parent" families, and that these include middle-class as well as impoverished homes. We should also recognize that there are two dynamic factors in contemporary American society which promise to make fathers even less available to greater numbers of children. The first is the incidence of divorce: between 1962 and 1971 the divorce rate increased by 68 percent, so that, during 1971, there was one divorce for every three marriages (1973 *World Almanac*, pp. 951–952). The second is the continuing migration to suburban residency, where low father availability has become almost normative. By 1970, more than half the population of metropolitan areas lived in suburban areas and the projection is that by the 1980s almost half the *total* population of the United States will be located in suburbs (*New York Times Almanac,* 1972, p. 482). Clearly, then, unacceptably large numbers of American children are experiencing permanent, temporary or intermittent separation from their fathers and, since there are also so few male teachers at the early grades, may be growing up in a world which is largely devoid of stable adult male influence.

In their recent review, Hetherington & Deur (1971) concluded that the effects of father absence are most disruptive when its onset takes place before five years of age, and that these effects are particularly detrimental for boys. They summarized that father-absent preschool boys were less assertive and aggressive, more dependent, less masculine in their game preferences and more like their female than their male peers in play patterns. Other studies have shown that early separation from their fathers interferes with young boys' intellectual performance, as well as inducing emotional problems. Blanchard & Biller (1971), for example, found that early father-absent boys and boys with relatively unavailable fathers received lower grades in school and scored significantly lower on the Stanford Achievement Test than did late father-absent boys and boys with highly available fathers. Hetherington (1972) has done the only first-rate study on the relationship between father absence and girls' development. She found that father-absent girls were more anxious than father-present girls, had a lessened sense of control over their lives, and were either very timid with, or inordinately open to, males during early and middle adolescence. Landy, Rosenberg and Sutton-Smith (1969) discovered a relationship between low father availability and low scores on girls' quantitative achievement tests, indicating that father availability is related to female as well as male intellectual development.

There is some evidence, however, that the presence of "father substitutes" can ameliorate some of the consequences of father absence and low father availability for both boys and girls. Santrock (1970) and Wohlford, et al. (1971) found that father-absent boys with a father substitute were less dependent than those who had none, and that boys and *girls* who had older brothers were less dependent and more aggressive than those who had only older sisters. A number of educators and psychologists have suggested that male teachers at the early childhood and early elementary levels might readily assume the role of substitute fathers (see Hetherington & Deur, 1971; Biller, 1970; Burtt, 1965), and Cortes & Fleming (1968) found that father-absent fourth grade boys expressed significantly greater preference for male teachers than father-present boys did. This small piece of evidence begins to make such suggestions sound like good common sense. Given that there is a great deal of separation between young children and their fathers in our society, and that such separation early in life has serious consequences for personal and intellectual growth, and that "substitute fathers" can counteract some of these consequences, then there is good reason to expect that stable, competent and reliable male teachers could make a vital contribution to the lives of young boys and restore some balance to the lives of young girls.

RESEARCH ON MALE TEACHERS IN THE EARLY GRADES

There has not been much research done on the differential effects of male and female teachers in the early grades and what little has been done has not been of outstanding quality. McFarland (1969), for example, assigned first grade children to one of two classes: the first combined a supervising female teacher with 26 male college juniors who were sequentially scheduled over the school year; and the second had a female supervisor and a female teacher. He found that the female teacher group performed significantly better on arithmetic than the male teacher group, and that both groups made approximately the same gains on tests of reading, personality and sex role identification. The flaw in this study was that the only constant and experienced adult in the "male teacher" group was the female supervising teacher. The "male teachers" were part-time transient, inexperienced apprentices who probably played a secondary role in their own "male teacher" group.

In another study, Kyselka (1966) placed four male high school seniors in a nursery school classroom for 45 minutes per day for 15 weeks. As might be expected, these adolescents reported that they were primarily concerned about discipline, respect and their own adequacy and confused as to their role in the classroom. If anything, Kyselka's sample of "male teachers" was even less equipped than McFarland's sample to handle a job which they barely understood. These college juniors and high school seniors were not representative of the kind of competent, professional male teachers one would hope to find in our classrooms.

Triplett (1968) reported a study on kindergarteners and first graders who were assigned to either all-male sections taught by male teachers or coeducational sections taught by female teachers. He found that while boys in both groups had the same school achievement, boys in the all male group scored higher on tests of self-esteem and attitudes toward teachers and school. The problem with this study is that the sex of the teachers was confounded with sex-grouping procedures. One does not know if the male teacher or the male peers, or the combination of both, enhanced the attitudinal growth of the boys in the all-male group.

Unfortunately, all three studies suffer from serious methodological flaws and shed very little light on the differences between male and female teachers. Moreover, the focus in two of the three studies was on outcome rather than process. At this early stage of research on male teachers of young children, it probably makes better strategic sense to focus on their behavioral processes to see if they actually *do* anything different from female teachers. If, indeed, the behaviors of male and female teachers differ, then we can begin to identify and investigate selected outcomes which bear a logical relationship to what the teachers are actually doing.

In the following section we shall describe an observational and interview study conducted by the present authors. While this study is not free of defects, we think it is a good first attempt to identify some process differences between male and female teachers of young children.

A PRELIMINARY EMPIRICAL STUDY

In the present study we attempted to discover whether male teachers differed from female teachers in several respects. The following questions were raised:

1   Do male and female teachers distribute sanctions differently? That is, are there observable differences in the amount and direction of approvals and disapprovals or rewards and punishments distributed by male and female teachers to young boys and girls?

2   Do male and female teachers differ in their assignment of leadership positions, both explicit and implicit, to boys and girls?

3   Do male and female teachers differ in their grouping procedures? That is, do they differ in taking the initiative in forming groups, and does the sex composition of their groups differ?

4   Do male and female teachers differ in the kinds of activities they initiate or respond to in the classroom? Is there a greater tendency for male teachers to encourage "male" sex-linked activities, and for female teachers to encourage "female" sex-linked activities?

5   Do boys and girls have different attitudes toward teachers and themselves as a function of having male or female teachers?

Subjects

As might be expected, we had some difficulty in finding a sample of male head teachers of young children. For this reason, we were not able to use random sampling procedures, but used the head teachers we could find and added some male assistant teachers as well. We conducted our observations in 18 classrooms, of which six had two female teachers, six had a male and female teacher and six were taught by three teams, each consisting of a male and a female head teacher. The 18 classes ranged from preschool through second grade. Male and female teachers were matched according to grade taught and status as either head or assistant teacher. For the interview section of the study, we randomly selected three boys and three girls from each of the 12 classrooms which had both a male and a female teacher, for a total sample of 72 children.

Procedures

Each teacher and assistant teacher in the sample was observed for a total of two hours using an event sampling technique. The events observed corresponded to the first four questions stated above. The observations were recorded and yielded an overall interobserver reliability of 82.8 percent.

Each child in the sample was individually interviewed for approximately five minutes by a female graduate student. The interview consisted of 12 questions which were designed to gather information about the children's attitudes toward their teachers and their own status in the classroom setting (i.e., question number 5 above).

Findings

Teacher Sanctions: We observed and recorded every act of sanction or evaluation made by our sample of teachers. By this we meant any reward or punishment, any approval or disapproval a teacher communicated to a child, verbally and nonverbally, for his task performance or classroom behavior. In the following paragraphs we shall use the terms "approval" and "disapproval" to refer to positive and negative sanctions, respectively.

We found that female teachers gave almost twice as many sanctions as male teachers, that is, female teachers seemed to be generally more evaluative in their approach to children than male teachers were.

However, the ratio of approval to disapproval was approximately the same for male and female teachers.

Boys received about twice as many sanctions as girls, that is, boys were subject to more evaluation than girls were (z = 3.74, p = .01). There was a marginally significant relationship between sex of child and type of sanction (X^2 = 3.08, df = 1, p < .10). While boys received slightly more approval than girls, they received about two and a half times as much disapproval. Looked at in another way, girls' behavior was approved more often than disapproved, while the reverse held for boys.

When we looked at the relationship between sex of teacher and sex of child, we found a significant interaction on total sanctions (X^2 = 8.34, df = 1, p < .01). The male teachers were four times more evaluative toward boys than toward girls, while the female teachers were slightly more evaluative toward boys. Closer examination of *type* of sanction yielded some interesting results. Male and female teachers were equally disapproving of boys (X^2 = 2.46, df = 1, non-significant) but male teachers were very approving toward boys, while female teachers were slightly more approving toward girls (X^2 = 6.79, df = 1, p < .02). Female teachers, moreover, were inclined to be more disapproving toward boys than girls, while the opposite held for approvals (X^2 = 3.72, df = 1, p < .10).

Only 20 percent of the female teachers' sanctions included physical contact and it was equally distributed between boys and girls. On the other hand, male teachers used physical contact 30 percent of the time, and it was *all* directed at boys. It would seem that, in addition to being relatively non-evaluative with girls, male teachers were physically reserved with them.

In summary, our data indicate that female teachers were more evaluative than male teachers, that boys were evaluated more than girls and disapproved more than girls, and that female teachers were biased against boys in their evaluations. Male teachers, however, were unbiased in their evaluation of boys, and rather non-evaluative toward girls.

Assignment of Leadership Positions: For the most part, the teachers in our sample made explicit leadership assignments when they felt a group or an activity required a leader. Occasionally, however, they *implicitly* assigned leadership to a child by relating to him as though he were "spokesman" for a given group or activity. These latter assignments, while few in number, were added to the leadership data.

The female teachers made about 50 percent more leadership assignments than the male teachers, indicating a greater involvement in the selection of leaders. There was also a significant tendency for teachers to assign leadership positions to pupils who were members of their own sex (X^2 = 6.86, df = 1, p < .02). The male teachers designated boys as leaders about four times as often as girls, while the female teachers assigned leadership to girls about twice as often as to boys. It would seem from these data that male teachers provide boys with much more leadership experience than female teachers do and that, if anything, their bias against girls in this respect is even stronger than the female teachers' bias against boys.

Grouping Procedures: We observed three aspects of grouping practice: amount of grouping, teacher initiative in grouping and sex composition of pupil groups. Male and female teachers were equally inclined to relate to children in groups, but the male teachers almost always responded to groups which the children spontaneously formed, while they initiated groups very seldom, at a ratio of about 5:1. Female teachers, on the other hand, initiated groups about as often as they responded to them. The female teachers initiated groups about three times as often as male teachers did, while the male teachers were about twice as responsive to groups as female teachers were (X^2 = 24.29, df = 1, p < .001). Moreover, male teachers were much more inclined than female teachers to relate to single sex groups (X^2 = 5.58, df = 1, p < .05). These results could be a function of one or both of these practices: either male teachers approach single-sex groups more than female teachers do, or there is a tendency for male teachers to encourage, intentionally or otherwise, single-sex grouping in their classrooms. In either case, there appears to be an interaction between sex of teachers and sex composition of groups of children.

Sex Type of Classroom Activities: We recorded all classroom activities either initiated or responded to by our sample of teachers. We then typed brief descriptions of each activity on master sheets and had six graduate students (three men and three women) independently judge each activity as being either male, female or neuter. The six judges had no knowledge of which activities went with which teachers, nor did they have any knowledge of any of the teachers in our sample, nor had they ever been in any of the teachers' classrooms. We then combined the six judgments of each activity in order to get an overall "sex-role score" for each activity. Approximately one-third of the activities received mixed scores, thereby having no consensual sex linkage. Over one-third of the activities were consensually scored as "neuter," and somewhat less than one-third of the activities were consensually scored as either male or female.

We found, as with grouping practices, that male and female teachers related to approximately the same total number of activities, but that male teachers were inclined to respond to ongoing activities, while female teachers had a greater tendency to initiate activities ($X^2 = 20.50$, df $= 1$, p $< .002$). In estimating the "sex-role profile" of activities to which teachers related, we excluded those activities which received "mixed" scores. Since both male and female teachers had approximately the same number of mixed activities, this did not influence the sex-role activity profiles. Of those activities which were consensually scored by the judges, male teachers had 42 percent male-typed activities, 11 percent female-typed activities and 47 percent neuter-typed activities. Female teachers had 17 percent male-typed activities, 14 percent female-typed activities and 69 percent neuter-typed activities. These results indicated a marked relationship between sex of teacher and sex type of activities ($X^2 = 15.32$, df $= 2$, p $< .002$).

Male teachers related to male-typed activities, female teachers to neuter-typed activities, and there was a startling tendency for teachers, irrespective of sex, to become involved in very few female-typed activities. This last finding is particularly puzzling. It may be that there is a relatively narrow range of classroom activities which are clearly female typed. This does not correspond with the research of Kagan (1964) and Kellogg (1969) discussed earlier. Another possible explanation is that female teachers, since they were low on male- as well as female-typed activities, may have a strong preference for "sex-neutral" activities. In either case there appears to be an interaction between sex of teacher and sex-role profile of classroom activities.

Attitudes of Pupils: As mentioned above, we selected a random sample of 72 children, half boys and half girls, for brief individual interviews of about five minutes duration. We asked the children 12 questions, some of which were designed to establish rapport, and others designed to tap their attitudes about their teachers and their own status in the classroom.

Two of the questions attempted to discover which teacher had more salience, whether the children liked their teachers and whether there were sex-linked preferences. Female teachers appeared to have more salience for the children (z $= 1.97$, p $= .05$) but, when asked which teacher they *preferred*, boys made a significant shift toward the male teacher at a ratio of 2:1 ($X^2 = 5.40$, df $= 1$, p $< .05$), while girls expressed about equal preference for male and female teachers ($X^2 = 1.27$, df $= 1$, non-significant).

Four questions were designed to discover whether the children thought their teachers liked them and, again, whether there were sex-linked preferences. The vast majority of the subjects (85 percent) thought their teachers liked them and, with a modest drop-off, continued to feel this way even when asked to compare themselves with their favorite peer of the opposite sex. Moreover, there was a distinct tendency for both boys and girls to think their male teachers liked them better than their female teachers did (z $= 2.36$, p $= .02$), indicating an interaction between sex of teacher and pupil perception of positive feelings. The children's perceptions may have been a function of our earlier finding that the female teachers were generally more evaluative than the male teachers.

Finally, the subjects were asked two questions about whether they thought their teachers preferred boys or girls. In the abstract, children of both sexes saw the female teachers as preferring girls (z $= 2.09$, p $= .04$) and the male teachers as having no preference. However, when they were asked to name their teachers' favorite child, that is, when asked to think in concrete terms, a very different pattern emerged. The boys significantly reversed themselves and saw their male teachers as strongly preferring boys ($X^2 = 4.00$, df $= 1$, p $< .05$), while attributing neutrality to their female teachers. The girls also shifted significantly by maintaining that both male and female teachers preferred girls ($X^2 = 8.86$, df $= 1$, p $< .02$).

In summary, the interviews yielded these general conclusions: the children generally liked their teachers and saw the teachers as liking them; there was a tendency for boys to affiliate themselves with male teachers; and girls saw themselves as being preferred to boys by all teachers, while boys saw themselves as preferred only by male teachers.

Summary of Findings

The basic questions raised by this study were whether the male teacher does anything in the classroom different from female teachers, and whether these differences could reasonably be viewed as broadening the sex-role experiences of young children. We think our results would allow tentative affirmative responses to both questions.

While the present study confirmed previous findings that boys receive more disapproval than girls, and extended previous findings by indicating that both male and female teachers are more disapproving of boys than of girls, it also found that male teachers are generally more approving of boys than female teachers are. There was also a strong tendency for teachers to favor children of the same sex in leadership assignments and for male teachers to relate to male-typed activities, while female teachers focused on neutral activities. The boys' perceptions corresponded with these findings in that they strongly perceived themselves as affiliated with the male teacher; the girls' perceptions, however, cut across sex-role lines, in that they expressed more or less equal affiliation with male and female teachers.

The male teachers were different from the female teachers in several respects. Our male teacher sample seemed to be more reticent than our female teacher sample, in that they initiated fewer activities and groups and had less salience for the children. This may have been a result of our particular sampling procedure and it would be no surprise if other samples of male teachers did not share this characteristic. In spite of this reticence, however, the male teachers appeared to have a masculinizing influence on classroom activities, to be more balanced in their evaluations of boys, more inclined to give boys leadership positions and to set up affectional ties with boys and girls which were often different from those established by the female teachers.

One can tentatively conclude that the male teachers influenced classroom conditions such that they were more congenial to young boys. Moreover, with the exception of reduced leadership positions, this was not done at serious cost to the welfare of young girls. It should be kept in mind, however, that all-male teacher classrooms also had a female teacher and the conclusions of this study are clearly restricted to such situations. We do not have any feelings on classrooms with *only* male teachers and it may be that such classrooms would look rather different from the ones we studied. In the meantime, however, the male teachers bias against girls on leadership assignments was counterbalanced by the female teachers bias toward girls. It may be that the combination of male and female teachers is the optimal arrangement.

Concluding Remarks

There is one obvious reason for interpreting the results of the present study with caution: our male teacher sample was selected on a pragmatic basis, i.e., we used the ones we could find. For this reason, the sample may not be representative of the population of male teachers of young children. Nevertheless, we think our investigation has identified some tentative differences in the classroom behaviors of male and female teachers of young children, and has suggested fruitful directions for future research and inquiry. It is a first step toward identifying ways in which the male teacher may contribute to greater sex-role balance in the lives of young children.

REFERENCES

American Association of School Administrators and Research Division of NEA. Pupil promotion policies and rates of promotion. *Educational Research Service Circular*, 1958, No. 5, Washington, D.C.

Arnold, R. D. The achievement of boys and girls taught by men and women teachers. *Elementary School Journal*, 1968, 68, 367–372.

Bentzen, F. Sex ratios in learning and behavior disorders. *National Elementary Principal*, 1966, 46 (2), 13–17.

Biller, H. B. Father absence and the personality development of the male child. *Developmental Psychology*, 1970, 2, 181–201.

Blanchard, R. W., & Biller, H. B. Father availability and academic performance among third-grade boys. *Developmental Psychology*, 1971, 4, 301–305.

Burtt, M. The effect of a man teacher. *Young Children*, 1965, 21, 93–97.

Cortes, C. F., & Fleming, E. S. The effects of father absence on the adjustment of culturally disadvantaged boys. *Journal of Special Education*, 1968, 2, 413–420.

Davidson, H. H., & Lang, G. Children's perceptions of their teachers' feelings toward them related to self-perception, school achievement and behavior. *Journal of Experimental Education*, 1960, 29, 107–118.

Herzog, E., & Sudia, C. E. Families without fathers. *Childhood Education*, 1972, 48, 175–181.

Hetherington, E. M. Effects of father absence on personality development in adolescent daughters. *Developmental Psychology*, 1972, 7, 313–326.

Hetherington, E. M., & Deur, J. L. The effects of father absence on child development. *Young Children*, 1971, 26, 233–248.

Jackson, P. W. *Life in classrooms*. New York: Holt, Rinehart, & Winston, Inc., 1968.

Johnston, J. M. A symposium: Men in young children's lives, part 2. *Childhood Education*, 1970, 47, 144–147.

Kagan, J. The child's sex role classification of school objects. *Child Development*, 1964, 35, 1051–1056.

Kellogg, R. L. A direct approach to sex role identification of school-related objects. *Psychological Reports*, 1969, 24, 839–841.

Kendall, E. We have men on the staff. *Young Children*, 1972, 27, 358–362.

Kyselka, W. Young men in a nursery school. *Childhood Education*, 1966, 42, 293–299.

Landy, R., Rosenberg, B. G., & Sutton-Smith, B. The effect of limited father absence on cognitive development. *Child Development*, 1969, 40, 941–944.

Lippitt, R., & Gold, M. Classroom social structure as a mental health problem. *Journal of Social Issues*, 1959, 15, 40–49.

Madsen, C. Nurturance and modeling in preschoolers. *Child Development*, 1968, 39, 221–236.

McCandless, B. R., Roberts, A., & Starnes, T. Teachers' marks, achievement test scores, and aptitude relations with respect to social class, race, and sex. *Journal of Educational Psychology*, 1972, 63, 153–159.

McFarland, W. J. Are girls really smarter? *Elementary School Journal*, 1969, 70 (1) 14–19.

McNeil, J. D. Programmed instruction versus usual classroom procedures in teaching boys to read. *American Educational Research Journal*, 1964, 1, 113–119.

Meyer, W. J., & Thompson, G. G. Sex differences in the distribution of teacher approval and disapproval among sixth grade children. *Journal of Educational Psychology*, 1956, 47, 385–397.

Minuchin, P. P. Sex differences in children: Research findings in an educational context. *National Elementary Principal*, 1966, 46 (2), 45–48.

Murgatroyd, R. A man among six-year-olds. *Childhood Education*, 1955, 32, 132–135.

NEA Research Division (or Research Division of NEA). *Estimates of school statistics, 1971–72*, 1971-R13, NEA, Washington, D.C., pp. 13–14.

NEA Research Division. New profile of the American public school teacher. *Today's Education*, 1972, 61 (5) 14–17.

New York Times encyclopedic almanac. New York: The New York Times, 1972.

Oetzel, R. M. Classified summary of research in sex differences. In E. E. Maccoby (Ed.), *The development of sex differences*. Stanford: Stanford University Press, 1966.

Portuges, S. H., & Feshbach, N. D. The influence of sex and socioethnic factors upon imitation of teachers by elementary school children. *Child Development*, 1972, 43, 981–989.

Santrock, J. W. Paternal absence, sex typing, and identification. *Developmental Psychology*, 1970, 2, 264–272.

Triplett, L. Elementary education—a man's world? *The Instructor*, 1968, 78 (3), 50–52.

Wohlford, P., Santrock, J. W., Berger, S. E., & Liberman, D. Older brothers' influence on sex-typed, aggressive, and dependent behavior in father-absent children. *Developmental Psychology*, 1971, 4, 124–134.

1973 World almanac and book of facts. New York: Newspaper Enterprise Association, Inc., 1973.

Reading 43

The Milwaukee Project: Early Intervention as a Technique to Prevent Mental Retardation

Howard Garber
Rick Heber

The evidence that a certain population of disadvantaged children suffer depressing events through the early years is derived from the performance discrepancy typically exhibited between them and their counterparts, the "normal, middle-class, ad-vantaged child." Virtually all the studies of such early "deprivation" have attempted to ameliorate the intellectual deficiency that seems to attend developmental disadvantagement by using some sort of enrichment or compensatory education procedure. The enrichment procedure is intended to intellectually rejuvenate children who have been deprived of the stimulation appropriate for intellectual development. Moreover, it seemed entirely reasonable to attempt to close the performance gap for these children by implementing a "catch-up" compensatory program just prior to the time the children enter school.

Unfortunately, most gains in performance proved tenuous, as the discrepancy between the children reappeared after a few years of schooling. It appears that most of these attempts to rehabilitate the developmental process for such children did not begin intervention early enough to mitigate whatever depressing events occur most powerfully in the early environment, particularly since nearly all began after most of the critical periods. The human organism is an extremely complex organism and therefore cannot be expected to respond normally when the appropriate stimulation necessary for growth is not available. There is, rather, a biologically related sequence of critical periods in early life at which times both optimum nutrition and stimulation must be available—i.e., if development is to be normal.

There are both strong and weak aspects to this notion of compensation which is known more generally by the rubric: *social deprivation hypothesis.* Its strong points are that it has provided intellectual and nutritional benefits to otherwise disadvantaged children; and probably its strongest point is that it has helped children to adjust emotionally and attitudinally to the requirements of formal schooling, particularly since a major problem with the education of the disadvantaged in elementary school has been one of motivation, discipline, and maintenance of classroom decorum. The weak point is the fallacious notion that compensatory education would be a panacea for children with severe developmental histories.

The Milwaukee Project is at once similar in concept to the early education studies, but it is also *quite* different. It is because of its outward similarity that the difference in concept and design between the Milwaukee Project and other "early education studies" could be overlooked and even confused. True, the project is an intervention project concerned with the education of very young children who are quite disadvantaged: but the Milwaukee Project is much more than that.

The Milwaukee Project, as it has come to be known, represents an attempt to prevent intellectu-al deficits in "high-risk" children by early intervention. The intervention technique employs an intensive educational program for the very young high-risk child, beginning before six months of age. The label "high-risk" is a statistically based term which reflects that certain children have a critically high probability of being mentally retarded by the time they have reached maturity. This probability level is determined by a number of factors which include low maternal IQ, low socio-economic status (SES), low IQ of siblings, large-sized families, etc. Evidence from extensive survey work showed that the offspring of mentally retarded, low SES mothers, although testing at retarded levels on IQ instruments at maturity, test at normal levels very early in life. *The Milwaukee Project undertook to prevent this decline from occurring by having a group of children participate in an intensive early education program, beginning before six months of age.*

It is just this point that may not be well understood. The Milwaukee Project was designed as a study to prevent mental retardation—cultural-familial mental retardation—by intervening very early in life. The study was not designed to raise IQ levels, but to permit continued normal intellectual development by mitigating environmentally depressing events. . . .

Approximately ten years ago, faced with problems associated with early detection of mental retardation, the University of Wisconsin Research and Training Center established the High-Risk Population Laboratory. The main purpose of this effort was to provide opportunity for prospective longitudinal investigation into the problems of mental retardation, in contradistinction to the almost exclusive reliance upon retrospective techniques. Further, the intent of the laboratory was to bring into accessibility for research purposes the subpopulation of the mentally retarded labeled the cultural-familial retarded, which previously has been essentially unavailable to investigators. This group of retarded reside in the community and remain undetected for two reasons: (1) they have relatively mild intellectual deficits which are most difficult to detect in the very young; and (2) they are without major related physical problems. Ordinarily, neither of these characteristics alone would be sufficient to precipitate the attention of responsible agencies to these individuals.

The approach used by the High-Risk Population Laboratory in its search for a technique for early detection was to develop sufficient information to permit the diagnosis of cultural-familial retardation. In order to compile this information, a door-to-door survey was conducted in an area of the metropolitan community of Milwaukee which had previously been identified as having an extremely high prevalence of retardation. This area of the city has the lowest median educational level, the lowest median family income, the greatest population density per living unit, and the highest rate of dilapidated housing in the city. *Though the area comprises about 2 percent of the population of the city, it yielded approximately 33 percent of the total number of children identified in school as educable mentally retarded.* In our first survey, all families residing in this area who had a newborn infant and at least one other child of the age of six were selected for study. All members of the family, both children and adults, received an individual intellectual appraisal. In addition, extensive data were obtained on family history, including the social, educational and occupational history and status. This approach provided us with some key variables that appear to be sufficiently sensitive to the existence of cultural-familial retardation to be used as a signal for such.

The population survey data produced some striking data on the prevalence of retardation in depressed urban areas, on the distribution of retardation among families living in the high-risk area, and on trends in intelligence as a function of age of children and adults residing in the area. *For example, it was found that the high prevalence of mental retardation identified with Milwaukee's inner core population was strikingly concentrated among families where maternal intelligence was depressed, particularly where the family was large.* From our survey sample it was found that the prevalence of IQs of 75 and below was 22 percent, i.e. in these families where there was a newborn and at least one child of age six or greater. This selection procedure resulted in a sample of much larger than average families, and an increased prevalence of sub-75 IQs. However, it was found that 45.4 percent of the mothers who had IQs below 80 accounted for 78.2 percent of all children with IQs below 80. Moreover, it was found that depressed maternal intelligence was even a better predictor of depressed child intelligence for the older (above age six) than for the younger children. The most startling aspect of this data is that on infant intelligence tests, children of mothers above 80 IQ and below 80

IQ did about equally well. *After the infancy period, though, the children whose mothers had IQs greater than 80 appeared to maintain a fairly steady intellectual level, while the children whose mothers had IQs less than 80 exhibited a marked progressive decline in their intellectual level.* [See Figure 1] This trend toward a decline in measured intelligence for children in disadvantaged environments has wide acceptance as a general characteristic of a "slum" environment population, although this set of data indicates that this trend of declining intelligence as age increases is restricted to offspring of the "less bright" mothers.

SELECTION OF RESEARCH FAMILIES

As a consequence of the survey data, we have utilized maternal IQ as a basis for selection of a group of newborns, with confidence that a substantial percentage would be identified as mentally retarded. In other words, to identify the "high-risk" families within the "high-risk" residential area, the variable of maternal intelligence was utilized as a

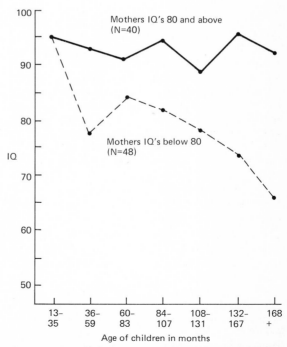

Figure 1 IQ change in the offspring of disadvantaged mothers as a function of maternal IQ. *(Heber et al. 1968).*

selection criterion since it proved to be the most efficient predictor of low school-age offspring intelligence.

The High-Risk Population Laboratory maintained a survey of births in the high-risk area. By first screening and then administering individual tests of intelligence, we identified those mothers of newborns who were mentally retarded, i.e. who had full-scale WAIS IQs less than 75. From this pool of candidates, accumulated over an eighteen-month period, we drew 40 mentally retarded mothers and randomly assigned them to either the Experimental or Control condition, after they had been invited to participate in a study of child development being conducted by the University of Wisconsin. All of the families selected were of Negro extraction.

The Experimental group, beginning within the first few months of life, was to undergo a comprehensive intervention in their social environment, the objective of which was to displace all of the presumed negative factors in the social environment of the infant being reared in the slum by a mother who is herself retarded. We are, thereby, testing the "social deprivation" hypothesis of etiology by seeing whether it is possible to prevent retardation from occurring in the offspring of these retarded mothers.

Should the Experimental children enter school and exhibit normal intellectual functioning we will know that it is possible, through our experimental program, to prevent mental retardation from occurring at the present high frequency of children raised in these circumstances. If the children are assigned to classes for the retarded at the rate of those without training, our program has not been successful.

The experimental intervention is comprised of two components: (1) the maternal rehabilitation program and (2) the infant stimulation program which are described below.

THE MATERNAL REHABILITATION PROGRAM

A two-phase program was initiated to better prepare the experimental mothers for employment opportunities and to improve their homemaking and child-rearing skills. Through improved employment potential, increased earnings, and self-confidence, it was hoped that positive changes in the home environment would occur. The rehabilitation program consisted of adult education classes to teach the mothers basic academic tools necessary for vocational adaptability, and finally, an occupational training program to teach specific vocational skills.

The job training program utilized two large, private nursing homes in Milwaukee. The choice of the nursing homes as a site for training was made because of the appropriate job skill areas represented in these facilities, the availability of professional staff with some understanding of rehabilitation problems, and the employment opportunities available in nursing homes and other chronic care facilities.

During the educational phase of the program, the basic academic skills of reading, writing and arithmetic were emphasized. In addition, their curriculum included community-oriented social studies, home economics, interpersonal relations, and child care.

While the occupational habilitation component of the maternal program appears to have been quite successful to date, major problems with respect to adequacy of homemaking skills and care and treatment of children remain to be resolved with a number of experimental families. With many of the mothers now successfully employed, the maternal program is shifting to an increased emphasis on training in general care of family and home, budgeting, nutrition, and food preparation.

THE INFANT STIMULATION PROGRAM

The program is, in its most basic sense, designed to facilitate intellectual development of very young children. The plan is concerned with (1) a physical location which promotes learning, (2) a staff to manage and arrange instruction for children, and (3) the educational program.

Physical Plant

Over the years, the project has been located in several facilities. When all of the children were around six months of age, a large fourteen-room duplex served our needs very well because of the many "nooks and crannies" where teachers could work with children on a more intimate one-to-one basis. . . . The entire program is now housed in a leased school facility located adjacent to one of the inner-city's churches. This building, complete with six classrooms, a gymnasium, office space, and a lunch room is well suited to the needs of the program.

The Staff

At the onset of the stimulation program we chose to employ a para-professional staff. The persons chosen were, in our judgment, language facile, affectionate people who had had some experience with infants or young children. The majority of these "teachers" resided in the same general neighborhood as the children, thus sharing a similar cultural milieu. The teachers ranged in age from approximately eighteen to forty-five with most of the teachers in their mid-twenties. Their educational experience ranged from eighth grade to one year of college. The teachers were both black and white.

The teacher of an infant had the major responsibility of establishing initial rapport with the infant's mother. This was done during a brief period, ranging from two to eight weeks, when the teacher worked with her child in the home until the mother expressed enough confidence in the teacher to allow the child to go to the center. . . .

Educational Program

When the children first entered the project (by six months of age), they were each assigned a teacher. If the match proved satisfactory, the child remained with her as his primary teacher until he reached twelve months of age. At that time the child was gradually paired with other teachers and children. By the time he was fifteen to twenty months old, depending on the child, he was grouped with two other children and came into contact with three different teachers. This situation held for just his academic-learning environment. Actually each child was in contact with most of the other children and teachers.

The teacher who was assigned to an infant was responsible for his total care, including: feeding and bathing, cuddling and soothing, reporting and recording general health as well as organizing his learning environment and implementing the educational program. Within the context of the educational program, the teacher was expected to follow and expand upon a prescribed set of activities. Her job was to make these activities interesting, exciting and varied. She was also required to "objectively" evaluate and report the child's progress, pointing out areas of apparent difficulty.

The present groupings and teacher-pupil ratios vary with the age level of the child, but are flexible to allow for individual child needs. Under most circumstances, the infant remained with a teacher on a one-to-one basis up to twelve months, at which time another teacher and child were paired with him to encourage the expansion of relationships. Around fifteen months of age, a transition period began during which two children were assigned to one teacher. By age eighteen months we began to form the children into small groups so that by about 24 months all children of the same age level (about a five-month span) were grouped together with enough teachers to provide a one-to-three teacher-child ratio. During structured learning periods, the teacher-pupil ratio may be 1:2, 1:3, 1:4 depending on the age and the ability of the children. Within each age group, behavioral and educational evaluations were made by the teachers, teacher supervisor, and curriculum supervisors in bi-monthly conferences, at which time decisions on whether to regroup children, provide individual instruction or curriculum changes were made.

To facilitate learning and teacher effectiveness, a structured program was planned for each age group. The schedule remained constant to aid the child in developing realistic expectations and time orientation. For children under 24 months of age, the teacher varied the schedule in consideration of the child's moods and attention, while teachers of children older than 24 months followed the schedule somewhat more closely, gradually increasing the demands made on the child's attention span. The daily schedule for each child was as follows:

8:45	Arrival
9:00–9:30	Breakfast
9:30–10:00	First structured learning period
10:00–10:30	Second structured learning period
10:30–11:00	Self-directed activities in free play environment
11:00–11:30	Third structured learning period
11:30–12:00	Sesame Street
12:00–12:30	Lunch
12:30–1:45	Nap
1:45–2:00	Snack
2:00–2:30	Fourth structured learning period
2:30–3:00	Fifth structured learning period
3:00–3:30	Sixth structured learning period
3:30–4:00	Motor period
4:00	Departure

Though a child was never forced to remain in a learning area, the teacher was encouraged to make it exciting for him to do so. . . .

The intent of the education program was to provide an environment and a set of experiences which would allow children to develop to their potential intellectually as well as socially, emotionally, and physically. The specific focus of the educational program was to prevent from occurring those language, problem-solving, and achievement motivation deficits which are associated with mild mental retardation and severe disadvantagement.

The general educational program is best characterized as having a cognitive-language orientation implemented through a structured environment by prescriptive teaching techniques on a daily basis (seven hours per day, five days per week). This program and schedule was coupled with a high teacher-child ratio, affording an opportunity to present a variety of cognitive tasks, to evaluate their effectiveness, and to provide both direct and nondirect teaching within both small and large groups.

Although there are many theories which have implications for an educational program; e.g., Skinner, Piaget, Montessori, Bruner; none is complete while all are relevant. By necessity the theory which has guided the development of the curriculum for the Milwaukee Project's Educational Program is eclectic yet structured in its presentation. There were no suitable programs available as guides for intervention the first few months of life. Consequently, the project staff has continually adapted existing methods and materials for the purposes of our program.

The educational program had two major emphases: (1) language and (2) cognition. We considered language not only as essential to social communication, but essential to the ability to manipulate symbols, the tool by which one stores and recovers information and a major influence on how one interprets his environment. It was our intent that tasks or experiences be presented to the child with considerable emphasis on verbal expressiveness in order to facilitate this development.

The cognitive development of the children was of primary concern because we did not want to simply identify and provide children with those facts which are the supposed elements for success in school. A child must have at his disposal the technique not only to incorporate, integrate, refine,

and utilize this information, but (and most importantly) to be able to act spontaneously whenever the situation changes.

Thus while a handle for the term cognitive developments is difficult to find, there were certain identifiable developmentally important cognitive skills, e.g., classification, association, generalization, integration, interpretation. We have focused on these and have attempted to facilitate their development by incorporating into the educational program specific tasks, which were begun as soon as the children entered the program.

Importantly, although language was emphasized as a tool for processing information as well as for communication, and cognitive development was emphasized for the development of thinking creatively as well as providing the child with a repertoire of responses, we recognized that the energy to make this system work is the desire to utilize these skills. Therefore, a third area of concern was motivation. We attempted to develop achievement motivation by both designing tasks and creating an atmosphere which would maximize interest, provide success experiences, provide supportive and corrective feedback from responsive adults, and to gradually increase the child's responsibility for task completion.

The educational program took place within a structured learning environment. By utilizing a structured learning approach, the emphasis was on educating the teacher to plan and present relevant and organized learning situations. The content of instructional units was presented in small logical steps. The children's progress was evaluated and corresponding program adjustments made as part of an ongoing process. Yet within this structured environment, we still emphasized flexibility as essential in order to meet the needs of the children and the teacher. Opportunities could be provided for both directed and non-directed instruction. There was greater opportunity for direct child-teacher intervention.

Thus the Milwaukee Project attempted to change the expected course of children who were at high-risk for mental retardation. The plan was to implement a comprehensive family intervention, beginning in the home.

The program for the retarded mothers was designed to modify those aspects of the environment which the mother herself creates or controls. Each day, her child was picked up at home and brought to the Infant Education Center for the entire day. These children are the Experimental group. The Control group is essentially the same kind of children whose mothers were in the original pool of high-risk families from which were drawn both the Experimental and Control group families. The children in the Control group are seen only for testing, which is done on a prescribed schedule for both groups of children.

ASSESSMENT OF DEVELOPMENT

In order to assess the effects of the kind of comprehensive intervention we have made with the natural environment of the infant reared by a retarded mother, we have undertaken an intensive schedule of measurements.° Our schedule of measurement includes measures of physical maturation, standardized and experimental measures of developmental schedules of infant adaptive behavior, standardized tests of general intelligence, an array of experimental learning tasks, measures of motivation and social development, and a variety of measures of language development.

Both the Experimental and Control infants are on an identical measurement schedule. Infants are scheduled for assessment sessions every three weeks. The particular measures administered at a given session depend upon the predetermined schedule of measures for that age level. A particular test or task is administered to both Experimental and Control infants by the same person; the testers are not involved in any component of the infant stimulation or maternal program.

In the first 24 months of life, the measurement schedule was largely restricted to general developmental scales and emerging vocalization and language.

Gesell Data

The Gesell Developmental Schedules were administered to Experimental and Control infants at the ages of six, ten, fourteen, eighteen, and 22 months. Through six, ten, and fourteen month testings, both groups appeared reasonably comparable on the four schedules: Motor, Adaptive, Language, and Personal-Social. These data can be seen in the

*Because of the obvious limitations of this report, only a portion of the measurements are reported here.

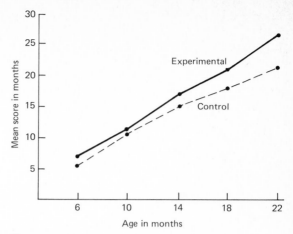

Figure 2 Composite of four Gesell scores.

graph [Figure 2] which is a composite of the four schedules plotted in terms of the mean scale developmental age norms for each age level tested. There is some divergence in performance at fourteen months, due mainly to the significant ($p < .05$) difference on the Motor and Adaptive schedules in favor of the Experimental group. The Control group at this time also performs above average. At eighteen months the Control group begins to fall three to four months below the Experimental group, although still performing at or close to Gesell norms. The Experimental group at eighteen months is significantly ($p < .001$) ahead of the Controls on all but the Personal-Social Gesell Schedule. At 22 months the Experimental groups scores are from four and one-half to six months in advance of the Control group ($p < .001$) on all four schedules, while the Control group has fallen below the Gesell norms on the Adaptive and Language schedules.

In summary, the Gesell data is roughly comparable for both groups to fourteen months with performance on all scales slightly in advance of test norms. At 22 months, performance of the Experimental group is clearly accelerated while the Control group performs at or slightly below norms for the four scales.

Learning

Beginning at 24 months, increased emphasis was given to experimental, direct measures of learning and performance, as well as to the standardized tests of general intelligence.

The learning tasks chosen were those that, on the one hand, would characterize the developmental learning process and on the other hand were tasks that could be repeated yearly. By repeating tasks we could keep pace with the increasing CA's of our Ss and yet maintain a continuity of task which would permit evaluation of developmental changes in performance. *Obviously, the exceedingly complex nature of cognitive growth required more than a single measure of intellectual development, such as is obtained from IQ tests. Thus, a more comprehensive picture of the growth of cognitive abilities was attempted by an array of experimental learning tasks (see, e.g., Stevenson, 1972).*

Most importantly, we were concerned with delineating some of the characteristics of early learning behavior that are either facilitating or interfering with learning. We wanted information on the response patterns or behavior style, and we wanted information about the role of attention in early learning. These tasks, therefore, not only provided a measure of the differential development of the learning process in the children, but measured our understanding of how certain performance variables relate to cognitive growth.

One experimental task has been concerned with development of the child's attention to color and form and the response strategy employed. It is a color-form matching task in which the child may respond consistently according to one of the dimensions: color or form. He cannot respond consistently if he does not attend to one dimension or the other, especially if he uses a response strategy such as position responding or alternation responding. In this case, responding to the dimension of either color or form is more developmentally advanced than ignoring the color-form dimension and responding, e.g., to position. This test has been administered four times. During the third year of life, none of the Controls demonstrated a dimensional response (i.e., in terms of color or form). By contrast, over half of the Experimental group (55 percent) showed unidimensional responding. In the fourth year of life and during the fifth and sixth years as well, this differential performance was maintained. There are two notable points: (1) three-fourths or more of the Experimental group showed unidimensional responding at each successive testing, while even at the fifth and sixth year testings the percentage of the Control group showing unidimensional responding was comparable

only to the Experimental group's first test performance, nearly two years before; and (2) the Experimental group showed a significant shift to form, which is quite consistent with other research indicating advanced developmental performance. Quite interestingly, of those children in both groups who did not show dimensional preference, by far a greater percentage of the Controls, at each testing, showed response perseveration. In other words, little or no attempt was made, it seems, to attend to either color or form since most (over two-thirds) responses were made purely to position. As of the last testing (when children are between the ages of five and six) only twenty percent of the Experimentals showed such responding, as compared to nearly two-thirds of the Control group.

Additional evidence for perseverative responding and the development of strategies was gained from a probability learning task. In this task no response is always correct, but a strategy of responding can help to increase the child's percentage of payoff. In fact, although both groups were reinforced at about the same rate (i.e., payoff)—they were very different in their use of strategy. The Control group showed a greater tendency to perseverate, i.e., they continued to respond to either a stimulus or position irrespective of the consequence of their previous response. Further, whereas only one-third of the Experimental group showed a tendency to perseverate, 80 percent of the Controls perseverated. By the second testing, nearly two years later, nearly three-fourths of the Control children continued to perseverate as compared to only one-fourth of the Experimental group. This tendency to perseverate suggests that the children are insensitive to the reinforcement contingencies—i.e., they do not seem to appreciate the feedback to be gained from their response and therefore perseverate their response to position.

Thus, we feel that in spite of the apparent simpleness of these tasks, they demonstrate the association of early intellectual development with an ability to impose order on the environment—an ability which is basic and essential to intellectual development. This difficulty in the performance of various learning tasks may be similar to the input phenomena found in studies of short-term memory (Calfee, 1969). In that kind of an experimental paradigm, and perhaps in ours as well, there appears to be a critical lack in the ability to organize stimulation for input where there is sub-average intellectual functioning.

A deficiency in this critical ability becomes quite apparent in the performance of various problem-solving and concept formation tasks. For example, we have studied the performance of the children in an oddity discrimination task. The child is presented with a horizontal array of three stimuli, each of which has four component dimensions: color, form, size, and number. In order for the child to be able to select the odd stimulus on each trial, he must first separate the dimensions into relevant, irrelevant, and quiet. This is an extremely complex conceptual task for very young children.

This task has been presented three successive times, and the data show superior performance by the Experimental children. We have analyzed the data further by a breakdown of the concept categories. These results show a superior performance on all dimensions and particularly on the form dimension for the Experimental children, which is consistent with their performance on our most recent replication of the matching study. Obviously this preference can facilitate performance, but it is just this point that underscores our earlier remark regarding the development of attentional processes. Though it may be that dimensional preferences lead in some situations to response biases, it can also index the developmental process of selective organization of the stimulus environment, especially for very young children. The earlier that such behavior occurs, the greater the facilitation of learning performance on just such kinds of tasks. In our case, the data point obviously to a developmentally related facilitation of performance as a function of the degree to which the early dimensional preferences have been established.

Language Development

A child's acquisition of language occurs in a surprisingly short period of time. Although grammatical speech rarely begins before eighteen months of age, the basic process appears complete by the age of three and one-half. Furthermore, at this age level, it is probably language facility which most clearly differentiates the cultural-familial retardate from his non-retarded peers. It is for this reason that we have given so much emphasis to both the development of the children's language abilities and the measurement of this aspect of behavior. Our concern is both with the quantitative and qualita-

tive differences in the developing language structures of these two groups.

The development of language depends on a number of organic and environmental factors. The main variable in the social environment critical to language development in the child is the primary responsible adult: usually the mother. Brown and Bellugi (1964) suggest three processes operating in the learning of language. The first process is one of imitation with reduction by the child of the adult utterances in the environment. The young child seems to reduce adult utterances to a form which is much like that of a telegram, i.e., it utilizes the high content, low-function words of the adult utterance. Thus, where an adult might say something like, "I see the big chair," the child might say, "See chair." This telegraphic language can communicate a situation known to the adult and the child.

The second process appears to involve the imitation of the child's utterances by the adult. What might happen is, when a child says something, the adult repeats the utterance and expands it slightly. The resulting utterance is a perfectly formed model sentence in the adult language which apparently has, as its purpose, the effect of saying to the child, "This is the way you could have said what you just said." Thus, where a child might say something like, "There doggie," the adult might say, "Yes, there is a doggie." This type of imitation occurs in about 30 percent of the utterances.

The third process is one of induction of the latent structure: this requires that the child learn the rule of language, which he appears to do in some covert manner. The basic learning of the language system is usually complete by the time the child enters school. It is obvious, therefore, that if the responsible adult in a child's environment is language deficient and somewhat nonresponsive, there can be serious retardation in a child's language development.

The first statistically significant difference in language development appeared at eighteen months on the Language scale of the Gesell Developmental Schedule. At this testing age the Experimental children were two months above the norm and three months ahead of the Controls. By 22 months the Experimental children were over four months ahead of the norm and six months ahead of the Controls. This trend of differential language development has continued, and perhaps in even a more dramatic way. In fact, some of the most striking differences in the performance of the Experimental and Control children are reflected in the research measures of language performance.

Research in developmental psycholinguistics usually divides language into three areas: imitation, comprehension, and production. We are using both tests developed in our laboratory and such standardized instruments as the Illinois Test of Psycholinguistic Abilities (ITPA), in order to assess language development. Imitation, the child's ability to repeat certain grammatical structures presented to him as models, is tested through a sentence repetition test; comprehension, the understanding of grammatical structures, is assessed through a grammatical comprehension test; while production, spontaneous language facility, is measured through gross feature tabulation of free speech samples. Together, the results of these measures have provided us with a comprehensive picture of the children's language development for five years.

Samples of conversation between each child and our language tester (a black, middle-aged woman) have been analyzed since the child's eighteen-month birthday. The free speech sampling technique is quite useful with such young children since the situation is relaxed, unstructured, and the child is quite comfortable in conversation. Structured test situations, on the other hand, particularly at these very early ages, tend to restrict the behavior of the child and thereby reduce the validity of the speech sample somewhat.

The analysis of this language sample indicated that the Experimental children between the ages of one and one-half and three say a lot more in conversation. Using this measurement technique, we find that it is not until three years of age that the Control group produces the same amount of utterances as the Experimental children. However, since the measure provides a rather gross picture of language as language becomes more complex, it actually masks the considerable linguistic differences that exist between the children. These differences show up in the group's performance on the more sophisticated language measures.

Still, we feel that this considerable early difference in language behavior is basic to the more sophisticated language skills yet to come. We are not quite sure why, but the repetition and verbal expressiveness characteristic of the Experimental group between one and one-half and three seems fundamental to the continued differential development of language skills by the E group over the C group. The amount of utterances at the eighteen-month level for the Experimental group is not achieved by the Control group until nearly a year later.

The mean number of unique words, lexical growth in free production, was also measured. Vocabulary range is always greater on the part of the Experimental group. This is so even when the Control group produces more utterances than the Experimental group; the Experimental group still produces more unique words.

At the age of three we began to test imitation by means of a sentence repetition test. It is an easily administered instrument: you ask the child to repeat what the tester says. The children's replies are analyzed for omissions, substitutions, and additions. The omissions are significantly greater for the Control group at every age level from 36 months on while there is a significant decrease in omissions by the Experimental group every six months. Also, the Experimental group has made significantly fewer substitutions and additions to the repetitions. The Experimental group by the age of four has significantly more exact repetitions than the Control group, whose performance is comparable to the Experimental group's performance at three. This same performance differential continues through age five.

Also at age three we tested grammatical comprehension with a modified version of a test developed by Dr. Ursula Bellugi-Klima (Fraser, 1963). It is a game in which the child manipulates objects in order to demonstrate his ability to comprehend various grammatical constructions, such as the active and passive voice. In this test you might have, for example, two toy animals and you ask the child to show "the pig chases the cow" and then you ask the child to show you "the pig is chased by the cow." The child is expected to act out these situations, which requires just comprehension, not production. The game is played with the child across sixteen syntactic areas: e.g., active-passive voice, embedded sentences, singular-plural, possessive nouns, and prepositions. The results show that the Experimental group's performance is significantly superior at all age levels tested (three, four, and five). Their grammatical comprehension is at least one year (and more) in advance of the Control group.

Our standardized language instrument has been

the ITPA, which has been administered to all children over four and one-half. The results have, basically, supported the differential performance of the Experimental and Control groups on our other measures. The mean psycholinguistic age of the Experimental group is 63 months (measured at 54 months) as compared to a mean of 45 months for the Control group, a difference in favor of the Experimental group by over a year and one-half.

In describing the language behavior of the Experimental children one would find them volubly expressive, verbally fluent, and according to the ITPA linguistically sophisticated. They speak their own dialect and they are proud of their own speech and yet their performance is developmentally advanced on sophisticated tests of the English language.

MOTHER-CHILD RELATIONSHIP

Each mother . . . creates an environment for her child which is quite different from that created by other mothers, even though all live in the same environment. Indeed, it is the very nature of the environment created by the mother which influences social, emotional, and cognitive development. The investigation of this relationship has been studied in detail by Hess and Shipman (e.g., 1968). They found that the mother's linguistic and regulatory behavior induces and shapes the information-processing strategies and style in her child and can act to either facilitate or limit intellectual growth.

Mildly retarded mothers tend to regulate behavior by using imperatives and restricted communication—a behavior control system which can [limit] *intellectual growth in her child.* Furthermore, the nature of this interaction is such that it induces a passive-complaint attitude by weakening the child's self-confidence and dampening motivation. We are quite concerned, therefore, in determining the nature of the mother-child relationship, especially after having intervened in this critical process.

In the mother-child interaction most sophisticated behavior—such as the initiation of problem-solving behavior by verbal clues and verbal prods, or the organization of tasks with respect to goals in problem-solving situations, etc.—is done by the mother. However, where the mother is of low IQ, the interaction is more physical, less organized, and less direction is given to the child. Indeed, while this was the case in the Control group mother-child

dyads, it was quite different in the Experimental dyads.

We used a specially prepared mobile laboratory for all experimental sessions. The testing room was equipped with videotape and sound recording equipment, so that the entire session with each family was recorded for later analysis. The mother and child are brought to the laboratory and seated at a table. Part of this research involved explaining to the mother the tasks she and the child were to perform. First, she was to tell the child a story based on a picture, which afforded us the opportunity to measure the mother's language facility. Second, the mother was told to teach the child a block sorting task and how to copy three designs on a toy Etch-A-Sketch. The behavior between the mother and child was rated on a scale with rating categories divided into various kinds of physical and verbal behaviors, with additional categories to indicate whether the behavior was active or passive.

We found that the Experimental dyads transmitted more information than the Control dyads, and this was a function of the quality of the Experimental child's verbal behavior. The Experimental children supplied more information verbally and initiated more verbal communication than found in the Control dyads. The children in the Experimental dyad took responsibility for guiding the flow of information—providing most of the verbal information and direction. The mothers of both dyads showed little differences in their teaching ability during the testing session. However, in the Experimental dyads, the children structured the interaction session either by their questioning or by teaching the mother. As a result, a developmentally more sophisticated interaction pattern has developed between the Experimental children and their mothers, which contributed to faster and more successful problem completion.

It is apparent from this description of a portion of the data of the mother-child interaction, that the intervention effort has effectively changed the expected pattern of development for the Experimental dyads. Moreover, the result of what might be termed a reciprocal feedback system, initiated by the child, has been to create a more sophisticated and satisfying interaction pattern in the Experimental dyad. In fact, there is some evidence that the Experimental mothers may be undergoing some changes in attitude and self-confidence. The Experimental mothers appear to be adopting more of an "internal locus of control"—an attitude that 'things happen' because of their decisions and actions and not purely by chance or fate. Thus, the intensive stimulation program, undergone by the Experimental children, has benefited both the Experimental child and the Experimental mother by broadening their verbal and expressive behavioral repertoire.

MEASURED INTELLIGENCE TO 66 MONTHS

The standardized tests of intelligence included the Cattell, Stanford-Binet, and Wechsler Preschool-Primary Scale of Intelligence (WPPSI). The Cattell test, extending into the Binet, was scheduled at three month intervals beginning at CA 24 months and at six month intervals from CA 48 months on. The graph illustrates the course of intellectual development for the two groups from twelve months until 66 months of age. The data presented use scores derived from the Gesell schedules from 12 to 21 months, and Cattell and Binet scores from 24 to 66 months. The mean IQ at the upper age level of 66 months is based on approximately half of the group, because at this time not all of the subjects have reached this age.

The mean IQ for the Experimental group based on the means at each age interval from 24 to 66 months is 123.4. For the Control group, mean IQ for all testing is 94.8. At the latest point the Experimentals are just above their mean, at 125 (s.d. = 8.5) while the Controls have slipped below their overall mean to 91 (s.d. = 9.1). The discrepancy between Experimental and Control group performance at each three month test interval varies from a minimum of 23 IQ points at 24 months to over 30 IQ points at 66 months.

These data summarize the present differential development between the Experimental and Control groups. The dotted line on the graph [Figure 3] represents the mean IQ's of offspring of mothers with IQ's below 75, taken from our original population survey. This is referred to in our study as the Contrast group. It depicts the pattern of development expected for our actual Control group. You will recall that our hypothesis was in terms of preventing the relative decline in development of the Experimental group which we see in the Contrast group and which we can begin to see in the Control group. In sharp contrast is the Experimental group's performance, to date, on the stadardized tests of measured intelligence, indicating a remark-

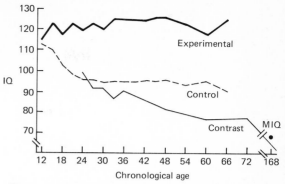

Figure 3 Mean IQ performance with increasing age for the experimental and control groups in comparison to the high risk survey contrast group.

able acceleration of intellectual development on the part of these children exposed to the infant stimulation program. Further, their performance is quite homogeneous as contrasted with that of the Control group where less than one-fourth of the Ss test at or above the norms with the remainder trending toward sub-average performance.

It is important to point out that there is reason for caution in the interpretation of such data, particularly when one considers the numerous pitfalls and hazards of infant measurement. The Experimental children have had training, albeit fortuitously, on items included in the curriculum which are sampled by the tests, while the repeated measurements have made both groups test-wise. It is well to point out, however, that curriculum materials and tests used are standard fare for early education programs everywhere. All in all, it does seem that the Experimental group has benefited from the intensive training program, a program to which no comparable group of infants has ever been exposed, to the best of our knowledge. We have tried very hard to answer whether it has been simply a matter of training and practicing specific skills. In fact, extraordinary precaution has been taken to separate the development of the curriculum and the assessment program. Two separate staffs have been employed. It is obvious to most researchers that, to some extent, infant intelligence tests must contain material which approximates material used in preschool curricula, primarily because of the limited variety of material for this age. To circumvent this problem somewhat, we have employed other measures of performance, which minimized the stock item, and thereby afforded additional insight into the differential development of these children. As could be seen in the measures of learning and language development, the differential performance descrepancy is consistent with the IQ measures, indicating advanced intellectual development of the Experimental group. What is more, there is considerable difference in the pattern or style of behavior between the groups—particularly the tendency to stereotypy of response exhibited by the Control group, which certainly in antagonistic to successful learning performance.

Thus, infant testing difficulties notwithstanding, the present standardized test data, when considered along with performance on learning tasks and language tests, indicate an unquestionably superior present level of cognitive development on the part of the Experimental group. Also, the first "wave" of our children are now in public schools. *None* have been assigned to classes for the retarded and we are collecting data on school performance generally.

CONCLUSION

We are particularly concerned with the social-emotional development of our children, which was encouraged through the interpersonal relationship developed between the teachers and the children and their families. We felt that this was fundamental to developing intellectual strength in children. Intellectual strength we defined as the ability to meet new experiences with not only considerable creativeness and ingenuity, but with self-confidence and the kind of motivation that is based on the natural curiosity to learn. The child who feels himself to be intellectually strong enters new learning situations with eagerness, unafraid of failure, and filled with curiosity and excitement with each new adventure in knowledge gathering. Unfortunately, this natural desire to pursue and discover and learn about our world, that is within each of us, can be dampened or shut down by negative learning experiences. In all too many cases a child's failure to learn is due to the restricted learning environment created for him in early life. As a result, children who have such developmental histories develop a behavior system which is antagonistic to the learning they must do for successful school performance.

Learning need not be forced if there is excite-

ment. Experiences must not be restricted, opportunities for learning must be varied, solutions must have alternatives, and discovery must be shared in. The environment for preschool age children must be at once so rich, so varied, so intriguing, and so organized that a child has before him considerable opportunity to learn and make use of his own natural tendencies to discover.

It appears, however, that the mitigation of the environmental influences for which cultural-familial retardation is a consequent can be accomplished, though not by any single source. Most importantly, though, help must be given to that large population of mothers who are unaware of the critical nature of early childhood and also unaware of their own needs during pregnancy. *In large part, it is these mothers who consequently contribute to the growing number of children so poor in development that they are at high risk for mental retardation.* Therefore, existing early stimulation programs notwithstanding, there is considerable need for a comprehensive, nation-wide program for the prevention of mental retardation. The implementation of this program with any consideration for success will require an active community service program for which there probably is no previous model, but there is now available information of the kind we have just presented to you. Indeed, if our country is to seriously challenge the problem of cultural-familial retardation, we must do so at its doorstep and that will require a strategy for prevention, with increased emphasis on early detection and early intervention.

REFERENCES

Brown, R. and Bellugi, U. Three processes in the child's acquisition of syntax. *Harvard Educational Review,* 1964, 34, 133–151.

Calfee, Robert C. *Short-term Retention in Normal and Retarded Children as a Function on Memory Load and List Structure.* University of Wisconsin Center for Cognitive Learning, Technical Report No. 75, 1969.

Fraser, C., Bellugi, U., and Brown R. Control of grammar in imitation, comprehension and production. *Journal of Verbal Behavior,* 1963, 2, 121–135.

Heber, R., Dever, R., and Conry, J. The influence of environmental and genetic variables on intellectual development. In H. J. Prehm, L. A. Hamerlynck, and J. E. Crosson (Eds.) *Behavioral Research in Mental Retardation,* Research and Training Center, Monograph 1, University of Oregon, 1968, 1–22.

Hess, R. D. and Shipman, V. C. Maternal influences upon early learning. In R. D. Hess and R. M. Bear (Eds.) *Early Education,* Chicago: Aldine, 1968, 91–103.

Stevenson, Harold W. The taxonomy of tasks. In F. J. Monks, W. W. Hartup, and Jan de Wit (Eds.) *Determinants of Behavioral Development,* New York: Academic Press, 1972, 74–88.

Reading 44

Research on *Sesame Street:* Some Implications for Compensatory Education

Samuel Ball
Gerry Ann Bogatz

It was probably a weak moment when the first-named author unilaterally sent off the title of this paper some months before the paper itself had to be written. At least there was a prolonged pause when we both later set about writing and the second author asked: "And what did you mean by compensatory education?" Well, we did reach consensus, at least as the term relates to preschoolers, but it took awhile.

The first reaction to the question was: "What a silly question. Compensatory means making amends or making up for a loss, so compensatory education is the education you give disadvantaged children. More or less, that is."

Then came the reaction to the reaction. "What about *Sesame Street?* It was telecast throughout the country—not specifically to the disadvantaged. And what if both middle class and lower class children learn a great deal from the program? Does this mean that the program is not compensatory? Does it mean that it is compensatory only if we can somehow persuade middle class children *not* to watch it? Or, does this mean that the middle class too had lacked something that they could be compensated for?" The first-named author did not respond this time. Sometimes it is wiser to cut your losses.

Names and titles are important, as any member of the peer group will tell you. But you do not have to be introduced in order to start a conversation. So without indicating yet what we decided we meant by the term compensatory education, let us present our paper—and then think again about the meaning of the word "compensatory." First, the background to the paper, and this is provided by a brief description of our work over the past few years.

We began our work as independent evaluators of *Sesame Street* in the summer of 1968. At that time the goals for the first year of *Sesame Street* were established. The meetings brought together television writers and producers, authors of children's books, librarians, Madison Avenue executives, educational researchers, child psychologists and psychiatrists, movie moguls, and even teachers of preschool children. These meetings themselves provided compensatory education with the educators learning about the world of research and of television, the academic researchers learning about the world of television and about how young children behave, and the television specialists learning about the wonderful worlds of education and research.

Some goals were selected following those meetings; they were couched in behavioral terms and grouped in four sections:

1 Symbolic Representation (letters, numbers, geometric forms).
2 Cognitive Processes (perceptual discrimination, relational concepts, classification, sorting).
3 The Natural and Physical Environment (animals, machines).
4 The Social Environment (social skills such as cooperation and sharing, community members).

Some of these goals were established as those to be emphasized and were given greater time on the show. They were mainly in the cognitive area of symbolic representation and cognitive processes, and almost all of them were assessed in the first-year evaluation.

Two major principles guided us in the evaluation. First, we felt it important to look for unintended as well as intended outcomes. That is, the goals of the show were important, and we certainly hoped to assess the effects of viewing the show in relation to those goals. But that was not enough. The medical model of evaluation tells us that concentrating on achieving intended outcomes and ignoring side-effects can lead to some horribly wrong overall evaluations—for example, in the original testing of thalidomide (Scriven 1967). So in addition to looking for intended changes in children such as the learning of the alphabet, we also looked for changes in the children's TV viewing habits and in the parents' attitudes toward school.

A second major principle we considered was that interactions might tell us more in an evaluation than main effects. That is, in a worthwhile evaluation we must discover not only if the educational intervention, in general, works (an important question, of course) but also for which children it works best, for which children it does not seem to work, and the conditions under which it operates most efficiently. Too often evaluations have concluded that a new program is of little consequence, when in fact it is a boon to some children and a ruin to others, but when averaged over all children, its effectivensss seems little different from that of the old program.

The application of these two principles in the summative research for *Sesame Street* caused us to assess at pretest and posttest times not only progress toward some thirty-six primary goals of the show but also transfer effects, home background variables, parental attitudes, and socioeconomic factors. We decided to sample children from middle class suburbia, lower class northern and western urban ghettos, and lower class sections of a southern town; rural children; Spanish-speaking children; children at home and children in Head Start and nursery schools; boys and girls; black children and white children; and three-, four-, and five-year-old children. You will, of course, notice that these categories are not necessarily mutually exclusive.

Initially we tested over 1,300 children in five sites across the country. Then we observed many of them viewing the show, made a content analysis of the show itself, administered a questionnaire to teachers whose classes viewed the show, and assessed the amount of viewing for all the subjects in the study, using four different assessment techniques. When evaluating a program in which side-effects and interactions are considered important, the study has to be wide-ranging, the sampling

extensive, and the statistics multivariate (Freeman 1963).

Nonetheless, despite the decision to spread our attention to different groups of preschool children, we also noted that *Sesame Street was primarily intended for disadvantaged children, at home, without benefit of Head Start or similar formal educational experience.* Therefore, our major concentration in the sampling was on this particular subpopulation.

Our experimental design in the evaluation of the first year of *Sesame Street* was much better in prospect that in retrospect. We randomly assigned children to either an encouraged-to-view group or a not-encouraged-to-view group in each of the five field sites. Unfortunately, we had expected, on good evidence, that few children would view unless specifically encouraged to do so. In fact, however, most children viewed the show at least some of the time, irrespective of our assignment to experimental or control conditions. Thus, we were forced to analyze our data in a number of different ways from those originally planned. We think that the analyses we carried out provided convincing evidence to allow us to draw a number of specific and more general conclusions indicating the merit of the show for all groups of children studied. Our report on the first year is available (Ball & Bogatz 1970) and an extensive review of the report is being published under a grant from the Russell Sage Foundation (Cook 1972).

We also carried out a major evaluation of the second year of *Sesame Street,* including a follow-up study of those subjects who were disadvantaged and at home (not in school) during the first year of the show (Bogatz & Ball 1971).

The second year of *Sesame Street* saw an expansion of the show's goals to achieve somewhat wider curriculum coverage and to include more difficult topics in goal areas already established in the first year. For example, classification on the basis of a single criterion was a goal in both years, but in the second year double classification was also included. Similarly, counting from one to ten was extended to from one to twenty, and simple addition and subtraction became goals for the first time in the second year. The replication element in the second year study took us to two new sites where we sampled only at-home disadvantaged children who had not viewed the show in its first year. We were interested in seeing if effects noted in the first year were also seen in the second year, and whether the new and extended goals were achieved. In one site, the only means of obtaining access to the show was through cable, and we assigned cable to only half our subjects. The other site had an ultra high frequency (UHF) television channel that attracted few viewers from ghetto areas unless a special effort was made to encourage viewing a specific show. The result was that in the second-year study the encouraged-to-view (experimental) subjects did view, and a major proportion of the not-encouraged-to-view (control) subjects did not view. Our subsequent analyses of the second-year data were easier to interpret than those of the first-year data. They supported the general finding that the show benefited the viewer over a range of goals; we also found, however, that the new, extended goals were not well learned in comparison to the more basic goals carried over from the first year.

Another aspect of the second-year study was the follow-up of at-home disadvantaged children from the first year. About half of them went on to school in the second year, while the others did not. We tested both these groups of children in October 1970 and May 1971, coinciding with the beginning and ending of the second year of the *Sesame Street* series. We also obtained from the teachers of those who went on to school a ranking of our subjects in relation to the other children in the class on seven criteria. We found that a second year of viewing had positive effects over just one year of viewing, but mainly in the areas of the new, extended goals. Thus, the producers of the show have the dilemma of deciding whether to concentrate on simple and basic goals to the benefit of the younger children viewing for the first time or to put effort into extended goals, thereby benefiting somewhat older children viewing for a second year.

So far we have not been particularly specific about our measures, our field operations, or our results and conclusions. The purpose has been mainly to sketch a general outline upon which to base our implications for compensatory education. As we present the implications, the sketched outline of the evaluation will doubtless be given greater detail, and if the reader becomes really interested there is always recourse to the two reports (Ball & Bogatz 1970; Bogatz & Ball 1971).

We again have to confront the problem of what compensatory education is. One way of looking at it, and the one that we suspect most of us fuzzily use, is to regard compensatory education as education specifically provided for disadvantaged chil-

dren. Examples would be the Head Start program or Title I programs of the Elementary and Secondary School Education Act. Then, we might legitimately ask: What does our *Sesame Street* research tell us that has implications for such education? Given this approach, there are some major implications.

MEASURES

Perhaps because we were conducting an evaluation pointed toward assessing a number of specific goals, we were interested in using measures that would provide a clear picture of status with respect to a specific goal. At least among the arsenal of tests available for use with young children, we found the situation appalling. Take, for example, items such as: "Put the green marbles in the square box." If the child gets it wrong, is it because he does not know the meaning of "green," "marbles," "square," or "box"? Or, what if the child is given a stimulus triangle and asked if she can find another one just like it embedded in a larger drawing? The child is asked to trace around it. If she cannot perform the task correctly, does this mean that she did not find it, that she has poor motor coordination, or that she does not want to play games with the tester? In one well-known standardized test for five-year-olds, we found that the percentage passing national norms for a particular counting item were lower than we had obtained at pretest with four-year-old disadvantaged children. Then we looked at the administration manual, where we found the instruction for the children was: "We are now going to play a number game. Look at the pictures of the fish bowls at the top of the page. Let's pretend that there are five tables in your class and each table has a fish bowl on it. See the large letters above the fish bowls. These letters are A, B, C, D, and E. Listen carefully. In which bowl do you see just three fish?" What happens to a child who does not understand words like "pretend" and who has never seen a fish bowl?

The point that we are trying to make is this. If we are to develop and improve compensatory education we must have measures that will allow us to learn with reasonable clarity what we are accomplishing. Frankly, our experience as we developed the test battery for *Sesame Street*, and again as we developed our tests for *The Electric Company* (The Electric Battery), was that many tests of young children currently in use are defective: they are unnecessarily difficult to administer; often they lack face, content, and construct validity; and, peculiarly, they seem to assume that if they are individually administered tests they had better involve the tester in making loose subjective and clinical judgments about the child's performance. It does not surprise us, therefore, that our understanding of compensatory education remains at a low level. Science can hardly be expected to flourish without adequate measuring instruments.

RACE

At a time when genetics, race, and education were becoming mixed into a rather emotional stew, we had the interesting experience of meeting poverty groups in order to obtain their cooperation in our evaluation of *Sesame Street.* More than once we were pointedly asked by black community leaders whether we were simply again trying to prove that their children were dumb; and more than once we argued that it was *Sesame Street* we were trying to evaluate and not their children. The fact is that we did collect a lot of data on disadvantaged children, both black and white. It was our intention not to make black versus white comparisons and indeed we kept our resolution during the preparation of our first report. We analyzed the data from our disadvantaged sample in terms of amount of viewing and eschewed the additional, possibly independent, factor of race. Our major reasons were that we had already indicated to those community groups who had cooperated with us that this was the kind of analysis that would take place, and that we were not certain at all that the black disadvantaged in our study were comparable to the white disadvantaged. Thus, we sought to avoid the problem of unfair and invidious comparisons.

After the publication of our first-year study we did look at our data to see if disadvantaged black viewers gained more compared to disadvantaged black nonviewers, and if disadvantaged white viewers gained more compared to disadvantaged white nonviewers. As we surveyed these groupings of the data we were struck by the similarity of the scores of the disadvantaged black children and the disadvantaged white children within each site at pretest, and we were also struck by the similarity of gains made in relation to their degree of viewing. Subsequent multivariate analyses of variance confirmed our impression that among the disadvantaged in our study there were no significant effects due to race.

A curious exception deserves some reflection. Most of our tests were specially developed to assess status and growth on the goals being sought on the show. Here the pretest and gain scores of black and white children were quite similar. However, in the first-year evaluation we also used, at pretest only, a standardized test, the Peabody Picture Vocabulary Test (PPVT), in order better to describe our subjects and as a covariate in covariance analyses of gains. To our surprise, there were systematic differences between black and white disadvantaged children on this test to the degree of about half a standard deviation. In IQ terms there was about a ten-point difference favoring the whites. Note that, of the pictures in the test, only two are of blacks (a spear carrier and a porter). Look too at the specific vocabulary called for. Of course, it could be that our black sample study had a poorer vocabulary than our white sample, but it could also be a function of the test used; this seems a perfectly reasonable assumption, since scores on the other tests did not differ in this way.

In general then, black and white disadvantaged preschool children from within the same testing sites seemed to be quite comparable at pretest and gained similarly, given similar amounts of viewing over the six months of the show. The exception was their present status on the PPVT, and we consider this to be probably a function of the test rather than an indication of lower vocabulary levels by the black children. Thus, apparently serious proposals to use different forms of education for disadvantaged black children than for disadvantaged white children have no substantiation from our *Sesame Street* data. Rather, race was shown to be an unimportant factor in determining the degree to which a child could learn from the show.[*]

NONTRADITIONAL EDUCATION

The traditional form of education used with preschool children has been to provide small group settings with one or two adults to usually no more than fifteen or so children. Play and fun have often been advocated as an important if not essential element in the process; we can look back to the writings and work of Pestalozzi, Froebel, and perhaps even Plato to show that these ideas are not exactly new. Similarly, experts in early education

*Some readers will want to compare these findings with those of Bereiter, Weikart, and McAfee in Stanley (1972). [Ed.]

have usually stressed the need for a close relationship between adult and child for optimal learning to occur.

Sesame Street had objectives that were much more limited than a good nursery school or Head Start program. Nonetheless, the objectives and some of the gains were by no means trivial. We remember the air of somber, sober, and scientific pessimism that pervaded its advisory boards before the show began telecasting for the first time. How could an hour a day on television have much effect? If a teacher in a school all day with her class accounts for so little of the variance of scores among classes (Wolf 1965), how would an object with a mean diagonal measurement of twenty-one inches do better and without personal contact? We were also told that preschoolers have very short attention spans and that disadvantaged preschoolers have even shorter ones.

The facts are that the show was seen to have a marked effect, not only in areas of rote learning of basic skills, such as counting, and in simple contiguity association learning, such as learning the names of letters and numbers, but also in higher areas of cognitive activity, such as sorting and classifying pictorial representations and, as far as we could tell, in attitudinal areas such as attitude toward the race of others. Furthermore, these effects were obtained with boys as well as with girls, yet many studies suggested that boys are the ones who present the majority of the learning problems.

Thus, the implication seems clear that we should put greater effort into nontraditional means of educating young disadvantaged children, not to supplant but to supplement older ways. It also seems clear that the cherished ideas of some educators about what is essential in early education in order for children to learn might not stand close scrutiny. For example, while close emotional ties might be important for learning in the emotional and interpersonal areas, they might not be so important for learning in the cognitive areas.

DELIVERY PROBLEMS

There is a couplet in a song with the words, "Ain't We Got Fun?" which has the interesting social comment that the rich get rich and the poor get children. An analogous problem is that educationally rich middle class parents tend to make use of the educational opportunities that are available for their children, whereas the educationally impoverished lower class tends not to do so. Thus, when *Sesame Street* appeared on the television screen and the educational scene, it quickly acquired a large audience. It was disproportionately larger, though, for the middle class than for the lower class. Furthermore, within the disadvantaged group, it was the most disadvantaged who viewed least. Educators with a sense of social justice similarly note that the ghetto children they would most like to reach are the ones hardest to reach.

In our evaluation of the second year of *Sesame Street*, we assigned children to encouraged-to-view and not-encouraged-to-view conditions. We assessed the amount of viewing for all children, because it was impossible to ensure that all encouraged children would view all the shows, just as it was impossible to ensure that all not-encouraged children would view none of the shows. In fact, the distribution of subjects looked like this:

	Non-viewers	Moderate viewers	Frequent viewers	Total
Encouraged	9	43	78	130
Non-encouraged	99	46	8	153

We were interested in extracting the encouragement effect from the viewing effect, since both effects were somewhat confounded, and since both effects seemed to be positive. We carried out a univariate analysis of covariance on the grand total gain score and obtained the following results: The regression of viewing on total gain was similar for the encouraged and not-encouraged groups. That is, amount of viewing affected both groups similarly.

This regression was significantly different from zero, indicating that amount of viewing was positively associated with gains. There was a definite encouragement effect, irrespective of the amount of viewing.

From other analyses we could conclude that the disadvantaged gained as much as the more advantaged, if they viewed as much. However, the tendency was for them not to view as much. The important question was: What would happen if disadvantaged children were to view the show as much as the advantaged, because of some conscious effort to get them to do so? The answer seems to be that such encouraged viewers will do at least as well as children who view entirely of their own volition. Furthermore, the act of encouragement itself may have beneficial effects. For example, the child's mother is more likely to view with the child and then talk about the show with the child if encouragement to view occurs.

The implication we draw from this is, we hope, now clear. While it is true that the more disadvantaged tend to avail themselves less of educational opportunities, it also seems to be true that a conscious program of encouragement is worthwhile. We should spend money on providing compensatory educational programs; we should also spend money on delivery systems to ensure that those who need these programs receive them.

IQ

We have already discussed the peculiar results obtained with the PPVT in our first-year evaluation (i.e., black disadvantaged children performed less well than white disadvantaged children on this test). In other respects, however, the test proved useful in that it enabled us to describe our sampled children and compare them to those in other studies, and it enabled ut to examine, if imprecisely, the moderating effects of vocabulary size on learning.

Soon after the close of the first-year series, a number of unsolicited letters arrived at our office from school teachers and school psychologists in which the thought was expressed that the new groups of children reaching their schools were "brighter" than in the past and that almost invariably the mothers were mentioning *Sesame Street* as the causal agent.

We also realize that the PPVT, despite the fact that it provides IQ conversions, is basically the oral receptive vocabulary test. However, vocabulary is traditionally seen as one slice (though a thin one) of the pie we call intelligence. Therefore, with, I hope, uncharacteristic foolishness we gave the PPVT as a posttest as well as a pretest in the second-year evaluation, both to the follow-up subjects and the new replication subjects. In almost all of our analyses of the second-year data a clear trend emerged. Viewing of *Sesame Street* affected scores on the PPVT, and, therefore, if one had the faith to make the conversion, affected IQ scores. Since teachers commonly misinterpret IQ scores, then children with higher IQ scores on their permanent records might conceivably be treated differently from children with lower scores.

This finding, that *Sesame Street* affects IQ scores

as determined by one particular test, is not so different from other studies (though the medium of television has never before been accused of raising the intelligence of the viewer). Compensatory programs can have positive general cognitive effects, just as failure to provide educational programs can have negative ones.

AGE

The final implication we wish to draw, using this model of compensatory education as it applies to preschoolers, deals with age. In our *Sesame Street* evaluations we studied three-, four-, and five-year-old disadvantaged children. We subdivided each age group by amount of viewing. The results from the *Sesame Street* test battery at pretest and again at posttest are presented graphically in Figure 1. Before *Sesame Street* went on the air, older children almost invariably performed higher on the test than younger children. After *Sesame Street, however, three-year-olds who watched most (Q4) scored higher at posttest than three of the four-year-old groups and two of the five-year-old groups, although these three-year-olds had pretest scores lower than all five-year-olds and all but one of the four-year-old groups. In other words, the placement of the children along the scale measuring the goals of Sesame Street was very dependent on age at pretest, while at posttest it was much more related to amount of viewing.*

If the viewing of *Sesame Street* were not effective and the gains noted in the first-year study among the four viewing groups were primarily a matter of differential growth rates noted at pretest, then the juxtapositions of age groupings at posttest would be difficult indeed to explain.

The implication here is that disadvantaged three-year-olds were quite capable of learning much of the material and many of the skills taught on the first year of *Sesame Street*. Perhaps in compensatory education we aim too low at too high an age level. More positively, perhaps we should think of beginning with younger than four-year-old children, and perhaps we should raise our expectations of what these very young children can learn.

An effort has been made in the preceding pages to draw implications for compensatory education, where compensatory education has been defined in terms of disadvantaged children. We did include in

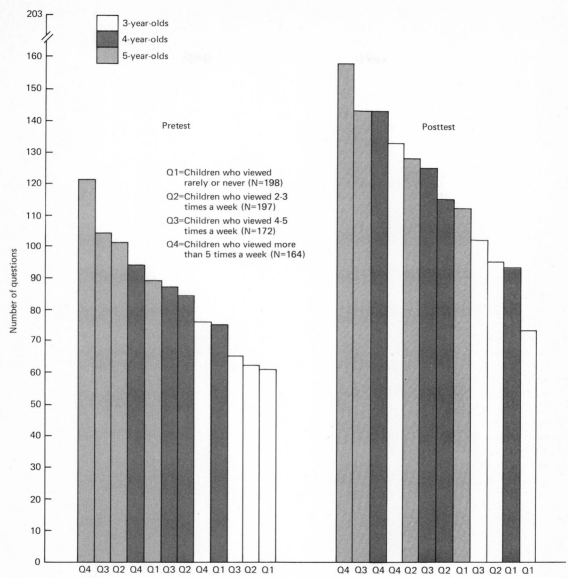

Figure 1 Pretest and posttest scores of 3-, 4-, and 5-year-old disadvantaged children.

our first-year evaluation a group of advantaged middle class children from suburban Philadelphia. We had purposefully chosen a site where we were not studying disadvantaged children, because we were not initially interested in comparing these two groups. Rather, we were making internal comparisons (viewing versus non-viewing) within each group.

However, we were rather surprised by our re-

sults. Figure 2 presents pretest and posttest scores of advantaged and disadvantaged children. The frequent-viewing, disadvantaged children not only outgained but surpassed the infrequent-viewing, middle class children. This was the point that interested us, and it was also the point that drew criticism upon us. In one sense the gap between middle and lower class children was being diminished from pretest to posttest; but it should also be

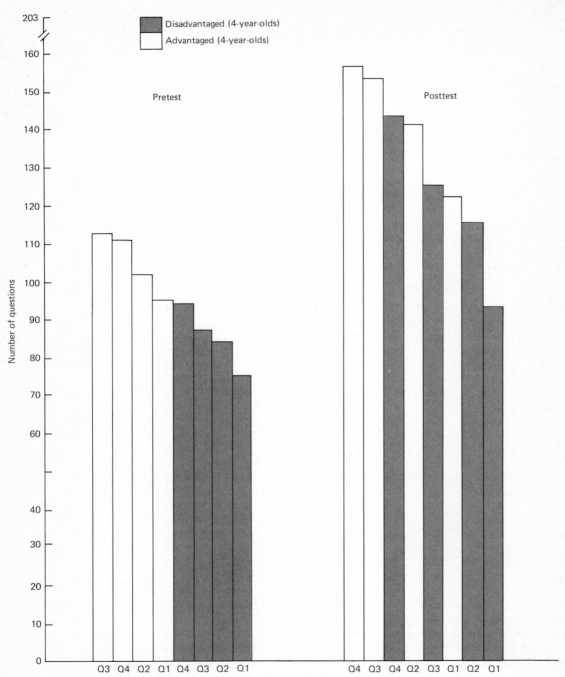

Figure 2 Pretest and posttest scores of disadvantaged and advantaged 4-year-old children.

noted that the middle class children tend to gravitate to the frequent-viewing groups, whereas disadvantaged children tend toward the less-frequent-viewing groups. Some kind of weighting, therefore might lead us to a different conclusion. We reject, however, the analysis of our data (Sprigle 1971, repeated by Ingersoll 1971), in which nonviewers were included in the comparison in order to show middle class children widening their distance from lower class children. Predictably, lower class nonviewers are going to learn less than middle class nonviewers. Would we argue that Head Start is ineffective because lower class children who do *not* attend are increasingly disadvantaged in comparison with middle class children?

The major point here, however, is not the one we have been presenting. What is worth noting is that the effects of the show can be clearly discerned on middle class, advantaged children too. Note that this group included children attending nursery school. This suggests to us that while for good, socially responsible reasons we spend much of our time concerning ourselves at the preschool level with disadvantaged children, we might legitimately be concerning ourselves with middle class children too. Perhaps even with these children their educational input is by no means optimal.[*]

If compensatory education is related to what are Webster's Dictionary second and fourth definitions ("to make proper payment to" or "to offset an error, defect, or undesired effect"), then we may well decide that many children need compensatory education, including a large proportion we fail to recognize when we conventionally think of the term "compensatory."

We began by asking: What is compensatory education? We begged the question first by briefly describing the evaluations of *Sesame Street* that we have carried out; then we took one possible definition of compensatory education as extra education for disadvantaged children and drew six implications, assuming the validity of the definition; finally, we took an alternative definition, which suggests that almost all children need compensatory educa-

tion in some areas, and pointed out the implication for preschool education if this were true. Actually, however, like most semantic arguments, it does not matter which definition we take. Preschool education needs better programs, a greater variety of programs (including nontraditional ones), better delivery systems so that the vast majority of children receive their benefit as opposed to the current minority who do, and better methods of assessing the value of the programs. This may seem to be a rather somber note on which to end this first paper in the series being presented here; but it also carries the message that improvements in all these areas can be effected, for our *Sesame Street* evaluations tell us so. We know, too, that the subsequent papers in this volume will provide heartening examples of progress in early childhood compensatory education—and this means a potential benefit in the education of all young children.

REFERENCES

Ball, S., and Bogatz, G. A. 1970. *The first year of Sesame Street: An evaluation.* Princeton, N.J.: Educational Testing Service.

Bogatz, G. A., and Ball, S. 1971. *The second year of Sesame Street: A continuing evaluation.* Princeton, N.J.: Educational Testing Service.

Cook, T. 1972. Untitled manuscript. A report to be presented on the Educational Testing Service evaluations of *Sesame Street.* New York: Russell Sage Foundation.

Freeman, H. E. 1963. Strategy of social policy research. In H. E. Freeman (ed.), *Social welfare forum.* New York: Columbia University Press.

Ingersoll, G. November 1971. *Sesame Street* can't handle all the traffic. *Phi Delta Kappan* 53(3): 185–87.

Scriven, M. 1967. The methodology of evaluation. In R. E. Stake (ed.), *Perspectives of curriculum evaluation. AERA Monograph Series on Curriculum Evaluation,* No. 1, pp. 39–83.

Sprigle, H. A. March 1971. Can poverty children live on *Sesame Street? Young Children* 26(4): 202–17.

Stanley, J. C. (ed.). 1972. *Preschool programs for the disadvantaged.* Baltimore: The Johns Hopkins University Press.

Wolf, R. M. 1965. The measurement of environments. In *Proceedings of the 1964 Invitational Conference on Testing Problems.* Princeton, N.J.: Educational Testing Service, pp. 93–106. Reprinted in W. H. MacGinitie and S. Ball (eds.), *Readings in psychological foundations of education.* New York: McGraw-Hill, 1968, pp. 186–97.

---

[*]One must consider, however, that most advantaged children will probably in time master the basic skills without special help, whereas a considerable number of the disadvantaged might not. Whether or not precocity resulting from *Sesame Street* permanently benefits middle class children seems to be, as yet, an open question. [Ed.]

Reading 45

The Role of Male and Female in Children's Books—Dispelling All Doubt

Mary Ritchie Key[1]

. . . Bill said, "I will sit in front and steer the sled, Joan, You sit in the back so that you can hold on to me."[2]

Textbooks and children's literature are under scrutiny these days by persons interested in the full potential of both male and female. It is being discovered that the above quote appears to be typical of the general atmosphere in children's literature today:*Boys do; girls are.*

In general, children's books show that boys: climb, dig, build, fight, fall down, get dirty, ride bikes, and have many adventures, while girls sit quietly and watch. Boys are taught to express themselves; girls to please. According to an infamous little book called *I'm glad I'm a boy! I'm glad I'm a girl* (Windmill, 1970), "Boys invent things," and "Girls use what boys invent." Illustrations showing a little boy inventing a reading lamp and a little girl in an easy chair reading under his lamp are captioned by these phrases.

The theoretical basis behind this is, of course, Freud's hackneyed "biology is destiny," without regard for a balanced consideration that psychology can also be destiny."

At this point it is difficult to judge how much influence children's books have in shaping the child's life. One cannot be certain whether the structure of society is simply reflected in the books, or whether the books are further determining the structure of society. Leah Heyn, for one, speaks of the role in child growth that children's books have and feels that books do, indeed, have an influence in terms of the development of the senses, idea

reinforcement, knowledge expansion, and the liberation from the child's born-into environment.

In any case, it is clear that the prejudices and myths held by the majority of the members of society are perpetuated in children's literature. For example, John P. Shepard's study[3] in 1962 showed that the characters "strongly tend to be clean, white, healthy, handsome, Protestant Christian, middle-class people. Villains much more often turn out to be ugly, physically undesirable persons of non-Caucasian races, often either very poor or of the wealthy classes." In this study however, the categories investigated did not include the sex variable which is under investigation today.

One of the earliest statements in the recent acknowledgement of sex prejudice in children's books was made by the well-known anthropologist John Honigmann, in *Personality in Culture* (1967):

Reflecting a poorly concealed bias in American society, central characters in the stories are male more than twice as often as they are female. Surely this confirms the reader's belief that one sex is more important than the other, even if that isn't the only way he finds it out. Stories frequently differentiate male and female roles, just as our culture does. They generally leave female characters to display affiliation and nurturance and to flee danger; rarely do girls display traits of activity, aggression, achievement, or construction; seldom do they win recognition. In other words, girls are pictured as kind, timid, inactive, unambitious, and uncreative. Furthermore, characters in the story who are nurtured by a central character are mostly female, suggesting that females are likely to be in a helpless position. . . . The school readers portray males as bearers of knowledge and wisdom, and also as the persons

[1]The Research Committee of the Gamma Epsilon Chapter of Delta Kappa Gamma took the topic expressed in the title as a study project. Members of the committee collected materials and made analyses of several series of books. As chairman of the committee, I compiled the reports and worked them into this larger study. References to these analyses will be made by name only, since none of this was previously published. The contributions were from the following members: Marguerite Pinson, coordinator of library services; and Laura Wright.

[2]Glenn McCracken and Charles E. Walcutt. *Basic Reading* (Lippincott, 1963), California State Department of Education, 1969, p. 41.

[3]John P. Shepard, "The treatment of characters in popular children's fiction," *Elementary English* 39 (November 1962), pp. 672–676.

through whom knowledge reaches a child [pp. 203–204].

This statement was, in part, based on a 1946 study by Irwin Child and others.[4]

The idea that sex prejudice is the only prejudice now considered socially acceptable seems remarkably applicable to the books found in the field of education, one of our most respected institutions. One writer, Marjorie U'Ren, notes that textbooks written for co-education early in this century present a much more favorable picture of women and girls than do textbooks written from 1930 on. The atmosphere has changed since then, In 1946 Child did a content analysis and concluded that "the most striking single fact of all . . . about the differences between the sexes is that the female characters do simply tend to be neglected."

Studying the Studies

During the last two years over a dozen different studies have been made on children's books: picture books, early childhood books, teen-age books, general library books, a series for minority groups, and California textbooks, which *every* child in California is exposed to. The remarkable thing about these studies is that, although they often make statements which are identical or similar and they reinforce the conclusions of one another, there appears to be no awareness between them of the other studies. They seem to have sprung up spontaneously across the nation, from student, mother, writer, professor, administrator, teacher, and librarian. The studies overwhelmingly document discrimination and prejudice against females in children's books.

Before proceeding further to the focus of our statement, let us stop here to evaluate other recent studies which seem to indicate opposite conclusions, namely the studies of first-grade reading books by Blom, *et al*; Waite, *et al*; Wiberg and Trost; and others which these articles quote. For example, the Wiberg and Trost article concludes that children's books have "a tendency to denigrate the masculine role." Blom, Waite, and Zimet show that "A large number of stories were in the boy-girl activity category (46 percent) as compared to boy

activity (26 percent), and girl activity (28 percent) . . . " "Active Play, Outings, Pranks, and Work Projects were related to boy activity. Quiet Activities, School, Folk Tales, and Real Life with Postive Emotions were related to girl activity." Such statements are somewhat misleading and must be tempered with other facts and other perspectives. In addition, the terminology of studies such as these obfuscates. What is meant by "ambiguity in sex role, sex role appropriateness, oedipal conflict, sex of activity, sex preference"?

Other facts to be considered, for example, are how many boys and how many girls figure as the central character of those so-called "boy-girl activities" comprising 46 percent of the studies mentioned above. Worley counterbalances with other facts:

In most of the stories examined, the central character was a boy and the plot development reflected male circumstances . . . there were twice as many stories reflecting male story situations as there were stories reflecting female story situations.

He suggests that:

A larger proportion of basal reader stories should involve a female as the central character. The heavy emphasis given male figures creates a distorted and perhaps harmful sex role image for all readers. (p. 148)

Other perspectives to be considered concern the judgments made about what, indeed is a girl-activity and what is a boy-activity. It is highly possible that *all* activities that six-year-olds participate in could be either boy or girl activities, if the youngsters weren't socialized to what adults *think* they should do. There don't seem to be great differences in muscular ability, and this age is still a long way from child-bearing functions—two activities which are, indeed, not culturally learned. It would appear from the evidence presented in the studies I am summarizing that a significant number of scholars, persons in education, and lay people disagree with the stereotyped roles assigned to boys and girls in the foregoing studies. Apparently females also like to climb trees, explore caves, go fishing; feel invigorated with accepting responsibility; and can accept leadership with equanimity.

We Needn't Have Feared!

This present paper is a result of a two-fold approach: a survey of studies already made, and an

[4]Irvin L. Child, Elmer H. Potter, and Estelle M. Levine, "Children's textbooks and personality development," *Psychological Monographs* 60.3 (1946) pp. 1–7, 45–53.

analysis of some actual books to confirm statements made. In our committee discussions while formulating plans for the project, we were concerned about how one would come to conclusions as to whether or not the text pictures showed discrimination. How would one avoid subjective, biased statements? We needn't have feared! In many cases, there was no analysis to do because of the absence or the paucity of females either as protagonists or supporting characters. It would appear that modern children's literature follows true to the tradition of early English literature. George K. Anderson commented on the place of women in Old and Middle English literature:

Indeed, the relative insignificance of women in the social scene marks the Old English period as different even from the Middle English. Women had a harsh enough time of it at best in the Middle Ages, partly because they had no opportunity to do much of anything except in the domestic sphere and partly because Christian tradition traced the fall of man to a woman. . . . If we were to judge by Old English literature alone, we would conclude that only queens, princesses, abbesses, a few wives, and a scattering of mistresses comprised the female population of England at that time.[5]

In the *Be a Better Reader* series for the seventh grade, story after story unfolds without any female in existence. It is the exception when a female is a real part of any scene, such as in a farm story in which the mother and daughter are depicted as more thoughtful and intelligent than the boy and husband.

The absence or almost absence of females is also typical of *The Roberts English Series: A Linguistics Program* (Books 3 to 8), especially the later books. In Book 6, out of thirty main sections, only two focus on the female. One section discusses a poem of comparison between the jaded and weary hill-country wife (not woman, but *wife*) and the prairie wife who owns "one last year's dress" and whose life is a series of long, dull, lonely hours (pp. 132–133). The other section treats a humorous (?) poem about a remarkable (neurotic?) little girl

"who didn't let things bother her very much." The "Things" she deals with are an enormous bear, a wicked old witch, a hideous giant, and a troublesome doctor (Ogden Nash, in Book 6, pp. 262–264). Book 8 has three sections out of thirty in which females dominate the scene. One is "The Solitary Reaper," another is a story about a crotchety old aunt. The book, and the series, end with the third and final piece about a female, "The Hag," a witch who rides off with the Devil to do their mischief.

Some of the other recent textbooks adopted or recommended for second through sixth grade in California were analyzed by U'Ren, Gail Ann Vincent, and our committee. In these books at least 75 percent of the main characters are male. The stories about females are not as lengthy. Often the stories about males include no mention of a female, although the stories about females include males with whom the females interact. The mother figure is typically presented as a pleasant, hardworking, but basically uninteresting person:

. . . she has no effect upon the world beyond her family, and even within the family her contribution is limited to that of housekeeper and cook. . . . She enters a scene only to place a cake on the table and then disappears. Or she plays foil to her husband by setting him up for his line. It is mother who asks, "What shall we do?" and by doing so invites a speech from father (U'Ren, p. 7).

Librarian Marjorie Taylor confirms this: "Daddy is the predominant character. His are the ideas, the main portions of the conversations, where the action is."

Vincent's study concentrates on the socialization of the female in the California textbook series. References are made to previous studies on sex-role concepts. Lawrence Kohlberg's[6] study, for example, is said to show that children age five to eight "award greater value or prestige to the male role." "He also finds that identification with the father and other male figures increases dramatically for boys during these years, whereas preferential orientation to the mother in girls declines." Fe-

[5]George K. Anderson, *Old and Middle English Literature from the Beginnings to 1485*, Vol. 1 of *A History of English Literature*. New York: Collier Books, 1962.

[6]Lawrence Kohlberg, "A cognitive-developmental analysis of children's sex-role concepts and attitudes," in Eleanor Maccoby, ed., *The development of sex differences*, Stanford University Press, 1966.

males are not seen interacting together as are males. In the one instance where girls are grouping together and excluding boys ("I *never* play with boys"), they are ridiculed by the boys. Vincent observes that the reverse, i.e., girls ridiculing boys for similar behavior, never occurs. Taylor also documented stories where high value is put on all male activity. In *All Through the Year* by Mabel O'Donnell (Harper & Row, 1969), when the children are going to play detective, Mark shouts, "Boy, this is going to be fun. . . . No girls can be in on this. Just boys. . . . "

With regard to physical tasks, Vincent observes that boys are more competent than girls in the California textbooks: the boy fixes his bike and rides it while the kneeling girl admires him; the boy shoots a basket, while the girl tries and misses.

In creative activities the males also excel: a boy is the best painter; a boy is the best storyteller; father is the best at riddles; a boy wins a contest in snow-sculpting.

In children's books, females do not have the freedom to inquire, explore, and achieve. Margaret Mead is quoted as saying, "Man is unsexed by failure, women by success." This indoctrination starts early. Vincent analyzes the repeated theme of a female not succeeding and notes that when a girl does initiate a tree-climbing episode, punishment is the result (a broken leg for one boy), and a grandmotherly character scolds her for shameful behavior: "What's wrong with you?"

With regard to pictures and illustrations, U'Ren found that many California textbooks included females in only about 15 percent of the illustrations. In group scenes, invariably the males dominate. In *The Roberts English Series: A Linguistic Program,* which includes a great deal of poetry, many of the poems are written with pronoun referent unspecified as to sex, e.g., "I, me, we, they." The pictures accompanying the poems, however, with the exception of Book 3, are almost all male-dominated. In Book 4, eleven poems are illustrated thus, with none illustrated by a female or female-dominated picture. The prose story of Daphne (p. 65) is illustrated by three pictures in which Apollo and Cupid hold the scenes. Daphne is shown only as the transformed laurel tree. In the text, which is presented in three sections, Daphne doesn't enter the story until the second section. Thus, even when a story is supposed to be about a female, the actual pictorial and textual presentation may diminish the female.

THE AWARD WINNERS

Alleen Nilsen analyzed the winners and runners-up of the Caldecott Award during the last twenty years. Presented annually by the Children's Service Committee of the American Library Association for the most distinguished picture book of the year, this exclusive award makes for wide distribution of these books across the country. Of the eighty books analyzed, Nilsen found that the titles included names of males over three times as often as names of females. One-fourth of the books had only token females. In the last twenty years, the presence of females in the Caldecott books is steadily decreasing. This statistic parallels other statistics which are commonplace today, such as the percentage of women in administrative positions in education and the percentage of women professors, which is less now than it was in the 1930s. Among the forty-nine Newbery Award winners of 1969, books about boys outnumber books about girls some three to one.

Elizabeth Fisher studied books for young children found in bookstores and libraries. There were five times as many males in titles as there were females. The fantasy worlds of Maurice Sendak and Dr. Seuss are almost all male.

In children's books, there is a significant reversal of the usual use of "she/her" for animals and inanimate objects. I have discussed pronoun referents in another study of the linguistic behavior of male and female.[7] Grammar rules and usage indicate, among other things, that large animals are "he," small animals are "she," and other inanimate objects are usually "she." Admittedly there is a great deal of confusion and inconsistency in rules and usage, which I point out in the paper. Storybook animals in our children's books, however, are almost all male, and female animals tend to carry names of derogation or are objects of derision: Petunia the Goose, Frances the Badger, and the sow who entered the Fat Pigs contest (Wodehouse, in *The Roberts English Series 8*). Personifications of the inanimate are invariably male; for example, in *The Roberts English Series.* While no sailor worth

---

[7]Mary Ritchie Key, "Linguistic behavior of male and female," to be published in *Linguistics: An International Review.*

his salt in real life would refer to a ship as "he," our children's books have boats, machines, trains, and automobiles which carry only male names and gender. This contradicts T. Hilding Svartengren's study[8] where he showed that these items were referred to in literature by the referents "she/her."

THE BUTT OF THE JOKE

The treatment of females in comedy is another area of concern in children's books. Too often the butt of the joke in poems and stories is a female. *The Roberts English Series: A Linguistics Program* is chock full of such "funny" poetry by writers such as Belloc, Nash, and Thurber.

As far as role identity is concerned, when women are mentioned or pictured, they are usually shown in relation to men or as accouterments to men. Virginia Woolf pointed out that in literature as a whole this is the situation. In one of the Newbery Award winners, our next generation was advised, "Accept the fact that this is a man's world and learn how to play the game gracefully."

Books written for teen-age boys often tell them that females do not exist; life moves on without girls or women. The worlds of Mark Twain (*The Roberts English Series 7*) and Robert Louis Stevenson (*The Roberts English Series 8*), without a single mention of a female, are being reiterated in contemporary literature. The *Field Educational Checkered Flag Series,* written for boys, is such an example (Henry A. Bamman and Robert Whitehead, California State Text, 1969). When females do occur in books written for young people approaching adulthood, the girls and women are not like the people whom young men will meet in real life.

What Do Big Girls Do?

The following list, compiled from one of *The Roberts English Series,* written for junior high students, gives a comprehensive covering of what females do in Book 8:

- Count votes for males who were nominated;
- Accompany men to the hunt;
- Find their beauty is short-lived;
- Sit with their fans in their hands and gold combs in their hair;

[8]T. Hilding Svartengren, "The use of the personal gender for inanimate things." *Dialect Notes* (1925), 1928–1939, pp. 7–56.

- Put cream on their faces and "lie in bed staring at the ceiling and wishing [they] had some decent jewelry to wear at the . . . Ball";
- Poison their husbands;
- Die because they "never knew those simple little rules . . .";
- Get eaten up by alligators;
- Cut and gather grain and sing to no one;
- Listen to men give speeches;
- Rear children;
- Do silly, ridiculous things (James Thurber);
- Ride with the Devil.

Diane Stavn analyzed for attitudes about girls and women novels which are known to be popular with boys. She made two observations: ". . . the sweeping, sometimes contradictory" incidental comments about the female sex, and "the fact that the girlfriends and mothers are almost always unrealized or unpleasant characters—one-dimensional, idealized, insipid, bitchy, or castrating—while sexually neutral characters, such as little sisters and old ladies, are most often well conceived and likable." For example, the girlfriend of jazz freak Tom Curtis turns out to be "merely a mouthpiece to relate information about other characters in the book and a sounding board for their ideas and problems." In general, the girls accompanying these teenage boys are inadequately fleshed out, tinny, paper thin, made of the stuff of angels, gentle, feminine, fairly quiet, doomed to be unreal. Good old Mom, on the other hand, often is depicted as "an insipid lady who flutters around chronically worrying and inanely commenting."

Stavn does discuss a few books where boys can come away with pretty good feelings about girls and women. The following quotes, however, seem to outweigh the good attitudes:

Women in the States . . . have forgotten how to be women; but they haven't yet learned how to be men. They've turned into hippies, and their men into zombies. God, it's pitiful!

Remember—she's a female, and full of tricks.

Men . . . liked to talk about women as though they had some sort of special malignant power, a witch-like ability to control men.

Polly . . . says "I'm a witch . . . I was being nasty . . . Girls just do those things, I guess. . . . "

Even old girls like my mother. If she hadn't

torpedoed my father's idea to buy a garage, he might not have taken off.

[Polly] . . . began to think she should run the show. That's where I had to straighten her out. And after I got her straightened out she seemed happier.

Boys and young men are reading quotes such as these at the time of their lives when their thoughts of female relationships are predominant, and they are formulating ideas about the kind of woman they want as a partner—or are developing patterns of rejection altogether.

After reviewing the current lists of girls' books, one anonymous observer noted that a preponderance of stories about love, dating, and romance occurred among the themes identified. According to her literature, a female has no alternate life styles, but lives in a limited world with no control over her future. Nilsen calls this the "cult of the apron" and notes that this conditioning starts early. Of fifty-eight picture books which happened to be on a display cart of children's literature at Eastern Michigan University last year, twenty-one had pictures of women wearing aprons. Even the animals wore aprons!—the mother alligator, mother rabbit, mother donkey, and mother cat.

It is well known nowadays that 40 percent of all mothers work, and yet many studies indicate that there is not one mention of a working mother in the particular group of books reviewed. A notable exception is Eve Merriam's *Mommies at Work* (Knopf, 1961). And a notable discrepancy is the *Bank Street Readers,* a series designed for the inner-city child. In the three books, only one mother is shown as a working mother, a woman who serves in a cafeteria.

Social Studies Texts

In Jamie Frisof's analysis of social studies textbooks, men are shown in or described in over one hundred different jobs and women in less than thirty, and in these thirty jobs, women serve people or help men to do more important work. Men's work requires more training; men direct people and plan things; men go places and make decisions; at meetings men are always the speakers; men make the money and are the most important members of families. The pictures in these social studies books show men or boys more than seven times as often as women or girls. Rarely are men and women

working together or seen in equally competent roles. In short, these socializing books "do their part in preparing girls to accept unquestioningly their future as unimportant, nonproductive, nonadventurous, and unintelligent beings."

Regarding professional persons depicted in children's books, Heyn points out that among the several books in the field of health and medicine, without exception the doctor is portrayed as a white male—nurses and receptionists as female.

U'Ren and Vincent report that one of the California textbooks gave an account of Madame Curie, where she appears to be little more than a helpmate for her husband's projects (Eldonna L. Evertts and Byron H. Van Roekel, *Crossroads,* Harper and Row Basic Reading Program, Sacramento: California State Department of Education, 1969). "The illustration which accompanies this section reinforces that view of her. It portrays Madame Curie peering mildly from around her husband's shoulder while he and another distinguished gentleman loom in the foreground engaged in serious dialogue."

DIALOGUE

It might be well at this point to examine other examples of dialogue which occur in children's literature. Linguistic behavior is culturally taught, as are other expressions of behavior. In surveying the dialogues which occur in these books, one notes a pathetic lack of conversation with bright, adventurous females of any age. Rarely is there a give-and-take dialogue in which a female is shown to be capable of making a decision or where the input of the female is intelligent and useful information. The things which girls and women say in these books too often reflect the stereotypes of society: "Women are emotional."

In *The Story of Mulberry Bend* (William Wise, Scott Foresman, 1965), we read, "One little girl thought they were so beautiful she began to cry."

During a scene about fishing and baiting the hook, the girl says, "I can't . . . I don't want to touch those things." "Of course you don't, here I'll do it for you." And then she would have lost the pole but Johnny grabbed it in time (Nila Banton Smith, "Cowboys and Ranches," *Be a Better Reader Series,* Foundation A, Prentice Hall, 1968).

Peter said, "You can't do it, Babs. You will get scared if you do." "No I won't," said Babs. "Yes, you will. You will get scared and cry," said Peter (Mae Knight Clark, *Lands of Pleasure,* Macmillan, California State Department of Education, 1969).

The Little Miss Muffet syndrome, which depicts females as helpless, easily frightened, and dreadfully dull, occurs over and over again in the literature. If one compares this image, which crystallizes in the formative years of child development, with the potential of woman in adulthood, it becomes apparent that both male and female have difficulty in participating in equal sharing dialogues at the professional level. Males who have grown up learning dialogues such as are in children's books today are not able to listen to a female in adult life. Males paralyze when a rare female makes a constructive suggestion. Likewise females are trained not to take their share, or hold their own in decision-making interchange. There are no linguistic models in this early literature for females to take active parts in the dialogue nor for males to respond with dignified acceptance and a willingness to listen. With such indoctrination as this, is it any wonder, then, that doctors don't permit women on the surgical team and women scientists are excluded from projects and from the laboratory, where a female is thought to be useless or a nuisance?

It must also be realized that in some sense male stereotypes are also projected in these books. Future research could be undertaken on these aspects: Is a male permitted to be a whole person? Is he permitted the whole range of emotions that all human beings should have in their repertoire? Must he always be aggressive? Must he always be taller than the females in his circle? Is he allowed to make mistakes and still be accepted?

It is likely that the discrimination and obtrusive imbalance which occurs in the books is unintentional for the most part. But, as Vincent says, this does not mitigate its destructiveness. The results may be of much wider consequence than one might imagine. One of the studies (Anon., "A Feminist Look . . .") asks, "Is depression in the adult woman perhaps linked to the painful suppression of so many sparks of life?" It cannot be said, moreover, that all this treatment is out-of-awareness. For example, Nilsen reports that in a course entitled "Writing for Children" the instructor advised: "The wise author writes about boys, thereby insuring himself a maximum audience, since only girls will read a book about a girl, but both boys and girls will read about a boy." And Nilsen reports that the

prize-winning *Island of the Blue Dolphins* was initially rejected by a publisher who wanted the heroine changed to a hero.

In order not to end on a blue note, it might be well to point out that remedies are in the offing. The National Organization for Women (NOW) initiated a bibliography[9] of children's books showing females in nonstereotyped roles—females "who assume a balanced role during the growing-up process. Traits such as physical capability, resourcefulness, creativity, assertiveness, ingenuity, adventuresomeness, and leadership are emphasized, in addition to literary quality." Thousands of copies of this bibliography have been sold, and authors are already writing material which is more equitable to both male and female. We might expect, then, that the new dialogues will take other forms and that "A Ride on a Sled," the story of Joan and Bill, might sound something like this:

. . . Joan then spoke up, "It's my turn to steer, Bill. Hang on, 'cause we're going a new way!"

REFERENCES
SOURCES AND SELECTED BIBLIOGRAPHY

Anon., "A feminist look at children's books," by the Feminists on Children's Literature, *School Library Journal* (January 1971), pp. 19–24.

Anon., "Little Miss Muffet fights back," *School Library Journal* (November 1970), pp. 11, 14.

Anon., *Little Miss Muffet Fights Back,* by Feminists on Children's Media, P.O. Box 4315, Grand Central Station, New York, N.Y. 10017.

Gardner, JoAnn, "Sesame Street and sex-role stereotypes," *Women: A Journal of Liberation* 1.3 (Spring 1970).

Heyn, Leah, "Children's books," *Women: A Journal of Liberation* 1.1 (Fall 1969), pp. 22–25.

Honigmann, John J., *Personality in Culture.* New York: Harper and Row, 1967, pp. 203–205.

Howe, Florence, "Liberated Chinese primers: (let's write some too)," *Women: A Journal of Liberation* 2.1 (Fall 1970), pp. 33–34.

Meade, Marion, "Miss Muffet must go: a mother fights back," *Woman's Day* (March 1971), pp. 64–65, 85–86.

Anon., *Report of the Advisory Commission on the Status of Women, California Women,* "Textbooks," p. 16, 1971.

Anon., "Sex role stereotyping in elementary school read-

---

[9]Anon., *Little Miss Muffet Fights Back,* comp. by Feminists on Children's Media (P.O. Box 4315, Grand Central Station, New York 10017), p. 48.

ers," pp. 13–18 in *Report on sex bias in the public schools,* NOW, New York City, 1971.

Anon., "Sugar and spice," editorial, *School Library Journal* (January 1971), p. 5.

Child, Irwin L., Elmer H. Potter, and Estelle M. Levine, "Children's textbooks and personality development," *Psychological Monographs* 60.3 (1946), p. 54.

Eliasberg, Ann, "Are you hurting your daughter without knowing it?" *Family Circle* (February 1971), pp. 38, 76–77.

Fisher, Elizabeth, "Children's books: The second sex, Junior Division," *The New York Times Book Review,* Part II (May 24, 1970), pp. 6, 44.

Frisof, Jamie Kelem, "Textbooks and channeling," *Women: A Journal of Liberation* 1.1 (Fall 1969), pp. 26–28.

Miles, Betty, "Harmful lessons little girls learn in school," *Redbook* (March 1971), pp. 86, 168–169.

Nilsen, Alleen Pace, "Women in children's literature," *College English* 32.8 (May 1971), pp. 918–926.

Schlaffer, Maria, "Sexual politics: Junior division," *All*

Worley, Stinson E., "Developmental task situations in stories," *The Reading Teacher* 21.2 (November 1967), pp. 145–148.

You Can Eat, reprinted in *Sherwood Forest: Orange County People's Press* 1.20 (October 1970), p. 10.

Stavn, Diane Gersoni, "The skirts in fiction about boys: a maxi mess," *School Library Journal* Book Review (January 1971), pp. 66–70.

Stefflre, Buford, "Run, Mama, run: women workers in elementary readers," *Vocational Guidance Quarterly* 18.2 (December 1969), pp. 99–102.

U'Ren, Marjorie, "Sexual discrimination in the elementary textbooks" (unpublished manuscript, 14 p.), to be published in *51%: The Case for Women's Liberation,* Basic Books.

Vincent, Gail Ann, "Sex differences in children's textbooks: a study in the socialization of the female." (unpublished manuscript, 20 p.).

Reading 46

Aggression in Childhood: The Impact of Television

Robert M. Liebert
Emily S. Davidson
John M. Neale

How does watching violent television programs affect children? This question has been posed continually since the advent of television sets as a common fixture in American and European homes almost two decades ago. Answers to it, based both on simple opinion and on research which reflects varying degrees of sophistication, have ranged from confident statements that television's influence is uniformly pernicious to equally glib assertions that merely watching entertainment fare can do little to shape children's social behavior.

Although literally hundreds of studies have been focused directly or indirectly on television and its effects upon youngsters, the series of investigations commissioned by the Television and Social Behavior Program of the United States National Institute of Mental Health constituted one of the first systematic and purposefully coordinated attempts to employ the efforts of a large group of researchers with relevant expertise and diverse viewpoints. As psychologists specializing in children's development—both normal and abnormal—each of us contributed to the Television and Social Behav-

ior inquiry. This involvement gave us an opportunity, over the past few years, to read and study all of the technical documents, research reports, and summaries as they were prepared and to evaluate them in the light of past and other recent research.

For concerned citizens the task of keeping informed of this work has been unfortunately complicated by the fact that the Television and Social Behavior Program generated almost 5,000 pages of technical material; the official summary (Cisin et al., 1972), while considerably shorter, is clouded by the participation of five network representatives who persistently minimized the effects of television and confused the significant issues (cf., Boffey and Walsh, 1970; Morgenstern, 1972; Paisley, 1972). A full account of the Program's work and related evidence has been presented elsewhere (Liebert, Neale, and Davidson, 1973). The purpose of this paper is to summarize briefly the state of our present knowledge as it has grown out of these and later investigations and to reflect on some possibilities for the future.

OBSERVATIONAL LEARNING AND TV AGGRESSION

The scientific issue most fundamentally related to the particular question of the effects of television revolves around the nature of *observational learning,* the way in which the behavior of children and adults changes as a function of exposure to the behavior of others. Regardless of their other theoretical views, social scientists have virtually all acknowledged that a child's values and behavior are shaped, at least in part, by observational learning. Research has shown that the simple observation of others can be very potent in changing such widely varied aspects of social behavior as a child's willingness to aid others, his ability to display self-control, and his learning of language. Young children's observation of others on film has been shown to increase sharing and to markedly reduce fear reactions—if, of course, the content is designed to teach these lessons.

This list represents only a few examples from the impressive body of evidence which suggests that learning by observation is a critical aspect of the social learning process through which the child is informed about the world around him and molded into an adult member of his society. It is in this context that social scientists asked whether viewing violent television entertainment has a significant impact on the young. In answering, they had to consider four points: How much violence is shown on television? How much violent entertainment is actually seen by children? What do they learn from this exposure? And, finally: Does such learning lead to changes in real-life behavior?

HOW MUCH VIOLENCE IS SHOWN ON ENTERTAINMENT TELEVISION?

Although violence has always been part of American entertainment in television, its frequency has increased steadily over the past twenty years. In 1954, for example, violence-saturated action and adventure programming accounted for only 17% of prime time network offerings; by 1961 the figure was 60% (Greenberg, 1969). Translating such figures into concrete terms, during one week of television in 1960 there were 144 murders, 13 kidnappings, 7 torture scenes, 4 lynchings, and a few more miscellaneous acts of violence, all occurring before 9:00 p.m. By 1968 the National Association for Better Broadcasting estimated that the average

child would watch the violent destruction of more than 13,400 persons on television between the ages of five and fifteen (Sabin, 1972).

The most accurate estimate of current levels of violence on television during prime time and Saturday morning has been provided by Gerbner et al. (1972a; 1972b), who define violence as:

> The overt expression of physical force against others or self, or the compelling of action against one's will on pain of being hurt or killed (1972a: 34).

In Gerbner's work, carefully trained observers watched a full week of network entertainment programs on all of the major networks, with striking results. In 1969 about eight in ten shows contained violence, and the frequency of violent episodes, as defined above, was almost eight per hour. Further, the most violent programs of all were those designed exclusively for children—cartoons.

> The average cartoon hour in 1967 contained more than three times as many violent episodes as the average dramatic hour. The trend toward shorter plays sandwiched between frequent commercials on fast moving cartoon programs further increased the saturation. In 1969, with a violent episode at least every two minutes on all Saturday morning cartoon programming (including the least violent and including commercial time), . . . the average cartoon hour has nearly six times the violence rate of the average adult television drama hour, and nearly twelve times the rate of the average movie hour (1972a:36).

Gerbner has continued his analysis of network television dramas, and the data for 1970 and 1971 have recently been made available. He summarizes the new findings: ". . . New programs in 1971 spearheaded the trend toward more lethal killers by depicting record high proportions of screen killers" (1972b:3).

The level of violent programming over the five-year period studied by Gerbner can be seen in Figure 1, which shows the percentage of programs containing violence, and the number of violent incidents per program hour.

Clearly, violence on television is not decreasing at any appreciable rate. Prime time drama was still, in the 1971-72 season, overwhelmingly violent. The new figures are of special interest since they reflect

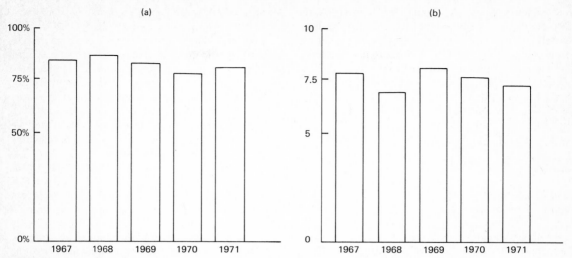

Figure 1 Percentage of network programs containing violence (a) and average number of violent episodes per program hour (b) over the period 1967–71. *(Source: Drawn from data appearing in Gerbner, 1972b.)*

a long history of unfulfilled network promises. In the mid 1960s network officials had promised a sharp decrease in TV violence and then claimed that the promise had been met. Gerbner's 1967 and 1968 data showed that it had not. The promise was reissued, but, again, the appearance of Gerbner's 1969 data (published in 1972 because considerable time is required for sophisticated data processing) showed little change. It was then claimed that substantial changes had certainly occurred during the 1970 to 1971 seasons. Now, again, the facts have answered with unfortunate monotony: little change.

HOW MUCH TV VIOLENCE DO CHILDREN SEE?

Portrayals of violence on television cannot produce an effect unless they are seen. Therefore, we must ask about the frequency with which children actually view such shows. Lyle and Hoffman (1972) conducted an extensive survey of media use among more than one thousand children from widely varied backgrounds. They concluded that "television saturation was almost total; only 2% of the students stated that there was not a working TV set in their home." The data also showed that more than one-third of the first-graders are still watching television at 8:30 p.m. on weeknights, and more than one-half of the sixthgraders are doing so. Likewise, Stein and Freidrich (1972) reported that

in a sample of about 100 preschool children, television viewing was among the most frequently reported waking activities. Indeed, exposure to television is, for children, so pervasive that Lesser (1970) contends that a child born today will, by the age of 18, have spent more of his life watching television than in any other single activity but sleep.

The impact of television can be seen even more clearly by moving from percentage figures to absolute numbers. McIntyre and Teevan (1972), citing the Violence Commission staff reports of 1969, remind us that "on one Monday during the period covered, over five million children under the age of 12 . . . were still watching between 10:30 and 11:00 p.m. . . ." They also point to the Commission's observations that "there is a great deal of violent content available, at all times of the day, for all manner of intended audience."

Moreover, cartoons, the most violent of all types of TV entertainment, are among those most often watched by young children. In the Lyle and Hoffman reports, for example, 24% of the first grade children said that cartoons were their favorite type of program. A similar pattern was found in Stein and Friedrich's study of preschoolers, whose parents reported that they watched cartoons an average of more than seven hours per week; even adult violent programs were watched more than a full hour per week by these three-to-five-year-old children.

It is important to note, though, that high exposure to violence is more a result of saturation by broadcasters than a strong preference for this type of programming by youngsters. Among first graders, for example, the two most popular programs are situation comedies ("My Favorite Martian" and "I Love Lucy"); preschoolers prefer "Sesame Street" to violent cartoons (Lyle and Hoffman, 1972a; 1972b).

WHAT DO CHILDREN LEARN FROM TV VIOLENCE?

There is little doubt that children can learn novel forms of behavior—both words and actions—from simply watching others. It is, however, only through systematic research that we are able to see the degree to which this form of learning is effectively mediated by television and televisionlike formats.

Studies by Bandura (summarized in Bandura, 1973), designed to show that brief exposure to novel *aggressive* behaviors can lead to their acquisition by quite young children, have uniformly shown that this influence is potent indeed. In one study, for example, 88% of the children (three-to-five-year-old boys and girls) who saw an aggressive television program displayed imitative aggression in a play situation even though they had not been asked to do so and were free to play with attractive, nonaggressive toys such as a tea set, crayons, cars and trucks, plastic farm animals, and the like.

Further, there is evidence that behavior acquired in this way may be recalled for long periods of time. Hicks (1965) found that children shown a simulated television program similar to those used by Bandura and his associates learned many new aggressive behaviors after a single viewing and could still produce them when tested again, without further exposure, six months later. So there is no doubt that children learn, with the level of repeated exposure which takes place, a good deal of the aggressive repertoire that they see in televised violence.

Beyond teaching specific ways of perpetrating aggression and mayhem, contemporary TV entertainment conveys a more general lesson: violence succeeds. In an early investigation (Larsen, Gray, and Fortis, 1963), for example, eighteen programs were studied, six in each of three categories: adult programs, "kidult" programs (programs where the child or teenage audience comprises at least 30% of the total audience), and children's programs—usually cartoons. In all three program types, violent methods were the ones most frequently used in goal attainment. And, when goal achievement methods were further analyzed for degree of success, it became clear that the most successful were *not* those in the socially approved category. Simply, then, television programming—aimed both at children and at adults—is presenting an antisocial system of values.

Network officials, though, have sometimes justified television violence because the "bad guy" is usually punished for his misdeeds. The argument deserves a closer look. The usual sequence involves aggression or other antisocial behavior by the villain, through which he achieves his immediate objectives (the plans for the latest missile or the crown jewels of England). Next, the hero catches up with and vanquishes the villain—by virtue of exemplary performance in the final brawl or shootout. The hero's reward is a raise, a blonde, or a bottle of champagne; if he is lucky, he may get all three plus a vacation in the sun. The lesson is thus that aggression, while reprehensible in criminals, is acceptable for those who have right on their side. But all of us, children and adults, rich and poor, on any side of any legal statute, feel we have right on *our* side. "Every man," William Saroyan wrote many years ago, "is a good man in a bad world—as he himself knows."

DOES EXPOSURE TO TV VIOLENCE SHAPE CHILDREN'S REAL-LIFE BEHAVIOR?

There are now numerous documented instances of direct imitation of TV violence by children which have been truly unfortunate, such as the case of a lad who was stabbed while he and his friends reenacted scenes from the movie *Rebel Without a Cause* which they had seen as a televisoin rerun or the youngster who laced the family dinner with ground glass after observing this tactic used successfully on a television crime show (cf. Liebert, Neale, and Davidson, 1973). A more generalized influence upon children of televised aggression can be seen from experimental studies.

An Example

To illustrate the logic that underlies some of this research, let us examine a study conducted independently of the Television and Social Behavior Program. This study by Steuer, Applefield, and Smith (1971) was designed to show the absolute degree of control which television violence can have on naturally occurring aggressive behavior and involved children enrolled in the preschool of the University of North Carolina's Child Development Center. The youngsters, boys and girls, knew each other before the study began. First, they were matched into pairs on the basis of the amount of time they spent watching television at home. Next, to establish the degree to which aggressive behavior occurred among these youngsters *before* any modification of their television "diets," each was carefully observed for ten sessions in play with other children, and the frequency of aggressive responses were recorded.

Steuer and her associates used a demanding measure of physical interpersonal aggression including (a) hitting or pushing another child, (b) kicking another child, (c) assaultive contact with another child, such as squeezing or choking him, and (d) throwing an object at another child from a distance of at least one foot. Only these severe acts of physical aggression were recorded. The initial measure, or baseline, established a remarkable degree of consistency within each pair prior to the modification of their television diet. No one could say, then, that the children differed from one another in aggression before the controlled television experience began.

Next, Steuer and her associates asked about the effects of television. One child in each pair observed, on eleven different days, a single aggressive television program taken directly from Saturday morning program offerings, while the other member of the pair observed a nonaggressive television program. Subsequent observations of the children at play provided continuous measures of interpersonal physical aggression by each child. Changes from the original measures, if any, would have to be caused by television's effects since the children were entirely alike before the television treatment began.

By the end of the eleven sessions, the two groups had departed significantly from one another in terms of the frequency of interpersonal aggression. In fact, for every pair, the child who had observed aggressive television programming became more aggressive than his mate, who had watched neutral fare. In several of the cases, these changes were

truly striking, with youngsters showing increases of 200%-300% in aggressiveness. These results are not new or unique.

More than fifty studies have been conducted, involving more than 10,000 children from every type of social background. With remarkable consistency, these studies regularly lead to one conclusion: *there is a clear and reliable relationship between the amount of violence which a child sees on entertainment television and the degree to which he is aggressive in his attitudes and behavior.*

Converging evidence for the conclusion comes, for example, from correlational field studies which relate viewing of violence on television to various measures of aggressive behavior. Working with adolescent subjects, McIntyre and Teevan (1972) reported to the United States government that they had found a consistent relationship between objective ratings of the amount of violence on programs which youngsters reported watching and many kinds of deviant behavior. Moreover, these investigators found a positive relationship between the violence rating of the child's favorite progams and the degree to which he expressed approval of violence by others. For example, they said "those adolescents whose favorite programs are more violent more frequently approve of a teenage boy punching or knifing another teenage boy."

In another study, involving 434 nine-to-eleven-year-old boys, exposure to television violence was related to the boys' approval of and willingness to use violence themselves (Dominick and Greenberg, 1972). Measures were also obtained of the degree to which the boys perceived violence as effective and the degree to which they suggested violent solutions to conflict situations when presented with open-ended questions. Again, exposure to aggressive television was significantly related to the boys' stated willingness to use violence and to their perceptions of its effectiveness when used. The investigators then used the same methods to relate television violence viewing and aggressive attitudes for girls. The results closely paralleled those for boys, with exposure to such aggressive fare making a "consistent, independent contribution to the child's notions about violence. The greater the level of exposure to television violence, the more the child was willing to use violence, to suggest it as a solution to conflict, and to perceive it as effective" (1972:329).

In yet another study conducted for the Television and Social Behavior Program the relationship between viewing televised violence and a variety of measures of aggressive behavior were obtained in two relatively large samples of older adolescents. The investigators reached the following conclusions:

> Our research shows that among both boys and girls at two grade levels [junior high and senior high] the more the child watches violent television fare, the more aggressive he is likely to be. . . . Adolescents viewing high levels of violent content on television tend to have high levels of aggressive behavior, regardless of television viewing time, socioeconomic status, or school performance (McLeod, Atkin, and Chaffee, 1972a:187-91).

Another correlational study in the Program was longitudinal, designed to determine whether the amount of television violence watched by children at age nine influenced the degree to which they were aggressive ten years later at age nineteen. The findings indicated clearly that, for boys, such a relationship did exist. The investigators reported to the United States government that on the basis of their research ". . . the most plausible single causal hypothesis would appear to be that watching violent television in the third grade leads to the building of aggressive habits" and ". . . that a substantial component of aggression at age nineteen can be predicted better by the amount of television violence the child watched in the third grade [age nine] than by any other causal variable measured . . ." (Lefkowitz, Eron, Walder, and Huesmann, 1972: 51-6).

Finally, consider a uniquely important investigation conducted by Stein and Friedrich (1972). They employed the experimental method in a relatively naturalistic situation in order to examine directly some of the effects of observing television upon quite young children. Participants were fifty-two boys and forty-five girls between $3^{1}/_{2}$ and $5^{1}/_{2}$ years of age, who were systematically exposed to television programs of differing content while attending a summer nursery school.

This carefully designed experiment involved an initial measurement period in which the free play of children in the nursery school was observed and rated according to a variety of categories; a four-week experimental period in which children were systematically exposed either to aggressive cartoons ("Batman" and "Superman"), neutral television programming (children working on a farm and the like), or prosocial programming (episodes from the program "Misterogers' Neighborhood"); and a two-week postviewing period in which effects could be observed and assessed.

The children were exposed to the programs for approximately twenty minutes per day, three times a week during a four-week period. During this time, and during the two-week postviewing period, the children's behavior was again systematically observed in the naturalistic preschool situation. Behavior ratings included measures of aggression, interpersonal prosocial behavior, and self-control. They were checked carefully for reliability and collected by raters who were "blind" to the children's treatment.

Stein and Friedrich found that children who were initially in the upper half of the sample in interpersonal aggression subsequently showed greater interpersonal aggression if they were exposed to the aggressive programming than if they were exposed to either the neutral or prosocial programming. The investigators emphasize that:

> These effects occurred in naturalistic behavior that was removed both in time and in environmental setting from the viewing experience. They occurred with a small amount of exposure, particularly in relation to the amount the children received at home, and they endured during the postviewing period (p. 247).

Social scientists are carefully trained to avoid statements of certainty. In fact, even in the physical and biological sciences, professional and scientific reports are always couched in terms of probabilities rather than absolutes. Notwithstanding this tradition, it seems to us that it has been clearly demonstrated that watching television violence, sometimes for periods of only a few hours, and in some studies even for a few minutes, can and often does instigate aggressive behavior that would not otherwise occur.

SOCIAL SIGNIFICANCE AND IMPLICATIONS: SOME RECURRING QUESTIONS

If TV violence can instigate aggressive behavior—and the data leave little doubt that it can—then we are left with two questions: How socially significant or *important* are the findings? What action, if any, should be taken and by whom? Each of these broad questions can be answered only by considering more specific ones regarding both the data themselves and larger political and social considerations.

HOW IMPORTANT ARE THE FINDINGS?

Let us address this question in several ways that may shed light on the major issues.

For What Types of Children Has an Effect Actually Been Shown?

The "official" report of the Surgeon General's Scientific Advisory Committee on Television and Social Behavior states that TV violence might affect ". . . a small portion or a substantial proportion of the total population of young television viewers. We cannot estimate the size of the fraction, however, since the available evidence does not come from cross-section samples of the entire American population" (p. 12).

It is easy to misunderstand this statement, and many commentators have been confused by it. In point of fact, the studies of the Television and Social Behavior Program involved children and adolescents from every type of background. White, black, and Asian American youngsters all participated. They came from both urban and rural homes; from families in which the breadwinners were physicians, lawyers, plumbers and laborers—as well as from families where there was no breadwinner at all. Large samples participated from Maryland, Wisconsin, California, and New York, while other studies were done in Tennessee, Louisiana, and Ohio. No region, ethnic group, or type of economic circumstance is unrepresented in the data collected to date. One team described its results as revealing that "for relatively average children from average home environments, continued exposure to violence is positively related to acceptance of aggression as a mode of behavior" (Dominick and Greenberg, 1972, pp. 331–32). Most of the other researchers could—and did—describe their findings in the same way.

Is the Effect Limited Only to Children Who Are "Aggressively Predisposed"?

The official report implied repeatedly that the effect of TV violence occurs only among children who are predisposed to it. The suggestion has led to much confusion.

At times, for a variety of reasons, each of us is somewhat more or less predisposed to work hard, eat a steak, or go to a football game; similarly, since not every child will become more aggressive after watching a particular sequence of television violence, we might say that some children are more "predisposed" to show the effect at a particular time than are others. It is presumably in this vein that we should take the committee's observation that the causal sequence is very likely applicable only to those who are predisposed to it. But if we so view the remark, then we must be careful to understand what has been said. As Dr. Steven Chaffee, who made substantial contributions to the research and overviewed the correlational studies, astutely noted:

> The "predisposition to aggression" limitation is to some extent a near universal or tautological proposition, in that most children almost surely have at least some latent aggressive tendencies and are thus "predisposed" to aggression if so stimulated. At the other extreme, it could be taken as a statement that only "a few bad kids" (presumably not yours or mine) can be influenced by media violence . . . "(1972, p. 12).

Going on to discuss other evidence, Chaffee concludes: "Perhaps a more defensible conclusion would be that there is a small subgroup of habitually passive and unaggressive children who will *not* be stimulated to perform aggressively regardless of what they see on television." The research clearly favors Chaffee's analysis; the effects are not limited to a small number of peculiarly predisposed children.

Equally important, we must remember that aggressive actions are by their nature social phenomena; continually watching television violence is not the only way an average, normal child can be harmed. Suppose, for example, that a particular youngster either never watches aggressive television shows or is for some reason unaffected by them. He may still be influenced profoundly as the *target* of aggression: one or more of his playmates who has become more aggressive as a result of television violence may select him as a victim. For this reason, there is an important sense in which we can say with confidence that any and every child can be affected adversely by the present TV violence offerings.

How Much Contribution to the Violence in Our Society Is Made by Extensive Television Violence Viewing by Our Youth?

The question was first posed by Senator John Pastore in his original charge to initiate the Program. The answer appears, to us, to be that such viewing makes a significant contribution. It is not, of course, the only contributing factor to aggression. Cigarette smoking is by no means the only (or even the most influential) factor contributing to heart disease; moderate exercise is not the only factor contributing to good health. No one would doubt the role of the family, the school, and the entire social milieu in contributing to whether or not a child will act aggressively. But would anyone say that it is any of these other factors, alone, which causes aggression? All are important; and concern for one should never deflect societal attention from the others—but neither should the complexity of aggressive behavior mask the social significance of television's demonstrably great impact on children from widely varied backgrounds.

WHAT SHOULD BE DONE?

Some might conclude that television itself is bad for children. We do not. It has been shown, quite unambiguously, that violence on television has an adverse effect. But something else has come from the accumulated research, a finding which is much more fundamental:

> Any steady diet of television, regardless of its content, can exert a powerful influence on children.

Television, we have now discovered, functions for the young as their earliest window on the world, through which they learn, from the repeated examples shown on the screen, how to cope with many aspects of life. *What* they learn depends, quite simply, on what we show them through this window. *How* they learn is a process which we now understand quite well.

Television rests technologically on a complex of twentieth-century electronic inventions, but psychologically its effects are not based on any new or mysterious process. Television influences children through the inevitable, natural consequences of observing the behavior of others. Purposely or inadvertently, television is foremost a teacher, and its potential can be harnessed to shape our society in directions we deem more desirable. Indeed, evidence for this enormous potential has already begun to emerge. The Stein and Friedrich (1972) study, mentioned earlier, showed how selective viewing can have positive effects on a wide range of behavior in normal preschool children. Recall that each group watched television for approximately twenty minutes, three times a week for four weeks. The first group watched aggressive programs, the second watched so-called neutral programs, and the third watched programs that showed prosocial behavior. It is the last group which is of interest now. The children who had watched the positive programs now showed more self-control, in a variety of ways, than did the children who watched either the aggressive programs or the neutral ones. These significant changes were achieved after only four weeks—and even though children in all three groups continued to watch regular television at home.

In our own work we have begun to redirect our efforts toward investigating the potential of television for the teaching of positive lessons, focusing on three related tasks. The first is the development of a code defining prosocial behavior, now proceeding in our laboratory. Several complex issues surround the undertaking, the most important being the nature of *prosocial behavior* as a construct. "Prosocial behavior" does not permit an inclusive, yet specific definition; it is, instead, a class which must be divided further into categories so that each can be defined more precisely. Our code presently includes seven such behavior categories, shown in Table 1, and is being tested and refined with network programs.

With the code, we will be able to assess the whole spectrum of network dramatic offerings, including information such as that collected by Gerbner about violence: who is involved, as actor and recipient, under what circumstances, and with what results? What types of programs contain the most prosocial actions? What is the ratio between aggression and prosocial behavior in any particular program or series?

The second task is more extensive exploration of the *effects* of prosocial programming. Except for successful "therapeutic" uses of television with specialized programs and audiences (e.g., O'Connor, 1969), this job is just recently begun. Our own effort is two-pronged, involving both the identification of existing commercial programs which have positive effects and—more importantly—the cre-

Table 1 Types of Prosocial Behavior That Can Be Shown on Television and a
Definition of each

Terms	Definitions
1. Providing aid or assistance to another	Spontaneous gift or loan of one's possessions to another; giving aid (instructions, physical assistance) to another. Includes two or more people helping each other to achieve either a mutual goal or independent goals.
2. Control of aggressive impulses	Demonstrations or suggestions of alternatives to aggression in frustrating situations.
3. Making up for bad behavior	Verbal apology, including admission of mistake, or some other behavior (e.g., sharing) which is clearly intended as reparation.
4. Delay of gratification	Putting off or foregoing completely some smaller reward for the sake of a larger reward later. Will usually involve some verbalization of this intent. Includes taking time on tasks so that product will be better, and task persistence.
5. Explaining feelings of others	Teaching, explaining why someone acts the way he does, what other people think and feel.
6. Sympathy	Verbalizing concern for others and their problems. Distinct from friendliness. May also include a specific nonverbal behavior.
7. Resistance to temptation	Resisting opportunity to engage in prohibited behavior that would be of some benefit to the individual.

ation of new programs which teach a variety of such lessons.

For networks to change their programming policy, they must be assured that new shows with prosocial themes woven in will have high ratings; the commercial structure of American television dictates that prosocial programs must be able to earn their share of the TV audience. Learning more about preferences and reactions to programs is our third task. In our laboratory we are now conducting studies in which, while a child watches television, a camera watches and records his behavior. Subsequently, the video tape of the child's facial reactions can be coded along dimensions such as interest and enjoyment. This information has already assisted us greatly in the initial design of new programs which can have beneficial effects *and* be commercially viable.

REFERENCES

Bandura, A. Aggression: A Social Learning Analysis. Englewood Cliffs, New Jersey: Prentice-Hall. 1973.

Boffey, P. M., and J. Walsh. Study of TV violence. Seven top researchers blackballed from panel. Science, May 22, pp. 949–52. 1970.

Chaffee, S. H. Television and growing up: Interpreting the Surgeon General's report. Paper presented to Pacific chapter, American Association for Public Opinion Research, Asilomar, California, March 1972.

Cisin, J. H., T. E. Coffin, I. L. Janis, J. T. Klapper, H. Mendelsohn, E. Omwake, C. A. Pinderhughes, I. de Sola Pool, A. E. Siegel, A. F. C. Wallace, A. S. Watson, and G. D. Wiebe. Television and growing up: The Impact of Televised Violence. Washington, D.C.: U.S. Government Printing Office. 1972.

Dominick, J. R., and B. S. Greenberg. Attitudes toward violence: The interaction of television exposure, family attitudes, and social class. In G. A. Comstock and E. A. Rubinstein, eds., Television and Social Behavior. Vol. III: Television and Adolescent Aggressiveness. Washington, D.C.: U.S. Government Printing Office, pp. 314–35. 1972.

Gerbner, G. Violence in television drama: Trends and symbolic functions. In G. A. Comstock and E. A. Rubinstein, eds., Television and Social Behavior. Vol. I; Media Content and Control. Washington, D.C.: U.S. Government Printing Office, pp. 28–187. 1972a.

———. The violence profile: Some indicators of the trends in and the symbolic structure of network television drama 1967–1971. Unpublished manuscript, the

Annenberg School of Communications, University of Pennsylvania. 1972b.

Greenberg, B. S. The content and context of violence in the mass media. In R. K. Baker and S. J. Ball, eds., Violence and the Media. Washington, D.C.: U.S. Government Printing Office, pp. 423–52. 1969.

Hicks, D. J. Imitation and retention of film-mediated aggressive peer and adult models. Journal of Personality and Social Psychology 2:97–100. 1965.

Larsen, O.N., L. N. Gray, and J. G. Fortis. Goals and goal-achievement methods in television content: Models for anomie? Sociological Inquiry 8:180–96. 1963.

Lefkowitz, M. M., L. D. Eron, L. O. Walder, and L. R. Huesmann. Television violence and child aggression: A followup study. In G. A. Comstock and E. A. Rubinstein, eds., Television and Social Behavior. Vol. III: Television and Adolescent Aggressiveness. Washington, D.C.: U.S. Government Printing Office, pp.35–135. 1972.

Lesser, G. S. Designing a program for broadcast television. In. F. F. Korten, S. W. Cook, and G. L. Lacey, eds., Psychology and the Problems of Society. Washington: American Psychological Association, 208–14. 1970.

Liebert, R. M., and J. M. Neale, and E. S. Davidson. The Early Window: Effects of Television on Children and Youth. New York: Pergamon Press. 1973.

Lyle, J., and H. R. Hoffman. Children's use of television and other media. In E. A. Rubinstein, G. A. Comstock, and J. P. Murray, eds., Television and Social Behavior. Vol. IV: Television in Day-to-day Life: Patterns of Use. Washington, D.C.: U.S. Government Printing Office, pp. 129–256. 1972a.

———. Explorations in patterns of television viewing by preschool-age children. Ibid., pp. 257–73. 1972b.

McIntyre, J. J., and J. J. Teevan, Jr. Television violence and deviant behavior. In G. A. Comstock and E. A. Rubinstein, eds., Television and Social Behavior. Vol. III: Television and Adolescent Aggressiveness. Washington, D.C.: U.S. Government Printing Office, pp. 383–435. 1972.

McLeod, J. M., C. K. Atkin, and S. H. Chaffee. Adolescents, parents, and television use: Adolescent self-report measures from Maryland and Wisconsin samples. In. G. A. Comstock and E. A. Rubinstein, eds., Television and Social Behavior. Vol. III: Television and Adolescent Aggressiveness. Washington, D.C.: U.S. Government Printing Office, pp. 173–238. 1972a.

———. Adolescents, parents, and television use: Self-report and other report measures from the Wisconsin sample. Ibid., pp. 239–313. 1972b.

Morgenstern, J., The new violence. Newsweek, February 14. 1972.

O'Connor, R. D. Modification of social withdrawal through symbolic modeling. Journal of Applied Behavior Analysis 2:15–22. 1969.

Paisley, M. B. Social Policy Research and the Realities of the System: Violence Done to TV Research. Institute for Communication Research: Stanford University. 1972.

Sabin, L. Why I threw out my TV set. Today's Health, February. 1972.

Stein, A. H., and L. K. Friedrich. Television content and young children's behavior. In J. P. Murray, E. A. Rubinstein, and G. A. Comstock, eds., Television and Social Behavior. Vol. II: Television and Social Learning. Washington, D.C.: U.S. Government Printing Office, pp. 203–317. 1972.

Steuer, F. B., J. M. Applefield, and R. Smith. Televised aggression and the interpersonal aggression of preschool children. Journal of Experimental Child Psychology, 11:442–47. 1971.

Acknowledgments

Chapter 1

A. Rosenfeld, "If Oedipus' parents had only known." *Saturday Review/World,* September 7, 1974. Copyright 1974 *Saturday Review/World.* Reprinted with permission of A. Rosenfeld and *Saturday Review.*

Berry Brazelton, "Effect of prenatal drugs on the behavior of the neonate." *American Journal of Psychiatry,* vol. 126, pp. 1261–1266, 1970. Copyright 1970, the American Psychiatric Association. Reprinted by permission of the author and publisher.

Marshall Klaus and John Kennell, "Care of the mother." From Marshall H. Klaus, M.D., and Avory A. Fanaroff (Eds.), *Care of the high-risk neonate,* Philadelphia, W. B. Saunders Company, 1973, pp. 98–107. Reprinted by permission of the author and publisher.

Henry N. Ricciuti, "Malnutrition and psychological development." From biological and environmental determinants of early development. Research Publication A.R.N.M.D., Vol. 50. Copyright © 1973, Association for Research in Nervous and Mental Disease. Reprinted with permission of the author and publisher.

Anke A. Ehrhardt and Susan W. Baker, "Fetal androgens, human central nervous system differentiation, and behavior sex differences." From Richart Friedman and Vande Wiele (Eds.), *Sex differences in behavior.* New York, 1974, pp. 33–51. Copyright 1974 by John Wiley & Sons, Inc. Reprinted by permission of the authors. Reprinted by permission of John Wiley & Sons, Inc.

Chapter 2

Sandra Scarr-Salapatek, "Unknowns in the IQ equation." *Science,* Vol. 174, pp. 1223–1228, December 17, 1971. Copyright 1971 by the American Association for the Advancement of Science. Reprinted with permission of the author and publisher.

Sandra Scarr-Salapatek and Richard A. Weinberg, "The war over race and IQ: When black children grow up in white homes. . . . ," *Psychology Today,* December 1975. Copyright © 1975 Ziff-Davis Publishing Company. Reprinted by permission of *Psychology Today Magazine.* Reprinted with permission of the authors and publisher.

Mary Jo Bane and Christopher Jencks, "Five myths about your IQ." *Harper's,* February, 1973, pp. 32–34, 38–40. Copyright February, 1973 by Harper's Magazine. Reprinted from the February, 1973 issue by special permission. Reprinted with permission of the authors.

Chapter 3

Tom Bower, "Competent newborn." *New Scientist,* March 14, 1974, Vol. 61, pp. 672–675. From *Child alive!,* edited by Roger Lewin. Copyright © 1974, 1975 by IPC Magazines, Ltd. Reproduced by permission of Doubleday & Company, Inc. Reproduced also by permission of the author.

Daniel G. Freedman, "The social capacities of young infants." From Daniel G. Freedman, *Human infancy: An evolutionary perspective,* Copyright © 1974 by John Wiley & Sons, Inc., and Erlbaum Associates. Reprinted by permission of the publisher and author.

Michael Lewis and Jeanne Brooks-Gunn, "Self, other, and fear: The reaction of infants to people." Reprinted by permission of the authors.

Arnold J. Sameroff, "Early influences on development: Fact or fancy?" Abridged from *Merrill-Palmer Quarterly,* 1975, Vol. 21, No. 4, pp. 267–294. Reprinted by permission of the author and publisher.

Jerome Kagan and Robert E. Klein, "Cross-cultural perspectives on early development." From *American Psychologist,* Vol. 28, No. 11, November, 1973, pp. 947–961. Copyright 1973 by the American Psychological Association. Reprinted by permission.

Chapter 4

Roger Brown, "Development of the first language in the human species." *American Psychologist,* Vol. 28, No. 2, 1973, pp. 97–106. Copyright 1973 by the American Psychological Association. Reprinted by permission. Reprinted also by permission of the author.

Dan I Slobin, "Children and language: They learn the same way all around the globe." *Psychology Today,* July, 1972. Copyright © 1972 Ziff-Davis Publishing Company. Reprinted by permission of *Psychology Today Magazine* and the author.

Kathryn P. Meadow, "Language development in deaf children." *Review of Child Development Research,* Vol. 5, E. M. Hetherington, ed., pp. 450–459, 466–467. Copyright © 1975 by the University of Chicago Press. Reprinted by permission of The University of Chicago Press and the author.

Jean Berko Gleason, "Code switching in children's language." From T. E. Moore (Ed.), *Cognitive development and the acquisition of language,* pp. 159–167. Copyright 1973 by Academic Press, Inc. Reprinted by permission of the author and publisher.

Barry Silverstein and Ronald Krate, "Cognitive-linguistic development." From B. Silverstein and R. Krate, *Children of the dark ghetto,* Chapter 7, pp. 143–169, New York, Praeger University Series, 1975. Copyright © 1974 by Praeger Publishers, Inc. Reprinted by permission of the publisher and author.

Chapter 5

David Elkind, "Giant in the nursery—Jean Piaget." *The New York Times Magazine.* May 26, 1968. © 1968 by The New York Times Company. Reprinted by permission. Reprinted also by permission of the author.

Scott A. Miller and Celia A. Brownell, "Peers, persuasion, and Piaget: Dyadic interaction between conservers and nonconservers." *Child Development,* 1975, **46,** 992–997. Copyright © 1975 by The Society for Research in Child Development, Inc. Reprinted by permission of the publisher and authors.

Anne C. Bernstein, and Philip A. Cowan, "Children's concepts of how people get babies." *Child Development,* 1975, **46,** 77–91. Copyright 1975 by The Society for Research in Child Development, Inc. Reprinted by permission of the publisher and authors.

Albert Bandura, "Analysis of Modeling Processes." This selection is an abridged version of an article which originally appeared in A. Bandura (Ed.), *Psychological Modeling: Conflicting Theories,* 1971. Reprinted by permission of the author. Reprinted by permission of the publishers, Lieber-Atherton, Inc., Copyright © 1974. All rights reserved.

Ross D. Parke, "Some effects of punishment on children's behavior—Revisited." Reprinted by permission from *Young Children,* Vol. XXIV, No. 4 (March 1969). Copyright © 1969, National Association for the Education of Young Children, 1834 Connecticut Avenue, N.W., Washington, D.C. 20009. Revised and updated for this volume.

Earle S. Schaefer, "Parents as educators: Evidence from cross-sectional, longitudinal, and intervention research." Reprinted by permission from *Young Children,* Vol. XXVII, No. 4 (April 1972), pp. 227–239. Reprinted by permission of the author. Copyright © 1972, National Association for the Education of Young Children, 1834 Connecticut Avenue, N.W., Washington, D.C. 20009.

Chapter 6

Corrine Hutt, "Sex differences in human development." *Human Development,* **15:**153–170 (Karger, Basel, Switzerland, 1972). Reprinted by permission of S. Krager AG, Medical and Scientific Publishers, Basel, Switzerland. Reprinted also by permission of the author.

Willard W. Hartup, "Aggression in childhood: Developmental perspectives." *American Psychologist,* 1974, **29,** 336–341. Copyright © 1974 by the American Psychological Association. Reprinted by permission. Reprinted also by permission of the author.

Michael J. Chandler, "Egocentrism and antisocial behavior: The assessment and training of social perspective-taking skills." *Developmental Psychology,* 1973, **9,** 326–332. Copyright 1973 by the American Psychological Association. Reprinted by permission. Reprinted also by permission of the author.

Carol Dweck, "Children's interpretation of evaluation

feedback: The effect of social cues on learned helpless-ness." *Merrill-Palmer Italy,* Vol. 22, No. 00, 1976, 000–000. Reprinted by permission of the author and publisher.

Marian Radke Yarrow and Carolyn Zahn Waxler, "The emergence and functions of prosocial behaviors in young children." Reprinted by permission of the authors and the National Institute of Mental Health.

Miriam M. Johnson, "Fathers, mothers and sex typing." *Sociological Inquiry,* 1975, 45, **1,** 15–26. Reprinted by permission of the author and publisher.

Chapter 7

Richard Q. Bell, "Contributions of human infants to caregiving and social interaction." From M. Lewis and L. Rosenblum (Eds.), *The effect of the infant on its caregiver.* New York: Wiley, 1974, pp. 1–19. Reprinted by permission of the author.

Diana Baumrind, "Socialization and instrumental compe-tence in young children." Reprinted by permission from *Young Children,* Vol. XXVI, No. 2 (December 1970). Copyright © 1970, National Association for the Education of Young Children, 1834 Connecticut Ave-nue, N.W., Washington, D.C. 20009. Reprinted also by permission of the author.

Ross D. Parke and Douglas B. Sawin, "Father-infant interaction in the newborn period: A re-evaluation of some current myths." Reprinted with the permission of the authors.

E. Mavis Hetherington, Martha Cox, and Roger Cox. "Beyond father absence: Conceptualization of effects of divorce." Reprinted with permission of the authors.

Urie Bronfenbrenner, "The changing American family." Reprinted with permission of the author.

David B. Lynn, "Cultural experiments in restructuring the family." From *The father: His role in child develop-ment,* by D. B. Lynn, pp. 45–61. Copyright © 1974 by Wadsworth Publishing Company, Inc. Reprinted by permission of the publisher, Brooks/Cole Publishing Company, Monterey, California, and the author.

Chapter 8

Willard W. Hartup, "Peer interaction and the behavior-al development of the individual child." From E. Schopler and R. J. Reichler (Eds.), *Child development, deviations, and treatment.* Copyright 1976 by Plenum Publishing Corporation, New York. Reprinted by per-mission of the author and publisher.

Steven R. Asher, Sherri L. Oden, and John M. Guttman, "Children's friendships in school settings." From L.

Katz (Ed.), *Current Topics in Early Childhood Educa-tion,* Volume I. Copyright 1976 by L. Erlbaum Associ-ates. Reprinted with permission of the authors and publisher.

Daniel G. Freedman, "The development of social hierar-chies." From L. Levi (Ed.), *Society, stress and disease,* Vol. 2: *Childhood and adolescence,* pp. 303–312. Lon-don, Oxford University Press, 1975. Reprinted by per-mission of the author and publisher.

Paul V. Gump, "Big schools-small schools." *Issues in Social Ecology,* 1965–1966, pp. 276–285. Reprinted with permission from Chronicle Guidance Publications, Inc., Moravia, N.Y., and the author.

Pamela C. Rubovits and Martin L. Maehr, "Pygmalion black and white." *Journal of Personality and Social Psychology,* 1973, Vol. 25, No. 2, 210–218. Copyright 1973 by the American Psychological Association. Re-printed by permission of the publisher and the author.

Patrick C. Lee and Annie Lucas Wolinsky, "Male teach-ers of young children: A preliminary empirical study." Reprinted by permission from *Young Children* Vol. XXVIII, No. 6 (August 1973). Copyright © 1973, Na-tional Association for the Education of Young Chil-dren, 1834 Connecticut Avenue, N.W., Washington, D.C. 20009. Reprinted also by permission of the au-thors.

Howard Garber and Rich Heber, "The Milwaukee proj-ect: Early intervention as a technique to prevent mental retardation." Reprinted with permission of the authors and the University of Connecticut from National Lead-ership Institute-Teacher Education/Early Childhood, University of Connecticut Technical Paper, March 1973.

Samuel Ball and Gerry Ann Bogatz, "Research on Sesa-me Street: Some implications for compensatory educa-tion." In J. C. Stanley (Ed.), *Compensatory education for children ages 2 to 8,* pp. 11–24. Copyright 1973 The Johns Hopkins University Press. Reprinted by permis-sion of the authors and publisher.

Mary Ritchie Key, "The role of male and female in children's books—Dispelling all doubt." Reprinted by permission from the October 1971 issue of the *Wilson Library Bulletin.* Copyright © 1971 by the H. W. Wilson Company.

Robert M. Liebert, Emily S. Davidson, and John M. Neale, "Aggression in childhood: The impact of televi-sion." In Victor B. Cline, ed., *Where do you draw the line?* Provo, Utah: Brigham Young University Press, 1974. Reprinted by permission of the authors and publisher.